2004

# The Origins of World War I

This work poses an easy but perplexing question about World War I: Why did it happen? Several of the oft-cited causes are reviewed and discussed. The argument of the alliance systems is inadequate, lacking relevance or compelling force. The argument of an accident (or "slide") is also inadequate, given the clear and unambiguous evidence of intentions. The arguments of mass demands, those focusing on nationalism, militarism, and social Darwinism, it is argued, are insufficient, lacking indications of frequency, intensity, and process (how they influenced the various decisions).

The work focuses on decision making, on the choices made by small coteries, in Austria-Hungary, Germany, Russia, France, Britain, and elsewhere. The decisions made later by leaders in Japan, the Ottoman Empire, Italy, the Balkans, and the United States are also explored.

The final chapters review the "basic causes" once again. An alternative position is advanced, one focused on elites and coteries, their backgrounds and training, and their unique agendas.

Richard F. Hamilton is Professor Emeritus of Sociology and Political Science and Research Associate of the Mershon Center at the Ohio State University. He has published nine books, including *Who Voted for Hitler?* (1982) and *The Bourgeois Epoch* (1991).

Holger H. Herwig is Professor of History and Canada Research Chair in Military and Strategic Studies at the University of Calgary. Among the many books he has written are the *Biographical Dictionary of World War I* (1982), coauthored with Neil M. Heyman; *The First World War* (1997); and *The Destruction of the Bismarck* (2001).

# The Origins of World War I

Edited by

**RICHARD F. HAMILTON**
*Ohio State University*

**HOLGER H. HERWIG**
*University of Calgary*

**CAMBRIDGE**
UNIVERSITY PRESS

PUBLISHED BY THE PRESS SYNDICATE OF THE UNIVERSITY OF CAMBRIDGE
The Pitt Building, Trumpington Street, Cambridge, United Kingdom

CAMBRIDGE UNIVERSITY PRESS
The Edinburgh Building, Cambridge CB2 2RU, UK
40 West 20th Street, New York, NY 10011-4211, USA
477 Williamstown Road, Port Melbourne, VIC 3207, Australia
Ruiz de Alarcón 13, 28014 Madrid, Spain
Dock House, The Waterfront, Cape Town 8001, South Africa

http://www.cambridge.org

© Cambridge University Press 2003

First published 2003

Printed in the United Kingdom at the University Press, Cambridge

*Typeface* Sabon 10/13 pt.     *System* LATEX 2$_\varepsilon$   [TB]

*A catalog record for this book is available from the British Library.*

*Library of Congress Cataloging in Publication Data*

The origins of World War I / edited by Richard F. Hamilton and Holger H. Herwig.
p.   cm.
Includes bibliographical references and index.
ISBN 0-521-81735-8
1. World War, 1914–1918 – Causes.   2. World War, 1914–1918 – Diplomatic
history.   3. World War, 1914–1918 – Historiography.   I. Title: Origins of
World War One.   II. Title: Origins of World War I.   III. Hamilton, Richard F.
IV. Herwig, Holger H.

D511 .O68   2003
940.3'11–dc21          2002067092

ISBN 0 521 81735 8 hardback

*For Irene and Lorraine*

# Contents

# List of Tables and Maps

## Tables

## Maps

# Contributors

John Milton Cooper, Jr.
University of Wisconsin
Madison, WI

Frederick R. Dickinson
University of Pennsylvania
Philadelphia, PA

Richard C. Hall
Georgia Southwestern State University
Americus, GA

Richard F. Hamilton
The Ohio State University
Columbus, OH

J. Paul Harris
Royal Military Academy
Sandhurst, United Kingdom

Holger H. Herwig
University of Calgary
Alberta, Canada

Eugenia C. Kiesling
U.S. Military Academy
West Point, NY

**Geoffrey P. Megargee**
Center for Advanced Holocaust Studies
U.S. Holocaust Memorial Museum

**David Alan Rich**
U.S. Department of Justice
Washington, DC

**Ulrich Trumpener**
University of Edmonton
Alberta, Canada

**Graydon A. Tunstall, Jr.**
University of South Florida
Tampa, FL

# Acknowledgments

This work was supported by the Mershon Center of the Ohio State University. We are much indebted to Richard Ned Lebow, the center's director, and to Mershon's superb staff, most especially to Wynn Kimble. Special thanks are due also to two very capable and diligent research assistants, Young Ho Kim and Byoung Won Min.

The project began with a conference at the Mershon Center in October of 1999. Our original expectation was for a "short campaign" with the chapters ready for the publisher by December. But like the war itself, the "home by Christmas" expectation proved illusory. Many people have helped the editors and our eight coauthors by providing insights, guidance, suggestions, and, most important, corrections. We thank all of them and trust they will understand if we omit the several pages that would be required to give them the credit they deserve.

Richard F. Hamilton
Holger H. Herwig

# World Wars

## *Definition and Causes*

## Richard F. Hamilton and Holger H. Herwig

It is only fair to ask: *Why* another book on 1914? Surely, the origins of that war have been studied, reviewed, and revised almost beyond any reader's endurance. Vladimir Dedijer, arguably the leading expert on the Sarajevo assassination, claimed that already in 1966 more than 3,000 books had been published on that subject alone. And the torrent of ink spilled on that tragic murder has never abated. Hence, why more?

The short answer is that many of us have missed several key elements in the vast literature on 1914. First, who precisely *were* the decision makers? Monarchs, presidents, foreign ministers, staff chiefs, or a combination of these? And what were their mindsets in July 1914? How had the experiences of the recent past (and especially of the two Balkan Wars of 1912–13) shaped their outlooks? Second, *how* did those governments go about declaring war? In other words, was there a constitutional definition of war powers? Were cabinet and parliamentary approval required in all cases? Or could war be declared simply by royal fiat? Third, *which* "social forces" or extraparliamentary lobbies had input into the decision for war? And fourth, what *were* the reasons? What were the justifications for the decisions to go to war? Why did those decision makers do it? Were there common or similar justifications? Or is a differentiated reading needed? In short, we sought answers to questions that had troubled us from previous readings on July 1914. We hope in this volume to have provided not only answers, but, above all, stimulus for further thought and research.

*Richard F. Hamilton and Holger H. Herwig*

## The Road to 1914

World War I, once called the Great War, seems to defy explanation: Why did it happen? Numerous books on the subject carry the words "causes" or "origins" in their titles. The literature on the subject is extensive, probably the largest for any war in human history.[1] To address that question, we begin with a definition of what constituted a world war and then proceed to a discussion of possible causes regarding July 1914. It is our argument that the numerical suffix established in 1919 for the "war to end all wars" (1914–18) as constituting the "first" world war is flawed. Rather, we see it in terms of the *longue durée*, of five centuries of conflicts that transcended "normal" or "short" wars in terms of both intensity and globalization. We offer this overview to place the "Great War" in historical perspective, fully aware that our selections are open to debate (precisely our intention).

We define a world war as one involving five or more major powers and having military operations on two or more continents. Wars of such extent are costly ventures. The principal "actors" therefore have to be rich nations and ones with substantial intercontinental outreach. Rich, of course, is a relative term. The masses in a given nation might have been poor, but that nation, relative to others, could be rich, sufficiently so as to allow it to sustain large armies and navies in distant struggles for extended periods. For example, The Netherlands could do that in the seventeenth century when it was a rich nation. In the eighteenth century, when relative to others it was not so rich, that nation was no longer a "great power." China, a rich nation, presents the opposite experience. It was a rich nation with a demonstrated ability to reach out, but then in 1433 by imperial decree the voyages ceased, overseas trade was severely restricted, and the construction of ocean-going ships stopped. Confucian-trained officials, it seems, "opposed trade and foreign contact on principle."[2] China's foreign involvement ended at that point.

Since central Europe tore itself apart during the Thirty Years' War (1618–48), eight wars fit our definition of a world war. They are: the

---

[1] For a partial listing, see the first section of the bibliography, Appendix C.

[2] John King Fairbank, *China: A New History* (Cambridge, 1992), pp. 138–9; and Louise Levathes, *When China Ruled the Seas: The Treasure Fleet of the Dragon Throne, 1403–1433* (New York, 1994). Levathes reports a more extended transformation: "In less than a hundred years, the greatest navy the world had ever known had ordered itself into extinction" (p. 175). In the course of the fifteenth century, she reports, "China's tax base shrank by almost half" (p. 178).

War of the Grand Alliance (sometimes called the War of the League of Augsburg), 1689–97; the War of the Spanish Succession, 1701–14; the War of the Austrian Succession, 1740–48; the Seven Years' War, 1756–63; the French Revolutionary Wars, 1792–1802; the Napoleonic Wars, 1803–15; then, after a ninety-nine-year interlude, World War I, 1914–18; and, two decades later, World War II, 1939–45. The participating powers and measures of battle fatalities are given in Table 1.1.[3] Following our definition, within this time span the "Great War" was actually World War VII.

A few cautionary remarks should be noted. The "severity" figures in the table considerably understate the total wartime deaths: Neither civilian deaths nor the deaths – military and civilian – suffered by smaller countries (i.e., not great powers) are included. One source gives World War I deaths as 14,663,000 and World War II as between 41 and 49 million.[4] Seen in relative terms (losses per 1,000 of population), some other wars were much more destructive. The victorious Athenians put to death "all the grown men" of Melos in 416 B.C. The destruction of Carthage in 146 B.C., it is said, "was essentially total." Taking an unlikely high estimate of European losses in World War I, one author suggests a loss of "about 4.1 percent." The German states lost one-fifth of their population in the Thirty Years' War; Prussia, one-seventh of its population in the Seven Years' War. A very destructive war, one that receives little attention, was a civil war, the Taiping Rebellion in China (1851–64), with a loss of some 20 million lives. We routinely focus on wars as the big killing events but neglect another even more lethal one. In March 1918 an influenza epidemic broke out among army recruits in Kansas. Subsequently

---

[3] In Britain's North American colonies, the first three wars are known as King William's War, Queen Anne's War, and King George's War. The Seven Years' War is known there as the French and Indian War; in Germany it is called the Third Silesian War.

The table suggests a level of knowledge and degree of precision that, as seen below, is not warranted. The severity/intensity numbers are rough estimates best interpreted as involving fair-sized margins for error. The dates vary somewhat from source to source. The War of the Spanish Succession, for example, ended with the Peace of Utrecht, 1713, but that was supplemented with other treaties in 1714. For brief reviews, see Stanley Chodorow, MacGregor Knox, Conrad Schirokauer, Joseph R. Strayer, and Hans W. Gatzke, *The Mainstream of Civilization*, 6th ed. (Fort Worth, 1994); Donald Kagan, Steven Ozment, and Frank M. Turner, *The Western Heritage*, 7th ed. (Upper Saddle River, N.J., 2001); and R. Ernest Dupuy and Trevor N. Dupuy, *The Encyclopedia of Military History from 3500 B.C. to the Present*, 4th ed. (New York, 1993). For brief reviews of those wars in North America, see John M. Blum, Edmund S. Morgan, Willie Lee Rose, Arthur M. Schlesinger, Jr., Kenneth M. Stampp, and C. Vann Woodward, *The National Experience: A History of the United States*, 8th ed. (Fort Worth, 1993).

[4] Dupuy and Dupuy, *Encyclopedia of Military History*, pp. 990 and 1198.

TABLE I.I. *World Wars*

| War | Dates | Number of great powers | Countries[a] | Severity[b] | Intensity[c] |
|---|---|---|---|---|---|
| Grand Alliance | 1689–97 | 5 | ABFNS | 680 | 6,939 |
| Spanish Succession | 1701–14 | 5 | ABFNS | 1,251 | 12,490 |
| Austrian Succession | 1740–48 | 6 | ABFPRS | 359 | 3,379 |
| Seven Years' War | 1756–63 | 6 | ABFPRS | 992 | 9,118 |
| French Revolutionary Wars | 1792–1802 | 5 | ABFPR | 663 | 5,816 |
| Napoleonic Wars | 1803–15 | 5 | ABFPR | 1,869 | 16,112 |
| All European wars, 1815–1913 (N = 18) | 1815–1913 | 3 or fewer | A: 6; B: 1; F: 8; R: 5 | Fewer than 217 | Fewer than 1,743 |
| World War I | 1914–18 | 8 | ABFGIJRU | 7,734 | 57,616 |
| World War II | 1939–45 | 7 | BFGIJRU | 12,948 | 93,665 |

[a] Countries participating in war: A: Austria-Hungary; B: Britain (England); F: France; G: Germany; I: Italy; J: Japan; N: Netherlands; P: Prussia; R: Russia; S: Spain; U: United States.
[b] Severity of war: total battle fatalities suffered by great powers, in thousands.
[c] Intensity of war: total battle fatalities suffered by great powers, per million European population.
*Source:* Joshua S. Goldstein, *Long Cycles: Prosperity and War in the Modern Age* (New Haven, 1988), pp. 236–37. Reprinted with the permission of Yale University Press.

called the Spanish flu, it spread, within a year, to all continents. Estimates of total deaths range from 25 to 39 million, more than twice the World War I total. The rates would be equivalent to the above-mentioned wartime losses of Prussia and the German states.[5]

The eight world wars were initiated by well-off, indeed, rich European nations. Five or more major powers were involved in those struggles. Most history textbooks, understandably perhaps, emphasize the battles fought on the European continent. But in each case, the wars were fought also in Asia, Africa, and the Americas. In three of those wars, the English and French fought in India, with France ultimately losing out. And in four of them, the same contenders fought in North America. In the last of those

[5] For the comparisons with other wars, see John Mueller, "Changing Attitudes Towards War: The Impact of the First World War," *British Journal of Political Science* 21 (1991): 1–28. On the "Spanish flu," see K. David Patterson and Gerald F. Pyle, "The Geography and Mortality of the 1918 Influenza Pandemic," *Bulletin of the History of Medicine* 65 (1991): 4–21.

struggles, in 1763, the British gained the vast territories of New France. In the course of the same war, the British "took" Martinique, Grenada, Havana, and Manila (all later returned).

World wars, as defined here, require extensive economic, technological, and political development. Five or more nations had to generate considerable wealth, create capable naval forces, and acquire overseas empires. Basically, they had to establish and maintain relatively large military forces and send them enormous distances. That initially meant transport with large seagoing vessels armed with effective cannons. Later, in the nineteenth and twentieth centuries, railroads, motor vehicles, and air transport came to be the decisive factors.[6]

A military revolution occurred in the seventeenth century.[7] The most important of the many changes was a considerable growth in the size of the armies. Those large forces could no longer "live off the land": steal supplies from the populace. That change forced the creation of "the train," a large number of horse-drawn wagons to carry foodstuffs (for men and animals), munitions, medical supplies, and so forth. The size of military operations increased accordingly, with armies marching over several roads and converging later, it was hoped, at the site of battle. For several reasons, the military was forced to give much greater emphasis to drill and discipline; much more elaborate arrangements for command and control became necessary.

---

[6] Carlo Cipolla, *Guns, Sails, and Empire: Technological Innovation and the Early Phases of European Expansion* (New York, 1965). For more extensive treatments, see Martin van Creveld, *Supplying War: Logistics from Wallenstein to Patton* (Cambridge, 1977); William H. McNeill, *The Pursuit of Power: Technology, Armed Force, and Society since A.D. 1000* (Chicago, 1982); Paul Kennedy, *The Rise and Fall of the Great Powers: Economic Change and Military Conflict from 1500 to 2000* (New York, 1987); and John Keegan, *A History of Warfare* (New York, 1993).

There are always complications and specifications. Russia was a rich and powerful nation with a sizable army. But it had a small navy, one with limited ocean access. In the 1880s Russia's leaders viewed Britain as their implacable enemy but were frustrated by their inability "to strike back at London in any meaningful way. How indeed could the elephant exert pressure on the whale?" From William C. Fuller, Jr., *Strategy and Power in Russia 1600–1914* (New York, 1992), p. 332.

[7] See Michael Roberts, *The Military Revolution, 1560–1660* (Belfast, 1956); Geoffrey Parker, *The Military Revolution: Military Innovation and the Rise of the West, 1500–1800* (Cambridge, 1996); Brian M. Downing, *The Military Revolution and Political Change: Origins of Democracy and Autocracy in Early Modern Europe* (Princeton, 1992); Clifford J. Rogers, *The Military Revolution Debate: Readings on the Military Transformation in Early Modern Europe* (Boulder, 1995); and MacGregor Knox and Williamson Murray, eds., *The Dynamics of Military Revolution, 1300–2050* (New York, 2001).

The increase in the size of armies and their growing complexity required the development of trained professional leaders, changes that came about in the next two centuries. No longer did it suffice to send aspirants to cadet schools at Lichterfelde in Germany, Sandhurst in Britain, St. Cyr in France, or West Point in the United States. Now, staff officers were formally educated at academies (*écoles militaires*) in Berlin, St. Petersburg, Vienna, Woolwich, Santiago de Chile, and Nanking. Likewise, naval colleges were created in Brest, Kronstadt, Newport, and Etajima. While Maximilien Robespierre's experimental École de Mars eventually failed, the French Revolution was highly successful with its new engineer officer training academy (École polytechnique) as well as its advanced gunnery school at Châlons and its military engineering school at Metz. At the end of the Napoleonic period, the Prussians founded a special advanced war academy (Kriegsschule, later called Kriegsakademie) in Berlin.

War offices and admiralties were created to provide both the training and the command structures. Those rich modern states were able to create the disciplined and organized forces that allowed the conduct of coherent and effective military operations over long periods not only in Europe, but also, as indicated, across broad expanses of the world's oceans.

Although often overlooked, economic costs are a constant factor in military and diplomatic affairs. The military revolution increased those costs considerably. There were more soldiers to be housed, clothed, fed, armed, and trained. The number of infantry and artillery pieces required grew, and with the technological advances, the unit costs of those weapons also increased. The sources of wealth allowing this revolution were diverse: New World gold and silver as well as trade and commerce (tea, coffee, cocoa, sugar, silk, spices, slaves, woolens, and, later, cotton goods). Machine manufacture had a considerable impact, increasing national wealth and making new weapons possible. This innovation came first in the production of cotton goods, and then in that of iron and steel. The latter industry produced the steam engines for cotton manufacture, pumps for the mines, rails and locomotives for the railways, and ever more effective cannons.

A nation's military capacity, at all times, is limited by its economic strength, by its ability to pay. One can increase taxes and borrow money to pay the costs. But ultimately, an end point would be reached, forcing that nation out of the struggle. Histories generally focus on monarchs and generals when discussing wars. But that overlooks another important figure: the finance minister. When the tax monies reach their limit and no further loans are possible, the war ends. Austria's participation in the Seven Years' War is a classic case in point. Campaigns were budgeted for 10 to 12 million florins per annum, but a single campaign in 1760 cost 44 million florins. Overall, the costs for the Seven Years' War came to 260 million florins. The war ended in large part when the finance minister told Maria Teresa that Vienna had reached its financial limit.[8]

A curious interpretative bias appears in this connection. Many writers focus on the military outcome: Who won the war? But the economic consequences are often markedly different. The Seven Years' War ended in 1763. But the debts incurred continued and, in the case of France, subsequently had very serious impacts, especially with the added costs of its involvement in the American Revolution. An important lesson was restated here: that wars can contribute to revolution.

Another economic linkage should be noted. Britain was likely the richest of the European nations on the eve of the French Revolution. Though maintaining only a small army, Britain's wealth allowed the hiring of mercenaries and the payment of subsidies to its allies. Above all, Britain's wealth, combined with its insular position and command of the seas, allowed it to participate in as much or as little of a European war as it desired. In raw figures, Britain spent £1,657 million on wartime expenditures between 1793 and 1815, up more than £1,400 million from the period 1776 to 1783. Much of that was to finance the various coalitions it formed against Napoleon Bonaparte.[9]

The above paragraphs deal with necessary conditions, with the prerequisite factors that make world wars possible. One must also consider

---

[8] Christopher Duffy, *The Army of Maria Theresa: The Armed Forces of Imperial Austria, 1740–1780* (Vancouver and London, 1977), p. 124. For a brief account of the struggles between the ministries of war and finance in Russia, see Fuller, *Strategy and Power*, p. 329. For the problems facing the chancellor of the exchequer in Britain in the years before the Great War, see David Lloyd George, *War Memoirs*, 6 vols. (London, 1933–6), vol. 1, pp. 8–10. The nations differed also in the efficiency and the sensed justice of their taxation arrangements. In these respects, Britain was well ahead of France, its most important continental rival. See John Brewer, *The Sinews of Power: War, Money and the English State, 1688–1783* (Cambridge, Mass., 1990); J. F. Bosher, *French Finances, 1770–1795* (Cambridge, 1970); and Kennedy, *Rise and Fall*, chs. 3 and 4.

[9] Kennedy, *Rise and Fall*, pp. 81, 136. British subsidies kept Prussia and other mercenary states involved in the struggle during the Seven Years' War. Ibid., pp. 85, 98. John M. Sherwig, *Guineas and Gunpowder: British Foreign Aid in the Wars with France, 1793–1815* (Cambridge, Mass., 1969), makes the point that these subsidies, though large in aggregate, constituted only a small percentage of the military outlays of Britain's continental partners.

the sufficient conditions, the circumstances that would lead five or more great powers to engage in such a war. Some of these world wars (1688, 1701, 1803) were fought by coalitions to thwart the ambitions of a dominant power; others (1740, 1756, 1792) were fought to *create* a dominant power or hegemon once a war had started. Louis XIV had obvious expansive ambitions; in response, combinations of English, Dutch, Austrian, Spanish, Swedish, and German principalities allied at various times to resist the Sun King's aspirations. In 1688 Louis XIV invaded and laid waste to the Palatinate. In what we have termed the first world war, the Grand Alliance sought to block his ambitions. The war involved five major powers and lasted nine years. It raged from Belgrade to Bantry Bay (Ireland), and from Lagos to the British and French settlements in America.

In 1700, the Spanish monarch, Carlos II, died without heir. Both Habsburgs and Bourbons had claims to the succession. If the Bourbons gained the crown, the French-Spanish linkage (with their massive overseas connections) would produce a very formidable power. Once more, Louis XIV chose war (our second world war) to pursue his hegemonic aspirations. And once more, the other European powers – England, Austria, The Netherlands, Portugal, Prussia, and many of the smaller German states – combined to thwart that possibility. Again, the struggle reached beyond the European continent: from Cartagena to Mallorca, and from Port Royal to St. Augustine to Quebec. After twelve years of war, a compromise was reached. The Bourbons retained the Spanish throne, but the settlement excluded joint occupancy. France and Spain would continue as two separate nations.

In 1740, Frederick II of Prussia, who had just recently taken the throne, on the flimsiest of pretexts took Silesia from Austria. Maria Theresa understandably responded, which led to the War of Austrian Succession (our fourth world war). It involved six powers (Austria, Britain, France, Prussia, Russia, and Spain) and lasted eight years. Overseas, the war witnessed two mainly Anglo-French wars, one in India and the other in North America.

But the War of Austrian Succession solved little. From 1756 to 1763, Austria and Prussia (and later Britain, France, Sweden, Russia, and most small German states) fought the Seven Years' War. Again, the six major powers fought in Europe. Elsewhere the war was fought in the Atlantic and Indian Oceans, in India and in the Americas. For eight years, six major powers mounted seven major campaigns. In India, Robert Clive drove the French under Thomas Lally off most of the subcontinent. In the Americas, the French were driven out of Canada in 1760 and out of Martinique in 1762.

Our fifth world war took place between 1792 and 1802, as the French revolutionary forces, like Louis XIV before them, tried to establish dominion over the Continent. In this case, five major powers (but mainly France and Austria) fought for ten years. The non-European component of the war extended from Egypt to Ceylon, and from the West Indies to Mysore and Bangalore.

Of particular interest in the French Revolutionary Wars is a second revolution in military affairs: the engagement of the citizenry in the effort. For the first time, rulers dared arm their subjects in vast numbers. Nationalism and patriotism rather than impressment and bad fortune would, presumably, prompt young men to take up arms. The concept of the *levée en masse*, of the "nation in arms," was formulated by the Committee of Public Safety and passed by the Convention on 23 August 1793. It declared that:

From this moment until that in which every enemy has been driven from the territory of the Republic, every Frenchman is permanently requisitioned for service with the armies. The young men shall fight: married men will manufacture weapons and transport stores: women shall make tents and nurse in the hospitals: children shall turn old linen into lint: the old men shall repair to the public squares to raise the courage of the warriors and preach the unity of the Republic and hatred against the kings.[10]

Military practice was dramatically altered, as the number of men directly involved escalated considerably. Some words of caution should be added. Achievement fell far short of aspiration. Legislative decrees do not easily transform mass sentiments. Monarchists did not become Jacobins; faithful Catholics did not become ardent secularists.

Napoleon Bonaparte put the new principle into practice in his imperial wars from 1803 to 1815, the sixth of the world wars. For twelve years, the emperor and his subjugated allies fought wars against the Revolution's major-power opponents. Once again, the conflict extended well beyond the European continent: to the West Indies, to Turkey, and to Egypt, with indirect effects in the United States and Canada (War of 1812), and in Latin America (the wars of independence). With a single stroke of the pen (and for a good deal of cash), Napoleon in 1803 sold much of a continent,

---

[10] Gunther E. Rothenberg, *The Art of Warfare in the Age of Napoleon* (Bloomington, Ind., 1980), p. 100.

the Louisiana Purchase, which gave the United States claim to lands from Louisiana to Alberta. Politics, strategy, and finances were all combined in a single operation.

The first six of these world wars depended on "executive decisions": A ruler (or rulers) initiated and others responded. The decision makers typically consulted within an immediate circle of advisors. Imperialism, or intercontinental outreach, was clearly involved (although it differed in character from the later efforts). The causal factors that appeared in the course of the nineteenth century – nationalism, militarism, newspapers, public opinion, and insurgent "masses" – are notably muted in discussions of the causes of the first six of these world wars.

## The Men of 1914

Of the eight wars, World War I poses the most serious challenges with regard to explanation. The heir presumptive to the Austro-Hungarian throne was assassinated on 28 June 1914. The Austrian government alleged official Serb involvement, issued an ultimatum, and, rejecting negotiation, began hostilities with a bombardment of Belgrade. In a linked series of decisions, four other major powers – Russia, Germany, France, and Britain – joined the struggle. In all instances, the decision makers recognized the hazards involved. They knew their choices could enlarge the conflict and significantly escalate the dimensions of the struggle. A key notion, as one German participant, Kurt Riezler, put it, was that "[w]ars would no longer be fought but calculated." The assumption underlying this "calculated risk" was that one power could enter the conflict without motivating the next power to make the same choice. Bluff, or offensive diplomacy, could be played, forcing other possible participants to desist just short of a major war.[11] Ultimately, however, twenty-nine nations would be involved.[12]

The notion of the "calculated risk" requires further comment. It evokes an image of calm, reasoned deliberation, effectively a scientific judgment.

---

[11] Andreas Hillgruber, "Riezlers Theorie des kalkulierten Risikos und Bethmann Hollwegs politische Konzeption in der Julikrise 1914," *Historische Zeitschrift* 202 (1966): 333–51. See also Chapter 5.

[12] This count is based on a listing of declarations of war contained in Ian V. Hogg, *Historical Dictionary of World War I* (Lanham, Md., 1998), pp. 57–8. Our total indicates participants rather than declarations (thus eliminating double counts). Most accounts, understandably, are selective, passing over the declarations by, among others, San Marino, Siam, Liberia, Guatemala, Nicaragua, Costa Rica, Haiti, and Honduras.

But in fact, the decision makers in the major European capitals were beset by doubts, fears, emotions, even panic as they considered their various choices and reached their decisions for war. Chaos and confusion, rather than reason and rationality, reigned. All of Carl von Clausewitz's "irrational" factors came into play: interaction, escalation, friction, chance, and the proverbial "fog of war." The German chancellor, Theobald von Bethmann Hollweg, perhaps was closest to the mindset of decision makers in July 1914 when he spoke of a "leap in the dark." The "calculated risk" proved more like playing *va banque* against the house dealer at Monte Carlo.

To understand the origins of this war, we must know who was involved in the decision making. Specifically, we need to know who were the leaders of the five major European powers. In each case we are dealing with a coterie of some six, eight, or ten individuals. The coterie, in most cases, consisted of the monarch, a prime minister, a foreign minister, a war minister, an army chief of staff, and possibly a finance minister. Several other persons appeared in ancillary roles, in most cases as ambassadors to the other major powers.

And we need to know the grounds for their decisions. What factors led them to make the choices they did? How did the decision makers see the events of the immediately preceding years and those of July 1914? How did they define their nations' interests? What logic or rationale led them to their decisions?

The decision making is best seen as involving "small group dynamics" as opposed to the notion of hierarchy and authority. The British monarch, George V, took no significant part in the discussions. Emperor Franz Joseph had only a peripheral role (although the final decision was his). In those two instances, the British Foreign Secretary Sir Edward Grey and the Austro-Hungarian Chief of Staff Franz Conrad von Hötzendorf, determined "subordinates," led the other participants to the ultimate decisions. In all cases, it was the combination of "information" (of perception, fact, logic, and rationale) and "group dynamics" that produced the result, the decision to become involved.

Most university-level history and social science courses reviewing the causes of the war focus on "big" events, processes, or structures. Most accounts of the war's origins begin with the alliance system and continue with discussions of nationalism, imperialism, and militarism. All of these factors are "big" and all are routinely assumed to have had powerful impacts. They are, accordingly, treated as appropriate or acceptable causes. Accounts focused on individuals – on Emperor Franz Joseph,

Kaiser Wilhelm II, or Tsar Nicholas II; on their outlooks, whims, and fancies; and on their closest advisors – are viewed as "small." The peculiar traits of an individual or the chance presence of a given person, in short, are treated as somehow unacceptable.

The big-cause preference was anticipated by Alexis de Tocqueville in his most famous work. "Historians who write in aristocratic ages," he wrote, "are inclined to refer all occurrences to the particular will and character of certain individuals: and they are apt to attribute the most important revolutions to slight accidents. They trace out the smallest causes with sagacity, and frequently leave the greatest unperceived." Historians writing "in democratic ages exhibit precisely opposite characteristics. Most of them attribute hardly any influence to the individual over the destiny of the race, or to citizens over the fate of the people: but, on the other hand, they assign great general causes to all petty incidents."[13]

Tocqueville did not analyze modern societies in either/or terms, either general or particular causes or, to use current terms, either structure or contingency. "For myself," he wrote, "I am of the opinion that, at all times, one great portion of the events of this world are attributable to very general facts and another to special influences. These two kinds of cause are always in operation: only their proportion varies." As may be seen in any of Tocqueville's writings, his main concern was to sort things out, to generalize where it was appropriate, and, where it was not, to particularize. The obvious imperative is that one should be guided by evidence, by the "facts of the case." This is also our position.

The above discussion may be summarized with four generalizations.

First: World War I resulted from the decisions taken by the leaders of five nations, those referred to as the great powers: Austria-Hungary, Germany, Russia, France, and Britain.

Second: In those nations the decision to go to war was made by a small number of men, basically by coteries of five, eight, or ten persons. A considerable element of chance or contingency was involved in each of the decisions. Three of those nations were authoritarian regimes, and, accordingly, their decision making is best viewed, in Tocqueville's terms, as resulting from "the particular will and character of certain individuals." France and Britain, with parliamentary regimes, had somewhat

---

[13] Alexis de Tocqueville, *Democracy in America*, 2 vols. (New York, 1963), vol. 2, pp. 85–8. This brief chapter is entitled "Some Characteristics of Historians in Democratic Times." The bias in favor of "general causes" is found, with even greater insistence, in the social sciences.

more complicated procedures, but even there the decisions rested with very small numbers of individuals.

Third: Explanations for the war's origins must center on the considerations that moved the members of those five groups of decision makers. One must delineate the information, perceptions, and motives involved in each case. The key question: What were the concerns that moved those groups? Put differently, what were their agendas? If the review of motivations reveals a common tendency – that the five coteries were moved by nationalism, imperialism, and militarism – then a general conclusion, a focus on those big causes, might be warranted. If the agendas differed, then some other explanatory strategy is appropriate.

The drive for generalization is often defended in terms of intellectual economy, with reference to William of Ockham's "razor," that is, his caution against unnecessary complication. The aim, it is said, should be simplification, the discovery of a small number of powerful general statements. But another central aim of scientific presentations is accuracy. If economy brings distortion or, worse, misinformation, it must be avoided. If the causal process is complicated – for example, if the five major powers had separate and distinct agendas – then a more complicated formulation is necessary.

The fourth generalization is concerned with constitutional arrangements: All countries have procedures, formal and informal, that specify who will participate in the decisions to go to war. A curious gap appears in many narrative histories: The question of war powers is rarely addressed.[14] How did it happen that a given set of, say, seven individuals made "the decision"? A few others may have played ancillary roles, but everyone else (persons, groups, or elites) in the nation was "out of it." The procedures specifying the war powers provide the cast of decision makers. They stipulate which individuals (or office holders) will be present. And each of those arrangements, in turn, would have an impact on the agenda brought to bear on the decision. A narrowly based coterie consisting of the monarch, his chosen political leaders,

---

[14] Most narrative histories bypass this important question, proceeding to report the actions of various individuals without asking, "Why them?" Comparative government textbooks rarely discuss war powers. The same holds for international relations textbooks. Apart from the work of a small band of specialists, sociology is indifferent to the entire subject of war and the military. Perhaps most surprisingly, many historians view the subject with disdain, some with evident hostility. On the latter point, see John A. Lynn, "The Embattled Future of Academic Military History," *Journal of Military History* 61 (1997): 777–89.

and the heads of the military might readily agree on a given agenda. Other elites – bankers, industrialists, press lords, clergy, or intellectuals – might have different concerns and, if present, might favor quite different options.

It is easy, especially for Americans, to think in terms of written constitutions with fixed jurisdictions and specifications of powers. Four of the five major powers did have written constitutions, but their importance should be neither assumed nor exaggerated. Russia had a constitution after the 1905 revolution, but the tsar announced he would pay it little attention.[15] The actual arrangements in those nations were loose, informal, and easily altered depending on ad hoc needs or personal fancy. A determined ruler could at will bring others into the decision making. A lazy monarch could, by either plan or indifference, delegate power. An aggressive and/or astute minister could significantly enhance his power or, at minimum, could cajole an easily influenced ruler.

Many present-day accounts of late nineteenth- and early twentieth-century history have been written in terms of newly enfranchised masses, the advance of responsible government, and an insistent loss of old regime privileges. But the image of irrepressible movement is misleading. The constitutions were not as "progressive" as one might think.[16] And the authoritarian regimes showed unexpected capacities to resist the "advance of democracy" and, in some instances, to reverse the movement.[17]

Among the powers that remained, unambiguously, in the hands of old-regime elites in Austria-Hungary, Germany, and Russia was the power to declare war. The German constitution specified that the powers "to declare war and to conclude peace" rested solely with the kaiser. His decision for war required the approval of the Federal Council, or Bundesrath, the Upper House of the legislature. In republican France, the

---

[15] Dominic Lieven, *Nicholas II: Emperor of all the Russias* (London, 1993), p. 152.

[16] The Russian constitution of 1906 is routinely viewed as a "step ahead," as an important progressive achievement. The text, however, tells a different story: "Article 4. To the All-Russian Emperor belongs the Supreme Autocratic Power. To obey his power, not only through fear, but also for the sake of conscience, is commanded by God Himself"; "Article 9. Our Sovereign the Emperor shall sanction the laws and without his sanction no law may go into effect"; "Article 12. Our Sovereign the Emperor shall be the supreme leader of all external relations of the Russian State with foreign powers ..."; "Article 13. Our Sovereign the Emperor shall declare war and conclude peace as well as treaties with foreign states." From Albert P. Blaustein and Jay A. Sigler, eds., *Constitutions That Made History* (New York, 1988), p. 259.

[17] See Arno Mayer, *The Persistence of the Old Regime: Europe to the Great War* (New York, 1981).

decision makers, officially, were the premier, the cabinet, and the Chamber of Deputies. In fact, however, the decision was largely the work of the president and the premier. Britain was a constitutional monarchy with cabinet government. Formally, the prime minister and the cabinet, some fifteen or twenty of his appointees, had "the power." The decision for war required a majority vote in cabinet, and a tiny minority led by Edward Grey, the foreign secretary, generated that majority and brought about the final decision. The American constitution stipulates that "Congress shall have the Power ... to declare War." However, the decision in 1917 was largely the work of one man, Woodrow Wilson.

Another constitutional factor deserves some consideration. Over the long term, the "power of the purse" came to be vested with a representative legislature. In Germany, for example, the Reichstag had the authority to say "no" to the war budget. It is one of the great "what ifs" of history: What if a majority had voted "no" on 4 August? But that did not happen, a problem that deserves some attention. The issue comes up regularly in leftist historiography, the Socialist parties, presumably, being the most likely nay-sayers.[18]

One important implication follows from our guiding assumptions. A decision for war made by individuals, by a small coterie, means that contingency is very likely. Misinformation, weak nerves, ego strength, misjudgment of intentions, misjudgment of consequences, and difficulties in timing are inherent in the process. Put differently, diverse choices are easy to imagine.

Arguments focused on the "big" causes, on the so-called structural factors, assume highly determined processes. Those "ineluctable" forces would yield a given outcome regardless of the character or concerns of the decision makers. Nationalism, for example, would be an irresistible force. Its "power" would be felt by any and all decision makers. But the choice of interpretative options, whether coterie and contingency or powerful

---

[18] None of the 78 Socialist deputies voted against war credits on 4 August (although 14 had indicated opposition in the prior caucus). See Richard N. Hunt, *German Social Democracy 1918–1933* (New Haven, 1964), p. 22. The Prussian police had carefully investigated the party, checking for likely Socialist initiatives, but eventually shelved plans to arrest the party's leaders. See Dieter Groh, *Negative Integration und revolutionärer Attentismus: Die deutsche Sozialdemokratie am Vorabend des Ersten Weltkrieges* (Frankfurt, Berlin, and Vienna, 1973). For comparable investigations in France, see Jean-Jacques Becker, *Le Carnet B: Les Pouvoirs publics et l'antimilitarisme avant la guerre de 1914* (Paris, 1973). See also Georges Haupt, *Socialism and the Great War: The Collapse of the Second International* (Oxford, 1972), ch. 9; and James Joll, *The Second International 1889–1914*, rev. ed. (London, 1974), ch. 7.

compelling structures, should not depend on a priori stipulation. Both logic and evidence should be central to the decision.

## The "Big" Causes

One of the earliest works dealing with the origins of the war, the compendious revisionist history, *The Origins of the World War*, by Sidney Bradshaw Fay (1928), begins with a chapter on the "Immediate and Underlying Causes."[19] Fay discusses the early readings on the subject, reviews and comments on recently published documents, and finally considers the underlying causes. He reviews five of these: the system of secret alliances, militarism, nationalism, economic imperialism, and the newspaper press. Four of those causes appear routinely in present-day histories, but the argument of newspaper agitation has largely disappeared.[20] Many accounts add another cause, social Darwinism, to the basic list. And some authors offer still another, the argument of "domestic sources." This holds that the powers, some or all of them, chose war to head off or to quell internal dissent. Another option, one that appeared immediately after the war's end, is the argument of a "slide." The Great War, it is argued, was an accident; it was neither intended nor foreseen by any of the decision makers. This argument, clearly, differs significantly from the others on our list.

Some initial comment on Fay's and subsequent "causes" is appropriate. We first discuss the alliance-systems argument, and then consider the others in the following sequence: nationalism, social Darwinism, imperialism, militarism, the newspaper press, domestic sources, and the argument of a "slide." Some authors understandably offer a ninth possibility, that of multiple causation, or combinations of the above. Social Darwinism, for example, stimulated imperialism, which in turn justified the expansion of armies and navies.

[19] Sidney Bradshaw Fay, *The Origins of the World War*, 2 vols. (New York, 1930). This is the second, revised edition, later reprinted by the Free Press–Macmillan in 1966. The first volume provides a detailed history of the alliances. The other factors are considered but without the same system and detail. On Fay's importance in the historiography of the war, see Holger H. Herwig, "Clio Deceived: Patriotic Self-Censorship in Germany After the Great War," *International Security* 12 (1987): 5–44; and John W. Langdon, *July 1914: The Long Debate, 1918–1990* (New York, 1991), ch. 2.
[20] See, e.g., Richard Goff, Walter Moss, Janice Terry, and Jiu-Hwa Upshur, eds., *The Twentieth Century: A Brief Global History*, 4th ed. (New York, 1994), pp. 102–10. Their discussion begins with the Sarajevo assassination, then proceeds to the "combustible atmosphere" that led to the "all-consuming fire." They review four background factors: nationalism, imperialism, militarism, and the alliance system.

The "alliance system" refers to the network of mutual obligations, a set of treaties that presumably determined the August 1914 choices. As of 1907, Europe was divided between two power blocs: the Triple Alliance of Germany, Austria-Hungary, and Italy and the *entente cordiale* of France, Russia, and Great Britain. Some readings, following the 1920s revisionism, talk of the binding character of those obligations. Some, the more relaxed formulations, talk only of their constraining character. Again, some differentiation is needed.

A brief analysis of the various alliances is necessary either to validate or to deny the deterministic character (or power) of this argument. First, the "purely defensive Agreement" between Austria-Hungary and Germany of 7 October 1879 pledged the two contracting parties to "come to the assistance one of the other with the whole war strength of their Empire" in case "one of the two Empires be attacked by Russia." In case one of the contracting parties was attacked by "another Power," the other "binds itself not only not to support the aggressor," but also "to observe at least a benevolent neutral attitude towards its fellow Contracting Party."[21] Since there was no Serbian attack on Austria-Hungary in June–July 1914, Germany was not contractually bound under the Dual Alliance of 1879 to issue the famous "blank check" to Austria-Hungary on 5 July.

In May 1882, Berlin and Vienna extended their alliance to include Italy. The Triple Alliance bound all three states to observe "a benevolent neutrality" in case one was threatened by a "Great Power nonsignatory to the present Treaty." In case France attacked Italy, Austria-Hungary and Germany promised "to lend help and assistance with all their forces"; in case France attacked Germany, "this same obligation shall devolve upon Italy." Article III of the treaty stated that if one or two of the "High Contracting Parties" were attacked and engaged in a war "with two or more Great Powers nonsignatory to the present Treaty, the *casus foederis* will arise simultaneously for all the High Contracting Parties."[22] Thus, in 1914 France and Russia would have had to attack Austria-Hungary and Germany for the *casus foederis* (literally, a case within the stipulations of the treaty) to have applied for Italy. The Triple Alliance was renegotiated in 1887, 1891, 1902, and 1912.

---

[21] From Alfred Franzis Pribram, ed., *The Secret Treaties of Austria-Hungary 1879–1914*, 2 vols. (New York, 1967), vol. 1, pp. 25–31. The treaty was renewed in March 1883 and then became part of the Triple Alliance.

[22] Ibid., pp. 65–9.

In October 1883, Austria-Hungary signed an alliance with Romania. The "High Contracting Powers" agreed not to enter into an alliance "directed against any one of the States"; more specifically, Austria-Hungary promised "help and assistance" against any aggressor that threatened Romania.[23] Germany acceded to the treaty later that same year; Italy in May 1888. The Romanian extension of the Triple Alliance was renegotiated in 1892, 1896, 1902, and 1913. In 1914, Romania was attacked by no "aggressor" and hence there was no cause to invoke the 1883 treaty.

Many historians have focused on Austria-Hungary's annexation of Bosnia-Herzegovina in 1908 as a key step on the road to war in 1914. Under Article 25 of the Treaty of Berlin, 13 July 1878, the two Turkish provinces were to be "occupied and administered by Austria-Hungary," but to remain officially Ottoman. But that changed, in June 1881, when Austria-Hungary, Germany, and Russia agreed under the terms of the Three Emperors' League that Vienna "reserves the right to annex [Bosnia and Herzegovina] at whatever moment she shall deem opportune."[24] While the Three Emperors' League eventually lapsed, in May 1897 Austria-Hungary and Russia signed an agreement whereby St. Petersburg accepted Vienna's right, "when the moment arrives," to "substitute" for the present status of occupation and garrisoning of Bosnia-Herzegovina "that of annexation."[25] Then, in October 1904, Austria-Hungary and Russia negotiated a "Promise of Mutual Neutrality." Both signatories agreed to "persevere" in their "conservative policy to be followed in the Balkan countries." In case one of the "two Powers" found itself in a war with a "third Power," that is, with a non-Balkan power, the other would "observe a loyal and absolute neutrality."[26]

In 1908, Alois Lexa von Aehrenthal, Austria-Hungary's foreign minister, proceeded with the annexation, but only after first securing the agreement of his Russian counterpart, Alexander Izvolskii. Subsequently, however, other members of the Russian government, shocked at what they saw as a betrayal of the Serbs and the Slav cause, and thus of Russian public opinion and prestige, forced its repudiation. Izvolskii then denied any agreement, and Austria-Hungary, understandably, threatened to expose the lie. In this case, annexation was "authorized" by the prior secret

[23] Ibid., pp. 79–83.
[24] Ralph R. Menning, ed., *The Art of the Possible: Documents on Great Power Diplomacy, 1814–1914* (New York, 1996), p. 201.
[25] Pribram, ed., *The Secret Treaties*, vol. 2, pp. 185–95.
[26] Ibid., pp. 237–9.

treaty. But for Russia the practical realities of the moment – rather than any hard treaty calculus – effectively nullified that "understanding." Finally, the murder at Sarajevo on 28 June 1914 demanded absolutely nothing of (and certainly constituted no *casus foederis* for) the signatories of the treaties discussed above: Austria-Hungary, Germany, Italy, Romania, and, by special extension, Russia.

With regard to the Allies, their several "alliances" were of disparate character. The Military Convention between France and Russia of August 1892 – cemented by the Franco-Russian Alliance of January 1894 – was a firm pledge of support. Russia promised to attack Germany if France were attacked by Germany "or by Italy supported by Germany"; France, for her part, promised to attack Germany if Russia were attacked by Germany "or by Austria supported by Germany." In case one or all of the powers of the Triple Alliance mobilized, France and Russia "without the necessity of any previous concert" would also mobilize. France promised to put 1.3 million and Russia 700,000 or 800,000 men into the field at once.[27]

Great Britain abandoned its policy of "splendid isolation" in January 1902 by concluding an agreement with Japan, whereby both powers, should they become involved in a war with another power, pledged to "maintain a strict neutrality." Furthermore, the two states promised to come to the "assistance" of one another in case "any other Power or Powers should join in hostilities against that ally."[28]

Beyond that, Britain had no binding alliance commitments. The links to France and to Russia established in 1904 and 1907 had a limited focus. In fact, they were rather imprecise, a series of bilateral agreements eventually called the *entente cordiale*. In April 1904, Britain and France buried long-standing colonial rivalries in a convention whereby France agreed to cooperate with the British occupation of Egypt while Britain agreed to support France in Morocco. Article 9 stated that London and Paris would "agree to afford one another their diplomatic support."[29] It was, as the name indicates, an "understanding" as opposed to a firm commitment. In August 1907, Great Britain signed a convention with Russia relating to Persia, Afghanistan, and Tibet. The two powers agreed

---

[27] Michael Hurst, ed., *Key Treaties for the Great Powers 1814–1914*, 2 vols. (Newton Abbot, U.K., 1972), vol. 2, pp. 668–9; and Menning, ed., *The Art of the Possible*, p. 247.
[28] Hurst, ed., *Key Treaties*, vol. 2, pp. 726–7.
[29] Convention of 8 April 1904. *British and Foreign State Papers*, 170 vols. (London, 1841–1968), vol. 99, p. 229.

to divide Persia into Russian, British, and "neutral" zones. But the convention's real importance lay in two areas: first, in the fact that London and St. Petersburg decided "to settle by mutual agreement" their often conflicting claims "on the Continent of Asia"[30] and, second, that the two clearly intended to exclude Germany from Persia and Central Asia and to limit its penetration of the Middle East. The convention did not include a single word about military matters, nor did it use the word "alliance" to describe the new Anglo-Russian relationship.

As of 1 August 1914, neither France nor Russia had attacked either Austria-Hungary or Germany. But at that point, Germany declared war on Russia, the first such move by a major power, that being followed by a second declaration, on 3 August, against France. Berlin was treating the French and Russian mobilizations as equivalent to an attack. The "without direct provocation" clause also leaves room for interpretation. Pointing to Austria-Hungary's forceful behavior with regard to Serbia, Italy "opted out," that is, chose not to join with her alliance partners.[31] Italy's leaders then solicited and received offers from both sides and ultimately entered the war on the side of the *entente*.

Russia was not obliged by any alliance to come to the aid of Serbia. The Russian response had no "contractual" basis. The Franco-Russian alliance of 1892–94, as previously shown, did have a binding character: Both powers agreed to mobilize their forces in case those of the Triple Alliance, or of one of the Powers composing it, mobilized. Quite apart from "the letter" of the agreement, the leaders of the two nations were generally disposed to accept those terms. But even in this relationship, there were sources of concern and anxiety. Each needed the other, but it was a relationship filled with unsettling moments. Would the partner honor the commitment? Or would fear and anxiety obviate formal contractual agreements? When Britain and France signed their *entente* in 1904, for example, St. Petersburg feared this accommodation might prompt Paris to renege on its treaty obligation in the case of a Russian clash with Britain. In the wake of the Russo-Japanese War, there was deep-seated fear in Petersburg whether the French might reassess the value of the alliance in the wake of Russia's humiliating defeat. Thus, during joint staff talks held at Paris in April 1906, the tsar's General Staff "consistently" but

---

[30] Convention of 31 August 1907, in Hurst, ed., *Key Treaties*, vol. 2, pp. 805–9.

[31] Italy's leaders based their decision, in part, on the provocation clause. The alliance also required that the partners be given information prior to any aggressive action. But Italy was not told beforehand of the ultimatum to Serbia. For more detail, see Chapter 11.

"fraudulently" reassured their French counterparts that the war and the resulting revolution had not reduced Russia's defense capabilities.[32]

Finally, one of the most famous of all the various treaties also deserves mention. Austria, Britain, France, Prussia, and Russia in April 1839 had agreed to respect and defend recently created Belgium as "an Independent and perpetually Neutral State."[33] For a decade prior to 1914, however, Germany's key strategic plan involved the violation of that neutrality, a plan that was ultimately implemented. France's strategic planning at various points also involved an incursion into Belgium. In the days just before the German invasion, leaders in Berlin made two attempts at negotiation, offering to reward Belgium and Britain in some way if the passage of German troops through Belgium were permitted. Both offers were refused. Germany's leaders were surprised at the lack of "realism" in those responses.[34]

At a key cabinet meeting in late July 1914, British Foreign Secretary Grey presented an array of documents intended to generate support for intervention. One item presented, probably unintended, was an excerpt from a William Gladstone speech from 1870 in which the then prime minister declared that he was

> not able to subscribe to the doctrine ... that the simple fact of the existence of a guarantee is binding on every party to it irrespectively altogether of the particular position in which it may find itself at the time when the occasion for acting on the guarantee arises. The great authorities upon foreign policy to whom I have been accustomed to listen – such as Lord Aberdeen and Lord Palmerston – never, to my knowledge, took that rigid and, if I may say so, that impracticable view of a guarantee.[35]

An even more telling comment on the merit of treaties was made by Italy's king, Vittorio Emmanuele III. Angered by Austria-Hungary's takeover of Bosnia-Herzegovina in 1908, he told the American ambassador, commenting on the Triple Alliance: "I am more than ever convinced of the utter worthlessness of treaties or any agreements written on paper. They are worth the value of the paper. The only real strength lies in

---

[32] Fuller, *Strategy and Power*, pp. 414–15.

[33] Menning, ed., *The Art of the Possible*, p. 43.

[34] See V. R. Berghahn, *Germany and the Approach of War in 1914* (Basingstoke and London, 1993), pp. 218–19.

[35] Quoted in Keith Wilson, ed., *Decisions for War, 1914* (New York, 1994), ch. 7 (by Wilson), "Britain," p. 189.

bayonets and cannon."[36] For both men, clearly, the immediate context and resulting interests counted for more than the obligations of any treaty.

One further observation with respect to the treaties is needed. Most postwar accounts provide what might be described as "open-book" narratives. But many of the treaties were secret or, more precisely, were intended to be secret. The analysis of the August 1914 decisions therefore must also ask the following questions: How much was known? And how accurate was that knowledge?

The next four causes – nationalism, social Darwinism, imperialism, and militarism – all supposedly have cultural roots. All four demands begin with attitudes or preferences said to be widely held among "the masses." In that respect, then, they may be subjected to some common lines of criticism. Each of these causes should be considered at three "levels": those of mass belief, the advocacy groups, and the decision makers' responses.

The key problem with respect to the mass outlooks is their indeterminacy. Many assertions put forth with respect to these factors appear in what might be termed the "declarationist" mode, that is, unsupported statements of frequency and weight or importance. The problem is that with no serious public opinion surveys prior to the mid-twentieth century, we have no satisfactory indication of the prevalence, intensity, or import of any "mass" attitude. It is easy to declare that "fervent nationalist" views were held by some tens of millions. But given the lack of serious evidence, the appropriate response to such judgments is another declaration, an unambiguous "don't know." Unsupported declarations of frequency and intensity, especially if widely shared, hide ignorance. Worse, still, they discourage thought and investigation.[37]

---

[36] William A. Renzi, "Italy's Neutrality and Entrance into the Great War: A Reexamination," *American Historical Review* 73 (1968): 1414.

[37] Although obviously problematic, the single-minded advocacy of favored theses is a persistent problem in the academic world. As a corrective, see the important article by T. C. Chamberlin, "The Method of Multiple Working Hypotheses," *Science* 148 (1965): 754–9.

When faced with apodictic declarations of frequency, one useful response is to consider alternative substantive possibilities. As opposed to the implicit 70 to 80 percent claims (the portion of ardent nationalists), one might suggest (or declare) 2 or at best 4 percent and invite presentation of contrary evidence. A similar problem appears with regard to divisions of opinion, a frequent assumption being sharp opposition with high levels of commitment on both sides – all persons either pro or con. Contemporary public opinion polls routinely find large numbers of other choices – "don't know" or "no answer." Another familiar possibility is "none of the above." In *Romeo and Juliet*, Mercutio's last comment on the contention in Padua was "a plague 'o both your houses."

We have better evidence with respect to the supportive associations – the advocacy groups – although even here the quantity is limited and the quality often questionable. We can often find data on total membership of such organizations. But rarely do we find indications of intensity, of how many of the members were active, how many inactive, how many lapsed. We rarely find a time series showing membership trends over the course of key decades. Associations, with rare exceptions, inflate the membership figures and exaggerate their influence.[38]

Another frequent problem appears in this connection: partial or one-sided presentations. Information on nationalist sentiments and organizations is reported at length, but no equivalent account of internationalist tendencies is provided. The same holds with respect to the militarism-pacifism pair. Social Darwinism was widespread, to be sure, but opposition to those views was probably also widespread, especially in the major religious bodies.

In contrast to our knowledge of "mass sentiment" and of the organizations, our knowledge of the decision-making coteries is extensive. But here too one finds a serious gap. Were the members of the coteries responding to the demands of the masses? Or to the demands of organizations representing them? Or were they fending off mass demands? Or – another possibility – were they simply indifferent to such importunities? The German kaiser, very upset by the July Crisis, referred to the coming struggle as one between "Teutons and Slavs." Was he simply mouthing a common cliché? Or was he moved by social Darwinist beliefs when he made the key decision for war? Or was his decision based on some strategic concerns, on Germany's place within Europe? The basic problem here is the failure to specify the connections: How did the alleged cause, those "mass" sentiments, affect the decision makers in July 1914?

Nationalism, the second of the causes reviewed here, appears in all countries of Europe, and those sentiments clearly gained importance in the course of the nineteenth century.[39] Textbooks routinely cite two principal

---

[38] Most accounts stressing the size or impact of a given belief do not provide even the most rudimentary estimates of strength – membership as percentage of the eligible population, of all adults, or, if routinely gendered, of all adult males. For further discussion and evidence on these questions, see Richard F. Hamilton, *Mass Society, Pluralism, and Bureaucracy: Explication, Assessment, and Commentary* (Westport, Conn., 2001), ch. 2.

[39] For an amazing assemblage of relevant quotations on this theme, see L. L. Farrar, Jr., "Villain of the Peace: Nationalism and the Causes of World War I," *Canadian Review of Studies in Nationalism* 22 (1995): 53–66. Roughly 400 sources are cited. As presented, however, those quotations "stand alone," i.e., without any indication of evidence in their support, e.g., that in Germany "the tide of patriotism engulfed the whole country."

sources for this development: the extension of compulsory education and, apart from Britain, the requirement of universal military service. Those "broad brush" depictions, however, are best seen as plausible but untested hypotheses.

Basic literacy increased considerably in the course of the previous century, a fact often cited as a source of the "new" nationalism. Teachers and textbooks did probably help to create a national sense, imposing a common language (as opposed to local or regional dialects) and giving some sense of a larger shared heritage. For France, Eugen Weber has suggested that schools were very effective at creating "cultural homogeneity" by the turn of the century and instilling patriotic sentiments in their pupils. But even Weber concedes that no broad survey of "national consciousness and patriotism" was ever undertaken in the nineteenth century, and that hence he is working with "rather thin evidence."[40]

One should consider some additional questions. How many of those schooled in the early '90s would have been enthusiastic supporters of a national cause in 1914? How many would have given primacy to "the national interest," putting it ahead of the lives, health, and well-being of their immediate families? How many would have been indifferent – or opposed – to involvement in those distant locations, in Bosnia, Serbia, Alsace, or East Prussia? In July 1913, France passed a law increasing the period of military service from two to three years. Weber thinks that majority opinion in France was opposed to the change. The subsequent issue, paying the costs, brought strenuous opposition, the theme, in elections fought out in the spring of 1914, being "no new taxes."[41]

Some accounts focus on nationalistic social movements and pressure groups, Pan-Germans and Pan-Slavs receiving much of this attention. One might consider an alternative hypothesis: For every member in Pan-Slav or Pan-German organizations, there were 100 nonorganized "localists," persons who would put family welfare above all else.[42] Again, even if

---

[40] Eugen Weber, *Peasants into Frenchmen: The Modernization of Rural France 1870–1914* (Stanford, 1976), pp. 99–104, 332–8. See also Weber's *The Nationalist Revival in France, 1905–1914* (Berkeley, 1968). The nationalism of 1905–14, he writes, "was a product of Paris. It never went much beyond, and, even in Paris, it remained a minority movement, trying to compensate in violence and vociferation for the paucity of its numbers" (p. 145).

[41] Weber, *Nationalist Revival*, chs. 11 and 12.

[42] For some sense of the complications involved, see Barbara Jelavich, *Russia's Balkan Entanglements, 1806–1914* (Cambridge, 1991), pp. 34, 93, 135, 157–8, 170, 208–10. Panslavism, a diverse and changing set of plans, she writes, had an influence on public opinion "among the educated sections of Russian society." Those ideas "did play a role in foreign policy in both a positive and negative direction" (p. 34). See also Roger

the numbers could be determined, one must still ask about the flows of influence: Were the decision makers responding to the organizations? Or were they moved by different, more immediate concerns? Again, information on the specific lines of influence and the possible effects is routinely omitted.

It is possible that military service helped generate nationalist outlooks. But an opposite hypothesis should also be considered, namely, that service in the military generated hostility, resentment, or disdain. Civilian careers were interrupted, the learning of job skills, apprenticeship, and on-the-job training were postponed. Marriage was delayed. For a couple of years, one had to suffer the daily importunities of officers and noncommissioned officers. Unfortunately, we have little serious evidence dealing with "mass" reactions to military experience.

We do have one unambiguous bit of "hard" evidence on this subject: No nation had universal military training. In the North German Confederation, Otto von Bismarck in an "iron" army law in 1867 put a limit of 1 percent (of the total population) on the numbers called up for service, a limit that was generally accepted, welcomed even, by Germany's military leaders.[43] Universal service would have brought in hundreds of thousands of working-class sons who, so the leaders thought, might be persons of questionable loyalty. In 1914, out of a potential of 10.4 million men between the service ages of twenty and forty-five, almost 5.4 million (52 percent) had not served, primarily because the state found it too expensive to train all of its eligible males. In August 1914, accordingly, there would have been much opportunity for volunteers, and thus such figures provide another measure of nationalist sentiments. The German press, on

---

Chickering, *We Men Who Feel Most German: A Cultural Study of the Pan-German League 1886–1914* (London, 1984). The founders thought the Pan-German League would be "a massive organization." Shortly after the turn of the century, however, "the number of members began to decline steadily after reaching a peak of a little over 23,000" (pp. 103–4). Most of the members were from the upper or upper middle class. Gustav Schmoller estimated that Germany's upper middle class contained 2.75 million families (p. 107). The Navy League, by far the largest of the patriotic societies, is said to have had "well over 300,000 members" in 1913 (p. 205). An obvious question is, Is that a credible number? The league's paper, *Die Flotte*, puts the number for 1914 at 331,493. Although presumably a powerful organization, naval appropriations had recently been cut and the funds shifted to the army. In 1914, the German Peace Society had but 10,000 members. *Die bürgerlichen Parteien in Deutschland: Handbuch der Geschichte der bürgerlichen Parteien und anderer bürgerlicher Interessenorganisationen vom Vormärz bis zum Jahre 1945*, 2 vols. (Berlin, 1968), vol. 1, pp. 364, 432.

43 Wiegand Schmidt-Richberg, "Die Regierungszeit Wilhelms II," *Handbuch zur deutschen Militärgeschichte 1648–1939*, 5 vols. (Munich, 1979), vol. 3, pp. 55–8.

11 August, stated that "over 1,300,000 men" had volunteered. But the actual numbers were considerably smaller. In Prussia, which contained roughly three-fifths of Germany's population, the number of volunteers as of that date was 260,672 (of which 143,922 were accepted).[44]

A third cause, one not included on Sidney Fay's list, is social Darwinism. Put simply, the "men of 1914" were smitten with the notion that Charles Darwin's theories of natural selection could be transferred to the development of human society. From Herbert Spencer in Britain to Ernst Hackel in Germany, from Ludwig Gumplowicz in Austria to Jakov A. Novikov in Russia, and from Georges Vacher de Lapouge in France to William Graham Sumner in the United States, the social Darwinists argued that life was a constant struggle to survive. Those most fit did survive, and the others perished. The history of nations and empires, as they saw it, was a constant pattern of "rise and fall." To stand still meant to decline – and to die.[45]

Central and critical to the social Darwinist debate were the glorification of war, the notion of its inevitability, and the concept that nations constituted distinct and separate "races." Men as diverse in their upbringing and education as Cecil Rhodes of Britain, Theodore Roosevelt of the United States, and Friedrich von Bernhardi of Germany all to varying degrees embraced Rudyard Kipling's notion, to "Take up the White Man's Burden." For some, God himself had created the trial of peoples, the test of war. Thus, the Great Moralist, Woodrow Wilson, could send troops to Mexico to uphold western civilization (and God). In Germany, Hunold von Ahlefeld, one of Admiral Alfred von Tirpitz's department chiefs, stated the position clearly in a private letter in 1898. "The struggle for life exists among individuals, provinces, parties and states. The latter wage it either by the use of arms or in the economic field – we cannot help this – ergo we wage it; those who don't want to, will perish."[46] In Britain, Nathaniel Barnaby in his *Naval Development of the Century* (1904) reminded his countrymen of the harsh connection between natural selection

[44] Jeffrey Verhey, *The Spirit of 1914: Militarism, Myth, and Mobilization in Germany* (Cambridge, 2000), p. 97.

[45] See Winfried Baumgart, *Imperialism: The Idea and Reality of British and French Colonial Expansion, 1880–1914* (Oxford, 1982), pp. 82–90; Paul Crook, *Darwinism, War and History: The Debate over the Biology of War from the "Origin of Species" to the First World War* (Cambridge, 1994); and Mike Hawkins, *Social Darwinism in European and American Thought, 1860–1945* (Cambridge, 1997).

[46] Cited in Volker R. Berghahn, *Sarajewo, 28. Juni 1914: Der Untergang des alten Europas* (Munich, 1997), p. 49.

and trial by war. "While injustice and unrighteousness exist in the world, the sword, the rifled breechloader and the torpedo boat become part of the world's evolutionary machinery."[47]

But again one must put the critical question: How did this "background factor" lead to the decisions of August 1914? What were the mechanisms linking the ideology and the decisions? Were the various coteries driven by that belief or were they moved by more immediate political concerns?

The imperialism argument, our fourth cause, also requires some additional consideration. A first observation: One must differentiate.[48] Britain had the world's largest empire. Russia, the second largest, also had immense holdings. France had a much smaller empire, one-tenth the size of Britain's. Germany had some modest holdings, most of them economic losers. Austria-Hungary had no off-continent empire and showed no serious interest in gaining one. The lessons are, first, that the five major powers would have had markedly different imperial agendas and, second, that any analysis focusing on impacts must specify the "interests" or "needs" sensed by the various groups of decision makers.

One can point to advocacy groups, to the Empire League and the German Kolonialverein. But, as with the other factors discussed here, one must again ask about weight, importance, and impact. As opposed to an insistent magnification bias, one should again consider an alternative hypothesis: 100 nonmembers for every one so engaged. Put differently, that would mean a hundred indifferent or opposed persons for every member wishing to see the nation's presence in Fashoda, South Africa, Southwest Africa, China, the Philippines, or Ethiopia.

Obviously, the decision makers of most of the powers (and those of some minor powers or aspirants) were driven by some imperialist concerns: Most of them wanted colonies. That "interest" often proved an astonishing mistake. The colonies, on the whole, were not profitable. The returns, typically, were limited, and the costs of policing, administration, and defense against other contenders were often enormous. This conclusion was argued in Britain by important liberals, by Jeremy Bentham, Richard Cobden, John Hobson, and many others. James Mill described the empire as "a vast system of outdoor relief for the upper classes."[49]

[47] Baumgart, *Imperialism*, p. 88.

[48] Richard F. Hamilton, *Marxism, Revisionism, and Leninism: Explication, Assessment, and Commentary* (Westport, Conn., 2000), ch. 4.

[49] A. P. Thornton, *The Imperial Idea and Its Enemies: A Study in British Power* (London, 1959); C. J. Lowe, *The Reluctant Imperialists: British Foreign Policy, 1878–1902* (New York, 1969); and Lance E. Davis and Robert A. Huttenback, *Mammon*

Again, Imperial Germany provides a convenient test. Its colonies never fulfilled their promise as the new El Dorado: The aggregate value of Berlin's commerce with its colonies between 1894 and 1913 remained less than what was spent on them. Kiaochow alone received more than 200 million Goldmark in subsidies. Of the Reich's total trade, a mere 0.5 percent was with its colonies. Only one in every thousand Germans leaving the homeland chose to go to the colonies (5,495 people by 1904).[50] Colonies, in short, were mainly a sign of German power and prestige.

But few appreciated the logic and evidence of colonial ventures, and the ruling coteries, with rare exception, continued their "forward movement." Russia's leaders were true believers, effectively agreeing with V. I. Lenin's later publication on the subject. At enormous cost, Russia pushed to the East, building the world's longest railway line (single track), developing Pacific ports, and, ultimately, taking over an important Chinese province, Manchuria. William C. Fuller summarizes the result as follows:

Russia had carelessly acquired a new Eastern empire but lacked the manpower and revenue to maintain it. Attempts to encourage Russian colonization in Manchuria were unsuccessful. [Sergei] Witte's expectations about the monetary gains Russia would realize from its special position there also proved illusory. Despite all the efforts that Petersburg made to make Manchuria a captive market for Russian goods, Russia still continued to run a huge trade deficit with China.... Nor did Manchuria prove to be conspicuously fertile soil for Russian industrial enterprise.... [Russia] failed utterly to integrate the population of Manchuria into its economy: since Russia had gotten involved in the provinces, only two Russian factories had been started there, and those were distilleries that produced liquor mainly for the Russian army of occupation.[51]

We are regularly invited to think about informed, rational, calculating elites. But opposite hypotheses are always useful; in this case, for example, that the decision-making coteries were uninformed or ignorant. One might also consider a social-psychological possibility, that some kind of "groupthink" was operating. The logic of imperialism seemed plausible; "everyone" was doing it. Bismarck, interestingly, was an exception to this rule, one not moved by such peer pressure. Recognizing the costs, he ended Germany's limited imperialist effort (while recommending it to

*and the Pursuit of Empire: The Political Economy of British Imperialism, 1860–1912* (Cambridge, 1986).

[50] Holger H. Herwig, *"Luxury" Fleet: The Imperial German Navy 1888–1918* (London and Atlantic Highlands, 1987), pp. 105–8.

[51] Fuller, *Strategy and Power*, p. 374.

others, e.g., to France).[52] Subsequently, Wilhelm II was an ardent advocate of *Weltpolitik*, calling for naval expansion and for overseas empire.

An important lesson about the causal dynamics appears in the Austro-
Hungarian experience. The interest there, in 1912–14, came largely
from political leaders, specifically, from Foreign Minister Count Leopold
Berchtold, who saw some opportunity in Anatolia. But his plans faced
a serious difficulty: "the almost complete lack of interest on the part of
commercial circles in the Monarchy." Those circles evidenced "absolutely
no pressure to found colonies – this had to be stirred up artificially by the
government." The Anatolian venture, F. R. Bridge states, "was based on
the old quest for prestige, or, rather, on that concern to avoid losing prestige which was to become a neurotic obsession in Vienna in the last years
of peace."[53]

The imperialism argument exploded anew in 1961 when, with specific
reference to the German context, the Hamburg historian Fritz Fischer published his provocative book *Griff nach der Weltmacht*, wherein he posited
that Germany in July 1914 had embarked on an explicit "grab for world
power."[54] The book shattered the calm of Germany's historical profession
because Fischer had reopened the wound of Imperial Germany's "guilt"
in starting World War 1. Coming on the heels of the ashes occasioned
by Germany's second "bid for world power" in 1939–45, Fischer's opus
outraged his colleagues and ushered in two decades of debate concerning
both the origins of the war in 1914 and the place of German imperialism
therein.

Fischer's argument was as brutal as it was simple. From 1890 on, he
argued, Germany had pursued world power. In its drive for colonies
and imperial trade, it had offended established powers such as Britain
and France, but also other upstarts such as Japan and the United States.
This course of *Weltpolitik* was deeply rooted within German economic,

[52] On Bismarck's brief and puzzling imperialist efforts, see Woodruff D. Smith, *The German Colonial Empire* (Chapel Hill, N.C., 1978); and John Lowe, *The Great Powers: Imperialism and the German Problem, 1965–1925* (London, 1994). For Bismarck's encouragement of French imperialism, see Allan Mitchell, *Bismarck and the French Nation 1848–1890* (New York, 1971), pp. 93–5; and Fritz Stern, *Gold and Iron: Bismarck, Bleichröder, and the Building of the German Empire* (New York, 1977), pp. 330–1.

[53] F. R. Bridge, "*Tarde venientibus ossa*: Austro-Hungarian Colonial Aspirations in Asia Minor 1913–1914," *Middle Eastern Studies* 6 (1970): 319–30, esp. pp. 322 and 319.

[54] Fritz Fischer, *Griff nach der Weltmacht: Die Kriegszielpolitik des kaiserlichen Deutschland 1914/18* (Düsseldorf, 1961). The third, revised edition was translated into English under the innocuous title, *Germany's Aims in the First World War* (New York, 1967).

political, military, and social structures. Both moderates and annexation-
ists, both civilian and military leaders, Fischer suggested, had steered a
course of aggressive imperialism under Wilhelm II. The German government's infamous 1914 "September program" of war aims – which ranged
from bases in both the Atlantic and the Pacific oceans to colonies in the Far
East and in Africa – was but the formal enunciation of desires and aims
present well before then. More, Fischer suggested that this "imperialism"
dominated Germany's wartime drive for expansion and refusal to mediate
that conflict, that it survived the Great War largely intact, and that it found
new vigor in the barbaric racial and settlement policies of the Third Reich
in the East. In other words, there existed continuity in the course and
shape of German imperialism from Wilhelm II to Adolf Hitler. Neither
the outbreak of World War I nor that of World World II were "industrial
accidents" (*Betriebsunfälle*), as some of Germany's more conservative historians had argued. In the wake of the Fischer debate, no historian could
ignore his emphasis on the centrality of imperialism among the causative
factors behind the decision for war in July–August 1914.[55] We return to
Fischer's "imperialism" argument in Chapter 5.

Militarism is the next factor on what might be termed the standard list
of causes.[56] The nations of Europe were engaged in a serious arms race,
escalating the size and capacity of their armed forces. This hypothesis
obviously has two aspects: one mass and one elite. The masses were mobilized perhaps by those nationalist or social Darwinist sentiments, perhaps by a xenophobic press. Some, as indicated, might have been moved
by direct experience, as members of the armed forces and, later, by their
involvement in the reserves. As for the elites, they made decisions with
respect to the arms outlays.

Discussions of militarism ordinarily begin with a review of the arms
race, of the competition between the powers in the years before 1914.
Many of those discussions come without benefit of numbers, such as
figures on army appropriations, the size of the military, and the capacity
of weapons. Again, the first point of critique is the need for differentiation.

[55] The ferocity of the "Fischer controversy" was first summarized by John A. Moses, *The War Aims of Imperial Germany: Professor Fritz Fischer and His Critics* (Queensland, 1968). Fischer's main critic was Gerhard Ritter, "Eine neue Kriegsschuldthese?," *Historische Zeitschrift* 194 (1962): 657–68. Ritter later devoted the entire third volume of his magisterial *The Sword and the Scepter: The Problem of Militarism in Germany*, 4 vols. (Coral Gables, 1969–72), to rebutting Fischer.
[56] For a review of views on the subject, see Volker R. Berghahn, *Militarism: The History of an International Debate 1861–1979* (Leamington Spa, U.K., 1981).

The five powers were doing different things. Germany was the most zealous in its effort, first with naval expansion, then, between 1911 and 1913, with a shift to the army. In 1913, it spent £118 million on defense, while Britain spent £76 million. One of the powers, Austria-Hungary, made no serious increase in the decades before 1914. Russian army effectives actually declined slightly between 1911 and 1913. Between 1910 and 1913, France increased its army expenditures by 7.6 percent, Russia by 21 percent, and Germany by 105 percent.[57] The "broad brush" depiction suggests a commonality of response, as if to say "they were all doing it." But obviously there was a striking diversity in their efforts.

All of the great powers faced important constraints on their ability to finance naval and military expansion, and none more so than Austria-Hungary. In terms of per-capita expenditures on the defense budget of 1906 in Austrian Kronen, for example, Britain spent 36, France 24, Germany 22, Italy 12, Russia 10, and Austria-Hungary 10. As late as 1903, Habsburg subjects spent as much on tobacco and more on beer and wine than on defense. Hungarian bureaucrats, ever wary of Habsburg military power, constantly denied Kaiser Franz Joseph the requisite funds to modernize his armed forces. And in the Austrian half of the Dual Monarchy, bitter ethnic debate forced Premier Count Karl Stürgkh to prorogue parliament (Reichsrat) just before the war. As a result, the Dual Monarchy each year trained only between 22 and 29 percent of draft-eligible males (compared with 40 percent in Germany and 86 percent in France). In 1914, only one in four of the 1.8 million men available for service in Austria-Hungary had ever been on active duty.[58] The undifferentiated portraits of "the arms race" fail to note the obvious significance of these important considerations. The powers faced markedly different financial and political restraints. Insufficient attention, moreover, is paid to the opposite camp, to the Socialists, the liberal internationalists, the

---

[57] David G. Herrmann, *The Arming of Europe and the Making of the First World War* (Princeton, 1996), pp. 234, 237. The aggregates can be misleading. Two Russian alliances relieved pressures, allowing a regrouping of forces. The Anglo-Russian *entente* of 1907 provided an "amiable settlement" of the central Asia colonial conflicts. One signed with Japan "defined the interests of the two powers in Mongolia and Manchuria." See Fuller, *Strategy and Power*, pp. 416–17. Defense spending in 1913 from David Stevenson, *Armaments and the Coming of War: Europe, 1904–1914* (Oxford, 1996), p. 4.

[58] Holger H. Herwig, *The First World War: Germany and Austria-Hungary 1914–1918* (London, 1997), pp. 12–14. On military service and its possible impacts, see M. R. D. Foot, *Men in Uniform: Military Manpower in Modern Industrial Societies* (New York, 1961); and Margaret Levi, *Consent, Dissent, and Patriotism* (Cambridge, 1997).

anti-imperialists, and pacifists, those who argued that war was no longer an option by 1914.[59]

Some dissent was registered also in circles where one might have anticipated support for both arms outlays and their use. In 1911 in a private conversation, Heinrich Class, leader of the Pan-Germans, pleaded for a preventive war. His partner in the conversation was Hugo Stinnes, a leading figure in the steel industry and Germany's most aggressive industrialist. Stinnes counseled restraint: After "3–4 years peaceful development" Germany would be "the undisputed economic master of Europe."[60] The influential Hamburg banker, Max Warburg, was shocked by Wilhelm II's rhetorical question at dinner, one week before the Sarajevo murders, whether it was not better "to attack now rather than to wait" for Russia to complete her rearmament. Warburg counseled the kaiser not to draw the sword. "Germany becomes stronger with every year of peace," he declared. "We can only gather rewards by biding our time."[61] Obviously, some influential capitalists preferred economic to military competition.

Admiral von Tirpitz, the architect of the High Sea Fleet, had so squeezed private shipbuilders out of profits that by 1914, they were on the verge of open rebellion against the Navy Office.[62] Nor should it be overlooked that most farmers, shopkeepers, small businessmen, civil servants, and workers would pay more taxes but stood to gain nothing from armaments

---

[59] See A. C. F. Beales, *The History of Peace* (New York, 1931); Charles Chatfield and Peter van den Dungen, eds., *Peace Movements and Political Cultures* (Knoxville, 1986); John Mueller, *Retreat from Doomsday: The Obsolescence of Modern War* (New York, 1989), chs. 1 and 2. Also, Roger Chickering, *Imperial Germany and a World without War: The Peace Movement and German Society, 1892–1914* (Princeton, 1975); and Keith Robbins, *The Abolition of War: The "Peace Movement" in Britain, 1914–1919* (Cardiff, 1976), ch. 1. The most incisive treatment of the German Socialists remains Groh, *Negative Integration und revolutionärer Attentismus*.

Membership figures and activity levels, as always, cannot be established with any certainty. Chickering, *Imperial Germany*, pp. 62–3, reports that by 1914 there were 98 local peace groups with a membership of "just under ten thousand." But, he adds, "the concept of membership was nebulous" and no one was certain how many "actively belonged." At an earlier point, one of the leaders estimated that "no more than a third of the local groups carried on any activity at all, and even this was probably a liberal estimate." The Navy League was said to have had 30 times as many members (note 42 above).

[60] Cited in Wolfgang J. Mommsen, *Großmachtstellung und Weltpolitik: Die Außenpolitik des Deutschen Reiches 1870 bis 1914* (Frankfurt and Berlin, 1993), p. 293.

[61] Max M. Warburg, *Aus meinen Aufzeichnungen* (Glückstadt, 1952), p. 29; cited in Fritz Fischer, *Krieg der Illusionen: Die deutsche Politik von 1911 bis 1914* (Düsseldorf, 1969), pp. 658 and 684.

[62] Michael Epkenhans, *Die wilhelminische Flottenrüstung 1908–1914: Weltmachtstreben, industrieller Fortschritt, soziale Integration* (Munich, 1991), pp. 266–90.

or wars. In France, the need for increased taxes to pay the costs of the three years of service, as noted, provided the central issue for the legislative elections in the spring of 1914.

Many accounts point to the "war euphoria" that gripped the European capitals in August 1914, this presumably showing the militarization of the masses. Many people saw the war as a chance at rejuvenation. Others depicted it as a cleansing "thunderstorm," many having grown tired of the long Bismarckian peace. In Vienna, for example, even the pacifist writer Stefan Zweig was impressed. Thirty years later, he still remembered the enthusiasm: "The trains filled with freshly arrived recruits. Flags waved, music boomed. I found the entire city of Vienna in a state of intoxication. . . . And to be truthful, I must admit that I found something great, magnetic, irresistible, and even seductive in this first popular awakening."[63] Elsewhere, crowds chanted "*à Berlin,*" "God save the tsar," and "*auf nach Paris.*" But the euphoria came after the fact, after the key decisions had been made. And that means it could not have caused those decisions.

While the observed enthusiasm was no doubt genuine, again the questions of frequency and typicality need consideration. There were, at the same time, demonstrations by tens if not hundreds of thousands of workers against the war.[64] Jeffrey Verhey's review of a cross-section of German newspapers and periodicals, some eighty-five of them, reports the evidence of euphoria, most of it found not among "the masses" but among intellectuals, students, and the upper middle classes. He also discovered a wide range of responses, with mixed feelings, dismay, fear, and anxiety much more frequent than ever suspected. There were frequent reports of tears. Theodor Wolff, editor of the *Berliner Tageblatt,* writing in 1916 on the anniversary of the outbreak, denied the mass euphoria claim, declaring as "false" the notion that "the German people greeted the outbreak of war with joy." "Our people," he declared, "had heavy hearts; the possibility of war was a frightening giant nightmare which caused us many sleepless nights. . . . Only a few talked of a 'fresh, wonderful war.'" The censors forbade "indefinitely" further publication of such denials.[65]

[63] Zweig is cited in Wolfgang Michalka, ed., *Der Erste Weltkrieg: Wirkung, Wahrnehmung, Analyse* (Munich and Zurich, 1994), pp. 8–9. For a recent description of the euphoria, see Roger Chickering, *Imperial Germany and the Great War, 1914–1918* (Cambridge, 1998), pp. 13–17.
[64] See Herwig, *The First World War*, pp. 33–7.
[65] Verhey, *Spirit of 1914*, pp. 7–8. For a comprehensive account of intellectuals' reactions, see Roland N. Stromberg, *Redemption by War: The Intellectuals and 1914* (Lawrence, Kans., 1982). See also the discussion in Chapter 15.

The euphoric crowd in Berlin, the "centerpiece" of the myth, appeared there on 25 July, at first waiting for news of Serbia's reaction to the Austrian ultimatum. Verhey describes the event and attempts some quantification: "That evening 'Germany' had not paraded. Only a small minority of the Berlin population had participated – no more than 30,000, or less than 1 percent of the population of greater Berlin. This was far, far fewer, as [the Socialist newspaper] *Vorwärts* noted the next day, than the hundreds of thousands who had demonstrated for Prussian suffrage reform in 1910." Verhey's 30,000 figure is based on "the most generous estimates" given in police and newspaper reports. The war-euphoria imagery, he argues, was a useful myth. The aim was to justify the initial decision and, as late as October 1918, to mobilize a weary citizenry for still another effort.[66]

One can easily agree that the four just-discussed sentiments were increasing: There was more nationalism, more social Darwinism, more imperialist sentiment, and more militarism than at some earlier time. That said, however, some qualifications, some specification must be added. We know little about the prevalence of these outlooks. What was the extent of the infection in the general population? Was it 10 percent, 30, or 75? We also know little about the strength or virulence of those views. What percent of the adherents expressed their views? What percent made demands in their support? How many joined appropriate pressure groups? And what of the members? Were they active or were they quiescent dues-payers? The members of voluntary associations are drawn, typically, from the upper and upper middle classes, which means the sentiments of other classes, those forming the vast majority, remain unheard.[67] Advocacy

---

[66] Verhey, *Spirit of 1914*, pp. 26–33. For evidence on reactions in France, see Jean-Jacques Becker, *1914: Comment les Français sont entrés dans la guerre* (Paris, 1977); and P. J. Flood, *France 1914–18: Public Opinion and the War Effort* (Houndsmills and London, 1990), ch. 1. The latter work is mistitled; it deals with reactions in the Department of Isère, southeast of Lyon. See also the two comprehensive studies by E. Malcolm Carroll, *French Public Opinion and Foreign Affairs 1870–1914* (Hamden, Conn., 1964 [1931]), esp. ch. 13; and his *Germany and the Great Powers 1866–1914: A Study in Public Opinion and Foreign Policy* (New York, 1938), esp. ch. 14.

[67] Voluntary association membership is always positively related to class, that is, much more frequent in the upper and upper middle classes. For an overview, see Hamilton, *Mass Society, Pluralism, and Bureaucracy*, ch. 2. That tendency was clearly the case with the patriotic organizations studied by Chickering. The leaders of the Pan-German League were "overwhelmingly urban and middle class," the latter clearly being high on the social scale. Nearly half of the local leaders, Chickering reports, "were on the public payroll [almost half being] university and high-school teachers...." *We Men Who Feel*, p. 104. See also his further discussion and comparisons with other organizations, pp. 104–8.

groups, at all times, show a persistent magnification bias. They exaggerate their membership, the urgency of their message, and their influence.[68] One key question about these advocacy groups typically remains unanswered: How were they viewed by the nation's leaders? Were they seen as valued supporters or as a troublesome nuisance?

The focus on "mass attitudes" and demands poses still another difficulty. Those arguments imply some "bottom-up" dynamics: irrepressible popular demands ultimately forcing responses by those nations' leaders. Those causal arguments, clearly, need elaboration. We need a specification of the mechanisms involved.

There is a need also for consideration of alternative hypotheses about "mass attitudes." As opposed to the ardent-enthusiasm claim, we have an easy alternative: voiceless masses. One should consider the substantive possibilities, what those "voices" would have said had they been asked, "What are your priorities?" One possibility might be expressed as follows: "my family and my family's welfare, first and foremost."[69] The refusal on the part of scholars from the "broad-brush" school of history to come to grips with such everyday matters reflects academia's persistent preference for the "big" thesis. Put differently, it reflects a general disdain for the "little things," for the facts of everyday life.

The sixth of the traditional "cause-of-war" arguments under review focuses on the popular press, on the newspaper agitation that generated the mass sentiments that in turn forced the political leaders to their choices. Some sixty years ago, Oron J. Hale, at the outbreak of what we classify here as the eighth world war, made a passionate plea that the press lords and their minions be included in the pantheon of warmongers.[70] There

---

[68] At one time or another, Chickering reports, the Pan-Germans had almost 400 chapters. But "the majority or these groups – more than two-thirds – existed only on paper or were dormant on all but select occasions" (p. 136). Alfred Fried, a leader of the German Peace Society, reported that most of their local organizations existed "on paper only." He estimated that "no more than a third of the local groups carried on any activity at all, and even this was probably a liberal estimate." Chickering, *Imperial Germany*, p. 63.

[69] For elaboration and evidence on this position, based on surveys from the 1970s, see Richard F. Hamilton and James D. Wright, *The State of the Masses* (New York, 1986), ch. 3, "The Persistence of Traditional Goals and Concerns." For discussion of mass sentiment in an important historical case, the English civil war, see Richard F. Hamilton, *The Bourgeois Epoch: Marx and Engels on Britain, France, and Germany* (Chapel Hill, N.C., 1991), pp. 19–23.

[70] Oron J. Hale, *Publicity and Diplomacy with Special Reference to England and Germany 1890–1914* (London, 1940). But in his final chapter, he offers this summary statement: "For purposes of analysis it is assumed that the ultimate decision was made by the influential. The mass electorate had no opportunity to register its views; there were no

is no denying the bellicosity of much of the press, but to date, scholars have failed to discern its direct influence on decision making in 1914. This position, accordingly, has fallen into abeyance.

Here, too, there are many complications. A good deal of the press, especially on the Continent, was in fact in the sway (if not the pay) of political parties, central governments, or industrialists, thus making differentiation a necessity. Volker Berghahn states that none of Germany's 1,900 publications in 1912 was "ideologically neutral." About 870 followed the Conservatives, another 580 the National-Liberals, nearly 480 the Center party or the Catholic Church, and 90 the Socialists.[71] To assess influence, one would have to review the contents, have circulation figures, know the audience characteristics, know readers' reactions to those contents, and know something of their subsequent actions. One can research the contents, the easiest of those tasks, and here and there one can find circulation figures.[72] But beyond that, for all practical purposes, we have nothing. Another factor, basic literacy, also needs consideration. Illiteracy was still widespread in Europe in 1914, the rates everywhere being higher in the countryside and among older citizens. They were also higher in eastern Europe. For many people, a direct press influence was impossible.

Another problem is that of sequence. The argument holds that the press agitation led to the subsequent decision. There was much press agitation in Vienna in July 1914, much of it focused on provocative press comment in the Belgrade press. But that agitation came after Austria-Hungary's leaders had made the key decisions. In Germany, Verhey reports, the

public opinion polls for the discovery of the obvious. As a matter of fact, all governments in the crisis functioned autocratically, subject of course to influence and pressure from immediate centers of power" (p. 455).

  Sidney Fay gives just over two pages to this possibility, signaling it as a topic that (in 1930) was "only beginning to receive" the investigation it deserves. He points to the press feud between Austrian and Serbian newspapers in July 1914, this clearly his "best case." See his *Origins of the World War*, vol. 1, pp. 47–9.

[71] Volker R. Berghahn, *Imperial Germany 1871–1914: Economy, Society, Culture and Politics* (Providence and Oxford, 1994), pp. 187–8. For more detail on the major papers there, see E. Malcolm Carroll, *Germany and the Great Powers*, ch. 1.

[72] Jonathan French Scott argued that "the influence of public opinion in certain countries during the summer of 1914 was the most important factor in precipitating the war"; *Five Weeks: The Surge of Public Opinion on the Eve of the Great War* (New York, 1927), p. 19. Scott undertook an unsystematic review of contents of newspapers in the five major powers. At many points, however, he treats those contents as directly equivalent to "public opinion." But the book contains no direct measures of that opinion. And it provides no evidence on the linkages between that "public opinion" and the choices of the decision makers.

newspapers brought out many "extras" in the first days of August. The practice was a profitable one and also played some role in sustaining the enthusiasm. But that too came after the basic decisions had been made by the political and military leaders.

What is to be said of the seventh argument – a late entry in the field – that of domestic causes? Proponents of this school of interpretation see nationalism, armaments, and, ultimately, war as serving domestic needs. The argument, basically, is that conservative elites, facing serious internal threats, chose war to save their positions. Arno J. Mayer, a leading advocate of this position, states that war "may have been a by-product of the resolve by conservatives and ultraconservatives to foster their political position by rallying the citizenry around the flag." In Britain, France, and Italy, the "vital center" of parliamentary liberalism "was heavily besieged." In Germany, it was "almost completely emasculated." For conservative elites, then, the choice was either "armed repression at home" or "preventive war abroad – with the resolve of thereby arresting or reversing the course of history." It was the "spiraling political, economic, and social dysfunctions" within the Dual Monarchy that drove "Vienna's political class into trying to overcome its permanent internal crisis by recourse to external war." The argument, in short, is that the choice of war was counterrevolutionary; it was an attempt to counter very serious domestic threats.[73]

Subsequent research on the topic has found little support for this monocausal argument.[74] Some of the few remaining proponents of this view argue, rather vaguely, that the choice of war was to achieve the goal of "system maintenance." Most leaders, however, knew from previous experience the hazards involved. Mobilization alone brought severe

---

[73] For the basic statement, see Arno J. Mayer, "Domestic Causes of the First World War," in Leonard Krieger and Fritz Stern, eds., *The Responsibility of Power* (Garden City, N.Y., 1967), ch. 15; and Mayer's *Dynamics of Counterrevolution in Europe, 1870–1956: An Analytic Framework* (New York, 1971).

[74] Wolfgang J. Mommsen, "Domestic Factors in German Foreign Policy before 1914," *Central European History* 6 (1973): 1–43; Donald Lammers, "Arno Mayer and the British Decision for War: 1914," *Journal of British Studies* 12 (1973): 137–65; Michael R. Gordon, "Domestic Conflict and the Origins of the First World War: The British and the German Cases," *Journal of Modern History* 46 (1974): 191–226; David French, "The Edwardian Crisis and the Origins of the First World War," *International History Review* 4 (1982): 207–21; Jack S. Levy, "The Diversionary Theory of War: A Critique," in Manus I. Midlarsky, ed., *Handbook of War Studies* (Boston, 1989), ch. 11; and Niall Ferguson, "Public Finance and National Security: The Domestic Origins of the First World War Revisited," *Past and Present* 142 (1994): 141–68.

dislocations. Some sense of the problems may be gained from David French's account of the impact in Britain:

During the July Crisis, many of the Cabinet's worst fears about the domestic situation seemed about to come true. For several days, until the Government stepped in, the banking system and the shipping insurance markets were paralyzed. The price of food rose by an average of fifteen percent in the first week of August, and by the end of the month the Board of Trade estimated that nearly half a million workers had been thrown out of work because of the war. The idea of a general strike to stop the war was also abroad. On 2 August ... [Ramsey] MacDonald predicted that by November there would be bread riots and a socialist government.[75]

The lesson is clear: For conservative leaders, war was a very dangerous weapon, one more likely to destabilize than to maintain any "system."

The eighth argument might be termed the accident thesis. The Great War, in this view, was the unintended consequence of decisions aiming for some other outcomes. The most famous statement of this position, the argument of "inadvertence," came from David Lloyd George. Already in a speech of 23 December 1920, he had claimed, rather naively, that "no one at the head of affairs quite meant war" in July 1914. "It was something into which they [the statesmen] glided, or rather staggered and stumbled." Later, in his postwar memoirs, the British wartime prime minister took up the theme of inadvertence once more: "How was it that the world was so unexpectedly plunged into this terrible conflict? Who was responsible?" His reply became the classic statement of innocence for July 1914: "The nations slithered over the brink into the boiling cauldron of war without any trace of apprehension or dismay." The theme is developed, a few pages later, under this heading: "Nobody Wanted War."[76]

Lloyd George's postwar comments, it should be noted, stand in stark contrast to his "intentionalist" comments made during the British election of December 1918 and at the Versailles peace conference in 1919. During the election, Lloyd George and his supporters had demanded that the kaiser be prosecuted, indeed, be hanged, that the Germans "pay to the limit" for all war damages, and in general that the "pips" be squeezed until they "squeaked." During the peace conference, the prime minister

[75] French, "The Edwardian Crisis," p. 218.

[76] The December 1920 speech is from Scott, *Five Weeks*, p. 11; the postwar comments from Lloyd George, *War Memoirs*, vol. 1, pp. 49, 52. Most recent: Antony Lentin, *Lloyd George and the Lost Peace: From Versailles to Hitler, 1919–1940* (New York, 2001), p. 143.

had again suggested that the kaiser be tried for "war crimes," possibly in Britain.[77]

This remarkable shift from arguments of intention to those of inadvertence, one occurring within a few months, reflected new political concerns (as opposed to a concern for evidence). Lloyd George suggested his shift was based on his wide reading of diplomatic records, but in the late months of 1920, that seems unlikely. In the 1920s and early 1930s, political leaders and commentators advocated policies of reconciliation as opposed to the earlier effort, mobilization for war based on arguments of intent. The "slide" image found favor at that time with numerous scholars as well as politicians. It is central in Sidney Fay's *Origins of the World War*, the leading interwar revisionist work.[78]

Lloyd George's notion of the innocent or unintended "slide" stands sharply opposed to the evidence now available, evidence that is reviewed in later chapters. One should note, prior to that review, some initial problems with this argument. First, the inadvertence argument assumes an incredible, indeed, unbelievable, degree of probability: that all five coteries of decision makers in Vienna, Berlin, St. Petersburg, Paris, and eventually London "slithered" or "stumbled" into war. In any other context, such a "conjuncture" would seem ridiculous, for example, that five men hurrying to a meeting all stumbled en route. Apart from the question of improbability, there is a further problem, that of the implications: The "slide thesis" is the great equalizer or relativizer. King George V is as culpable as Wilhelm II, Sir Edward Grey as culpable as Count Leopold Berchtold. That some "men of 1914" found the argument attractive should have caused doubts.[79] "Interested parties" were pointing to the "boiling cauldron" and the "impersonal forces" they could not control; the argument made them innocent of the charge of having dragged their nation into the catastrophe.

[77] Lloyd George's position in 1918–19 is detailed in Kenneth O. Morgan, *Consensus and Disunity: The Lloyd George Coalition Government 1919–1922* (Oxford, 1979), pp. 39–41.

[78] Six decades later, U.S. Secretary of State Henry Kissinger offered the same conclusion, declaring that "nation after nation slid into a war whose causes they did not understand but from which they could not extricate themselves." See his speech of 11 March 1976, *New York Times* (12 March), p. 4. Also Marc Trachtenberg, *History and Strategy* (Princeton, 1991), p. 99.

[79] Even Lloyd George recognized some problem with his "Nobody Wanted War" claim, pointing on the same page (p. 52) to "one possible exception," that being "the foolish Berchtold." He cites a Berchtold dispatch that indicates, unambiguously, the man's bellicose intentions.

The use of metaphor, the talk of slides and cauldrons, is a digression, one that avoids the documentary record. The commentator simultaneously avoids the essence of decision making: human beings making choices. Nations simply do not "slither" into wars, driven by overpowering dark forces. Human beings at the highest levels, leaders, elites, decision makers, collect information, evaluate their chances, and make decisions. Their choices may have been mistaken, flawed, and ill-chosen. But their nation's involvement stems from a choice based on some kind of intention. As will be seen in later chapters, the leaders of the various governments in 1914 assessed their options, weighed the choices, and, fully aware of the most likely consequences, deliberately chose involvement.[80]

The equivalency problem appears also in many formulations of the other causes reviewed to this point. Many of them also relativize, indicating no differences between the responses of Austria-Hungary and France, between Germany and Britain. Nationalism and militarism were "rising" everywhere. The nations were all engaged in an arms race.[81] The "broad brush" depictions, however, avoid consideration of the amounts expended for armaments, the possible causes, or the sequence of events. The relativizing (or equivalency), to be sure, is most striking in the

---

[80] See Hew Strachan, *The First World War*, vol. 1: *To Arms* (Oxford, 2001): "What remains striking about those hot July weeks is the role, not of collective forces nor of long-range factors, but of the individual" (p. 101). This important work appeared too late for use in this book.

    Variants on the slithering, slide, or stumble argument appear, and are given credence, in some recent textbooks. One declares that the war "started because rulers and government officials blundered in the summer of 1914," Richard L. Greaves et al., *Civilizations of the World: The Human Adventure*, 2nd ed., 2 vols. (New York, 1993), vol. 2, p. 934. Another reports that "most historians believe that well-meaning unimaginative leaders in every capital stumbled into World War I.... They produced a result none had ever intended." This from Carter V. Findley and John A. Rothney, *Twentieth-Century World*, 2nd ed. (Boston, 1990), p. 56. Both works proceed to review other background factors. Another declares that "Europe stumbled in 1914 into disaster," R. R. Palmer and Joel Colton, *A History of the Modern World since 1815*, 8th ed. (New York, 1995), p. 695.

[81] Arno Mayer ("Domestic Causes," p. 288), writing of the problems facing "the major European polities" on the eve of the war, points to a presumed consequence, to "the 50 percent increase in military spending in the five prewar years...." David Stevenson's figures on defense expenditures, however, indicate wide variation in the growth for the powers in the years from 1908 to 1913. They range from 19 percent for Britain to 129 percent for Italy (then engaged in the Libyan war). France showed a relatively moderate increase – 30 percent – while Austria-Hungary, then worried about Balkan developments, showed a considerable 55 percent increase. Both Italy and Austria-Hungary, it should be noted, began with low base expenditures in 1908. The figures for the two other powers are: Russia, 31; and Germany, 45. From Stevenson, *Armaments and the Coming of War*, p. 4 (our calculations).

arguments of inadvertence, those that avoid consideration of actual decision making and instead depend on the familiar metaphors.

Two more options should be added to the eight hypotheses just reviewed. The ninth is the possibility of joint effects, that two or more factors – nationalism, militarism, and imperialism, for example – somehow worked in combination to generate a decision for war. Almost all accounts provide a "short list" of causes; almost all indicate multiple causes. The problems reviewed above apply also in this case. Those are: poor measures of incidence (extent and strength of views) and equivalence (they were "all doing it"). Here, too, there is a problem of weighting: How much importance should be assigned to factors A, B, C, and so forth?

Discussion of some of these causes presents another difficulty, the possibility of *post hoc ergo propter hoc* errors. The alliances, nationalism, imperialism, and social Darwinism all preceded the outbreak of war, but without further specification, it is not clear they had causal impact. A listing of factors that occurred prior in time is easy; establishing their causal significance is much more difficult. If a given factor was causal, it should figure in the thought and discussions of the July 1914 decision makers.

The tenth possibility, a routine scientific requirement, is the open-ended option usually referred to as "other hypotheses." We argue one such claim: that the decision makers of the five major powers sought to save, maintain, or enhance the power and prestige of the nation. We refer to this as the strategic argument.[82]

## A Summary

Analysis of the decisions made in the capitals of the five major powers that opted for war in 1914 must consider three components: the institutional arrangements, the persons involved, and the grounds or motives for their choices. Among the latter, we have their readings and assessments of the events of the previous two or three decades and their readings of events from 28 June onward.

Among the hundreds of items of information brought to the July 1914 decision makers, among the various grounds for their choices, were representations of mass attitudes, of public opinion, matters discussed in the preceding pages. One conclusion about those outlooks may be stated as

---

[82] Strachan takes a similar position: "By July 1914 each power, conscious in a self-absorbed way of its own potential weaknesses, felt it was on its mettle, that its status as a great power would be forfeit if it failed to act." Strachan, *The First World War*, vol. 1, p. 101.

an absolute: No precise measures of public opinion were available at that time. Every bit of information on this subject brought to their attention was a guess, an inference, a tenuous claim, or, to use later terminology, an unsubstantiated hypothesis. Precise knowledge of public opinion is not necessary for the analysis of the events reviewed here. Rather than pretending to have knowledge of the unknowable, the task is to discover what information was present among the coterie of decision makers and what use was made of it. That information, it should be emphasized, would consist of claims, beliefs, and hypotheses as opposed to documented empirical judgments. Here, too, one should keep an open mind with respect to the readings assigned such "facts." The decision makers might have proceeded independently of perceived mass opinion. The masses may have been opposed to war, but the leaders, indifferent to those views, chose engagement. The decision makers might have been moved by "larger" strategic considerations, by their conceptions of the nation's power and prestige, and accordingly paid no attention to mass opinion. Put differently, one should avoid gratuitous "democratizing" assumptions.

Our sense, clearly, is that a differentiated analysis is required. Nationalist sentiments had been aroused in each of the five major powers. They certainly had greater salience in 1914 than in the previous five, six, or seven decades. Stretching things a bit, one might point to imperialist concerns in each of the great powers. But the problems facing those "empires" were so diverse as to make any general analysis of this causal factor impossible. One might point to the needs of "capitalism" as somehow causing the catastrophe, but the specific form of those arrangements, the needs and interests of five sets of capitalists, also differed significantly from one nation to the next. Our hypothesis is that each of those nations was moved by a unique agenda, by a separate and distinct set of concerns.

After dealing with the July Crisis and the reactions of the five major powers, we turn to consideration of several important later participants in the struggle: Japan, the Ottoman Empire, Italy, Bulgaria, Romania, Greece, and the United States. In each, a small coterie made the decision for war. Some of these findings will come as no surprise. It has been known for years that in Austria-Hungary, Kaiser Franz Joseph acted on the advice of his foreign minister, chief of the General Staff, war minister, finance minister, and the premiers of the two halves of his empire. Similarly, in Germany the decision for war was made by Kaiser Wilhelm II and a small group of his close advisors: chancellor, foreign secretary, chief of the General Staff, chief of the Military Cabinet, and war minister. Likewise, in Russia, Tsar Nicholas II reached his fateful decision for war on the advice of a similarly small cadre of advisors: foreign minister, chief of the General Staff, war minister, and (somewhat of a surprise) agricultural minister.

But we find the same argument for coterie also made by our authors for some of the "lesser" or "later" combatants. At Constantinople the newly empowered Young Turks unsurprisingly took charge of national policy making: War Minister Ismail Enver Bey, Navy Minister Ahmed Cemal, Minister of the Interior Mehmed Talât Bey, among others. In Japan the decision for war was the product primarily of one man's political acumen: Foreign Minister Takō Takaaki, who in the process outmaneuvered both army and navy chiefs and the elder statesmen. In Italy the decision for war was made by Prime Minister Antonio Salandra and Foreign Minister Sidney Sonnino; and in the United States, after much soul searching and eventual congressional approval, by President Woodrow Wilson. In Bulgaria and Romania, the decisions for war rested solely in the hands of the monarch and a small ruling clique of royal officials. And in Greece, the tortuous decision for war on the side of the *entente* rested with Prime Minister Eleutherios Venizelos.

But also in the more progressive, more parliamentarian western powers, there was little wider participation in the decision making. In Britain, Foreign Secretary Grey watched the July Crisis unfold in splendid isolation, seeking the counsel neither of fellow cabinet ministers nor of senior Foreign Office professionals – not even naval and military leaders. In France, where both President Raymond Poincaré and Premier/Foreign Minister René Viviani spent much of the July Crisis aboard the battleship *France* steaming between Le Havre and Kronstadt, the nation was moved closer to war not by the Chamber of Deputies or the press, but rather by the relatively unknown and inexperienced Minister of Justice Jean Baptiste Bienvenu-Martin. And in the world's oldest and most open democracy, the United States, President Wilson, in the words of his official biographer, exercised "almost absolute personal control" over foreign affairs. Wilson routinely bypassed the State Department via private agents, conducted negotiations behind the backs of his secretaries of state, and generally "acted like a divine-right monarch in the conduct of foreign relations."[83]

Finally, we need to point out that in making the case first and foremost for coterie and contingency, for what Tocqueville called "the particular

[83] Arthur S. Link, *The Higher Realism of Woodrow Wilson and Other Essays* (Nashville, Tenn., 1971), p. 83.

will and character of certain individuals," we are *not* overlooking the importance of social history, of the "big" factors. We are sensitive to the mindset, the *mentalité* of that coterie. How did they interact with both the head of state and fellow decision makers? Did certain common, long-term patterns of education, training, and public rhetoric contribute to the "mood of 1914"? Put differently, what assumptions, both spoken and unspoken, did they bring to the table in 1914?[84] For, in the words of that super-determinist, Karl Marx, "Men make their own history, but they do not make it just as they please; they [make it] under circumstances directly encountered, given and transmitted from the past."[85]

As well, we are keenly aware of the question: To what degree do disciplines such as economics, psychology, and sociology shed additional light (beyond that provided by diplomatic, military, and political history) upon what George F. Kennan called "*the* great seminal catastrophe of this century"?[86] We strove to be sensitive (where possible and applicable) to the role of such nonprimary agencies as public opinion, financial institutions, academic leaders, church fathers, and press lords. And in the case of the Balkan states, the numerous secret societies that maintained ties to governments that could not at all times control their agenda.

---

[84] See the seminal studies by James Joll, *1914: The Unspoken Assumptions* (London, 1968); and his *Origins of the First World War*, 2nd ed. (London, 1992), ch. 8, "The Mood of 1914."

[85] Karl Marx, "The Eighteenth of Brumaire of Louis Bonaparte," in Karl Marx, Friedrich Engels, *Collected Works*, 48 vols. (New York, 1975– ), vol. 11, p. 103.

[86] George F. Kennan, *The Decline of Bismarck's European Order: Franco-Russian Relations, 1875–1890* (Princeton, 1979), p. 3.

## 2

# The European Wars

## 1815–1914

### Richard F. Hamilton

Many accounts of the Great War's origins, understandably, focus on the short term, 28 June through to early August 1914. Others, also for good reason, look at the longer term, beginning with 1866 or 1870. The decisions of July and August 1914, after all, were made against a background of several decades of experience.

It is useful to consider an even longer term, the entire period from 1815 to mid-year 1914, the ninety-nine years following the last major conflagration, the world war generated by Napoleon Bonaparte. Twenty-three international wars were fought on the European continent in that period. Roughly half of them were small wars, ones with 10,000 or fewer battle fatalities. Most sources report the Crimean War (1853–56) as the largest of these struggles, with roughly half a million combat-related fatalities. If accurate, it would mean the number of lives lost in that war would have been roughly one-twentieth the number lost in World War I. (One important source reports the Russo-Turkish War of 1877–78 as the largest of those wars, a discrepancy to be considered below in this chapter). The European wars fought in this ninety-nine-year span were relatively small, the four largest being, in sequence, the Russo-Turkish (1828–29), the Crimean (1853–56), the Franco-Prussian (1870–71), and the Russo-Turkish (1877–78). For almost a century, Europe had experienced no world war.

We routinely ask the "outbreak question": Why the war? But a prior question also deserves consideration: What circumstances made the ninety-nine relatively peaceful years possible? Some restraints, it is argued below, were operating in that period that helped to "keep the peace" or, more appropriately, to limit the extent of the wars. The restraints, as is also seen below, broke down at several points; the complete breakdown came in 1914. An examination of the "small wars" of this period provides some clues as to the "dynamics" involved. The key questions are: Why were the restraints generally effective for such a long period? And why, eventually, were they no longer operative in 1914?

This chapter does not follow the agenda spelled out in Chapter 1. It would take several volumes to review the decision making leading up to the twenty-three wars. The aims, rather, are to explain the absence of a major war (or, put differently, to explain the "relative" peace) and to provide background for the following chapters, those dealing with the outbreak of 1914.

### The Contenders and the Operating Principles

Throughout most of this ninety-nine-year period, Europe was dominated by five great powers: Britain, Austria (after 1867, Austria-Hungary), Prussia (after 1871, Germany), Russia, and France.[1] The first four were the victorious powers of 1815. At the Congress of Vienna they rearranged the map of Europe, reducing France to its pre-Revolutionary boundaries, putting Prussia in the Rhineland as a buffer, and putting Austria in northern Italy for the same purpose. France was present at the Congress, still treated as a major power. But at that point and throughout most of the following century, that nation was viewed with suspicion, as one harboring dangerous revolutionary tendencies.

Two lesser contenders were present on the European scene. The Ottoman Empire, once a formidable power, located in the southeastern "corner" of the Continent (and in the Near East, the Middle East, and across North Africa), was manifestly in decline, a condition that was key to much of subsequent history. A new state was created in 1861: a unified Italy, which, several decades later, toward the turn of the century, also sought "great power" status.

A first principle, the guiding concern for the victorious powers, was the maintenance of peace on the European continent. Having the disasters of the French Revolution and the Napoleonic era clearly in mind, the leaders

---

[1] A reference to five powers (or to any variation on the "great powers" theme) is an easy but misleading convenience. No two nations are ever "equal" in their power or capacity. The power of any nation, moreover, whether military, economic, political, or cultural, is always changing, always in flux. See Paul Kennedy, *The Rise and Fall of the Great Powers* (New York, 1987).

of the victorious great powers sought to prevent war through collegial discussion and agreement about any major actions to be taken. The underlying notion, necessarily somewhat diffuse, was called the Concert of Europe. The leaders were in substantial agreement on the basics, all favoring the established (or restored) monarchical regimes and opposing international conflict. The assumption of consensus, however, proved a tenuous one, since, as quickly became evident, the powers saw their interests somewhat differently.[2]

The great powers worked simultaneously with a second operating principle, that being the idea of a "balance" of forces, with power countering power. Consensus was the dominant concept in 1815, but, as mentioned, a set of buffer states was established along France's borders. The two guiding principles, consensus and balance, were used with varying emphasis until the ultimate collapse in August 1914. The idea of balance was that no one nation or combination of nations should be dominant.

A series of treaties (or informal understandings) were negotiated to attain and/or maintain that desired result. To achieve that balance, the principal options were, one, a promise of mutual support (if A were attacked, B would come to A's assistance), or two, a promise of neutrality (if A were attacked, B would stay out of the struggle). That sounds easy enough, but many of the treaties and terms were secret. And, more important, it was not certain that countries would honor the terms of the agreements. These were not binding contracts, since no agency existed to enforce compliance. Moreover, often the terms were open to interpretation. Was country A actually attacked? Or did A provoke the attack? There was another difficulty: The partners were not always honorable. In any given crisis, it was necessary, and a matter of utmost importance, for the partners to consult. They had to seek assurance that in the immediate circumstances the treaty partner would provide support or at least remain neutral.

The choices of coalition partners were not entirely free. Britain sought to remain free of continental ties, to maintain a continental balance

[2] René Albrecht-Carrié, ed., *The Concert of Europe* (New York, 1968); Carsten Holbraad, *The Concert of Europe: A Study in German and British International Theory 1815–1914* (London, 1970); F. R. Bridge and Roger Bullen, *The Great Powers and the European States System 1815–1914* (London, 1980); M. S. Anderson, *The Ascendancy of Europe 1815–1914* (London, 1985). For later developments, see Paul W. Schroeder, *Austria, Great Britain and the Crimean War: The Destruction of the European Concert* (Ithaca, 1972); W. N. Medlicott, *Bismarck, Gladstone, and the Concert of Europe* (London, 1956); and Richard Langhorne, *The Collapse of the Concert of Europe: International Politics, 1890–1914* (New York, 1981).

from outside, from its island base. British leaders, with evident pride, later referred to this stance as one of "splendid isolation." Continental leaders judged the practice differently, referring to the United Kingdom as "perfidious Albion."

There were, in addition, important political differences. Britain was a constitutional monarchy, one with a cabinet responsible to Parliament. Britain also offered occasional support for liberal insurgencies on the Continent. In sharp contrast, Louis Napoleon's *coup d'état* in 1851 brought eighteen years of rule by an ambitious and capricious dictator. Then, in the Third Republic, France abandoned monarchy entirely, choosing parliamentary rule and cabinet government. Tsarist Russia, an authoritarian regime, generally opposed all liberal tendencies. Austria and Prussia, especially under Otto von Bismarck's direction, showed the same disposition.[3] An alliance of the three authoritarian powers – Russia, Austria, and Prussia – would seem "a natural," but in time, that option, too, faced serious problems. After 1870–71, a German-French alliance was unlikely. An alliance of tsarist Russia and republican France seemed unnatural, but one was later formed and proved of decisive importance.

All nations must be concerned with internal affairs, with the problem of order, with "domestic tranquillity." This provided a third principle governing the behavior of the powers. A key question, at all times, is "which order?" At the outset, in 1815, all of the powers were conservative. They were old regimes, ones ruled by monarchs aided by supporting aristocracies. A basic aim, accordingly, was to maintain or stabilize the old order.

At the Congress of Vienna, the victorious powers, the original Concert of Europe, rearranged the map of the Continent and restored a few displaced monarchies. Among other things, they reunited The Netherlands after more than two centuries of division and installed a new monarch. Napoleon's creation, the Duchy of Warsaw, was abolished and Poland was again divided among three of the powers. There was an understanding, especially on the part of the three victorious continental powers, that they would oversee and protect the new arrangements. Faced with

---

[3] Prussia was generally opposed to political and social liberalism, but for several decades showed striking economic liberalism as exemplified in the Prussian Customs Union. This was a "national" liberalism, reforms within a larger trade area, as opposed to commitment to a world market. There was no "contradiction" here; economic liberalism provided considerably enhanced revenues for the illiberal regime. For further discussion, see Richard F. Hamilton, *Marxism, Revisionism, and Leninism: Explication, Assessment, and Commentary* (Westport, Conn., 2000), ch. 1.

a serious internal threat – political assassination – the German Confederation (comprising thirty-nine central European states) promulgated the Karlsbad Decrees in 1819, a collection of restrictive measures intended to thwart revolutionary movements (which included liberal or constitutional demands). On several occasions, when faced with insurgency, the powers undertook armed intervention to make appropriate correction. These police efforts were directed largely by the Austrian chancellor, Prince Clemens von Metternich. The arrangement, called the Metternich system, was generally successful. In the period from 1815 to 1847, apart from several efforts of insurgency and the Russo-Turkish War, the Concert managed to keep both domestic and international peace.

A fourth "principle" guiding the policies of the largest European nations was the maintenance of major-power status or, for some others, the achievement of that status. Britain was unquestionably a great power. The British Empire was the largest ever in the history of the world. France was a major power but, as shown in 1870–71, one of questionable strength. Russia was a major power, second after the British Empire in population and territory, but as demonstrated in the Crimean War, the Russo-Japanese War, and the 1905 revolution, there were serious grounds for doubt. Germany, once united, was clearly strong, a nation perhaps best described as "a comer," one looking for its "place in the sun." Austria-Hungary was widely viewed as a tottering power. Defeated by "upstart" Prussia in 1866 and facing serious internal divisions, it seemed destined to decline. Italy, a later arrival on the European scene, was also "a comer," an aspiring power, but its efforts were repeatedly thwarted. In 1896 at Adowa, it experienced a serious and humiliating defeat. Later, in Libya, a victory was achieved but came at a considerable cost.

The Ottoman Empire was clearly in decline. The Ottomans had crossed into Europe in 1345, first subduing the Bulgarians and then overwhelming the Serbs. A bypassed city, Constantinople, was taken in 1453, in another significant victory. The push into Europe continued with the capture of Belgrade in 1521 and the conquest of most of Hungary in 1526. The Ottomans almost took Vienna in 1529. But then in 1683, again at Vienna, the "forward movement" was halted, this time definitively. The Ottoman Empire had been in retreat ever since, a process that accelerated in the decades just before the Great War.

Elsewhere, toward the end of this period, two new powers emerged. Across the Atlantic, in 1898, the United States demonstrated that it, too, was a great and growing power. And on the Pacific rim, Japan, in the

Russo-Japanese War of 1904–5, demonstrated a considerable military capacity.

Great-power status usually brought with it some form of imperialism, gaining and maintaining some kind of control over other peoples and territories. Most of that "expansion," especially in the nineteenth century, occurred outside the European continent, that too being part of the general understanding. One peculiarity of the ninety-nine years of relative peace was a clear double standard: The major powers sought peace and civility "at home" in Europe (not always successfully), but war and rapacity was the accepted practice elsewhere, mostly in Asia and Africa.

The double standard is most striking in the case of Britain, the leading imperial power. The United Kingdom undertook four military interventions on the European continent in this period, the Crimean War plus three minor "police actions" in Greece, Portugal, and Belgium. In that same period, according to one account, Britain engaged in twenty-two conflicts elsewhere, that is, on other continents. Byron Farwell reports that there "was not a single year in Queen Victoria's long reign [from 1837 to 1901] in which somewhere in the world her soldiers were not fighting for her and for her empire."[4] The most notorious of these was the Opium War in China (1842). For Britain, the most alarming was the Indian mutiny (1857–58). The most serious was the Boer War in South Africa (1899–1902).

France engaged in six European struggles in this period, the two largest being the Crimean War and the Franco-Prussian War. The first of the nation's "new" imperialist wars, the Algerian effort, lasted with some interruptions from 1829 to 1847. Napoleon III sponsored the ill-fated Mexican venture (1862–67). Republican France fought a long war to take Indo-China. There was a war with China, one in Madagascar, and several escapades in Africa. In September 1898, British and French troops met at Fashoda on the Nile. The British force was much larger, and the French unit, 150 men, withdrew, leaving the Sudan in British hands.[5]

---

[4] J. David Singer and Melvin Small, *The Wages of War 1816–1965: A Statistical Handbook* (New York, 1972), pp. 60–9, 72–5. The Farwell quotation is from *Queen Victoria's Little Wars* (New York, 1972), p. 1.

[5] Ronald Robinson and John Gallagher, *Africa and the Victorians: The Climax of Imperialism* (1961; rpt., Garden City, N.Y., 1968), ch. 12; Winfried Baumgart, *Imperialism: The Idea and Reality of British and French Colonial Expansion* (New York, 1982); and David Levering Lewis, *The Race to Fashoda: Colonialism and African Resistance* (New York, 1987).

Prussia fought four wars in Europe, the last of these ending in 1871. Germany acquired four African territories and some Pacific holdings in the brief two-year span of 1884–86. Later, in 1898, Germany acquired the territory of Kiaochow along with various concessions in China's Shantung province. Early in the twentieth century, German forces crushed a rebellion by the Hereros in Southwest Africa, killing three-quarters of the tribe's population. Shortly thereafter, a second rebellion, in German East Africa, was put down, again with exceptional viciousness.[6]

Belgium fought no wars in Europe. That state broke away from the United Netherlands in 1830 and, with relative ease, created a constitutional monarchy, choosing as king a relative of the British royal house. The Concert powers, sensing possible complications, met in London and, in November 1831, signed a treaty that provided the basic terms for the new state's existence. The Dutch king did not accept the settlement and, accordingly, was not a signer. His agreement was secured in a subsequent treaty in 1839, this, too, arranged by the Concert powers again meeting in London. This treaty contained the following article: "Belgium … shall form an Independent and Perpetually Neutral State. It shall be bound to observe such Neutrality towards all other States."[7]

At a later point, in 1885, the second Belgian king, Leopold II, acquired a sizable African territory, this in an amicable agreement with the European powers (a representative from the United States also participated). The exploitation of King Leopold's personal possession, called the Congo Free State, was rapacious in the extreme. One author estimates the human costs at ten million lives; others put the figure much higher. One source reports

---

[6] The number of European wars fought involves some judgment calls, an issue to be discussed below. On Germany's wars in Africa, see Thomas Pakenham, *The Scramble for Africa 1876–1912* (New York, 1991), chs. 33 and 34. For more general consideration, see Woodruff D. Smith, *The German Colonial Empire* (Chapel Hill, N. C., 1978); W. O. Henderson, *The German Colonial Empire, 1884–1919* (London, 1993); and John Lowe, *The Great Powers, Imperialism and the German Problem, 1865–1925* (London, 1994).

[7] E. H. Kossmann, *The Low Countries 1780–1940* (Oxford, 1978), pp. 151–60, 164–78. For the treaties, see Edward Hertslet, *The Map of Europe by Treaty* (London, 1875), vol. 2, pp. 858–71 and 979–93 (quotation from p. 985).

The spirit of the Concert of Europe may be seen in an article of the 1831 treaty that announced: "In consequence of the stipulations of the present Treaty there shall be Peace and Friendship between their Majesties and the King of the United Kingdom of Great Britain and Ireland, the Emperor of Austria, the King of the French, the King of Prussia, and the emperor of all the Russias, on the one part, and His Majesty the King of the Belgians, on the other part, their heirs and successors, their respective States and subjects, for ever" (p. 970). If alliances had compelling force, there would have been no World War I.

that the slaughter by France and Germany in their colonies matched or
exceeded that seen in the Congo. The Belgian Congo received more attention by virtue of its size, the absolute number of victims being considerably
larger.[8]

The difference in practice, the double standard, may be summarized as
follows. A Lockean social contract would be applied by the five powers
on the European continent. No such restraint, however, would be imposed elsewhere. While not anarchic, not a "war of all against all," the
practice leaned in the direction depicted by Thomas Hobbes. Compartmentalization was not always possible, however, since the off-continent
ventures occasionally spilled over and threatened the European peace.
The Fashoda affair, for example, was "the worst crisis in Franco-British
relations since Waterloo."[9] The Boer War and the two Moroccan crises, as
seen below, also had very serious consequences for the European powers.
The European "social contract," the so-called Concert, was always tenuous, always in need of repair and adjustment. The strains became greater
with the scramble for further territory that began in the last decades of the
century. The basic problem in 1914 may be put as follows: The incentives
that had led the powers to maintain the contract were no longer operating. At that point, the leaders of several countries gave precedence to
their nations' interests, definitively rejecting the collective concerns, those
of the European Concert.

The European powers engaged in a series of attempts at reconciliation
of the two competing concerns: the maintenance of peace (or the limi-
tation of war) on the European continent and the maintenance, achievement, or extension of great-power status. The notion of the Concert, of
consensual arrangements, never disappeared. But, increasingly, bilateral
or multilateral agreements with *quid pro quo* trade-offs came to be the
basic operative procedure for maintaining the peace.

Most accounts of the war's origin focus on a series of steps, these
beginning with the assassination of Archduke Franz Ferdinand, followed
by the familiar series of mobilizations, and then the first episodes of actual
war. The reading of the war's origins offered here, in contrast, emphasizes
the breakdown of the restraints or, put differently, the failure (or refusal)
to either maintain or reestablish "the Concert." This two-sided reading

---

[8] Adam Hochschild, *King Leopold's Ghost* (Boston, 1998), pp. 280–3; Pakenham, *The
Scramble for Africa*, chs. 32–7. See also Kossmann, *The Low Countries*, pp. 375–97;
and Richard F. Hamilton, "A Neglected Holocaust," *Human Rights Review* 1 (2000):
119–23.

[9] John F. V. Keiger, *France and the Origins of the First World War* (New York, 1983), p. 17.

was stimulated by and is indebted to the insights and work of Paul W. Schroeder.[10]

## European Wars, 1815–1914: An Overview

Twenty-three European wars were fought in the ninety-nine-year span of 1815–1914 (see Table 2.1). This listing is based on my modification of J. David Singer and Melvin Small's important and influential work reviewing interstate conflicts. The analysis of "wars" involves no end of difficulties. One basic question is that of size: Struggles range from minor border skirmishes to major engagements, so some cut-off point is required. Singer and Small listed interstate wars in which an individual nation had a minimum of 1,000 fatalities. Defining a cut-off point is easy; obtaining accurate counts is much more difficult. The problem may be seen in the figures on Crimean War battle fatalities (including those through wounds and disease): Singer and Small report 264,200; R. Ernest and Trevor Dupuy 507,600; and Michael Clodfelter 615,378.[11] The two latter figures would make this easily the largest continental war of the period. Except

[10] This as communicated initially in personal conversations, then in his as yet unpublished article, "Stealing Horses to Great Applause: The International System, Imperialism, and Austria-Hungary's Decision in 1914," and in his "International Politics, Peace, and War, 1815–1914," ch. 5 of T. C. W. Blanning, *The Nineteenth Century: Europe 1789–1914* (Oxford, 2000). See also his *Austria, Great Britain and the Crimean War*.

[11] Singer and Small, *Wages of War*, pp. 30, 32; R. Ernest Dupuy and Trevor N. Dupuy, *The Harper Encyclopedia of Military History: From 3500 B.C. to the Present*, 4th ed. (New York, 1993), p. 907; and Michael Clotfelter, *Warfare and Armed Conflicts: A Statistical Reference to Casualty and Other Figures, 1618–1991* (Jefferson, N. C., 1992), vol. 1, p. 301. Another work, that of Jack Levy, reports 217,000 deaths, but that figure is for the major powers only: *War in the Modern Great Power System, 1495–1975* (Lexington, Ky., 1983), p. 91.

Alan Palmer, who reviewed several previous sources, agrees with the high estimates; see *The Banner of Battle: The Story of the Crimean War* (London, 1987), p. 244. David M. Goldfrank also gives very high figures: *Origins of the Crimean War* (London, 1994), p. 289. In private correspondence (29 February 2000), Goldfrank confirmed the numbers, based on his culling of many individual studies, and commented on the difficulties. Desertion was an important confounding factor. More agreement appears with regard to losses in the Russo-Turkish War (1877–8). Clotfelder gives a total of 218,000 (*Warfare*, p. 331).

The differences in procedure account for the discrepancy in the number of wars reported in our Tables 1.1 and 2.1, that is, 18 wars for the major powers (based on Levy) and 23 wars, including the wars of minor powers (based on Singer and Small).

The largest wars of this period, 1815–1914, were fought on other continents. These were in China (the Taiping Rebellion, 1851–66), in the United States (the Civil War, 1861–65), and in South America (the Paraguayan War, involving also Uruguay, Brazil, and Argentina, 1864–70). Clotfelder gives the losses of life as, respectively, 20 million, 600,000, and 350,000 (ibid., p. 392).

TABLE 2.1. *European Wars, 1815–1914: Severity and Intensity*

| War | Dates | Number of great powers[a] | Countries[b] | Severity[c] | Intensity[d] |
|---|---|---|---|---|---|
| Napoleonic Wars | 1803–15 | 5 | BFGARS | 1,869,000[e] | 16,112[f] |
| *First Period* | | | | | |
| Greek-Turkish[g] | 1821–28 | 3 | BFROGr | 15,000 | ? |
| Franco-Spanish | 1823 | 1 | FS | 1,000 | 23 |
| Russo-Turkish | 1828–29 | 1 | RO | 130,000 | 1,660 |
| *Second Period* | | | | | |
| Austro-Sardinian | 1848–49 | 1 | AI | 9,000 | 230 |
| First Danish-Prussian | 1848–49 | 1 | GD | 6,000 | 328 |
| Russo-Hungarian | 1848–49 | 2 | AR | 59,500 | 579 |
| Roman Republic | 1849 | 2 | FAI | 2,200 | 29 |
| First Turko-Montenegrin | 1852–53 | 0 | OM | 5,000 | 198 |
| Crimean | 1853–56 | 3 | BFRIO | 264,200 | 1,586 |
| Second Turko-Montenegrin | 1858–59 | 0 | OM | 3,000 | 115 |
| Austro-French Piedmontese | 1859 | 2 | FAI | 22,500 | 292 |
| Italo-Roman | 1860 | 0 | I | 1,000 | 40 |
| Italo-Sicilian | 1860–61 | 0 | I | 1,000 | 32 |
| Second Danish-Prussian | 1864 | 2 | GAD | 4,500 | 80 |
| Austro-Prussian | 1866 | 2 | GAI | 36,100 | 384 |
| Franco-Prussian | 1870–71 | 2 | FG | 187,500 | 2,193 |
| *Third Period* | | | | | |
| Balkan | 1875–77 | 0 | O | 10,000 | 355 |
| Russo-Turkish | 1877–78 | 1 | RO | 285,000 | 2,336 |

| | | | | | |
|---|---|---|---|---|---|
| Bosnian | 1878 | 1 | A | 3,500 | 91 |
| Greco-Turkish | 1897 | 0 | OGr | 2,000 | 75 |
| Italo-Turkish | 1911–12 | 0 | IO | 20,000 | 335 |
| First Balkan | 1912–13 | 0 | OYSeBgGr | 82,000 | 2,571 |
| Second Balkan | 1913 | 0 | OYSeBgRuGr | 60,500 | 1,609 |
| World War I | 1914–18 | 5 | BFGARIOUJ BePYSeBgGr | 9,000,000 | 14,137 |

[a] The Great Powers are Britain, France, Germany (Prussia), Austria, and Russia.

[b] Countries participating in war: A: Austria-Hungary; B: England; Be: Belgium; Bg: Bulgaria; D: Denmark; F: France; G: Germany (Prussia); Gr: Greece; I: Italy; J: Japan; M: Montenegro; H: Holland; O: Ottoman Empire (Turkey); P: Portugal; R: Russia; S: Spain; Se: Serbia; U: United States; Y: Yugoslavia.

[c] Severity of war: total battle fatalities suffered by all participating parties. Battle fatalities here mean the "battle-connected fatalities among *military* personnel only . . . include not only those personnel who were killed in combat, but those who subsequently died from combat wounds or from diseases contracted in the war theater" (Singer and Small, *The Wages of War*, pp. 48–9).

[d] Intensity of war: total battle fatalities suffered by all participating parties, per million population of all participating parties. As described in note d, the battle fatalities here includes those from wounds or diseases in the war theater.

[e] Severity here is total battle fatalities suffered by the great powers only. The figure is cited from Jack Levy, *War in the Modern Great Power System. 1495–1975* (Lexington, Ky., 1983), p. 90.

[f] Intensity here is total battle fatalities suffered by great powers only, per million European populations. The figure is from ibid.

[g] See text (p. 56) for explanation.

*Source:* J. David Singer and Melvin Small, *The Wages of War 1816–1965: A Statistical Handbook* (New York, 1972), pp. 60–69, 72–75, and app. C.

for the Napoleonic wars, all figures given in the table are based on Singer and Small. As the Crimean "results" indicate, they should all be viewed as approximate, rule-of-thumb figures.

Given Singer and Small's focus on interstate wars, civil wars were listed only if the requisite interstate involvement occurred. I have added the Greek-Turkish War (1821–28), a civil war, joining it with their listing of "Navarino Bay," a significant interstate involvement, treating this as a single struggle. Other civil wars occurred in the ninety-nine years and several of them brought outside interventions. Some of these apparently did not meet the Singer-Small level of severity. Austria, for example, intervened to put down revolts in the Kingdom of the Two Sicilies and in the Kingdom of Sardinia (Piedmont) in 1821, but they are not listed.

The twenty-three wars fall into three general categories depending on the causal dynamics. Some are best described as restorationist: one or more of the powers sought to put down political or national insurgency. Some wars were fought to either gain or enhance great power status (or, alternatively, to maintain it); these involved Italy, Prussia, France, and Austria. And some others involved what has been called "the eastern question"; these stem from problems posed by the decline of the Ottoman Empire. These wars, typically, were multilateral struggles involving the competing claims of some aspiring new states and of several interested empires, principally the Ottomans, Austrians, Russians, and Britain.

The twenty-three European wars have been divided here into three periods. With a few exceptions, each period is dominated by one of those distinctive causal patterns. The first, 1815 to 1847, is sometimes called the Metternich period. Two of those wars were restorationist in character (several other efforts, as noted, were too small to qualify for listing). The powers agreed to the insertion of troops to put down insurgency and to reestablish their preferred form of government. This arrangement collapsed with the revolutions of 1848. The first war on the list, the Greek-Turkish War, is an important exception, one with unusual dynamics (to be reviewed below). The Russo-Turkish War, a second exception, is perhaps best seen as involving "eastern question" issues.

The second period extends from 1848 to 1871. The first wars of this period were restorationist, or efforts to put down revolution. Most of the wars of this period, however, involved attempts to form or to reform national entities with a view toward achieving great-power status. A unified Italy was created in 1861 (with Venetia and Rome added later). And a unified Germany was created in 1871. The Crimean War was the most important exception to this great-power dynamic. By most accounts the largest war of the entire 1815–1914 period, it was fought over eastern-question issues and had unusually wide involvement. After German unification in 1871, central and western Europe experienced more than forty years of peace.

The third-period wars, those fought between 1875 and 1913, were all based in eastern Europe, and all involved the eastern question. The main contenders were the Ottomans, Russia, Austria-Hungary, and the emerging Balkan states. As the Ottomans retreated, or were beaten back, the question of succession arose. Which state (or states) would take its place?

The following narrative is intended to serve two purposes. First, it allows a limited consideration of the question posed at the outset: Why the relative peace? Second, it gives an overview of the major events in the years prior to 1914, events that provided the framework for decisions taken in August of that year.

## The First Period: 1815–1848

The restorationist efforts of the first period, as indicated, were developed through consultation among the rulers and ministers of the great powers. The guiding "principle of intervention" was drawn up at the Congress of Troppau. As formulated in Metternich's protocol of 19 November 1820, it reads:

States which have undergone a change of government, due to revolution, the results of which threaten other states, *ipso facto* cease to be members of the European Alliance, and remain excluded from it until their situation gives guarantees for legal order and stability. If, owing to such alterations, immediate danger threatens other states, the powers bind themselves, by peaceful means, or if need be by arms, to bring back the guilty state into the bosom of the Great Alliance.[12]

The development and implementation of Concert policy was not an easy task. Tsar Alexander I's thought processes were notoriously erratic. Metternich thought him unbalanced and dangerous and preferred intervention without Russian participation. Most of Europe's leaders opposed Greek independence, but, moved by a new force, "public opinion,"

---

[12] Frederick B. Artz, *Reaction and Revolution 1814–1832* (New York, 1934), pp. 164–5. He was quoting from W. A. Phillips, *The Confederation of Europe* (London, 1920), pp. 208–9. See also Henry A. Kissinger, *A World Restored* (New York, 1964), ch. 14; and Paul W. Schroeder, *The Transformation of European Politics 1763–1848* (Oxford, 1994), ch. 13; on Troppau, pp. 610–11.

a significant limited intervention was undertaken. The British, with an agenda closely linked to the needs of the empire, did not sign the agreement and distanced themselves from much of the work of the continental powers. France also did not sign.

The Troppau agreement was a response to two revolutions earlier in the year. Insurgent army units in Spain forced the king to proclaim the liberal constitution of 1812 and to accept wide-ranging constitutional reforms, including a broadly elected legislature. In July 1820 in Naples, the capital of the Kingdom of the Two Sicilies (an Austrian satellite), members of a secret sect, the Carbonari, together with army officers forced their king to accept the same constitution. Later, in March 1821 in Turin, the capital of Piedmont, a part of the army led by their general revolted and demanded a constitution. The royalists responded with an appeal for Austrian aid.

With the Troppau justification, Metternich sent Austrian troops into the Kingdom of the Two Sicilies and later to Piedmont to put down the insurgencies. Two years later, France, under Louis XVIII, the restored Bourbon king, sent troops into Spain for the same purpose. This brief summary may leave a misleading impression, that the counterrevolutionary effort was a simple and easy task. In fact, however, the discussions by the involved powers were complicated, cumbersome, and protracted.[13]

The uprising of Greeks against their Turkish overlords in 1821 posed a different set of problems and, ultimately, brought a different kind of intervention. This event dominated great-power discussions for more than five years. The rebels in this case gained the support of classically educated elites across Europe. Those Philhellenes clamored for intervention in favor of the descendants of Plato and Pericles. Metternich was opposed to intervention. The insurgents, in his view, aimed to overthrow the established order, just like those in Naples and Spain. The insurgency, however, was in the Ottoman Empire, outside the Concert's chosen jurisdiction. Still another consideration: Metternich feared the implications of a Russian involvement.

Eventually, an "unnatural" coalition was formed, and over Metternich's objections, Russia, France, and Britain sent naval forces to secure a compromise, one that would give Greece self-government but with continued tribute to the Empire. The intent was a nonviolent intervention to prevent resupply of the Ottoman forces. But the plan went astray and, in a four-hour exchange of fire, the Battle of Navarino Bay,

---

[13] For some sense of the complications, see Bridge and Bullen, *Great Powers*, ch. 2; and Schroeder, *Transformation*, pp. 606–14.

20 October 1827, the empire "suffered her greatest naval disaster since Lepanto."[14]

In 1832 in London, Britain, France, and Russia arranged a settlement, this without either Greek or Turkish participation. Greece was declared an independent nation, its existence to be guaranteed by the three powers. Much discussion was needed to establish its rather limited territory. The new nation was, of course, to be a monarchy. The allies sought and found someone willing to serve, the seventeen-year-old son of the Bavarian king, an "enthusiastic Philhellene," who became King Otto I.[15]

Accounts of international relations typically focus on political and military leaders and on businessmen, the dominant concerns being those of *Realpolitik* and "profits." The role of "ideal" factors in this instance is striking. The classically educated intellectuals, the romantic poets, and liberal forces moved the hard-headed realists, Lord Castlereagh and George Canning, to actions they would not have made on their own. Greek independence was a major achievement for Europe's liberals, their first post-Napoleonic victory over the forces of reaction. Except for this unique intervention by western Europe's Philhellenes, the Greek-Turkish War would have been restorationist, that is, a match for the other struggles of the period. Greek independence would have been postponed and Greece would have been a leading participant in "the Balkan struggles" that came later in the century.[16] The Greek civil war provided Russia with an opportunity for expansion. This led to the Russo-Turkish War (1828–29), which brought another defeat for the Ottomans and further loss of territory.[17]

---

[14] Artz, *Reaction and Revolution*, pp. 250–60; Schroeder, *Transformation*, pp. 614–21, 637–53; M. S. Anderson, *The Eastern Question 1774–1923: A Study in International Relations* (New York, 1966), ch. 3; Richard Clogg, *A Short History of Modern Greece* (Cambridge, 1986), ch. 3; David Brewer, *The Greek War of Independence* (Woodstock, N.Y., 2001).

In the Battle of Lepanto, 7 October 1571, a fleet assembled by Christian nations (Venice, Spain, the Pope, and several smaller states) defeated a Turkish fleet. It was "one of the world's decisive battles," from Dupuy and Dupuy, *Encyclopedia*, pp. 547–9.

[15] Artz, *Reaction and Revolution*, pp. 259–62; Schroeder, *Transformation*, pp. 637–53; Clogg, *Short History*, pp. 68–9.

[16] The success of this struggle is unique in that it depended on the efforts of those distant, foreign intellectuals. The later Balkan struggles were driven largely by indigenous leaders. For an account of the most famous instance, a direct intervention by a leading intellectual, see Elizabeth Longford, *The Life of Byron* (Boston, 1976), ch. 9.

[17] Tsar Alexander I died in 1825. His brother, who became Nicholas I, ruled until 1855. An arch conservative, he was both more capable and more independent than his predecessor. See Anderson, *Eastern Question*, pp. 68–73; Barbara Jelavich, *St. Petersburg*

In 1830, three revolutions disturbed the domestic peace. But all three were contained and yielded outcomes that, while not entirely pleasing, were nevertheless acceptable to the leaders of the major powers. The July revolution in Paris ousted the reactionary Bourbons and replaced them with the Orleanist branch of the same family. The new monarch, Louis Philippe, agreed to some modest constitutional restraints.

Later that year, Belgium broke away from the United Netherlands, this insurgency stemming from resentment over the monarch's anti-Catholic and pro-Dutch policies. The Dutch king sent troops to regain the lost provinces, and open hostilities followed. Ambassadors of the Concert powers met in London to counter the threat of a European war, a likely consequence if France intervened. They imposed an armistice and arranged the division of the unitary kingdom they had established fifteen years earlier. It, too, would be a monarchy, and through British influence, Prince Leopold of Saxe-Coburg was chosen as king. A kinsman by marriage of the British royal family, that choice gave important protection for the new nation. The Dutch king invaded again in August, a move that brought French and British interventions in support of the Concert agreement.[18] In 1839, as seen above, the great powers signed an agreement declaring that Belgium would be a "perpetually neutral" state.

The third revolution occurred in the Russian satellite state, Congress Poland, in November 1830. It was a military insurrection ultimately involving an army of 80,000. Some 100,000 Russian troops were required to defeat it, the struggle ending only in September the following year. It was clearly a major conflict, one that produced 15,000 battle fatalities. But, as a civil war, with a unilateral effort of restoration, it is not listed in our Table 2.1.[19]

## The Second Period: 1848–1871

The Metternich system collapsed in the course of the 1848 revolutions. The insurgencies all eventually failed, either finessed or defeated by force of arms. Some limited concessions were required in all instances. France adopted the republican form, this the short-lived Second Republic. A few

*and Moscow: Tsarist and Soviet Foreign Policy, 1814–1974* (Bloomington, Ind., 1974), chs. 2 and 3; and Barbara Jelavich, *Russia's Balkan Entanglements, 1806–1914* (Cambridge, 1991), ch. 2.

[18] Artz, *Reaction and Revolution*, pp. 270–6; Schroeder, *Transformation*, ch. 15. For more detail, David H. Pinkney, *The French Revolution of 1830* (Princeton, 1972); and John W. Rooney, Jr., *Revolt in the Netherlands: Brussels–1830* (Lawrence, Kans., 1982).

[19] Hugh Seton-Watson, *The Russian Empire 1801–1917* (Oxford, 1967), pp. 281–9.

years later, Louis Napoleon, a nephew of the great Napoleon, overthrew the republic and established a dictatorship called the Second Empire.

Although frequently portrayed as class struggles, several of the 1848 revolutions were national in character. The uprisings began in January in the city of Palermo in the Kingdom of the Two Sicilies. The Neapolitan army had to abandon Sicily, and three weeks later the king granted a constitution. Revolutions occurred in Paris, Brussels, Karslruhe, Munich, Dresden, Vienna, and Berlin, most of these involving demands for basic rights and constitutional reforms.[20] Insurgents in northern Italy, in Piedmont, battled the Austrians. National revolts occurred also in Bohemia and in Hungary. Insurgents in the largely German-speaking provinces of Schleswig and Holstein rejected Danish rule and gained support from the German states led by Prussia. Britain, for strategic reasons, exerted some pressure to reverse that move. The tsar's government threatened war, Prussia withdrew its forces, and the provinces were returned to Denmark.[21]

In June 1849, Russia came to Austria's assistance and sent troops into Hungary to suppress insurgency there. A revolutionary government appeared also in one corner of the Ottoman Empire, in Wallachia, southeast of Austria. In July, Russian troops entered neighboring Moldavia and, it was thought, would move on to Bucharest, the capital of the insurgent principality. But the tsar instead sought to work with the Ottoman government to contain the problem. Turkish troops entered Bucharest in late September. Nicholas I, dissatisfied with their pursuit of the revolutionaries, inserted his own troops a few days later. They remained until May 1849.[22]

The 1848–49 revolutionary efforts were all ultimately defeated. "Reform" involved, at best, some modest moves in the direction of constitutional monarchy. Overall, the immediate achievements, political, national, and social, are best described as meager.

Three major international conflicts were fought in the second period. These were the Crimean War, the wars leading to Italian unification, and those leading to German unification. A significant reordering of priorities was manifest in this period in that several nations now chose war in preference to the collegial peacekeeping efforts of the European Concert.

[20] Richard F. Hamilton, *The Bourgeois Epoch: Marx and Engels on Britain, France, and Germany* (Chapel Hill, N.C., 1991; Jonathan Sperber, *The European Revolutions, 1848–1851* (New York, 1994).

[21] Sperber, *The European Revolutions*, p. 213.

[22] See Keith Hitchens, *The Romanians, 1774–1866* (Oxford, 1996), pp. 245–9; Jelavich, *St. Petersburg and Moscow*, pp. 102–13; and Seton-Watson, *Russian Empire*, pp. 311–15.

In all three conflicts, for the first time since 1815, major European powers were fighting each other. The French dictator, Napoleon III, seeking to enhance his nation's status, was involved in all three. Britain and France fought Russia in the Crimean War. France joined Piedmont in the struggle against Austria that led to Italian unification. France actually did most of the fighting. Then Prussia, seeking to enhance its status, moved first against Denmark, then against Austria, and finally against France, inflicting serious defeats in the latter two wars. As of 1871, the relative positions of the European powers had been decisively altered.[23]

Austria was indirectly involved in the Crimean War and directly involved in the struggles for Italian and German unification that, to succeed, required Austria's defeat, loss of some territories, and its exclusion from "German" affairs. Austria was also a key participant in the events of the third period, those leading up to 1914. Because of its central importance, some detailed attention must be paid to its composition and geography. As of 1850, this multicultural empire extended from northern Italy and the Swiss border across to Moldavia (see Map 2.1). Since much of the action in the years to follow involved Austria's southern frontiers, Italy, and the Balkans, an extended review is essential.

In northern Italy, bordering on France, one found a small independent state, the Kingdom of Sardinia (also called Piedmont). Its lands extended from Switzerland to the Mediterranean and also included the island of Sardinia. It was ruled by the House of Savoy, the only Italian royal family in the Italian-speaking territories. Italian unification was in great measure the work of this kingdom's very capable prime minister, Camillo Cavour.

To the east of Piedmont was Lombardy and, further east, Venetia, both of these Austrian provinces since 1815. To the north of Venetia was South Tyrol (Trentino-Alto Adige), another Austrian possession. South of Lombardy and Venetia were three provinces, effectively satellite states ruled by Habsburg nobles: Tuscany, Modena, and Parma. South of these were the Papal states. And further south was the Kingdom of the Two Sicilies, which was ruled by a branch of the Spanish Bourbons. In a series of steps, through the combined efforts of Giuseppe Garibaldi and Camillo Cavour, the foreign rulers and the pope were dispossessed and the new state was created.

---

[23] A second Polish uprising occurred in this period. Stimulated by the prospect of conscription into the Russian army, this struggle, a guerrilla war, lasted two years and cost 5,000 lives. Like its predecessor, it was a civil war, one that did not require foreign intervention.

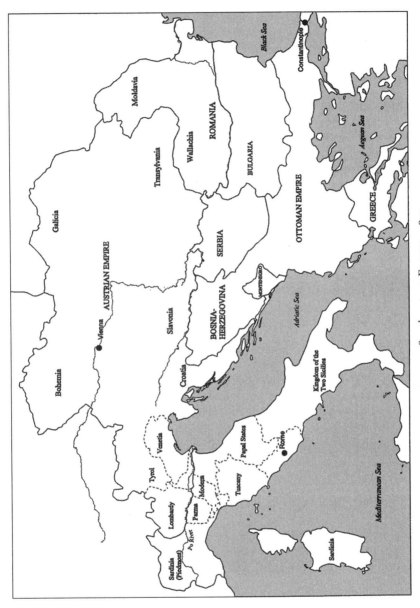

MAP 2.1. Southeastern Europe, 1850

To the east of Venetia, east of the Adriatic, were the Austrian provinces of Croatia and Slovenia (both actually part of the Hungarian realm). To the south was Dalmatia (also called Illyria), a long sliver of land stretching far along the Adriatic coast. The Sava River separated Croatia and Slovenia from Bosnia, an Ottoman province located to the south. The Sava flowed to the east, joining the Danube at Belgrade. For several hundred kilometers, these two rivers formed the border between Austria and Serbia. Although de jure still Ottoman territory, by 1857 Serbia was de facto an independent state. To the east, north of the Danube, were two Ottoman provinces (called the Principalities), Wallachia and Moldavia, the latter providing a buffer separating Austria from Russia. The Principalities were also involved in the state-making of the next decades. Together, they would form the core of the new Romania. In the northeast, another Austrian province, Galicia, faced Russia directly.

As of 1850, all of the territory south of the Sava and Danube rivers, apart from newly independent Greece and Montenegro, a tiny state that was never subjugated, belonged to the Ottoman Empire. With only minor changes, the Sava-Danube boundary had been stable for more than a century. In the course of roughly half a century, the Ottomans would lose all but a small corner of this territory, the area just to the north of the Straits – the waterway connecting the Black Sea with the Aegean and Mediterranean Seas – an area containing the capital city, Constantinople.

It was this "retreat" and the corresponding struggles over the Balkan succession that, as indicated, led to the 1914 eruption. Several new arrangements would be worked out for these territories, but the specifics, the units and their boundaries, were by no means "in the cards." At the outset, four principal options appeared likely. The first was direct rule by Austria or Russia. This was not a strong possibility, since the costs of direct rule were likely to be high and the returns modest. The second option was indirect rule, the creation of satellite states loyal to those powers. This was the option preferred by the two most concerned powers. Throughout much of the nineteenth century there was, among the great powers, a general understanding that Russia would be dominant in the east, in those territories facing the Black Sea, and that Austria would be dominant in the west, in those facing the Adriatic. A third option was new independent states, ones formed by the indigenous populations. A fourth option, of course, would be some combination of the previous three.

Along Austria's southern border, moving from west to east, one found Bosnia-Herzegovina, Serbia, and Wallachia. South of Wallachia was a territory that would become Bulgaria. Montenegro would continue as an independent state until incorporated into Yugoslavia in 1922. South of that state along the Adriatic was a population that would form Albania. Adjoining them, to the east, was a mixed-population territory, a center of major contestation, called Macedonia. And, finally, there was the recently created Greece, a small state that contained only a small minority of the area's Greek-speaking population.

Any new states formed out of that Ottoman territory would have to define (and defend) the new boundaries. Given the mixtures of populations, the centuries of war, and the subsequent migrations, the possibilities for dispute and contention were enormous. The Balkan strand of the history is continued below in the discussion of two later wars.

To the northwest, Austria (or, more precisely, its Czech province, Bohemia, along with Moravia) faced several German states, Bavaria, Saxony, and Prussia. This frontier would be the setting for the Austro-Prussian War (1866). To the northeast, as noted, Austria's province, Galicia, faced Russia. This was to be the setting for Austria's first major engagement in 1914. The internal composition of the empire, specifically, its dozen different nationalities, is considered at a later point.

To the south and east, Austria faced the Ottoman Empire, a tottering enterprise that, in the nineteenth century, was losing ground on all fronts, in Africa, Asia, and Europe. A central factor in the Ottoman decline was the Russian advance. From the late seventeenth century, Russia was expanding in all directions, moving mainly to the south, into Ottoman territory, to the southeast into central Asia, to the east across the Urals into Siberia, and into North America, establishing one outpost on the Russian River in northern California. The movement to the south produced eight Russo-Turkish wars over the span of two centuries; the first of these was fought in 1677–81, the second in 1735–39, the third and fourth, under Catherine the Great, came in 1768–74 and 1787–91.[24] In 1683, the Black Sea was effectively a Turkish lake. The north side of this lake formed the Khanate of the Crimea. To the east, Georgia and Armenia were also Ottoman territories. By the end of Catherine's reign, the northern and eastern territories were Russian possessions. Another Russo-Turkish war was fought in 1806–12, Napoleon Bonaparte having encouraged the Ottomans, effectively using them to occupy the Russians. Three Russo-Turkish wars were fought in the ninety-nine-year span

---

[24] For overviews, see Anderson, *Eastern Question*; Seton-Watson, *Russian Empire*; and William C. Fuller, Jr., *Strategy and Power in Russia, 1600–1914* (New York, 1992).

covered here, one in each of the three periods. These wars, understandably, had wide-ranging effects throughout the Balkans.[25]

The Crimean War, 1853–56, was a curious, unexpected, and unusual
conflict. It was the first time since 1815 that European powers fought
each other. Those powers, in other words, now disregarded or rejected
the understandings of the European Concert. Britain and France reached
across the Continent and together with the Ottomans (and later with
token support from Piedmont) fought a war against Russia. Judged in
terms of the losses incurred, the Crimean War was the largest European
war of the entire ninety-nine-year period.[26]

Tsar Nicholas I, recognizing the steady Ottoman decline and sensing
some possible advantage, demanded that the sultan recognize Russia as
the protector of Christian Holy Places within the empire. This transfer of
rights would enhance Russia's position at the expense of France, the previous protector. The demand was granted only to be followed by another,
this for a right to protect Orthodox subjects throughout the Ottoman Empire.[27] The Ottomans rejected the proposal, declaring it an infringement
of their sovereignty. Britain and France objected to Russia's aspirations
and, joined by Austria, sought to negotiate a peaceful resolution. But then,
in July 1853, Russia occupied Moldavia and Wallachia to put pressure on
the Ottomans. Austria was especially concerned since the possibility of
permanent occupancy would double the length of their common boundary. It offered mediation, but the Russians were unmoved.

To support the Ottomans, Britain and France sent naval units to the
Straits. Emboldened by this move, the Ottoman government demanded
evacuation of the provinces. Russia refused, and in October 1853, the
Ottomans declared war. In an initial engagement, a Turkish squadron was
annihilated. Then, in March 1854, violating international agreements,
Russian troops crossed the Danube and advanced further into Ottoman

---

[25] See Jelavich, *Russia's Balkan Entanglements*, plus the sources in the previous note.

[26] For explanation of the discrepancy between this judgment and the figures given in
Table 2.1, see note 11 above.

[27] This brief summary is based on Seton-Watson, *Russian Empire*, pp. 318–31; and Norman
McCord, *British History, 1815–1906* (New York, 1991), pp. 245–9. For more detail, see
Anderson, *Eastern Question*, ch. 5; Jelavich, *Russia's Balkan Entanglements*, pp. 115–42;
and Fuller, *Strategy and Power*, pp. 248–68. For still more detail, see Schroeder, *Austria,
Great Britain, and the Crimean War*; Andrew D. Lambert, *The Crimean War: British
Grand Strategy against Russia, 1853–56* (Manchester, 1990); Norman Rich, *Why the
Crimean War? A Cautionary Tale* (New York, 1991); Goldfrank, *The Origins of the
Crimean War*; and Winfried Baumgart, *The Crimean War, 1853–1856* (Oxford, 1999).

territory. France and Britain demanded that the Russians withdraw, but the advance continued. In response to these events and under heavy pressure from "public opinion," the two western powers declared war on Russia in March 1854. Sometime thereafter British and French troops landed at Varna in Bulgaria, where their principal enemy proved to be cholera.

In response to these moves, Russia withdrew its forces from the Danube provinces, effectively removing the immediate cause of the conflict. The Anglo-French forces, then, in September 1854, proceeded to the Crimea, their aim being to destroy the naval base at Sevastopol. Several major battles were fought and a long and difficult winter siege followed. Given the absence of prior planning, serious problems of supply and sustenance followed. Many more British soldiers died of disease and neglect than from enemy fire. Sevastopol fell in September 1855 and the fortifications were destroyed.

Hugh Seton-Watson sees the war as a result of "miscalculations and muddle rather than of deliberate aggression." Of the various factors involved, restoration of the balance of power was the most important. "Since 1849," he writes, "Russia appeared to dominate the Continent, a state of affairs to which even conservative British politicians traditionally objected."[28] The choice of target, however – Crimea, specifically the naval base at Sevastopol – and the insistence of the effort points to something other than muddle and miscalculation.

The central concern for the three major participants was the Straits. For Russia, it was the key to any naval effort in the Mediterranean or in more distant locations. Without the assurance of unhindered passage, Russia could have no serious impact. Britain was concerned with its connections to India and with other points in the East, some of that effort reaching across the Mediterranean and overland through the near- and middle-eastern territories. France claimed some rights in the eastern Mediterranean, that is, protection of Roman Catholics in the Holy Lands, rights that were more boldly asserted by Napoleon III than by his predecessors. Given their aims, both Britain and France saw the Ottoman Empire as a useful buffer state. Some elements of "realism," in short, a more compelling logic, underlay their involvement in this struggle. The tottering buffer state would be supported and the Russian naval threat would be limited or removed entirely.

---

[28] Seton-Watson, *Russian Empire*, pp. 320–21, and also 331.

Despite its manifest concern, Austria did not immediately participate in the struggle. In June 1854, Austria had demanded the withdrawal of Russian troops and at the same time concluded a secret agreement with the Ottomans, one that allowed Austria, following Russia's withdrawal, to occupy temporarily Wallachia and Moldavia. When Russia withdrew, neutral Austria undertook a "peaceful occupation" of the provinces, thus preventing further confrontation of Russian and Anglo-French forces. That move allowed the western allies to shift operations to Sevastopol, the center of Russian naval power. Russia's leaders saw Austria's action as a betrayal, no fit compensation for the aid provided in 1849 to pacify Hungary. This intervention irreparably damaged Austro-Russian relations. To make matters worse, in December 1854 Austria belatedly joined the allies in an arrangement involving the usual package of obligations and benefits.

Several major lessons should be noted. First, the Crimean struggle began with the Russian initiative, the Ottoman decline being seen as the occasion for an "advance" to the south. Britain and France, both sensing a threat to their interests in the Mediterranean and Near East, sought to block that advance, seeing the Ottoman presence as an effective buffer preventing or limiting Russian access in the region.

Second, the great powers made several attempts in the months prior to the outbreak to achieve a peaceful settlement, but these all failed. The Concert of Europe was no longer effective. In part this was due to misreadings and confusion, in part it was due to efforts of a new "actor." France, now led by Napoleon III, saw some advantage there. The conflict would break up the "reactionary" Austro-Russian alliance and allow greater opportunity for later French aggrandizement.

Enlarging the conflict, Piedmont subsequently joined with the allies, sending 15,000 men to the Crimea. That small state had no immediate interest in the distant struggle, but Cavour also anticipated some future benefits. His nation would gain prestige and would be represented at the future peace conference. There was also a quid pro quo: His allies would be under some obligation to Piedmont in subsequent conflicts.

Serious leadership deficiencies were shown by all parties at all stages of the conflict. The tsar misread and misjudged the signs provided by British leaders. The prior discussions of Turkey's future, beginning first in 1844, had been rather diffuse, providing no clear and obvious cues. The British military, following decades of neglect, was not prepared for combat, certainly not for the logistics involved in this one. And the British government did not have a clear line of policy at any point in the long struggle. Not surprisingly, perhaps, the House of Commons conducted an inquiry. Following its submission, Lord Aberdeen's government lost a vote of confidence by 305 to 148. Norman McCord describes it as "one of the greatest humiliations ever experienced by a British administration."[29]

"Public opinion" had an important role in the origins of the conflict. First seen in the struggle for Greek independence, in the demands of highly educated coteries, a much larger "mass opinion" was now operating, this mobilized by the reports appearing in large-circulation newspapers. The monarchs of the previous ages – Philip II, Louis XIV, Frederick the Great, and Maria Theresa – did not consult the general populace. They were not pushed or constrained in any serious way by mass sentiment. But the extension of education and the consequent growth of literacy provided the basis for a minor industry, mass-circulation newspapers, which could inform and mobilize opinion as in no previous era. The long dispute prior to the outbreak of hostilities stretched over some nine months, during which it was "continuously ventilated" in British and French newspapers. The Russian actions, it is said, "aroused a patriotic fervour."[30] Press reports and reader sentiments were constant factors in subsequent crises. Political and military leaders, accordingly, had to "stylize" the beginnings of conflicts in such a way as to make engagement seem plausible and justified.

In the Crimean War settlement, the Treaty of Paris, signed on 30 March 1856, the Russian protectorate of the two Ottoman Principalities was ended. Russia was required to cede the southern tip of Bessarabia located at the mouth of the Danube. Free navigation of the river was now guaranteed and put under the control of a European commission. The Russian claim to the protection of the Orthodox believers in the Ottoman Empire was denied. The Black Sea was neutralized; its waters were "to be open to merchantmen of all nations and closed to all warships. No naval arsenals or dockyards could in future exist on its shores." M. S. Anderson describes the settlement as "extremely harsh and indeed unprecedented." In a separate treaty, Britain, France, and Austria "guaranteed the independence and integrity of the Ottoman Empire."[31]

---

[29] McCord, *British History*, p. 249.

[30] Ibid., p. 246.

[31] Anderson, *Eastern Question*, pp. 143–4; Seton-Watson, *Russian Empire*, pp. 329–30; Jelavich, *Russia's Balkan Entanglements*, pp. 138–42; Fuller, *Strategy and Power*, ch. 7; and, for more detail, Winfried Baumgart, *The Peace of Paris, 1856: Studies in War, Diplomacy, and Peacemaking* (Santa Barbara, 1981), esp. ch. 3.

The settlement had formidable implications. In the words of the historian Anderson:

Its greatest single achievement was to make Russia a revisionist power, to end the stress on conservative solidarity and maintenance of the *status quo* ... and replace them by a concentration on purely Russian interests, many of which lay outside Europe.... Until 1853 the spirit of the Holy Alliance, though enfeebled, was still a force to be reckoned with in European politics. The Crimean War provided the death-blow.[32]

The outcome of the war brought a dramatic change in the perception of Russia by the other powers. Much of its influence in international affairs prior to the war, Barbara Jelavich writes, was "due to a gross overestimation of Russian military strength." From the Napoleonic Wars through to the early 1850s, it had faced no real test of that strength, and the empire's opponents accordingly "remained hypnotized by the mass of the Russian territory and the size of the Russian army." On the basis of that presumed strength, diplomatic victories continued to be won. The Crimean War, however, demonstrated the "weakness of her internal system and its effect upon her military potential." No longer able to act as the "gendarme of Europe," Russia was forced to withdraw from involvement in European affairs for many years to allow repair and reconstitution of its forces. With Russia's "restraining hand" removed, Napoleon III's France "was able to assist in the unification of Italy and play a generally disruptive role in regard to other national movements." In 1858, with some French assistance, Romania was created out of the two Principalities. Russia's leaders were opposed to this, but could do nothing to stop it.[33]

Austria's involvement in the Crimean War also had far-reaching implications. It had "prevented her encirclement by Russia in the southeast, yet at the price of permanent enmity." Subsequently, in the wars leading to Italian and German unification, Austria found itself without allies. Russia, the "natural" ally, did not intervene in 1859 or in 1866 when Austria was in serious difficulty. After 1856, Winfried Baumgart writes, Austrian isolation "was total."[34]

The Austro-French-Sardinian War was fought in 1859, three years after the Crimean War. In a prior secret agreement, Napoleon III arranged

[32] Anderson, *Eastern Question*, pp. 145–6.
[33] Jelavich, *St. Petersburg and Moscow*, pp. 111–12; and Jelavich, *Russia's Balkan Entanglements*, p. 146.
[34] In Baumgart, *Peace of Paris*, p. 203. See also Robert A. Kann, *A History of the Habsburg Empire 1526–1918* (Berkeley, 1974), pp. 263–7.

with Cavour to support the Kingdom of Sardinia (Piedmont) in its efforts to gain Lombardy and Venetia. Austria suffered two serious defeats, at Magenta on 4 June, then at Solferino on 24 June. In the final settlement, Lombardy, containing the Po River Valley and the city of Milan, passed to Sardinia. Austrian leaders were also removed from the three satellite states, Tuscany, Modena, and Parma. The French emperor backed out of a promise to liberate Venetia, and for a few more years that state remained with Austria.[35]

After further struggles, Italian unification was achieved in 1861 (more was to be gained later: Venetia in 1866, the Papal States in 1870, Trentino-Alto Adige in 1918). Italy experienced various internal adjustment problems in the first years of its existence. Several decades later, it too sought major power status and engaged in several episodes of "outreach."

Three other important wars occurred in this second period. They were all initiated by Prussia and are sometimes referred to as Bismarck's wars: the Danish-Prussian War (1864), the Austro-Prussian War (1866), and the Franco-Prussian War (1870–71). In the first, the smallest of the three, Prussia and Austria took Schleswig and Holstein from Denmark with Austria occupying Holstein. In the aftermath, Bismarck engineered a "falling out" with his Austrian partner and brought on the second war. Austria was quickly and definitively defeated. The decisive battle was fought at Königgrätz (opposite Sadowa) in Bohemia on 3 July 1866. The settlement, directed largely by Bismarck, had important implications, with Prussia gaining clear dominance among the German-speaking states. Austria, with a significant German-speaking population, was excluded from the new arrangement. Although generally called the Austro-Prussian War, it is also called the "German civil war," as most of the smaller German states were involved. Italy was also a participant and, in the settlement, was given Venetia.[36]

---

[35] Kann, *History of the Habsburg Empire*, pp. 267–70; and Denis Mack Smith, *Modern Italy: A Political History* (Ann Arbor, 1997), pp. 18–19.

By the terms of the settlement, Austria gave Lombardy to Louis Napoleon, who in turn handed it over to Sardinia. In exchange, the French emperor received Savoy and Nice. Italian nationalists, not too surprisingly, were outraged by these moves. Lombardy had been won with Italian lives. The Italian monarch, of the House of Savoy, had given away his own homeland.

[36] Geoffrey Wawro, *The Austro-Prussian War: Austria's War with Prussia and Italy in 1866* (Cambridge, 1996).

These few sentences cannot begin to report all of the complications. Venetia was surrendered to France, to Louis Napoleon, who in turn passed it on to the new Italian state. See Kann, *History of the Habsburg Empire*, pp. 273–7; Mack Smith, *Modern Italy*,

The war and the settlement had a further important consequence: It spurred the reorganization of the Austrian Empire. Prussia had, among other things, used subversion as a weapon in that conflict. Facing an ethnically diverse opponent, Prussia gave support to nationalist movements, specifically to the Hungarians, the aim being to fragment and immobilize its opponent. After the war, to address the same problem, Austria produced the Compromise (Ausgleich) of 1867, giving a wide range of powers to a newly created Hungarian government and Parliament. The empire at this point became Austria-Hungary, or the Dual Monarchy.

The 1869 Austro-Hungarian census reported that one-quarter of the nation's population was German and one-sixth was Hungarian. Combined, the two constituent groups formed only 41 percent of the total. This arrangement still left out the nation's majority, the other nine nationality groups. Austria-Hungary, an empire but not a nation, was the most fragile of the five major powers. In a period of growing nationalist sentiments, this multinational empire was a vulnerable entity.[37]

The Franco-Prussian War, 1870–71, the third of Bismarck's wars, was also brief. The result was a stunning and humiliating defeat for France, which, by the Treaty of Frankfurt, was obliged to pay enormous reparations. The sum fixed was "exactly proportionate with the one imposed by Napoleon I on Prussia in 1807."[38] One province, Alsace, and part of another, Lorraine, were taken from France and added to the new German Empire.

---

pp. 72–7; and A. J. P. Taylor, *The Struggle for Mastery in Europe 1848–1918* (London, 1971), ch. 8. Readings on the origins of this war differ. Taylor states that Louis Napoleon wished "to push Austria into war" and that the Austrians also "wanted to bring the war on." In the last resort, he states, "Austria and France themselves promoted the war which was to destroy their traditional grandeur in Europe" (*Struggle for Mastery*, pp. 164–5). Hajo Holborn states: "Whereas Austria was resigned to war, Bismarck wanted it and was only maneuvering to put the blame for its outbreak on Vienna," in *A History of Modern Germany 1840–1945* (New York, 1969), pp. 180–1. See also Kann, *History of the Habsburg Empire*, pp. 332–5; Gordon A. Craig, *Germany 1866–1945* (New York, 1978), pp. 3–7; James J. Sheehan, *German History 1770–1866* (Oxford, 1989), pp. 899–911; Thomas Nipperdey, *Deutsche Geschichte 1800–1866* (Munich, 1984), pp. 768–803; and Otto Pflanze, *Bismarck and the Development of Germany*, vol. 1: *The Period of Unification, 1813–1871* (Princeton, 1990), chs. 12–15.

[37] Earlier, in the 1859 war, France had used the nationality weapon against Austria; see Anderson, *Eastern Question*, p. 153. The census figures are reported in Vladimir Dedijer, *The Road to Sarajevo* (New York, 1966), p. 75.

[38] Keiger, *France*, p. 5. On the war, see Thomas Nipperdey, *Deutsche Geschichte, 1866–1918* (Munich, 1992), pp. 55–84; Pflanze, *Bismarck*, vol. 1, chs. 16–22; and, for more detail, Michael Howard, *The Franco-Prussian War: The German Invasion of France, 1870–1871* (New York, 1961).

The creation of that empire, of a unified Germany, was easily the most important result of the war. This occurred, officially, on 18 January 1871. The centuries-long history of German *Kleinstaaterei*, of small-state fragmentation, of lands with no great importance, was now ended. The new Germany, a large, unified nation with a rapidly growing economic base, would obviously be a major power, one of much greater importance than tottering Austria-Hungary.

All informed observers recognized the importance of this development. Benjamin Disraeli, the British Conservative Party leader, told the House of Commons that the struggle between France and Germany "is no common war" like the three preceding European conflicts. This war, he said, "represents the German revolution, a greater political event than the French revolution of last century.... Not a single principle in the management of our foreign affairs, accepted by all statesmen for guidance up to six months ago, any longer exists."[39] Lord Salisbury (later foreign minister and still later prime minister) foresaw a serious difficulty: "A ceded territory would be a constant memorial of humiliation." Its recovery would be "a holy cause" for France. "The French youth," he asserted, "will be brought up by countless teachers to long for the lost provinces, ... to look upon their recovery as the first of national duties, and to believe all means lawful, and all opportunities fitting for performing it." Recognizing France's weakness, that it could not do it alone, Salisbury declared: "She will not again attack Prussia single-handed." But the time must come, he said, when the ambitious dreams of the Germans "will cross the path of some power strong enough to resent them: and that day will be to France the day of restitution and revenge."[40]

Written in 1870, Salisbury's statement about French teachers and French youth might easily be counted as "telling" or "prescient," especially in the light of later events. But such judgments avoid, first, the question of validity, and, second, the question of mechanism, that is, the specific factors leading to the 1914 decision to engage. Two French observers commented on French attitudes after the 1870 war. Arthur de Gobineau saw the government trying to convince everyone that the French people were "burning" with patriotism. His sense, however, was that "the masses persisted in believing it was not their business." George Sand found Paris "braying with enthusiasm," but in the countryside she saw "little

[39] W. F. Monypenny and George Earl Buckle, *The Life of Benjamin Disraeli: Early of Beaconsfield*, 6 vols. (New York, 1910–20), vol. 5, p. 133.
[40] A. L. Kennedy, *Salisbury 1830–1903: Portrait of a Statesman* (London, 1953), p. 71.

enthusiasm" or – worse – outright opposition. The peasants, it is reported, "resented anyone and anything that threatened their security and homes." Eugen Weber reports that the schools were more effective at the turn of the century and better able to instill patriotic sentiments, but his evidence on this point is sparse.[41]

The war produced another change in European affairs, this involving the Eastern question. From 1856, Russia had sought revision, specifically, wishing the abolition of the Black Sea neutralization clauses of the Paris Treaty. The Franco-Prussian War provided Russia with the needed opportunity. In October 1870, after quietly securing Prussia's approval, Tsar Alexander II announced his rejection of the treaty articles. A subsequent big power meeting in London ratified the move, giving it post hoc legitimation. Russia's unilateral move was another demonstration of how far the powers had moved from Concert practice.[42]

The Concert of Europe, clearly, did not function well in this second period. The original understanding was that territorial changes required the consent of the great powers. But in this period, beginning with the Crimean War and ending with the Treaty of Frankfurt, that principle had been all but abandoned. Four states – Russia, France, Prussia, and the newcomer, Piedmont – had refused the consensual obligation and instead had chosen war as an instrument for their purposes.

The "balance sheet" as of 1871 reads as follows: Prussia, now Germany, had achieved significant gains; it was soon to be the major economic power of Europe and also a major military power. Piedmont, now Italy, also made major gains; the new unified nation would soon be "a power," although not of the same stature as the original Concert members. France had experienced major losses; it would never again have the stature held from the time of Louis XIV through to the Napoleonic period. A significant lasting heritage of the two Napoleonic regimes was the reduction of France to a second-rank power. Austria lost its long-standing dominant position in central European affairs, to be replaced by the Prussian "upstart." And Russia's weaknesses had been amply demonstrated in the Crimean War. From 1856 on, Russia was forced to abandon its previous role as the ultimate arbiter of central European affairs.

[41] Eugen Weber, *Peasants into Frenchmen: The Modernization of Rural France 1870–1914* (Stanford, 1976), pp. 99–104 and 332–8. Keiger also discusses the "myth of revenge" and cites appropriate evidence; see *France*, pp. 5–9, 15, 40, 72, 76, 119, and 163. That indifference changed at a later point; see Eugen Weber, *The Nationalist Revival in France, 1905–1914* (Berkeley, 1968).
[42] Anderson, *Eastern Question*, pp. 172–3; and Baumgart, *Peace of Paris*, pp. 191–4.

Those second-period losses provided new agendas, sets of concerns for great-power decision makers in the subsequent decades. Austria had experienced a series of losses. Unable to defeat the revolution on its own, it needed Russian assistance to recover Hungary in 1849. One important result of the Crimean War was that Russia was no longer an ally. In 1859, Austria lost a war to France and was deprived of some Italian territories. Then in 1866, it was defeated in the contest for dominance in central Europe, losing power, prestige, and more Italian territory. A few years later, Austria-Hungary sat out the Franco-Prussian War hoping, vainly, for gains if Prussia foundered. To maintain some semblance of its historic position as a great power, Austria-Hungary's leaders had to demonstrate the state's continuing political capacity.

Given its limited options, one might think that Austria-Hungary would seek to demonstrate that capacity through expansion into the Balkans, still largely under Ottoman hegemony. But that inference would be mistaken. Anderson declares that, in the 1870s, "the preservation of the Ottoman Empire as it stood was seen as a major Habsburg interest." Count Julius Andrassy, the foreign minister, summed up, in 1875, as follows: "Turkey is almost of a providential utility to Austria. Her existence is essential to our well-understood interests. She keeps the *status quo* of the small states and hinders their aspirations to our advantage. Were there no Turkey, then all these heavy duties would fall on us." Several decades later, with the continued Ottoman decline, Austria-Hungary was forced, as best it could, to undertake those "heavy duties."[43]

A similar claim has been made about Russia's Balkan aims. A. J. P. Taylor declared that Russia "had no ambitions in European Turkey nor interest in the Balkan states, except as neutral buffers versus Austria-Hungary and Germany." The prizes there "were trifling and hard to come by, compared to those in China or Persia." There were, he adds, "no Russian banks in the Balkans, no Russian-owned railways, virtually no Russian trade." The concern of Russian policy was the waterway, the "fear of being strangled at the Straits." Anderson offers a similar reading: "The Russian government did not wish to destroy the Ottoman Empire; but for a good many years Russian policy had envisaged the creation in its Balkan provinces of a series of autonomous states under Christian rulers somewhat on the lines of Rumania and Serbia." The Ottoman Empire, Anderson continues, "would be reduced, at least in Europe." Both Austria

---

[43] Anderson, *Eastern Question*, p. 180.

and Russia wished to see small and divided states in the region, ones that were allies (or satellites) or, at minimum, nonthreatening neutrals.[44]

The complexities of the Austro-Hungarian and Russian policies in the Balkans cannot possibly be captured in a few sentences. Dozens of options were proposed in the course of the years covered in this chapter. At one point, in 1844, Nicholas I and the Habsburg ambassador in St. Petersburg discussed the subject. The tsar suggested that "Austria should take Constantinople and, in fact, the entire Balkan heritage: 'I shall never cross the Danube ... and everything between this river and the Adriatic ought to be yours.' "[45]

## The Third Period: 1871–1914

This period is best characterized as one of small state insurgency. The powers attempted to hold onto the arrangements existing as of 1871. No military conflicts between the major powers occurred in this period until August 1914. The most serious problems appeared in southeastern Europe, where three unstable empires sought to maintain a "status quo." But a cluster of new (or aspiring) states sought other arrangements.

Recognizing the many sources of instability in the new Europe, Bismarck pursued several policies intended to alleviate the most obvious problems. First, he provided an easy peace for Austria after the 1866 war. He took no Austrian territory and imposed only a token indemnity. This left the door open for a reconciliation that came quickly and with relative ease. Second, to the other European powers he sought to demonstrate that Germany was "satiated," that it had achieved its goals and would now concentrate on internal development. Third, fearing a war of revenge, he sought to counter a possible French threat. The worst combination would be if France joined with Russia, leaving Germany, caught in middle, facing a two-front war. He therefore cultivated a Russian alliance and, simultaneously, encouraged the French to seek "glory" elsewhere, not in Europe but overseas. The French government and military did just that. Among other things, a long struggle in Indo-China followed, one not "settled"

[44] Taylor, *Struggle for Mastery*, p. 484; Anderson, *Eastern Question*, p. 180.
[45] Jelavich, *Russia's Balkan Entanglements*, p. 113. This thought, to be sure, appears to have been no more than a passing fancy. For some appreciation of the complexities, which included religious differences, nationalist sentiments, and "public opinion," see ibid., pp. 147–59.
 With respect to all of these subjects, one should remember the criticisms indicated in the previous chapter.

until 1887. Several decades later, a set of unexpected circumstances brought the focus of attention back to Europe.[46]

In 1873, the League of the Three Emperors, the Dreikaiserbund, was formed, joining Germany, Austria-Hungary, and Russia. It was, from one perspective, a "natural" combination, the three promising to "uphold legitimacy, order, and the monarchical principle." But the agreement was vague, toothless, and fragile; basically, the three agreed to consult. For the moment, however, it fit well with Bismarck's guiding rule: in a world of five powers, "try to be *à trois*."[47] But that combination proved unstable due to serious conflicts, mostly over the Balkans.

Bosnia and Herzegovina first appear in modern European affairs in an extended insurgency against their Turkish overlords, one that lasted from 1875 to 1877. The struggle was basically a guerilla war, similar to many such conflicts in the past (Serbia in 1804–13 and Greece in 1821–27) and many to come: the Boer War, the Cuban insurgency, the Philippines struggle, Vietnam, and Algeria. In 1876, Montenegro and Serbia, under considerable domestic pressure, came to the aid of their kinfolk and declared war on the Ottomans.

Six months later, in April 1877, after the Turks had defeated the Serbs and repressed a rising in Bulgaria, Russia joined the struggle. Overlooking much of the complexity, the conflict appears in most textbooks as "the Russo-Turkish War."[48] Russian forces, after some initial reverses, overwhelmed the Ottomans, swept through the Balkans, and approached the outskirts of Constantinople, where they bogged down. At this point, alarmed by the Russian advance, Disraeli, now prime minister, sent a British squadron to the Straits and mobilized troops elsewhere.[49]

---

[46] Donald Kagan, *On the Origins of War and the Preservation of Peace* (New York, 1995), pp. 101, 110–11. For more, see Keiger, *France*, pp. 8–10; Baumgart, *Imperialism*, p. 59; and Henri Brunschwig, *French Colonialism 1871–1914: Myths and Realities* (London, 1966). France's major foreign affairs crises in this period (Indochina, Fashoda, Morocco 1905 and 1911) were all linked to colonial aspirations – not to the recovery of Alsace and Lorraine.

[47] Craig, *Germany*, pp. 103–4; Holborn, *Modern Germany*, p. 236; Jelavich, *St. Petersburg and Moscow*, pp. 157–9; and Pflanze, *Bismarck*, vol. 2: *The Period of Consolidation, 1871–1880*, pp. 259–60.

[48] Jelavich, *Russia's Balkan Entanglements*, pp. 170–78; Fuller, *Strategy and Power*, pp. 308–27.

[49] A continued advance and the taking of Constantinople would have had world-historic implications. One possibility would have been an early end to the Ottoman Empire and its replacement with Russia now dominating the Straits. Or, another option, Britain and Austria-Hungary would have entered the war, this bringing a Russian defeat.

The British interest in the Near East, as noted earlier, was substantially enhanced with the opening of the Suez Canal in 1869, which then became the main route to India and the

The Russians, close to the end of their resources, quickly ended the war and, in the Treaty of San Stefano, dictated terms that would have driven the Ottomans from all but a tiny scrap of European territory. Russia planned a large Bulgarian satellite state, one reaching from the Black Sea to the Aegean Sea, thus blocking off Turkey from the rest of Europe. Several smaller states were to be created, or – seen from a different perspective – were to be reconstituted after centuries of subjection. This plan provides compelling evidence as to Russian intentions with regard to the Balkans, that is, creating satellite states as opposed to taking them over.[50]

Alarmed by this Russian success, the other European powers moved to rearrange the settlement and convened the Congress of Berlin in June 1878. Presided over by Bismarck, it was the most important international gathering to take place between the Congress of Vienna in 1815 and Versailles in 1919. The Congress substituted "a smaller, weaker, and divided Bulgaria," with a part remaining under nominal Turkish rule. Russia recovered the part of Bessarabia lost in 1856 and was allowed to keep some territories gained to the east of the Black Sea. Britain received some revisions of the Straits agreements. Turkey agreed to transfer Cyprus to Britain "for use as a base in the eastern Mediterranean" (for which Britain agreed to pay £98,000 per year).[51]

Earlier, in January 1877, Russia and Austria-Hungary had signed a secret agreement according to which the latter would remain neutral in the coming Russo-Turkish War. Russia promised it would create no large state in the Balkans. It agreed also that Austria-Hungary would be allowed to occupy the two Turkish provinces, Bosnia and Herzegovina, when it chose. Until then, those provinces, with their Croatian, Serbian, and Muslim populations, would be administered by Austria-Hungary, although officially they remained Ottoman possessions. The Austrian aim, apparently, was strategic; it would protect the long Dalmatian extension along the Adriatic and, simultaneously, would block a possible Serbian advance in that direction. The transfer of administration was the subject of

East. Shortly thereafter, Disraeli quietly arranged the purchase of a majority of the shares in the Suez Canal Company from Egypt's khedive. Within a few years, Egypt would pass to British rule, still another step in the dissolution of the Ottoman Empire. Robinson and Gallagher, *Africa and the Victorians*, chs. 4 and 5.

[50] For the war and San Stefano, see Anderson, *Eastern Question*, pp. 198–204 (for Russian and Austrian aims with regard to the region, see p. 180); Jelavich, *Russia's Balkan Entanglements*, pp. 170–8; and Fuller, *Strategy and Power*, pp. 320–2.

[51] From McCord, *British History*, pp. 275–7; Anderson, *Eastern Question*, pp. 205–18; Fuller, *Strategy and Power*, pp. 321–2; Pflanze, *Bismarck*, vol. 2, ch. 14.; and Dedijer, *Sarajevo*, pp. 54–63.

intense discussion at the Berlin Congress. The Ottomans, understandably, opposed it but were overruled. The Russians were divided but ultimately agreed to the change. Bismarck favored the move, since it gave Austria-Hungary some compensation for its 1866 losses and redirected its efforts away from central Europe. Publicly, Disraeli offered humanitarian arguments; privately, he thought the move would help break the League of the Three Emperors. The Berlin Congress did hasten its demise. From the start, it was an ineffective alliance; when the other powers denied Russia the fruits of victory further cooperation ended.[52]

Late in July 1878, a month after the Berlin agreement was signed, Austro-Hungarian troops entered Bosnia and Herzegovina. The Croats, mostly Catholic, greeted them; the Serbs viewed them with hostility; the Muslims were "in a state of ferment." Bosnian feudal lords roused the Muslim population and a "ferocious and sanguinary struggle" followed. It took some 200,000 troops three months to quell the insurgency. More than 5,000 Austro-Hungarian soldiers were killed, wounded, or missing. The rebel losses, which were probably considerably greater, were never recorded.[53]

Four years later, a second revolt occurred, following an order for conscription into the Habsburg army. This time, Muslims and Serbs fought on the same side. It took eight divisions six months to put down the rebellion. Austria-Hungary paid a heavy price for extending its rule. The newly subjected populations, obviously, paid an even greater price.

In October 1879, Bismarck opened the negotiations with Austria-Hungary that produced the Dual Alliance. This linkage of the two powers, which lasted to 1918, was to be of pivotal importance in European affairs over the next four decades.[54] In 1882, the alliance was extended to include Italy. Recognizing the unique problem stemming from Germany's central position in Europe, the nightmare of a two-front war, Bismarck subsequently arranged a highly secret treaty with Russia (June 1887). Called the Reinsurance Treaty, the parties agreed, for a three-year term,

---

[52] Anderson, *Eastern Question*, pp. 193–4, 210, 220–1. Also, Pflanze, *Bismarck*, vol. 2, pp. 430–1; Dedijer, *Sarajevo*, pp. 57–62; Taylor, *Struggle for Mastery*, ch. 11; and Tim Judah, *The Serbs: History, Myth and the Destruction of Yugoslavia* (New Haven, 1997), pp. 66–8. On the difficulties and demise of the Three Emperors' League, see Fuller, *Strategy and Power*, 293–4, 331–7.

[53] Dedijer, *Sarajevo*, pp. 64–6. Singer and Small's figure, shown in Table 2.1, clearly understates both the severity and intensity of this conflict.

[54] Pflanze, *Bismarck*, vol. 2, ch. 18.

to remain neutral in a war waged by the other. Two exceptions were specified: if Russia were to attack Austria or if Germany were to attack France.
Since those options seemed very unlikely, from one perspective the treaty
would appear pointless. But by separating Russia from France, by preventing joint initiatives, it was an important achievement. For Germany,
it avoided the threat of a two-front war.[55]

Gordon Craig judges Bismarck's foreign policy, on the whole, as a
success with the "warmongers in France and the Pan-Slavs in Russia ...
in eclipse."[56] The major powers of Europe were now focused on overseas
expansion. Bismarck had fended off the principal threats to Germany; he
initiated twenty years of peace in Central Europe.

Bismarck's achievement, however, was undone by events beginning in
1888. For Germany it was the year of the three emperors. Kaiser Wilhelm
I died that year and was succeeded by his son, Friedrich III, who was dying
of cancer. On 15 June 1888, Wilhelm II became kaiser. Unlike his grandfather, who rarely interfered with Bismarck, Wilhelm "was determined
to rule his empire himself." Bismarck, as seen, after 1871 had followed a
policy of restraint. Wilhelm II charted a "New Course," one focused on
*Weltpolitik*, the aim being to make Germany a great imperial power. As
opposed to the "structural" accounts of European affairs, Donald Kagan
writes, with complete justification, that it "is not possible ... to understand Germany's behavior in the years from 1888 to 1914 without taking
account of the ideas and personality of William II."[57]

Wilhelm II was an absolutist in a time of democratic aspirations. He
was also, Kagan reports, "a dedicated militarist, delighting in uniforms,
surrounding himself with a military entourage, and sharing in the ethic of

---

[55] A few sentences cannot satisfactorily deal with the many complex issues involved. For a
start, see Pflanze, *Bismarck*, vol. 3: *The Period of Fortification, 1880–1898*, pp. 248–53;
Craig, *Germany*, pp. 131–2; and Jelavich, *St. Petersburg and Moscow*, pp. 209–11.

[56] Craig, *Germany*, p. 134.

[57] Kagan, *Origins of War*, p. 119. Kagan's one-line conclusion about Wilhelm's personal influence is amply documented in Lamar Cecil's two-volume biography of the man, *Wilhelm
II: Prince and Emperor, 1859–1900* (Chapel Hill, N.C., 1989); and *Wilhelm II: Emperor
and Exile, 1900–1941* (Chapel Hill, N.C., 1996). Those who argue a determined history,
who point to powerful structural factors, and who deny "the role of individuals," should
read Cecil and then write a statement defending their position. On the year of the three
kaisers, see Cecil, *Wilhelm*, vol. 1, chs. 4–6.
    See also Isabel V. Hull, *The Entourage of Kaiser Wilhelm II, 1888–1918* (Cambridge,
1982); and John C. G. Röhl, *The Kaiser and His Court: Wilhelm II and the Government
of Germany* (Cambridge, 1994). Röhl is also producing a multivolume biography of the
man. The translation of the first volume is entitled *Young William: The Kaiser's Early
Life, 1859–1888* (New York, 1998).

the Prussian soldier. His military and naval officials had easier access to him than his chancellor." When things went badly, he would "think and talk of launching a military coup to abolish the constitution and restore absolute rule, although he never undertook such an action." Lamar Cecil reports that "his most pronounced – and most fatal – characteristic was his habitual inclination to act almost entirely on the basis of his personal feelings."[58]

In March 1890, Wilhelm compelled Bismarck to resign. The following week, under the new chancellor, General Leo von Caprivi, an action was taken, "the most crucial of all those made between 1890 and the outbreak of the First World War [one which] set in train the whole chain of calamity that led toward that catastrophe." On the unanimous advice of his advisors, Wilhelm II decided early in 1890 to let the Reinsurance Treaty lapse. The news was devastating for the Russians, who offered concessions to maintain the treaty, but these were to no avail.[59]

The kaiser's advisors were members of the Foreign Office, people who had worked for years under Bismarck's direction. That those experts, freed of Bismarck's dominance, unanimously advised dropping the treaty, points up a difficulty: There was something wrong with it. They thought it was "incompatible in spirit . . . with the Austro-German treaty and would compromise Germany's relationship with Vienna."[60] It is often said that Wilhelm, the starry-eyed amateur, "did it," that he dropped the treaty. In fact, it was the Foreign Office experts who "did it." But for their intervention and advice, Wilhelm II would probably have renewed it. The most serious immediate consequence was the development of the linkage that Salisbury had anticipated two decades earlier.

The Triple Alliance linking Germany, Austria-Hungary, and Italy was renewed in May 1891. At that time, it was widely believed that Britain had also joined, thus making the "three" into a "four." Both Russia and France accepted that claim, a reading that led their leaders to consider

[58] Kagan, *Origins of War*, p. 119; and Cecil, *Wilhelm*, vol. 1, p. xii. Europe's leaders had to deal with this man and with his idiosyncrasies. For Lord Salisbury's judgments, see Paul M. Kennedy, *The Rise of the Anglo-German Antagonism 1860–1914* (London, 1980), pp. 212, 219–20.

[59] Craig, *Germany*, pp. 230–9; Cecil, *Wilhelm*, vol. 1, pp. 189–91; and George F. Kennan, *The Fateful Alliance: France, Russia, and the Coming of the First World War* (New York, 1984), pp. 19–22.

[60] Cecil, *Wilhelm*, p. 189. This was the view, for example, of General Lothar von Schweinitz, the German ambassador to St. Petersburg. Bismarck claimed there was no incompatibility; if Franz Joseph learned of the treaty, he argued, "the result would not be uneasiness but relief," from Pflanze, *Bismarck*, vol. 3, p. 251.

joining together in an otherwise unnatural alliance. Signals were given: In July a French naval squadron visited Cronstadt; the tsar was present at the official reception; the *Marseillaise* was played and the tsar doffed his hat. Discussions were initiated, but these moved slowly and erratically. In December 1893, after a year and a half of negotiation, the tsar signed the agreement. The principal clause read: "If France is attacked by Germany, or by Italy supported by Germany, Russia shall employ all her available forces to attack Germany. If Russia is attacked by Germany, or by Austria supported by Germany, France shall employ all her available forces to fight Germany." As Kagan put it, "Bismarck's worst nightmare had become reality."[61]

The shift in alliances had serious implications for the eastern question. The Reinsurance Treaty gave Russia considerable freedom of action in the Balkans and – an important correlate – constrained Berlin's support for any of Vienna's initiatives in the region. But now, Wilhelm's move made Germany more dependent on its alliance partners, Austria-Hungary and Italy. The balance of incentives vis-à-vis Austria-Hungary, whether to constrain or to encourage, was now altered. The same conclusion held also for Russia; any sensed need for restraint was removed with the ending of Bismarck's alliance. For Germany, the move brought no evident gain and a considerable loss.

The new arrangement required important changes in Germany's military planning. Count Alfred von Schlieffen, who became chief of the General Staff in February 1892, devised the plan needed to counter the possible two-front war. With some important changes, it remained Germany's basic operational concept until its implementation in August 1914. The plan was based on the assumption that Russia, the stronger enemy, would be slow to mobilize. The aim, therefore, was a "one-two punch." The first, a powerful blow against France with overwhelming force, would yield a quick victory in the west. The second, with forces transferred from the western front, involved a concentrated attack on Russia. To defeat France, the plan called for an invasion of two neutral countries, Luxembourg and Belgium (Schlieffen's original version also included The Netherlands). Massive German armies would sweep through Belgium,

[61] Kagan, *Origins of War*, p. 126; Kennan, *Fateful Alliance*, ch. 13. The Triple Alliance and the Franco-Russian Alliance, it should be noted, were not "symmetrical" treaties. Geographic proximity allowed consultation in the former case, but since that was not possible for France and Russia, the latter provided for "automatic" responses. A separate military convention even specified the number of troops to be engaged.

cross into France, and then circle around the French forces then moving into Lorraine and Alsace. That sweep would allow the German forces to attack the French flank and rear. The conflict would be over in six weeks.[62]

Four separate lines of narration are required at this point: the first deals with Wilhelm II's subsequent efforts, the second with off-continent events, the third with Italian developments, and the fourth, moving back to the center of things, with events in the Balkans. Although overlapping in time, it is easier to deal with them separately.

One aim of the kaiser's "New Course" was to bring about an alliance with Britain, a goal that was never achieved. His bullying tactics certainly did not help. In 1894, Germany "challenged or quarreled with Great Britain about Samoa, the Congo, the Sudan, Morocco, Turkey, and Portugal's African colonies." The tactics were unpleasant, and the apparent lack of motive "confused and annoyed" the British without producing any serious gain for Germany. In 1896, the kaiser made a pointless and annoying intervention in the Transvaal, sending a telegram of support to President Paul Kruger after the Jameson raid. In the course of the South-African War, much of the German press was openly pro-Boer. It was easy to conclude that this anti-British content reflected the sentiments of the German government.[63]

Ideas of empire, of *Weltpolitik*, were propagated within Germany by political, military, and intellectual leaders and by pressure groups such as the Pan-German League, the Colonial League, and the Navy League. The advocates stressed both the supposed economic advantages and the prestige factor: A large empire was just and appropriate, something clearly owed to a great power. In 1897, Bernhard von Bülow, the state secretary of the Foreign Office (and later chancellor), provided a key slogan

[62] Gerhard Ritter, The *Schlieffen Plan: Critique of a Myth* (New York, 1958). Also, Craig, *Germany*, pp. 315–17; Holger H. Herwig, *The First World War: Germany and Austria-Hungary 1914–1918* (London, 1997), pp. 46–51; and Herwig, "Strategic Uncertainties of a Nation-State: Prussia-Germany, 1871–1918," in Williamson Murray, MacGregor Knox, and Alvin Bernstein, eds., *The Making of Strategy: Rulers, States, and War* (Cambridge, 1994), ch. 9. For further discussion and sources, see Chapter 5, below.

[63] The quotation is from Kagan, *Origins of War*, p. 130. See also Craig, *Germany*, chs. 7 and 9; and for a wealth of detail, Kennedy, *Rise of the Anglo-German Antagonism*, esp. pp. 239–43, 246–7. Kennedy writes that "the anti-Boer War literature in France, Russia and the Netherlands was almost as bad," but the British press expected more from Germany. The German government tried to restrain the anti-British press comment. At the same time, however, it encouraged some anti-British sentiment, this to help with the passage of naval appropriations. A more recent work argues that the German government at this time was pro-British; see Harald Rosenbach, *Das deutsche Reich, Grossbritannien und der Transvaal (1896–1902)* (Göttingen, 1993).

announcing that Germany demanded its "place in the sun." This expansionist agitation came without any clear focus or target. The aspirations at this point, moreover, were problematic, since most of the world was either "taken" or, if still "available," as in the case of China, would be hotly contested. Any new German colonies would have to be taken from the other powers, perhaps a declining one. A division of Portugal's African possessions came up for discussion.[64]

An overseas empire, presumably, would require a strong navy. The kaiser read and was much influenced by Alfred Thayer Mahan's *Influence of Sea Power upon History*. In June 1897, Alfred Tirpitz, a leading advocate of naval expansion, was appointed state secretary of the Navy Office, and under his direction Germany embarked on a major naval building program, one that caused Britain's leaders much concern. The aim, again, was not entirely clear; but Britain's navy seemed the obvious target.[65] One argument for imperialism emphasized the benefits it would bring, the wealth and glory, both helping to preserve "order" at home. The enormous costs, however, brought tax increases and of course serious domestic problems. Germany's naval program was one among several factors that brought about an important change in international relations: Britain, hesitantly, moved away from its long-term policy of "splendid isolation." In 1902, Britain reached an accommodation with Japan. And in 1904, it concluded a loose agreement with France called the *entente cordiale*. The agreement settled some continuing colonial disputes. At this point, it was not directed against Germany.[66]

The imperialist ambitions of the major powers, as seen, brought frequent conflicts that had long-term effects on both sentiments and alliances. Early in 1904, Russia was attacked and defeated by "upstart" Japan. For Russia, the outcome was both humiliating and costly. Apart from the

---

[64] Craig, *Germany*, pp. 119, 288, 307, and 325. For more detail on Germany's *Weltpolitik*, see William Roger Louis, *Great Britain and Germany's Lost Colonies 1914–1919* (Oxford, 1967), ch. 1; and Woodruff D. Smith, *The German Colonial Empire* (Chapel Hill, N.C., 1978). The division of the Portuguese colonies is discussed in Wolfgang J. Mommsen, *Großmachtstellung und Weltpolitik: Die Außenpolitik des Deutschen Reiches 1870 bis 1914* (Frankfurt, 1993), pp. 274–6; and in Richard Langhorne, "Anglo-German Negotiations Concerning the Future of the Portuguese Colonies, 1911–1914," *Historical Journal* 16 (1973): 361–87. For Salisbury's deprecating views on the Portuguese and their colonies, see Robinson and Gallagher, *Africa and the Victorians*, pp. 247–8.

[65] And as indicated in private statements, Britain was in fact the adversary; see Kennedy, *Rise of the Anglo-German Antagonism*, pp. 239–41.

[66] Craig, *Germany*, pp. 303–14; Keiger, *France*, 19–20; and Zara F. Steiner, *Britain and the Origins of the First World War* (London, 1977), pp. 29–30.

prestige loss, the army and navy were seriously damaged and in need of repair. A revolution broke out in 1905, and although ultimately put down, it too brought heavy costs for a floundering economy. Russia, accordingly, was judged to be "down." It would, presumably, take many years for it to recover.[67]

In 1905, the European powers struggled over Morocco. For a couple of centuries, Morocco had been a loosely managed, decaying feudal monarchy. Late in the nineteenth century, France and Spain intervened there, each taking a piece. Britain and Germany sought and secured guarantees of their rights to trade in these new protectorates. In 1905, the French government, in violation of a previous international agreement, moved to extend its control over Morocco. Having secured British, Italian, and Spanish consent, the aim was to present Germany with a *fait accompli*. But the German government challenged the move, and in March 1905, interrupting a Mediterranean cruise, a reluctant Wilhelm II made "a theatrical landing at Tangier" and asserted Germany's "demand for free trade and equal rights ... and confirmed the Sultan's status as ruler of an independent country." The kaiser "pointedly told the French consul that he knew how to defend German interests in Morocco and would expect the French to recognize that fact. The menace in these words was unmistakable." The resulting crisis, one involving an obvious threat of war, ended with the Algeciras Conference of 1906. This brought a humiliating defeat for Germany. The result, as summarized by Gordon Craig, was that "the French got exactly what they wanted, and the Germans found themselves isolated except for the support of Austria-Hungary." Italy, from the outset, sided against its Triple Alliance partner.[68]

After the Moroccan crisis, Germany's leaders were even more concerned with the problem of *Einkreisung*, of encirclement. Their reading, Germany-as-victim, was accentuated by the inherent weakness of the Triple Alliance. Italy, as seen, had not provided expected support. And Austria-Hungary, because of its internal weakness, was thought to be not entirely reliable. Hardly a "three," Germany, basically, was a partner in a not-so-certain "two," this in a system of five or six.

The German move, intended to break up the emerging alliance, had just the opposite affect. France solidified its relations with Russia and now

---

[67] Seton-Watson, *The Russian Empire*, pp. 582–607; Fuller, *Strategy and Power*, pp. 394–412.

[68] The quotations are from Craig, *Germany*, pp. 318–21; and Keiger, *France*, pp. 20–4. See also Cecil, *Wilhelm*, vol. 2, pp. 91–7, 107–9.

provided important financial support. The Anglo-French *entente cordiale* was also strengthened, this episode encouraging talks between their military staffs. London and Paris settled their long-standing colonial frictions in Persia, Afghanistan, and Tibet.

Some German leaders considered the possibility of a preventive war at this point. Russia was fighting its war with Japan and facing revolution at home. Britain had not yet recovered from the Boer War. A move against France at this time could, at little cost, remove that power and break up the developing alliances. At that point, however, no action was taken.[69]

Russia's leaders, recognizing the obvious facts, the empire's weakness and its "over-extension," in "rare unanimity" agreed to a rapprochement with Great Britain. The result was the Anglo-Russian *entente* of 1907 that sought to deal with their many points of contention along their central Asia frontiers. It spelled out settlements with respect to Tibet, Afghanistan, and Persia. This move, which was encouraged by France, was an important change from the long-standing hostility between the two powers.[70] A new alignment was being formed, a new *"trois"* – France, Russia, and, Britain – one ultimately to be called the Triple Entente or, for short, simply the *entente.*

In 1908, Austria-Hungary annexed Bosnia-Herzegovina, a move that again revealed the frailties of the Dual Alliance. Austria-Hungary had secured prior Russian agreement to this move but, significantly, failed to inform its alliance partners. The Ottomans, understandably, were upset. Germany's leaders, with growing economic ties to the Ottomans and the prospect of the Berlin-to-Baghdad railway connection, were "disagreeably surprised." But for the sake of the alliance, Germany's leaders continued to support their partner.[71]

This move had significant implications for Serbia and for Serbo-Austrian relations. To understand the linkages, it is necessary to backtrack and to review events in Serbia in the years immediately after the Congress of Berlin. It is easy to think that Orthodox Serbia would have had close traditional ties with Russia, but that was not the case. For more than two decades, Serbia had been an Austrian satellite, a role accepted by that nation's leaders. Prince Milan Obrenovich, Serbia's ruler from

[69] Craig, *Germany*, pp. 318–20.
[70] Fuller, *Strategy and Power*, pp. 415–16.
[71] Craig, *Germany*, pp. 321–4; Anderson, *Eastern Question*, pp. 278–86; Dedijer, *Sarajevo*, pp. 367–78; Jelavich, *Russia's Balkan Entanglements*, pp. 219–28; and F. R. Bridge, *From Sadowa to Sarajevo: The Foreign Policy of Austria-Hungary, 1866–1914* (London, 1972), pp. 301–20.

1868 to 1889, until San Stefano had been an extreme Russophile. But at that point, 1878, he "turned directly into the arms of Austria-Hungary" and "in a secret convention virtually put the conduct of Serbia's foreign affairs into Austro-Hungarian hands." The convention renounced Serbian rights to Bosnia and Herzegovina. It also stated that "Serbia will not tolerate" activities directed against the Austro-Hungarian monarchy, including Bosnia and Herzegovina.[72]

Those Austrophile policies ultimately helped bring the downfall of the dynasty. The Serbian metropolitan Mihailo was "the staunchest opponent" of the pro-Austrian direction. Some intellectuals also dissented, but the most decisive opposition came from within the army. King Milan was succeeded by his son, Alexander, who abolished the constitution and proceeded with despotic and erratic rule. A group of young officers organized an overthrow and, in June 1903, killed the king and his wife. Austrian dominance ended at that point. The new regime (Karadjordjević) again looked with favor to Russia. Serbia's new leaders now pushed their "larger" aspirations, unifying all those compatriots still ruled by the Habsburgs and the Ottomans.[73]

Austria-Hungary's annexation of Bosnia and Herzegovina in 1908 brought widespread internal opposition with major demonstrations by the Serb population. The annexation, as noted in the previous chapter, was in accord with previous treaty provisions. But those provisions were not widely known within the general populace. Even if known, Serbian nationalists would not have cared. Apart from A. P. Izvolskii, the foreign minister, Russia's leaders, as indicated, were angered by the move, but at that point still recovering from war and revolution, could do nothing about it. For them, it was a serious loss of prestige. The Serbian government, because of internal problems, was also forced to accept the outcome, even to the extent of being compelled to repress anti-Austrian movements.[74] This outcome left a heritage of unresolved tensions.

A second Moroccan crisis came in 1911 when France inserted troops there in a clear attempt at a takeover. Germany reacted by sending a

---

[72] Dedijer, *Sarajevo*, pp. 82–4; Anderson, *Eastern Question*, p. 231.

[73] Dedijer, pp. 85–7. The few sentences in the text cannot begin to summarize the complexities. The leader of the 1903 regicides was a young officer, Dragutin Dimitrijevich, who is better known by his pseudonym, Colonel Apis. Eleven years later, he was alleged, by Austria, to have been the instigator of the archduke's assassination.

[74] Dedijer, *Sarajevo*, pp. 370–71; Anderson, *Eastern Question*, p. 285. Once again, the complexities cannot possibly be summarized in a few sentences. The Serbs, under pressure, promised to carry out the Austro-Hungarian demands but then reneged.

gunboat, the *Panther*, which anchored off Agadir. The demands put forward were simple: Germany expected "some kind of territorial compensation," a demand later specified as "almost the entire French Congo." France resisted and Britain reacted with strong support. German leaders decided to back off and agreed to settle for "a large, but worthless, tract in Central Africa."[75] This demonstration of Germany's ambitions brought further moves to strengthen the British-French *entente*. The deprecating comments in Germany's nationalistic press made a "stronger" reaction necessary in the next crisis. One newspaper referred to the kaiser as "Guillaume le timide."[76] The Second Moroccan Crisis accelerated the arms race, led to more active British-French military planning, and stimulated the Italian government to pursue its ambitions in Africa, which in turn provided the occasion for the Balkan states to move against the Ottoman Empire.

Italy had undertaken several previous off-continent imperialist ventures. Reaching into Africa in 1890, it proclaimed a new colony, Eritrea, on the Red Sea. This was followed by an attempt to establish a protectorate over Ethiopia, one that ended with a major military disaster. Italy did retain Eritrea, but, as Denis Mack Smith put it, had acquired a desert at great expense. Italy also established a protectorate over much of Somaliland. Undaunted by the limited returns, Italy's leaders saw Libya as a next opportunity. But the resulting war of conquest, in 1911–12, proved very costly in men and money. Italy was ultimately successful, gaining Libya and the Dodecanese Islands in the settlement. Economically, however, this imperialist venture was also a complete disaster.[77]

The Libyan War again demonstrated Ottoman weakness, and this stimulated a war in the Balkans. In the summer of 1912, the newly formed Balkan League, a coalition of Serbia, Bulgaria, Greece, and Montenegro, moved toward war with the Ottoman Empire. Its goal, one of formidable importance, was "the destruction of Turkey-in-Europe." The major powers showed concern but, occupied with other matters, undertook no decisive action. A last-minute flurry of diplomatic activity produced a note,

---

[75] Craig, *Germany*, pp. 328–9; Keiger, *France and the Origins*, pp. 34–7; Kagan, *Origins*, pp. 167–75.

[76] Kagan, *Origins*, p. 173.

[77] Mack Smith, *Modern Italy*, pp. 134, 163–70, 241–9. One cannot cover all the details in a brief summary. Recognizing the hopelessness of the Eritrean colony, Prime Minister Luzzati thought of exchanging it for Cyprus. During the Boer War, some Italian newspapers "suggested aiding Britain in return for the gift of Malta and perhaps Egypt"; ibid., p. 241.

transmitted by Vienna, which announced the resolve of "the powers" that "no change of the status quo would be permitted." This was transmitted on 8 October, the day Montenegro declared war on the Ottomans. A few days later, Serbia and Bulgaria joined in. Unexpectedly, by the end of October the League had defeated every Turkish army in Europe. This conflict, the First Balkan War, was significant for several reasons. It was the first time in modern experience that small states had proceeded independently or, perhaps more appropriately, in defiance of the major powers.[78]

In November 1912, the Turks, in an important battle, stopped further Bulgarian advances. The Concert powers finally moved, and in mid-December peace talks began in London. The discussions dragged on for several months, the principal difficulty being Serb and Montenegrin intransigence over a small territory intended by the powers for Albania. As part of the settlement, the powers had planned a new state, Albania, and had decided on its boundaries. But Montenegro and Serbia besieged and took a tiny part of the planned state, Scutari, thus upsetting those arrangements. To force compliance, by mutual agreement, Austria-Hungary undertook a naval demonstration off the Montenegrin coast. Britain and Italy later added their ships to this "demonstration" and Russia agreed to "international coercion," all of this without effect. Under considerable pressure, Serbia withdrew its forces, but King Nikita held out. Ultimately, the threat of an Austrian military intervention brought a Montenegrin capitulation.[79] The final agreement was not signed until 30 May 1913.

In the course of this struggle, a serious confrontation occurred in central Europe. Russia, concerned about possible Austro-Hungarian intervention in the Balkans, announced a "trial mobilization" in the Warsaw military district. Vienna countered with troop increases in Galicia. Count Leopold Berchtold, Austria's foreign minister, sent a representative to Berlin to check on Germany's intentions should a conflict result. He was told Germany would not come to Vienna's support, not sensing sufficient cause. In early March the two contenders agreed to troop withdrawals, and tensions eased for the moment.[80]

---

[78] For brief summaries of the war, see Anderson, *Eastern Question*, ch. 10; Jelavich, *Russia's Balkan Entanglements*, pp. 229–35; and Samuel R. Williamson, Jr., *Austria-Hungary and the Origins of the First World War* (New York, 1991), ch. 7. For more detail, see Luigi Albertini, *The Origins of the War of 1914*, 3 vols. (London, 1952), vol. 1, ch. 7; and Richard C. Hall, *The Balkan Wars 1912–1913* (London, 2000).

[79] Williamson, *Austria-Hungary*, pp. 135–40.

[80] Ibid., pp. 132–5.

The settlement of the First Balkan War effectively pushed the Ottomans out of Europe, leaving that empire with only a tiny enclave on the north shore of the Straits. Some of the Aegean islands were transferred to new owners; the disposition of some others was to be undertaken by the great powers. The details involving Albania were also to be arranged by the powers. Austria-Hungary achieved two explicit demands: Serbia was denied an Adriatic port, and an independent Albania was established, a state that, in a small way, could help to counter possible Serb dominance in the area. But for Austria, the presence of an enlarged Serbia, now twice its previous size, was a source of alarm. A. J. P. Taylor describes the victory of Balkan nationalism as "a disaster beyond remedy for the Habsburg monarchy."[81]

In June 1913, a month after the signing of the peace, the Second Balkan War began. The members of the League were now struggling over the division of Macedonia. The Bulgarians attacked Serbia and Greece. Romania joined with the latter two and together quickly routed the Bulgarian forces. Turkey joined with them at that moment and regained Adrianople. Bulgaria agreed to a settlement, the Peace of Bucharest, which was signed on 10 August. The victors, understandably, gained territory and Bulgaria lost some. This settlement was arranged between the parties to the conflict without any great-power involvement.[82]

Austria-Hungary, understandably, was much concerned about this conflict. Initially, Austrian leaders welcomed the breakup of the League, anticipating a long drawn-out struggle in which all participants, most especially Serbia, would lose. As events developed, Vienna wished to help Bulgaria but found no support from Germany or Italy. The German position is worth noting – according to Samuel R. Williamson, Jr., Berlin did not see that "Serbia posed a fundamental threat to Austria-Hungary." Later, when Austria was considering a possible intervention, it again found that the "threat posed ... by Serbia remained unappreciated and minimized." The result was a "badly strained" relationship. The problem, as Williamson puts it, was one of discrepant agendas: "What was fundamental to Vienna was but part of a larger mosaic of German *Weltpolitik*."[83]

The August settlement did not end the episode. Serbia, it was discovered, had not evacuated Albanian territory as per the agreement but had occupied still more. Austrian leaders reviewed many possible responses.

[81] Taylor, *Struggle*, p. 491.
[82] Williamson, *Austria-Hungary*, pp. 143–50.
[83] Ibid., pp. 147–9.

One thread common to all of the options was agreement on a "military solution if diplomacy failed." Their outlook is summarized in a message from Count István Tisza, the Hungarian minister-president, to Berchtold, the Austrian foreign minister: The "border issue would show whether Austria-Hungary was a 'viable power' or had fallen into a 'laughable decadence.' "[84] Without informing Germany or Italy, their alliance partners, Austria sent an ultimatum to Belgrade. Serbia complied and withdrew the troops from Albania. This victory carried a lesson for the Austrian leaders: The threat to use force would win.

It was against this background that, on 28 June 1914, the assassinations of the Austrian heir-presumptive, the Archduke Franz Ferdinand and his wife, occurred.

[84] Ibid., p. 152.

# 3

# Serbia

## Richard C. Hall

Serbia, as seen in the previous chapter, was an Austro-Hungarian satellite state until the overthrow of King Alexander in 1903. At that point, the new government shifted its loyalties to Russia and undertook policies aiming to create a Greater Serbia. The principal events touching Serbia in the years leading up to August 1914 were a trade war with Austria-Hungary (called the "Pig War"), the Young Turk revolt of July 1908, the Austro-Hungarian takeover of Bosnia-Herzegovina in October of that year, and finally the two Balkan Wars of 1912–13. The latter included also Bulgaria, Greece, Montenegro, and of course the Ottoman Empire. For the inhabitants of these Balkan states war began in October 1912, and lasted, with short breaks, until October 1918.[1]

The "Pig War," which refers to Austria-Hungary's ban on a prominent item of Serbian commerce, ended Serbian economic dependence on Austria-Hungary.[2] It also exacerbated tensions between the two neighbors. These tensions increased still further as a result of the Austro-Hungarian annexation of Bosnia-Herzegovina soon after the Young Turks' assumption of power in Constantinople. The Austrians feared that the reform program of the Young Turks might cause the loss of Bosnia-Herzegovina, an Ottoman province under Austrian occupation since 1878. The Serbs coveted Bosnia because the largest single national

---

[1] This follows Joachim Remak's reading in his "1914 – The Third Balkan War: Origins Reconsidered," in H. W. Koch, ed., *The Origins of the First World War: Great Power Rivalry and German War Aims* (London, 1984), ch. 3.

[2] Michael B. Petrovich, *A History of Modern Serbia 1804–1918*, 2 vols. (New York, 1976), vol. 2, p. 571.

group in that province at that time was Serbian. They greatly resented the annexation.

In the two Balkan Wars of this period, the Serbs sought to enlarge their territories to include as many of their conationals as possible. They drew upon the recent Italian and German experience, seeking to emulate their national successes. Serb leaders saw the greater nation as a necessary precondition to economic and political success. That goal entailed, first and foremost, a direct confrontation with the Ottoman Empire where millions of Serbs were living long after the creation of an autonomous Serb nation in the previous century. Realization of that goal also required a confrontation with Austria-Hungary. Large numbers of Serbs lived under Austro-Hungarian rule in Bosnia-Herzegovina, Croatia, Dalmatia, and Vojvodina.

The human and physical geography of the Balkans stood in the way of these diverse national aspirations. Many people living in the Balkans lacked a clear sense of their national identities. Many peoples of different religions and/or languages dwelt close by, if not among each other. Furthermore, at one time or another during the Middle Ages the predecessors of the Balkan national states each had exercised an ephemeral domination over most of the peninsula. The Balkan leaders drew on dimly remembered recollections of these medieval empires to provide historic precedents for their national revivals.[3] These facts brought intense rivalries in the struggle for control of the remaining European portions of the moribund Ottoman Empire.

The major area of contention was Macedonia, a region with a mixed population of Slavs, Greeks, Turks, Albanians, and others. It became the object of Bulgarian, Greek, and Serbian aspirations. For much of the late nineteenth century, the national rivalries over Macedonia prevented the formation of a united Balkan effort directed against the Ottomans. Another intra-Balkan rivalry involved the competition between the rulers of Montenegro and Serbia for the leadership of the movement for a united Serbia. Both states aspired also to control Kosovo (Old Serbia) and other areas that had substantial Albanian populations.

The basic issues that led Serbs, Montenegrins, Bulgarians, and Greeks to confront the Ottoman Empire in October 1912 remained constant throughout this period, although the specific agendas differed

[3] Charles Jelavich, *South Slav Nationalisms: Textbooks and Yugoslav Union before 1914* (Columbus, Ohio, 1990); Tim Judah, *The Serbs: History, Myth and the Destruction of Yugoslavia* (New Haven, 1997).

significantly. A knowledge of the outbreak of fighting in the First Balkan War is important to an understanding of the "second round" of the struggle in July 1913, of the generalization of the conflict in August 1914, and of the intensification of the fighting in October 1915. The actions of the Serbs in the summer of 1914, certainly pivotal for the greater European struggle, were at the same time part of a larger Balkan constellation.

A small number of individuals in Serbia and Montenegro held political and military power, that is, had the power to direct and oversee the implementation of these national goals. These were the princes, later kings, the politicians, and the military leaders. The south Slavic states became monarchies after achieving autonomy from the Ottomans. In Serbia, two native families, the Karageorgeviches and the Obrenoviches, competed for the throne throughout the nineteenth century. Several constitutions were instituted by the dynasties in this period. Montenegro was ruled, without recourse to any constitution, by the Petrovich Njegosh family (which, for centuries, had also controlled the Orthodox bishopric of Cetinje).

In Serbia a small and active political class had developed from among the educated elite, one that included teachers, some merchants, and some lawyers. Since Serbia as well as the other Balkan countries lacked facilities for higher education, many politicians had been educated in western Europe. Nikola Pashich, for example, the Serbian prime minister from 1912 to 1918, had studied in Zurich, Switzerland. In western Europe, many of them had acquired "modern" ideas, notions of free expression, representative government, constitutional procedures, and nationalism. There were few fundamental differences in the foreign policy programs of these Serbian politicians after 1903 in that all sought national unification. All agreed in principle on the anti-Austrian direction of Serb affairs differing mainly on means and timing.[4] One key issue dividing Serb politicians at that point was whether to achieve the nationalist goals with or without a serious competitor, Bulgaria.

Political weapons alone, however, could not bring about the creation of an enlarged national state. Each of the Balkan states sought, therefore, to advance its goals through force of arms. The Balkan monarchs and political circles developed their military establishments, making them as strong as their weak economies allowed. In all of these settings, the military was

---

[4] Z. A. B. Zeman, "The Balkans in the Coming of War," in *The Coming of the First World War*, R. J. W. Evans and Hartmut Pogge von Strandmann, eds. (Oxford, 1988), ch. 2; and Mark Cornwall, "Serbia," in Keith Wilson, ed., *Decisions for War 1914* (New York, 1995), ch. 3.

responsible to the monarch, not to the parliamentary governments. The constitution of Serbia stipulated that the monarch was the commander-in-chief of the army.

None of the Balkan monarchs, however, sat comfortably on his throne. Nikola Petrovich Njegosh, the king of Montenegro, recognized increasing public dissatisfaction because of his autocratic rule and his failure to modernize his poor and remote country.[5] Peter Karageorgevich became king in Serbia after military plotters murdered his predecessor, Alexander Obrenovich, his wife, Draga, and several others, in 1903. The military gave the monarchs support vis-à-vis other contending forces within their countries. Clearly, the military establishment could also, with ease, overthrow and either exile or murder a troublesome monarch.

The Balkan military forces, prior to 1912, were not successful in their major tasks. Montenegrins and Serbs fought against the Ottoman Empire in 1876. The Greeks confronted the Ottomans in 1897. And the Macedonian revolutionary organizations, with Bulgarian support, revolted against Ottoman rule in Macedonia in 1903. All of those efforts failed. By themselves the Balkan states were not strong enough to defeat the Ottomans.

Secret societies were also active in these nations, also engaged in "the national struggle." The most important of these were found in Serbia and in the Ottoman Empire. They had support from active and reserve military officers and, not surprisingly, had close links with the military establishments. But operating outside the official hierarchies, their actions were not subject to the constraints that might be imposed upon public agencies.

These societies typically had rather murky origins and went through various incarnations. Some of the officers who overthrew and murdered King Alexander Obrenovich in 1903 formed the secret society Union or Death (Ujedinjenie ili Smrt) in 1911. Popularly known as the Black Hand (Tsrna Ruka), it bypassed the more moderate (actually, forcibly tamed) organization, National Defense (Narodna Odbrana), now basically a cultural and propaganda society. The constitution of Union or Death declared "the aim of realizing national ideas – the unification of Serbdom." It stated further that "the organization prefers revolutionary struggle to a cultural one."[6] The Black Hand had close ties with the Serbian military

[5] See John D. Treadway, *The Falcon and the Eagle: Montenegro and Austria-Hungary, 1908–1914* (West Lafayette, Ind., 1983) pp. 18–19, 52–55.

[6] David MacKenzie, "The 'Black Hand' and Its Statutes," in David MacKenzie, *Serbs and Russians* (Boulder, 1996), p. 357. Also, David MacKenzie, *Apis, the Congenial*

leadership. In 1913, the society's leader, Colonel Dragutin Dimitrijevich (called "Apis" because his bull-like physique recalled the ancient Egyptian god) became head of Serbian military intelligence. The latter organization, which was especially active in Bosnia and Macedonia, was to play a central role in the assassination at Sarajevo. A key question arising after that event was the involvement of the government. Were the assassins acting on their own? Or were they acting as agents of the Serbian government?

The nationalists of the Ottoman Empire had formed their secret society, the Committee for Union and Progress, beginning in the Macedonian port city of Salonika and quickly spreading with branches elsewhere. Popularly known as the Young Turks, it took power in Constantinople in July 1908 and forced the reinstitution of constitutional monarchy. The Young Turks' nationalist aims, modernizing and strengthening the decrepit empire, posed a direct threat to the aspirations of the Balkan states. A revived Ottoman state, one supported by European arms and military expertise, would never accept the loss of additional European provinces. The annexation of Bosnia-Herzegovina by Austria-Hungary in October that year posed a direct challenge to Serbian nationalist ambitions. These events are reviewed in greater detail in subsequent chapters.

The annexation of Bosnia-Herzegovina gave the Serb leaders an additional incentive to make arrangements with the other Balkan states. Serbian Foreign Minister Milan Milovanovich explained this to the Bulgarian war minister, General Stefan Paprikov, in 1909:

For us, there is another important consideration which speaks for the advantage of an agreement with Bulgaria. As long as we are not allied with you, our influence over the Croats and Slovenes will be insignificant. Outside of the differences of faith, these peoples have to a great degree the same culture we have. They do not see Serbia as a center, however, able to attract them. It will be something else all together, when you and we form a powerful bloc. Then all Orthodox and Catholic Serbs, Croats and Slovenes in the neighboring Monarchy [Austria-Hungary] will begin inevitably to gravitate towards us.[7]

The recognition of their individual weakness and the fear of the potential success of the Young Turks led the Balkan states to explore the possibility of a united effort against the Ottoman Empire. With the strong

---

*Conspirator: The Life of Colonel Dragutin T. Dimitrijevic* (Boulder, 1989), chs. 10–12; and, also by MacKenzie, *Violent Solutions: Revolutions, Nationalism, and Secret Societies in Europe to 1918* (Lanham, N.Y., 1996), ch. 11.

[7] Ministerstvo na voinata, Shtab na armiyata-voenno istoricheska komisiya, *Voinata mezhdu Bŭlgariya i Turtsiya*, 7 vols. (Sofia, 1933–37), vol. 1, p. 36.

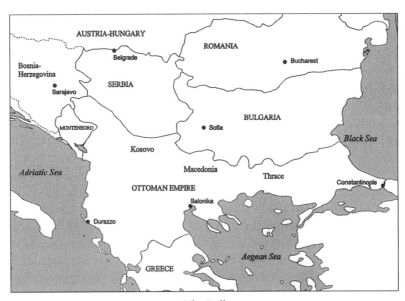

MAP 3.1. The Balkans, 1912

encouragement and support of the Russians, who wanted to strengthen their position in the Balkans, especially after the Bosnian fiasco, Bulgarian Minister President Ivan Geshov and Milovan Milovanovich, now the Serbian prime minister, began negotiations in the autumn of 1911.

After many difficulties, the Bulgarians and Serbs momentarily overcame their conflict over Macedonia and, in March 1912, signed an alliance.[8] This provided for mutual assistance against both Austria-Hungary and the Ottoman Empire.[9] A secret codicil provided for the partition of Macedonia, most of which would fall to Bulgaria, while Russia promised to arbitrate the disposition of the northwestern section, the so-called disputed zone, if Bulgaria and Serbia could not resolve the problem themselves (see Map 3.1).

The Serbian high command did not care for the arrangement. Even Nikola Pashich, who became the Serbian prime minister after the

---

[8] See Ernst Christian Helmreich, *The Diplomacy of the Balkan Wars 1912–1913* (New York, 1969), pp. 36–68.

[9] For the text of the treaty, see Mihailo Vojvodich, ed., *Dokumenti o spoljnoj politisi Kraljevina Srbije 1903–1914*, 7 vols. (Belgrade, 1985) (hereafter referred to as DSPKS), vol. 5, book 1, no. 168; B. D. Kesiyakov, *Prinos kŭm diplomaticheskata istoriya na Bŭlgariya 1878–1925* (Sofia, 1925–26), vol. 1, pp. 36–48; Ivan E. Geshov, *The Balkan League* (London, 1915), pp. 112–17.

premature death of Milovanovich on 1 July 1912, admitted, "[I]n my opinion we conceded too much, or better said, we abandoned some Serbian
areas which we should never have dared to abandon even if we were left
without an agreement."[10] That sense of things, the view shared also by
Serbian army leaders, made implementation of the treaty in its initial form
unlikely.

Russia had a different purpose in mind for this Balkan League. While
the Bulgarians and Serbs saw the alliance as a weapon directed against the
Ottoman Empire, the Russians saw it was a means to strengthen their position in the Balkans; they also saw it as directed against Austria-Hungary.
But the strong advocacy of Balkan national goals by Anatoli Neklyudov,
the Russian minister in Sofia, and Nikola Hartwig, the Russian minister
in Belgrade, complicated the policy of St. Petersburg.[11] Both men acted
more as advocates for their Balkan charges than as representatives of the
Russian government. This led the governments in Sofia and Belgrade to
overestimate Russian support for their actions.

In the spring and summer of 1912, the Bulgarian-Serbian arrangement
expanded with the addition of Greece and Montenegro into a loose arrangement called the Balkan League. Each country was bound to the other
by bilateral written or oral agreements backed by military conventions.
But again the arrangement was a fragile one. Because of the size of its
armies and because of its strategic location near the Ottoman capital,
Bulgaria was the most important of the partners. No provision was made
for division of Ottoman territory between the Bulgarians and Greeks, a
circumstance that caused immense difficulties from the start of the ensuing war.

In September 1912, the Ottomans mobilized. Eight days later the members of the Balkan League did the same. The Montenegrins declared war
against the Ottomans on 8 October, and on 17 October the Ottoman
Empire declared war on the Balkan allies. The following day, the other
members of the League declared war. Hartwig, the Russian minister to
Serbia, assured the other representatives of the great powers in Belgrade
that Russia would do nothing to prevent war against the Ottoman Empire.
If it did, he claimed, "armed revolution" would result.[12]

---

[10] Alex N. Dragnich, *Serbia, Nikola Pašić and Yugoslavia* (New Brunswick, N.J., 1971),
p. 101. All dates are given according to the Gregorian Calendar (new style), unless indicated as from the Julian Calendar then used in Bulgaria and Serbia (old style, or os).
[11] On this problem, see Edward C. Thaden, *Russia and the Balkan Alliance of 1912*
(University Park, Pa., 1965).
[12] Dr. Djordje Dj. Stankovich, *Nikola Pashich i Jugoslovensko pitanje* (Belgrade, 1985),
vol. 1, p. 110.

The Balkan allies achieved rapid victories over the Ottoman armies, but these came at a high price.[13] The Bulgarian Army sustained heavy casualties in its advance through Thrace to the Chataldzha lines, about twenty miles outside of Constantinople. The Serbs defeated the Ottomans in Macedonia and Kosovo with much lighter losses. After quickly occupying most of Macedonia, they advanced from Kosovo across northern Albania to the port of Durazzo on the Adriatic Sea, thus achieving a long-standing goal.

The presence of Serbian forces in Albania, however, aroused the concerns of Austria-Hungary. The Austro-Hungarian foreign minister, Count Leopold Berchtold, along with most others in the government, was strongly opposed to the prospect of a Serbian port on the Adriatic. He feared the Russians could utilize a Serbian port to cut off Austrian maritime access to the open seas. Berchtold also understood that a Serbian presence in northern Albania would undermine the viability of any Albanian state that could emerge from the Balkan War.[14] The heir-apparent to the Austro-Hungarian throne, Archduke Franz Ferdinand, shared this view.[15] To emphasize its opposition, the Dual Monarchy put its armies in Bosnia on a war footing and alerted troops in Croatia, Galicia, and Hungary.

The Austro-Hungarians appeared willing to fight Serbia and also to confront Russia to enforce their Balkan policy. At this point, Geshov assured Pashich that Bulgaria would uphold the obligation incurred in March 1912 and would support Serbia militarily on the Adriatic question.[16] Sensing the danger, the great powers now moved quickly and, on the invitation of Sir Edward Grey, the British foreign secretary, convened an ambassadors' conference in London in December 1912 to oversee the settlement of the Balkan War. The ambassadors readily agreed to the establishment of an independent Albania. Pashich accepted this solution, since the occupation of Kosovo and Macedonia had already stretched limited Serbian military resources. A sizable war, one that might have brought participation by two major powers, was thus narrowly averted.

---

[13] For the details of the First Balkan War, see Richard C. Hall, *The Balkan Wars 1912–1913: Prelude to the First World War* (London, 2000), pp. 22–68, 80–96.

[14] Samuel R. Williamson, Jr., *Austria-Hungary and the Origins of the First World War* (New York, 1991), pp. 124–5.

[15] Hugo Hantsch, *Leopold Graf Berchtold, Grandseigneur und Staatsmann*, 2 vols. (Graz, 1963), vol. 1, p. 347.

[16] Dr. M. Boghitschewitsch, ed., *Die Auswärtige Politik Serbiens 1903–1914* (Berlin, 1928–31), vol. 1, p. 210.

After a brief armistice lasting through most of December 1912 and January 1913, the war in the Balkans was resumed. As of January 1913, Ottoman control of Europe was limited to the besieged cities of Adrianople, Janina, and Scutari; the Thracian territory behind the fortified positions at Chataldzha; and the Gallipoli peninsula (Bulair). In March 1913, the Greek Army of Epirus took Janina. Later that month, the Bulgarians seized Adrianople. The defenders of Scutari, however, frustrated all Montenegrin assaults. In February 1913, King Nikola requested and received Serbian assistance in the form of troops and artillery.

Austria-Hungary's leaders saw the city as vital for the political and economic viability of the new Albanian state. By March 1913, they had secured the agreement of the other great powers for the inclusion of Scutari in Albania.[17] The Montenegrins, supported by Serbian troops, defied the resolution of the great powers that Scutari would go to Albania. Under great-power pressure, the Serbs once again agreed to withdraw. Pashich advised King Nikola: "The sacrifice is difficult, but it must be borne when the whole of Europe demands it. The same thing happened with Serbia in regards to the Adriatic Sea."[18]

The Montenegrin Army, however, continued the siege at Scutari alone. In April 1913, the Viennese government insisted that the siege end, and threatened war if it did not.[19] The great powers now decided upon a joint effort to enforce their decisions. A fleet including ships from Austria-Hungary, France, Germany, Great Britain, and Italy appeared off the Albanian and Montenegrin coast, and finally on 4 May, faced with the further threat of Austria troops, Montenegro withdrew from Scutari. For the second time in less than six months, the Viennese government had threatened war against a Serbian state over a Balkan issue. Again the great powers had moved, here in support of the Austro-Hungarian demands, to avert war.

The Serbs then focused their attention on Macedonia, most of which they had occupied by November 1912, but which, in the March 1912 treaty, they had acknowledged as Bulgarian. In February 1913, the Serbian government formally requested a revision of its terms.[20] The Bulgarians,

---

[17] Williamson, *Austria-Hungary*, p. 134.
[18] Dragnich, *Serbia, Nikola Pašić, and Yugoslavia*, p. 103.
[19] Ludwig Bittner et al., eds., *Österreich-Ungarns Aussenpolitik von der Bosnischen Krise 1908 bis zum Kriegsausbruch 1914: Diplomatische Aktenstücke des Österreichisch-Ungarischen Ministeriums des Äussern*, 9 vols. (Vienna, 1930) (hereafter referred to as ÖUA), vol. 5, no. 6253.
[20] Narodno sŭbranie, *Doklad na parlamentarnata izpitatelna komisiya*, 4 vols. (Sofia, 1918), vol. 1, pp. 405–8, no. 24, pp. 409–13, no. 25; DSPKS vol. 6, book 1, nos. 187, 271.

still fighting around Adrianople, ignored the request. Soon afterward armed clashes broke out between Bulgarian and Greek forces in southern Macedonia. On 11 April 1913, Pashich announced to the great powers that Serbia would go to war if she "did not receive the help of the Great Powers in delimiting the borders of Albania *and if they do not prevent Bulgaria from crossing the right bank of the Vardar and coming into contact through Ohrid and Bitola with Albania.*"[21] On 1 June, the Serbs and Greeks, who by then occupied most of Macedonia, signed a formal alliance directed against Bulgaria.[22] Although the Bulgarians had foreseen such an agreement, they did little to prevent its formation, instead choosing to rely on the Russian promise of arbitration and on the strength of the Bulgarian Army. Until a settlement was reached with the Ottomans, however, the Bulgarians had to maintain the bulk of their forces at the Chataldzha lines in Thrace.

Under pressure from the great powers, the Balkan belligerents finally reached a settlement at the end of May 1913. The Treaty of London of 30 May confined the Ottoman Empire in Europe to that part of eastern Thrace behind the Enos-Midia line.[23] This settlement, however, proved ephemeral. Within a month, the Balkan League collapsed and war began again, now between the previous allies. The key difficulty, the intractable problem, was the division of Macedonia. Both Serbia and Greece sought to retain the portions of Macedonia they had taken in the First Balkan War. On 1 June 1913, they concluded a formal alliance against Bulgaria.[24] In a rapid but costly campaign in July, the two nations, supported by Montenegro, overwhelmed Bulgaria. The Romanians, seeking to fulfill their self-proclaimed mission as "gendarme of the Balkans," and the Ottomans, attempting to recover some of their losses in the First Balkan War, also invaded Bulgaria, which made the catastrophe complete.

After a flurry of negotiations among the great powers and among the Balkan belligerents, all reached a consensus to hold peace talks at Bucharest.[25] There the great-power ambassadors attempted to influence the ensuing settlement, but they did not have much success. The Treaty of Bucharest, which ended the Second Balkan War, dramatically altered the dynamics of power in the Balkans. Serbia emerged as the biggest

---

[21] Stankovich, *Nikola Paschich*, vol. 1, p. 134. Emphasis in original. The Vardar River flows north to south through the middle of Macedonia.

[22] DSPKS vol. 6, book 2, nos. 186, 308.

[23] On the treaty, see Helmreich, *Diplomacy of the Balkan Wars*, pp. 326–40. For the text of the treaty see DSPKS vol. 6, book 2, no. 291.

[24] Ibid., no. 136.

[25] Helmreich, *Diplomacy of the Balkan Wars*, pp. 384–5.

MAP 3.2. The Balkans after the Peace Settlement, 1913

winner, nearly doubling its territory and increasing its population from 2,912,000 to 4,444,000.[26] Only Romania had a larger population and a stronger army at its disposal. But with the power of Bulgaria curbed, the Romanians could now concentrate their attention outside the Balkans, on Transylvania to the west and on Bessarabia to the east. For Austria-Hungary, this new Serbia, this large, aggressive, and antagonistic South Slavic state on their Balkan frontier, was seen, understandably, as a very serious threat to the integrity of the empire (Map 3.2). The threat was most acute in those regions with large Slavic populations, in Bosnia-Herzegovina, Croatia, and Dalmatia.

The Serb military successes and Montenegrin failures in the First Balkan War resolved the struggle between the Karageorgevich dynasty of Serbia and the Petrovich Njegosh dynasty of Montenegro over which house would lead the Serbian national movement. After the Treaty of London, Montenegro became, effectively, a Serbian satellite, and the continued existence of an independent Montenegro under the Petrovich Njegosh dynasty became problematical.[27] Montenegro and Serbia were

[26] Petrovich, *History of Modern Serbia*, vol. 2, pp. 603–4. On the Treaty of Bucharest, see Hall, *The Balkan Wars*, pp. 123–5.
[27] Treadway, *The Falcon and the Eagle*, pp. 174–7.

now joined physically after the division of the former Sandjak of Novi Pazar. In March 1914, King Nikola of Montenegro proposed a union of the two states. "Not only the people of Serbia and Montenegro," he declared, "but also Serbs under foreign domination will celebrate this agreement, as will all South Slavs whose hopes for the approaching union strengthen their spiritual fortitude."[28]

The Serbian victories, however, remained incomplete. The territories obtained in Kosovo, Macedonia, and the Sandjak of Novi Pazar contained considerable numbers of Albanians, Slavic Muslims, and Slavic Macedonians whose language, culture, and traditions differed from those of the Serbs. These conquests diluted the overall Serbian population of the Kingdom of Serbia. At the same time, large numbers of Serbs remained under Austro-Hungarian rule in Bosnia, Croatia, Dalmatia, and Slavonia. For the Serbs, the imperatives that led to war against the Ottoman Empire applied also to the Habsburg Empire.

The new state of Albania provided another source of conflict, with some Serb ambitions thwarted by the settlement. There were ongoing disputes about appropriate boundaries. Serbia continued to maintain strong forces in and around northern Albania to confront those Albanians who opposed their conquest of Kosovo. These troops also preserved Serb claims to northern Albania and for unimpeded Adriatic access. One consequence was that the newly acquired territories were administered by the Serbian Army rather than by the civilian authorities. This brought on a serious conflict between the government and the military, a conflict that lasted until May 1914. At that point, the Pashich government, with the support of Crown Prince Alexander and the Russian minister Hartwig, sought to reassert its authority over both the military and the Black Hand.[29] The government's efforts, however, were by no means complete and the two continued to operate with only limited government control.

The Serbian soldiers in northern Albania aroused a bellicose response from the local populations. They also brought reactions from leading figures among Albania's Austro-Hungarian protectors. During a visit to Vienna in October 1913, Pashich, reluctant to further antagonize his northern neighbor, especially after the exhausting Second Balkan War,

[28] Otto Hoetzsch, ed., *Die internationalen Beziehungen im Zeitalter des Imperialismus: Dokumente aus den Archiven der zarischen und der provisorischen Regierungen*, 8 vols. (Berlin, 1931–42), ser. 1, vol. 2, p. 169, enclosure 1.
[29] Cornwall, "Serbia," pp. 57–8; MacKenzie, *Serbs and Russians*, pp. 145–9.

attempted to calm matters. In a statement to the Austrian press, he declared: "I can assure you, that we have no intention of expanding over the borders assigned to Albania and us. We will only deal with the matter of obtaining the correct strategic border between the future principality of Albania and us in negotiations between an international commission appointed by the Powers and ourselves."[30]

Soon after returning to Belgrade, however, Pashich announced that the Serbs needed to reoccupy certain Albanian villages. On 13 October, replying to an Austrian note regarding Serbian intentions, he declared, somewhat obscurely, that the order "to halt the further advance of Serbian troops has already been given. The question as to when the Serbs already on Albanian soil will be withdrawn depends upon the circumstances."[31] In Vienna, the Serbian prime minister acted as a statesman; at home, however, having to contend with the Serbian military, he declared "military necessity" to be the primary basis for his policies.

The Dual Monarchy took a dim view of this "insolence" and, on 18 October 1913, issued an ultimatum demanding the withdrawal of Serbian forces from territories assigned to Albania by the London ambassadors' conference.[32] For the third time in less than a year, Vienna had threatened war against the Serbian states over a Balkan issue. And for the third time, the Serbian government accepted the Austro-Hungarian demands.[33] Exhausted from the Balkan Wars and still fighting in the south, Serbia was in no condition to confront Austria-Hungary. No help from Russia was forthcoming.[34] Thus, for the third time in the past year, great-power support for Austrian demands had prevented an Albanian war. Soon after this confrontation, the great powers established definitive Albanian frontiers. Neither the Albanians nor the Serbs were satisfied with the result.

Despite formal acquiescence to the Austro-Hungarian ultimatum, Serbian and Albanian forces continued to fight on both sides of their common frontier, and throughout the remainder of 1913 and into 1914, Albanians continued to resist Serbian rule in Kosovo. Pashich, in a note

---

[30] *Neue Freie Presse*, 3 October 1913, no. 317641, p. 1.

[31] *ÖUA*, vol. 7, nos. 8783, 8797, 8808, 8834.

[32] Ibid., 8850; DSPKS vol. 6, book 3, no. 425.

[33] *ÖUA*, vol. 7, nos. 8878, 8880. Helmreich pointed out that "[t]he whole procedure followed at this time was later duplicated in July, 1914: the warning to Serbia, the general promise of support from Germany, the independent presentation of the ultimatum, the subsequent notification of ally and rival." Helmreich, *Diplomacy of the Balkan Wars*, p. 426.

[34] Helmreich, *Diplomacy of the Balkan Wars*, p. 426.

to five of the great powers on 15 May 1914, explained the situation thus: "Serbia has experienced constant Albanian invasions. It is very difficult to protect this kind of frontier and Serbia is forced to make great sacrifices in men and money."[35] Given the Austro-Hungarian diplomatic and military support for the Albanians, he felt no need to address this note to Vienna. At the same time, Pashich requested Russian assistance in securing a revision of the Albanian frontier.[36]

While fighting in Albania and Kosovo, Serbia faced a serious revolt in Macedonia, where pro-Bulgarian elements and supporters of the Internal Macedonian Revolutionary Organization refused to accept the Serbian occupation. After the Treaty of Bucharest, these groups engaged in terrorism and direct military confrontation against the Serbian authorities and their sympathizers. Railway lines and bridges were bombed and small Serbian units attacked. The Sofia government provided material aid and sanctuary for the Macedonian insurgents. Not surprisingly, the insurgents also established contacts with the Albanians.[37] With enemies on its northern, eastern, and western borders, Serbia, like Germany, also faced a problem of *Einkreisung*, of encirclement. It had friendly frontiers only with its satellite Montenegro and with Greece. Romania, the erstwhile ally of the Second Balkan War, remained tied, by secret alliance, to Austria-Hungary.

The Balkan Wars brought great gains for Serbia, but the outcome, simultaneously, created enormous problems – most of them caused by Austria-Hungary. After the exhausting Balkan Wars, Serbia could not hope to deal single-handedly with the Dual Monarchy, thus making Russian support imperative. After the defeat of Bulgaria and the Treaty of Bucharest settlement, Serbia was Russia's only remaining Balkan ally. That circumstance allowed some freedom of action in regards to their great partner. A passive or defensive strategy was rejected by ardent nationalists, most especially by those of the Black Hand who thought in "larger terms." If the Dual Monarchy were eliminated as a factor in the Balkans, that would eliminate the problems in Albania and Macedonia and would allow the "return" of the Serb populations of Bosnia, Croatia, and Dalmatia. At the moment, however, that seemed a very distant possibility.

Early in 1914, Pashich and Crown Prince Alexander visited St. Petersburg. There, on 2 February, in a private audience, Tsar Nicholas II

35 DSPKS vol. 7, book 2, no. 13.
36 Ibid., no. 14.
37 Dimitŭr G. Gotsev, *Natsionalno-osvoboditelnata borba v Makedoniya 1912–1915* (Sofia, 1981), p. 135.

gave Pashich some very welcome assurances: "We will do everything for Serbia. Give my regards to your king and tell him, 'we will do every-thing for Serbia.' "[38] No assistance followed this bold assurance, and in the spring Pashich again appealed to St. Petersburg for aid against a pos-sible Austro-Hungarian attack. By June, "nothing had arrived," and on 18 June the Serbian legislature, somewhat reluctantly, "voted an extraor-dinary credit of 123 million dinars to re-equip the army."[39]

Ten days later, on the 28th, a group of young Bosnian Serb nation-alists with connections to the Black Hand assassinated Franz Ferdinand and his wife in Sarajevo. The archduke provided an appropriate target both because of his known hostility to Serbia and because of his sup-posed support for Trialism, a federalist plan with a South Slav state to be contained within the Austrian Empire.[40] Such a reform would undermine Serbian aspirations to unite with the Serbs of Austria-Hungary. It would also hamper attempts to create a Greater Serbia or a Yugoslav state that included the Croats and Slovenes.

The precise role of the Black Hand in the plot remains unclear. The organization did facilitate the acquisition of weapons for the plotters. Nevertheless, just as the Serbian government and the Serbian military were unable to control the Black Hand completely, so was the Black Hand unable to manage all of its agents.[41] The assassin, Gavrilo Princep, not a member of the Black Hand, subsequently claimed the plot had been his own idea.[42] Even if the Black Hand had wanted to prevent the killings, it would probably have faced the obstacles of youthful enthusiasm and obstinacy.

Princep was born in Obljaj, Bosnia, in 1894 to a poor Bosnian Serb peasant family. When a student in Sarajevo, he joined groups that ad-vocated South Slavic nationalist and modernist goals. Never a unified movement, these groups are often called collectively Young Bosnia (Mlada

---

[38] Nikola Pashich, "Pashicheva audijentsija kod Tsara Nikole II," in *Nikola P. Pashich* (Belgrade, 1937), p. 188.

[39] Dragnich, *Serbia, Nikola Pašić, and Yugoslavia*, p. 106; and Cornwall, "Serbia," p. 59.

[40] Joachim Remak, *Sarajevo: The Story of a Political Murder* (New York, 1959), p. 56. Vladimir Dedijer rejects this claim seeing trialism as a public position, one directed against Hungarians. Franz Ferdinand's private views, he argues, were markedly different; the archduke favored a unitary state with German dominance; see *The Road to Sarajevo* (New York, 1966), pp. 134–41.

[41] Mackenzie, *Apis*, pp. 149–53. Dedijer considered the plotters to have been independent idealists; see *Road to Sarajevo*, pp. 446–7.

[42] Dedijer, *Road to Sarajevo*, p. 393; Zeman, "The Balkans in the Coming War," pp. 24–5; MacKenzie, "The Black Hand and Its Statutes," p. 355.

Bosna).[43] Sharing the romantic nationalism of the period, Princep traveled to Serbia to volunteer for service in the First Balkan War but was rejected by the Serbian military authorities because of his small size.[44] Although Princep did not succeed in becoming a soldier, he remained in Serbia and made contact with the Black Hand, which provided him with some training. The organization later equipped Princep and his fellow Bosnian Serb, Nedjelko Chabrinovich, and five others with pistols and hand grenades, and on 1 June 1914, they crossed the Serbian-Bosnian border and traveled to Sarajevo. The bomb thrown by Chabrinovich at the archduke's automobile on the morning of 28 June bounced off the trunk and exploded under the following vehicle. Shortly thereafter, while returning from city hall en route to visit an officer wounded in the attack, Princep, given a second chance, shot Franz Ferdinand and his wife Sophie at point-blank range.

Since the beginning of June 1914, Pashich and several others in his government had been aware that a plot of some kind involving the Black Hand was under way. The government attempted to investigate but, because the military was implicated in the effort, failed to clarify the situation.[45] Pashich took some limited steps to frustrate the plot, but his vague words of warning to Vienna were ineffective.[46] Knowledge of the plot placed the Serbian government in a difficult position. If the plot were thwarted, it would uncover much of the Serbian intelligence network and there would be the risk of a coup d'état. If the plot succeeded, a punitive military response by the Dual Monarchy was likely.

Several other factors complicated any decision making at this point. On 24 June, King Peter temporarily retired due to ill health, and Crown Prince Alexander, then twenty-six years of age, became head of state, assuming the position of regent. New elections were scheduled at the same time, to fall on 14 August. In the midst of the August crisis, accordingly, Pashich was conducting an election campaign. When the Austro-Hungarian ultimatum was delivered in Belgrade on 23 July, Pashich was campaigning in the provinces. With national questions so passionately debated at home, moreover, Pashich had limited room for diplomatic maneuvering. He had to be conciliatory to Austria-Hungary but, at the same time, had to undertake a strong defense of Serbian national interests.

[43] Dedijer, *Road to Sarajevo*, p. 175.
[44] Zeman, "The Balkans in the Coming War," p. 25.
[45] Cornwall, "Serbia," p. 57.
[46] Dedijer, *Road to Sarajevo*, pp. 388–95.

In response to the killings, the Serbian government showed "correct respect," curtailing festivities (28 June was Vidovdan, the most important Serb national anniversary) and ordering mourning. A "flood of official condolences were [sic] dispatched to Vienna."[47] Personal condolences were sent to Emperor Franz Joseph.[48] Pashich also sent a circular to all Serbian embassies. This asserted that the Sarajevo assassination found the sharpest criticism throughout Serbian society; all official and unofficial circles were immediately aware of the bad reflection that this would have on the good relations between the neighboring monarchy and Serbia as well as the "position of our compatriots in Austria-Hungary."[49] In the same dispatch, Pashich stated that "anarchistic elements" may have been responsible for the crime. While doubtlessly referring to the Black Hand, he was clearly reluctant to identify them as the perpetrators.

The Austro-Hungarian authorities, with little hesitation, assigned responsibility to the Belgrade government. Under the circumstances, the key initiative rested with Vienna. The Serbian government quietly solicited support among the powers, great and small, requesting diplomatic efforts to moderate Austro-Hungarian demands. More important, it sought a promise of military support from Russia, its most likely ally. Whatever Vienna decided, the Serbs, still recovering from the losses of the Balkan Wars, had to rely on foreign and especially on Russian support. Despite the tsar's promises earlier in the year, no support was forthcoming.

Almost three weeks passed with no decisive move from Austria-Hungary. As the historian Mark Cornwall explained, "Vienna had been partially successful in lulling Belgrade into a false sense of security." Only on the 18th did Pashich have information, from several credible sources, indicating the seriousness of the forthcoming demands. At midnight on the 18th urgent telegrams were sent to all Serb legations (again, except for Vienna) asking them to request foreign governments to act for reconciliation.[50]

The Austro-Hungarian minister in Belgrade, Baron Wladimir Giesl, delivered the ultimatum at 6 P.M. on 23 July. It began as follows: "It is clear from the statements and confessions of the criminal authors of the assassination of the twenty eighth of June, that the murder in Sarajevo was

---

[47] Cornwall, "Serbia," p. 60.
[48] DSPKS vol. 7, book 2, no. 279.
[49] Ibid., no. 299.
[50] Cornwall, "Serbia," pp. 69–70.

conceived in Belgrade."[51] It then made ten demands on the Serbian government, including the suppression of anti-Austro-Hungarian propaganda; the removal from the Serbian military and government of all officials who had carried out anti-Austro-Hungarian propaganda; Serbian agreement to the cooperation of Austro-Hungarian authorities to suppress anti-Austro-Hungarian movements within Serbia; and the initiation, with the participation of Austro-Hungarian authorities, of judicial inquiries against every participant in the events of 28 June found on Serbian territory. The ultimatum imposed a forty-eight-hour limit for acceptance. These were by any measure imposing demands. Upon learning of the Austrian conditions, the British foreign secretary, Sir Edward Grey, pronounced them "the most formidable document" he had ever seen "addressed by one state to another that was independent."[52]

Pashich returned to the Serbian capital, arriving early the next morning. At this point the attitude of the powers, especially of Russia, toward Serbia was critical in the formulation of the Serbian reply. The Belgrade government realized that little sentiment in favor of Serbia existed in the *entente* capitals of London and Paris.[53] If Russia offered clear and forceful support, it would allow Serbia to reject much of what was demanded. Crown Prince Alexander telegraphed Tsar Nicholas II to indicate the Serb position: "We are prepared to accept those Austro-Hungarian demands which are in keeping with the position of an independent country as well as those which Your Majesty might recommend. We shall severely punish all persons who can be proven to have participated in the assassination." The message continued with an urgent statement: "[T]he Austro-Hungarian army is massing on our border. It is impossible for us to defend ourselves, and therefore we beg Your Majesty to hasten to our aid as quickly as possible."[54]

The last-minute Serbian efforts, however, were to no avail, for none of the powers "appeared to be doing anything definite to influence Vienna; all of them wanted Serbia's reply to be as conciliatory as possible, with a view to keeping the peace and then arranging some compromise."[55]

[51] Petrovich, *History of Modern Serbia*, vol. 2, p. 613; DSPKS vol. 7, book 2, no. 494. See also Luigi Albertini, *The Origins of the War of 1914*, 3 vols. (London, 1953), vol. 2, pp. 286–9.

[52] G. P. Gooch and Harold Temperley, eds., *British Documents on the Origins of the War 1898–1914*, 11 vols. (London, 1927–38), vol. 11, p. 91.

[53] For some sense of the complexities, see Cornwall, "Serbia," pp. 70–80.

[54] Petrovich, *History of Modern Serbia*, vol. 2, pp. 615–16.

[55] Cornwall, "Serbia," p. 78.

For Serbia's leaders, the most serious concern was the lack of any clear statement of support from Russia.[56] Romania, Serbia's ally in the war with Bulgaria, recommended acceptance of the Austrian ultimatum "without reservation."[57] That advice, along with some bland words from Greece, arrived after the expiration of the ultimatum.

Given those circumstances, the Serbian government's response was remarkably conciliatory. Pashich agreed to most of the demands, including the suppression of anti-Austrian propaganda. Most of the concessions were hedged, that is, pending presentation of appropriate evidence.[58] But Pashich refused the demand for Austro-Hungarian investigators empowered to act within Serbia, a point that, if accepted, would amount to a humiliating sacrifice of national sovereignty, one that would risk a backlash from the Serbian military and unpredictable actions from the Black Hand.

Pashich personally delivered the Serbian reply to the Austrian legation, just before the expiration of the time limit.[59] Baron Giesl, following his instructions, rejected the Serbian response and immediately left for Vienna. Three days later, on 28 July, Austria-Hungary declared war on Serbia.[60] On the 29th, at 5 A.M., gunboats of the Dual Monarchy began a bombardment of Belgrade that continued the entire day. This was the first act of war in the long struggle.

Many commentators, understandably, focus on the assassination of the archduke and his wife, centering discussion on the event of 28 June. In the familiar image, it was "the spark" that set off "the conflagration." But unlike a spark in the tinderbox, the killings, by themselves, caused nothing. It was the use made of this event, initially by Austria-Hungary, that brought the nations to war. The key event, one recognized by the decision makers of all the major powers, was the delivery of the Austro-Hungarian note to Serbia on 23 July. Leaders of all the great powers read the ultimatum and immediately saw the dangers. It was this note with its formidable demands that, through five distinct routes, brought about the involvement of five major powers.

---

[56] William Jannen, Jr., *The Lions of July: Prelude to War, 1914* (Novato, Calif., 1996), pp. 84–5, 134; Cornwall, "Serbia," pp. 79–81.

[57] ÖUA, vol. 8, no. 10664.

[58] See Albertini, *Origins of the War*, vol. 2, p. 371.

[59] For the Serbian reply, see DSPKS vol. 7, book 2, no. 538.

[60] Ibid., 616.

Austria-Hungary's leaders thought out and formulated this crucial document. They consulted with and received significant support for their effort from Germany's leaders. Those efforts are reviewed below in Chapters 4 and 5. The responses of Russia, France, and Britain are then considered.

There was a missed opportunity here, a "last chance" for avoiding the cataclysm. The great powers, specifically Russia, France, and Britain, could have exerted every possible influence on Austria-Hungary to urge restraint and conciliation. Failing that, they could have threatened "strong" reactions. To keep the peace, their task was to signal, unambiguously, the consequences that would follow from the Dual Monarchy's "calculated risk." This could have been done during the forty-eight hours or, even more emphatically, in the days immediately following Serbia's response to the ultimatum. But the Concert of Europe failed at this crucial moment. The collective effort to keep the peace did not occur.

Since the later Serbian experience is almost lost in most histories of the subsequent four years of war, a brief paragraph may prove useful. Anticipating a bellicose Austrian response, the Serbs had moved their government to the southern city of Nish on 24 July and had undertaken some basic military precautions. Serbia's Montenegrin satellite entered the war against the Dual Monarchy on 7 August 1914. At first, unexpectedly, the war went well for the Serbs. By the end of 1914, they had repelled three Austro-Hungarian invasions, albeit at heavy cost in men and material. In the summer of 1915, the Serbs and Montenegrins again occupied key positions in Albania, including Scutari. But at the same time, fighting intensified in Kosovo and Macedonia as the Albanians and Macedonians received support from Austria-Hungary and Bulgaria. In October 1915, Austro-Hungarian forces, reinforced by German and Bulgarian troops, invaded Serbia. By the beginning of 1916, all of Serbia and Montenegro were under enemy occupation, which would last almost two years.

# 4

# Austria-Hungary

## Graydon A. Tunstall, Jr.

Austria-Hungary's political and military leaders declared war on Serbia on 28 July 1914. The first act of hostilities came the next day with the bombardment of Belgrade. Using the assassination of Archduke Franz Ferdinand as the pretext, the leaders' aim was to end the Serbian agitation that, in their view, posed a serious threat to the Dual Monarchy. In the thirty days that intervened between those dates, the leaders in Vienna took a series of steps whose purpose was to bring about that war. The most important of these, one taken early in July, was to assure the support of Germany, their powerful ally. Some efforts were made to gain the support or sympathy of other nations or, alternatively, to discourage their active hostility. One central concern was to prevent Russian participation, to limit the conflict, to keep it a "localized" Austro-Serbian war. Decisions were made with regard to the call-up and use of the armed forces. Each of these decisions required planning with respect to timing and sequence. The question of timing led to some division of opinion between the allies, Germany's leaders pressing for an early response. But, as seen below, several considerations led the Austro-Hungarian leaders to delay.

Two conclusions deserve special emphasis, ones that might easily be lost in the complexities of this and the following chapters: In July 1914, Austria-Hungary's leaders were the first to opt for war, and they did so with plan and foresight. The latter point may be expressed negatively: Their action was not inadvertent, it was no accident, or, to use the most frequent cliché, this was no "slide into war."

Austria was easily the leading power of central Europe in the seventeenth and eighteenth centuries. But then, in 1805, came the humiliating defeat by Napoleon Bonaparte and the subsequent occupation. From

1815, for just over three decades, she was again the dominant power on the Continent. But another major defeat came in 1848, this in some ways even more humiliating, the work of insurgent citizens. In one important episode, in 1849, she required "rescue" by Russia. Austria was defeated again in 1859 in the war with Piedmont and France, this time losing most of her Italian holdings. A much more serious loss came in 1866. With the defeat by Prussia, she was now deprived of her centuries-old dominance in central Europe. One immediate result was the 1867 reconstitution of the empire to form Austria-Hungary, the Dual Monarchy, with sovereignty shared by the leaders of two dominant ethnic communities.

In a period of developing nationalism, this multiethnic empire was a highly vulnerable entity. New states (or aspiring ones) on its borders could appeal to fellow nationals living within the empire. Serbia and Romania were obvious threats; an emergent Poland would be another. Internal revolts, moreover, following the Hungarian example, could possibly lead to the secession of Bohemia or of Croatia or, alternatively, bring a demand for autonomy within the empire. A South Slav state, a "Yugoslavia," could bring the defection of millions of "Austro-Hungarians." The brutal 1903 regicide in Serbia of the head of the Obrenović dynasty transformed the docile satellite into an aggressive new nation, one with pronounced anti-Habsburg tendencies. A complicated series of moves followed, further exacerbating the strains. There was the Pig War, the Dual Monarchy's attempt to force Serbian dependency. Austria-Hungary took over Bosnia in 1908; and the two Balkan Wars followed in 1912–13. With Serbia now much larger, stronger, and presumably with even greater aspirations, the threat seemed enormous. See Map 4.1.

The Compromise of 1867 produced a peculiar and complicated system of government.[1] The emperor (who was simultaneously King of Hungary) ruled over the whole. But the state was now divided into two subentities, Austria and Hungary, with capitals in Vienna and Budapest, each with

---

[1] For brief overviews of the constitutional arrangements, see F. R. Bridge, *The Habsburg Monarchy among the Great Powers, 1815–1918* (New York, 1990), pp. 8–16; and Samuel R. Williamson, Jr., *Austria-Hungary and the Origins of the First World War* (New York, 1991), ch. 3. For a very detailed account, see Helmut Rumpler, "Die rechtlich-organisatorischen und sozialen Rahmenbedingungen für die Aussenpolitik der Habsburgermonarchie 1848–1918," in Adam Wandruszka and Peter Urbanitsch, *Die Habsburgermonarchie 1848–1918* (Vienna, 1989), vol. 6, part 1, pp. 1–121.

For general histories, see C. A. Macartney, *The Habsburg Empire, 1790–1918* (London, 1969); Robert A. Kann, *A History of the Habsburg Empire 1526–1918* (Berkeley, 1974); and Manfried Rauchensteiner, *Der Tod des Doppeladlers: Österreich-Ungarn und der Erste Weltkrieg* (Vienna, 1993).

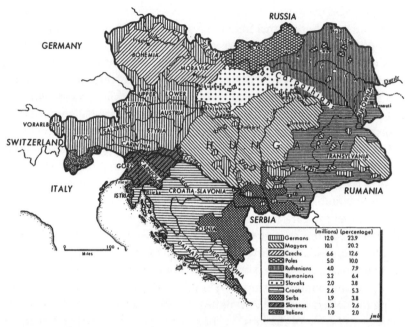

MAP 4.1. Ethnic Groups of the Habsburg Empire, 1910. *Source:* William McCagg, *History of Habsburg Jews, 1670–1918* (Bloomington: Indiana University Press, 1989), p. 168. Reprinted with permission of the publisher.

its own constitution, government, and parliament. The "halves" of the empire were governed by their respective German and Magyar aristocratic oligarchies, both of them facing serious problems stemming from the ethnic diversity of their states. Budapest's Magyarization policies were especially problematic, alienating its South Slav and Romanian subjects.

The Dual Monarchy was governed by a Common Ministerial Council, the highest agency in the empire's complicated governmental system. It ordinarily consisted of the emperor and five other individuals: the foreign minister (the highest official in the Dual Monarchy); two minister-presidents (or premiers), one Austrian, one Hungarian; the common finance minister; and the war minister. Officially, the emperor presided over the council's meetings, but more often it was chaired by his appointed foreign minister. This select group had the authority to summon others, such as the chief of the General Staff, to participate in their discussions as needed. At its disposal were all of the resources of the national government. For the July 1914 decisions, that meant effectively all the personnel of the Foreign and War Ministries.

The principal task of the Common Ministerial Council was to over-see the monarchy's dualistic governing arrangement. One authority, John Leslie, reports it was normally "more a discussion group than an executive cabinet." In fact, between the meeting on the Serbian-Albanian border cri-sis of 3 October 1913 and that on the war crisis of 7 July 1914, the council met only three times "and then only to discuss the rather narrow issue of the building of strategic railways in Bosnia-Herzegovina."[2] The council was not regulated by any constitution or laws. Apart from an ineffectual oversight agency, called the Delegations, it was not subject to any serious restraints. The Dual Monarchy was constructed so as to preserve, as best it could, the empire's previous absolutist character. But in the modern era it faced enormous problems, trying to reconcile the frequent differences that arose between the two halves of the empire and trying to fend off the insistent internal demands "from below" and those from its immediate neighbors. The Common Ministerial Council would make the decision for war against Serbia in July 1914.

A small coterie, not more than eight or ten persons, made the key decisions of July 1914. Some others played important ancillary roles, most of these as ambassadors to other nations, to Serbia and to the major powers. But they were more the tools rather than the creators of Habsburg foreign policy. The small coterie consisted of the emperor, Franz Joseph, the political leaders (basically, the members of the Common Ministerial Council), and the monarchy's top military leaders.

Franz Joseph was born in 1830 and became emperor at age eighteen in the midst of the tumultuous events of 1848. In July 1914, he was eighty-four years old; he had presided over the Habsburg heritage for sixty-five years. In that time he had witnessed a series of Austrian losses, those just reviewed, and now faced still another threat. Throughout his reign he had maintained close supervision and control of Habsburg foreign and military affairs. The historian F. R. Bridge writes that the emperor was "ultimately responsible" for the most momentous decisions taken during the seven decades of his reign, "either directly or through his choice of advisers [who] almost without exception were men after his own heart."[3] By 1900, however, that "ultimately responsible" phrase, while accurate,

[2] John Leslie, "The Antecedents of Austria-Hungary's War Aims: Policies and Policy-Makers in Vienna and Budapest before and during 1914," in Elisabeth Springer and Leopold Kammerhofer, eds., *Wiener Beiträge zur Geschichte der Neuzeit* 20 (Vienna, 1993), pp. 307–94; quotation from p. 309.
[3] Bridge, *Habsburg Monarchy*, pp. 4–5.

would be misleading. During the 1908 Bosnian crisis, Foreign Minister Count Alois Lexa von Aehrenthal and Chief of the General Staff Baron Franz Conrad von Hötzendorf continued to provide the monarch with memoranda, but they "increasingly behaved as if he were in virtual retirement." During the 1870 crisis, Franz Joseph presided over five ministerial conferences in twelve days; in the three and a half years prior to World War I, he attended none of the council's thirty-nine meetings. The governance of the empire, in short, was being delegated.[4]

The emperor appointed the members of the Common Ministerial Council and the leaders of the military, to be sure, after consultation with, and influence by, other officials. The foreign minister and most of the high-ranking officials at the Ballhausplatz (home of the Foreign Ministry) were members of the aristocracy, but, more important, they were graduates of either the Theresianum or the Consular Academy, and had long experience in the foreign service. Most important of all, they were chosen for their reliability and loyalty to the Habsburg family and the dynastic state.[5]

The emperor, as noted, often delegated the leadership of the Common Ministerial Council to the Imperial and Royal Minister of the Household and of Foreign Affairs. From 1906 to 1912, this was Aehrenthal, a man with a forceful personality, considerable charisma, and a sense of mission. His aim, basically, was to see the revival of the empire. The takeover of Bosnia-Herzegovina in 1908 was his work. It was, for better or for worse, his most important achievement. As he put it: "We have reconquered again the place that belongs to us among the Powers."[6]

Aehrenthal took on and trained the next generation of diplomats, imbuing them with his sense of purpose. They were staunch admirers of their mentor, serving as his loyal and devoted disciples. They had

---

4 Alan Palmer, *Twilight of the Habsburgs: The Life and Times of Emperor Francis Joseph* (New York, 1995), pp. 302, 322, 327. One specialist states that the emperor's position "on all decisive foreign policy questions in the final prewar year remains unfathomable"; Robert A. Kann, "Archduke Franz Ferdinand and Count Berchtold during His Term as Foreign Minister, 1912–1914," in Stanley B. Winter, ed., *Dynasty, Politics and Culture: Selected Essays* (Boulder, Colo., 1991), pp. 105–50; quotation from p. 146.

5 See Gary W. Shanafelt, *The Secret Enemy: Austria-Hungary and the German Alliance, 1914–1918* (New York, 1985), pp. 12–16; Ludwig Bittner, "Das österreichisch-ungarische Ministerium des Äußern: Seine Geschichte und Seine Organisation," *Berliner Monatshefte* 15 (1937): 819–43; and Friedrich Engel-Janosi, *Geschichte auf dem Ballhausplatz* (Vienna, 1963).

6 Bridge, *Habsburg Monarchy*, p. 295. For a sense of the man and his aims, see Solomon Wank, "Aehrenthal's Programme for the Constitutional Transformation of the Habsburg Monarchy: Three Secret *Mémoires*," *Slavonic and East European Review* 41 (1963): 513–36.

entered the diplomatic corps at the turn of the century and had served in varying capacities in the Balkans. They held social Darwinist viewpoints with respect to the "lesser Balkan peoples." Sometimes called the Young Turks or, more often, the Young Rebels (rebelling against Austria's casual, easy-going ways), they would have considerable influence on Aehrenthal's successor.

Aehrenthal died in February 1912 and was succeeded by Count Leopold Berchtold. He was forty-nine years old when appointed, the youngest foreign minister in Europe. Berchtold had served in the diplomatic corps from 1894 and for five years was Vienna's ambassador to Russia, where he served with distinction. But he lacked experience in the management of foreign affairs, never having served as a section chief in the ministry. He also lacked experience in domestic affairs and in military matters (this was a persistent problem for the monarchy, a result of its peculiar constitutional arrangements). A reluctant office holder, Berchtold served at what he once called the "simmering cauldron at the Ballplatz" against his own will and better judgment. One authority describes him as "intelligent and hard-working and possessed of a great personal charm," but "entirely lacking in that self-confidence that carried Aehrenthal through." Aehrenthal, it is said, always spoke "with a firm voice that brooked no opposition." Berchtold, in contrast, showed "indecisiveness and diffidence," and quick reversals of policy became serious problems.[7]

Berchtold's feelings of inadequacy made him heavily dependent on the advice and opinions of his personal staff at the Foreign Ministry, and he quickly adopted a "consultative" style to compensate for this. During the July crisis the leading officials met regularly with Berchtold late in the evening to discuss the day's events and prepare for the next. Some commentators have portrayed Berchtold as a pawn in the hands of Aehrenthal's aggressive disciples, but in the July Crisis that does not appear to have been the case. Samuel R. Williamson, Jr., writes that on this occasion Berchtold "commanded and managed the process."[8]

[7] Bridge, *Habsburg Monarchy*, pp. 312–13. Berchtold recognized his deficiencies as, for example, in this statement: "When I took over the ministry I had no notion of the southern Slav question," from Palmer, *Twilight of the Habsburgs*, pp. 312–13. See also Leslie, "Antecedents," pp. 375–84 and elsewhere.
[8] Williamson, *Austria-Hungary*, p. 191; and Hugo Hantsch, *Leopold Graf Berchtold. Grandseigneur und Staatsmann*, 2 vols. (Graz, 1963), vol. 2, pp. 644–5. See also John Leslie, "Österreich-Ungarn vor dem Kriegsausbruch: Der Ballhausplatz in Wien im Juli 1914 aus der Sicht eines österreichisch-ungarischen Diplomaten," in Ralph Melville, Claus

The leading members of that Ballhausplatz faction, the Young Rebels, constituted the most vocal prowar diplomatic cadre during the July Crisis. At their head stood the assertive Count Alexander Hoyos, a personal friend of Berchtold with diplomatic experience in Peking, Paris, Belgrade, and Berlin. After a tour of duty in Stuttgart and London, in 1912 he became *chef de cabinet* in Berchtold's ministry. At age thirty-six, "Alek" Hoyos headed the foreign minister's small immediate staff and thus was at the center of decision making at the Ballhausplatz. Early in July, Berchtold dispatched Hoyos to Berlin with Vienna's pleas for German support in its planned campaign against Serbia. As well, he recorded the minutes of the critical meetings of the Common Ministerial Council on 7 and 19 July 1914.

Just below Hoyos were the Foreign Ministry's five section chiefs. Count János Forgách had served as minister to Belgrade from 1907 to 1911. Thus, he played a significant role during the Bosnian crisis of 1908, but the following year discredited himself by providing forged documents for a highly publicized treason trial at Agram (Zagreb).[9] Sent into professional exile at Dresden, in the fall of 1913, Forgách nevertheless returned to the Foreign Ministry as chief of its Political Section (until 1917). The major participants in the July Crisis assign Forgách (along with Hoyos) a prominent role in those events. As head of the Political Section, he was responsible for preparing Berchtold's personal correspondence and material for Common Ministerial Council meetings. He also participated in numerous meetings with foreign envoys and ambassadors. During the July Crisis, Forgách maintained daily telephone contact with both Minister-President Count István Tisza at Budapest and Baron István Burián, the Hungarian emissary to Vienna.

Next in importance came Baron Franz von Matscheko, a senior section chief and Berchtold's Balkan expert. On 24 June, just four days before the killings at Sarajevo, Matscheko had counseled a more aggressive diplomatic policy, one that demanded the support of both Tisza and the Germans. Matscheko had spoken of Russia's "encirclement" of the Dual Monarchy and demanded "energetic" steps to break that alleged iron ring. As well, Matscheko identified Bulgaria as a potential ally and Romania

Scharf, Martin Vogt, and Ulrich Wengenroth, eds., *Deutschland und Europa in der Neuzeit* (Stuttgart, 1988), esp. pp. 663–4.

[9] Julius Szilássy, *Der Untergang der Donau Monarchie* (Berlin, 1931), pp. 254–5; József Galantai, *Hungary in the First World War* (Budapest, 1989). See also Ludwig Bittner, "Graf Johann Forgách," *Berliner Monatshefte* 13 (1935): 950–9.

(an ally) as a potential foe.[10] After Sarajevo, Matscheko replaced his strident call for a more militant diplomatic policy with one for an aggressive military policy. And finally, there was Baron Alexander von Musulin, diplomat and bureaucrat in the Foreign Ministry. Renowned for his penmanship, Musulin was entrusted by Forgách with drafting the ultimatum to Serbia in July 1914.

Among senior Habsburg ambassadors, the two most important were at Berlin and St. Petersburg. Count Frigyes Szápáry von Szápár had been Forgách's predecessor as head of the Political Section, having served in that position from 1909. Late in 1913, he was named ambassador to St. Petersburg, the first Russophobe to hold the position for some time. Personal problems forced Szápáry to leave St. Petersburg almost as soon as he had arrived, leaving much of the work to Legation Secretary Count Ottokar Czernin. During the first weeks of the July Crisis, Szápáry was again absent due to the illness of his wife, which of course hindered both intelligence and diplomatic efforts. But in Vienna during those weeks he participated in several important sessions dealing with the crisis. He returned to his post in the Russian capital in mid-July.[11]

The critical ambassadorship to Berlin had been held since 1892 by Count Ladislaus Szögyény-Marich. The most senior Habsburg ambassador, Szögyény loyally acted as a conduit for diplomatic messages rather than as a shaper of relations with Berlin. The arrival of Hoyos in Berlin as a special envoy of both Franz Joseph and Berchtold effectively reduced the ambassador's role during the most sensitive phase of the July Crisis.

The two minister-presidents, Count Karl Stürgkh of Austria and Tisza of Hungary, like Berchtold were also members of the Common Ministerial Council. Their primary concerns, ordinarily, were with internal affairs. In the matter of war, however, the minister-presidents had a veto power. If either refused consent, the entire effort would be halted.

Stürgkh was a professional bureaucrat, a man of limited vision whose career should have ended with his appointment as minister of education in 1908. Instead, he was appointed minister-president in November 1911. A bureaucrat of German centralist tendencies, Stürgkh proved to be a

[10] Memorandum of 24 June 1914, in Ludwig Bittner and Hans Uebersberger, eds., *Österreich-Ungarns Aussenpolitik von der Bosnischen Krise 1908 bis zum Kriegsausbrich 1914*, 8 vols. (Vienna and Leipzig, 1930), vol. 8, pp. 186–95. Hereafter cited as ÖUA.
[11] Leslie, "Antecedents," pp. 378–9; Ludwig Bittner, "Graf Friedrich Szápáry," *Berliner Monatshefte* 14 (Berlin, 1936).

disaster. In July 1913, he overthrew the Bohemian constitution, and in March 1914, he prorogued the Austrian parliament, the Reichsrat. As a result, Austrian politicians played no role in the events following the Sarajevo assassination.

Tisza was cut from a different cloth. Minister-president since June 1913, the Magyar aristocrat firmly believed in the Compromise of 1867 as the supreme guarantor of Hungarian rights against Germans, Romanians, and Slavs. Tisza was unwilling to make any concessions, such as the introduction of general suffrage, especially to the Slavs, who were a majority within Hungary. He ruled his half of the Dual Monarchy with an iron first. No decision could be reached at Vienna without his support. Early in the July Crisis, Tisza indicated some concerns, some grounds for dissent with respect to war with Serbia, but, as seen below, he eventually yielded.[12]

Tisza's activities, understandably, were based largely in Budapest. For this reason, his emissary in Vienna, István Burián, during the July Crisis was an influential participant in Council discussions. Burián had held many diplomatic appointments, in Moscow, Sofia, Bucharest, and Belgrade, and, from 1903 to 1912, had served as joint finance minister. In that capacity, after 1908, he had administered the newly annexed Bosnia-Herzegovina. His conciliatory approach to the populations of the new territories earned him the wrath of his fellow bureaucrats. Serious, unimaginative, and prone to strict legalistic approaches to issues, Burián in July 1914 was little more than Tisza's mouthpiece in Vienna.

The common finance minister, Ritter Leon von Biliński, was an avowed "hawk." Already during the Balkan Wars, he had demanded that Habsburg forces not only intervene in Montenegro, but also that they march against the Serbs – even if this brought about war with Russia. A victorious war against Montenegro-Serbia, Biliński counseled in May 1913, alone could bring new territories to the Dual Monarchy and arrest the forces of nationalism. During the July Crisis of 1914, Biliński, not surprisingly, reiterated his strident calls for military action against Serbia, with or without German support. After the Great War, he admitted to a friend that Austria had decided on a war course at the latest by 3 July.[13]

---

[12] Leslie, "Antecedents," pp. 323–47. Those pages discuss "The Hungarians," including Burián and others.

[13] Rauchensteiner, *Tod des Doppeladlers*, p. 68.

And finally, there was the minister of war, Ritter Alexander von Krobatin. The son of an army officer, he had been schooled exclusively in military institutions. He taught at the Technical Military Academy and later headed the Artillery Cadet School. From 1896, he served in the War Ministry and, in 1912, was named as its head. Krobatin worked tirelessly to modernize the Austro-Hungarian artillery. In July 1914, he vigorously supported the "hawks" in calling for an immediate military strike against Serbia.

The Council's consideration of war required the services of still other military specialists, the most important of whom was the chief of the General Staff, Conrad von Hötzendorf.[14] He too was the son of an army officer and had graduated from the Theresa Military Academy. He had participated in various campaigns, most notably in the Balkans, had taught at the War Academy, and had held regimental, divisional, and corps commands. Conrad met and became a friend of the heir apparent, Franz Ferdinand, who helped him acquire the chief of staff position late in 1906. Over the next five years, Conrad sought to update the antiquated Habsburg forces, especially the artillery. His advocacy of a preemptive strike against Serbia brought him into conflict with the emperor and with Aehrenthal in 1911. Later that year, following his call for a preemptive strike against Italy (an ally then engaged in the Tripolitanian War), Conrad was dismissed. Renewed difficulties in the Balkans in 1912 led to his return to the chief of staff position.

In his years as chief of the General Staff, Conrad was an insistent advocate of war against the empire's "congenital enemies." He counseled action against Italy, Serbia, Montenegro, and, on occasion, Romania and Russia – or combinations of the above. His prime targets, the objects of several plans, were Serbia and Montenegro. Conrad "argued repeatedly that the use of armed force alone could retard the centrifugal forces of nationalism in the 'multinational empire'...."[15] In July 1914, he was the most vigorous advocate of war with Serbia. In this matter, he received strong support from his close friend Krobatin, the minister of war.

Conrad was the empire's most revered as well as most overrated military commander. While one enthusiast considered him a military genius,

---

[14] A brief overview of Conrad is provided by Lawrence Sondhaus, *Franz Conrad von Hötzendorf: Architect of the Apocalypse* (Boston, Leiden, and Cologne, 2000).

[15] Holger H. Herwig, *The First World War: Germany and Austria-Hungary 1914–1918* (London, 1997), p. 9. For more detail, see Leslie, "Antecedents," pp. 310–23.

"the greatest Austrian commander since Eugene of Savoy," in fact, as
events would show, his policies and plans were very problematic. His
"strategic ideas and plans seldom, if ever, matched the manpower and
material of the Imperial and Royal Army. . . . Conrad consistently ignored
such critical factors as terrain, weather, season, or routes for supply or
movement."[16]

Most of these key decision makers were located either in the Foreign
Ministry or in the War Ministry. Most had spent their adult lives within
one of these organizations. Those two elites, as will be seen, in Austria-
Hungary and elsewhere, were driven by somewhat different concerns,
the diplomatic and military "necessities" not always converging. The emperor, of course, "stood above" those subordinates and, officially at least,
had the last word in all key decisions. Another lesson should be noted, a
negative one, namely, the groups that were not present. All other elites,
the leaders of industry, finance, church, universities, and the press, were
absent from the deliberations that led to war in 1914.

Before considering the actions taken following the assassination of 28 June
1914, a brief review of the empire's foreign affairs and military policy
in the period leading up to the crisis will prove useful. The annexation
of Bosnia-Herzegovina in 1908 was viewed, in most of the European
capitals, as a colossal error of judgment. The immediate consequence,
Bridge writes, was "the disgrace and isolation of Austria-Hungary." In the
years following, Foreign Minister Aehrenthal sought to repair the damage.
Vienna tried to conciliate Serbia, most notably by offering the free use of
a port on the Dalmatian coast and of railways to transport Serbian products through Bosnia to the Adriatic Sea. Aehrenthal's basic aim, Bridge
states, was to convince the powers that the annexation was "the final
rounding off of the Monarchy's southern frontiers; and that Vienna was
now genuinely desirous of maintaining the status quo."[17] Archduke Franz
Ferdinand objected to these conciliatory policies, since one implication

---

[16] Graydon A. Tunstall, Jr., "The Habsburg Command Conspiracy: The Austrian
Falsification of Historiography on the Outbreak of World War I," *Austrian History
Yearbook* 27 (1996): 181–98; quotations from pp. 191–2; and Leslie, "Antecedents,"
pp. 312–13.
    Kaiser Wilhelm, totally unaware of these problems, was a enthusiastic supporter. In
October 1913 he wrote his friend, Archduke Franz Ferdinand: "I am pleased that Conrad
stays in office. . . . He is a splendid character; they are rare nowadays." From Robert A.
Kann, "Emperor William II and Archduke Francis Ferdinand in Their Correspondence,"
*American Historical Review* 57 (1952): 323–52; quotation from p. 350.

[17] Bridge, *Habsburg Monarchy*, pp. 288, 293, 298–9. Serbia, incidentally, "flatly rejected
Aehrenthal's offer of commercial negotiations" (p. 294).

was that Aehrenthal would now oppose "any large expansion of the army or increase in its budget on the grounds that this would cause the Monarchy to be accused of aggressive aims. . . ."[18]

Most critically, Russia's leaders were not convinced by these concilia-tory efforts pointing to Austria-Hungary's Sanjak railway project, a line that would cross the Balkans to Salonika, on the Aegean Sea. They saw it as an attempt to extend Habsburg influence or frontiers, a view that in St. Petersburg acquired "the force of an immutable political law."[19] The rail line, first announced in January 1908, was also the work of Aehrenthal. A Vienna-to-Salonika line was already in existence, but it ran south from Budapest through Belgrade, while the new line would bypass Serbia. Aehrenthal does not seem to have had high hopes for the eco-nomic returns of the project, not expecting it to take business away from the existing line. His aim appears to have been political, to block Serbian, Balkan, and Russian aspirations, a threat seen as a *Drang nach Westen*. A countering project, a Danube-Adriatic line, was being considered, one that would bypass the Dual Monarchy entirely. Italy too was seen as a possible coconspirator in this connection. The original project, the Sanjak line, caused much concern, but it never materialized. In the course of the Balkan Wars, much of the planned route came into Serbian hands.[20]

The belief that Austria-Hungary had imperialist ambitions in the Balkans was widely shared, the view appearing in some accounts more than half a century later.[21] While the logic might be compelling, readily

---

[18] Lavender Cassels, *The Archduke and the Assassin: Sarajevo, June 28th 1914* (London, 1984), pp. 124–5.
[19] Bridge, *Habsburg Monarchy*, p. 298. For similar reactions in Belgrade, see Cassels, *Archduke and the Assassin*, p. 86.
[20] For a review of the complexities involved, see Solomon Wank, "Aehrenthal and the Sanjak of Novibazar Railway Project: A Reappraisal," *Slavonic and East European Review* 42 (1964): 353–69; and Wayne S. Vucinich, *Serbia between East and West: The Events of 1903–1908* (Stanford, 1954), part 8.
[21] One source of difficulty in interpreting Austro-Hungarian aims in the Balkans appears in Wank's article. He describes the Sanjak project as "an imperialistic policy of economic penetration of the Balkan peninsula" and as an "expansive programme of imperialism"; ibid., pp. 355, 368. Imperialism usually implies political control, actual takeover. Another option, however, would be economic penetration, an attempt to guarantee markets and raw materials, but without direct political domination (this being Aehrenthal's position, p. 363). Still another option would be "none of the above," the aim being mainly political, as is argued here. Wank reports that some Vienna officials thought the project would "open up boundless commercial prospects." Aehrenthal, however, recognized that "no private concessionnaire would assume the risk of constructing the railway through the Sanjak" (pp. 360, 365). The "boundless" prospects claim is a curious one. The region that would have been "served" was mountainous, rocky, and barren, the populations very poor. The leaders of Austria-Hungary's major banks were "unanimously opposed"

available evidence points to a different conclusion. Conrad was the most persistent advocate of the imperialist position, but he generally stood alone on this issue. In January 1909, with the Bosnian situation still smoldering, Conrad argued "that Serbia should be attacked in March and annexed." Aehrenthal, however, declared that the Dual Monarchy "could never absorb Serbia." Any action "must be restricted to consolidating the position in Bosnia and Hercegovina."[22] If Serbia could not be "contained," the preferred solution was division: Some parts would go to Romania, some to Bulgaria, some to newly formed Albania.

One prominent member of the leadership group, until 28 June, was the *Thronfolger*, the heir apparent, Archduke Franz Ferdinand. His hope, one communicated to Aehrenthal's successor, Berchtold, was that "the Monarchy could stay clear of Balkan entanglements." Conrad pressed again and again for a "settling of accounts" with Serbia, but the emperor and the archduke sharply rejected those demands. In one discussion, in early February 1913, Franz Ferdinand declared that war and a conquest of Serbia would be "nonsense." "Let us even assume," he added, "that no one else will contest us, [that we] can in peace and quiet settle accounts with Serbia." But, he asked rhetorically and most undiplomatically, what could Vienna gain thereby? "Only a pack of thieves and a few more murderers and rascals and a few plum trees. In other words, more rabble at the cost of so many soldiers lost and several billions spent. That most favorable case, that no one contests us, is more than unlikely." At a later point, commenting on another of Conrad's plans for war on Serbia, the archduke prophetically declared:

War with Russia means the end of us. If we take the field against Serbia, Russia will stand behind her, and we will have the war with Russia. Should the Austrian emperor and the Russian tsar topple one another from the throne and clear the way for the revolution? Tell Conrad that I categorically reject further suggestions in this vein.[23]

to the Sanjak project. See Bernard Michel, *Banques et Banquiers en Autriche au Debut du 20e Siècle* (Paris, 1976), p. 365.

[22] Cassels, *Archduke and the Assassin*, p. 99. Earlier, in October 1908, Franz Ferdinand wrote to his military aide: "Please *restrain* Conrad; he must stop agitating for war." If war with Serbia broke out, he argued, "Italy will attack us ... and we could have to fight on two fronts. That would be the end of the story" (p. 96). For more on the Conrad-Franz Ferdinand opposition, see Leslie, "Antecedents," pp. 316–17. The archduke, Leslie reports, "was opposed to any annexation of Serbian territory."

[23] Rudolf Kiszling, *Erzherzog Franz Ferdinand von Oesterreich-Este* (Graz, 1953), pp. 193, 196; and Franz Conrad von Hötzendorf, *Aus meiner Dienstzeit 1906–1918*, 5 vols. (Vienna, Leipzig, and Munich, 1921–5), vol. 3, pp. 125ff. For a discussion of the

Because of its importance, an extended quotation on the subject is useful. These are the words of Archduke Franz Ferdinand from a letter of 1 February 1913, directed this time to Berchtold:

It would be a misfortune if we were to get involved in a big war with Russia. Who knows whether we can count on protection for our left and right flank; Germany has its hands full with France, and Romania will use the Bulgarian threat as an alibi. So this is a very unfavorable time. Suppose we wage a separate war against Serbia. In no time at all, we will overpower it, but what then, and what good will it do us? First of all, we will have all of Europe after us and viewing us as a disturber of the peace. And God save us from annexing Serbia: a country over its head in debts, brimming with regicides and scoundrels, etc. As it is, we cannot even cope with Bosnia, and that nonsense alone is costing us huge sums of money and creating a host of constitutional problems. And Serbia will be far worse! We can throw away billions there and still be faced with a terrible irredenta.

Over and over, the archduke advised the Ballhausplatz along similar lines. His conclusion: "The best policy is to remain an onlooker while others bash in each other's skulls, *egg them on in their quarrels, and keep the monarchy at peace.*"[24]

For most of Austria-Hungary's decision makers, the preferred arrangement for the Balkans was fragmentation, not takeover. They wished to see a cluster of small, nonthreatening states, either harmless neutrals or docile satellites. Any additions of new Balkan populations to the Dual Monarchy would only add to the problems of what already was a nearly unmanageable multinational empire. That was also the view in Budapest.

The transition from Aehrenthal to Berchtold brought no immediate change in the Dual Monarchy's Balkan policies. The new minister, one authority writes, "was no expansionist, but, like Aehrenthal, a firm believer in the Monarchy's role as a conservative, status quo power." The "cadets," the Young Rebels, continued their mentor's basic directions. One of those directions, however, was to have considerable significance: Forgách, Hoyos, Matscheko, and Musulin were "all advocates of a tough, confrontational approach towards the Monarchy's opponents." Berchtold responded to the difficulties posed by the Balkan wars by resort to "concert" principles, calling on intervention by the European powers,

archduke, of his growing influence, and the significance of his removal, see Samuel R. Williamson, Jr., "Influence, Power, and the Policy Process: The Case of Franz Ferdinand, 1906–1914," *Historical Journal* 17 (1974): 417–34.

[24] Kann, "Archduke Franz Ferdinand," pp. 122–3.

hence the initial settlements in London. But, as circumstances worsened, Vienna's decision makers shifted to the use of that "tough, confrontational approach."[25]

The Dual Monarchy was poorly prepared for such an approach. Throughout the prewar period, its military expenditures lagged far behind those of the other European powers. One major problem was legislative reluctance, the Hungarian parliament being most unwilling. In 1911, as the arms race was heating up, Germany, Russia, and Britain had the largest defense budgets. At that point, Austria-Hungary's expenditures were less than a third of those of Germany and barely more than a third of those of Russia and Britain. Its defense outlay was less than half that of France and only marginally greater than that of Italy. The monarchy's expenditures, moreover, had been comparatively modest from the turn of the century, and that meant a serious deficit in the quality of weaponry vis-à-vis any likely opponents.[26] This circumstance had profound implications for any Austro-Hungarian military initiative. The obvious preferred option would be limited war, the monarchy versus one or two minor contenders. A more problematic next-best option would be a war fought with German support.

There were other difficulties. The Habsburg military was not a single unified body but instead consisted of three distinct organizations: the Imperial and Royal Army, which drew its recruits from throughout the monarchy; the Landwehr, comprised of the Austrian National Guard; and the Honvéd, the royal Hungarian National Guard.[27] The Habsburg Army was critical to maintaining a unified empire and keeping its multinational populace *kaisertreu*. Although dominated by Germans, that army also

---

[25] Bridge, *Habsburg Monarchy*, p. 312. For the larger context, see R. J. Crampton, "The Decline of the Concert of Europe in the Balkans, 1913–1914," *Slavonic and East European Review* 52 (1974): 393–419.

[26] David Stevenson, *Armaments and the Coming of War: Europe, 1904–1914* (Oxford, 1996), p. 4. Those figures include naval expenditures. The disparity is less if we examine only army expenditures, but even there the Dual Monarchy was in a difficult position; ibid., p. 8, and David G. Herrmann, *The Arming of Europe and the Making of the First World War* (Princeton, 1996), pp. 236–7. See also Rauchensteiner, *Tod des Doppeladlers*, pp. 41–7.

[27] Judged by expenditures, the common army was by far the largest of the three components, the Honvéd the smallest. Expenditures for the latter declined steadily between 1909 and 1912. Expenditures for the navy increased dramatically between 1907 and 1912, the total far exceeding monies for the Landwehr and Honvéd; see Stevenson, *Armaments*, p. 136.

faced serious nationality problems. In the event of an armed conflict, the Habsburg Army would have to mobilize its reservists, which, depending on the character of the conflict, would add further elements of uncertainty. One additional difficulty: The most likely opponents, Serbia and Russia, had armies with recent combat experience. Austria and Hungary had not fought a major war since 1866.

The creation of the Balkan League in 1912, exploiting Turkey's weakness stemming from the Tripolitanian War with Italy, was followed immediately by a war in the Balkans. Vienna was very much concerned about this development, sensing that enlarged and more aggressive Slavic states would threaten the integrity of the monarchy. Worse still, during both Balkan wars, Berlin proved indifferent to what Vienna viewed as its vital interests. As a result, all Berchtold could do was to adopt a "wait and see" attitude and to keep Habsburg forces in a state of readiness. At a Common Ministerial Council meeting on 3 October 1913, not only the military but also the Young Rebels in the Foreign Ministry voiced preferences for a more forceful approach, especially to Serbia. The Treaty of Bucharest in August 1913, which ended the Second Balkan War, was a severe diplomatic defeat for Berchtold. He tried unsuccessfully to influence its final decisions, only to learn that his major ally, Germany, had boldly backed both Greece and Romania. Most important for the events of July 1914, Vienna's leaders were now even more convinced that the South Slav "problem" could be resolved only by Serbia's demise.

In the aftermath of the Balkan Wars, the Dual Monarchy's leaders again found cause for alarm. Albania, Berchtold's major achievement, was a flimsy construction, one posing many difficulties, both internal and external. The Triple Alliance faced some very serious difficulties. Romania was a fourth member of the alliance, albeit a secret one. But there were signs of a possible defection and, worse, that the nation might join with Russia and the *entente* powers. Given the substantial Romanian population within Hungary and the ever-present irredentist threat, this posed a major problem. But the military implications were even more serious. Austria-Hungary and Russia had a relatively small common boundary on the Galician (Polish) frontier. If Romania defected, one way or another, whether as enemy or as neutral, the threatened frontier would be doubled in size. This concern became acute when a visit to Romania by Tsar Nicholas II and his wife was announced for mid-June 1914. The visit, described as a "process of courtship," was accompanied by "profusions" of goodwill on both sides. One additional source of alarm: During the visit,

Sergei Sazonov, the Russia foreign minister, "conspicuously crossed into Transylvania to show support for the Romanians who lived under Magyar rule."[28]

The possibility of Romania and Serbia as allies with Russian backing gave rise to many worries for Austria-Hungary's political and military leaders. Ottokar Czernin, then the monarchy's ambassador to Romania, communicated his sense of things in a long letter to Berchtold on 22 June, just after the tsar's visit. "Primarily," he wrote,

the hatred of Romania for Budapest ... which since last year has come to include Vienna, is a powerful factor in the wish to swing over to the *Entente*. But it is not the only one. Since last year and the behavior of Austria-Hungary during the war, the firm conviction has grown here, as in many other parts of Europe, that the Monarchy is an entity doomed to downfall and dissolution, that at the partition of Turkey we have inherited nothing from her but her fate – that, in other words in the near future the Habsburg Monarchy will be put up to European auction."[29]

Czernin summarized with a hypothetical statement, with "the lesson" that the French and Russians would give to the Romanians:

"Do not tether yourselves to a death-stricken carcass" – "leave the sinking ship while there is still time" – "do not cast in your lot with that of the Monarchy; Vienna can only drag you down into its own destruction, whereas the *Entente*, at the sharing out of the spoils, will reward you with the gift of Transylvania."

The ambassador's final conclusion was laced with ultimate pessimism: "Before our eyes in broad daylight, plain for all to see, the encirclement of the Monarchy proceeds glaringly, with shameless effrontery, step by step.... And we stand by with folded arms interestedly observing the carrying out of this onslaught."[30]

Italy presented the Dual Monarchy with still another source of concern. There was uncertainty as to whether Italy would stay in the Triple

---

[28] Williamson, *Austria-Hungary*, ch. 9, esp. pp. 170–2.

[29] This passage and those in the following paragraphs are from Luigi Albertini, *The Origins of the War of 1914*, trans. and ed., Isabella M. Massey (London, 1952), vol. 1, pp. 527–34; quotations from p. 531 (spellings changed).

[30] The sense that Austria-Hungary, like the Ottoman Empire, was a "target" for division was not fanciful. See Eurof Walters, "Franco-Russian Discussions on the Partition of Austria-Hungary, 1899," *Slavonic and East European Review* 28 (1949–50): 184–97. This article also describes the efforts of another irredentist movement, the Dual Monarchy's Pan-Germans, one of whom described himself as "a high traitor." In a Reichsrat debate, he declared: "Our ideal has nothing to do with the Austrian State idea.... What we do, we do solely for the German people in this state. To us, the dynasty and the Austrian state are matters of complete indifference" (pp. 186–7).

Alliance or, in an attempt to regain Trentino and Trieste and possibly some advantage in the Balkans, would move against the monarchy. If that happened, Austria-Hungary would face a very difficult two- or even three-front conflict.[31]

Countering these evident or feared losses were two possible gains. Germany was cultivating relations with the Ottoman Empire. And Bulgaria, once a dependable Russian satellite, now showed signs of defection. Austria-Hungary did what it could to facilitate this move. As seen below, both of these nations did eventually join the war on the side of the Triple Alliance. Although providing some consolation, definite "plusses" for the position of the Dual Monarchy, those two nations were off at some distance to the southeast. Of greater importance, by far the more urgent concern, were the nations close at hand, those on the borders to the north, east, and south.

The newly enlarged Serbia was a central problem. The Austrian military attaché in Belgrade sent Berchtold a summary of "Easter Greetings" that appeared in the Serbian press. These promised "the Resurrection," that is, "the liberation of the Slavs in the Monarchy." One of them read as follows: "We Serbs in the Kingdom who need to celebrate no resurrection, must today meditate what must be the longing of our brothers beyond the Danube, Save, and Drina. Liberation! They long for what our brothers on both banks of the Vardar longed for two years ago."[32] The problem was made worse by its manifest – or apparent – Russian backing. The Russian minister in Belgrade, Nicholas Hartwig, was an "ubiquitous presence" in Serbian politics and an active supporter of Pan-Slav groups there. His support of Serbian Minister-President Nikola Paschich in the May–June civil-military struggle was crucial to the success of the politicians. Especially galling to the Austro-Hungarian leaders were his "frequent references" to the Dual Monarchy as "the next sick man of Europe."[33]

A further complication was that the two allies, Austria-Hungary and Germany, had markedly different readings of Balkan affairs. The German leaders thought that Romania, if properly cultivated, would remain loyal to the alliance. They also thought that Serbia could be enticed to affiliate if the right incentives were provided and if the Dual Monarchy made appropriate friendly overtures. If successful, the expanded alliance,

---

[31] Williamson, *Austria-Hungary*, pp. 177–8.
[32] Albertini, *Origins of the War*, vol. 1, pp. 532–3.
[33] Williamson, *Austria-Hungary*, pp. 173–4.

with Italy remaining loyal to it, would form a solid bloc within central Europe. The Russian threat would be removed from the Balkans and its "presence" forced well to the east of the Austrian-Hungarian border. The leaders of the Dual Monarchy viewed this reading of things as hopelessly unrealistic. It was, not too surprisingly, a source of great concern for them.[34]

In reaction to these developments, Berchtold and his staff prepared a memorandum calling for and justifying a new and more aggressive policy in the Balkans. Called the Matscheko Memorandum, as noted above, it was completed on 24 June and intended for Franz Joseph, Franz Ferdinand, Tisza, and the Germans. The hope was to bring all four recipients around to recognition of the new and urgent necessities. Its most striking feature, Williamson reports, was the "fixation on Russia's more active, assertive foreign policy." Matscheko's new threat assessment held that "St. Petersburg would press every advantage. Vienna wanted the Germans to realize just how dangerous the Russian threat had become … and that some action now, rather than later, might be preferable."[35] Surprisingly, in terms of both past and future events, Serbia was not the focus of Matscheko's position paper. Rather, he trained his diplomatic guns on Russia – and on Italy. Chaos reigned in Albania, Matscheko argued, largely because the former Turkish commander, Essad Pasha, now in the pay of the Italian consul at Durazzo, incited the populace against the new Austrian ruler, Prince Wilhelm zu Wied. Put differently, Albania, Berchtold's major triumph in the Balkan Wars, seemed threatened by alleged Italian disloyalty.

Unsurprisingly, the assassination of the archduke and his wife brought the focus back to Serbia. Austria-Hungary's tough, aggressive responses had proven successful in previous episodes, in 1908–9, in December 1912, in May 1913, and again in October 1913. To halt the sensed loss of position, to fend off the threat, the need now was for a more decisive action, this time for the definitive punishment for Serbia.

The steps taken by the Dual Monarchy's leaders in the thirty days following the assassination were rather complicated. Leaving aside many

---

[34] For an overview, see R. J. Crampton, "The Balkans as a Factor in German Foreign Policy, 1912–1914," *Slavonic and East European Review* 55 (1977): 370–90. See, esp., p. 386, where the German plan for a new Balkan League is reviewed, this to include Romania, Greece, and, "if possible," Serbia.

[35] Williamson, *Austria-Hungary*, pp. 164–79 (quotations from pp. 165, 174–5); Albertini, *Origins of the War*, vol. 1, pp. 534–9; and Hantsch, *Graf Berchtold*, pp. 545–51. The original is cited in note 10 above.

of the complexities, "the basics" may be summarized as follows:

| | |
|---|---|
| 28 June–3 July | General agreement achieved on war with Serbia; preparation of two key documents. |
| 4–5 July | Hoyos mission to secure German backing. |
| 7 July | Common Ministerial Council meets and agrees, with one qualified dissent, to continue the course. Further details planned: the ultimatum, the date of delivery. |
| 8–17 July | Some ten days of quiet follow, during which hopes and expectations for peace rise; this is a period of deception on the part of Austria-Hungary and Germany. |
| 18–20 July | Some disconcerting reports appear. |
| 19 July | Common Ministerial Council meets: agreement on last details about the note for Serbia. |
| 23 July | The note delivered to Serbia. |
| 25 July | The Serbian response is rejected. |
| 28 July | Franz Joseph signs declaration of war. |
| 29 July | Belgrade bombarded. |

What we have here, basically, is a series of steps, all conscious and calculated, all designed to bring about war with Serbia. The few objections, the few signs of demurral were largely over tactics and timing, the concern being for alternatives that would put "a better face" on things. One serious difficulty was posed by the scheduling of the empire's reaction. The delay stemmed from two insurmountable problems: the needs of the economy and those of the military. Apart from these questions of implementation, the most striking feature of Austria-Hungary's decision making was the substantial consensus on the immediate goal, war with Serbia, even in the face of a very serious threat, that of a Russian intervention.

When news of the assassination arrived in Vienna late on 28 June, most of the monarchy's leaders were away for a long weekend or on vacation, scattered about the empire. There was neither panic nor even a sense of great grief. Franz Ferdinand was not a beloved figure: The emperor and the court had been scandalized by his morganatic marriage to Sophie Chotek; the Magyars detested what they perceived to be his anti-Hungarian stance; the imperial bureaucracy was concerned about his alleged reform plans for the empire; and Conrad von Hötzendorf feared for his job as long as the archduke was alive. There was no hard evidence that the Serbian government had a hand in the assassination – the Vienna press, in fact, presented its readers with a host of possible "conspiracies" to commit murder by the likes of German intelligence, Freemasons, and even Minister-President Tisza of Hungary! Almost unanimously, the sympathy of Europe's royal families (only France was a republic) was squarely with Austria-Hungary; regicide appealed to few crowned heads. Moreover, members of royal houses and aristocratic families had been murdered in public in the past. Recent wars in the Balkans and in northern Africa had not led to a wider war. Why should 28 June 1914 be different?

What makes the Austrian case so interesting is that a great power, without certain knowledge of the regicides and their putative handlers, decided almost immediately upon war. There was much informal debate about "punishing" Serbia for its alleged support of the archduke's murderers, but the real discussions at the Ballhausplatz focused almost immediately on using the assassination to advantage. As one senior Habsburg diplomat, Baron Leopold von Andrian-Werburg, indelicately stated, "precious fruits for the Monarchy were to ripen" from Franz Ferdinand's spilled blood.[36] Put differently, the leaders in Vienna quickly grasped the fact that an aggressive stance against Belgrade could change the perception of Austrian weakness, decadence, and decline that was present not only in Serbia but also in much of the rest of Europe. Two of the so-called Young Rebels at the Foreign Ministry, Forgách and Matscheko, met right after news of the assassination arrived in Vienna. They rewrote Matscheko's 24 June memorandum, which called for a more aggressive diplomatic policy at the Ballhausplatz, and instead counseled a military solution to the Serb "problem."

In revising their stance, the Young Rebels were prompted primarily by perceptions and illusions. Serbia to them was the center of what they perceived to be a monstrous plot to dissolve the empire both from without and from within. They ignored some patently obvious realities. The Serbian Army, while battle-hardened and experienced, was also exhausted and in need of respite. Serbia had emerged from the Balkan Wars with major gains, but also with major losses. The newly acquired territories and their diverse nationalities had to be incorporated into Serbia. The treasury was depleted. A bitter civil-military struggle in June 1914 revealed to all interested parties that Serbia was politically unstable. And, of course, Belgrade could never be sure of St. Petersburg. In the past, the Russians had been readily at hand with promises of undying support; when in need,

[36] Cited in Rauschensteiner, *Tod des Doppeladlers*, p. 68.

however, those verbal assurances had never quite translated into divisions and corps. No one knew this better than the Ballhausplatz, given that a mere signal from Berlin had forced the Russians to back down during the Bosnian annexation crisis of 1908. In other words, Russia remained as unpredictable a component of Serbian policy as Germany did of Austrian policy.

Foreign Minister Berchtold "commanded and managed" the decision making at Vienna in the aftermath of the killings at Sarajevo. His primary concerns were, first, to learn more about the event itself and, second, to learn others' reactions, principally those of Franz Joseph, István Tisza, and of Kaiser Wilhelm II. Several members of the Common Ministerial Council, most notably Austrian Minister-President Stürghk, Common Finance Minister Biliński, and War Minister Krobatin, pressed for immediate action against Serbia. Chief of the General Staff Conrad von Hötzendorf announced that the murder was "Serbia's declaration of war on Austria-Hungary [and that] the only possible response to it [was] war."[37] Conrad wished to mobilize on 1 July without any further discussions with Serbia. Berchtold later summarized Conrad's views during the July Crisis with three words: "War, war, war." Despite those pressures, the foreign minister moved cautiously in the first days after the assassination.[38]

On Tuesday, 30 June, Berchtold met with Franz Joseph. Both agreed that they should "await the judicial investigation," that they should learn Tisza's views, and, most important, that they should inquire about Berlin's attitude and support. They learned, the same day, that Tisza opposed an immediate military confrontation. That step, he argued, should come only after further investigation and exploration of diplomatic measures. Tisza, who feared any new annexation of Slav subjects to Hungary, wrote letters to Franz Joseph on 1 July and later on 8 July to seek assurance that diplomatic actions preceded any military effort. Berlin's attitude and

---

[37] Williamson, *Austria-Hungary*, pp. 190–1; Conrad von Hötzendorf, *Aus meiner Dienstzeit*, vol. 4, pp. 16–17, 30–1, 33–7.

[38] Williamson, *Austria-Hungary*, pp. 191–2; Rauchensteiner, *Tod des Doppeladlers*, pp. 67–70; Hantsch, *Berchtold*, 557–8.

For an accessible 1,200-page collection of relevant documents, see Imanuel Geiss, ed., *Julikrise und Kriegsausbruch 1914*, 2 vols. (Hanover, 1963); on the initial reactions, see vol. 1, pp. 55–78. Some of this work, about 300 pages, has been translated; Geiss, ed., *July 1914: The Outbreak of the First World War* (New York, 1967). See also ÖUA, vol. 8, pp. 343–51; and Karl Freiherr von Macchio, "Momentbilder aus der Julikrise 1914," *Berliner Monatshefte* (Berlin, 1936), p. 772.

Tisza's reservations provided one of the principal immediate agenda items for the next couple of weeks.[39]

By Thursday, the 2nd, some information had been received, based on interrogation of the conspirators, that revealed links to Serbia. Three of them, Gavrilo Princip among them, had just returned from Belgrade, where they had been given the pistols and the bombs. Complicity by several members of Serbian military intelligence – most notably by Colonel Dragutin Dimitrijević ("Apis") – was suspected. This incomplete report (which said nothing of Serbian leaders' involvement) helped reinforce the already existing consensus. Oskar Potiorek, the governor-general of Bosnia (and the man most responsible for the failure of security at Sarajevo), also argued for an attack on Serbia, to help put down the alarming and pervasive "unrest" he now, with generous distortion, reported in the recently annexed provinces.[40]

As previously stated, Berchtold had the Matscheko memorandum rewritten to stress the now even more urgent imperatives for submission to Germany's leaders. He also had a private letter, from Franz Joseph to Wilhelm, drafted on 2 July for presentation to the Germans. The letter placed the blame for the assassination on Russia and on Serbian Pan-Slavs. Although not specifically calling for war, it stated that "the band of criminal agitators in Belgrade" should not go "unpunished."[41]

Berchtold had made clear his bellicose stance on 3 July in conversation with Heinrich von Tschirschky, Germany's ambassador to Vienna, by speaking of the need for a "final and fundamental reckoning" with Belgrade. But Tschirschky reacted with great caution, asking first what Vienna intended to do with Serbia, once conquered. And then, how would Italy and Romania react to war with Serbia?[42] Kaiser Wilhelm II fully endorsed Berchtold's demand with the marginalia "now or never." The kaiser sharply opposed his ambassador's call for moderation. His comment on Tschirschky's warning against "precipitate steps" was "nonsense."[43] Tschirschky would later be censured by Berlin for his "laxity."

[39] Gábor Vermes, *István Tisza: The Liberal Vision and Conservative Statecraft of a Magyar Nationalist* (New York, 1985), pp. 221–35, esp. 222–3; Williamson, *Austria-Hungary*, pp. 192–3.

[40] Ibid., pp. 193–4. There was much "unrest" following the assassinations, most of it directed against Serbian properties.

[41] Franz Joseph to Wilhelm II, 2 July 1914; ÖUA, vol. 8, pp. 250–61.

[42] Berchtold-Tschirschky discussion, 3 July 1914, ibid., pp. 277–8.

[43] Tschirsky to Bethmann Hollweg, 30 June 1914, in Imanuel Geiss, ed., *Juli 1914, in Die europäische Krise und der Ausbruch des Ersten Weltkrieges* (Munich, 1965), pp. 39–40.

Ordinarily, the monarchs of Europe would have come to Vienna for a state funeral, at which time some discussion of appropriate responses could have occurred. But, because of Franz Joseph's advanced age and infirm condition, other arrangements were made. That change meant that the Dual Monarchy's leaders had to make a special effort to ascertain Germany's response. A member of the Foreign Ministry was sent, secretly, to Berlin for this purpose. The undertaking is usually referred to as the Hoyos mission.[44] Count Hoyos, Berchtold's personal friend and *chef de cabinet*, volunteered for this mission.[45] Described as one of the most articulate "hawks" in Berchtold's circle, "Alek" Hoyos would be a most competent advocate of the "prowar" position. The mission was a brilliant ploy on the part of the foreign minister. By choosing Hoyos, Berchtold made sure that the Germans would hear of Vienna's resolve to strike at Serbia; that the aged and unimaginative Ambassador Szögyény at Berlin would, as much as possible, be bypassed; and that any further intrusions by Tisza into the diplomatic process would be preempted.[46] Thus, the secret mission had only one purpose: war. There was no talk of deterrence, much less of peace.

Ambassador Szögyény was alerted late on the 4th, told of Hoyos's imminent arrival and purpose, and instructed to request interviews with the kaiser and chancellor. On the next day, Sunday, 5 July, Hoyos reviewed the

---

[44] On origins of the mission, see Fritz Fellner, "Mission Hoyos," in Wilhelm Alff, ed., *Deutschlands Sonderung von Europa 1862–1945* (New York, 1984), pp. 283–316.
 There are different readings on the question of the absent state funeral. Hoyos was told by Berchtold that the emperor's age was the decisive factor; Fellner, "Mission," p. 309. Rauchensteiner, *Tod des Doppeladlers*, p. 68, claims the Foreign Ministry did not want the Russian, British, or French heads of state in Vienna. Williamson, *Austria-Hungary*, p. 191, says rumors of a threatened Serb attack on Kaiser Wilhelm led that monarch to abandon the visit. See also ÖUA, vol. 8, pp. 235–6; Karl Kautsky, *Die deutschen Dokumente zum Kriegsausbruch* (hereafter *DDI*), 3 vols., vol. 1: *Vom Attentat von Sarajevo bis zum Eintreffen der serbischen Antwortnote in Berlin 1919* (Berlin, 1919), no. 3, p. 72; and Haus-, Hof-, und Staatsarchiv (hereafter HHStA), Vienna, Politische Archiv, Fasz. 496.

[45] On 1 July, Hoyos had been interviewed by a German publicist, Viktor Naumann, who declared that both the German government and public "stood as one man at the side of the ally and would view war as a liberating act." There has been some dispute over the significance of this conversation. The basic questions: Was Naumann an emissary, somehow representing the German government? Or was he a pretentious journalist suggesting more than was warranted? See Hoyos's "top secret" notes on a conversation with Naumann, 1 July 1914, in Geiss, ed., *Juli 1914*, pp. 40–2. Also, Viktor Naumann, *Dokumente und Argumente* (Berlin, 1928), p. 7.

[46] Williamson, *Austria-Hungary*, p. 195. See also H. Bertil A. Petersson, "Das österreichisch-ungarische Memorandum an Deutschland vom 5. Juli 1914," *Scandia* 30 (1964): 138–90.

two documents with the ambassador. Szögyény then had lunch with the kaiser at Potsdam. Hoyos had lunch with Arthur Zimmermann, the under-secretary of the Foreign Office (Gottlieb von Jagow, the foreign secretary, who had just married, was away on his honeymoon). At 10 P.M. Szögyény cabled Berchtold about the kaiser's pledge of "full German backing" in any action that Vienna took, requesting only that it proceed promptly.[47] It would be deplorable, Wilhelm had counseled Szögyény, if Vienna did not exploit "the present situation which is so favorable to us." The kaiser's only reservation was that he would have to consult with the chancel-lor, Bethmann Hollweg, before taking a final decision. Independently, Zimmermann conveyed much the same sense to Hoyos.

Late that afternoon, the kaiser and the chief of his Military Cabinet, Baron Moritz von Lyncker, met with Bethmann Hollweg and Erich von Falkenhayn, the Prussian minister of war. These four men reviewed the previous discussion and the options facing them. In this brief meeting, they "considered the question of Russian intervention and accepted the risk of a general war."[48] The discussions, it was agreed, would continue the following day.

On the 6th, Bethmann Hollweg and Zimmermann ratified the commit-ments made by Wilhelm II. Ambassador Szögyény cabled Berchtold that evening that Bethmann regarded Austria-Hungary's "immediate interven-tion" against Serbia as the "most radical and best solution" of its "dif-ficulties in the Balkans."[49] More, Bethmann Hollweg offered Berchtold "a major concession," declaring it unnecessary that he alert their allies, Romania and Italy.

These declarations of support for Austria-Hungary, for that country's imminent war on Serbia, have been referred to as the "blank check." The Dual Monarchy could "fill in" the contents when it chose, although, to be sure, those issuing "the check" urged them to do so quickly. These promises of backing were of immense importance. Without them, Austria-Hungary could not have moved to war. Some other option, something less punitive, would have been required.

Upon his return to Vienna on 6 July, Hoyos met, secretly, with Berchtold and the two minister-presidents, Stürgkh and Tisza. The

---

[47] Szögyény to Berchtold, 5 July 1914. ÖUA, vol. 8, pp. 306–7.
[48] Williamson, *Austria-Hungary*, p. 196. See also Geiss, *Julikrise*, vol. 2, pp. 79–117; ÖUA, vol. 8, pp. 250–61, 319 ff., 381; DDI, 15; and Fritz Fischer, *Griff nach der Weltmacht: Die Kriegszielpolitik des kaiserlichen Deutschland 1914/18* (Düsseldorf, 1964), p. 64.
[49] Szögyény to Berchtold, 6 July 1914, ÖUA, vol. 8, pp. 319–20.

German ambassador, Tschirschky, also participated in their discussion and informed the Austrians of what they already knew – namely, that Chancellor von Bethmann Hollweg considered the present moment to be more suitable for action than a later occasion.

The following day, Tuesday, 7 July, the Ministerial Council met ostensibly to consider disorders in Bosnia but actually to determine the next steps to be taken with respect to Serbia. The promise of German backing strengthened the predominant sentiment, the agreement on "settling accounts with Serbia."[50] Over four hours, the ministers (Berchtold, Biliński, Stürgkh, Tisza, Krobatin) as well as a guest, Conrad von Hötzendorf, deliberately examined each option. The decisions taken, in the words of Samuel Williamson, were "carefully evaluated choices." The possibility of a surprise attack on Serbia was rejected, mainly because of Tisza's objections: It would alienate other European governments. A consensus developed on the possibility of a "strongly worded ultimatum to Belgrade," one which Serbia would have to reject, thus providing the justification for a "local" war. In the afternoon, Conrad reviewed the military plans, including the possibility of Russian intervention. He minimized the risks involved and, to Tisza's objections, repeated his "better now than later" phrase.[51]

The steps discussed and generally agreed to at the 7 July meeting were those actually followed later in the month. In relatively quick order, both Franz Joseph and, subsequently, Tisza agreed to the steps to be taken against Serbia. Those steps led to the initiation of hostilities.

Both events, the Hoyos mission and the 7 July Ministerial Council meeting, figure prominently in accounts of the origins of the war. Both subsequently became, effectively, "open book" events. But in July and August 1914, at the outbreak of the war, few members of the general public, in Austria-Hungary, Germany, or elsewhere, would have known of those events or of the decisions taken. The "mass" reactions later in the month and in early August were, necessarily, based on different factors, perceptions, and considerations. For most people, for those who followed public affairs, those understandings would have been based on newspaper reports.

---

[50] The protocol of the 7 July meeting, recorded by Hoyos, is in Miklós Komjáthy, ed., *Protokolle des Gemeinsames Ministerrates der Österreich-Ungarischen Monarchie (1914–1918)* (Budapest, 1966), pp. 141–50.

[51] Williamson, *Austria-Hungary*, pp. 197–9; Vermes, *István Tisza*, pp. 222–3; Geiss, *Julikrise*, vol. 1, pp. 104–15; and *ÖUA*, vol. 8, pp. 343–51.

The decisions taken by Austria-Hungary's leaders had implications for their subsequent efforts. Given the decisions taken on 7 July, it follows that they would seek to avoid or block any later peacemaking efforts. Those decisions, moreover, were taken prior to any serious effort of inquiry, before any official Serbian role in the assassination had been established. And despite that problem, the decisions enjoyed the full support of the German Foreign office. On 8 July, Zimmermann informed the Austrians that "now was the right moment – a moment, which might not ever reappear under such favorable conditions – energetically to move against Serbia."[52]

The period of quiet came at this point. The length of that period varies depending on one's "social location." The ordinary citizen would have read of the assassination in Monday morning newspapers on 29 June. The next major event, signaling the alarm, would be the delivery of Austria-Hungary's ultimatum to Serbia on 23 July, three and a half weeks later. For many European leaders, the "quiet period" ended on the weekend of 18–19 July, when news of Austria's impending action spread to several governments. For Germany's leaders, the "quiet period" would have begun on the 6th with the ending of the Hoyos mission. Given their understandings, that period of quiet became a source of concern: Why was the move against Serbia being delayed?

Three factors led to the postponement of the monarchy's response. Tisza, as indicated, wished that an effort be made to establish Belgrade's role in the assassination so as to legitimize the Austro-Hungarian response. His concern led to the dispatch of an investigative body to Sarajevo, headed by a prominent lawyer and member of the Foreign Ministry, Ritter Friedrich von Wiesner. This source of the delay, however, does not appear to have been decisive. Tisza's biographer, Gábor Vermes, suggests he had converted by mid-month, by 14 July, but does not indicate Wiesner's investigation as a cause. At that point, Tisza was in full agreement with the steps decided on at the 7 July Council meeting. Wiesner's report had been cabled to Berchtold from Sarajevo on 13 July. Vermes states only that Tisza had "certainly" been notified. That brief report posed serious difficulties of interpretation, but these problems appear to have been largely bypassed. Other factors appear to have been the decisive causes of the delay.[53]

---

[52] Szögyény to Berchtold, 8 July 1914. ÖUA, vol. 8, p. 357.
[53] Many discussions of this investigation provide a truncated and seriously misleading account of the findings. Quoting from Wiesner's report, one authority has it that investigation found "no evidence to show or even suspect that the Serbian Government

A second and more compelling consideration was that the monarchy's troops were not immediately available. As a concession to agrarian interests, Conrad had instituted a policy of harvest leaves, allowing men in the military to return home on temporary leave to help harvest the crops. On 6 July, Conrad "discovered" that many units were on leave and not scheduled to return until 25 July. To cancel those leaves would disrupt the harvest, upset railroad schedules, and, most importantly, Williamson writes, would "alert Europe to Vienna's possible military intentions."[54]

A third factor was the scheduled visit of France's President Raymond Poincaré and Premier René Viviani to St. Petersburg. To block a concerted response by the two *entente* partners, Vienna's leaders planned to deliver the ultimatum on 23 July, after the visit ended and when the French leaders would, literally, be at sea. The second and third factors meant that "settling accounts" with Serbia could not begin before the last week of July. Since a general mobilization would take some time, the "settlement" could not possibly begin until at least mid-August.

Several important events occurred in this quiet period. From an early point, as seen, most of Austria-Hungary's decision makers favored "decisive action" against Serbia, this including Tisza's personal representative, Burián.[55] One of Tisza's main concerns was a fear of a possible invasion of

was involved.... On the contrary there is far more to indicate that this is to be regarded as out of the question." Cassels, *Archduke and the Assassin*, pp. 187–8. That is the conclusion of the first section, which comments on the knowledge and involvement of the "Serbian government." The second section, the very next paragraph, implicates lower-level Serbian officials, naming them, reporting the provision of weapons and smuggling across the border, and so forth. See Geiss, *Juli*, vol. 1, pp. 154–5. Rauchensteiner, *Tod des Doppeladlers*, pp. 75–7, reviews the history of this document, including the postwar use of the truncated version. For more detail, see Friedrich Würthle, *Die Spur Führt nach Belgrad: Die Hintergründe des Dramas von Sarajevo 1914* (Vienna, 1975), pp. 136, 139–40.

Wiesner had joined the Ministry in 1911. Although not a South Slav expert, he was asked, in early July, to review a mass of accumulated material on Belgrade's activities. He was then sent to Sarajevo to investigate further, arriving on the morning of the 11th and asked to report on the 13th. His report went off in two installments, one early, one late on that afternoon. For some sense of the complications, of the task facing Wiesner, see Barbara Jelavich, "What the Habsburg Government Knew about the Black Hand," *Austrian History Yearbook* 22 (1991): 131–50, esp. her summary on p. 136.

54 Williamson, *Austria-Hungary*, pp. 199–200. For a brief review of the considerations involved in the delay, see Samuel R. Williamson, Jr., "Confrontation with Serbia: The Consequences of Vienna's Failure to Achieve Surprise in July, 1914," *Mitteilung des österreichisches Staatsarchiv* 43 (1993): 168–77, esp. 170–2.

55 István Diószegi, "Aussenminister Stephen Graf Burián. Biographie und Tagebuchstelle," *Annales: Universitatis Scientiarum Budapestinenses de Rolando Eötvös Nominatae* 8 (Budapest, 1966), pp. 161–208.

Transylvania by Romania during the Serbian engagement. A letter from King Carol of Romania to Franz Joseph, dated 9 July, offered assurance of Romanian neutrality in the event of a Serbian war. This relieved much of Tisza's concern. A meeting between Burián and the emperor on 12 July led to further stiffening of the Hungarian's resolve. Franz Joseph admonished Burián to avoid any further delays and asked Tisza to compromise on his position. By the 14th, as indicated, Tisza had withdrawn his objections, and the planning of the next steps proceeded accordingly.[56]

At a meeting on 14 July, Berchtold, Tisza, Stürghk, and Burián reviewed matters again and agreed on the content and overall plan of the ultimatum to Serbia. The document was to be delivered to Belgrade with a forty-eight-hour time limit for a reply. Tisza accepted the harsh ultimatum with its unacceptable demands and short deadline, but only on two conditions: There was to be no annexation of Serbian territory following a Habsburg victory, and defensive military measures were to be initiated immediately along the Transylvanian frontier.[57]

One crucial aspect of the Austrian decision making deserves special note. Emperor Franz Joseph had "the last word" with respect to all of these fundamental decisions. But he was not present at any of the discussions of the Common Ministerial Council where these policies were being formulated. On the morning of 7 July, prior to the key Council meeting, he left Vienna for his summer estate, the Kaiservilla, located in Bad Ischl, five hours by train from Vienna, where he remained for the next three weeks. Since all key decisions had to be ratified by the emperor, Berchtold on 9 July had to travel there to review the Council's decision. He made the journey again on the 19th for the emperor's review of the text of the ultimatum. Berchtold, Krobatin, and Biliński were there with the emperor on the 25th to await word of the Serbian response. Franz Joseph was in complete agreement with the directions chosen but had, clearly, delegated all further questions to his immediate subordinates.[58]

Vienna's leaders at this point, as Williamson puts it, were engaged in a "policy of deception." They were "lulling Europe." The aim was to suggest that no exceptional measures would be taken against Serbia. The local press was asked to curtail its comments about Serbia. Attempts were made to obtain more favorable treatment in the foreign press. To allay possible fears of impending war, Generals Krobatin and Conrad left

[56] Dioszegi, "Burian Tagebuch," 9 July 1914.
[57] Notes of Berchtold's audience with Franz Joseph, 14 July 1914, ÖUA, vol. 8, pp. 447–8.
[58] Palmer, *Twilight of the Habsburgs*, pp. 327–31.

Vienna "with conspicuous fanfare," ostensibly on leave. "No military moves were undertaken," Williamson reports, "and Habsburg officers on leave were left undisturbed."[59]

On the weekend of 18–19 July, three weeks after the assassination, information regarding Austro-Hungarian intentions began circulating in the European capitals. The "trail," as far as can be determined, was a rather circuitous one. The members of the Triple Alliance were obliged to inform their partners of any warlike moves. But for reasons touched on earlier, the Dual Monarchy was hesitant about informing Romania and Italy. Even communications with Germany were rather sparse. The "leak" began on 11 July, when the German foreign secretary, Jagow, informed the German ambassador in Rome of "the general thrust of Habsburg intentions." The ambassador then "mentioned" the substance of this message to the Italian foreign minister, Antonio di San Giuliani, who passed this information, on 16 July, to the Italian embassies in St. Petersburg, Vienna, and Belgrade. Austrian cryptographers had broken the Italian codes and thus discovered that this information was available in the four capitals, two of them "unfriendly." It is likely that Russian cryptographers also broke the code. Another possibility, of course, is that the Italian ambassadors passed the information directly to their hosts in St. Petersburg and in Belgrade.[60]

The reactions of the European nations changed dramatically at this time. On 18 July, Serbia began calling up army reservists. On the same day, Vienna received a memo from the Russian minister of foreign affairs, Sazonov, warning that an attempt against Serbia's independence would not be permitted.[61] The Habsburg ambassador in St. Petersburg, Count Szápáry, apparently allayed Sazonov's concerns at that point, convincing him that Vienna "planned nothing unusual." Three days later, however, Poincaré, in St. Petersburg, sought out the same ambassador and "left no doubt of France's support of Russia and Russia's support of Serbia." The conclusion is that "before the French delegation had ever left St. Petersburg, the two allies were able to shape the broad outlines of their policy for the approaching crisis."[62]

---

[59] Williamson, *Austria-Hungary*, pp. 200–1.

[60] For a brief summary, see ibid., p. 201. For more detail, including a second leak, beginning with Berchtold on 16 July, see Williamson, "Confrontation with Serbia," pp. 173–4.

[61] Otto Hoetzsch, ed., *Die internationalen Beziehungen im Zeitalter des Imperialismus*, 26 vols. (Berlin, 1934), vol. 4, p. 272; vol. 1, pp. 5, 19. Also, Rauchensteiner, *Tod des Doppeladlers*, pp. 80–1.

[62] Williamson, "Confrontation with Serbia," pp. 174–5. For the two Szápáry telegrams to Berchtold, *ÖUA*, vol. 8, pp. 495, 567–8.

On Sunday, 19 July, the Council of Ministers met at Berchtold's home, the members arriving in unmarked vehicles. The tasks were simple: to review again the terms of the ultimatum (those spelled out here in Chapter 3), to confirm the dates of delivery and reply, and to review the steps that would follow Serbia's anticipated rejection of the demands. Conrad reviewed the military situation focusing on his Plan B, the attack on Serbia, largely neglecting the likely Russian response. The ministers "did not probe further." Both to assuage Tisza (who wished "no more Slavs" in the monarchy) and to fend off possible criticism by other nations, the group pledged that Austria-Hungary would take no Serbian territory. Conrad was not pleased by that decision but assumed it would be altered after the coming victory.[63]

On 21 July, Berchtold traveled to Bad Ischl, where he again briefed the emperor. And again, Franz Joseph assented to the plan of action. The same day, a sealed copy of the ultimatum was delivered to the Habsburg ambassador in Belgrade, Baron Wladimir Giesl von Gieslingen. The final version of the ultimatum was delivered to Berlin on 22 July.[64] And following the plan, Ambassador Giesl handed the note to the acting head of the Serbian government at 6 P.M. the following evening. At about the same time, copies of the ultimatum were delivered to the governments of the major European powers. All of the recipients, as seen below, recognized the seriousness of the move. On the 25th, the Dual Monarchy sent the same governments a lengthy statement spelling out the grounds for its action.[65]

Serbia had commenced full mobilization measures three hours prior to receipt of the Austro-Hungarian note. On the following day, 24 July, the tsar ordered a "period preparatory to war," a partial mobilization of four military districts bordering the Dual Monarchy to defend against Habsburg military activity if necessary. Franz Joseph ordered a partial mobilization against Serbia on 25 July, shortly after the Serbian rejection of the Austrian note.[66] The first official day of mobilization would be 28 July. Before then, however, reports of accelerating Russian military measures,

---

[63] Komjáthy, ed., *Protokolle des Gemeinsamen Ministerrates*, pp. 150–4; ÖUA, vol. 8, pp. 511–14; Williamson, *Austria-Hungary*, pp. 202–3; Oskar Wertheimer, ed., *Graf Tisza, Briefe* (Berlin, 1928), vol. 1, pp. 93–4, 115–20.

[64] The text is in ÖUA, vol. 8, pp. 515–18.

[65] DDI, vol. 1, no. 120. The lengthy statement, 57 printed pages, was prepared by Wiesner. It had little impact. Delivery was slow, in some instances taking three to five days. By then the dominant concern was war itself, not the justifications. See Würthle, *Die Spur*, pp. 231–4.

[66] The Serbian reply is in ÖUA, vol. 8, pp. 660–3.

initiated on 25 and 26 July, arrived in Berlin and Vienna. Although Russia had openly warned Austria-Hungary that it would mobilize if Habsburg troops crossed the Serbian frontier, Berchtold asked that Franz Joseph sign a declaration of war against Serbia. Again the emperor assented and the Dual Monarchy declared war on 28 July.[67] On 29 July, the first hostile action occurred when Austria-Hungary bombarded the Serbian capital.[68] The Russian decision for a general mobilization came shortly thereafter.

The Austrian decision for war, as seen, was the end result of a careful, well-thought, and very rational process. Early on, they sought and secured a promise of support from their major ally. Then Vienna's senior ministers, diplomats, and military leaders met twice in planned formal sessions to review the issues and to weigh their options. On 7 July and again on 19 July, they reached the same conclusion, namely, that the empire's "Balkan problems" could be solved only by war against Serbia. They then sought, and received, formal approval for their decision from the ultimate decision maker, Emperor Franz Joseph. But then, curiously, having decided on war, they failed utterly in planning for the implementation and execution of that decision.

The impact of the assassination itself should be noted. A rash, impetuous act of murder committed by a teenager at Sarajevo on 28 June 1914 removed the Dual Monarchy's most influential and outspoken opponent of war with Serbia and, consequently, with Russia, Archduke Franz Ferdinand. The killing allowed Conrad von Hötzendorf to remain chief of staff and it emboldened Count Berchtold to act on the "hawkish" advice of Conrad and of the so-called Young Rebels at the Foreign Ministry. Princip, seeking to eliminate what he considered to be an archenemy, instead removed the key decision maker who would have prevented the general European war.

For the past four decades, Fritz Fischer's powerful indictment of the German decision for war (reviewed in the next chapter) dominated research into the origins of the Great War. Fischer's arguments, first in *Griff nach der Weltmacht* (1961) and then in the follow-up work *Krieg der Illusionen* (1969), were so radical, so powerful, and so devastating to German conservative historians that attention was riveted almost exclusively on Germany. Austria-Hungary's part in starting the "great seminal

---

[67] Ibid., p. 811.
[68] For the opening campaigns against Serbia, see Rauchensteiner, *Tod des Doppeladlers*, pp. 128–36.

catastrophe" of the twentieth century was glossed over: Berlin, Fischer brazenly stated, had merely taken Vienna "on the leash." Gradually, however, scholarly judgment has shifted to a more complex, more nuanced view. The initial decision for war, after all, was made in Vienna, not Berlin.

Today, serious scholarship into the origins of the war focuses, unambiguously, on Austria-Hungary. That country's government, Samuel R. Williamson writes, "clearly initiated the violence in July 1914." Later, in another forceful statement, he declares that "Vienna plunged Europe into war."[69] With regard to relations between Vienna and Berlin, Vienna made the original decision for war, approached its ally for support, decided the pace and the timing of events, and eventually foreclosed all options other than war.

We have numerous statements by Habsburg diplomats involved in the July Crisis supporting Williamson's claims. "Alek" Hoyos openly admitted to Josef Maria Baernreither, a German-Austrian politician: "We want the war, that is why we composed the note [to Serbia] that way."[70] Another senior Austrian diplomat, Leopold von Andrian-Werburg, writing in December 1918, declared: "We started this war, not the Germans, and certainly not the Entente...."[71] Also attesting to that clear intention are the various rejections by Vienna's decision makers of the last-minute peacemaking efforts, of those originating in London. When Foreign Minister Berchtold on 27 July asked the emperor to sign a declaration of war, he openly stated that he did so because "he did not consider it impossible that the Triple Entente might yet undertake an attempt to reach a peaceful resolution of the conflict, if a clearing of the air was not attained by way of a declaration of war."[72] Berchtold's German counterpart, Jagow, that same day informed Ambassador Szögyény that Berlin would "decisively reject" rumored last-minute peace overtures from London.[73]

---

[69] Williamson, *Austria-Hungary*, pp. 1 and 6; and Williamson, "Vienna and July 1914: The Origins of the Great War Once More," pp. 9–36, esp. pp. 29–30; Williamson and Peter Pastor, eds., *Essays on World War I: Origins and Prisoners of War* (New York, 1983); also, Herwig, *First World War*, p. 18.

[70] Leslie, "Antecedents," p. 381. The text gives the date of this statement as 28 July. The footnote refers to a diary entry of 21 July.

[71] Leslie, "Oesterreich-Ungarn," p. 675. Finance Minister Biliński later stated that they had decided for war on 3 July; Rauchensteiner, *Tod des Doppeladlers*, p. 68. Fellner sees 7 July as the appropriate date. Everything that followed hinged on the decision taken that day; "Mission Hoyos," p. 297.

[72] Ibid., p. 300; *ÖUA*, vol. 8, p. 811.

[73] Szögyény to Berchtold, 27 July 1914, *ÖUA*, vol. 8, pp. 778–9.

The Austro-Hungarian leaders, moreover, determined on war from an early point, effectively from the 7 July meeting. The minutes of that meeting are revealing:

All those present, with one exception [Tisza], were of the opinion that a purely diplomatic victory, even if it ended with a striking humiliation of Serbia, was worthless; and that therefore such demands should be made upon Serbia as to secure their rejection so that the way for a radical solution along the lines of a military intervention could be opened up.[74]

In other words, as the historian Fritz Fellner writes, "in Vienna one decided on a war against Serbia on 7 July and all deliberations and subsequent diplomatic actions up to the declaration of war on 28 July were only consistent executions of the basic decision made on 7 July 1914."[75]

Austria-Hungary's leaders sought a limited war, one in which, they hoped, the Dual Monarchy would eliminate, definitively, a troublesome Serbia. Their intention, effectively, was a Third Balkan War. Those leaders knew that Russia was very likely to intervene, in which case the war, obviously, would be a much larger enterprise. In the course of those key discussions in Berlin, Under-Secretary Zimmermann gave Hoyos his estimate: "Yes, 90% probability for a European war if you undertake something against Serbia."[76] Although the decision makers knew this, it is curious,

---

[74] Komjáthy, ed., *Protokolle des Gemeinsamen Ministerrates*, p. 148.

[75] Fellner, "Mission Hoyos," p. 297. The enthusiastic reactions of several Austrian leaders are reported on the same page.

Another member of the Foreign Ministry who appears in some accounts of the decision making is Baron Alexander von Musulin, Forgách's intimate associate at the Ballhausplatz. He had been ambassador to Moscow; later to Belgrade; back to Moscow, 1901. But he was not directly involved in the early discussions and even later served only an instrumental function: An accomplished writer, he was called on to draft the ultimatum. Later, he was asked to write a response to the Serbian comments on the monarchy's note, this also to be circulated to the European capitals. His memoir, published in 1924, gives a report that is sharply at variance with the account given here in the text. The most striking statement: "At the Foreign Ministry one did not think that the ultimatum would lead to war." In Alexander Musulin, *Das Haus am Ballplatz: Erinnerungen eines österreich-ungarischen Diplomaten* (Munich, 1924), p. 227. Musulin's memoir contains several other curiosities: "The Monarchy's leading statesmen believed that the solidarity of European conservatives and dynastic interests would manifest themselves also in the year 1914, and they believed this especially with regard to Russia" (p. 228).

[76] Fellner, "Mission Hoyos," p. 296. Forgách provides a detailed (if disingenuous) review of the Austro-Hungarian intentions in a letter (16 July) to Kajetan Mérey von Kapos-Mére, the monarchy's ambassador in Italy; Hantsch, *Graf Berchtold*, vol. 2, pp. 592–4. The letter states: "If at all possible, we naturally wanted to avoid a world war, even though Germany was fully prepared to wage it on her own."

astonishing even, that at the Common Ministerial Council meeting of 19 July they "did not even bother to discuss the chances of Russian intervention." Later, when Franz Joseph saw the key document, he recognized the implication: "Russia cannot possibly swallow this note."[77] Those, to be sure, were the German and Austrian readings. But France and Russia also read matters the same way. President Poincaré, as indicated, "left no doubt" about the French and Russian positions.

But as seen, Austria-Hungary's leaders proceeded with a single-minded focus on Serbia, neglecting entirely Russia and its implications. Apart from a couple of brief mentions, the minutes of the Common Ministerial Council of 7 July, in the words of William Jannen, "show no serious discussion of what war with Russia might mean." Apart from Tisza's proposal, that they reject any annexation of Serbian territory, the minutes of the 19 July meeting show "no discussion of the possible consequences of Russian intervention." Their decision making, described as "peculiarly blinkered," differed from that of the other major powers. The other powers saw themselves as "having no choice" but sensed that their opponents were free to back down or compromise. Their policies were built on those assumptions. But the Dual Monarchy's leaders, in striking contrast, centered their discussions on the threat to their empire; they "paid virtually no attention to the likely response of other powers or to the monarchy's ability to sustain a Great Power war." When considering military capabilities, "they tended to measure themselves against Serbia and Bulgaria rather than against France and Russia."[78]

The initial military operation, Plan B (Balkans), directed the monarchy's forces to the south, to Serbia, a move that brought disaster (see Map 4.2). John Leslie summarizes this effort as follows: "Conrad's obsession with his vendetta against Serbia led to one of the worst military blunders of modern history." It was a classic case of emotions driving strategy. Although Conrad had ample evidence from both the German military attaché to Vienna and from his own attaché to St. Petersburg that Russia had commenced its mobilization measures against Austria-Hungary on

---

[77] Robert A. Kann, *Kaiser Franz Joseph und der Ausbruch des Weltkrieges* (Vienna, 1971), p. 12.

[78] William Jannen, Jr., "The Austro-Hungarian Decision for War in July 1914," pp. 55–81 (quotations from pp. 58–60), of Williamson and Pastor, ed., *Essays On World War I*. Jannen offers some explanation, effectively a social psychology of the decision-making peculiarities. Observers commented on one of its distinctive qualities: These decision makers showed evident euphoria on the completion of their task.

MAP 4.2. Austria-Hungary, Germany, and Russia

25 July and ordered a general mobilization on 30 July, Conrad nevertheless ignored this intelligence. Obsessed with destroying what he called
"dog" Serbia, he deployed the bulk of his forces for his long-planned
offensive against Serbia. In the process, he sent to Serbia units essential
to holding off Russia in the initial stage of the German Schlieffen plan
and gave priority only to the Galician-Polish theater of war on 4 August,
"after frantic appeals from the German chief of staff." By this time, the
radical change of direction from Serbia to Poland threw Habsburg plans
and forces into chaos. With the Russians advancing into Galicia much
sooner than expected, the Serbian campaign had to be broken off prematurely. The troops involved had to be turned about for what proved to be
"a hopelessly mismanaged offensive against Russia ... which led directly

to the catastrophic defeat of the Austro-Hungarian army by the Russians in Galicia in the first half of September 1914 and the loss of one third of its strength."[79]

But even this devastating verdict is too charitable. Conrad did not respond to those "frantic appeals" on 4 August. In fact, the orders for the change of direction did not reach the Austro-Hungarian divisions in the Serbian theater until forty-eight hours later.[80] Thus, only two corps of Conrad's Second Army arrived in Galicia by 28 August.

Unlike social or intellectual history, military history often provides a clear verdict concerning decisions made or omitted. This was certainly the case with Austria-Hungary in 1914. The price for Conrad's mobilization disaster was paid by hundreds of thousands of Austrian and Hungarian soldiers both in Serbia and in Galicia. In the south, General Potiorek invaded Serbia with 460,000 troops, many of them inexperienced Landsturm brigades, and 500 mobile guns. He charged across the Drina and Save rivers and headed for Belgrade. But the wily Serbian commander, Field Marshal Radomir Putnik, simply allowed the enemy to advance until dogged by supply problems – and then counterattacked its flanks at Jadar on 16 August. In ten days, Potiorek lost 600 officers and 23,000 men. Belatedly, Conrad conceded that he had concentrated his forces in the south for "political reasons," that is, "the need to slap Serbia."[81]

Worse was to come in the north. Conrad refused to wait for the arrival of the Second Army from the south and, instead, now following Plan R (Russia), rushed available forces on foot on a broad sweep against the advancing Russians from the Dniester to the Vistula Rivers – a salient 250 miles wide and 90 miles deep. He experienced first-hand the cost of faulty planning and execution: 100,000 dead, 220,000 wounded, 100,000 prisoners of war; Austrian Galicia in Russian hands; the great fortress of Przemyśl and its garrison of 100,000 invested by the enemy; and the Carpathian passes leading down onto the Hungarian plain exposed

[79] Leslie, "Antecedents," pp. 320–1.
[80] Norman Stone, "Moltke-Conrad: Relations between the Austro-Hungarian and German General Staffs, 1909–14," *Historical Journal* 9 (1966): 201–28. Conrad's belated efforts to cover up his mishandling of both the mobilization of 1914 and the writing of its official history have been exposed by Tunstall, "The Habsburg Command Conspiracy," esp. pp. 186–8.
[81] Notes of 14 September 1914 of the German military attaché at Conrad's headquarters, Colonel Karl von Kageneck. Cited in Herwig, *First World War*, p. 89.

to assault.[82] It is not too far off the mark to state that the backbone of the venerable Habsburg Army was broken in Serbia and especially in Galicia in August and September 1914.

The narrative to this point has centered on Austria-Hungary, the decisions taken by its leaders and the implications of those decisions. The decisions, as seen, aimed to bring about "a little war," one involving two nations. That "localized" war would be fought in the Balkans, probably to the south of the Save and Danube rivers. But a separate set of decisions changed that plan dramatically. In a second, but linked causal sequence, the decision makers of Germany, Russia, and France initiated events that would bring about a much larger war. That larger war forced the redirection of the Austro-Hungarian effort. From this first episode, the Dual Monarchy found itself in the tow of its more powerful ally.

---

[82] Edmund Glaise von Horstenau and Rudolf Kiszling, eds., *Österreich-Ungarns Letzter Krieg 1914–1918*, 7 vols. (Vienna, 1931–38), vol. 1, pp. 319–20; Norman Stone, *The Eastern Front 1914–1917* (London, 1975), pp. 70–91; Graydon A. Tunstall, Jr., *Planning for War against Russia and Serbia: Austro-Hungarian and German Military Strategies, 1871–1914* (New York, 1993), pp. 237–59.

# 5

# Germany

## Holger H. Herwig

> Even if we go under as a result of this, still it was beautiful.
>
> General Erich von Falkenhayn, 4 August 1914

These almost surrealistic words, uttered by the Prussian war minister in the wake of the July Crisis, in many ways encapsulate the mood that prevailed among Germany's political and military elite as July yielded to August 1914. In fact, Falkenhayn had played a decisive role in pushing for war. At 5 P.M. on the afternoon of 1 August, he had made his way through a throng of thousands of cheering Germans into the Neues Palais at Potsdam, and had witnessed Kaiser Wilhelm II sign the order for "war mobilization" on a desk made of planking from Admiral Horatio Nelson's flagship HMS *Victory*. "Thereupon," Falkenhayn stated, "the kaiser shook my hand for a long time; tears stood in both of our eyes." It was to be "war sans phrase," as Falkenhayn recorded in his diary.[1]

Historians since then have hotly debated the *why* of the decision to go to war. Was it, as John C. G. Röhl has suggested, to establish German hegemony over the Continent? Was it, in the well-known words of Fritz Fischer, a decided "bid for world power"? Or was it, as Andreas Hillgruber has posited, nothing more than an effort to secure the Reich's tenuous position as a European great power? Whatever their argument, these scholars have interpreted the decision for war within the twin parameters of the "cult of the offensive" and the "short-war illusion." In

---

[1] Excerpt from Falkenhayn's diary, 1 August 1914. Bundesarchiv-Militärarchiv (BA-MA), Freiburg, Bestand Kriegsgeschichtliche Forschungsanstalt des Heeres, W-10/50635 Tagebuch v. Falkenkayn.

other words, Germany decided to go to war secure in the knowledge that the struggle would be fought offensively beyond the Reich's borders, and that it would be of short duration. The kaiser's declaration that the troops would be home "before the leaves fell from the trees" simply echoed such sentiments.[2] Still, we remain with the complex question of *why* Otto von Bismarck's successors were willing to unleash what the diplomat George F. Kennan called "*the* great seminal catastrophe of this century."[3]

### The Great Gambit

By the time that the Germans made the decision to mobilize, their ally, Austria-Hungary, had already begun what leaders in Vienna hoped would be a localized war against Serbia by bombing Belgrade on 28 July. With resolute purpose, those leaders had decided to use the murder of Archduke Francis Ferdinand at Sarajevo on 28 June not just to "punish" Serbia, but also to solve the Dual Monarchy's "Balkan problems." On 1 August, a second causal sequence, or a second decision-making process, unraveled at Potsdam. It would lead to a very different, though obviously linked, war. Few, if any, German leaders paid much attention to the Austrian plan B (Balkans) and instead focused almost exclusively on the great blueprint for victory in the West.

Any discussion of the German decision for war in 1914 must give attention to the Schlieffen plan, for historians by and large still see in the inflexibility of the plan in general and of its railroad time tabling in particular one of the major causes of the great folly of 1914.

What, in fact, had Schlieffen committed to paper? Despite a recent provocative article, in which Terence Zuber declared, "There never was a 'Schlieffen plan,'" the available evidence clearly disputes that radical assertion.[4] In the July Crisis of 1914, General Helmuth von Moltke the

---

[2] Cited in *Deutschland im Ersten Weltkrieg*, ed. Autorenkollektiv des Zentralinstituts für Geschichte der DDR, 3 vols. (Berlin, 1970), vol. 1, p. 309.

[3] George F. Kennan, *The Decline of Bismarck's European Order: Franco-Russian Relations, 1875–1890* (Princeton, 1979), p. 3.

[4] Terence Zuber, "The Schlieffen Plan Reconsidered," *War in History* 6 (July 1999): 262–305. Zuber bases much of his argument on an unpublished manuscript by Wilhelm Dieckmann entitled "Der Schlieffenplan." After studying all available documentation (since destroyed or lost) in the 1920s, Dieckmann came to the conclusion that there in fact existed a Schlieffen plan. In any case, Dieckmann's manuscript ends with the year 1904–5 and hence does not address the critical winter 1905–6 Schlieffen memoranda. BA-MA, W-10/50220. As well, Zuber's claim that Schlieffen planned frontally "to break the great French fortress line" flies in the face of all available evidence.

Younger, chief of the General Staff, reminded Kaiser Wilhelm II that Germany had but one operations plan, Schlieffen's blueprint. Early in August, Moltke enacted precisely that grand design – altered only at the edges. Every German corps and army commander in 1914 (and thereafter) fully believed that he was conducting what General Wilhelm Groener termed the "great symphony" of the Schlieffen plan.

Austria-Hungary, as seen in the preceding chapter, was most concerned with how to delay the Russian "steam-roller," once the tsar's vast armies had begun to mobilize. Schlieffen showed little concern for either Austria-Hungary or Russia. He distrusted the former and ignored the latter. Instead, his attention focused on how to defeat the "archenemy," France. Already in his first year as chief of the General Staff, 1891, Schlieffen had broken with his predecessors, Helmuth von Moltke the Elder and Alfred von Waldersee, concerning a "Russia-first" strategy. Seen from Berlin, Russia constituted an inverted funnel: With every hundred miles they advanced, German armies would face an ever-widening front and the attendant need to administer ever-greater tracts of land and hostile populations. Spectacular but ultimately meaningless victories – what General Ludwig Beck later called "gusts of air" – would bring no decision.[5] Thus, Schlieffen had in August 1892 arrived at his well-known France-first concept. For the next five years, he set his staff to work on the problem of overcoming the French double line of fortresses from Belfort to Dunkirk that stood in the way of the planned march to Paris. Memories of the slaughter at Gravelotte-St. Privat (1870) were too fresh for Prussian generals to risk a bloodbath at the start of any war.

On 2 August 1897, Schlieffen first came up with the simple but seductive plan of avoiding altogether the French fortresses by advancing along a northern route through Luxembourg, southern Holland, and Belgium. He set his staff to work for another seven years on this high-risk operational concept. While it solved Germany's operational dilemma, "an offensive which seeks to wheel around Verdun" entailed violation of Belgium's "perpetual neutrality" and thus ran the risk of escalating any future war to include the signatories of the 1839 Twenty-Four Articles. In the critical war games of 1905, Schlieffen decreed as unacceptable protracted position warfare featuring weeklong battles.

In two famous memoranda of the winter of 1905–6, Schlieffen arrived at his final operational concept.[6] The vast bulk (hammer) of the German

---

[5] See Ludwig Beck, *Studien*, ed. Hans Speidel (Stuttgart, 1955), p. 173.

[6] Given that Schlieffen's war mobilization plans for 1905–6 were destroyed by Allied bombing raids on the Prussian Army Archives in April 1945, this discussion

armies would assemble around Aachen, punch through the Maastricht Appendix and the Ardennes, and then wheel through Belgium around the French armies and fortresses to the south, before falling into the Seine basin in order to drive the disoriented French onto the anvil of the German forces anchored in Lorraine.[7] A giant *Kesselschlacht*, or battle of envelopment and annihilation akin to the earlier battles of Cannae (216 B.C.), Leuthen (1757), or Sedan (1870), would break the French Army. This 450-kilometer advance – truly a classic "best-case scenario" – was to be done in forty-two days from first mobilization. A single army corps composed mainly of "greenhorns and grandfathers" was to fight a holding action in the East.[8] Schlieffen simply assumed that Austria-Hungary would hold the Russians at bay long enough for his armies to defeat the French.

All was predicated on speed: "The offensive must never be allowed to come to a standstill."[9] A delay of just seventy-two hours in railway mobilization and deployment could spell disaster. The German armies would have to force the pace of the war, never allowing the enemy to seize the initiative, but only to react. The main French forces would be crushed in a single *Kesselschlacht*; the escape of even a part of the French armies would translate into what Schlieffen called an "endless" war. "The French Army must be annihilated."[10] Schlieffen tested his operational design year after year in General Staff studies and in the annual fall maneuvers. In its final version, the Schlieffen plan was little more than a staff college tour de force. At that, the document was permeated with hedge words such as "if," "when," "perhaps," and "hopefully."[11]

Finally, Schlieffen argued, only a short war would allow Germany to avoid a breakdown not just of its economic and financial system, but perhaps of its social and political fabric as well. Put differently, only a short war would alleviate his nagging fears about what he called the "red ghost," that is, workers' revolts and possible revolution.[12] The general had studied carefully Imperial Germany's first war in Southwest Africa and concluded that negotiation with the rebellious Hereros alone had

rests on reconstructed fragments mainly of the great memorandum of 28 December 1905.

[7] Gerhard Ritter, *Der Schlieffenplan: Kritik eines Mythos* (Munich, 1956), pp. 145–95.

[8] Dennis E. Showalter, *Tannenberg: Clash of Empires* (Hamden, Conn., 1991), p. 68.

[9] Ritter, *Schlieffenplan*, p. 156.

[10] Ibid., p. 157.

[11] Ibid., pp. 146–55.

[12] Alfred von Schlieffen, "Der Krieg der Gegenwart," BA-MA, Nachlass Schlieffen, N 43, vol. 101, manuscript of 1908, published in *Deutsche Revue* (January 1909): 13–24; and in *Gesammelte Schriften*, 2 vols. (Berlin, 1913), vol. 1, pp. 11–22.

spared Germany the debacle of a prolonged campaign;[13] the African war simply reconfirmed the short-war illusion.

This tunnel vision, whereby all attention was focused on the great operational campaign in the West, was perhaps Schlieffen's major legacy. Flexibility, exploitation of local breakthroughs, and partial envelopments – the hallmarks of the earlier Prussian *Auftragstaktik* – were cast overboard. Clausewitzean concepts such as friction, interaction, the "genius of war," and the "fog of war" were jettisoned as well. Nor did Schlieffen ever press the issue that he lacked eight army corps for the critical right wing when he penned his great *Denkschrift*; that testy item was left for his successors to tackle.[14] Until his death in January 1913, Schlieffen lectured his successors on the need to keep any future war short. "A strategy of attrition," he wrote in 1910, "will not do if the maintenance of millions [of people] requires billions [of Mark]."[15] Schlieffen apparently chose to ignore the fact that France in 1913 fielded only 82,000 soldiers fewer than the Reich, and Russia half a million more.[16]

Schlieffen's great adventure was not without its critics. At the same time that the chief of the General Staff devised his France-first concept, Chancellor Leo von Caprivi, a Prussian general and admiral, cautioned that "war just against France" would be "tenacious and protracted."[17] Senior distinguished commanders such as General Colmar von der Goltz gradually came round to share Caprivi's sentiment, airing their doubts about the short-war scenario and warning that future wars would be long-drawn-out affairs involving nations and not just cabinets.[18] As is well known, the Elder Moltke had used his last speech in the German parliament, or Reichstag, on 14 May 1890 to caution the nation that the next European conflict would most likely be a "Seven or Thirty Years' War."[19]

[13] Schlieffen to Bülow, 23 November 1904, cited in Horst Drechsler, *Südwestafrika unter Deutscher Kolonialherrschaft* (Berlin, 1966), pp. 192ff.

[14] See Holger H. Herwig, *The First World War: Germany and Austria-Hungary 1914–1918* (London, 1997), pp. 46–7.

[15] Schlieffen, "Der Krieg in der Gegenwart," BA-MA, Nachlass Schlieffen, N 43, vol. 101. See n. 12 for publications.

[16] See David G. Herrmann, *The Arming of Europe and the Making of the First World War* (Princeton, 1996), p. 234.

[17] Reichsarchiv, *Der Weltkrieg 1914 bis 1918: Kriegsrüstung und Kriegswirtschaft*, 2 vols. (Berlin, 1930), vol. 1, p. 327.

[18] See Colmar von der Goltz, *Das Volk in Waffen* (Berlin, 1899), pp. 286–90. The 1883 edition had much less to say about the power of defense (pp. 340–1).

[19] Germany, *Stenographische Berichte über die Verhandlungen des Reichstages, 1890/91*, vol. 114, pp. 76–7.

Perhaps most critically, Schlieffen's quartermaster-general, Ernst Köpke, when reviewing his chief's notes, had warned that France's numerical superiority in troops and its excellent network of fortresses had made a repeat of Sedan (1870) unlikely. "We cannot expect quick, decisive victories," General Köpke lectured Schlieffen. The war of the future would feature "a tedious and bloody crawling forward step-by-step," that is, "siege-style" warfare. Ominously, he concluded, "army and nation will slowly have to get used to these unpleasant perspectives if we wish to avoid a worrisome pessimism already at the outset of [the next] war, one that could lead to grave danger regarding its outcome." While Schlieffen found Köpke's critique convincing and could produce no counterarguments, he declined to revise his *va banque* operations plan accordingly.[20] Nor did he heed the warnings of the wily Field Marshal Gottfried von Haeseler, who warned that one could not simply "carry off the armed forces of a great power [France] like a cat in a sack."[21] Schlieffen's staff, however, treated the proposed *Westaufmarsch* as official policy.

But Schlieffen's critics lacked a viable alternative. Their vision (or fear) of a peoples' war lasting anywhere between seven and thirty years was unacceptable – to kaiser, generals, parliament, and nation. The Second Reich was not the Third; total mobilization for total war was anathema to one and all. Thus, simply to reject Schlieffen's blueprint of a short war for limited aims – a strategy deeply rooted in Prussian military annals – was to deny the very validity of what the historian Gerhard Ritter called *Kriegshandwerk*.[22] Put bluntly, to concede that the vaunted Prussian General Staff could no longer conduct short wars of annihilation was to admit that war had ceased to be a viable option by the start of the twentieth century. There were few takers in Germany for such a radical notion.

---

[20] BA-MA, W-10/50220, unpublished manuscript, "Der Schlieffenplan" (Dr. Wilhelm Dieckmann), pp. 53–7.

[21] Cited in Lothar Burchardt, "Operatives Denken und Planen von Schlieffen bis zum Beginn des Ersten Weltkrieges," *Operatives Denken und Handeln in deutschen Streitkräften im 19. und 20. Jahrhundert* (Hamburg, Berlin, and Bonn, 1988), p. 61. While the French had clear indications of Schlieffen's grand design, Chief of Staff General Joseph Joffre refused to allow intelligence to undermine his own planning. See Jan Karl Tanenbaum, "French Estimates of Germany's Operational War Plans," in Ernest R. May, ed., *Knowing One's Enemies: Intelligence Assessment before the Two World Wars* (Princeton, 1984), pp. 150–71.

[22] Dennis E. Showalter, "German Grand Strategy: A Contradiction in Terms?," *Militärgeschichtliche Mitteilungen* 48 (1990): 65–102. Also by Showalter, "From Deterrence to Doomsday Machine: The German Way of War, 1890–1914," *Journal of Military History* 64 (2000): 679–710.

In the final analysis, it is fair to state that the Schlieffen plan was little more than a blueprint for the opening operations in an uncertain campaign – a design for a *battle* of annihilation rather than a *war* of annihilation. Moreover, Schlieffen's incomplete plan failed to address the question of how to deal with Fortress Paris or what to do after a French collapse. War termination rested on two political propositions: a French government sufficiently strong to conclude peace, and a Russian regime willing to return to the status quo ante bellum.

## The Cast of 1914

The German decision to go to war in 1914 must be seen as the result of coterie or contingency, as the actions undertaken by a small cadre of decision makers at Berlin in July 1914. The all-too-clever argument that vast but indirect social movements and serious class, political, and regional antagonisms limited the freedom of German decision makers in 1914 begs the question of causality and responsibility.[23] Without descending into the quagmire of "war guilt," it might be instructive to recall the cold, hard logic of a Berlin insider on the issue of responsibility for the Great War. Philipp Prince zu Eulenburg-Hertefeld, once a trusted member of Wilhelm II's inner circle and kept informed by senior military advisors in 1914, pointed to the central problem with Germany's decision making during the July Crisis:

Serbia *is* Russia. If Austria marches against Serbia, and *if Berlin does not prevent Austria's belligerent action*, then the great breaking wave of World War rolls irresistibly towards us. I repeat: Berlin *must* know that, otherwise *idiots* live in the Wilhelmstrasse. Kaiser Wilhelm *must* know that.[24]

Thus, the decision makers of 1914 and their choices deserve close scrutiny.

The process of decision making – and, in the case of July 1914, of crisis management – in Imperial Germany was restricted to the small coterie of high-level political and military advisors that surrounded Wilhelm II.

---

[23] For this line of argument, see Dieter Groh, " 'Je eher, desto besser!' Innenpolitische Faktoren für die Präventivkriegsbereitschaft des Deutschen Reiches 1913/14," *Politische Vierteljahresschrift* 13 (1972): pp. 501–21; also, David E. Kaiser, "Germany and the Origins of the First World War," *Journal of Modern History* 55 (1983): 442–74.

[24] Letter of 22 September 1919, cited in John Röhl, *1914: Delusion or Design? The Testimony of Two German Diplomats* (London, 1973), p. 134. The Wilhelmstrasse was the site of the German Foreign Office.

In fact, the "war powers" rested exclusively with a single individual: Wilhelm II. Under Article 11 of the Constitution of 16 April 1871, the power "to declare war and to conclude peace" was accorded solely with the kaiser; not the Reichstag, nor the Foreign Office, nor the General Staff could exercise that power. The only possible curb on the kaiser's "war powers" was the Upper House (Bundesrath), which had to approve a decision to go to war. Consisting of the diplomatic representatives of the various German states, the Upper House by 1914 had, in the words of the constitutional scholar Ernst Rudolf Huber, become little more than "an aristocracy of princes" that readily gave consent to all imperial legislation. Article 68 further granted the Supreme War Lord the authority unilaterally to declare a "state of war" to exist in case the "security of the Reich" was threatened.[25] The Lower House (Reichstag) could not interfere in foreign policy or military affairs; its powers were restricted under Article 23 to "suggesting" legislation to the chancellor and the Bundesrath.[26] The General Staff, it should be noted, was but an advisory bureau for the monarch.

The kaiser alone enjoyed the "power to command" (*Kommandogewalt*) and to promote and/or assign each of the nearly 30,000 officers of the Prussian Army.[27] Whatever influence the General Staff could wield derived from its history and traditional procedures – and from the force of personality of its chief. Since Imperial Germany never developed an organization analogous to the Committee for Imperial Defence, National Security Council, or Conseil Supérieur de la Guerre, the kaiser's chambers remained the final venue of decision making.

The inner circle of Germany's crisis management team in July 1914 consisted of Kaiser Wilhelm II, Chancellor von Bethmann Hollweg, War Minister von Falkenhayn, and chief of the General Staff von Moltke. State Secretary for Foreign Affairs Gottlieb von Jagow as well as State Secretary of the Navy Office Alfred von Tirpitz were absent from the capital early in July; the former, on his honeymoon in Italy, was represented by Permanent Under-Secretary Arthur Zimmermann and the latter, at his summer home

[25] Ernst Rudolf Huber, ed., *Dokumente zur deutschen Verfassungsgeschichte*, vol. 2: *Deutsche Verfassungsdokumente 1851–1918* (Stuttgart, 1964), pp. 293, 304. The reference to the Upper House as a *Fürstenaristokratie* is in ibid., vol. 3: *Bismarck und das Reich* (Stuttgart, 1963) p. 849.

[26] Ibid., vol. 2, p. 295.

[27] See Wilhelm Deist, "Kaiser Wilhelm II in the Context of His Military and Naval Entourage," in John C. G. Röhl and Nicolaus Sombart, eds., *Kaiser Wilhelm II: New Interpretations: The Corfu Papers* (Cambridge, 1982), pp. 170ff.

of St. Blasien in the Black Forest, by Deputy-Secretary Admiral Eduard von Capelle.

Wilhelm II was a tragic example of a ruler who could not accept and much less live within the range of his limited talents. The kaiser's formal education consisted of high school at Kassel and two years at Bonn University; his informal education came by way of the Prussian Guards, the Bonn Borussen fraternity, and a plethora of sycophants. As soon as he ascended the throne in 1888, Wilhelm announced that he wanted to be his "own Bismarck," to be the "captain of the ship of state." While intelligent, he was weak and vacillating, unable to do sustained work. He admired Great Britain, the home of his mother, yet yearned to supplant it as the premier naval power. He consistently gave bloodthirsty speeches and loved to rattle the saber, yet was unable to steer a steady course in the decisive weeks of July 1914. The kaiser's influence on German politics and history was mostly negative. King Edward VII accurately assessed his nephew as "the most brilliant failure in history."[28] A recent biographer has depicted the pattern of the kaiser's career as descendant, moving from martial pretension to political obtuseness, and from diplomatic maladroitness to military inconsequence.[29]

Chancellor von Bethmann Hollweg was a highly competent bureaucrat who should have reached the pinnacle of his career as state secretary of the Interior in 1907. The complexity of the July Crisis of 1914 (and later of war leadership) was beyond the limited talents of this lawyer.[30] A Hamlet-like figure, Bethmann Hollweg all too often fell victim to indecision and half-measures. He was unable to chart a clear course for his country and unable to restrain either his blustering sovereign or the military. In July 1914 he fell victim to the theoretical speculations of Kurt Riezler, his principal advisor. Bouts of moroseness and dark depression haunted Bethmann Hollweg at the best of times.

---

[28] This and the following capsule biographies are from Holger H. Herwig and Neil M. Heyman, eds., *Biographical Dictionary of World War I* (Westport and London, 1982).

[29] Lamar Cecil, *Wilhelm II*, vol. 2: *Emperor and Exile, 1900–1941* (Chapel Hill, 1996), p. 356. See also Thomas A. Kohut, *Wilhelm II and the Germans: A Study in Leadership* (New York, 1991); and John C. G. Röhl, *Young Wilhelm: The Kaiser's Early Life, 1859–1888* (Cambridge, 1998), the first of a trilogy.

[30] For Bethmann, see Eberhard Vietsch, *Bethmann Hollweg: Staatsmann zwischen Macht und Ethos* (Boppard, 1969); and, more apologetically, Konrad Jarausch, *The Enigmatic Chancellor: Bethmann Hollweg and the Hubris of Imperial Germany* (New Haven, Conn., 1973).

General von Moltke was perhaps the most complex figure among the German decision makers.[31] The nephew of the victor of Königgrätz and Sedan nurtured serious doubts ("too reflective, too scrupulous") about his military abilities, yet he accepted the post of chief of the General Staff when it was offered in 1906. Within five years, Moltke had gravitated into the camp of the hawks. During the Agadir crisis of 1911, for example, he wrote to his wife, "If we slink out of this affair again with our tail between our legs . . . then I despair of the future of the German Reich." He advised use of "the sword" or, failing that, sarcastically suggested placing the Reich under "the protectorate of Japan."[32] While Moltke had serious misgivings about the Schlieffen plan, once in command of the General Staff he was content merely to tinker with some of its features. Dour and pessimistic at heart, Moltke speculated in Oriental studies, theology, theosophy, and stereoscopic photography. His wife, Eliza, imbued him with a strong veneration for spiritualism and the occult. The July Crisis of 1914 would reveal fully his shortcomings.

In terms of social origin, the ruling elite came from a homogeneous and ancient aristocratic class. Bethmann Hollweg's family could trace its roots to Goslar in the year 1416; Falkenhayn's ancestors were noted in Silesia since 1504; Jagow's descendents had been in the Mark Brandenburg since 1268; and the German branch of Moltke's clan had first been recorded in Mecklenburg in 1254. Moltke's deputy, Georg von Waldersee, even had Hohenzollern ancestors, and they had come to Brandenburg in 1415.

With regard to the generals, most had been born the sons of East Elbian army officers and landed squires; almost all had attended first the Prussian Cadet School and then the War Academy; and all but a few had served with the General Staff.[33] Of Prussia's highest-ranking officers – field marshals, colonel generals, and the twenty-five corps commanders – 77 percent belonged to the ancient nobility of the sword, and 23 percent to the newer titled nobility. Six out of every ten lieutenant generals and more than half the major generals were noble. Service was frequent and consistent. In

---

[31] See Annika Mombauer, *Helmuth von Moltke and the Origins of the First World War* (Cambridge, 2001), for the most recent analysis of Moltke and the coming of the war.

[32] Moltke's letter of 19 August 1911, in Eliza von Moltke, ed., *Generaloberst von Moltke: Erinnerungen Briefe Dokumente 1877–1916. Ein Bild vom Kriegsausbruch, erster Kriegsführung und Persönlichkeit des ersten militärischen Führers des Krieges* (Stuttgart, 1922), p. 362.

[33] See Wiegand Schmidt-Richberg, "Die Regierungszeit Wilhelms II.," in *Handbuch zur deutschen Militärgeschichte 1638–1939*, vol. 3, pt. 5: *Von der Entlassung Bismarcks bis zum Ende des Ersten Weltkrieges 1890–1918* (Munich, 1979), p. 71.

1914, among active officers from noble families, there were 49 Puttkamer, 44 Kleist, 34 Zitzewitz, 30 Bonin, and 20 Kameke. During the Great War, 33 Bülow died, as did 26 Arnim, 24 Wedel, 21 Puttkamer, 19 Schwerin, and 18 Prittwitz.[34] These same families had shed their blood on Frederick the Great's battlefields; most had intermarried and all were closely related both by birth and by mentality.

The Reich's diplomats came from similarly narrow social strata, but of course with a different education. Of the 548 Imperial German diplomats between 1871 and 1914 studied by Lamar Cecil, 69 percent bore titles of nobility – as did all ambassadors to European states. Of Cecil's cohort, 21 percent were fraternity men – Jagow was Wilhelm II's fraternity brother in the Bonn Borussen – and 57 percent had military service. Almost all had degrees in jurisprudence – Bethmann Hollweg, for example, had read the law at Straßburg, Leipzig, and Berlin. Given the social homogeneity of the officer corps and the diplomatic corps, it is not surprising that their professional ties were as close as their social bond. Senior officers, on retiring, were sometimes called straight into ambassadorial positions; subalterns not infrequently bounced back and forth between the army and the diplomatic corps.[35] Regardless of their institutional home or their diplomatic agendas, they were devout supporters of the monarchy and its policies.

## Unspoken Assumptions

Operations plans – including the Schlieffen plan – do not cause wars. Nor do General Staff timetables, economic rivalries, alliance structures, or imperial adventures. Nor do so-called structural forces, the "big" causes often touted by historians seeking to explain decision making in 1914. Wars, as detailed in Chapter 1, are in fact caused by human beings who weigh their options, calculate the risks, and eventually decide that the recourse to arms is in their best interest. In the case of July 1914, the decision for war in Germany was made by a small coterie of perhaps half a dozen leaders. Coterie, of course, makes contingency highly likely. Weak nerves, misinformation, misjudgments, and misperceptions all take their place at the table.

---

[34] See Walter Görlitz, *Die Junker: Adel und Bauer im deutschen Osten: Geschichtliche Bilanz von 7 Jahrhunderten* (Limburg, 1964), p. 319. For reduced estimates of nobles, see Ulrich Trumpener, "*Junkers* and Others: The Rise of Commoners in the Prussian Army, 1871–1914," *Canadian Journal of History* 14 (April 1979): 29–47.

[35] Lamar Cecil, *The German Diplomatic Service, 1871–1914* (Princeton, 1976), pp. 66, 68, 84, 110, 112.

In reaching the decision for war in July 1914, German planners were motivated by a complex set of assumptions, both spoken and unspoken. They did not come to the table with the slate of the past wiped clean, as a tabula rasa or a fresh data bank. Rather, they were the product of their times, of the history they had learned at school, of the stories about the national past they had been told, in short, of the popular *mentalité* of their age. Political and military leaders, as James Joll has percipiently argued, at times of crisis fall back on their instinctive reactions, traditions, and patterns of behavior.[36] They are motivated in reaching their decisions by certain beliefs, certain rules, and certain objectives. Thus it is not at all contradictory to argue for coterie, on the one hand, and then to suggest the influence of unspoken assumptions, on the other.

First and foremost among these assumptions was the conviction that war was part of the natural order, a legitimate extension of politics by other means. As strange as it may seem looking back on the violent twentieth century, Europeans around 1900 considered war to be but one of the many arrows that statesmen had in their quivers. Most nations had been forged in war. Most had consolidated that gain and then expanded overseas by way of war. And most anticipated that the twentieth century would also see its share of wars. On New Year's Eve, 1899, in Berlin, for example, artillery salutes joined fireworks displays in announcing the new century. The bells of overfilled churches pealed throughout the land. Ships' horns pierced the chill night air in the Hanseatic ports. Addresses by university rectors and editorials in leading newspapers prophesied that the breakup of the British Empire would be the most important event of the coming century. And Germany had to be prepared to do battle for its share of this "inheritance."[37] As General von der Goltz put it most crassly in 1900, "But I could do with a war, with a truly hard, invigorating, joyful war."[38] In short, be they wars lasting a month, a year, seven years, or even thirty years, wars were part and parcel of great-power relations. Thus, the recourse to arms in 1914 was not an aberration, but the norm.

Second, a good number of politicians and writers viewed war as a cure-all for what they perceived to be the evils of an age of bourgeois

[36] James Joll, *1914: The Unspoken Assumptions* (London, 1968).

[37] The various New Year's declarations have been brilliantly analyzed by Michael Salewski, " 'Neujahr 1900': Die Säkularwende in zeitgenössischer Sicht," *Archiv für Kulturgeschichte* 53 (1971): 335–81.

[38] Goltz to Colonel von Morgen, 10 February 1900, BA-MA, N 227, Nachlass Curt von Morgen, vol. 34. The reference to a *"frisch und fröhlich"* war was derived from a popular hunting call, and it would be repeated later by the German Crown Prince.

materialism: lethargy, emasculation, and moral rot. The Conservative Party leader Ernst von Heydebrand und der Lasa even suggested that war "will lead to a strengthening of the patriarchal order and mentality."[39] In other words, a "jolly, little war" could turn back the clock in domestic politics and end the dangerous process of modernization. The National Liberal Party leaders Rudolf Bassermann and Gustav Stresemann shared Heydebrand's willingness to draw the sword, but in their case to launch a "realistic world policy" based on German military strength and potential.[40] They wanted the Reich not simply to defend Bismarck's gains of 1864–71 but to take the next step: to build a fleet, to secure colonies, and to expand overseas – all that came to be encapsulated by the slogan *Weltpolitik*.

Among the German literati, the novelist Thomas Mann stated that he was "tired, sick and tired" of Bismarck's peace, and instead yearned for war as "a purification, a liberation, an enormous hope." His colleague, Hermann Hesse, suggested that it would be salutary for Germans "to be torn out of a dull capitalistic peace." The philosopher Max Scheler thought that a war would once again bring out the "noble beast" in German youth. Gertrud Bäumer sought to rally the half-million members of the Federation of German Women with the argument that the "great alternative: to win or to die, a greater fatherland or death," would raise the concept of "nation above all other treasures of life." Magnus Hirschfeld, leader of the homosexual movement, depicted the omnipresent uniforms, guns, and rifles of 1914 as sexual stimulants. The Austrian draft-dodger Adolf Hitler was hardly alone when, upon hearing the order for mobilization at Munich, he fell down on his knees and thanked Heaven for "the good fortune to be alive at this time."[41] Unlike Edwardian England, where the pacifist groups were gaining in strength after the Liberal victory at the polls in 1905–6, in Wilhelmian Germany the nationalism of the middle class grew ever shriller and drowned out the minuscule pacifist movement.

Third, German leaders viewed a future war as a contest among "rising" and "falling" races. In December 1912, Wilhelm II twice gave expression to this sentiment. On 8 December, while acknowledging a report from Ambassador Karl Prince von Lichnowsky that London could not possibly

---

[39] Cited in Wolfgang J. Mommsen, "The Topos of Inevitable War in Germany in the Decade before 1914," in Volker R. Berghahn and Martin Kitchen, eds., *Germany in the Age of Total War* (London, 1981), p. 26.

[40] Ibid., p. 28.

[41] Herwig, *The First World War*, p. 35.

stand by and allow Berlin to establish its hegemony in Europe, the kaiser nevertheless argued that such a perfidious British balance of power policy could only lead to war. More, that such a "struggle to the bitter end between Slavs and Germans" would find "the Anglo-Saxons on the side of the Slavs and Gauls."[42] To make certain that the message was not lost on Berlin diplomats, Wilhelm that same day telegraphed the state secretary for foreign affairs, Alfred von Kiderlen-Wächter, his belief that "the struggle for survival that the Germans in Europe (Austria, Germany) would have to conduct against the Romans (Gauls) supported by the Slavs (Russia), would find the Anglo-Saxons on the side of the Slavs."[43] One week later, Wilhelm informed Albert Ballin, a confidante and head of the Hamburg-America Line, that a *"racial war"* was in the offing between the "Germans" and the "presumptuous Slavs." This *"racial war"* was for nothing less than "the survival of the Habsburg Monarchy and the *existence* of our fatherland."[44] To be sure, such racial musings were restricted neither to the monarch nor to Germans. They were also expressed in Reichstag debates and by foreign leaders such as Cecil Rhodes and Theodore Roosevelt.

The popular press gave wide circulation to the kaiser's racialist views. That same December 1912, for example, a lead article in the *Hamburger Nachrichten* warned the nation of the "unavoidable clash between the Germanic and Slavic peoples."[45] In short order, right-wing papers such as the *Post*, the *Berliner Neueste Nachtichten*, and the *Rheinisch-Westfälische Zeitung* took up the clarion call of the inevitable future war of cultures – as did more moderate papers such as the semi-official *Kölnische Zeitung* and the Catholic *Germania*.

General von Moltke, chief of the General Staff since 1906, thought along similar lines. In a letter to his wife of November 1914 entitled "Observations and Remembrances," Moltke argued that the "Romance peoples," such as the French and the Italians, had passed their peak of historical creativeness and were in the process of decline and decay. "England pursues only material goals." The "Slavic peoples, first and foremost the Russians," were on the "rise," but not yet ready to lead the Continent. A Slavic victory would subject Europe to "intellectual barbarism" under

---

[42] Cited in John C. G. Röhl, "An der Schwelle zum Weltkrieg: Eine Dokumentation über den 'Kriegsrat' vom 8. Dezember 1912," *Militärgeschichtle Mitteilungen* 21 (1977): 85.

[43] Cited in ibid., p. 101.

[44] Wilhelm II to Ballin, 15 December 1912, cited in ibid., pp. 112–13.

[45] See Klaus Wernecke, *Der Wille zur Weltgeltung: Außenpolitik und Öffentlichkeit im Kaiserreich am Vorabend des Ersten Weltkrieges* (Düsseldorf, 1970), pp. 185–6.

the "Russian whip." That left the Germans as "the only people who at this time can lead humanity towards higher goals."[46]

The chancellor joined in this chorus of doomsday prognostications. In a speech to the Reichstag in 1913, Bethmann Hollweg, much like Wilhelm II and Moltke, couched the prospect of war in racial terms, as an "inevitable struggle" between Slavs and Teutons.[47] Indeed, the diplomatic and political records in Berlin as well as in Vienna by 1914 were filled with references to "Germanic loyalty," *Nibelungentreue*, and standing "shoulder-to-shoulder" with Austria-Hungary against the Anglo-French-Russian *entente*.

Fourth, wide circles of Germany's ruling elite were besotted with the ideas of social Darwinism, of the need to either rise to world power status or to decline. As Chancellor von Bethmann Hollweg reminded Jules Cambon, the French ambassador to Berlin, early in 1914, France had pursued a "grandiose policy" of "immense empire" for the past forty years; now Germany needed its own "place in the sun." Germany's growing population, burgeoning commerce, and industry, as well as navy, cried out for overseas expansion. The Reich, the chancellor averred, "is in a sense condemned to spread outwards."[48] Educated Germans were familiar with the works of Houston Stewart Chamberlain, Joseph Comte de Gobineau, Richard Wagner, and Friedrich Nietzsche – whether in the original or in abridged versions – who popularized the case for natural selection and survival of the fittest. One of those Germans, General Erich von Falkenhayn, used the English-language term "struggle for life" in his private correspondence.[49] Even Liberals such as Theodor Heuss and Conrad Haussmann deemed war to be a test of "moral strength" and a struggle "of the will to assert oneself." The economist Johann Plenge depicted the war of 1914 as a clash of civilizations: between the German "ideas of 1914" – duty, order, justice – and the French "ideas of 1789" – liberty, fraternity, equality.[50]

Fifth, European leaders were gripped by what the historian Wolfgang J. Mommsen has called "the topos of inevitable war" – a topos heavily

[46] Moltke, ed., *Generaloberst Helmuth von Moltke*, p. 14. Already on 22 July 1913, Moltke had spoken of the coming war as "a clash between Germanic and Slavic civilizations." Ibid., p. 374.
[47] Speech of 7 April 1913, *Verhandlungen des Reichstages*, vol. 189, pp. 4512–13.
[48] Cambon's report of 28 July 1914. Cited in Kaiser, "Germany and the Origins," p. 463.
[49] Falkenhayn to Hanneken, 20 October 1904, cited in Holger Afflerbach, *Falkenhayn: Politisches Denken und Handeln im Kaiserreich* (Munich, 1994), p. 52.
[50] Herwig, *The First World War*, p. 35.

tainted by a "home-made" fatalism that eventually turned into a self-fulfilling prophecy.[51] Beginning with the first Moroccan crisis of 1905–6, Europe proceeded from one crisis to the next: the Bosnian annexation crisis in 1908, the second Moroccan crisis in 1911, the Tripolitanian War that same year, and the Balkan Wars of 1912–13. The Foreign Office at Berlin was unable to mount a consistent foreign policy, and instead hastily extemporized responses. Popular pundits saw the beginnings of a *finis Germaniae*. Most ominous of all, Russia in October 1913 passed its "Large Program for Strengthening the Army," which would provide an additional 11,000 officers and 468,000 men by 1917 for what already was the largest army in Europe. The Russian "great program" quickly became the key obsession of the decision-making coterie in Berlin, for it added a timeline to the growing feeling of falling behind.

The general pessimism shared by Germany's leaders may be seen in one of Schlieffen's last published articles. He painted a frightening future for an "encircled" and endangered Germany. "At the given moment, the gates will be opened, the drawbridges let down, and armies of millions of men will pour into Central Europe across the Vosges, the Meuse, the Königsau, the Niemen, the Bug, and even across the Isonzo and the Tyrolean Alps in a wave of devastation and destruction."[52] In 1912, Friedrich von Bernhardi published his blockbuster two-volume opus, *Germany and the Next War*, in which the general called for nothing less than "the total destruction of France" by war. The book went through six editions by 1913, and it posited a clear choice for Germany: either "world power or decline."[53]

Nor were retired military leaders alone in this desperate feeling that time was running against Germany and that war alone could rejuvenate the Reich. Foreign Secretary von Jagow perhaps best captured the fear of Russia that dominated decision makers in Berlin at the height of the July Crisis. He pessimistically informed Ambassador von Lichnowsky at London that while the Berlin-Vienna partnership was "growing steadily weaker," Russia would soon be "ready to strike" and to "crush us."[54] Chancellor von Bethmann Hollweg had already concluded, in

---

[51] Mommsen, "The Topos of Inevitable War," pp. 23–44. Topos refers to a stock rhetorical theme or topic.

[52] Alfred von Schlieffen, "Der Krieg in der Gegenwart," BA-MA, Nachlass Schlieffen, N 43, vol. 101. The manuscript was written in 1908. For its later publication, see note 12.

[53] Friedrich von Bernhardi, *Deutschland und der Nächste Krieg*, 2 vols. (Stuttgart, 1912).

[54] Cited in *Die Deutschen Dokumente zum Kriegsausbruch 1914*, ed. Max Graf von Montgelas and Walter Schücking, 4 vols. (Berlin, 1919), vol. 1, p. 72.

1911, that the German people were "in need of a war."[55] In July 1912, while showing Ambassador Hans von Flotow the park of his estate Hohenfinow on the Oder River, he had wistfully mused, "whether it made sense to plant new trees; the Russians would be here in a few years in any case."[56] In July 1914, at the very moment at which Vienna asked Berlin to back its play in the Balkans, Bethmann Hollweg instructed the Austrians that because Russia "grows and grows and weighs on us like a nightmare," he felt the "present moment" to launch a war "more advantageous than a later one."[57]

The Younger Moltke likewise felt war to be inevitable. As early as December 1911 he had lectured the General Staff: "All are preparing themselves for the great war, which all sooner or later expect."[58] One year later, at the so-called war council of 8 December 1912, at which the issue of solving Germany's strategic problems by way of a preventive strike against France and Russia had been raised, this at the highest levels, the general had forthrightly counseled war, "and the sooner the better."[59] During his last meeting in May 1914 with his Austro-Hungarian counterpart, General Franz Conrad von Hötzendorf, Moltke again demanded war: "to wait any longer meant a diminishing of our chances."[60] Returning to Berlin from Karlsbad, the general informed State Secretary von Jagow that time was running against Germany, that "there was no alternative but to fight a preventive war so as to beat the enemy while we could still emerge fairly well from the struggle."[61] On 1 June 1914, he apparently told the diplomat Hermann von Eckardstein, "If things would only finally boil over – we are ready; for us, the sooner, the better."[62] Moltke's deputy, General Georg von Waldersee, as late as May 1914 argued that Germany had "*no* reason whatever *to avoid*" a European war, "but *quite*

[55] Entry for 30 July 1911, in Kurt Riezler, *Tagebücher, Aufsätze, Dokumente*, ed. Karl Dietrich Erdmann (Göttingen, 1972), p. 180.

[56] Egmont Zechlin, "Deutschland zwischen Kabinetts- und Wirtschaftskrieg: Politik und Kriegführung in den ersten Monaten des Weltkrieges 1914," *Historische Zeitschrift* 199 (1964): 400. Private communication to Zechlin from Bethmann Hollweg's son.

[57] Herwig, *The First World War*, p. 21.

[58] Memorandum of 2 December 1911, Auswärtiges Amt, Politisches Archiv (AA-PA), Bonn, Deutschland Nr. 121 geh., vol. 1.

[59] Fritz Fischer, *Krieg der Illusionen: Die deutsche Politik von 1911 bis 1914* (Düsseldorf, 1969), p. 233.

[60] Discussion of 12 May 1914, Conrad von Hötzendorf, *Aus meiner Dienstzeit 1908–1918*, 5 vols. (Vienna, Leipzig, and Munich, 1921), vol. 4, p. 670.

[61] AA-PA, Nachlass Jagow, vol. 6, pp. 69 ff. Scholars debate whether the discussion took place on 19 May or 3 June 1914; in any case, it was well before the Sarajevo regicide.

[62] Hermann Frhr. von Eckardstein, *Lebenserinnerungen und politische Denkwürdigkeiten*, 3 vols. (Leipzig, 1921), vol. 3, p. 184.

*the opposite*, [good] prospects *today* to conduct a great European war
quickly and victoriously."[63]

Sixth, Chancellor von Bethmann Hollweg had developed a model for
war based on the writings of his principal advisor, the political scientist
Kurt Riezler. According to the latter's so-called calculated-risk theory,
future wars would be fought not on the battlefield but around the negotiating table. War had become too expensive and too dangerous for
states to risk. "The more one arms," Riezler wrote (under the pseudonym
J. J. Ruedorffer), "the more the relationship between the advantages and
disadvantages of going to war shift in favor of the latter, and thus in favor
of peace." War or, better, the threat of war, had become a game of bluff.
"Wars will no longer be fought," Riezler stated, "but calculated." Guns
would no longer fire, "but have a voice in the negotiations." In a Europe
divided between two antagonistic camps, the game of bluff (offensive
diplomacy) could be played all the way up the escalatory ladder, stopping just short of war. But it was critical that the two antagonistic camps
could at the flash point back down and avail themselves of a great-power
mediator – for Bethmann Hollweg, this meant Great Britain.[64] Hence the
chancellor planned, throughout the July Crisis, to make use of the "British
card."

Finally, playing directly against Riezler's and Bethmann Hollweg's
model of the calculated risk was the military's dedication to professionalism and its obsession with mobilization timetables – in short, its inflexibility. By 1914, the General Staff possessed only one contingency war plan:
Schlieffen's notes for a short campaign in France. Germany had to be the
first to mobilize, first to take the field, and first to victory. Delay meant defeat. Men who had spent their careers shaving minutes and miles from an
operations timetable, the historian Dennis E. Showalter has argued, were
unlikely to scrap that work while the politicians and diplomats played the
dangerous and time-consuming game of bluff.[65]

[63] Herwig, *The First World War*, pp. 20–1. Even "liberal imperialists" such as Paul
Rohrbach and Ernst Jäckh were alert to the "inevitability" of war in Europe; in the
spring of 1914 they founded the journal *Das größere Deutschland* to prepare the
German people "for the impending war." Paul Rohrbach, *Zum Weltvolk hindurch*
(Stuttgart, 1914), p. 4.

[64] J. J. Ruedorffer [Kurt Riezler], *Grundzüge der Weltpolitik der Gegenwart* (Stuttgart and
Berlin, 1914). Riezler's model has been analyzed by Andreas Hillgruber, "Riezlers Theorie
des kalkulierten Risikos und Bethmann Hollwegs politische Konzeption in der Julikrise
1914," *Historische Zeitschrift* 202 (1966): 337–42.

[65] Dennis E. Showalter, "From Deterrent to Doomsday Machine: The German Way of War,
1871–1914," *Journal of Military History* 64 (2000): 679–710.

That military-technocratic mindset was fully revealed on 1 August 1914, when the kaiser, falsely believing that Britain would stay out of the war if Germany did not invade France, ordered Moltke to deploy the entire field army in the East. Moltke was flabbergasted. Schlieffen had left behind no operations plan concentrating against Russia. As late as December 1912, the former chief of the General Staff had laconically noted that the tsar's armies would not invade Galicia before the die were cast in the West; "Austria's fate will be decided not on the Bug but on the Seine!"[66] As a result, Schlieffen had seen no need to coordinate his strategy with that of the Viennese ally. Obviously, *Nibelungentreue* had its limits. The "deployment of a million-man army," Moltke lectured his Supreme War Lord, could not be "improvised." Any change in the *Große Aufmarsch* he had inherited from Schlieffen would cause chaos and result "in a disorderly heap of confused armed men without supplies" charging aimlessly toward the advancing Russians.[67] Professional education, technical knowledge, and mathematical accuracy ruled the General Staff in 1914.[68]

## Public Assumptions

Right-wing pressure groups by and large advocated bellicose policies both before and during 1914. The Pan-German League, almost two-thirds of which was composed of university-educated men, of whom half were in public service, was a firm supporter of an aggressive foreign policy and of the need to back that policy with force, if necessary. Driven by social Darwinism and a militant, largely Protestant theology, the Alldeutsche repeatedly announced their willingness to sacrifice "blood and treasure" for the future of Reich and Volk.[69] One of the league's leaders, Ernst Hasse, year after year assured his followers that war was imminent, and that the Pan-Germans were prepared "to manufacture a war threat" in case the vacillating Wilhelm ("Guillaume le timide") II or the Reich's

---

[66] Ritter, *Schlieffenplan*, p. 174. Moltke used these exact words with Conrad in February 1913.

[67] Moltke, ed., *Generaloberst Helmuth von Moltke*, pp. 19–20. The kaiser's retort that Moltke's great uncle would have given him a "different answer" hardly steadied the younger Moltke's nerves at this critical juncture.

[68] Arden Bucholz, *Moltke, Schlieffen and Prussian War Planning* (New York and Oxford, 1991), p. 317.

[69] On the Pan-Germans, see Roger Chickering, *We Men Who Feel Most German: A Cultural Study of the Pan-German League 1886–1914* (London, 1984).

"weak and sleepy people" should lapse into a false sense of permanent peace.[70]

The various veterans groups, formally organized into the Kyffhäuser Bund with its registered 2.8 million members by 1913, were perhaps the most servile of nationalistic Germans. Their leaders adored uncritically the Reich and its Hohenzollern masters. Born at "hour zero" on the battlefields of Gravelotte, Mars-la-Tour, and Sedan in 1870, the veterans groups saw themselves as "the kaiser's army in civilian frock[s]." Parades, military tattoos, martial music, and battlefield recreations honed their rhetoric, if not their skills. Politically, they offered themselves as a "well-armed wall" or "bulwark" against the Social Democrats' "divisive" influence on German society.[71] In December 1911, many joined a new German Defense League under General August Keim to lobby for increased defense spending and a more aggressive foreign policy; in 1914 they rallied behind "Kaiser, Folk and Fatherland."

Germany's university professors, widely regarded as a cultural-educational elite and as public-opinion makers, had long championed the national cause. The fact that professors yearned to don reserve officers' tunics, those noted badges of honor, and that fraternities by and large had turned to conservatism, if not downright reaction, is well known. Moreover, various disciplines had rallied behind national ventures. Thus, geographers joined the German Colonial Society. Historians and sociologists embraced social Darwinism, racialism, and acceptance of war. Economists gravitated toward "cultural" and "armed" nationalism. The German *civitas academica* supported the Hohenzollern Monarchy, founded the Prussian school of history, and clamored for global expansion.[72]

Of Germany's two major religions, Protestants most openly announced their prowar convictions. The dominant features of Protestant theology by 1914 have been summarized as "militarization of thought," growing acceptance of the "necessity of war" and willingness to participate enthusiastically, and preparing the flock for the "inevitable" war. Many Protestant theologians accepted social Darwinistic "laws" such as the

---

[70] Cited in Stig Förster, *Der Doppelte Militarismus: Die Deutsche Heeresrüstungspolitik zwischen Status-Quo Sicherung und Aggression 1890–1913* (Stuttgart, 1985), pp. 183–4.

[71] See Klaus Saul, "Der 'Deutsche Kriegerbund': Zur innenpolitischen Funktion eines 'nationalen Verbandes' im kaiserlichen Deutschland," *Militärgeschichtliche Mitteilungen* 2 (1969): 95–159.

[72] See Rüdiger vom Bruch, " 'Militarismus,' 'Realpolitik,' und 'Pazifismus': Außenpolitik und Aufrüstung in der Sicht deutscher Hochschullehrer (Historiker) im späten Kaiserreich," *Militärgeschichtliche Mitteilungen* 39 (1986): 37–58.

"rise and fall" of peoples – that is, the "rise" of Germany and the "fall" of France. Countless others depicted the July Crisis not only as a god-given time of national awakening, but also as a new "German Pentecost." When war came in August 1914, Lutheran theologians celebrated it as a "holy war," as a great "educator and leveler" that would sweep away all that was "unjust, superficial and wrong."[73]

Among Catholic theologians, the *Leitmotif* of July 1914 centered on the notion of a just war. They depicted Germany, "the hearth of peace," as the "victim" of an evil armaments race. The Reich, "encircled" by a ring of hostile powers, had no choice but to defend itself. Catholic leaders did little to warn their flock about succumbing to the siren calls of war, but generally eschewed the extreme chauvinistic declarations of their Protestant brethren. In the end, they, too, rallied behind the official motto, "with God for Kaiser, Folk and Fatherland."[74]

At another level, it is generally assumed that most captains of industry rallied to the flag. To be sure, armaments firms such as Krupp, Mauser, and Ehrhardt stood to gain from a war, but even here there exists a need for differentiation. While Alfred Hugenberg, chairman of the board of Alfried Krupp, demanded a more aggressive German foreign policy – read expansion – Carl Duisberg, director-general of Friedrich Bayer and Co. of Leverkusen, favored a rapprochement with Great Britain. Again, while the influential Karl Helfferich, director of the Deutsche Bank, sought German expansion not by trade and investment but, rather, by military strength, his fellow director at the Deutsche Bank, Arthur von Gwinner, like Duisberg wanted Berlin to find a diplomatic arrangement with London.[75]

Some captains of industry and banking even attempted to curb Wilhelm II's blustering rhetoric and expansionist aims. Hugo Stinnes, one of Germany's most dynamic entrepreneurs, hardly was in the camp of the hawks before 1914. When Heinrich Claß, head of the Pan-German League, in September 1911 demanded that Germany take advantage of the First Balkan War and launch a preventive war against the *entente*, Stinnes was not amused. After "3–4 years peaceful development," the Rhineland

---

[73] Martin Geschat, "Krieg und Kriegsbereitschaft im deutschen Protestantismus," in Jost Dülffer and Karl Holl, eds., *Bereit zum Krieg: Kriegsmentalität im wilhelminischen Deutschland 1890–1914. Beiträge zur historischen Friedensforschung* (Göttingen, 1986), pp. 35–6, 46–7, 48, 50.

[74] August-Hermann Leugers, "Einstellungen zu Krieg und Frieden im deutschen Katholizismus vor 1914," in ibid., pp. 56–73.

[75] Fischer, *Krieg der Illusionen*, pp. 657–8.

magnate lectured Claß, Germany would be "the undisputed economic master of Europe."[76] Walther Rathenau, the chairman of General Electric (AEG), likewise counseled trade rather than war. Economic rivalry to Ballin was a "positive" response to an expanding world market. Armaments, on the other hand, argues Ballin's biographer, Lamar Cecil, was a "negative" policy "grounded in fear, vanity, and megalomania," one conducted by "misguided princes, ambitious admirals, and inept diplomats."[77] And just one week before the Sarajevo assassination, the Hamburg banker Max Warburg rejected Kaiser Wilhelm's bellicose query of whether, in the face of the rapid pace of the Russian rearmament program, "it would not be better to attack rather than to wait" until 1916–17. Warburg instead tendered the sage advice that there was no cause to draw the sword in the immediate future. "Germany becomes stronger with every year of peace. We can only gather rewards by biding our time."[78]

But such sagacious counsel fell upon deaf ears. There is no record of a direct response to Gwinner, Ballin, Stinnes, or Rathenau on the part of the kaiser, chancellor, or foreign secretary. Nor is there any indication that their warnings against drawing the sword were discussed in depth by the Foreign Office or the General Staff. The "men of 1914" measured great power status not in terms of financial ledgers but rather in land and military might.

There were few direct links between the various Wilhelmian pressure groups, university professors, religious leaders, and industrialists, on the one hand, and the Reich's small political and military elite, on the other. There is no question that men such as Bethmann Hollweg and Moltke were concerned with the views of the Reich's public opinion makers.[79] But there is no evidence to suggest that any time during the July Crisis they shaped their policies according to the perceived interests of those groups. No political leaders, no eminent bankers, no captains of heavy industry

---

[76] Cited in Wolfgang J. Mommsen, *Großmachtstellung und Weltpolitik: Die Außenpolitik des Deutschen Reiches 1870 bis 1914* (Frankfurt and Berlin, 1993), p. 293.

[77] See Lamar Cecil, *Albert Ballin: Business and Politics in Imperial Germany, 1888–1918* (Princeton, 1967), pp. 165–6; and Hartmut Pogge von Strandmann, ed., *Walther Rathenau: Industrialist, Banker, Intellectual, and Politician: Notes and Diaries 1907–1922* (Oxford, 1985), pp. 183–4.

[78] Max M. Warburg, *Aus meinen Aufzeichnungen* (Glückstadt, 1952), p. 29; Alfred Vagts, "M. M. Warburg and Co. Ein Bankhaus in der deutschen Weltpolitik," *Vierteljahrsschrift für Sozial- und Wirtschaftsgeschichte* 45 (1958): 353; and Fischer, *Krieg der Illusionen*, pp. 657–8.

[79] See Bernhard Rosenberger, *Zeitungen als Kriegstreiber? Die Rolle der Presse im Vorfeld des Ersten Weltkrieges* (Cologne, 1998).

were consulted in the final considerations for war. Nor were Germany's academics, theologians, or veterans groups consulted.

Once having opted for war, the "men of 1914" certainly wanted to carry the broad public with them. And they wanted to be certain of the support of the labor movement in general and of its political arm, the Social Democratic Party of Germany (SPD), on the other. Thus, Bethmann Hollweg personally sounded out the party's leaders late in the July Crisis. The chancellor was delighted with the result and shelved existing plans to arrest the SPD's leaders at the start of war. Yet at the very moment at which Bethmann Hollweg was working to establish the Social Democrats' intentions, War Minister von Falkenhayn was cynically urging his Bavarian colleagues to "use the prevailing public euphoria before it goes up in smoke."[80]

The role of public opinion in July 1914 remains nebulous. To be sure, Imperial Germany had a rich newspaper culture: There were weekly and daily editions; some had but small circulation, others upwards of half a million; and Berlin boasted no fewer than fifty papers, with a few published three times a day. But German newspapers, by and large, did not create public opinion; rather, they trumpeted the view of their owners, which often were political parties or pressure groups. Thus, moving from left to right, the SPD had *Vorwärts*, the Progressive Party the *Frankfurter Zeitung* and *Vossische Zeitung*, the National Liberals the *Kölnische Zeitung* and *Magdeburgische Zeitung*, the Center Party the *Kölnische Volkszeitung* and *Germania*, the Conservatives the *Neue Preußische* (or *Kreuz-*) *Zeitung* and *Deutsche Tageszeitung*, and the radical right or Pan-Germans the *Tägliche Rundschau* and *Rheinisch-Westfälische Zeitung*. Readers tended to take their political instructions from these party papers, the lead articles of which during the July Crisis were as consistent as they were predictable.[81] The Social Democratic press, for example, called for peace and brotherhood, repeatedly showed the horrors of war, and argued that Germany should not fight for Austria-Hungary in the Balkans. The Pan-German papers, not surprisingly, called for what they termed a "preventive war," from which they hoped to get not only a strengthening of the Viennese ally, but also an "inner cleansing" of the

[80] Cited in Herwig, *The First World War*, p. 35. For Bethmann and the SPD, see Dieter Groh, *Negative Integration und revolutionärer Attentismus: Die deutsche Sozialdemokratie am Vorabend des Ersten Weltkrieges* (Berlin, 1973), pp. 628–34.

[81] The best survey of the Wilhelmian press remains Wernecke, *Der Wille zur Weltgeltung*, pp. 11–25; for the newspapers and the July Crisis, see Rosenberger, *Zeitungen als Kriegstreiber*.

German nation. The bulk of middle-class papers saw the coming war both as being inevitable and as a defensive struggle against the *entente*'s "encirclement" policies; at best, they hoped that it could be localized in the Balkans. Most Germans read the smaller provincial press, which tended to present the views of the government.

A recent survey of the "spirit of 1914" suggests that the lead articles of most German newspapers reveal neither a broad war enthusiasm nor a nation unified for war.[82] Moreover, many historical accounts indicate that the "war euphoria" of August 1914 was most pronounced among students and the upper middle class, and least among urban workers. The majority of Germans, raised through the nationalistically oriented school system, still nurtured a degree of social deference and accepted military service and leadership as a form of national identity and cohesion. Most were willing to follow whatever course their government charted for them.[83] Still, recent studies of Darmstadt, Freiburg, Hamburg, Saarbrücken, and Wesel have shown that tens (if not hundreds) of thousands of workers took part in peace demonstrations in late July. An Austrian scholar has suggested that some of the prowar demonstrations – and especially those in front of the Chancellery in Berlin – may have been organized by the chancellor's cousin, Dietrich von Bethmann Hollweg.[84] Whatever the case, available documentary evidence does not allow the conclusion that the "men of 1914" were responding to public opinion in deciding for war.

### The Essence of Decision Making

How and why, then, was the decision for war reached? Again, it is necessary to return to that small cadre of decision makers surrounding Kaiser Wilhelm II. Many feared that the coming war would be a prolonged, bloody, exhausting, and possibly unwinnable undertaking. Yet, they opted for war in an almost exuberant manner. As General Karl von Wenninger, the Bavarian military plenipotentiary to Berlin, noted upon visiting the Prussian War Ministry, "[e]verywhere beaming faces, shaking

[82] Jeffrey Verhey, *The Spirit of 1914: Militarism, Myth, and Mobilization in Germany* (Cambridge, 2000), p. 20.
[83] Thus, Michael Howard, "Europe on the Eve of the First World War," in R. J. W. Evans and Hartmut Pogge von Strandmann, eds., *The Coming of the First World War* (Oxford, 1988), p. 15.
[84] Fritz Fellner, ed., *Schicksalsjahre Österreichs, 1908–1919: Das politische Tagebuch Josef Redlichs*, 2 vols. (Graz and Cologne, 1953–4), vol. 2, p. 44.

of hands in the corridors; one congratulates one's self for having taken the hurdle."[85] Perhaps what Wenninger noted can be attributed to cognitive dissonance, or the joyous relief at the end of weeks of anxiety and uncertainty.

The steps taken by senior decision makers in Germany during the July Crisis were complicated and followed a punctuated rhythm rather than a broad, steady, ever rising movement. The "basics," parallel to the listing of events in the previous chapter, may be summarized as follows:

| | |
|---|---|
| 28 June | Assassination of Archduke Franz Ferdinand. |
| 5–6 July | Critical phase in Berlin; Hoyos mission; meetings with the kaiser and chancellor; Wilhelm II and then Bethmann Hollweg issue Vienna a "blank check" to proceed against Serbia, even if "European complications" arise as a result. |
| 6–25 July | Quiet days; the kaiser leaves for a three-week northern cruise; Germany denies to all that any aggressive moves are afoot; on 25 July, Germany delays passing on to Vienna Britain's mediation proposal until after the Serbian ultimatum's deadline has passed. |
| 26–27 July | Days of decision in Berlin; the Foreign Office rejects the proposal for a four-power conference to mediate the Serbian dispute; Wilhelm II returns to Berlin; Foreign Secretary von Jagow presses Vienna not to delay the action against Serbia; Jagow disassociates himself from another British proposal for mediation. |
| 28–30 July | Chaos in Berlin: On 28 July, the kaiser announces all cause for war removed in light of Serbia's cordial response to the Austrian ultimatum; on 29 July, Bethmann offers London a deal: British neutrality for a German promise not to annex French lands; on 30 July, Britain firmly rejects the German proposal; Moltke presses for mobilization and urges speed of action on Vienna. |
| 31 July | Germany declares a "state of imminent danger of war" (*Kriegsgefahrzustand*). |
| 1 August | Germany declares mobilization, and war on Russia. |

Of all the German decision makers, General von Moltke harbored no illusions about the coming war. On 28 July 1914, about to orchestrate the

[85] Cited in Bayerisches Hauptstaatsarchiv, Kriegsarchiv, Munich, HS 2546, Tagebücher General von Wenninger.

"great symphony" of the Schlieffen plan, he penned a secret "Evaluation of the Political Situation" for Bethmann Hollweg. In it, Moltke spoke of the coming war as a "world war" – well before Europe's leaders had taken the fateful decisions for this eventuality. He foresaw "Europe's civilized nations" about to embark on a "mutual tearing to pieces" (*Zerfleischung*) of one another. An undefined "fate," Moltke argued, was about to unleash a war "that will destroy civilization in almost all of Europe for decades to come."[86] Still, the nephew of the victor of 1866 and 1871 saw no alternative but to launch the Schlieffen plan – Moltke had no problem identifying Germany's one operations plan in 1914 as such – to provide Germany with a strategic advantage at the start of what he believed would be a long, hard war. On 29 July, Moltke instructed Wilhelm II that Germany would "never hit it again so well as we do now with France's and Russia's expansion of their armies incomplete."[87]

This was hardly the vision of war that prevailed at the chancellor's palace. There, Bethmann Hollweg after 28 June began to play his game of "calculated risk." Instead of immediately initiating diplomatic discussions concerning the Sarajevo murder and holding back the military option as a trump card, the chancellor eschewed negotiations and conducted his game of diplomatic bluff. Might this not be the last chance, he mused, to alter the strategic balance in the Balkans by exploiting the assassination and supporting an Austro-Hungarian strike against Serbia? Should the war come "out of the East," that is, if Germany appeared to be "fighting for Austria-Hungary and not Austr[ia]-Hungary for us," the Reich stood a very good chance "of winning it." But should Russia back down, Germany stood an equally good chance of having "maneuvered the entente into a parting of the ways."[88]

The arrival at Berlin on 5 July of the Austro-Hungarian special emissary, Count Alexander Hoyos, with a request for German backing of Vienna's planned actions against Serbia must be seen against this background. Around noon that day, Ambassador Count László Szögyény-Marich visited Kaiser Wilhelm II at Potsdam. Concurrently, Hoyos called on Under-Secretary Zimmermann (State Secretary von Jagow being on his honeymoon in Italy) at the Foreign Office in Berlin. According to

---

[86] Moltke to Bethmann Hollweg, 28 July 1914, BA-MA, Nachlass Groener, N 46, vol. 40. The letter was reprinted in Moltke, ed., *Generaloberst Helmuth von Moltke*, pp. 3–7.

[87] Imanuel Geiss, ed., *Julikrise und Kriegsausbruch 1914: Eine Dokumentensammlung*, 2 vols. (Hanover, 1964), vol. 2, p. 299.

[88] Entry of 8 July 1914, Riezler, *Tagebücher*, p. 184.

the ambassador's account of his meeting with Wilhelm II – the only
record of the discussion at Potsdam – the kaiser encouraged a harsh
policy vis-à-vis Serbia, "even if serious European complications" arose
as a result. Wilhelm counseled Austria-Hungary "not to delay its action." Russia was unprepared for war. And even though its posture was
sure to be "hostile," Germany "had been prepared for this for years."[89]
The kaiser's only caveat was that he be granted time to consult his
chancellor.

At 5 P.M. that afternoon, the kaiser called Bethmann Hollweg,
Zimmermann, War Minister von Falkenhayn, and Chief of the Military
Cabinet Moriz von Lyncker to Potsdam. Wilhelm II apprised them of the
"blank check" that he had just issued the Habsburg government, reaf-
firming that he would stand by the Viennese ally in case Russia were to
intervene in an Austro-Serbian war. All present fully concurred, accepting the risk of Russian intervention leading to a general war.[90] On 6 July,
Bethmann and Zimmermann formally conveyed Berlin's unequivocal support for Vienna to Szögyény and Hoyos. The Austrians immediately cabled the good news to the Ballhausplatz, home of the Foreign Ministry in
Vienna.

Knowing that under the Constitution of 1871 a decision for war would
require the consent of the Bundesrath, Under-Secretary Zimmermann at
once informed the Bavarians that Berlin saw the moment as "very propitious" for Vienna to launch a "campaign of revenge" against Serbia, "even
given the danger of further entanglements." When the Bavarian plenipotentiary inquired what these "entanglements" might be, Zimmermann
was perfectly candid: "War with Russia."[91]

Thus, a small coterie of four decision makers – Wilhelm II, Bethmann
Hollweg, Falkenhayn, and Lyncker – in a most offhand manner decided to
escalate the crisis up to and including war. Even this can hardly be called
a meeting of peers – the only voice that counted was that of the kaiser, in
whose hands the "war powers" alone rested. Not until the next morning,
just before departing for his annual cruise off Norway, did Wilhelm II,

[89] Szögyény to Berchtold, 5 July 1914, *Österreich-Ungarns Aussenpolitik von der Bosnischen Krise 1908 bis zum Kriegsausbruch 1914: Diplomatische Aktenstücke des
Österreichisch-Ungarischen Ministeriums des Äussern*, eds. Ludwig Bittner and Hans
Uebersberger, 8 vols. (Vienna and Leipzig, 1930), vol. 8, pp. 306–7. Hereafter cited as
ÖUA.
[90] Fischer, *Krieg der Illusionen*, pp. 688–91.
[91] Bayerisches Hauptstaatsarchiv, Munich, MA 3076, Militär-Bevollmächtigter Berlin, 9
and 17 July 1914.

having exercised his constitutional *Kommandogewalt*, get around to notifying the General Staff of this decision. Even then, the kaiser called to Potsdam not Moltke, who was on vacation at Karlsbad, or his deputy, General von Waldersee, but rather General Hermann von Bertrab, a surveyor and cartographer who was not a member of the inner planning group at the General Staff.[92] Unfortunately, the destruction of the General Staff records by two Allied air raids in 1944 and 1945 does not allow insight into why the kaiser chose a cartographer for such an important discussion. This notwithstanding, Bethmann Hollweg's mentor, Riezler, slyly summarized the decision of 5 July for a quick strike against Serbia as follows: "Fait accompli and then friendly [face] toward the entente; then we can sustain the shock [of war]."[93]

But reality refused to conform to Riezler's "model." As early as 7 July – that is, a mere twenty-four hours after having issued Vienna the famous blank check and thereby initiating his policy of the "calculated risk" – Bethmann Hollweg realized that his room to maneuver was incredibly restricted. Any "action" against Serbia, he confided to Riezler, "can lead to a world war." Like Moltke, Bethmann Hollweg regarded "a war, regardless of how it ended," as anything but a forty-day march to Paris. The chancellor, in Riezler's words, equated armed conflict with "the overthrow of everything that exists."[94] Under-Secretary Zimmermann at the Foreign Office agreed with Austrian diplomats that an attack on Serbia meant a "European war ... with a probability of 90 percent."[95] In other words, the German Foreign Office regarded a "calculated risk" of one chance in ten for peace to be acceptable. Leaders in Berlin, like their counterparts in Vienna, and as evidenced by the kaiser's comments to Szögyény-Marich at Potsdam on 5 July, fully expected a "hostile" Russian reaction (read armed intervention) to any Habsburg military play in the Balkans. Finally, Zimmermann's comment makes mockery of the "slide-into-war" theory later propounded by politicians and historians alike.

Still, what to do? Bethmann Hollweg escalated the game of bluff. For the period immediately following the Hoyos mission, that is, from about 7 to 25 July, while Austria-Hungary was making the key decisions that

---

[92] See Ulrich Trumpener, "War Premeditated? German Intelligence Operations in July 1914," *Central European History* 9 (1976): 62–3.

[93] Comment of 8 July 1914, Egmont Zechlin, "Zur Beurteilung Bethmann Hollwegs," *Geschichte in Wissenschaft und Unterricht* 15 (1964): 536.

[94] Entry of 7 July 1914, Riezler, *Tagebücher*, p. 183.

[95] Fritz Fellner, "Die Mission Hoyos," in Wilhelm Alff, ed., *Deutschlands Sonderung von Europa, 1862–1945* (Frankfurt, 1984), p. 296.

led to war, Bethmann Hollweg adamantly refused all suggestions to involve Great Britain as a mediator in the Serbian matter. Rather, he pressed Vienna to act against Belgrade, assuring the Austrians of Germany's full support. To act otherwise would cost the Reich "the last real ally."[96] As well, Bethmann Hollweg, widely viewed in nationalist circles as a dove, was determined to show strength in the face of danger. To have abandoned Austria-Hungary in July 1914, he later wrote, would have been tantamount to "castration" on Germany's part.[97] Such "*Selbstentmannung*" would have translated into "capitulation" in the face of the Russian threat, and this the chancellor was not about to condone. Rather than "capitulation," he doggedly pursued his policy of the "calculated risk," a policy that historians such as Fritz Fischer, Imanuel Geiss, and John Röhl, among others, have termed one of "deception." On 14 July, Bethmann Hollweg informed Riezler that he would stay the course, even if it constituted "a leap into the dark."[98] Indeed, in the days that followed, Berlin escalated the calls for armed action against Serbia. On 25 July, Ambassador Szögyény cabled Count Leopold Berchtold, the Habsburg foreign minister, that German leaders saw danger in delay; they advised Vienna "to press forward immediately [with war against Serbia] and to confront the world with a fait accompli."[99]

It would be a classic case of academic overkill to retrace the tortuous steps that eventually led to war – the hour-by-hour petty bickering that began behind the scenes on 29 July among Wilhelm II, Moltke, Falkenhayn, and Bethmann Hollweg concerning the timing of an official proclamation of premobilization (the so-called declaration of "imminent danger of war"[100]). These have been told and retold ad nauseam. Rather, it seems more profitable first to concentrate on Bethmann Hollweg's and Moltke's motivations during the last week of peace and, second, to examine the chaos and confusion that reigned at German headquarters during the last days of July. This is now possible due to the recently discovered diary

---

[96] Entry of 7 July 1914, Riezler, *Tagebücher*, p. 183.
[97] Theobald von Bethmann Hollweg, *Betrachtungen zum Weltkriege*, 2 vols. (Berlin, 1919–21), vol. 2, p. 133.
[98] Entry of 14 July 1914, Riezler, *Tagebücher*, p. 185.
[99] Szögyény to Berchtold, 25 July 1914, ÖUA, vol. 8, p. 704.
[100] "Imminent danger of war" was stage three of German mobilization and the first to be made public. Leaves would be canceled, reserve staffs ordered to report for duty, the state of siege law proclaimed, and 11 of the 25 army corps bulked up by way of a call-up of their first-line reserves. Bucholz, *Moltke, Schlieffen and Prussian War Planning*, pp. 300–2.

fragment of War Minister von Falkenhayn, starting on 27 July 1914. The diary was given to the Reichsarchiv by Falkenhayn's widow in November 1927 and marked "confidential, not to be made public." It resurfaced in former East German archives after the "accession" of 1990.

Bethmann Hollweg, the central political figure of the July Crisis, revealed that he was no Bismarck. On 27 July the chancellor still imagined that he could manage the crisis. During a meeting with Wilhelm II and Moltke, to which Falkenhayn was not invited, chancellor and kaiser agreed "to see the matter through [to war] no matter what the cost." Bethmann Hollweg informed Riezler that he saw "a fate larger than [what] human power" could control "descend over Europe" – a shocking abdication of politics.[101] When news of the decision for war was leaked to Falkenhayn, he ordered that all troops be confined to barracks and that Germany "purchase wheat in great quantities."[102] Obviously, war, and a long one, was just around the corner.

On 28 July, Austria-Hungary commenced military operations against Serbia, whereupon Russia moved toward partial mobilization. Falkenhayn pressed for additional military measures. Moltke pushed hard for war, informing Bethmann Hollweg, "We shall never hit it again so well as we do now."[103] But Bethmann Hollweg could not decide. On the one hand, he deemed the time for negotiations with London still to be premature; on the other, he sought to rein in the military's war fever. Wilhelm II, the ultimate arbiter, at this point allowed that he "now no longer wanted war." A desperate Falkenhayn openly warned Wilhelm II that he had "lost control over events."[104]

When news confirming Russian partial mobilization of the military districts of Moscow, Kazan, Odessa, and Kiev arrived in Berlin on 29 July, panic ensued. What did the Russians know about the Schlieffen plan?[105] What details of Austro-Hungarian mobilization had the traitor Colonel Alfred Redl passed on to the Russians in 1913? Chancellor von Bethmann Hollweg was the first to push the panic button. His one remaining hope

---

[101] Entry of 27 July 1914, Riezler, *Tagebücher*, p. 192.
[102] Falkenhayn's diary entry for 27 July 1914, BA-MA, W-10/50635 Tagebuch v. Falkenhayn.
[103] Geiss, *Julikrise*, vol. 2, p. 299.
[104] Diary entry of 28 July 1914, BA-MA, W-10/50635 Tagebuch v. Falkenhayn.
[105] According to William C. Fuller, Russian military planners had received "many indicators" concerning the design of the Schlieffen plan, but remained paranoid about the possibility that German planners had a variant plan for a major offensive in the East. See his *Strategy and Power in Russia 1600–1945* (New York, 1992), p. 442.

was to pass responsibility for the coming "European conflagration" on to Russia.[106] Thus, he dictated several telegrams for "Willy" to dispatch to his cousin "Nicky," Tsar Nicholas II, at St. Petersburg. Both rulers merely suggested that the other take the first steps to mediate the conflict. It is difficult to escape the conclusion that neither was sincere; both were by then heavily under the influence of their respective diplomatic and military leaders. The telegrams at best served to maintain the policies of deception.

The Russian partial mobilization also moved other senior decision makers in Berlin. Falkenhayn and Moltke rushed to Bethmann Hollweg's residence, where the war minister demanded that the decree for premobilization be issued at once. Next, the two generals raced out to Potsdam, where they were later joined by the chancellor, to convince the kaiser of the urgency of the moment. Wilhelm II, having declared all threat of war to have dissipated with Serbia's cordial response to the Austrian ultimatum on 28 July, now undertook one of his customary about-faces and, after a series of what Falkenhayn termed "confused speeches," decided again in favor of war. "The ball that has started to roll," Falkenhayn stated in fatalistic terms, "can no longer be stopped." Falkenhayn reiterated the need to begin premobilization. But then, in an astounding turn-around, Bethmann Hollweg, now assisted by Moltke, urged caution and restraint.[107]

Late that night, the two generals again visited the chancellor at Berlin to assess the Russian partial mobilization. Once again, Falkenhayn pushed for proclaiming a state of "imminent danger of war." Once again, Bethmann Hollweg and Moltke stood firm in their opposition, arguing that the Russian action "did not mean war." Both Moltke and Bethmann Hollweg were eager to let St. Petersburg take the lead so that Russia could be depicted as being "responsible for the great debacle."[108] In the end, Falkenhayn bowed to their wishes, arguing – incredibly – that "a few hours more or less" were of no importance to German premobilization.

In truth, Bethmann Hollweg had been less than forthcoming that day. After the generals departed, the chancellor decided to play his "trump" card. Shortly before midnight, Bethmann Hollweg called the British ambassador to his residence. He assured Sir Edward Goschen that

---

[106] See Fritz Fischer, *Griff nach der Weltmacht: Die Kriegszielpolitik des kaiserlichen Deutschland 1914/18* (Düsseldorf, 1964), pp. 87–103.

[107] Diary entry of 29 July 1914, BA-MA, W-10/50635 Tagebuch v. Falkenhayn.

[108] Ibid. The German term they used was "*Kladderadatsch.*"

were Britain to remain neutral in the coming war, Germany would offer London a neutrality agreement, guarantee the independence of The
Netherlands, and promise not to undertake "territorial gains at the expense of France."[109] Goschen, and later Secretary for Foreign Affairs Sir
Edward Grey, rejected these proposals as "shameful."

It never dawned on Bethmann Hollweg that the "calculated risk" and
the Schlieffen plan (whose basic contours he knew by December 1912)
were diametrically opposed to one another. For an advance through neutral Belgium would not directly affect Russia, the power that according
to the "calculated-risk" model the chancellor hoped to deter but, rather,
Great Britain, the very power he needed to maintain as final arbiter in the
crisis.[110] Thus, Bethmann Hollweg's single-option plan, the "calculated
risk," collapsed in the wake of Goschen's rejection of the "neutrality" offer. There was no longer any hope for a British "miracle" at the eleventh
hour. Nor was there a fall-back position.

The 30th of July, in Falkenhayn's words, was a day of "endless discussions." At a session of the Prussian Ministry of State, Bethmann Hollweg
allowed that "the hope for England [was now] zero." Later he confessed
that "all governments" simply had "lost control" of the July Crisis. "The
stone has begun to roll."[111] The seeming rationality of the "calculated
risk" had yielded to the irrationality of a war *à outrance*. Later that
evening, Bethmann Hollweg called Moltke and Falkenhayn to his residence, not to reassess the July Crisis but to launch a bitter debate with
Moltke concerning personal responsibility "for the coming war." The
generals seized the opportunity to convince the chancellor of the need
to declare a state of "imminent danger of war," at the latest by midday,
31 July. Moltke now undertook another 180-degree turn and demanded
war "*sans phrase*," that is, without circumlocution. Falkenhayn was
"at a loss" to explain Moltke's abrupt about-face.[112]

The reason for the chief of the General Staff's sudden *volte-face* became
apparent on 31 July, another day of panic at Potsdam. That morning,
Moltke received news from intelligence units at Allenstein in East Prussia
that Russia seemed to be mobilizing its forces in Poland. But there was no
hard confirmation of this action. "Unfortunately, Moltke very nervous,"
Falkenhayn noted in his diary. Then, during a meeting with Bethmann

---

[109] Herwig, *The First World War*, p. 27.
[110] Hillgruber, "Riezlers Theorie," p. 343.
[111] Geiss, *Julikrise*, vol. 2, p. 373.
[112] Diary entry of 30 July 1914, BA-MA, W-10/50635 Tagebuch v. Falkenhayn.

Hollweg, both Moltke and Falkenhayn demanded premobilization. Finally, around noon, a telegram arrived from Ambassador Friedrich Count von Pourtalès in St. Petersburg stating that Russia had mobilized its entire army. Wilhelm II, in his constitutional capacity as Supreme War Lord, immediately telephoned orders that a state of *Kriegsgefahrzustand* existed. France and Russia were to be given ultimatums calling upon them to declare their intentions.

The moment of decision finally was at hand. Falkenhayn arrived in the Star Chamber of the Neues Palais at Potsdam by 2 P.M. An intense discussion ensued, during which it was decided "to attribute the entire responsibility for war to Russia." Wilhelm II, in Falkenhayn's view, at long last rose to the occasion: "His bearing and his words are worthy of a German kaiser." Falkenhayn signed the decree declaring a state of "imminent danger of war" and Moltke read an emotional appeal entitled "to the German people." For that action, Bethmann Hollweg accused Moltke of meddling in political affairs and lectured the chief of the General Staff that the chancellor's office alone could issue such a proclamation. Bethmann Hollweg and Wilhelm II then engaged in a bitter exchange of words over who was responsible for the nation's political future.[113] Later that night, after a last-minute plea by Tsar Nicholas II to preserve the peace, Falkenhayn visited Bethmann Hollweg and demanded that the order proclaiming German "war mobilization" be issued at once.

The first day of August brought yet another bizarre turn in their crisis management. Afraid that Germany might lose the psychological edge by declaring war on Russia first, Falkenhayn visited Foreign Secretary von Jagow and then Bethmann Hollweg to head off such a "foolish" declaration. Falkenhayn's last-minute attempt to bring Moltke and Tirpitz into the discussion was cut short by Wilhelm II's order that his political and military leaders prepare the "war mobilization" document and come to Potsdam at once. The order for "war mobilization" was signed at 5 P.M. on 1 August 1914. Then, a telegram arrived from London, wherein Ambassador von Lichnowsky suggested that Britain might remain neutral if Germany pledged "not to set foot on French territory." Another moment of chaos and recriminations ensued. Falkenhayn caught the moment thus:

After excited exchanges between the chancellor and Moltke, I dictate the telegram of reply to Jagow on orders from the kaiser. Moltke telephones Trier that the

[113] Ibid., diary entry of 31 July 1914.

16$^{th}$ Division for the moment is not to march into Luxembourg. [Moltke] claims to be completely broken, because this decision by the kaiser shows that the latter still hopes for peace. I console Moltke.

The final turn in the July Crisis came around midnight, when another telegram arrived from Lichnowsky, this one stating that Britain's price for neutrality was the inviolability of Belgian territory. "It is decided," Falkenhayn recorded, "not to answer the 2. telegram." Moltke persuaded Wilhelm II to order the occupation of Luxembourg.[114]

Just as Austria-Hungary had engineered "its" war against Serbia, so Germany now launched "its" war under the auspices of the Schlieffen plan. Senior decision makers could be well pleased with their efforts. Admiral Georg Alexander von Müller, chief of the Navy Cabinet, caught the euphoria of that 1 August 1914 in his diary. Müller recorded his "happiness" that the government had "managed brilliantly" to shift the blame for the war onto Russia, and to make Germany "appear the attacked."[115]

It is hard to escape the conclusion that the small political and military elite in whose hands the future of the German nation rested was utterly incapable of shouldering that responsibility. Far from conjuring up what Fritz Fischer called a "bid for world power," that elite was beset by doubts, petty bickering, confusion, and lack of vision. Their discussions at the end of July and the beginning of August centered only on managing the immediate crisis; there was no discussion of how that crisis related to the nation's future, to the Tirpitz plan, or to global power aspirations. *Balkanpolitik* had replaced *Weltpolitik*.

General von Falkenhayn's diary, while it differs in minor details with the later accounts by the major players at Potsdam and certainly enhances the war minister's claim to have been the one steady pole during the July Crisis, nevertheless reinforces the suspicion that Berlin was a house without direction. Orders were issued, countermanded, then reactivated. Wilhelm II and Moltke undertook radical, sometimes daily, shifts in their war policies. Each telegram from London and each piece of intelligence from East Prussia occasioned acrimonious debate and fundamental shifts in policy. Chaos and confusion rather than direction and design were the hallmarks of German decision making in late July 1914.

114 Ibid., diary entry for 1 August 1914.
115 Walter Görlitz, ed., *Regierte der Kaiser? Kriegstagebücher, Aufzeichnungen und Briefe des Chefs des Marinekabinetts Admiral Georg Alexander von Müller 1914–1918* (Göttingen, 1959), p. 38.

Finally, neither Moltke nor Bethmann Hollweg understood the full implications of their policies of war on the German economy or finances. In 1914, there existed ammunition for only a few opening battles, and raw materials for just between two and six months. The war materials that the General Staff now demanded in eight weeks could not be produced in less than six months. Ammunition reserves for most guns were only at 20 to 50 percent of requirements.[116] Few government agencies appreciated that 49 percent of the workers at the Imperial Shipyards, 61 percent of those in the Royal Prussian Armories, and half of those in the vital metal trades were draft-eligible. Financially, the Reich's gold reserves stood at 120 million Mark. The Berlin banker Jakob Riesser that same year warned that mobilization alone would cost 1,800 million Mark. In fact, the Great War cost 45.7 billion Mark per annum.[117]

Most critically, there existed no common planning for war. While Generals von Bernhardi and von der Goltz had joined the bankers Warburg and Riesser in demanding the creation of an "economic general staff," nothing of the sort had happened. Only in the summer of 1906 did government agencies – under indirect pressure from the General Staff, which possessed no constitutional basis for raising the matter – turn their attention to securing the nation's food supply in case of war. By and large, both Prussian and Imperial ministries were content to exchange a flurry of memoranda, with each office seeking to place responsibility for feeding civilians and soldiers alike on the other. State Secretary of the Interior Clemens von Delbrück refused to interfere in what he considered to be a private-sector matter; in case of war, he cheerily suggested, the potato "can and must" make up for any grain shortages. Prussian ministries considered the food supply to be a "military measure." The Imperial Treasury countered that it was a "public welfare" matter. While Delbrück argued that the costs of victualing the nation be borne by the Reich, treasury officials countered that such outlays devolve to the individual states.[118] Not even the creation in December 1912 of a "Standing Commission for Economic Mobilization" brought relief: The commission was to meet but once a year and possessed neither a budget nor a mandate. It is interesting to note that the state secretary of the treasury, Hermann Kühn, was conspicuously absent from these

---

[116] Manuscript, "Die Vorbereitungen des deutschen Heeres mit Munition vor Ausbruch des Krieges" (Dr. Wilhelm Dieckmann), dated 1939, BA-MA, W-10/50777.

[117] Burchardt, *Friedenswirtschaft*, pp. 8, 225–6.

[118] Ibid., pp. 140, 201, 214, 242.

discussions. Apparently, he did not consider war financing to fall within his domain.

While Moltke canceled Schlieffen's proposed march through the Maastricht Appendix to keep Holland open as a "windpipe" for food imports – in case of a long war? – he failed to suggest concrete steps to put this option into play. In April 1913, the Prussian Ministry of War rejected as unrealistic a proposal by the Ministry of Finance to lay 2.5 million tons of food in store – largely because this would require a one-time expenditure of 440 million Mark.[119] A spur-of-the-moment suggestion by the General Staff in February 1914 that the Reich purchase the entire Argentine grain harvest and store it in ships on the Rhine River likewise was rejected on budgetary grounds.[120] The mayor of Berlin bitterly complained on 28 July and again on 30 July 1914 that Silesian grains were still being shipped to Austria and Russia.[121] In short, none of Germany's leaders had the slightest inkling of the implications of "total war."

### In Retrospect

Where does the debate concerning Germany's role in launching the First World War stand? Almost four decades after Fritz Fischer first put forth the explosive thesis that Germany had gone to war in 1914 as part of a bold "bid for world power," it seems incontrovertible that this is stretching the available evidence. For, such an audacious "bid" would have required careful planning, detailed preparation, and coordinated action – in short, a firm and resolute monarch, a rational and efficient government at Berlin, and extensive detailed planning. Nothing of the kind can be detected in what the historian Stig Förster has called "the polychratic chaos of the imperial system of government."[122] One could almost argue that in Berlin there existed *no* government in control of events in July 1914. Schlieffen had refused to share his blueprint for victory even with the Prussian war minister. Neither the treasury nor the interior ministries had been prepared to undertake steps to assure the nation's supply of food in case of war. Neither ammunition nor raw materials had been stockpiled. Nor had the war effort been coordinated with the ally at Vienna.

---

[119] Reichsarchiv, *Kriegsrüstung*, vol. 1, p. 364.
[120] BA-MA, Nachlass Groener, N 46, vol. 51, "Zum Schlieffenplan."
[121] Burchardt, *Friedenswirtschaft*, pp. 210, 239.
[122] Stig Förster, "Der deutsche Generalstab und die Illusion des kurzen Krieges, 1871–1914: Metakritik eines Mythos," *Militärgeschichtliche Mitteilungen* 54 (1995): 92.

In July 1914, there never took place a grand council of state to decide the critical issue of war or peace in a rational, coordinated manner. Each branch of government pursued an independent agenda. Wilhelm II failed abysmally in his assigned constitutional task of coordinating German foreign and military policies. Men as diverse as the journalist Maximilian Harden and General Erich Ludendorff concurred that Wilhelm II was incapable of decisive leadership. Five successive war scares in the immediate prewar period had gone without the recourse to arms. In short, what is striking about Berlin during the July Crisis is the lack of government direction and resolution.

Yet, Imperial Germany went to war. Why? Senior decision makers in Berlin were convinced that time was running against them, and hence they developed a "now-or-never" attitude toward a European war – what we have called the strategic argument. Moltke, looking back on July 1914, still expressed this mindset. First, he argued that war had been a desirable option in 1914, even if its outcome and its duration could not be predicted with certainty. Next, he combined fatalism with social Darwinism to suggest that Germany had gone to war simply to "fulfill its preordained role in the development of the world." For the Reich could not "fulfill its role in civilization . . . without conflicts, as time and again opposition has to be overcome; this can only be done by way of war." Even if Germany should lose the war, Moltke argued in 1915, and in the process see its culture snuffed out, such was the iron law of history, whereby the "epochs of civilization" proceeded according to preordained postulates. "We live in colossal times."[123]

However one "gamed" the available options in the run-up to the July Crisis of 1914 at Berlin, only the recourse to arms seemed to offer a future that included Germany as one of the great powers. All other options were ruled unacceptable. First, the Elder Moltke's successors rejected his suggestion that a policy of "deterrence" alone was feasible – given both the unlikelihood of another short war as in 1866 or even 1870, and the realization that Germany could not win a protracted war against Britain, France, and Russia. Such a policy would deny the existence of their profession and the validity of their craft. Second, various government agencies dismissed the call by retired military men and civilian bankers that the Reich prepare itself financially, economically, and psychologically for a long war as too costly to answer.[124] The General Staff could coordinate

---

[123] Moltke, ed., *Generaloberst Helmuth von Moltke*, pp. 13–14.
[124] Förster, "Der deutsche Generalstab," pp. 80, 90.

little beyond the initial operational concept of the Schlieffen plan; it possessed no constitutional basis on which to force government agencies to articulate policies that would enhance the military tour de force. Thus, in 1914, only the third option, the gamble with a modified version of Schlieffen's 1905 concept, remained. Thereby, Germany could hope to win a great opening battle in the initial campaign of the war and at best gain an advantage for the ensuing peace negotiations. To wait any longer, given German fears of war once the Russian "big program" of rearmament was completed by 1917, entailed almost certain failure for the Schlieffen option, hence the "strike-now-better-than-later" mentality that dominated Berlin during the July Crisis. In the process, Germany's decision makers transformed Austria-Hungary's "localized" Balkan war into a general European war.

The recent work by Stig Förster and others concerning the "delusion" of the "short-war illusion," however, suggests an even darker side to the German decision for war. For, if the minuscule political and military elite resorted to arms in 1914 with the knowledge and conviction that the coming conflict would be a protracted "peoples' war" of perhaps two or three years; if they were convinced that short, successful wars à la 1864 and 1866 were out of the question; if they saw no alternative to their strategic dilemma but apocalyptic war; if they failed to prepare the army, the economy, and the nation for this eventuality; and if they were content to launch a war they knew was sure to destroy *belle époche* Europe – while all along paying mere lip-service to Schlieffen's short-war panacea – then their actions amounted to "an almost criminal lack of responsibility."[125]

---

[125] Ibid., p. 94. Schlieffen's original plan had German forces reaching the English Channel and, in a grand sweep, moving south of Paris. The 1914 operation was less ambitious, passing to the north of Paris. Two useful maps showing German and French *intentions* in August 1914 may be found in Robert Asprey, *The First Battle of the Marne* (Philadelphia, 1962), p. xiii.

# 6

## Russia

### David Alan Rich

Austria will, in the perhaps not too distant future face a choice between two paths: either fundamental reconstruction of the state structure on the basis of federation of the different nationalities, or a desperate struggle aimed at the final confirmation of the predominance of the German-Hungarian minority over all the other peoples in the Empire. . . . At a given moment, especially if Germany were disposed towards this, the warlike tendency might come out on top in Austria-Hungary, and its supporters are already pointing out that war is perhaps the only way out of insoluble internal difficulties.

G. N. Trubetskoi to Nicholas II, January 1914

Imperial Russia bore a special burden for the origin of the Great War. This was an idée fixe in both popular understanding and academic thought for half a century after the outbreak of that war. During the July Crisis, German policy attempted to manage the unfolding of events in such a way as to make German mobilization, when it came, appear to be the consequence of Russia's prior declaration. In the 1920s, German scholarship and diplomatic publication (no less so than French or even British) "documented" the crisis in terms that explained (i.e., cautiously justified) its entry into the war. The interests of the young and militant Soviet regime, however, lay in discrediting the actions of its tsarist and bourgeois predecessors. Soviet central archives made public (and German publishers eagerly translated and republished) many of the most compromising historical documents they held on St. Petersburg's policy and actions of the prewar period. A vast quantity of other documentation, however, remained hidden from independent examination until 1991.

The perspective of German scholarship at least up to 1961 was that "Russia, Austria-Hungary, and Germany – in that order – were to blame for the conflict," even though most non-German scholars, led by Luigi Albertini, had concluded since the early 1950s that the weight of responsibility lay with Germany.[1] In the 1970s, L. C. F. Turner believed that Russia's declaration of mobilization severely foreshortened possible diplomatic intervention from London, which might have changed Germany's course.[2] Indeed, a recent work of an Oxford historian revived the war-by-timetable charge against Russia, declaring that the origins (and thus the blame) lay with St. Petersburg "the moment [it] decided on full mobilization."[3] Human agency in the business of making war did not inform interpretations that favored the "slide-into-war" view. A certain fatalism or, better, human impotence in the face of mobilization systems and mechanisms had pushed the actions of decision makers from the stage of history: Every nation failed to prevent the war, but Russia failed first and most disastrously.[4] The concrete ways that Russia's leaders made their decisions during the crisis and the way their mobilization mechanisms actually operated in 1914 provide the counterpoint to such imaginative speculation and are the principal concerns of this chapter.

The choices Russian statesmen and general staff officers faced during the July Crisis were, paradoxically, simple and unaffected by decades of modernization, and yet clearly constrained by diplomatic and military choices made in preceding years. Statesmen, including Tsar Nicholas II, would struggle with the hour-by-hour development of the crisis, particularly after 24 July, without apparent reference to Russia's political and military crises of 1904–5, the national embarrassment of 1908, or the strategic sea-change of 1911–12. Yet each of these points, and many others that preceded and accompanied them, constituted a matrix in which decision making evolved in the Russian capital throughout the July Crisis. Fear of an outcome such as Russia faced three years later – revolutionary disintegration of the army and home front – did not guide the government's reaction to Austrian and German coercive diplomacy in mid-1914.

---

[1] Fritz Fischer, *Germany's Aims in the First World War* (New York, 1967), pp. x–xi. To the extent possible this chapter cites materials available in English and major European languages. See the Suggested Readings for additional literature.

[2] L. C. F. Turner, "The Russian Mobilization in 1914," in *The War Plans of the Great Powers, 1880–1914*, ed. Paul Kennedy (London, 1979), ch. 11.

[3] Niall Ferguson, *The Pity of War: Explaining World War I* (London, 1999), pp. 154–8.

[4] In describing the July Crisis, Ferguson, for instance, mentions neither the chief of Russian mobilization (Danilov) nor the chairman of Nicholas's Council of Ministers (Goremykin); War Minister Sukhomlinov receives passing mention, but only in connection with his dismissal in spring 1915.

Various groups of government servitors, and even individuals within those groupings who could influence the advice given to men with power in Russia, shared certain sentiments about Russia's interests and political means in mid-1914. Even as Russia's government stumbled from one decision to the next from 24 July onward, now excluding experts then consulting them and changing course, St. Petersburg's fundamental position – to resist Austro-German demands against Serbia – was consistent. There is little record of dissension among the men who formulated Russia's response to the Sarajevo assassination crisis.

It has been said that a salient characteristic of the political system known as Russian autocracy was its emphasis on unity of decision making: The tsar-autocrat authorized his servitors (ministers, generals) only grudgingly to exercise power independent of him and insisted they were subordinated to him alone. This was true in times of crisis or normalcy, the latter a rare circumstance indeed during imperial Russia's final two decades.[5] The isolation in which ministers and generals worked in St. Petersburg, without reference to those of their colleagues who also had some responsibility for Russia's actions (for instance, in matters of war and peace or foreign policy), hindered the operation of government as the July Crisis brought the empire closer to war. Although these generals and ministers carried out their responsibilities largely independent of each other, the declaration of war was the decision all had concluded would be necessary in the circumstances. Nicholas II had certainly worked as vigorously to avoid the development of coordinated cabinet government during his reign as he had to resist the growth of responsible parliamentary activity after 1905. Ultimately, however, this did not contribute to alleged fatal mistakes in July 1914. Russia's choices were by then stark, as they had been virtually from the turning point of the crisis on 24 July 1914.

Remarkably, any student of Russia's stepwise progress into the crisis from 24 July onward cannot help but be struck by the apparent absence of close communications between policy adjudicators and military officers responsible for mobilization. Foreign Minister S. D. Sazonov, a rather excitable man, communicated throughout the crisis with his emperor,

---

[5] The "crisis of autocracy" school is represented in the works of David MacLaren McDonald, *United Government and Foreign Policy in Russia, 1900–1914* (Cambridge, Mass., 1992); Andrew M. Verner, *The Crisis of Russian Autocracy: Nicholas II and the 1905 Revolution* (Princeton, 1990); and Frank William Wcislo, *Reforming Rural Russia: State, Local Society, and National Politics, 1855–1914* (Princeton, 1990).

ministerial colleagues, and War Ministry counterparts, only as necessary. Quartermaster-General Iu. N. Danilov, the officer directly responsible for mobilization preparations and intelligence collection on the General Staff, fretted nervously as the days passed in late July 1914, and yet had tarried weeks into the crisis before returning to the capital from the Caucasus. Once back in St. Petersburg, he operated with apparent detachment from both War Minister V. A. Sukhomlinov and Chief of General Staff N. N. Ianushkevich (neither with mobilization planning background). Choices made by these participants and others during the years leading up to 1914 had long before set the trajectory of their actions and Russia's policy choices that July. That segmentation of action and the knowledge on which it depended is the focus of the first portion of this chapter. Their convictions concerning Russia's failings as a great power, acquired during the decade between the Russo-Japanese War (1904–5) and the outbreak of the Great War, determined the framework in which they exercised judgment in July 1914, and constitutes the final part.

## Government and War Powers in Nicholas's Russia

Russia's General Staff and War Ministry had been making preparations for war with Prussia-Germany since 1870, if not earlier. Of this work, Russia's Foreign Ministry and tsar were largely oblivious. From about 1870 onward, key staff planners had considered both Germanic empires, Germany and Austria-Hungary, as an indivisible unit, a unitary threat, as far as Russian contingency planning was concerned. And from their strategic perspective, Otto von Bismarck's Reich was clearly the partner with the most vitality. But successfully checking the military bureaucratic center, the Finance Ministry sought to recover Russia's economic solvency following the Russo-Turkish War (1877–78), foremost by containing any rearmament and modernization programs promoted for Russia's land and naval forces. Strategic railroad construction (the arterial system of mobilization planning) likewise slowed dramatically between the 1880s and the new century. The General Staff had plans and ideas but few resources with which to see them through.

The diplomatic corps meanwhile attempted to weave consistency into foreign policy toward the rest of Europe and to promote the goals it perceived as Russia's vital interests, in particular that of finding accommodation with the new German empire. The Foreign Ministry, led by men with a real interest in bringing Russia and Germany into alignment, if not alliance, fashioned secret agreements that included Germany (the

Three Emperors' League and the Reinsurance Treaty) up to 1890. This, to a degree, aided Bismarck's ambition of binding Berlin, Vienna, and Petersburg so tightly that war among them would be impossible. The Russian Foreign Ministry, however, could find its policies undone (or superceded) by a sovereign who made his own diplomacy, by generals on far-flung frontiers who exercised "initiative" on their sovereign's behalf, by renegade ambassadors who received a nod from the court, or by powerful interests close to the throne with schemes to benefit themselves. At other times, the war and foreign ministries, locked in bureaucratic disagreements, paralyzed each other's attempts to strengthen the empire's position in Europe. Thus, the two ministries most directly responsible for Russia's security and international relations operated instead as divergent and competing power centers up to the outbreak of the Great War.

Russia, to be sure, possessed not a ministerial government but an autocracy. The tsar ultimately held the levers of government in his hands, delegating authority or seizing it, as his own sense of personal responsibility moved him. One of Nicholas's most competent finance ministers (and a man of towering ego), S. Iu. Witte (Vitte), wrote of this exotic model of state operation and authority: "The tsar is an autocrat because it depends upon him to impart action to the machine, but since the tsar is a man, he needs the machine for the administration of a country of 130 million subjects, as his human strength cannot replace the machine." Essentially, the Russian empire pursued policies on two bases: according to the tsar's expressed will, and according to the confidence (*doverie*) that he extended to a particular state servant to exercise independent authority on his behalf.[6]

Forces beside the tsar and his ministers also touched the course of state policy and security. Individuals of no official standing, who by reason of tradition or social station had access to the tsar, brought their opinions on policy into view; their real influence is difficult to credit in a concrete way, although the course of Russian policy on the eve of the Russo-Japanese War offers a striking exception.[7]

After 1905, yet another factor was present in the empire's policy making. Russia's educated liberal-left elite leveraged from Nicholas a limited

---

[6] McDonald, *United Government*, pp. 5–8 (quote from pp. 5–6). There was nothing to prevent the tsar from extending his "confidence" (and thus, authority) to someone with no standing in the ministerial government, which essentially bypassed the entire system of policy.

[7] Ibid., chs. 2 and 3.

imperial grant of representational government (through the body in which they served, the Duma) during the disturbances late in the war. The men who entered the first Duma added "public opinion" (i.e., their own class opinions) to the forces influencing the course of Russian policy. It was their control of funding of government programs, narrowly prescribed though that was under the Fundamental Laws, which gave them the medium through which to express alternative views on Russia's position in the world.[8]

This depiction of the men in the top positions of government during the regime's final decade suggests "class rule," but that impression is misleading, hiding their lack of real authority.[9] With war powers (and security and foreign policy matters in general) concentrated in the tsar's hands, and the heads of the military and diplomatic services subordinated directly to him, Nicholas II had in his Council of Ministers something less of a unified cabinet than a bureaucratic collegium. Nicholas trusted his government perhaps only slightly more than he did the Duma and expected it loyally to restrain its impulses toward independent decision-making initiatives. Even so, after the ruinous outcome of his foreign minister's secret 1908 contacts with Austria (for the Bosnian annexation crisis, see below), Nicholas conceded that his council (if only its chairman) needed at least passing acquaintance with the empire's foreign policy. During the First Balkan War (1912), a rash and potentially disastrous mobilization proposal put by the General Staff directly to Nicholas likewise proved the same thing true of strategic planning. In that instance, however, mobilization planners were not expected to have communications with Nicholas's ministers.

Thus, in July 1914, when Petersburg received Vienna's ultimatum to Serbia, Nicholas personally led his council in full session to discuss Russia's response and to advise him. This it did on the grave diplomatic

[8] D. C. B. Lieven, *Russia and the Origins of the First World War* (New York, 1983), pp. 119–38.

[9] Recent work on Russia's government has tended to steer clear of pointed characterization of the statesmen who kept the empire afloat. The description of Russia's "system" of government presented here, however, might incline contemporary students to expect great profit from prosopographical or psychological study of that cast. Certainly, vivid personal descriptions have brought to life some of the works on 1914, such as Turner, "Russian Mobilization." There is little reliable evidence, however, that the vanity of these statesmen and officers (Nicholas II excepted) clouded their judgment or aggravated their passions during the July Crisis. Well rehearsed in pursuing Russia's interests, they made the choices that they perceived as representing the state's vital interests, unfired by intemperate hatred of their rising enemies.

and political issues that Sarajevo presented – but completely in ignorance of what Russia's mobilization planners could deliver.[10] Dominic Lieven's assessment – that Nicholas "preferred heads of departments to confine themselves to their own specific spheres and that he regarded foreign affairs as being peculiarly the business of himself and those to whom he chose to turn for advice" – summarized the tsar's notion of proper ministerial government.[11]

Nicholas's Council of Ministers on the eve of war was led by I. L. Goremykin, a conservative servitor about whom few contemporaries have good things to say. A doyen of Russian history described Goremykin as "a cynical bureaucrat and a believer in the comforting theory that except the will of the tsar, nothing mattered in Russia and that representative institutions and public opinion were but 'nonsense' and 'idle talk.'"[12] Formerly head of Russia's police, Goremykin believed that "the whole government is the tsar alone, and what he will say is what we will execute, but as long as there is no clear instruction from him we must wait and be patient."[13] Passivity ensured that Goremykin would play little role during the July Crisis.

The man who controlled Russia's economy from 1906 to 1914, Finance Minister V. N. Kokovtsov, was both more powerful and important to governmental deliberations. A brilliant bureaucratic in-fighter who believed that the new Duma was an expendable element in government operation (even though its only real power was over budgets), he possessed Nicholas's complete confidence. His major achievement before the Great War was to bring Russia's foreign debt into line with its means to pay by following policies that helped spark rapid economic growth after about 1907. In achieving that, he cut investment in security to a dangerous (if not fatal) level.

The Foreign Ministry on the eve of the war was led by S. D. Sazonov. Rising rapidly from minor diplomatic posts to be foreign minister in 1910, Sazonov brought intelligence to the post, which he exercised relatively

---

[10] Lieven, *Russia and the Origins*, pp. 140–4, presents a masterful account of the council's debate on 24 July 1914.

[11] Ibid., p. 60.

[12] Michael T. Florinsky, *Russia: A History and an Interpretation*, 2 vols. (New York, 1953), vol. 2, p. 1190. A former premier noted that Goremykin "took no pains to conceal the little respect he had not only for the Duma but even for the Council of Ministers, considering the institution a useless innovation...." Quoted in McDonald, *United Government*, pp. 95–6.

[13] Characterization of Goremykin's philosophy by another chairman, P. A. Stolypin, quoted in McDonald, *United Government*, p. 99.

cautiously for the half-decade before 1914. Ill health restricted his effectiveness, as it did other ministerial appointees such as A. V. Krivoshein, minister of agriculture (who also played an important role in ministerial discussions during the July Crisis). Lack of a chancellery background, the traditional prerequisite to lead the ministry, hobbled Sazonov during his tenure. Indeed, his promotion was due to the influence of Nicholas's powerful premier at the time, P. A. Stolypin, who believed that Russia needed "twenty years of peace," the best guarantee of which would be détente with Germany and holding fast to the French alliance.[14] Stolypin nominated men of his choosing for most ministerial appointments, which gave him considerable control over policy but ultimately cost him Nicholas's confidence. His violent death in September 1911 removed that moderating hand from Russian foreign policy and left Sazonov to face the insubordination of Russia's overseas diplomatic representatives.[15]

In the military establishment, General Sukhomlinov was not Premier Stolypin's creature, but Nicholas's own man. His later reputation, shaped in the 1920s by military critics from both sides of Russia's Civil War, was of a shallow military thinker and the man who helped produce the disaster of Tannenberg in 1914.[16] He was also a sturdy bureaucratic infighter who eventually brought the General Staff and War Ministry under his centralized leadership in the years before the outbreak of the Great War. In July 1914, the Chief of General Staff was a well-regarded military academic, General N. N. Ianushkevich, an officer who knew little about core staff work (i.e., mobilization planning). He had little preparation for the challenges he faced in the third week of July 1914.

Ianushkevich's subordinate, General Iu. N. Danilov, on the other hand, epitomized the mobilization planning technician par excellence. He strongly advocated centralized control of war planning and strategy formulation, and proved to be an important actor in War Ministry

---

[14] Ibid., pp. 157–9.

[15] Stolypin was at once a brilliant modernizer (instituting an extraordinary attack on traditional peasant land tenure) and a deeply despised disciplinarian (for his bloody role in suppressing revolution in 1905). Right-wing conservative noblemen charged him with "grand vizierism" for his presumptive command of government, and hatched political conspiracies against him. Revolutionaries made repeated attempts on his life, including a bombing in August 1906 that killed family members and numerous servants. His moral stature grew in the wake of the attack, thanks to his equanimity and control during the incident.

[16] The so-called Sukhomlinov Effect – that the side whose generals are most opulently dressed will lose the war – encapsulated the derisive evaluation of the war minister, not entirely with justification.

deliberations in July 1914, once the minister and chief of staff recognized their own ignorance of Russia's mobilization capacity.

Superficially, these men shared the characteristics of their social class, the Russian noble educated elite. What mattered to their actions, however, during the denouement of the July Crisis was their shared experience of the preceding decade. They had together passed through Russia's military humiliation, revolutionary upheaval, and economic weakness after 1904 and believed that Russia's great power status would depend on its ability to counter or divert the Austro-German challenge in central and southeastern Europe.

## Consequences of the Russo-Japanese War

Embarrassment abroad and enfeeblement at home induced Emperor Nicholas II, autocrat of Russia, to accept the demands from Russia's politically restive liberal elites for an active role in governing. As a result, Russia received its first hesitant, truncated representative political institutions in the aftermath of the East Asian war and accompanying domestic unrest. Lacking traditions of self-government, political parties, or experience of compromise politics, the men who ushered Russia into the family of states with representative government faced a particularly challenging task: to find a workable division of authority between themselves (in the Duma) and their sovereign. Nicholas's October 1905 Manifesto (prepared by his former finance minister, Witte) formed the constitutional basis for the Fundamental Laws, issued in April 1906, which reinforced the tsar's formidable power over legislation and gave him absolute power over all issues of national security.[17]

Russia's new constitutional framework posited various changes in the functioning of the state, touching civil rights, press freedom, police powers, and the prerogatives of the new Duma. Imperial security and war powers remained securely and solely in Nicholas's hands: He held supreme command over the armed forces and direction of Russian diplomacy (insofar as he was interested in exercising those areas). The Duma's powers in the area of security were restricted to approval of military budgets (which it did not, in any event, have the authority to reject) and the right to question ministers about those budgets. Especially after 1907, some Duma members found novel ways to influence military matters by

---

[17] Russia's transition to constitutional government is described in numerous works, including Florinsky, *Russia*, vol. 2, ch. 40.

forming confidential alliances with powerful War Ministry officials. Young reformist military officers also attempted to skirt ministry resistance to their schemes by conspiring with Duma confederates. In the end, however, the emperor (or those in whom he placed his confidence) made Russian foreign policy and decided issues of war and peace. So it was in July 1914. Nicholas asserted his imperial and constitutional prerogatives vigorously, though not necessarily consistently nor in the best interest of his state. As the October Manifesto put the issue of subordination:

[Those] matters relating … to the defense of the state and to external policy are submitted to the Council of Ministers where there is an Imperial command to this effect, when the heads of the relevant departments see this as necessary, or when the affairs in question concern other departments.[18]

Thus, the ministers of war, navy, and foreign affairs reported directly to the tsar, and they received instructions the same way, usually without reference to their council colleagues or the chairman. As long as Nicholas's confidence rested with just one man (ideally, the chairman of his Council of Ministers), then all state policy was unified in that man. If, however, Nicholas's trust extended to more than one, Russia's policies could go badly astray, as they had in 1903 before the East Asian war and as they would again before the 1908 and 1912 Balkan crises.

In the Russo-Japanese War, Russia suffered 400,000 casualties, lost two of its three fleets, denuded its western frontier fortifications of troops and armaments (fortunately, with German and Austro-Hungarian assurances to remain sympathetically neutral), and had seen its army repeatedly bloodied at the hands of "Asiatic inferiors." Combat leadership at unit level, though fiercely courageous, was unimaginative, inflexible, and prone to vast wastage of lives and material; army operational and strategic direction was generally beyond incompetent. Mobilization and logistical support of armies 5,000 miles from their European bases exceeded in complexity anything staff planners had attempted before. In spite of terrible losses, the Russian army in East Asia had risen by 1905 to the size necessary to defeat Japanese forces there, just as the Japanese army was approaching exhaustion. However, the human cost and duration of that reinforcement exceeded the patience of the nation. The war was brought to a halt by revolutionary action, both at home and in the army strung out along the Trans-Siberian railroad line from the Urals to the Pacific.

---

[18] Article 14, Law of 19 October 1905 [old style], quoted in Lieven, *Russia and the Origins*, p. 59.

The Finance Ministry's calculation of extraordinary outlays due to the war was in its own way even more disturbing. The empire's twenty-month tangle with Japan and subsequent demobilization had cost more than 3 billion rubles – more than the combined ordinary outlays for the war and navy ministries from 1900 to 1905, inclusive. The losses in naval hardware alone cost another 250 million rubles. Former Finance Minister Witte, whom Nicholas had dismissed on the eve of the war, concluded in 1907 that the war had "completely destroyed the entire economic organism of the country."[19] Battlefield failure and fiscal impoverishment shattered Imperial Russia's international standing as a great power, humbled its ruling elite, burdened the treasury with huge debts to German and French financiers, and encouraged social elements eager to overturn the lot. From the point of view of national security, the most serious casualty was Russia's liquidity, and with the loss of that, its ability to repair and modernize its defenses.

Rank inefficiencies such as had characterized the state's administration of its late war prompted a series of changes in security decision making. Nicholas's concern for fundamental battlefield performance was closely linked to his own criticism of the highest levels of national leadership. Nicholas experimented with two reforms that he supposed would address the array of military malfunctions. And the strictly military issues were indeed numerous. Army doctrine, standing in the shadow of decades-old institutional rivalries, had failed to produce coordinated infantry and artillery operations; generals commanding defensive operations had no knowledge of military engineering; and the army and navy so distrusted each other that their plans for operations made no reference to their common objectives. Most important, Nicholas and his General Staff and army leadership understood that the recent bloodletting would almost certainly characterize Russia's next war as well, and that Japan had succeeded in spite of horrendous losses because of the individual national convictions of each soldier.

To strengthen the influence and authority of the army's war planning apparatus to deal with these problems, Nicholas liberated the General

---

[19] Peter Gatrell, *Government, Industry and Rearmament in Russia, 1900–1914: The Last Argument of Tsarism* (Cambridge, 1994), Witte quote: p. 66; ordinary/extraordinary expenditures: pp. 92 and 140, table 3.1; William C. Fuller, Jr., *Strategy and Power in Russia 1600–1945* (New York, 1992), pp. 402–7, for the interlocking crises produced by military reversals, domestic unrest, fiscal exhaustion, and military-administrative incompetence.

Staff's war planning (intelligence and mobilization) parts from War Ministry control, consolidated them as the Main Directorate of the General Staff (known by its awkward initials, GUGSh), and subordinated this new organization to himself.[20] He also created in 1905 a Council of State Defense (GSO) to fashion a unified security policy for the empire. The new organization was supposed to reconcile the competing strategies and the incompatible funding priorities they entailed, and to provide central leadership in matters of national security. GSO membership consisted of the war and navy ministers, the chiefs of the general and naval staffs, and the grand dukes who ran the main army inspectorates (cavalry and artillery), under the chairmanship of the emperor's uncle, Nikolai Nikolaevich, an astute reformer in his own right and an advocate of army modernization.[21]

Russia's immediate security challenge was to restore its military forces. Arsenals and units across the western front had been stripped of everything they had: small arms, automatic weapons, stocks of ammunition, artillery and shells, horses, uniforms, and personnel equipment. Refurbishment of the army, however, was constrained by three considerations. First, mutiny within the ranks that lasted through 1906, and tied down forces in the countryside somewhat longer, occupied very large numbers of army units in unpleasant internal policing actions. Second, national bankruptcy brought on by the war allowed the new finance minister, V. N. Kokovtsov, who enjoyed the particular confidence of the tsar, to limit the War Ministry's spending as long as he thought Russia's fiscal liquidity was in danger. Finally, Russia's alliance partner, France, demanded first attention to its strategic objectives, which simply was not possible. For instance, plans for the peacetime dispersal of army regiments throughout European Russia, in contrast to their prewar concentration in agriculturally weak Poland, could save the state vast sums in annual upkeep of men and horses. It would also, however, cripple Russia's capacity to mobilize rapidly against Germany (and Austria-Hungary) in accordance with the French agreement. Before the GSO could decide on whether to

---

[20] The Main Directorate possessed all the elements usually associated with the Prussian paradigm of General Staff responsibility – mobilization planning, intelligence collection, etc. – and some others as well.

[21] Fuller, *Strategy and Power*, pp. 408–9; Bruce W. Menning, *Bayonets before Bullets: The Imperial Russian Army, 1861–1914* (Bloomington, Ind., 1992), pp. 217–18; M. Perrins, "The Council for State Defense, 1905–1909: A Study in Russian Bureaucratic Politics," *Slavonic and East European Review* 58 (1980): 370–98.

rebuild the army or the navy – for Russia could not afford to do both after 1905 – it needed a strategic consensus, approved by the tsar, on just how Russia would face the world.[22]

Thus, not mere penury crippled Russia's reinstatement as a respectable great power. With their ministries unable to prioritize even their own spending after 1905, the army and navy found their return to readiness retarded for half a decade and more. This followed logically from the shifting, unguided political process that determined strategic priorities during Nicholas's reign, but factions within the officer corps contributed also. The officers who led the General Staff after the Russo-Japanese War were themselves divided between two groups. On the one side were those who, like their predecessors, saw Germany and Austria-Hungary as the only serious security threat to Russia.[23] On the other were officers who directed their attention toward Asia in spite of Russia's recent experiences there. After the Russo-Japanese War, some believed that in fact Japan posed a more serious threat to Russia than did any European power. One prominent statesman imagined circumstances in which Japanese forces, surging out of Manchuria, would sever the Trans-Siberian Railroad and detach Vladivostok and the Pacific maritime from Russia. Russia's eastern frontier would then rest on Lake Baikal.[24] Naturally, senior officers with responsibility for Russia's East Asian security joined those "westerners" in the officer corps who were converted to an eastern disposition by the recent humiliation in Manchuria.

Russia's turn to the East had very long antecedents, even though the overriding importance of the western frontier had been an article of faith in strategic planning for more than forty years. The General Staff had seventy years of engagement around the entire Asian periphery, and

---

[22] Menning, *Bayonet before Bullets*, pp. 218–21, 238–40. William C. Fuller, Jr., *Civil-Military Conflict in Imperial Russia, 1881–1914* (Princeton, 1985), pp. 133ff., examines the strain that internal policing imposed on all military reform and readiness after 1905; in 1906 the army was ordered to deploy company-sized units in over 15,000 actions against peasant unrest. Also, John Bushnell, *Mutiny amid Repression: Russian Soldiers in the Revolution of 1905–1906* (Bloomington, Ind., 1985), details the involvement of army troops in the disintegration of civil order during and immediately after the Russo-Japanese War.

[23] See the discussion in David Alan Rich, *The Tsar's Colonels: Professionalism, Strategy, and Subversion in Late Imperial Russia* (Cambridge, Mass., 1998), pp. 151–65, 194ff.

[24] A. A. Abaza, an elder statesman and member of the Council of State who had joined A. M. Bezobrazov in promoting the aggressive penetration of Manchuria and northern Korea just before the Russo-Japanese War, was hardly a disinterested observer. For his memorandum, see Fuller, *Strategy and Power*, p. 423. Japanese forces subsequently occupied Russian territory as far west as Lake Baikal during the Civil War (1918).

its members, such as the dashing Colonels N. M. Przhevalskii and Karl Mannerheim (future president of independent Finland) and scores of others, had undertaken missions of exploration, ethnographic observation, and geographic and cartographic surveying from the Tienshan to Manchuria since the 1840s.[25] Such men eagerly played the "great game" with their English counterparts across the Hindu Kush, Persia, and anywhere else that was not Europe (although that game's allure faded after the 1907 colonial agreement with Britain, aimed precisely at defusing those peripheral tensions). Indeed, one of the fissures that defined Russian educated society divided those with western-oriented values from others, categorized loosely with conservative Slavophiles and the later pan-Slavs, who saw brighter prospects in Russia's East and Central Asian spheres. Military men holding the latter prejudice had some ascendancy in the War Ministry and General Staff after 1905, when postwar contraction coincided with political and strategic disarray. These tensions were not finally resolved until the strategic reorientation of 1911–12 and the military rebuilding programs of 1912–14 were begun.

The two orientations, westward- or eastward-looking, demanded quite different military tools. An active eastern policy required a large, modern, effective blue-water navy (such as Russia's premier flotilla, the Baltic fleet, which in 1905 lay at the bottom of Tsushima Strait) that would have to be able to face the Imperial Japanese Navy and squadrons from Germany, the United States, and clearly the Royal Navy as well. It would not require an expensive system of fortresses in Poland or an enormous field army equipped to take the fight to the Germanic powers. The maritime strategy would encompass reconstruction of the Pacific and Baltic fleets and creation of a new Black Sea squadron, altogether accounting for dozens of battleships, scores of destroyers, and large numbers of submarines.[26] Such an orientation would necessarily have run counter to Great Britain's and Japan's interests and would have brought Russia

[25] For a highly readable work on Russian military engagement in East Asia, and on Przhevalskii in particular, see Dave Schimmelpenninck van der Oye, "Ex Oriente Lux: Ideologies of Empire and Russia's Far East, 1895–1904," Ph.D. dissertation, Yale University, 1997. See also the observations in David Alan Rich, "Imperialism, Reform and Strategy: Russian Military Statistics, 1840–1880," *Slavonic and East European Review* 74 (October 1996): 621–39.
[26] The commissioning of HMS *Dreadnought* in 1906 further burdened Russia's naval finance plans by rendering obsolete the empire's few surviving capital vessels and raising exponentially the cost of their replacement with state-of-the-art hulls. The best works on this subject are in Russian, foremost the studies of L. G. Beskrovnyi, well known to specialists in the field. See the discussion in Fuller, *Strategy and Power*, p. 410.

and the Central Powers onto better terms. The traditional western orientation, on the other hand, would demand a massive program of replacement and modernization of small arms, automatic weapons, and
artillery; the reorganization of field units; rapid and dense development
of strategic railroad lines; the stockpiling of war reserve material; and perhaps a very expensive program of modernization of the citadel fortresses
along the Vistula. In 1906, Russia's fundamental international alignments
and relationships predicated only the latter, with Russia allied to France
for confrontation with Germany. Each strategy had its price, and the
combined cost of reconstruction along both lines – new fleets and army
rearmament – was beyond the capacity of the Russian state, economy, and
people.[27]

The tsar's GSO, formed to decide fundamental issues of national security such as these, was incapable of performing that role. Indeed, it became
the bureaucratic center of "interest group politics run amok," as historian William C. Fuller, Jr., has put it. Finance Minister Kokovtsov cleverly
played off the GSO's priorities against other ministerial and General Staff
agendas and blocked funding for any military reforms he thought too expensive. Under the reformist leadership of Nikolai Nikolaevich, GSO had
the temerity to attempt to block the tsar's pet project, construction of a
new navy, a split into which the Finance Ministry drove a very big wedge
to prevent much spending at all until 1908.[28] On the other hand, the
council culled the officer corps vigorously of dead wood: By 1907, some
7,000 "unsuitable and superannuated" officers had been pensioned off,
making room for promotion of younger men whose Manchurian service
had not discredited them.[29]

The independent war planning apparatus (GUGSh) that Nicholas had
set up in June 1905 proved to be a misguided reform, as well. Separation
of those elements from War Ministry control merely encouraged a breakdown in cooperation between them and caused pointless duplication of
effort and unnecessary expense. The War Ministry, GUGSh, and the GSO
were locked in a perpetual struggle for influence over matters of strategic importance. By the turn of 1909, both "reformist" institutions ceased

---

[27] Gatrell, *Government, Industry, and Rearmament*, pp. 95–102, traces the limitations on
decision making that fiscal constraints placed on GSO and the military ministries, particularly in 1906–7.

[28] Ibid., pp. 125–38.

[29] Bruce Menning, "Mukden to Tannenberg: Defeat to Defeat, 1905–1914," in *The Military
History of Imperial Russia*, ed. Frederick Kagan and Robin Higham (New York, 2001),
ch. 10.

operation: Nicholas disbanded the GSO and reincorporated GUGSh into the War Ministry.[30] The appointment of Sukhomlinov, formerly commander of the vital Kiev Military District and a western-oriented officer, as war minister in early 1909 completed the postwar reorganization of strategy-making organizations in the Russian army.[31]

Organizational paralysis in GUGSh and GSO reached their climax at precisely the time that Russia's relations with the Central Powers cast the entire basis for imperial security – the Franco-Russian military agreement – into doubt. In September 1908 Foreign Minister A. P. Izvol'skii learned that Vienna intended to annex Bosnia-Herzegovina, the south Slavic provinces in the western Balkans that it had administered under the terms of the 1878 Treaty of Berlin. At a secret meeting with his Austrian counterpart, Izvol'skii attempted to secure something profitable for Russia that it had neither the power nor right to demand. He told Foreign Minister Count Alois Aehrenthal that in exchange for Russia's assent to the annexation, Austria-Hungary must commit itself to support Russia in revocation of the Turkish Straits clauses of the 1878 Berlin treaty, by which that passage was closed to the warships of any power. Izvol'skii undertook these negotiations with the secret authorization of the tsar – just the sort of disunity of government that Nicholas found appealing. Izvol'skii's agreement involved leaving to their own devices the Balkan south Slavs, most particularly the Serbs, who had the strongest national interest in opposing any extension of influence in the peninsula by Austria. (See Chapter 4 for further discussion of Austria's Balkan interests after 1908.)

The whole plan blew up in October, when Aehrenthal prematurely announced the annexation. Izvol'skii, without time to prepare, now faced domestic Russian outrage over his duplicitous dealings. In the Council of Ministers, the ministers of war, marine, finance, and interior denounced Izvol'skii and his initiative. A Russian threat of war to prevent the Austrian annexation was out of the question, the war minister said, because the army could not even defend the western frontier against invasion. Militarily, the outcome would depend on the reaction of Russia's and Austria's allies. In the event, France did not consider itself bound to assist Russia militarily in the embarrassing fiasco that Izvol'skii's policy had produced

[30] Menning, *Bayonets before Bullets*, pp. 218–21.
[31] See Menning, "Mukden to Tannenberg," for a nuanced biographic characterization of Sukhomlinov, an officer whose reputation has suffered considerably since 1914, and who will undoubtedly benefit from balanced reconsideration of his decision making between 1909 and 1914.

(as he and the rest of the government knew); Petersburg would find no assistance there. The War Ministry confirmed that from mid-1908, Austrian forces had been concentrating on the border with Serbia and in Austrian Galicia; alarming news came from the Russian military attaché in Vienna that German forces were ready to take up positions beside Austrian units in Galicia to keep Russia in check. When Berlin cast its lot with Vienna, St. Petersburg lost whatever hope it may have had of bullying its way into a graceful exit. Russia acquiesced to Germany's March 1909 ultimatum, accepted Austria's new annexations, and disassociated itself from Serbian objections.

Russia's humiliation was a by-product of dysfunctional government: If Izvol'skii had vetted his plan with council colleagues, he might have learned sooner of the army's precarious condition and the considerable risks his demarché entailed. (The shoe was on the other ministerial foot in 1912, when a naive and risky mobilization plan already presented to the tsar produced shock in the council when Nicholas brought it to his assembled ministers' attention.)[32] In 1908, a council discussion would at least have forced Izvol'skii to reconcile his hard-headed opinion of Russia's obligations to its south Slav "cousins" with those public sentiments that identified Russia's interests with those of the pan-Slavs. While objectively Russia had little direct national interest in the fate of the south Slavs per se, and Izvol'skii was right to place the state's interest in the status of the Turkish Straits ahead of such sentiment, the scheme of "buying" something for nothing and of expecting to achieve a political triumph over Austria in the bargain was naive at best. Russian attitudes toward the Germanic powers never improved after the Bosnian retreat, and suspicion reappeared dramatically in 1913–14.

The Bosnian retreat reduced Russia's European policy alternatives to two. Petersburg could recognize German preeminence and come to terms with Berlin at the possible expense of its French alliance, and activate Germany to restrain Austria from further Balkan adventures. Or Russia could cleave more closely to France (and Britain) in the expectation of nudging their policies toward the Ottoman Empire and the Balkans closer to its own. Petersburg explored first the Berlin course (to the great satisfaction of Germanophiles such as the conservative Petr Durnovo), then swung decisively back to its alliance orientation.

---

[32] Turner, "Russian Mobilization," pp. 253–4. Turner's inability to use Russian-language sources and the inaccessibility of archival materials at the time he prepared his essay limit its usefulness.

A new government in Berlin under Chancellor Theobald von Bethmann Hollweg seemed to offer hope of improvement in relations, and in
November 1910, the tsar and Foreign Minister Sazonov visited Wilhelm II
and his chancellor in Germany. In their final agreement, Russia dropped
objections to German plans for the Berlin-to-Baghdad railroad. Bethmann
promised Sazonov that Berlin would not participate in any future Austrian
"aggressive posturing" in the Balkans, a vow he reiterated two years later
at another imperial meeting.

The Russian press (and hence some foreign military attachés assigned
to Russia) made much of Russia's "historic mission" in the Balkans (and
to a lesser extent, in the Near East). Modern historians likewise have
attended closely to the pan-Slavic impetus behind Russian policy, particularly from the 1860s onward.[33] Indeed, many segments of Russian
educated opinion found assurance in popular slogans about unity among
all Slavs in the face of the "German danger." The right-wing press, some
officers in army Guards and line regiments, aristocratic salon society in
Petersburg and especially Moscow, certain branches of the imperial family, and some industrialists all shared sentimental (if patronizing) views
about the "small" Slavic peoples.

To assert, however, that any of those elements exercised influence over
government policy toward the Balkans – for instance, leading to the
1877–78 Russo-Turkish War, as is frequently postulated – simply ignores
the evidence of how policy was made in St. Petersburg. Even when influential personages with strong pan-Slavic ideas commanded imperial
confidence, there was little they could do to direct the course of policy
toward the Balkan states. Both the General Staff and Foreign Ministry
had entire sections of experts devoted to formulating plans and policy
toward the peninsula. Furthermore, Russia's course (like those of Austria
and other great powers) was tangled in the dense thicket of international
guarantees of Ottoman integrity and the Balkan status quo that had developed since the Münchengrätz Agreements (1833), if not before.[34] Finally,
Russia was a toothless power after 1905, unable to raise the funds to

[33] Dietrich Geyer, *Russian Imperialism: The Interaction of Domestic and Foreign Policy,
1869–1914* (New Haven, 1987), has proposed a dramatic interpretation of Russian
foreign policy as the reflection of "extra-governmental forces" such as the right-wing
nationalist press and certain industrial and elite circles that frolicked in the waters of
Slavic unity.

[34] By two of the three Münchengrätz agreements, Austria and Russia pledged to sustain the
status quo in regard to the Ottoman Empire and their adjacent parts of Poland. A. J. P.
Taylor, *The Struggle for Mastery in Europe 1848–1918* (Oxford, 1954), pp. 2–3.

rebuild its armed forces, much less settle on how they should look. That all changed with the beginning of an economic boom and resolution of the policy struggles that had occupied the War Ministry and foreign policy establishment.

## Military Reformation and the Great Program

In spite of Foreign Ministry agreement with Britain and Japan in 1907 that established workable *modi vivendi* among the powers in Asia, the chief of GUGSh, General A. A. Palitsyn, wrote in early 1908:

Our [army] deployment was developed with war with the powers of the Triple Alliance in mind and the need, resulting from this, for the swift concentration of our troops on the western frontiers. But after the distribution of forces had already taken form there arose in the Far East a terrible military power which could open hostilities against us at any minute.[35]

Palitsyn, with the assistance of Major-General M. V. Alekseev (army over-quartermaster, or head of mobilization and intelligence), and Colonel S. K. Dobrorol'skii (GUGSh's chief mobilization technician), and the chiefs of staff of the western military districts (Warsaw, Kiev, and Vilna) crafted Mobilization Schedule No. 18. That plan held the army to strictly defensive dispositions during the first phase of war with the Central Powers, and shifted to active operations only when forces were fully mobilized and concentrated. Palitsyn argued to Grand Duke Nikolai Nikolaevich that the persistent danger in East Asia necessitated this fundamentally defensive strategy and its concomitant peacetime army deployment: the transfer of 138 battalions from the western military districts to the central and eastern parts of the empire, not a strategic deployment intended to reassure Russia's ally, France.[36]

Until about 1911, Russia's formal relations with France evolved little, from the perspective of the two states' conventions and agreements. When viewed through the reporting of Colonel V. P. Lazarev, Russia's military attaché in Paris to the General Staff in Petersburg, however, a fundamental reorientation of Russia's strategic perspective was taking shape during the previous four years. As early as summer 1907, Lazarev reported "stubborn" French positions on various Baltic issues of interest to Russia. This resistance, in his view, reflected "if not the subscription,

---

[35] Quoted in Fuller, *Strategy and Power*, p. 425.
[36] Menning, *Bayonets before Bullets*, pp. 220–1, 238–40. Also, Menning, "Mukden to Tannenberg."

then at least the preparations for a convention and a plan of combined Anglo-French action in the event of war with Germany. Moreover, some signs point toward the conclusion that our agreement with France has been communicated to the English government." Lazarev's intelligence reports also noted "secret Anglo-French discussions" that had begun in April 1905 and continued from January to March 1906 on the question of military cooperation between London and Paris. By late 1906, he continued, it was clear that the German army was not strong enough to carry off its planned swing through Belgium, because "a British corps" would land on the Channel coast around Ostend and threaten the entire German right flank.[37] Palitsyn passed the military attaché's August 1907 report on these matters to Nicholas.

Within a year of his arrival in Paris, the military attaché reported (as the Bosnian annexation crisis reached its climax) that important segments of France's political and, especially, financial leadership were agitating for an agreement with Germany to secure those two states' neutrality in the event of an Austrian-Russian war (the aim being to protect the Third Republic's strategic and investment interests).[38] Russia and France, however, continued their previous course and began intensive exchanges of staff officers and intelligence information. The cooperation led, on 16 July 1912, to agreements formalizing Franco-Russian military and naval cooperation and coordination. The next month, French military negotiators made their priority quite clear to the Russian side: strategic railroad construction from the Russian interior to the army's assembly points along the German frontier.

Strategic railroads had preoccupied mobilization planners in Petersburg from 1868 onward. But Russia's two handicaps – penury and vast spaces – rendered its investments in mobilization lines perpetually insufficient. By the turn of the century, Russian railroad mileage exceeded that of every other European power (only the United States possessed greater mileage), even as the opening of the Trans-Siberian system was drawing

---

[37] Lazarev served in Paris from March 1901 to May 1908. For his report of August 1907 and discussion of Anglo-French planning coordination of 5 October 1906, see: E. Yu. Sergeev and R. A. Ulunian, *Ne Podlezhit' oglashenii: Voennye agenty Rossiiskoj imperii v Evrope 1900–1914 gg.* (Moscow, 1999), pp. 142–3.

[38] Colonel G. I. Nositz succeeded Lazarev in late summer 1908. Previously an attaché assigned to Berlin, Nositz then served in Paris between August 1908 and March 1912. His reporting on French mobilization preparations, politics, and labor conditions, if tinted with strong anti-Masonic and even anti-Semitic tones, was crucial to Petersburg's understanding of evolving Franco-British military relations. See Sergeev and Ulunian, *Ne Podlezhit' oglashenii*, pp. 144–50.

off greater and greater amounts of development capital. By 1910, Russia could boast only ten lines from the interior into the frontier Warsaw Military District, and only six of those were double-tracked. This severely restricted the number of troop trains per day that could be moved to the border zone upon mobilization. France's concerns were justified, in view of their general knowledge of the Schlieffen Plan. Yet by April 1913, Sukhomlinov could still tell Kokovtsov that he lacked 4,000 locomotives and 3,900 miles of track necessary to meet Russia's and France's mobilization goals.[39]

The bright forty-three-year-old staff planner, Major-General Danilov, and Colonel Dobrorol'skii consumed the intelligence information coming from their French counterparts.[40] Danilov was a strong proponent of the virtues of centralized control of war planning, in contrast to Palitsyn, who showed deference to military district staffs. They concluded by late 1910 that Franco-British "coordination" in a war with Germany was virtually an accomplished fact: They presumed a combined Russian-French-British alliance in the event of general war on the Continent and began reworking Russia's mobilization plans accordingly.[41]

Nicholas dismissed Palitsyn in November 1908 before the defensive Alekseev/Palitsyn strategy could mature, and placed Sukhomlinov at the head of GUGSh. Four months later, Sukhomlinov also took over as war minister, resubordinated the independent General Staff to the War Ministry (with Nicholas's approval), and elevated Danilov to quartermaster-general. By December 1909, Sukhomlinov and Danilov had adopted parts of the Alekseev/Palitsyn plan (to shift many regiments out of Poland to interior dispositions) as their own.[42] Historians have

---

[39] A useful if dated overview of Russia's strategic railroad dilemma is D. N. Collins, "The Franco-Russian Alliance and Russian Railways, 1891–1914," *Historical Journal* 16 (1973): 777–88. Strategic and economic dimensions are precisely discussed in Fuller, *Strategy and Power*, pp. 338–42, 362, 380–1, 439–40. On origins of Russian awareness of railroads' significance and the frustration of building plans: Rich, *Tsar's Colonels*, pp. 78–86, 94–103.

[40] As first over-quartermaster (*Ober-kvartirmeistr*), Danilov was both chief of the general staff's operations department and head of military intelligence, which oversaw the 5th Department (*Deloproizvodstvo*), "Intelligence"; Sergeev and Ulunian, *Ne Podlezhit' oglashenii*, p. 139.

[41] I am grateful to Bruce Menning for this insight, which he elaborates in "Mukden to Tannenberg." The connection between Anglo-French discussions and a reorientation in Russia's plans around the time of the Agadir crisis is perceived (vaguely) by Turner, "Russian Mobilization," p. 252.

[42] Other elements of Sukhomlinov's plan, contributed by Danilov and other technicians involved in strategic planning, included abandonment of Russia's fortress system (a costly

disagreed on whether a search for greater strategic flexibility to contain future threats from Japan or a lingering concern for domestic order and development (through reducing of military expense, depriving the "Poles and Jews" of army expenditures in Poland, and distributing army units more evenly among the population) motivated the strategic redeployment plan.[43] Palitsyn and Sukhomlinov both raised such justifications. In any case, the 1910 mobilization schedule (designated No. 19) placed greater emphasis on depth of deployment in the west and transferred some 150,000 troops and almost 400 additional artillery pieces from Siberian military districts for concentration in the west. Mobilization in any future war with the Central Powers would occur in the Russian heartland, and forces would then be transported for concentration and battle. This strategy could not satisfy France's persistent demand for some sort of Russian offensive action against Germany within two weeks of declaration of mobilization, simply because Russia did not have the railroads to carry it out quickly. If Schedule No. 19 were implemented, Russia would be able to take the fight into Prussia on about the twentieth day after declaration of general mobilization (M+20). Russian statesmen soon felt the stinging reproof of the French press, politicians, and officers of the État Major (as the French General Staff was called) for its alleged appeasement of Germany and neglect of its alliance obligations.[44]

Sukhomlinov's mobilization Schedule No. 19 (also called the "Danilov plan" or the "1910 Plan") anticipated concentration of the mass of Russia's active army in the relative safety of northern Belarus (east of the Bug River and north of the Pripet Marshes). There, it would be less exposed to disruption during the chaos of mobilization than it would have faced if deployed along the Vistula River in Poland. After units from

and ultimately useless drain on fiscal resources), and advocacy of foresaking additional battleships in favor of intense further railroad network construction and building of submarines, torpedo boats, and aircraft.

[43] Fuller, *Strategy and Power*, pp. 423–33, credits the significance of strategic considerations; Menning, *Bayonets before Bullets*, pp. 238–40, argues that although Russian planners felt nervous about the Empire's eastern exposure, they ultimately believed that Germany posed the greatest threat. The subsequent 1910 redeployment plan to move units from that frontier reflected a more nuanced sense of the balance between offensive and defensive possibilities that derived from its sophisticated military-theoretical thinking on force, mass, space, and time in modern warfare.

[44] Menning, *Bayonets before Bullets*, pp. 240–1. Although the Russians went to lengths to hide the implications of Schedule No. 19 from their ally, French staff officers appear to have been especially well informed of Palitsyn's and Sukhomlinov's "new direction." See Pertti Luntinen, *French Information on the Russian War Plans, 1880–1914* (Helsinki, 1984), ch. 5.

the general reserve arrived from central Russia, the force would drive northward, into the open flank of an anticipated German offensive toward Petersburg. The risks were huge, for the new schedule simply could not account for the additional time needed to move units from the Volga River and Siberia back to the western part of European Russia. In that time, the war might already be lost.[45]

In 1912, new and much better intelligence about Anglo-French military coordination, observation of British behavior during the 1911 Agadir crisis, intense lobbying by the commanders and planning staffs of the western frontier military districts (Warsaw, Vilna, and Kiev), as well as objections from defense circles in the Duma led the General Staff to modify the strategic precepts of Schedule No. 19. No less important, Russia had entered a period of intense economic expansion and growth around 1908, and Finance Minister Kokovtsov's economies and strictures were no longer sustainable on fiscal grounds.

Danilov shifted Russia's mobilization planning to favor a muscular strategy, "to go over to the offensive against the armed forces of Germany and Austria-Hungary with the objective of taking the war into their territory." Nicholas signed the plan into effect in May 1912. Designated "Mobilization Schedule No. 19 (Revised)," the plan had two alternatives. Variant "A" envisaged placing the army's mass against Austrian Galicia, Variant "G" against Germany. Under "A," two armies of twenty-nine divisions would attack into East Prussia to seize an "assembly area for future operations." At the same time, four armies (forty-five divisions) would fall on Galicia, strike across the Carpathian Mountains, and spread out across the Hungarian Plain. In contrast, under Variant "G," the armies on the northeast front were almost doubled (to forty-three divisions), while the southwestern armies, comprised thirty-one divisions, would screen the rear of the advance into Prussia.[46] The presumption

---

[45] Although intelligence from the Austrian General Staff "was as abundant as ever" (in Fuller's words), Russia's general staff remained essentially blind to the shape of German strategy. Observing Germany's summer maneuvers, mobilization planners in Petersburg could gauge how quickly Germany might mobilize and concentrate its armies for operations, but the shape those operations would take was largely inscrutable. Fuller, *Strategy and Power*, p. 441.

[46] The evolution of the Russian mobilization schedule from the 1880s forward, an important but tedious topic, is described in numerous, sometimes contradictory accounts. See, e.g., S. K. Dobrorol'skii, *Mobilizatsiia Russkoi armii v 1914 godu. Podgotovka i vypolnenie po materialam Voenno-Istoricheskogo arkhiva* (Moscow, 1929), part 1 (esp. pp. 63–81); Menning, *Bayonets before Bullets*, ch. 7 (quotes here from pp. 242–3); Fuller, *Strategy and Power*, ch. 9; and Rich, *Tsar's Colonels*, ch. 7.

of British subscription to the Franco-Russian alignment liberated Russia (prematurely) to consider its strategic dilemmas in central Europe resolved.[47]

Any lingering fears of Japanese intentions toward Russia's East Asian territory also receded as far more serious troubles appeared in Europe and the Ottoman Empire. In early 1912, naively encouraging an anti-Austrian defensive league among the Bulgarians, Serbs, and later Greeks, Russia discovered that an alliance it had encouraged – the Balkan League – possessed aggressive appetites it could satisfy without reference to its sponsor. The league's members turned their considerable military power against the Turks in October 1912, with great success in the First Balkan War. Unhappy with the division of spoils among themselves (by the terms of the London Treaty, May 1913), Bulgaria turned on Serbia and Greece. Turkey and Romania then entered against Bulgaria and now, in the Second Balkan War, each took a piece of Sofia's recent gains.

These developments brought threats from Vienna, not least against Serbia, whose forces had demonstrated some effectiveness on the battlefield. Vienna shifted five army corps to its border with Serbia in early 1913, prompting Sazonov and the General Staff to be concerned with Vienna's threatening attitude toward its neighbor, "upstart" Serbia. But, lacking German backing in both Balkan wars, Vienna was forced to back down and the threat of war was temporarily removed. The Russian government could not tolerate the arrival in October 1913 of a German military mission led by General Liman von Sanders, who was placed in command of an Ottoman army corps in Constantinople. The Russian protests were initially dismissed by Berlin. Further protests brought a promotion of Sanders to Turkish Field Marshall (thus rendering him ineligible for field command), which relaxed the tension.

By 1910, Russia's economic recovery could support a modest program of rearmament, called the "Small Program," which allocated

---

[47] Menning notes that a version of Schedule No. 19 (Revised) that incorporated elements of the new Schedule No. 20 (planned for implementation in autumn 1914) pertained in July 1914. The default variant in the event of war was "A," unless the "Russian high command" noted German troop concentrations above certain unspecified levels. Menning, *Bayonets before Bullets*, p. 243. By 1913, Germany was aware of Russia's enthusiastic expectations of Britain's cobelligerency in the event of a war with Germany, even if that enthusiasm might be misplaced. See comments in J. P. T. Bury's contribution to "The Shifting Balance of World Forces, 1898–1945," *New Cambridge Modern History*, vol. 12, citing Egmont Zechlin, "Deutschland Zwischen Kabinettskrieg und Wirtschaftskrieg," *Historische Zeitschrift* 199 (1964): 350–553.

additional spending to the army and navy.[48] Predicated on the strategic
reorientation of Schedule No. 19, however, War Minister Sukhomlinov
began reversing in 1912 some of its spending goals (e.g., demolition of
fortresses). The War Ministry then launched an urgent examination of
military reorganization and rearmament. The "Great Program" of defense spending was the result. Its approval by Nicholas in October 1913
was merely a preliminary clue that the Russian government – War Ministry, General Staff, and Foreign Ministry – had put its house in order for
the first time since the Russo-Japanese War. In 1912, with implementation of Mobilization Schedule No. 19 (Revised), Sukhomlinov responded
halfway to the anxious appeals of the French General Staff for a return to
Russia's traditional strategic dispositions that were tightly bound to the
western frontier and more certainly focused on active operations against
East Prussia. In the course of secret staff talks in 1912 and again in 1913,
the Russians promised to attack Germany with 800,000 men fifteen
days into a general mobilization (M+15). Chief of General Staff Ia. G.
Zhilinskii went so far in 1913 as to promise the same performance by
M+13 within another year (no matter how unconvincing such promises
were, in view of the chronic shortcomings in strategic railroad network
development in the western provinces).[49]

To carry out the revised mobilization plan, Russia also needed immediately a vast arsenal of new and reorganized field artillery, tactically more
agile units, better organized logistical infrastructure, and, most important,
a massive new program of strategic railroad construction to move troop
units from central Russia to their concentration points in Tsarist Poland.
Much of this Sukhomlinov and the army was promised with the Great
Program.

Modernization of artillery was a vast and complex undertaking. The
War Ministry called for replacement of much obsolete field and mountain
artillery with large numbers of the newest pieces, as would be expected,
at great cost. Sukhomlinov and his predecessors had planned for years
to introduce a new organization to army artillery that would have the
instantaneous effect of increasing by 25 percent the number of batteries
deployable (by the deceptively simple measure of equipping each battery

---

[48] Fuller, *Strategy and Power*, pp. 436–7. The extra spending in fact supplemented very
    limited ordinary spending on the armed forces that had gradually restocked arsenals
    but did not include such major items as new fleets or modernization of artillery. The
    best discussion (in any language) of defense spending after the Russo-Japanese War is
    Gatrell's *Government, Industry and Rearmament*, particularly ch. 3.

[49] Fuller, *Strategy and Power*, pp. 439–40.

with six guns instead of more cumbersome eight guns). However, this step alone would require many additional artillery subalterns, more artillery personnel, more magazines, larger numbers of reserve rounds, more horses, and the like.

Nicholas in March 1913 responded to Sukhomlinov's appeal for emergency funding of reform and reequipping with approval of immediate expenditures totaling 225 million rubles (including 181 million for artillery alone). In July, he approved a five-year program just for artillery modernization and reorganization. Finally, the next year military reform received the infusion it needed for comprehensive modernization at a total cost of 433 million rubles. The Great Program consisted of funding in four principal areas:

1. 500,000 additional men (266,000 infantry, 126,000 gunners, and miscellaneous other technical troops);
2. reorganization of unit mobilization structures to absorb troops more rapidly and to create more numerous units (e.g., by the creation of a "secret cadre" system by which a designated portion of the standing army would fall out of each peacetime unit on M-Day to form the skeleton of 560 additional battalions);
3. a large-scale investment in all caliber of artillery, including new heavy field batteries (the fortress- and trench-busters), intended to be completed by 1917;
4. systematic investment in military aviation (a first for the Russian army).[50]

Russia could probably have implemented the program, if inefficiently, by the end of the decade, if left alone. The program would not have overcome Germany's lead in heavy artillery (a lead that would doubtless have increased, even as Russia undertook its own belated entry into the field). And fielding just under two million men, while impressive as a raw figure, hardly could make up for the material deficiencies Russia faced.

The Great Program marked the final triumph within the Russian General Staff of the "Germany first" school. Russia could just as readily have contemplated its decades-old predisposition to throw its weight against

---

[50] See the superior work on the birth and evolution of Russian military aviation: Gregory Michael Viterbo, "'The Power, Strength and Future of Russia': Aviation Culture and the Russian Imperial Officer Corps, 1908–1914," Ph.D. dissertation, University of Michigan, 1999.

Austrian Galicia instead of East Prussia in the event of war, without need-
ing such a large and costly program of modernization. The behavior of
the Central Powers, however, had drawn the attention of mobilization
planners back to central Europe, where alliance politics and Britain's
quiet "commitment" to intervention had convinced most Russian planners that they had little choice but to operate within the structure of their
French obligations. The effect of the Great Program, its architects may
have hoped, was to conjure up for the Germans the specter of a credible quick mobilization to deter aggression against France. (Of course,
to what ends Russia's newfound strength may have been turned after the
program's completion in 1917, absenting a German attack on the *entente*,
is inscrutable.)

The Great Program and, indeed, the rest of Russia's military preparations prior to the July Crisis, were not intended to provide Russia with
a rapid victory; Germany and Austria-Hungary both continued to enjoy
considerable advantage in the pace of their mobilization. As one insightful
observer put it, "reorganization of troop units, recruitment of additional
troops, provision of extra firepower – these were hardly the stuff of which
dreams of military grandeur were made."[51] Russian statesmen, including
the tsar, knew in July 1914 that the program had not even begun (it had
been funded by the Duma only weeks before), a fact which dampened
any irrational enthusiasm for belligerency during the crisis. The knowledge that would have informed their decision making was, instead, recol-
lection of Austro-German coercion during the 1908–9 Bosnian crisis, an
acute awareness of Russia's military ill-preparedness, and the firm belief
that Russia would no longer be seen as a great power if it allowed Serbia
to be "chastised" as Vienna intended and the path to the Turkish Straits
opened to the Triple Alliance.

## The July Crisis

Until relatively recently, students of Russian government activity during the weeks following the Sarajevo assassination on 28 June 1914 believed that St. Petersburg had little inkling of the crisis rapidly unfolding

---

[51] Gatrell, *Government, Industry and Rearmament*, p. 134. For data on the defense expenditures of the six leading European powers, see David Stevenson, *Armaments and
the Coming of War* (Oxford, 1996), pp. 2, 4; and David G. Herrmann, *The Arming of
Europe and the Making of the First World War* (Princeton, 1996), appendices A and B.

in Vienna and Berlin.[52] In fact, the Russian council of Ministers under Premier I. I. Goremykin was well apprised of the unfolding crisis and settled on Russia's response at an early stage. From the very start, the council saw war as the "inevitable outcome." On 11 July, Foreign Minister Sazonov reported to his colleagues on his ministry's estimation of the situation and the policy it proposed to follow.[53] He placed responsibility squarely at Germany's doorstep for the danger, which he saw deepening in each report that arrived from Russia's missions in the European capitals. His and the government's knowledge of events rested also on intercepted foreign diplomatic cable traffic transmitted to or from embassies in Petersburg.[54] Later, Sazonov described the impression that Austria's strident response to the assassination crisis left on him:

> The moment had come when Russia, faced with the annihilation of Serbia, would lose all her authority if she did not declare herself the defender of a Slavonic nation threatened by powerful neighbors.... If Russia failed to fulfill her historic mission she would be considered a decadent State and would henceforth have to take second place among the powers.[55]

A. V. Krivoshein, the influential conservative minister of agriculture, then declared that "opinion" (public and parliamentary) would accept nothing short of bold action. Russian statesmen had reinvigorated the empire's economic development and rebuilt its military establishment since 1907. Those men felt that their sovereign, Nicholas II, could face the Germanic powers if Russia's vital interests demanded a showdown. Finally, the

[52] Lieven, *Russia and the Origins*, pp. 140–1, argues that "when the crisis broke on 24 July [date of the Austrian ultimatum to Belgrade] the Russians therefore both felt gulled and were taken by surprise." James Joll, *The Origins of the First World War* (London, 1984), p. 14, thought that it was only on 24 July, "nearly four weeks after the assassination of Franz Ferdinand ... that the scale and implications of the crisis began to be realized outside of Berlin and Vienna."

[53] Russia's Julian calendar was thirteen days behind the western (Gregorian) calendar from the start of the century.

[54] On code breaking, see Joll, *Origins of the First World War*, p. 12; William C. Fuller, Jr., "The Russian Empire," in Ernest R. May, ed., *Knowing One's Enemies: Intelligence Assessment before the Two World Wars* (Princeton, 1984), pp. 98–126; and Rich, *Tsar's Colonels*, pp. 175–6. The virtually continuous collections of daily intercepts are stored now in the Imperial Foreign Ministry Archive (AVPRI), Moscow. Although analysis of these materials is not complete, the impression one takes from them is of high cryptographic competence and, hence, well-informed leaders in the Russian Foreign Ministry. The influence of these diplomatic reports on Petersburg decision makers, however, has not yet been established by specialists.

[55] Quoted in McDonald, *United Government*, p. 204.

stability of Russia's internal order – its restive urban proletariat and the revolutionary cadres at work within it – would not be a threat to the regime in the event of war, thanks to generally improving working conditions from 1910 onward.[56] Three days later, Sazonov departed for his estate for a brief rest before the arrival in the Russian capital of France's President Raymond Poincaré and Premier René Viviani, expected on 20 July.[57]

On 16 July, Vienna received a quiet but unmistakable warning from the Russian Foreign Ministry, transmitted through Italian intermediaries: With "unquestionable resolution," Russia would stand by Serbia in the face of Austro-Hungarian aggression. Italy's ambassador in St. Petersburg characterized Vienna's reception of the warning for the benefit of the Foreign Ministry: "Austria was capable of taking an irrevocable step with regard to Serbia based on the belief that, although Russia would make a verbal protest, she would not adopt forcible measures for the protection of Serbia," a report echoed by Russia's minister in Vienna the same day.[58] The allies' response to Austria's and Serbia's battle of accusations dominated discussions between Sazonov and the French guests, who arrived four days later.[59]

The Balkan crisis was apparently low on the agenda of points that the French had intended to discuss (as it was on the agendas of most European

---

[56] Ibid., pp. 204–5. McDonald described the trajectory of Russian policy thus: "The traditional formula connecting war and revolution had been completely inverted by the summer of 1914." Even Geyer, who perhaps uniquely sees social revolution and its counteraction, pan-Slavism, underlying most Russian policy crises after 1861, flatly rejects governmental fear of a "revolutionary situation" in the decision making it followed during July 1914. Geyer, *Russian Imperialism*, p. 314. For a well-established alternate view attributing rising radicalism to workers in 1914, see Leopold Haimson, "The Problem of Social Stability in Urban Russia," *Slavic Review* 23 (1964): 619–42, and ibid., 24 (1965): 1–22, as well as his revisitation of the subject (buttressed with new documentation), "'The Problem of Political and Social Stability in Urban Russia on the Eve of War and Revolution' Revisited," *Slavic Review* 59 (2000): 848–75.

[57] The midsummer departure of government officials from the Russian capital (no less than in other European countries) was and remains conventional practice. Throughout the crisis preceding the 1877–78 Russo-Turkish War the tsar traveled around Poland and then spent weeks in the Crimea, greatly complicating Russian war planning. Rich, *Tsar's Colonels*, pp. 120–42.

[58] Quoted in Luigi Albertini, *The Origins of the War of 1914*, 3 vols. (Oxford, 1952–7), vol. 2, p. 184.

[59] S. D. Sazonov, *Vospominaniia* (Paris, 1927), pp. 180–2. The content of the consultations between the French and Russian sides remains something of a mystery; see, however, discussion in Chapter 7, below. Nicholas's speech at a banquet welcoming the French dignitaries, however, anticipated the reassuring outcome of those negotiations.

cabinets before Austria presented its ultimatum to Serbia).[60] Nevertheless, by the end of the visit Sazonov and Viviani shared what they euphemistically termed a "perfect community of views" on the maintenance of peace in Europe and especially the Balkans. That nebulous diplomatic term in all likelihood meant that they had decided to take action against Vienna to forestall Habsburg intervention in Serbian affairs (i.e., to prevent an attack on Serbian sovereignty). Most important, the two powers solemnly affirmed the mutual obligations imposed by their alliance: France would stand by Russia against Austria in the Balkan crisis.[61] Unfortunately, the absence of precise documentation of the Franco-Russian discussions prevents more detailed analysis.

Throughout the three-day visit, rumors of impending Austrian action against Serbia surfaced in the Russian capital. When the crisis erupted on 24 July – just after France's chief executive and head of state departed aboard a French battleship – Russia was awkwardly positioned to craft a quick, consistent policy toward Austria-Hungary and Germany. Key Russian diplomats, including the ambassadors to Paris, Vienna, Berlin, and Belgrade, on whose diplomatic reports, intelligence collection activities, and foreign liaison the Foreign Ministry relied, were away from their posts on summer vacation. The chief of the General Staff's operations section, Quartermaster-General Danilov, and the Foreign Ministry's chief of the Near Eastern desk, Prince G. N. Trubetskoi, were out of the Russian capital as well.[62]

Foreign Minister Sazonov was not surprised when the Habsburg ambassador, Count Friedrich Szápáry, presented him the formal text of the ultimatum Vienna had dispatched to Belgrade at 10 A.M. on 24 July. During the twenty-four hours preceding Austria's demarché, Sazonov had received six warning indicators about the turn Austrian policy was about to take. The Foreign Ministry's *camera noir* (literally "black chamber,"

---

[60] See the discussion of this point and most of what is known of the French visit in Albertini, *Origins of the War*, vol. 2, pp. 188–94.
[61] Sazonov and French minister Maurice Paléologue together informed Sir George Buchanan (minister of Great Britain to Russia) of the summit results, which Buchanan reported to his foreign minister on 24 July. *British Documents on the Origins of the War*, ed. G. P. Gooch et al., 11 vols. (London, 1926), vol. 11, no. 101, Buchanan to Grey, 24 July 1914; hereafter BDOW. Paléologue confirmed to Buchanan that France would "fulfill all the obligations imposed on her by the [Franco-Russian] alliance."
[62] Lieven, *Russia and the Origins*, p. 140. Danilov was leading a General Staff "ride" in the Caucasus at the moment the crisis broke; with him also was the chief of the general staff's operations section for the western front, Colonel Shcholov. Jurij Daniloff, *Rußland im Weltkriege 1914–1915* (Jena, 1925), p. 14.

the ministry's cryptographic section) provided two alerts that Vienna was on the brink of taking action. On 23 July, Sazonov read Count Szápáry's "secret" report to Austrian Foreign Minister Count Leopold Berchtold concerning the mood in Russia, as well as news from Szápáry's counterpart in Berlin on the German Foreign Ministry's position on the crisis.[63] From Russia's diplomatic agents in other capitals, Sazonov acquired further alarming news. His chargé in Vienna reported news circulating there of a "sharp note" to be presented in Belgrade that day, rumors underscored by Szápáry's urgent telephoned request to Sazonov on the evening of 23 July for an early appointment the next morning. Sazonov also heard, from the Italian ambassador in Petersburg, that Austria intended to present Serbia with "an unpleasant ultimatum" that very day, and learned by cable that evening from the Russian chargé in Belgrade that Vienna had, in fact, presented Belgrade with an ultimatum having a forty-eight-hour deadline.[64] Count V. N. Strandtmann (Strandman) in the Serbian capital cabled Petersburg that the Austrian minister in Belgrade had not only delivered the ultimatum, but had also verbally informed the Serbs that the Austro-Hungarian Empire intended to break off diplomatic relations if Serbia did not meet its demands within the mandated time period.[65] In other words, Russia's principal foreign policy decision maker and the tsar's closest adviser was well informed from a variety of sources about the events precipitating the crisis.

Even so, when Szápáry informed Sazonov of the ultimatum's terms, Sazonov declared, "It's the European war!" – not because it came unexpectedly, but because the brash, undiplomatic bellicosity of Vienna's address to Belgrade signaled to him the extremity of Austria's position in the crisis. Sazonov understood that the ultimatum involved an enormous risk, one that Vienna was inexplicably willing to undertake. "You want to go to war with Serbia," Sazonov declared to Szápáry. In unusually forthright terms for a diplomat, he continued:

I see what is going on. The German papers are adding fuel to the fire! You are setting fire to Europe. It is a great responsibility you are assuming, you will see

---

[63] *Die internationalen Beziehungen im Zeitalter des Imperialismus: Dokumente aus den Archiven der Zarischen und der Provisorischen Regierung*, ed. Otto Hoetzsch, 5 vols. (Berlin, 1934), series I, vol. 5, nos. 4, 7; hereafter IB.

[64] IB, vol. 5, nos. 5, 6, 10. Note that Italy remained Austria-Hungary's and Germany's nominal ally until the outbreak of hostilities.

[65] Ibid., no. 10.

what sort of an impression you will make in London and in Paris and perhaps elsewhere. It will be considered an unjustified aggression.[66]

The Foreign Ministry hurriedly recalled all members of its chancellery and the Near East desk, while Sazonov began a cycle of meetings with Ambassadors Sir George Buchanan (Great Britain) and Maurice Paléologue (France). Sazonov already knew that Russia was scarcely in a position to act militarily against Austria, even in response to aggression against Serbia. In the immediate term, Russia had little opportunity to begin preparations for a military crisis (all Russian strategic planning since 1878 had been built on the assumption of some extended period of crisis before hostilities), and the state's long-term plans for military modernization and rearmament remained years from completion. Even the large-scale strategic railroad expansion would not approach completion until 1918. Thus, Sazonov hoped that if the crisis could be drawn out, if Austrian action could be delayed, the other European powers might defuse the tensions. His goal was to forge sufficient unity among the other powers to dissuade Austria from pressing ahead with its ultimatum, and to buy the time necessary to deflect Vienna from its apparent course. He made those goals clear to the foreign ambassadors in Petersburg, appealing directly to Buchanan to activate Britain's influence in Berlin and Vienna for moderation of the Austrian ultimatum and, foremost, to extend the deadline. Although Sazonov said that the Russian government had yet to consider whether an Austrian invasion of Serbia constituted a *casus belli*, Buchanan sensed that France and Russia together intended to stay the course – with or without Britain's open cooperation.[67] Put differently, Russia was prepared to block with military means any Habsburg offensive against Serbia while France prepared to meet the expected German attack (Schlieffen Plan).

Late that same morning, Austria's Foreign Minister Berchtold assured the Russian chargé, Prince N. A. Kudashev, that Vienna understood the real consequences of a policy of humiliation toward Serbia – that Vienna would face "repercussions" from Russia – and declared the matter one of balance of power and dynastic politics. Kudashev asked what Austria's actions would comprise in the event that Serbia failed to comply with the ultimatum. Berchtold replied that the Habsburg Mission would depart Belgrade – to which Kudashev declared, *"Alors! C'est la guerre!"*

[66] *July 1914: The Outbreak of the First World War: Selected Documents*, ed. Imanuel Geiss (New York, 1967), no. 49, Szápáry to Berchtold, the contents of which were presumably known to the Russian Foreign Ministry as well.

[67] IB, vol. 5, no. 25; BDOW II, no. 101.

and reported the exchange to Petersburg.[68] When the tsar's Council of Ministers met at about 12:30 that Friday afternoon, Sazonov had already learned most of what the Russian government would know about the crisis before it turned into war, and much of the diplomatic thinking of Russia's antagonists in Vienna and Berlin.

The Council of Ministers under Goremykin (guided by Sazonov) proposed five resolutions for Tsar Nicholas II's consideration, to defuse the crisis and protect Russia's interests:[69]

1. that the great powers had to be involved in examination of the conspiracy surrounding the assassination at Sarajevo;
2. that Serbia's fate would be entrusted to the great powers;
3. that Nicholas II authorize declaration of mobilization in four military districts and the Baltic, based on the subsequent unfolding of events;
4. that the War Ministry build up material stockpiles in preparation for a possible mobilization; and
5. that Russia take steps immediately to reduce its sums of exchange on deposit in Germany and Austria-Hungary.[70]

According to the minutes of the meeting, the *partial* mobilization would achieve two objectives. First, it would send an unmistakable signal to Vienna that Russia's "verbal protest" would be backed with steel. Second, it would send pacific signals to Berlin because Russian reservists would not be mobilized within any military district adjacent to Germany.[71] Nicholas approved the preparations for this partial mobilization and directed War Minister Sukhomlinov and the recently appointed Chief of General Staff Ianushkevich to begin those the next day. The tsar also had the resolutions, which, upon his agreement, became the official Russian policy statement, transmitted to the Serbian ambassador for relay immediately to Belgrade.[72]

[68] Geiss, *1914*, no. 48; IB, vol. 5, nos. 31, 32.
[69] Following the full session, Sazonov continued in special session with the ministers of war, marine, and finance, who prepared the imperial submission.
[70] IB, vol. 5, no. 42; also in Geiss, *1914*, no. 76, in English translation.
[71] Fuller, *Strategy and Power*, p. 446, citing the Foreign Ministry document.
[72] Ibid., p. 446; Gale Stokes, "The Serbian Documents from 1914: A Preview," *Journal of Modern History* 48 (1976): 69–84. Stokes cites Serbian diplomatic materials that make clear the complex maneuvering that was taking place among the Russian and Serbian representatives on 24–25 June, and the probable wishful thinking that gripped Serbian reporting out of Petersburg.

In Vienna, the diplomatic representatives of Russia, Britain, and France were in continuous consultation. Kudashev reported information that corroborated Strandtmann's earlier cable: Austria intended to sever diplomatic relations with Belgrade if the Serb response was inadequate. "The Austro-Hungarian government plainly ... is prepared to risk armed conflict in the event of rejection."[73] Strandtmann further reported Austria's stake in the matter of Serbia: The ultimatum would serve the purpose of "clarifying" Austro-Serb relations, a matter of vital interest to Vienna, on which it considered its status as a great power to depend. According to Strandtmann's cable, Berchtold believed that St. Petersburg ought properly to share Austria's interest in defending the monarchial principle and the balance of power.[74]

Late on Friday evening, 24 July, the Austro-Hungarian Chief of General Staff, Franz Conrad von Hötzendorf, informed the Italian military attaché in Vienna that the orders were ready "for instant mobilization" as soon as the ultimatum's time limit expired. The British military attaché in Vienna was also well informed of Austrian military activity. He reported that siege trains loaded with heavy howitzers were already departing Vienna's South Station at 0300 and mobilization had *so far* affected at least five Austrian corps, some Honvéd divisions, and units associated with the Galician corps facing Russia. Russia's penetration of the Austro-Hungarian staff and military infrastructure could hardly have yielded less alarming intelligence for the mobilization planners in Petersburg.[75]

Shortly before noon on Saturday, 25 July, Nicholas approved the Council of Ministers' proposal for partial mobilization, affecting 1.1 million men in the Odessa, Kiev, Moscow, and Kazan military districts and in the Black and Baltic sea fleets. He also declared that, if Austro-Hungarian

[73] IB, vol. 5, nos. 102, 31; also in Geiss, *1914*, no. 63.
[74] IB, vol. 5, no. 32; also in Geiss, *1914*, no. 64.
[75] BDOW, vol. 11, no. 124. There is little published information from archival sources on the extent of Russian military attaché reporting from Vienna during the crisis. Dating back into the 1870s at least, Russian officials (General Staff officers and military attachés) had bribed, bought, stolen, and otherwise scraped together important military intelligence from Vienna. Petersburg's most famous asset in Vienna, the renowned Colonel Alfred Redl (chief of staff of Austria's VIII Corps) who sold Austrian mobilization secrets to the Russians for years, was caught in 1913 and forced to commit suicide. However, information undoubtedly continued to flow eastward. This intelligence was for use by the general staff's mobilization planning section (which also oversaw that collection work). As with the sources on diplomatic cable intercepts, this topic awaits a careful examination.

troops violated Serbia's borders, Russia would declare mobilization, and war preparations would begin – but those steps would not be taken until Austria attacked Serbia, and no mention was made of declaring war. Even then, he said, it would proceed only in those districts adjacent to Austria. Russia would in any case enter the "period preparatory to war" during the night of 25–26 July. All troops would return to winter quarters from leave or furlough; the Kronstadt, Reval, and Sveaborg fortresses would begin to rearm; and all fortresses on the western frontier would transition to a war footing.[76]

Ianushkevich ordered his planners (still without Danilov's leadership) to activate plans for the transition to "the period prior to mobilization," a military phase of the "period preparatory to war." This required officers to return to their regiments from leave and instantly converted all probationary general staff officers (men who had graduated from the staff academy in Petersburg but not yet been inducted into the "General Staff Corps" itself) to permanent General Staff status, if they were serving in staff officer billets. He next prepared the draft declaration of partial mobilization for the tsar's signature.[77]

Neither the war minister nor his Chief of General Staff had any background in the rarified business of mobilization planning. Neither was familiar with the intricacies of Russia's mobilization schedule nor with the assumptions on which it had developed. They possessed limited understanding of the relative inflexibility of Russia's mobilization plan and thus the limitations on their choices in ordering partial mobilization. Together, they misjudged the ability of the General Staff to craft a customized mobilization plan on the spot, and in particular to deliver a partial mobilization order. And they certainly did not anticipate the stridency of the professional staff's technical arguments *against* partial mobilization when it learned of their recommendation to the tsar. War Minister Sukhomlinov had depended on the inexperienced chief of staff, Ianushkevich, when he put forward the proposal for partial mobilization to Foreign Minister Sazonov and the tsar. The mobilization wizards in the General Staff greeted the tsar's order for just such a mobilization with horror.

---

[76] IB, vol. 5, no. 42; also in Geiss, *1914*, no. 76; IB, vol. 5, no. 79 [GUGSh Journal, 2000 hr, 25 July 1914].

[77] BDOW, vol. 11, no. 124. A lesson of Russia's previous two wars (with Japan and Turkey) was that a shortage of General Staff–qualified officers could severely hamper the transition to hostilities. In previous conflicts, the army's insufficiency of General Staff officers slowed mobilization, concentration, and the opening of combat operations. Nicholas's order addressed that "lesson."

General Danilov was head of the quartermaster-general's section, which since the beginning of the century had sole responsibility for mobilization planning, Schedule No. 19 (Rev.) being in effect in July 1914. He attempted to explain the military reasons for jettisoning the bizarre partial mobilization choice. (Like Germany's, Russia's mobilization planning made no allowance for mobilization against only one potential enemy; unlike Germany's, however, Russian mobilization did *not* lead automatically to war.)[78] Danilov and his planners, and indeed almost all of their predecessors, had viewed war with the Dual Monarchy as the trigger for German mobilization – theoretically from the 1880s at the latest and, concretely, since Germany's actions during the Bosnian annexation crisis of 1908. Thus, partial mobilization, regardless of any usefulness it might serve as a "diplomatic telegram," threatened to paralyze Russia's war fighting ability *when* (rather than *if* ) Germany declared mobilization. Furthermore, Schedule No. 19 (Rev.) comprised a single, integrated, general mobilization; parts could not be pried off and jettisoned. Theoretical possibilities of partial mobilization aside, to carry out Nicholas's order would have required the preparation of an entirely new schedule that addressed only select military districts, and with no assurance that the partial measure would "fit" with Schedule No. 19 (Rev.), should Germany subsequently take offense and the sovereign have to declare general mobilization.

Even if hostilities could by some miracle be limited to Austria-Hungary, from an operational point of view the theater of war necessarily included both Central Powers: The most important Russian military district, Warsaw, abutted both states. To leave it out of a partial mobilization (in deference to German sensitivities) would leave it unprepared for the Austro-Hungarian offensive that planners knew to be the central element of Vienna's general war plan.

---

[78] This factor is salient in evaluating the unfolding crisis: Repeatedly, Sazonov informed German Ambassador Pourtalès that *politically*, Russian mobilization did not mean war, that the tsar would arrive at a decision for war separately, and that Russia "would doubtless be able to remain under arms [i.e., mobilized] for weeks to come without crossing the frontier" (A.M., 29 July: IB, vol. 5, no. 218; also Geiss, 1914, no. 124a (quote)). In his memoirs Danilov likewise asserted that "all knew" that Russian mobilization could never be mistaken for a declaration of war: Daniloff, *Rußland im Weltkriege*, p. 28. Danilov published his memoirs of 1914–15 in Russian and then German, as an émigré in the west, and expanded the work for French publication: *La Russie dans la Guerre Mondiale (1914–1917)* (Paris, 1927). See also Lieven, *Russia and the Origins*, pp. 146–7. The Central Powers refused to take heed of those differences.

The final act of the drama began on 28 July, when Austria-Hungary declared war on Serbia, an act that committed Russia to proceed. The General Staff technicians believed general mobilization was essential, and thus the urgency of advising Nicholas of the implications of a partial mobilization became acute. The planners under Danilov drafted two imperial orders, one for partial and one for general mobilization. The following day, 29 July, Petersburg learned that Austria's riverine gunboats had bombarded Belgrade. Count Friedrich von Pourtalès, Germany's ambassador to Petersburg, warned that if Russia did not cease and reverse all military activity immediately, Germany would mobilize. Sazonov, already doubting the wisdom of partial mobilization before that threat, wrote: "As we cannot fulfill Germany's desires, it remains for us to speed up our armament and count on the true inevitability of war."[79] On 30 July, Sazonov, Sukhomlinov, and Ianushkevich agreed together to urge Nicholas unequivocally to declare general mobilization.

Nicholas sustained the hope that through direct communications with his German cousin, Wilhelm II, the emperors together could eliminate the disagreements into which their respective governments had seemingly locked the empires. And even at that crucial moment, Sazonov, Sukhomlinov, Ianushkevich, and the military and diplomatic staffs behind them understood that even *general* mobilization by no means implied war with both Vienna and Berlin. The lethargy of Russia's shift to a wartime footing – twelve to sixteen weeks for completion, in the best staff estimates – in their view offered the state extensive room for maneuver and negotiation before declaring war. Danilov later wrote that, in principle, a declaration of general mobilization affected only the empire's ability to defend itself and to place its forces in readiness, an observation born out by five decades of General Staff study and field exercises. Russia's survival would depend on the rapidity with which it could bring its army to readiness to defend itself.[80]

Powerful as the military imperative for mobilization might have appeared, it did not convince Nicholas on 30 July, when, in a series of meetings with Sazonov and others, the tsar labored long over the decision. Nicholas refused to take any of the urgent telephone calls from the General Staff that morning as he ruminated over a telegram from his cousin:

---

[79] Quoted in Fuller, *Strategy and Power*, p. 447.

[80] For the more accessible version, see Daniloff, *Rußland im Weltkriege*, pp. 8–32. On Russia's military apprehension (if not pessimism), see Fuller, *Strategy and Power*, ch. 8; Menning, *Bayonets before Bullets*, chs. 3 and 4; and Rich, *Tsar's Colonels*, pp. 88ff.

The kaiser declared that the decision for European war rested solely on Nicholas's shoulders! Wilhelm II assured him that he would not be able hold back events if Nicholas's government took unilateral military steps. It is scarcely imaginable that the gravity of this warning could have rested more heavily on any other European statesman that July day.

That afternoon, Nicholas's ministers urged him to act. Sazonov noted that Berlin had demanded "from us a capitulation to the Central Powers, for which Russia would never forgive the Sovereign, and which would cover the good name of the Russian people with shame." Krivoshein argued that Russia was not the weakened state of 1908, but could again assert itself with confidence as a great power. Krivoshein's strong conservative position, balancing considerations of strategic danger and domestic stability, gave him de facto leadership of the council, eclipsing Goremykin, whose deferential views of council authority would lead to continued inaction.[81]

Sazonov knew of Berlin's diplomatic threats to Paris of the previous day and communicated this news to Nicholas. When confronted with this, his German cousin's apparent betrayal and deception, Nicholas II agreed to order general mobilization. Sazonov immediately called Ianushkevich with the imperial order – and told him to smash his telephone, to forestall any imperial second thoughts. The order went into effect on 31 July, and Germany declared war the following day.

### Conclusion

Did Russian leaders have a realistic grasp of the implications of their mobilization? And did they comprehend the nature of Germany's policy sufficiently clearly to choose the best course for imperial Russia in 1914? An important distinction should be noted here: Russia mobilized; Germany declared war. Furthermore, neither Russia's entry into war with Germany nor the empire's eventual collapse from within were overdetermined by the political, economic, and social crises that occupied the country before 1914 – nor even by the very fact of war and military setback. At the beginning of 1915, much of Austrian Galicia was in Russian hands, as was a part of East Prussia. A year into the war, Russia's military prospects, if not sanguine, were far from bleak, in spite of setbacks on the battlefield. The German army had advanced no more than a few score kilometers

[81] McDonald, *United Government*, pp. 204–5.

from the East Prussian border and had not reached the Bug River boundary between tsarist Poland and the Russian heartland. Even after the disastrous loss in the 1915 Gorlice campaign and even in December 1917, when Germany extracted a punitive armistice from Russia's new Bolshevik regime, the front still had yet to reach the Russian core.[82]

The conservative statesman and Germanophile Petr Durnovo had written directly to Nicholas in early 1914 of the danger Russia faced if it confronted Germany. He declared that, "in the event of defeat, the possibility of which in a struggle with a foe like Germany cannot be overlooked, social revolution in its most extreme form is inevitable." Yet his superficial prophecy obscures just how little mastery Russian statesmen (and the public) had of the quarter from which danger to the dynasty and state would come. The government's gross inability to govern through the usual means available to a "well-ordered state" in times of either peace or war meant that its enemies, external or internal, would ultimately profit as crises turned to chaos. Russia's policy makers in fact suffered, as many of their number had for decades, under the double illusion that Russia's resources would allow it to pursue its political goals and that it could simultaneously guard against a preeminent external danger. Although similar charges of myopia may be laid at the doorstep of other powers involved in the July Crisis, only Russian power rested on a brittle social system from which the government could expect little loyalty or sacrifice in a crisis as severe as it faced in 1914–16. The government's dysfunctionality and isolation were products of autocracy itself. Reform of the mechanisms of governing could defy all efforts of even the state's most powerful servitors. In spite of societal malaise and government fragmentation, Petersburg's freedom of action in the 1914 crisis was at once stabilized by half a century of decision making in the General Staff and Foreign Ministry and liberated from that stability by the unlimited power of the sovereign, Nicholas II.

---

[82] This point is made by John P. LeDonne, *The Russian Empire and the World, 1700–1917: The Geopolitics of Expansion and Containment* (Oxford, 1997), pp. 366–7.

# 7

# France

## Eugenia C. Kiesling

### Introduction

France had a central role in the origins of the First World War. A long-standing hostility toward Germany led to the Dual Alliance with Russia and the *entente cordiale* with England, these providing the framework for Germany's diplomatic isolation. The two Moroccan crises brought serious strains and more nationalist rhetoric that exacerbated international tensions. After 1911, as war seemed more and more likely, French financial support for a massive Russian military program to be completed in 1917 gave Germany's military leaders reason to fight sooner rather than later. In the immediate crisis of July 1914, with French support assured, Russia mobilized against the Central Powers, Germany declared war, and an Austro-Serbian conflict turned into European war.

These many French contributions notwithstanding, numerous studies of the events of 1914 have portrayed France as a minor player.[1] The most important role attributed to France is a supposed inciting of Russia to

---

[1] France is almost invisible in most studies of the war's origins. Five of the six references to French President Poincaré in one typical account refer to his Russian trip as keeping him out of the action; see Laurence Lafore, *The Long Fuse* (Philadelphia, New York, and Toronto, 1971), p. 282. The fifty-page introduction to Geiss's document collection gives France less than a paragraph; Imanuel Geiss, ed., *July 1914: The Outbreak of the First World War: Selected Documents* (New York, 1967), pp. 26–7. Only twelve of Geiss's 188 documents are French. Keegan, like Lafore, mentions only the Poincaré-Viviani cruise; John Keegan, *The First World War* (New York, 1999), pp. 55–6. Richard Cobb's imaginative "France and the Coming of War," in R. J. W. Evans and Hartmut Pogge von Strandmann, eds., *The Coming of the First World War* (Oxford, 1988), ignores French policy in favor of fascinating observations about national mood.

war against Austria-Hungary, this appearing in works intended to ex-
onerate Germany.[2] More often, France takes the stage as the incidental
victim of German war plans against Russia.[3] Yet another version of the
script ignores France in favor of her partner in Western Europe's military
affairs. Great Britain, not France, should have prevented war by creating
an army capable of rapid intervention on the Continent and by advertis-
ing her willingness to defend neutral Belgium.[4] Moreover, Britain would
not have been placed in the position of having to deter a European war
over Serbia had her policies not undermined the stability of the Austro-
Hungarian Empire in the first place.[5] The only recognition France receives
is for championing the "spirit of the offensive." The conviction that saber
and bayonet would win the next war was not uniquely French, but no
nation accepted it more whole-heartedly.[6] In short, historians who are
focused on the "war-guilt" question or who are fascinated by the complexities of Balkan politics tend to reduce French policy to nationalism and
*revanchism* and, given the Schlieffen plan, deny that French intentions –
and therefore French decisions – mattered at all.

Adding to the temptation to ignore France's contribution to the outbreak of the Great War is the fact that its government made surprisingly
few decisions in July 1914. Indeed, France appears to have abdicated
the opportunity to participate in the great events of the day. The Senate

[2] A flurry of works by French Leftists charging their nation with warmongering ended after
the publication of the French diplomatic documents in 1929; on this, see Luigi Albertini,
*The Origins of the War of 1914*, 3 vols. (London, New York, and Toronto, 1952), vol. 1,
pp. ix–xi. Two Americans, Elmer Harry Barnes and Robert L. Owen, accused France
and Russia of planning a Balkan war to secure Alsace-Lorraine and the Dardanelles; in
Barnes, *The Genesis of the World War: An Introduction to the Problem of the War Guilt*
(New York, 1926), and Owen, *The Russian Imperial Conspiracy 1891–1914* (New York,
1923). Frederick L. Schuman, *War and Diplomacy in the French Republic* (New York,
1931), also emphasizes the Franco-Russian role.
[3] Thus, "the French entered the war because they had no alternative. The Germans had
attacked them. It was that simple." Joachim Remak, *The Origins of World War I 1871–
1914* (New York, 1967), pp. 142–3.
[4] Thus, Kagan, whose conclusions about the origins of the First World War also ignore
France: Donald Kagan, *The Origins of War and the Preservation of Peace* (Ithaca, N.Y.,
1995), pp. 86–93, 205–14.
[5] Paul Schroeder, "World War I as Galloping Gertie: A Reply to Joachim Remak," *Journal
of Modern History* 44 (1972): 319–45.
[6] See Michael E. Howard, "Men against Fire: Expectations of War in 1914," and Steven
Van Evera, "The Cult of the Offensive and the Origins of the First World War," in Steven
E. Miller, ed., *Military Strategy and the Origins of the First World War* (Princeton, 1985),
pp. 41–57 and 58–107.

and Chamber of Deputies, which had to approve any declaration of war, began their summer recess on 15 July 1914 and were reconvened only on 4 August – after the German declaration of war.[7] President Raymond Poincaré and Premier/Foreign Minister Paul Viviani, the key French leaders, put themselves out of the action by embarking on a long-planned visit to St. Petersburg and Scandinavia.[8] At sea from 16 July until their arrival in Russia on 20 July, they were again in touch only by radio during the return voyage of 24–29 July.[9] In the absence of Viviani, his responsibilities fell on the inexperienced Minister of Justice Jean Baptiste Bienvenu-Martin.[10] Effectively, there was no one in Paris to make decisions.

In many respects, France's goal in July 1914 was to avoid making decisions. Any action taken in that highly incendiary situation could contribute to igniting a conflagration that France did not want and for which it did not wish to be responsible. Against this motive for inaction, however, were the countervailing imperatives of the Franco-Russian alliance. Crucially, France had to avoid arousing Russian fears that French support was in any sense uncertain. To treat support for Russia as a matter for decision was to imply that France had the option of abandoning its ally and, conversely, that Russia was free to abandon France. Given that Russian military cooperation was vital to French hopes of deterring or

---

[7] Gordon Wright, *Raymond Poincaré and the French Presidency* (Stanford, 1942), p. 140. On 15 July the Senate finally voted to establish an income tax; D. W. Brogan, *France under the Third Republic 1870–1939* (New York and London, 1940), p. 450. Tax reform aroused far more public attention than foreign affairs.

[8] To have abandoned the trip, planned in January 1914, would have further tarnished a presidency already embarrassed by the difficulty of forming a cabinet; Wright, *Poincaré*, p. 313. Poincaré, however, stressed the risk of "alarming Europe" and inconveniencing the Scandinavian monarchs on his itinerary; Poincaré, *Au service de la France*, vol. 4: *L'Union Sacrée* (Paris, 1926–33), pp. 211, 301–2.

[9] J. F. V. Keiger's excellent recent biography, *Raymond Poincaré* (Cambridge, 1997), p. 164, argues that the voyage reduced French influence on events. It determined the timing of the Austrian ultimatum, which Foreign Minister Berchtold wanted to reach Belgrade after Poincaré's party had reembarked for France and could no longer coordinate a result with the Russians. Letter from Heinrich Leopold von Tschirschky to Gottlieb von Jagow, 11 July 1914, quoted in Geiss, *July 1914*, pp. 108–9.

[10] Bienvenu-Martin "came to spend three-quarters on an hour each day at the [Foreign] Ministry in a mood of some indifference." Jules Ferry quoted in Christopher Andrew, "France and the German Menace," in Ernest R. May, ed., *Knowing One's Enemies: Intelligence Assessment before the Two World Wars* (Princeton, 1984), p. 143. Austro-Hungarian Ambassador Imre Szecen noted after meeting with the acting foreign minister that "Monsieur Bienvenu-Martin has of course no influence whatever on the course of foreign policy in France," Szecsen to Berchtold, 24 July 1914, Geiss, *July 1914*, p. 179.

surviving a conflict with Germany, France had to adhere whole-heartedly to the alliance and to act, therefore, as if the nation had no options at all.[11]

Concern for foreign and domestic opinion also weighed in against visible decision making. It was important to the French government that both the British government and its own people recognize that France was being dragged by Austria-Hungary and Germany into an unwanted war.[12] Discussions of whether or how much to assist Russia would give the impression that France had more choices than it chose to admit. Not only was the most important French decision preordained, but France denied that there was even a decision to be made.

### Internal Politics and Policy Makers

Still, even decisions not to decide require decision-making procedures. The general interpretation of the Third Republic's ambiguous constitution is that power rested with the two legislative assemblies, either of which could oust a government by rejecting essential legislation.[13] The Senate, originally conservative because of a system of indirect election overrepresenting rural communities, had come by 1914 to mirror the directly elected chamber of deputies. Sitting together, the two houses chose the Republic's president, whose limited role was to influence rather than govern.[14] The law that charged the president with the direction of the armed forces required that a minister countersign every presidential order.

---

[11] For an analysis emphasizing not Russia but Great Britain in French thinking, see S. R. Williamson, "Joffre Reshapes French Strategy, 1911–1913," in Paul M. Kennedy, ed., *The War Plans of the Great Powers, 1871–1914* (London, 1979), pp. 133–54. Douglas Porch deprecates French reliance on Russia, but his evidence reflects the situation before 1911; Douglas Porch, *The March to the Marne: The French Army, 1870–1914* (Cambridge, 1981), p. 228.

[12] Poincaré's "obsession" with British opinion and French unity is the centerpiece of Keiger's analysis; *Poincaré*, pp. 165, 183, 187.

[13] The "constitution" of the Third Republic consists of separate laws passed in 1875. English texts are in David Thompson, ed., *France: Empire and Republic, 1850–1940, Historical Documents* (New York, 1968), pp. 58–68. For the original French and an insightful discussion of how the system actually worked, see Schuman, *War and Diplomacy*, pp. 423–5.

[14] For more on the constitutional arrangements, see Wright, *Poincaré*, pp. 1–17. Wright's description of the president as the "pin boy in the bowling alley, whose only function it was to pick up fallen cabinets as the Chamber knocked them down" does not, however, apply to Poincaré. Wright, *The Reshaping of French Democracy: The Story of the Founding of the Fourth Republic* (New York, 1948), p. 10.

He could declare war only with the previous consent of the two chambers.[15] The president's greatest power lay in foreign policy, as he was empowered to make treaties and to conceal them from the chambers in the "interest and security of the state."[16]

The day-to-day governance of France fell to the council of ministers (in English, the "cabinet"). The chief voices in the council were the president of the council (the "prime minister" or "premier") and the foreign minister. Crucially, the council had the authority to mobilize the armed forces. Since the ministers served at the sufferance of the legislative assemblies, policy conflicts, which might have remained largely submerged in a presidential system, resulted in frequent reshuffling of ministerial portfolios. "Between 1907 and 1914," one scholar stated, "there were nine ministers of foreign affairs, eight ministers of finances, seven ministers of the navy, nine war ministers and twelve presidents of the council."[17]

Weak institutions rendered personalities important. Constitutionally, the key figure in July 1914 should have been Premier and Foreign Minister Viviani.[18] But Viviani had attained the premiership under conditions promising him little control over French policy. His selection was a by-product of the contentious general election of May 1914, fought largely over the 1913 three-year military service law and proposals for a progressive income tax. The elections returned more than 260 Radicals and 100 Socialists, obliging an unhappy Poincaré to look to the left for the next premier.[19] The president bowed to general pressure to select the

---

[15] "Constitutional Law on the Organization of the Public Powers," (25 February 1875), Article 3; and "Constitutional Law on the Relations of the Public Powers," (16 July 1875), Article 9; both in Walter Fairleigh Dodd, *Modern Constitutions* (Chicago, 1909), pp. 287 and 293.

[16] Ibid., p. 61. Since the Franco-Russian military and diplomatic agreements and those that created the Dual Alliance were signed only by Chief of Staff Boisdeffre and Foreign Minister Ribot, respectively, they should not have been binding on France, but French institutions were nothing if not flexible; Schuman, *War and Diplomacy*, p. 149.

[17] Paul de la Gorce, *The French Army: A Military Political History* (New York, 1963), p. 86.

[18] Viviani's left-wing credentials included having been a founding member of the SFIO, the French Socialist Party. Political groupings in the Third Republic were as unstable as cabinets, but a basic pattern remained fairly constant. The major parties of the left were the SFIO and the Independent Socialists. The center comprised a wide range of "republican" parties extending from the Radical Socialists through the Radical Republicans to the Moderate (or Opportunist) Republicans of the center right. Further to the right were a variety of Catholic and/or monarchist groups. Although the Radicals and Radical Socialists had some ideological differences, they combined as the Radical and Radical Socialist Party during the prewar period.

[19] The implications of the election were ambiguous. Socialist gains superficially suggested popular hostility to three-year service, but careful analysis reveals an electorate willing

independent ex-socialist, who promised not to overturn the three-year military service law. But Viviani proved unable to find men of the left willing to serve in a cabinet committed to defend the military law against which their parties had just campaigned. Poincaré turned then to Alexander Ribot, whose center-right cabinet failed to win the approval of the chamber. Faced with the alternate of dissolving the chamber and repeating the elections, Poincaré offered Viviani a final chance to form a government. Advertised by Viviani as "an elegant mosaic," the resulting cabinet was a motley collection united only by a willingness to serve and an agreement not to give up the three-year law, at least not too precipitously.[20]

Although often portrayed as a moderate counterweight to the bellicose Poincaré, Viviani was actually incapable of maintaining a policy of his own. He began his first premiership with a shaky cabinet and unprepared for his foreign affairs portfolio. Poincaré noted Viviani's "complete ignorance of foreign affairs" and accordingly "spent the four-day voyage to Kronstadt giving foreign affairs lessons to Viviani."[21] During the trip to Russia, the premier was incapacitated by nervous strain and abdicated his role to Poincaré, whose diaries suggest that he was not at all loath to assume control of the negotiations.[22] Once war started, Viviani moved quickly from the stage, on 3 August yielding the foreign ministry to Gaston Doumergue.

While Viviani was too weak to handle the considerable powers of the premiership, Poincaré's authority reflected his personal resolve rather than his limited constitutional power. Indeed, he chose Viviani to head the cabinet in a time of crisis not only in deference to electoral arithmetic but because Viviani was suitably pliable. Poincaré had previously arranged cabinets so as to extend his own influence, especially over foreign affairs.[23] Upon his election to the presidency in January 1913, Poincaré had insured the selection of an inexperienced foreign minister, Charles Jonnart, who accepted the president's guidance. Though forced in December 1913 to accede to a Radical government under Gaston Doumergue, Poincaré

to sacrifice for national defense. Workers expected the "blood tax" to be balanced by the levy on incomes. Hence the strident calls for progressive taxation. J. V. F. Keiger, *France and the Origins of the First World War* (New York, 1983), p. 142.

[20] Poincaré, *L'Union sacrée*, pp. 145–51, 165; Keiger, *Poincaré*, pp. 170–1.

[21] The diaries also lament Viviani's preoccupation with the Caillaux trial and his own mistress's infidelity; Keiger, *Poincaré*, pp. 166–7, 170–1.

[22] For Keiger's discussion of Albertini's misjudgment of Viviani, see ibid., p. 170.

[23] The suggestion that Poincaré saw Viviani as a usefully malleable foreign minister is not incompatible with his undoubted relief to see him go on 3 August (Kreiger, *Poincaré*, 184). Viviani apparently proved not merely plastic but stupid and mentally fragile.

insisted on dictating foreign policy to the new cabinet. He also conducted foreign policy directly by communicating with foreign ambassadors.[24]

After the war, Poincaré would exploit the formal weakness of his office in denying his own responsibility for the events of 1914, but his complaints of "helplessness and isolation" were much exaggerated.[25] He had shaped the Viviani cabinet so as to maximize his own control over French policy. During the period between his return from Russia and the outbreak of war, moreover, Poincaré chaired virtually constant cabinet meetings, keeping a firm hand on the smallest elements of French policy.[26]

Since Poincaré was the Frenchman best placed to make key decisions in July 1914, his politics demand attention. Traditional descriptions of Poincaré as a conservative Lorrainer and of partisan vituperation against "*Poincaré la Guerre*" misrepresent the Moderate Republican. Typically for a man on the right side of the Republican center, Poincaré was anti-clerical but not antireligious, nationalist but not bellicose, a defender of property rights, free markets, and small government. No ideologue, he was a practical politician willing to work with any true Frenchman but adamant in defending France from the Socialist left, the Catholic right, and, of course, Germany.[27]

Though often treated as *revanchist*, this native Lorrainer's policy toward Germany was pragmatically defensive. Poincaré's famous warning about the German "menace" and his calls for rectification of past injuries inflicted by the Germans were not cries for war but rejection of the appeasement proposals of Joseph Caillaux and Jules Cambon.[28] Poincaré objected to concessions to Germany because he believed that conciliation would not work. In his diary for March 1914, he tellingly described France's posture toward Germany as "no longer a question of revenge, it is a question of threat."[29]

---

[24] For Poincaré's unusual personal diplomacy, see ibid., pp. 151–2 and 159. Keiger denies that Poincaré selected Paléologue as ambassador to St. Petersburg (ibid., p. 172), but it seems improbable that Poincaré was not involved in his old friend's appointment. Poincaré's ambiguous account is in *L'Union sacrée*, pp. 29–30.

[25] For a balanced discussion, see Wright, *Poincaré*, pp. 126–41.

[26] Keiger, *Poincaré*, p. 185.

[27] For Poincaré's politics, see ibid., pp. 36, 62–63.

[28] Poincaré, 16 January 1912, quoted in Eugene Weber, *The Nationalist Revival in France, 1905–1914* (Berkeley, 1959), p. 100; Poincaré to Jules Cambon, 27 March 1912, Commission de publication des documents relatifs aux origines de la guerre de 1914, *Documents diplomatiques français, 1871–1914*, 41 vols. (Paris, 1929–59), vol. 2, p. 263. Hereafter cited as DDF.

[29] Stevenson, *Armaments and the Coming of War: Europe 1904–1914* (Oxford, 1996), p. 308.

Poincaré believed that it was possible to deal with Germany on specific issues, but that moving too close to Germany would be dangerous and costly.[30] It was dangerous because such a move would unnerve Russia and undermine the Dual Alliance. It was costly because Germany would sell her friendship only for colonial concessions. And it was costly for Poincaré because it would undermine his support on the French right. On the other hand, boyhood memories of the Franco-Prussian War left Poincaré with no desire for conflict.[31] Though a champion of military preparedness, Poincaré, "despite his ardent patriotism and his ancestral links with the lost provinces, found the idea of war repulsive."[32] Under Poincaré, "[t]he grand designs of French foreign policy continued to be motivated by the need to strengthen France's position on the international stage through reinforcing her militarily, through tightening the links of the Triple Entente, and through refusing any penetration of the alliance systems."[33]

Central to all three elements of this deterrent design was solidarity of the Russo-French alliance. Signed while he was serving as a young minister of education in his first cabinet, the Franco-Russian pact was one of the foundations of Poincaré's political world. The Russians had no doubt about his convictions. Ambassador Alexander Izvolskii reported to Foreign Minister Sergei Sazonov after Poincaré's inauguration: "Russia can count, not only on the armed co-operation of France in the case provided for in the Franco-Russian agreement, but on her most vigourous and effective diplomatic assistance in all the enterprises of the Russian government on behalf of those States."[34]

This pro-Russian orientation notwithstanding, until the time came to write self-exculpatory histories, not even the Germans viewed Poincaré as bellicose. The first Poincaré government, formed on 13 January 1912

---

[30] On the 1911 Morocco agreements, he commented, "I never thought that loyalty to our memories dictated, in relation to our neighbours, a sort of chronic animosity and prohibited us, them as much as us, on all points of the globe from hope of specific agreements"; Keiger, *Poincaré*, p. 125. Also, Keiger, *France*, pp. 70, 81.

[31] M. B. Hayne, *The French Foreign Office and the Origins of the First World War, 1898–1914* (Oxford, 1993), p. 238; also, Keiger, *France*, p. 44.

[32] *Pace* Lafore, *Long Fuse*, p. 105, who sees Poincaré's election as evidence of the strength of French *revanchism*. See Keiger, *Poincaré*, p. 16. Hayne, *French Foreign Office*, insists that Poincaré "rarely lent his name to the more strident forms of nationalism." Note that Poincaré discouraged Russia from going to war during the Balkan crisis of 1912; Keiger, *France*, pp. 99–100.

[33] Ibid., p. 118. For Poincaré's support of the Dual Alliance, see Albertini, *Origins*, vol. 1, pp. 413–15.

[34] Letter from Izvolski to Sazanov, quoted in Albertini, *Origins*, vol. 1, p. 413.

with Poincaré at the foreign ministry, met with general approval in Berlin. Apparently, Germany respected the man who described his own policy as based on "a sincerely pacific spirit, courteous and frank relations, inspired by a mutual respect of interests and dignity." Poincaré's election to the presidency in the tense diplomatic atmosphere of 1913 aroused no concern in Germany.[35]

Poincaré's reputation for bellicosity stemmed from his exhortations for military preparedness, his warnings about the German threat, his Lorraine background, and campaign slanders from elements of the French left about "*Poincaré la Guerre.*" Such political invective hides the more important point that the Socialists, though ever alert to opportunities to charge nationalists with warmongering, helped Poincaré to win the presidency in 1911 by failing to throw their support behind the Radical Party's candidate, Caillaux. The historian J. F. V. Keiger tellingly observes that "at no point between 1912 and 1914 did the left-wing Radicals even accuse him of being a warmonger, let alone oppose his candidacy on those grounds."[36]

If Poincaré's statements occasionally contributed an undeserved reputation of bellicosity, his official declarations during the July Crisis have created misunderstandings in the opposite direction. Keiger, in particular, exaggerates the importance of Poincaré's repeated references to keeping the peace. For Keiger, Poincaré's objective was to avoid war by restraining Russia, though he had to support Russia sufficiently to keep it in the alliance. Thus, "Poincaré was constantly at pains to maintain the fine balance between too much, or too little support for France's ally, either of which could have dire consequences."[37] Although Poincaré did not want war, avoiding it was secondary to two pragmatic concerns. The first was to maintain the integrity of the Franco-Russian alliance, essential as both a deterrent against war and a source of strength should deterrence fail. The second was to ensure that, if war broke out, France would appear to be an innocent victim of German aggression. Otherwise, Poincaré could not count on British support and would find it difficult to mobilize his own people. To sacrifice Russia's interests in the slender hope of averting war was to risk finding oneself in unwanted conflict beside an aggrieved and therefore unreliable ally.

[35] Keiger, *Poincaré*, pp. 128–30, 150.
[36] Gerd Krumeich, *Armaments and Politics in France on the Eve of the First World War: The Introduction of Three-Year Conscription 1913–1914* (Leamington Spa and Dover, N.H., 1981), pp. 40–2; Keiger, *Poincaré*, p. 147.
[37] Keiger, *Poincaré*, pp. 147, 168–72.

Aside from the president and premier/foreign minister, the minister of war had the greatest role in decisions of war and peace. Few of the thirty-one French war ministers from 1871 made much of a mark, but ex-soldier Adolphe Messimy of the Radical Party was better than most. As war minister in Caillaux's cabinet from July 1911 to January 1912, Messimy was responsible for the ouster of defensive-minded Chief of Staff General Victor Michel. Reacquiring the portfolio in the Viviani government of June 1914, he authorized all French military measures during the July Crisis and proved willing to act unilaterally during Poincaré's and Viviani's absence in Russia. Upon the French leaders' return from Russia, however, Messimy fell into line behind Poincaré. Later, Messimy took credit for the decision to shift three corps to defend Paris and, consequently, for making possible the "miracle of the Marne." His subsequent weakness in the face of the army's wartime accretions of authority worried the government. In August, Poincaré reluctantly shifted the War Ministry from Messimy to Alexandre Millerand as part of the price for bringing the Moderates into the cabinet.[38]

The cast of characters listed so far – the determined president, the weak premier, and the obedient minister of war – adhered consistently, but not always clearly and never explicitly, to a policy of deterrence through alliance solidarity. Clarity and explicitness were politically impossible for fear of appearing to push (rather than support) the Russians. This diffuse "line" inevitably made French policy look uncertain and, therefore, weak. Other elements, such as fragmented legislatures and ephemeral governments, introduced genuine uncertainties. Another destabilizing factor was the power of the professional diplomats in the Quai d'Orsay and also of the ambassadors in foreign capitals to push their own varied agendas. The Quai d'Orsay was generally anti-German, but the ambassadors operated independent fiefdoms. Paul Cambon, who served as ambassador to the Court of Saint James from 1898 to 1920, had far more influence than any foreign minister over Franco-British relations. An advocate of amity with Britain, Cambon was the most important author of France's refusal to support Russia in 1908.[39] In 1912, however, Cambon insisted on strengthening the Russian alliance so that the *entente* could counter Austria's supposed ambitions in the Balkans.[40] His brother Jules, who was

---

[38] Poincaré, *Au service de la France*, vol. 5: *L'Invasion*, pp. 169–76; Sewell Tyng, *The Campaign of the Marne, 1914* (New York, 1935), p. 350. For Poincaré's role, see Keiger, *Poincaré*, p. 180.

[39] Hayne, *French Foreign Office*, p. 196.

[40] Albertini, *Origins*, vol. 1, p. 415.

France's ambassador to Berlin from 1907 to 1914, sought to nourish the Russian alliance while pursuing Franco-German détente. Jules suggested that France support German interests overseas "in areas likely to divert her gaze from the European continent and from the French Empire."[41] When Jules worked to prevent war with Germany in 1911, he was acting against the anti-German policies of his colleagues in the Quai d'Orsay.[42]

The role of French ambassadors to St. Petersburg in furthering the Dual Alliance is discussed below, but it is useful here to mention one extraordinary attempt by a French ambassador to dictate national policy. On 5 June 1914, Ambassador Maurice Paléologue returned from St. Petersburg to announce that he would resign his post if the proposed Viviani Cabinet failed to retain the three-year military service law.[43]

The only other claimant to an important role in the decision-making process in 1914 is the French Army, or, more precisely, Chief of Staff General Joseph Joffre, its sole spokesman. Joffre's denial that the army could guarantee victory was enough to prevent France from going to war in 1911. His insistence on mobilization ensured that France could not stay out of war in 1914. Joffre's actions in 1914 reflected one overwhelming concern: the importance of acting wholly in accordance with French obligations under the terms of the Russian alliance. He was also confident that France was better prepared to fight the Germans than was the case three years earlier.[44] Although Joffre's opinions mattered greatly, on the issue of whether France would fight, he remained subject to War Minister Messimy and the cabinet as a whole. On the different but critically important question of how France should conduct military operations against Germany, Joffre's was the decisive voice. His role in assessing German war plans and designing the French response is discussed below.

The navy, incidentally, had no voice in French policy. Two strong navy ministers, Vice Admiral Augustin Boué de Lapeyrère and Théophile Delcassé, oversaw naval improvements from 1909 to 1913. But their successor, Armand Gauthier, the historian Gordon Wright reports, "had shown incompetence, even negligence, and was replaced on 3 August on 'health grounds.'"[45]

---

[41] Keiger, *France*, pp. 37–9. Jules Cambon did not want to undermine the *entente* but had little faith in Russia's military capabilities; Hayne, *French Foreign Office*, pp. 189, 193.

[42] Hayne, *French Foreign Office*, pp. 222–3.

[43] Wright, *Poincaré*, pp. 120–1.

[44] Stevenson, *Armaments*, p. 388.

[45] Wright, *Poincaré*, p. 184. Barbara Tuchman reports that at the start of the war Gauthier "forgot" to deploy French torpedo boats; see, *The Guns of August* (New York, 1962), p. 106.

Absent from this list of key actors in 1914 are many of the "usual suspects" – military leaders, arms manufacturers, press lords, pressure groups – those who, presumably, represent the forces of militarism, capitalism, and nationalism and are often blamed for the outbreak of the Great War. None of these, however, had a role in French decision making in 1914 nor influenced the men who did. Only the military leaders had clearly identifiable opinions on foreign policy.

Some French officers published opinions more bellicose than the army's official position. There was a faction that welcomed war with Germany as an opportunity to restore its honor and regain France's lost provinces. In John Cairn's words, "Sure that war was both imminent and in the long run desirable [the soldiers] struggled to combat all internal weakness and to place France in a material and psychological position where she would be able and ready to choose the most favorable moment to fight for her life, her honor, and the restoration of her former greatness."[46]

These men, however, were a minority even within the army, and their domestic agenda tended to discredit their foreign policy. Their struggle was not against Germany alone but also against the internal weaknesses of France: socialism, pacifism, and parliamentary government. An extreme proponent of these views proclaimed that war would "deliver Alsace-Lorraine from the Germans and France from the 'parliamentary yoke.'"[47] However much such men welcomed war in 1914, they had no influence over the parliamentary system they detested.

As for the notorious "merchants of death," arms manufacturers had little power in a country where most munitions contracts went to government arsenals. David Stevenson's exhaustive study of arms races before World War I offers not the slightest suggestion that that French manufacturers urged their government to go to war.[48]

The argument that the French people as a whole desired war rests on superficial assumptions about the persistence of French *revanchism*

---

[46] John Cairns, "International Politics and the Military Mind: The Case of the French Republic, 1911–1914," *Journal of Modern History* 25 (1953): 274. Soldiers in the most extreme circles hoped that war would bring an end to the detested parliamentary institutions of the Third Republic; ibid., pp. 282–5.

[47] Ibid., pp. 285, 284.

[48] Stevenson, *Armaments*. David G. Herrmann provides a sweeping general statement: "There is no evidence that lobbying by armaments manufacturers for large new contracts for, say, artillery or fortress construction played an influential part in the actual spiral of armaments increases," in his *The Arming of Europe and the Making of the First World War* (Princeton, 1996), p. 228.

and misunderstandings of the significance of Poincaré's election by the French parliament. As the memory of the Franco-Prussian War faded, ever fewer Frenchmen yearned to die for the return of the "lost provinces," while the inhabitants of Alsace-Lorraine came to accept German rule.[49] A contemporary analyst stated that "the very idea of war had disappeared from the popular mind" and that the French people believed war to be impossible.[50] And a recent study of French policy bluntly asserts that by 1911, "France had not only renounced revenge but even begun to believe that there would never be another war."[51] Although Germany claimed to fear French *revanchism*, Ambassador Wilhelm von Schoen's reports from Paris reveal that he knew better. As late as 18 July 1914, Secretary of State for Foreign Affairs Gottlieb von Jagow denied that France was "anxious for war at the present time."[52]

Swayed by reported national manifestations of "sacrificial joy" in July 1914, some historians have projected backward an exaggerated French desire for war.[53] The method is suspect, for such manifestations may have been less a reflection of genuine feeling than an emotional defense against fear and despair. Long before Jean-Jacques Becker's demolition of the fiction that most Frenchmen marched to war with zeal and optimism, Paul de la Gorce pointed out that "songs and warlike slogans helped to make the moment of leave-taking bearable" and that "in the villages ... there was no crowd, no band, no popular enthusiasm to hide the simple truth that the men were going."[54]

[49] So the realistic Jules Cambon had informed Paris; Keiger, *France*, p. 72. In his study of French war aims, Douglas Johnson dismisses the lost provinces: "[O]ne does not need to stress the fact that the idea of revenge for 1870, or the idea of liberating Alsace-Lorraine, were not important factors in impelling any French government to go to war." Douglas Johnson, "French War Aims and the Crisis of the Third Republic," in Barry Hunt and Adrian Preston, eds., *War Aims and Strategic Policy in the Great War 1914–1918* (London, 1977), pp. 42–3.

[50] Jacques Civray, *L'avant guerre: Comparée en Allemagne et en France* (Paris, 1919), pp. xvii, xviii. Civray even attributes the inadequacy of prewar French intelligence about German military plans to the government's conviction that war would not befall a country determined to avoid it; ibid., p. 122.

[51] Jean Doise and Maurice Vaïsse, *Diplomatie et outil militaire 1871–1991* (Paris, 1992), p. 193.

[52] Reports of Ambassador Schoen, 10 November 1912 and 15 November 1913, cited in Geiss, *July 1914*, p. 27; Jagow to Prince Karl Lichnowsky, 18 July 1914; ibid., 123.

[53] For an overblown wartime account of the French spirit ("never, perhaps, in the long centuries of her historic existence has France experienced the single-hearted enthusiasm that swept the country"), see Anna Bowman Dodd, *Heroic France* (New York, 1915), p. 2.

[54] De la Gorce, *French Army*, p. 95.

Although the years before the war in France, as elsewhere in Europe, saw a substantial outpouring of romantic, nationalist prose exalting the morally pure and mystical experience of battle for *la patrie*, the militarism often identified as endemic in European populations had little hold on French policy makers and even less on the general population.[55] For every nationalist intellectual declaiming in Paris about the virtues of self-abnegation, heroism, and war, thousands of Frenchmen faced war with trepidation.[56]

This survey of French policy-making institutions in July 1914 suggests that, while few Frenchmen wanted war, there was little agreement about how to avoid it. Policy confusion in Paris was exacerbated by the unregulated activities of French diplomats abroad. Those who understood the importance of the Russian connection said nothing. Although President Poincaré stepped in to fill a leadership vacuum, he had to do so by stealth. Wary of overstepping his constitutional prerogatives, he was even more concerned to avoid any appearance of French aggression. To make a policy decision was to risk shattering his nation's brittle unity. Because political concerns demanded that France be pushed into war, Poincaré would eschew any action even suggestive of jumping.

Recent events in Franco-German relations ensured that any signals given by the French government in 1914 would have a hostile edge. Since the beginning of the century, French leaders had struggled to advertise their nation's importance as a great power in the face of repeated challenges from a psychologically insecure Germany. At the same time, those leaders knew the nation was not ready for a military confrontation. Cabinet instability exacerbated both the desire for diplomatic success and the hesitancy to fight. In short, concern for prestige and deep-rooted fear of war combined to create the diplomatic style disparaged by Jules Cambon in 1911 as "aggressive on minor issues and platitudinous on major ones."[57]

---

[55] Ibid., pp. 91–2.

[56] Even Weber, who argues for the importance of nationalism in the period 1905–14, admits that "if the nationalist revival was influential, its scope was very limited"; Weber, *National Revival*, p. 101. Cobb presents a convincing picture of the "subdued" mood and the *"mourne résignation"* with which rural France faced the prospect of war; Cobb, "France and the Coming of War," p. 139. A study focusing on the Department of the Isère contrasts the fear and anguish manifested in rural France with the greater "resolution" of the urban centers; see P. J. Flood, *France 1914–18: Public Opinion and the War Effort* (New York, 1990), pp. 5–12. The crucial study of French attitudes is Jean-Jacques Becker, *1914: Comment les Français son entrés dans la guerre: Contribution à l'étude de l'opinion publique printemps-été 1914* (Paris, 1977).

[57] Keiger, *France*, p. 41.

France's rhetoric was anti-German and its specific policies suscepti-ble to such interpretation. To the extent that the Russian alliance, colo-nial *rapprochement* with Britain, and efforts to reconcile her Russian ally with her new British friend strengthened France, they naturally aroused German resentment. The very existence of the *entente cordiale* angered Germany's francophobic elements, and French actions sometimes seemed to vindicate German paranoia.

Most competition was over prestige rather than any vital interest, but that in no way lessened the importance of the consequences. There was, for example, nothing in Morocco worth a Franco-German war, but German efforts to assert their "rights" against France in Morocco led to con-frontations in 1905 and 1911. During the 1905 incident, the French cab-inet rejected Premier Delcassé's intransigent line and replaced him with the proappeasement Maurice Rouvier. Such conciliation did not mollify Germany's leaders, who brought on the Second Moroccan Crisis by dis-patching the gunboat *Panther* to Agadir in 1911. This time even a cabi-net headed by Rouvier's fellow appeaser Caillaux was willing to go war rather than swallow further insult. Popular opinion, antiwar in 1905, now reflected what the German military attaché in Paris described as a deep-rooted chauvinism fueled by hatred of Germany.[58] What held France back in 1911 was General Joffre's statement that he could not guarantee a 70 percent chance of victory.[59] War did not come closer in 1911 than in 1905 because Morocco had become more valuable or French leaders more warlike. It came closer because the repetition of the German assault on French dignity constituted an additional insult in itself.

If the two countries could come to the brink of war over colonial prestige, it is hardly surprising that Germany took umbrage at the gen-uine threat implied in France's encouragement of a substantial Russian military buildup. The Russian military reforms planned for completion in 1917 and railroad construction program financed by French loans provoked reasonable fears that France and Russia would eventually have the resources for a coordinated offensive against their common enemy.[60]

Having done its share to inflame European tensions, France had no reliable strategy for avoiding war in July 1914. It could only hope to deter

---

[58] Weber, *National Revival*, p. 99.

[59] Marshal Joseph Joffre, *Mémoires du Maréchal Joffre 1910–1917*, vol. 1 (Paris, 1932), pp. 15–16.

[60] For Russian military expansion, see William C. Fuller, Jr., *Strategy and Power in Russia: 1600–1914* (New York, 1991), pp. 436–8; and Stevenson, *Armaments*, pp. 146–59; for the railroad program, see ibid., pp. 323–6.

Germany by manifesting military readiness and maintaining the Russian alliance. This had to be deterrence "in a low key," however, as the need to maintain national unity militated against threatening language. Neither deterrence nor the other foundations of French policy – prestige and adherence to the Franco-Russian Dual Alliance – was suited for public discussion. Debate about whether France would defend itself strengthened neither deterrence nor prestige. Worse was any hint that France would renege on its obligations to Russia. Indeed, a key to understanding French actions in 1914 is the passage in Joffre's *Mémoires* noting that

> one can affirm that the Russian General Staff's certainty about our offensive plans and our commitment to the clauses of the military agreement, a certainty reinforced at every contact with our General Staff, strongly contributed to leading the Russian General Staff to intensify its effort. If it had sensed on our part any less firmness, there is no doubt that our allies would have been more cautious at the beginning of the war.[61]

Reassuring the Russians was crucial for French security, but so too was avoiding talk or action likely to generate public antiwar sentiment. On this score, the government was fortunate. French voters, who had recently returned a Socialist and Radical Socialist majority to the Chambre des Deputés, could trust Socialist-Republican Viviani's government to take all reasonable measures to avoid war. It has been alleged, moreover, that Russian subsidies encouraged Parisian newspapers to incite anti-German feelings.[62] Richard Cobb describes the government's "cool, intelligent, and rather machiavellian approach" as "suggesting that it had full confidence in the common sense and loyalty of provincial opinion." So well did the French government handle the crisis that the French public saw the war as "forced upon a peaceable Republic as a result of German aggression."[63]

Perhaps French policy worked too well. Imanuel Geiss suggests that French passivity after Franz Ferdinand's murder may have exacerbated the crisis by allowing Germany to believe in the possibility that a

[61] Joffre, *Mémoires*, vol. 1, p. 130. Unless otherwise noted, all translations are by the author. Cairns argues that the French Army advertised the alliance to reassure not only the Russians but also the people of France; Cairns, "International Politics," p. 274. Joffre's testimony is presumably honest since his insistence that France encouraged Russian military action was hardly helpful in the postwar period.

[62] Schuman, *War and Diplomacy*, pp. 221–2, assumes Russian influence over the French press. Owen, in *Russian Imperial Conspiracy*, pp. 75–83, cites alleged telegrams from Isvolskii offering names, dates, and amounts. The issue clearly demands further study.

[63] Cobb, "France and the Coming of War," pp. 140–1.

conflict between Austria-Hungary and Serbia could remain confined to the Balkans.[64]

The assassination of the Austrian archduke aroused little interest in a country that was deeply engrossed with the consequences of a much more interesting murder. Frenchmen cared much less about the European response to Gavrilo Princep's deed than about the fate of Mme. Caillaux, wife of Radical leader Caillaux, for emptying a revolver into *La Figaro*'s editor Gaston Calmette. Mme. Caillaux's trial from 20 to 29 July, which overshadowed such events as the Austrian ultimatum to Serbia and Poincaré's state visit to St. Petersburg, constituted France's "July Crisis."[65] But as Becker puts it, "one may suspect that Mme. Caillaux's trial did not divert public opinion from the crisis; rather public opinion, largely unconscious of the danger, had no reason to shift its attention from the trial."[66]

This general survey of France on the eve of the Great War suggests a country little interested in current international events but fearful of potential calamities. Both war and diplomatic embarrassment were to be avoided. In the best of all possible worlds, the crisis would go away without French action. In pursuing its policy of avoiding war while defending national prestige, France's main tool, and therefore the centerpiece of this discussion, was the "fateful alliance" created by the Franco-Russian military convention of 1893.[67]

## The Russian and British Connections

The history of Franco-Russian relations after 1893 illustrates the general themes of French foreign policy: fear of Germany, general uncertainty, defense of French prestige. Just as French foreign policy contained conflicting elements of appeasement, deterrence, and efforts at national aggrandizement, the Dual Alliance contained major internal contradictions. Each country saw the importance of maintaining a unified stand against Germany but contained a pro-German faction willing to explore other diplomatic possibilities. Each saw the other's military support as crucial against German aggression, but neither, understandably, wished to be

[64] Geiss, *July 1914*, p. 61. On this view, a more active response to events by France, Britain, and Russia might have deterred Austria-Hungary and/or Germany. For one important reading of likely French and Russian reactions, by Germany's ambassador to France, see Schoen to Hertling, 18 July 1914; Geiss, *July 1914*, p. 130.

[65] Becker, *1914*, pp. 131–3, 145.

[66] Ibid., p. 135.

[67] George F. Kennan, *The Fateful Alliance: France, Russia, and the Coming of the First World War* (New York, 1984).

drawn into war by an ally's adventurism. Joint military plans were obviously necessary to prosecute a successful war against Germany, but neither France nor Russia had much faith in the other's military capabilities. Obligations remained vague and subject to constant negotiation.

In 1906, an especially depressing year in Franco-Russian relations, Russia felt betrayed by France's retreat from three- to two-year compulsory military service, while France resented Russia's refusal of military support in the event of a Franco-German conflict over Morocco.[68] France could certainly take no comfort from the outcome of the Russo-Japanese War. As General Louis Moulin, the French military attaché in St. Petersburg, argued in 1906, Russia had no effective military aid to offer France, but staff talks were important in keeping the alliance alive.[69]

The annual military conversations between the French and Russian chiefs of staff, however, normally concluded with nothing more impressive than a reaffirmation of the need for regular meetings and, accordingly, were consistently disappointing. In 1908, General Moulin accused the Russians of failing to strengthen the alliance militarily, while France showed no interest in supporting Russia during the Bosnia-Herzegovenia affair. In 1910, without consulting its dismayed French ally, Russia began to decommission Polish fortifications and to withdraw its troops eastward. The Russian war plans presented to the French delegation during staff talks held in September 1910 were so manifestly improbable that French political leaders insisted on more information.[70] As the withdrawal from Poland denied the possibility of immediate Russian help in the event of a German attack on France, the Dual Alliance appeared doomed. Fearing that the Russians were beginning to look toward better relations with Germany, in 1911 France sent a colonel to attend the Russian Staff College, whence he sent a depressing report about the health of the alliance.[71] Also, in 1911 Russia offered France no encouragement during the Second Moroccan Crisis (Agadir).

The mere existence of regular conversations and the development of strong relationships among the military attachés, however, gave the alliance international credibility and allowed French soldiers to hope for

---

[68] France also resented Russia's objections to France's *rapprochement* with Great Britain; Pertti Luntinen, *French Information on the Russian War Plans 1880–1914* (Helsinki, 1984), p. 107.

[69] Ibid., 108. Luntinen stresses the role of the French attachés, especially General Moulin, whose 28 years in St. Petersburg (1880–1908) gave him unique access to the Russians; ibid., pp. 120, 166, 169–70.

[70] Ibid., pp. 111, 14, 122–5.

[71] Ibid., pp. 127–8.

substantive Russian support. While relations reached their nadir in 1911, they improved remarkably thereafter as a result of Poincaré's policy of strengthening France vis-à-vis Germany. Joffre sent General Auguste Dubail to St. Petersburg in August 1911 to urge the Russians to commit to an immediate offensive in case of war. The staff talks resulted in an agreement that Russia would launch an offensive by the sixteenth day of the war and expect to engage five or six German corps. Visiting Russia in 1912, Poincaré described French plans in the event of a war against Germany and encouraged his ally to plan for a coordinated offensive. In the same year, chiefs of staff Joffre and Y. G. Zhilinskii made considerable progress in coordinating operational plans. Most important was the agreement that Russia and France would mobilize in response to German mobilization without waiting for consultation, a process that would have been difficult after hostilities cut the main lines of communication through Europe. The two powers also decided to remedy the communications problem by constructing radio stations beyond the reach of the two Germanic powers.

Given the state of Russia's army and railways, the rapid Russian offensive required by French plans was chimerical, but now the Russians acceded to French proposals for improvements in both areas. For its part, France passed the three-year service law largely to reassure Russia of her own capabilities for a rapid offensive.

In sum, France's ability to deter Germany from war rested on the capabilities and reliability of its Russian ally. Both were doubtful in the first decade of the century, but France worked to strengthen Russian military power and resolve. Nothing was certain in 1914, except that France could not survive a war without Russia's active engagement against Germany. Thus, the most important decision that France had to make during the July Crisis – whether to support Russia's policy – was predetermined by the imperative of alliance solidarity.

France's prewar ambassadorial appointments in St. Petersburg reinforced her military commitment to the Dual Alliance. In 1912, the vehemently anti-German Delcassé replaced the "calm, reasonable and conciliatory" Ambassador Georges Louis. Since Delcassé's policies as foreign minister had sparked the First Moroccan Crisis and cost him the portfolio in 1905, his appointment by Foreign Minister Poincaré was viewed as significant.[72] Delcassé, in poor health and with diminishing mental stability, lasted only into early 1914 before being replaced by Poincaré's friend

---

[72] The description of Louis comes from his Austrian counterpart Count Thurn, who saw Delcassé's appointment as a threat to peace; Albertini, *Origins*, vol. 1, p. 418. Hayne argues that Delcassé's increasingly vehement Germanophobia made his appointment a mistake (Hayne, *French Foreign Office*, pp. 265–6), but it did serve to affirm France's

Paléologue. The latter claimed to have been surprised to hear Delcassé report that "his sole aim would be to ensure that the Tsar's armies would be prepared to make any necessary offensive in fifteen days."[73] But, given France's desire for firm adherence to the Dual Alliance, Paléologue was presumably less surprised by his predecessor's policy than by his candor.

Paléologue's journal attests that Gaston Doumergue had told him in January 1914, "The safety of France will depend on the energy and promptness with which we shall know how to push [our allies] into the fight."[74] Paléologue's promises to Russian Foreign Minister Sergei Sazonov on 25 and 28 July 1914 of "unequivocal French support" matched Delcassé's protestations of French loyalty.[75] They were also entirely in line with Poincaré's admonition to the Austrian envoy in St. Petersburg on 21 July that France would support Russia and Russia support Serbia.[76]

Historians who see a conflict between, on the one hand, Viviani's telegram of 27 August about "neglecting no effort to resolve the conflict" and acting "in the interest of the general peace," and, on the other, the assurances offered Russia by the ambassador on 28 August, treat Paléologue as a loose cannon, whose Germanophobia led him to exceed his authority.[77] That interpretation, however, misconstrues both the intent and the authorship of "Viviani's" communications. By 27 August, Viviani's nerves had given out. Any telegram sent over his name contains the views of Poincaré. More to the point, it is difficult to believe that after several days of personal contact with the ambassador in St. Petersburg,

---

loyalty. The Viennese newspapers got the message: "Not a paper [reported the French ambassador in Vienna] has failed to attribute some more or less disquieting significance to the sending of so important a representative to St. Petersburg"; Albertini, *Origins*, vol. 1, p. 417.

[73] Keiger, *France*, p. 138.

[74] Cairns, "International Politics," p. 285.

[75] For 25 July, see Schuman, *War and Diplomacy*, pp. 219–20; for 28 July, Sazanov to Alexander Isvolskii, 29 July 1914, Geiss, *July 1914*, p. 295 (*Die Internationalen Bezeihungen im Zeitalter des Imperialismus.*, Ser. 1, v. 5, p. 221); D. C. B. Lieven, *Russia and the Origins of the First World War* (New York, 1983), p. 141.

[76] Samuel R. Williamson, "Confrontation with Serbia: The Consequences of Vienna's Failure to Achieve Surprise in July 1914," *Mitteilungen des Österreichischen Staatsarchivs* 43 (1993): 174.

[77] Typical of the "loose cannon" school is Keiger, *France*, p. 160, while Schuman, *War and Diplomacy*, pp. 219–33, portrays Paléologue as all but amok. Lieven is more persuasive in arguing that Paléologue's words reflected French policy rather than personal inclination; Lieven, *Russia*, p. 141. In *Poincaré*, Keiger offers a "less censorious" view of Paléologue but still treats him as too Russophilic for Poincaré's liking (pp. 172–4).

the French leaders would have relied on ship-to-shore radio to communicate the nuances of their foreign policy.[78] Surely, messages about conflict resolution and peace sent by such insecure means were intended for international consumption, not to undermine promises of unequivocal support given privately in St. Petersburg. That such messages were sent, effectively, by Poincaré is even more revealing, as, unlike Viviani, Poincaré has never been described as irresolute in 1914. In fact, neither the strong Poincaré nor the weak Viviani ever threatened to renege on France's obligations to the Dual Alliance. Wavering was too dangerous. In Keiger's summary, "to have held Russia back from entering the war, had that been possible, would have allowed Austria-Hungary to regain some of her prestige, while seriously reducing that of Russia, thus altering the balance between Triple Entente and Triple Alliance to the disadvantage of the former."[79]

Historians would be better placed to understand the role of Franco-Russian relations in the events of July 1914 if they knew the substance of the St. Petersburg conversations, but official document collections and the personal papers of the participants are equally devoid of pertinent material.[80] The unusual silence suggests a concerted effort at concealment.[81] Since France could not be seen to be encouraging Russian action against Austria, the absence of evidence about the talks reinforces the theory that Poincaré's message to the Tsar was one of alliance solidarity. Thus the British ambassador to St. Petersburg cabled Foreign Secretary Sir Edward Grey that "secure of support of France, [Russia] will face all the risks of war."[82] Behind these assurances was the fact that, since nothing frightened France more than facing the German Army alone, her leaders worked to bind Russia to her obligations. If France's willingness to back Russia's play against Austria increased the risks of embroilment in a war she did not want, at least she would not have to fight alone. In the uncertainty of the moment, France clung to the course of action that avoided the worst possible outcome.

---

[78] Viviani to Paléologue, 27 July 1914, *DDF*, p. 138. Paléologue's account of what he told Sazanov quotes Viviani's message of 28 July verbatim; Paléologue to Bienvenu-Martin, 29 August 1914, *DDF*, p. 248.

[79] Keiger, *France*, p. 167.

[80] Albertini, *Origins*, vol. 2, p. 189.

[81] Any purges of the archives must have happened soon after the event, before changes of government destroyed Franco-Russian consensus about the need to hide French encouragement of Russia.

[82] Sir George Buchanan to Sir Edward Grey, 25 July 1914, telegram 169, Geiss, *July 1914*, pp. 213–15 (*British Documents on the Origins of the War 1898–1914*, p. 125).

Not only did both Paléologue and Poincaré adhere to the same policies in supporting Russia and warning Austria-Hungary, but they did so with reasonably good information about the possible consequences. Although Vienna intended its ultimatum to reach Belgrade only after the French leaders had left St. Petersburg for Scandinavia, leaks in both Berlin and Vienna assured that every capital in Europe was forewarned. On the basis of intercepted communications, Russia queried the Austrians about their intentions on 18 July and Poincaré had his conversation with the Habsburg envoy on 21 July.[83]

Preventing war through a display of alliance strength was probably more hope than policy, but the Poincaré-Viviani mission took no military measures to ensure against a failure of deterrence. The meetings in St. Petersburg appear to have been purely political, with no discussion of how to fight a war against the Germanic powers. In the absence of military conversations, the Russian military attaché quite reasonably asked Joffre on 28 July whether France would mobilize against Germany if Germany moved against Russia alone.[84] Poincaré and Viviani had avoided the issue because war planning would have betokened political failure and, perhaps, encouraged Russia to act rashly. When the French leaders landed at Dunkirk on 29 July, both still believed that war would be avoided.[85]

The contrast between French promises of support and the absence of concrete plans made Russia understandably nervous. The tsar believed that the *entente* could keep the peace, but only if it demonstrated a willingness to use force.[86] Since French political leaders continued to express a desire to avoid war, Russia reasonably asked what France would do if deterrence failed. Suspicious Russians wondered whether France's encouragement of Russia's military buildup had been merely a French plot to compensate for her own weakness.[87] As late as 30 July, even after Russia had announced mobilization against Austria-Hungary, Premier Viviani continued to claim that France would not "neglect any effort toward a solution of the conflict in the interests of universal peace."[88] This

[83] Williamson, "Confrontation with Serbia," pp. 173–6.

[84] Joffre to Messimy, 28 July 1914, *DDF*, vol. 10, p. 233.

[85] According to Jules Ferry, quoted in Becker, *Comment*, p. 138. For French desire to avoid war, see ibid., p. 127. Poincaré had not yet abandoned the plan of spending the August holidays in the country; Cobb, "France," p. 131.

[86] Paléologue to Bienvenu-Martin, T.n.282, St. Petersburg, 24 July 1914, *DDF*, vol. 10, pp. 211–12.

[87] Lieven, *Russia*, p. 103.

[88] Viviani to Paléologue and Paul Cambon, 30 July 1914, quoted in Francis J. Reynolds, Allen Churchill, and Francis Trevelyan Miller, eds., *The Story of the Great War* (New York, 1916), vol. 1, pp. 457ff.

reiteration of French preferences for peace so worried Russia as to cause a brief suspension of mobilization.[89] Even at the last moment, on 31 July, President Poincaré tried to avert war by appealing to King George V to convince Germany "that the *entente cordiale*, would be affirmed, in case of need, even to the extent of taking the field side by side...."[90]

France's relationship with Great Britain was even more awkward than that with Russia. French diplomacy took British support for granted; its military plans assumed the presence of British troops on Joffre's left flank and of the Royal Navy to defend the Channel. Indeed, although the British government refused to commit itself to continental operations, Director of Military Operations General Sir Henry Wilson drew up contingency plans as if British intervention were certain. Ignoring political uncertainties, Wilson's staff was prepared in August 1914 to mobilize the British Expeditionary Force, transport it to France, and deploy it in a triangle formed by the towns of Hirson, Le Cateau, and Mauberge.[91] But no formal political agreements backed these assumptions, and if France was loath to plead for guarantees, Britain's Liberal government refused to abandon its traditional diplomatic "free hand" by offering them.[92] Promising efforts on the part of Lord Landsdowne and Paul Cambon to negotiate an understanding between the two powers in 1905 had stopped when Rouvier took over foreign affairs from Delcassé, and proved impossible to revive after a Liberal government took power in Britain.[93]

The years 1911 and 1912 saw important conversations between the two general staffs, but these arrangements had no political support. Ambassador Cambon, backed by Poincaré, urged Britain to make firmer arrangements, but at a meeting on 30 October 1912 the British Cabinet agreed only to an exchange of letters between Grey and Cambon expressing their governments' intentions of cooperating "to stop aggression or to keep the peace." These letters specified, moreover, that military and

---

[89] Poincaré, *L'Union sacrée*, pp. 438–9.

[90] Ibid., p. 467.

[91] Joffre, *Memoires*, vol. 1, p. 120. Samuel R. Williamson, *The Politics of Grand Strategy: Britain and France Prepare for War, 1904–1914* (Cambridge, Mass., 1969), pp. 311–14. Wilson's friendships with French generals, notably Ferdinand Foch, aided Anglo-French cooperation; Williamson, p. 168.

[92] The best study of British policy is Zara S. Steiner, *Britain and the Origins of the First World War* (London, 1977). For the military details, see Williamson, *Politics of Grand Strategy*.

[93] "Note sur les accords franco-anglais," 17 April 1914, *DDF*, vol. 10, p. 110.

naval conventions did not bind their governments to specific actions.[94] In the absence of formal political agreements between the two states, France could only avoid actions embarrassing to Britain and trust that London would fulfill its informal commitments.[95]

The political and diplomatic requirements of national unity and alliance solidarity that discouraged France from visible decision making in July 1914 also operated on the French Army, but with instructive differences. While the government's difficulties stemmed from efforts simultaneously to avoid war and to fight it on the most favorable terms, the army was much more inclined to welcome war as the means to restore France's lost glory.[96] But the need to impress friends and foes alike with French martial virtues does not explain the almost somnolent manner in which the French Army moved from peace to war. While the government denied the need to make any decisions, the army acted as if all relevant decisions had already been taken and as if their plans and premises required no further examination.

### The French Army

French soldiers seem to have been as oblivious as the rest of the country to the diplomatic crisis of summer 1914. The highest military coordinating agency, the Conseil Supérieure de la Guerre, devoted its meeting of 21 July to general issues such as France's defensive fortifications, artillery construction programs, and military aviation. Commander-in-chief-designate Joffre admitted to being distracted by the rumblings of war but not to the extent that the council changed its agenda.[97]

---

[94] Ibid. For further discussion of Anglo-French relations, see K. A. Hamilton, "Great Britain and France, 1911–1914," in F. H. Hinsley, ed., *British Foreign Policy under Sir Edward Grey* (Cambridge, Eng., 1977), pp. 324–41.

[95] In particular, concern for Britain's sensitivities led Poincaré to reject Joffre's proposal to attack Germany through Belgium in the event of war; Williamson, "Joffre," p. 139. For the frustrations experienced by the French ambassador in London, see Cambon to Viviani, 31 July 1914, Geiss, *July 1914*, pp. 327–8 (*DDF*, vol. 11, p. 459). Ferdinand Foch was foremost among those French soldiers who trusted in Britain rather than Russia; Cairns, "International Politics," p. 275. For efforts by Foch in 1911 to solidify Anglo-French military arrangements, see Williamson, *Politics of Grand Strategy*, p. 138. Even in the absence of an Anglo-French Treaty, the military cooperation between the two nations in 1914 was firmer than that between France and Russia or Germany and Austria-Hungary; ibid., p. 316.

[96] For the army's desire for war, see Cairns, "International Politics," p. 274.

[97] Joffre, *Mémoires*, vol. 1, p. 203: "...déja la guerre grondait." Among the rumors, presumably, were reports from "informant number three" in Vienna, who "confirmed Germany's

Only on the evening of 24 July did War Minister Messimy share with Joffre his concern that "we will perhaps have to go to war."[98] Learning on 25 July that Messimy had ordered generals and unit commanders to their posts, Joffre asked the minister the next day for permission to execute the entire contents of the *"Instruction sur la préparation à la mobilisation."* In particular, Joffre wanted to cancel troop movements and leave and to recall all officers and troops from leave or furlough. While agreeing to all of the other measures, the cabinet refused until late on 27 July to stir up public concern by curtailing agricultural furloughs.[99] That day, Joffre concluded that war was imminent and looked immediately toward the Russian alliance. He asked the minister of war to "insist of the Russian government by every possible means" that its army undertake the promised offensive in East Prussia.[100]

On 28 July, Joffre, to his surprise, learned from the minister of war that Jules Cambon had apprised the Quai d'Orsay of German preliminary steps toward mobilization as early as 21 July![101] Believing France to be "headed straight for war" and that Germany had achieved a week's head start, Joffre asked Messimy for permission to establish the *couverture* (frontier covering force), but Messimy preferred to await Poincaré and Viviani's return to Paris the next day. Thus, it was without political authorization that Joffre told the Russian military attaché (A. A. Ignatiev) of France's "full and active readiness faithfully to execute her responsibilities as an ally."[102] Only on 30 July did the cabinet finally authorize deployment of the *couverture* – and only to the extent that it could be accomplished without movement by railway, calling up reservists, or requisitioning horses. Moreover, to avoid unintentional contact with German troops, no French soldiers were to come within ten kilometers of the frontier.[103]

adherence [to the Austrian alliance]" and warned "look out! I know for sure that these pigs have evil intentions"; État Major de l'Armée n. 1719, "Les relations austro-Serbes," Vienna, 25 July 1914, *DDF*, vol. 11, p. 34. The note also contains its French author's sarcastic remark about Franz Joseph: "We always suspected that the opportunity to bury his nephew Franz-Ferdinand would rejuvenate him for months."

[98] Joffre, *Mémoires*, vol. 1, p. 206.
[99] Ibid., pp. 208–9.
[100] Ibid., pp. 210–11.
[101] Although he complained at not having been informed of Germany's action, Joffre also withheld important information from Messimy; Andrew, "France and the German Menace," p. 143.
[102] Quoted in Geiss, *July 1914*, p. 225.
[103] Joffre, *Mémoires*, vol. 1, pp. 216–18.

Convinced that war was imminent, Joffre continued to insist on the need to deploy the complete frontier covering force, reservists, horses, and all. In a strongly worded note, he warned his government that "beginning this evening, every twenty-four hour delay in calling up the reservists and sending the orders relating to the *couverture* will translate into a withdrawal of our areas of concentration. That is to say that we will have initially to abandon part of our territory, perhaps fifteen to twenty kilometers for every day of delay."[104] By 9 P.M., when Joffre received permission to establish the *couverture*, Russia had ordered general mobilization. Joffre insisted that France follow suit.[105]

Even given Joffre's legendary sang-froid, the sequence of events just described seems oddly calm. Joffre claims to have been unfazed by Messimy's first war warning, because "being accustomed continually to concern myself with preparations allowed me to contemplate this redoubtable eventuality without surprise."[106] But if the chief of staff had time to become inured to the prospect of war, he also had ample opportunity to identify the army's weaknesses. One would have thought that a commander-in-chief's responsibility at such a moment was to weigh the competing forces and offer guidance to the government about France's military prospects. Joffre had done just that during the Second Moroccan Crisis, but in 1914 he advised not caution but escalation to higher levels of military alert. The reasons for Joffre's change of stance are evident. In 1911, he had provided warnings of French weakness to discourage his government from an avoidable war. In 1914, however, hesitation would not prevent war but only alarm the Russians, encourage the Germans, concede the edge in a race to mobilize, and undermine the reputations of the French Army and its commander-in-chief.[107] In any case, the important decision, the formulation of the French war plan, had already been made. The significant question is, therefore, not what the French Army did in July 1914, but how it had developed the war plans on which it would rely so unreflectively.

Behind French planning lay, of course, estimates of German intentions. French military intelligence had long offered warnings that the

[104] Note du Générale Joffre 31 July 1914, approved by Viviani at 1715; ibid., pp. 221–2.
[105] Ibid., pp. 224–6.
[106] Ibid., p. 207.
[107] Another possible reason for restraint was to reassure Britain of France's benign intentions. That France chose the tougher line belies the arguments of those, like Williamson ("Joffre"), who see France as concerned about Britain's feelings but willing to take Russia's for granted. Williamson, *Politics of Grand Strategy*, pp. 122–4.

next war would not be the reprise of 1870 for which France had been preparing.[108] As early as 1900, the French military attaché in Berlin had reported on the German Army's emphasis on enveloping attacks against enemy flanks. The next year, the Belgian high command informed Paris that it expected any future German attack to come through the Ardennes, in southeast Belgium. A 1903 railroad construction agreement between Germany and Belgium adumbrated a German deployment into Belgium. A set of alleged planning documents provided by a disgruntled German officer foreshadowed the actual German movements of 1914. French intelligence could not determine the veracity of these so-called Vengeur documents but pronounced them to be "most interesting."[109] Moreover, German history from Frederick II's oblique order to the elder Moltke's encirclement victories at Königgrätz, Metz, and Sedan suggested the likelihood of a massive envelopment scheme. But nothing was definite. France's War Plan XVI, in force since March 1909, met strategic uncertainties by opening the war in a defensive stance. Only after the Germans had committed themselves to a clear axis of advance would the French Army counterattack.[110]

When Joseph Joffre assumed the combined posts of chief of staff and commander-in-chief-designate of the French Army on 28 July 1911, he shared the consensus about the threat via Belgium. In October 1911, he identified as a major strategic concern "the need to defend against a German violation of Belgium" and noted that Germany was more likely to violate Belgium neutrality than not. On 9 January 1912, he received approval from the Conseil Supérieur de la Défense Nationale for a French riposte into Belgium should German troops cross the Belgium frontier.[111]

But entering Belgium after the Germans was a pis aller. What Joffre really wanted was a diplomatic arrangement, tolerable to neither Belgium nor Britain, allowing preemptive entry into Belgian territory. Joffre was wholly pleased by one outcome of the 9 January meeting: President

---

[108] Tanenbaum, "French Estimates of Germany's Operational War Plans," in May, ed., *Knowing One's Enemies*, pp. 150–5. In 1870, the opposing armies had simply advanced to meet one another in Lorraine.

[109] Ibid., pp. 150–2.

[110] Joffre, *Mémoires*, vol. 1, pp. 17–18. In early 1911, then Chief of Staff Victor Michel proposed a wholly defensive strategy; ibid., 19.

[111] Ibid., vol. 1, pp. 114–16, 124. For a thorough analysis of Joffre's thinking, see Robert A. Doughty, "French Strategy in 1917: Joffre's Own," *Journal of Military History* (forthcoming).

Armand Fallières's repudiation of defensive thinking. "French soldiers,"
Fallières announced, were temperamentally suited to the offensive and
"would advance on the enemy without hesitation."[112]

Joffre was more gratified by Fallières's offensive-mindedness than he
was discouraged by the government's refusal to contemplate violating
Belgian neutrality. Strategic calculations interested him much less than
devising a campaign plan that put his army on the attack. Although Plan
XVI offered flexibility in the face of German options, Joffre rejected defense and counterattack in favor of a new Plan XVII, which called for
the French Army to advance against the foe – strategically, operationally,
and tactically.[113] As the regulations of 1912 specified, "The French Army,
reviving its old traditions, no longer admits for the conduct of operations
any other law than that of the offensive."[114]

Joffre's offensive predilections reflected his personality and strategic
judgment.[115] A career in the colonial army, "which saw itself as an ad-
venturous elite, achieving its conquests more through individual initiative
and force of character than force of arms," had left him contemptuous
of the cautious soldiers of the metropole.[116] Offensives were required
to win a short war, the only kind France would choose to fight.[117] More
concretely, the threat of coordinated French and Russian offensives would
upset German plans or possibly even deter them from attacking, while a
French defensive policy gave Germany the freedom to defeat Russia before turning her attentions westward. France relied on a Russian offensive
to pin down substantial German forces and could hardly expect Russia to

[112] Ibid., vol. 1, p. 118.
[113] Joffre believed that "incomplete study" of the Boer War had led to a "pernicious"
rejection of offensive tactics, while study of the Russo-Japanese War "restored a healthy
understanding of the general conditions of war"; *Mémoires*, vol. 1, pp. 31–2. For the
Michel Plan, see Tanenbaum, "French Estimates," p. 161.
[114] Ferdinand Foch, *The Memoirs of Marshal Foch* (Garden City, N.Y., 1931), p. lviii.
[115] Thanks to his unprecedented power as both peacetime chief of staff and wartime commander, Joffre's views were the only ones that mattered, and he offered the Conseil
Supérieure de la Guerre only "the vaguest hints" about the offensive details of Plan
XVII; Williamson, "Joffre," pp. 145–6.
[116] Howard, "Men against Fire," p. 519.
[117] Although Joffre emphasizes the universality of the short-war assumption (*Mémoires*,
p. 142), Paléologue claims that at a CSG meeting on 9 January 1912, Joffre prophesied
a long war regardless of which side gained the initial advantage; Doumergue, *Journal*,
quoted in Cairns, "International Politics," p. 282. The passage is also quoted in the
English version of Joffre's memoirs: Joseph Joffre, *The Personal Memoirs of Joffre,
Marshal of France* (New York and London, 1932), vol. 1, pp. 52–3.

fling her army against Germany without France agreeing to follow suit.[118]
Ready or not, France had to attack.

Plan XVII was authorized by the Conseil Supérieur de la Guerre on
18 April 1913 and by the minister of war on 2 May 1913; it was completed
in May 1914.[119] The plan placed the bulk of the French Army in the northeast theater with small forces screening the Alpine and Pyrenean frontiers.
The northeastern force comprised five armies: First Army around Epinal,
Second Army in the Toul-Nancy region, Third Army opposite Metz, Fifth
Army furthest north from Hirson to St. Menehould, and Fourth Army
in reserve near Bar-le-Duc.[120] In the event of war, these armies would
attack into Alsace and Lorraine, avoiding the political and geographical
obstacles imposed by Belgium and Luxembourg, respectively.

Given that French relations with Britain and Russia demanded, respectively, adherence to Belgian neutrality and an immediate offensive
operation in the event of war, Plan XVII is logical enough. What ought to
be of interest to the student of the decision-making process is how General
Joffre handled the mounting evidence that the plan would not work because Germany would not cooperate. He appears to have adopted two
techniques: ignoring unfavorable evidence and refusing to calculate the
likely outcomes of his planned detailed course of action.

Although Joffre had acknowledged Germany's ability to invade
Belgium in January 1912, he appears to have forgotten the whole issue
two years later.[121] What happened in the meantime was his fixation on
the offensively oriented Plan XVII. Encouraged in his offensive thinking
by the results of the 9 January meeting, he sent staff officers to Belgium
and Luxembourg to assess the suitability of the territory for a French
attack. The report being unfavorable, Joffre no longer regretted the political obstacles to advancing into Belgium.[122] Thus, the ill-fated Lorraine
offensive has to be understood as a decision by a general who preferred
for reasons of doctrine and alliance policy to attack in the wrong place
rather than not to attack at all.

---

[118] For the connection between offensive operations and the Dual Alliance, see Joffre,
*Mémoires*, vol. 1, p. 130.
[119] Ibid., p. 180.
[120] Ibid., p. 178.
[121] Senior French generals Joseph Galliéni, Charles Lanrezac, and Pierre Ruffy all believed
by early 1914 that the German assault would come through Belgium and then cross the
Meuse River; ibid., p. 154.
[122] Ibid., 141.

Having determined that Belgium was not a good place for an offensive campaign, the last thing Joffre wanted to hear was that the German Army intended to fight there. He persuaded himself, therefore, that Germany lacked the manpower to move west of the Meuse unless reserve troops combined with active ones.[123] Faced with mounting evidence, including reports from French, British, and Russian military observers, that the Germans intended exactly that, Joffre looked more skeptically at the intelligence reports than at his own premises.[124] For example, when the *deuxième bureau* acquired a copy of the October 1913 German mobilization plan specifying the use of reserve troops "with the active troops," the French General Staff interpreted the document as establishing separate, and relatively useless, reserve corps rather than as an expansion of spearhead forces.[125]

Joffre's dismissal of evidence about German intentions in Belgium was characteristic of his decision-making process. Instead of basing his strategic decisions on intelligence, Joffre interpreted his intelligence according to its repercussions for his strategy. Plan XVII was useless against a German sweep through Belgium, but the obvious alternative, a defensive deployment designed to react to several contingencies, contradicted both Joffre's public commitment to a short war and the demands of the Russian alliance. Rather than deciding on the best strategy, Joffre acted as if Plan XVII were the only possibility.

In addition to ignoring troubling intelligence reports, Joffre kept Plan XVII vague enough to hinder criticism. Though its political aim of fulfilling the Russian alliance was firm enough, the plan had no operational specifics. Plan XVII dictated only French deployment; the campaign plan would be devised as needed.[126] Joffre explained the omissions on the grounds that "it was impossible [to] define a specific maneuver plan in advance; one had to take into consideration all of the unknowns which complicated the problem." He would not commit to a specific line of advance until German intentions had become clear.[127] Given that the transport and supply of huge modern armies cannot be improvised, Joffre's

---

[123] Ibid., pp. 139, 248–9.
[124] Tannenbam, "French Estimates," p. 166. Joffre acknowledges the possibility, *Mémoires*, vol. 1, p. 161.
[125] Joffre, *Mémoires*, vol. 1, pp. 249–50.
[126] Joffre's concerns about an early draft of the plan calling for a two-pronged French offensive to envelop the German forces at Metz underscores the dangers of the offensive project; ibid., pp. 151–3.
[127] Ibid., pp. 143–4.

insouciance is astonishing. It was as if he had elevated to the operational level Colonel Louis Grandmaison's famous dictum, "it is more important to develop a conquering state of mind than to cavil about tactics."[128]

When Joffre decided to pursue Plan XVII in the face of contrary intelligence indications, he had no reason to share his strategic premises with France's civilian leaders. How else to explain Poincaré's diary entry for 3 July 1914: "We are expecting, of course, a German attack through Belgium, as our High Command has always predicted"?[129] The president of the Republic did not know that earlier, and sounder, predictions about German intentions had been revised to suit Joffre's plans.

Determined to stick to Plan XVII (and the military convention with Russia), Joffre abandoned efforts to predict Germany's intentions for a strategic version of *"système D,"* the *"débrouillage"* or improvisation for which the French Army was notorious. Moreover, lack of specific planning both on the French side and within the framework of the Dual Alliance may have eased Joffre's mind and fostered his remarkable insouciance in July 1914. Nonexistent plans could not be evaluated, and no one was responsible for explaining why the concurrent French and Russian offensives would succeed.

Another upsetting possibility finessed by Joffre was that the French Army, admittedly unready for war in 1911, was not yet prepared in 1914. After all, Joffre had warned that the "superior" offensive form of war required the "intellectual and moral preparation of the army" and material of high quality.[130] Although the army had made considerable progress during Joffre's three-year tenure, could he believe that the correlation of forces between France and Germany had shifted between 1911 and 1914 so as to justify a French offensive?

In terms of doctrine, the signs do not appear, on Joffre's admission, to have been promising. Two years of hard work had produced new, offensive-oriented military regulations, but there had not been time to assimilate the new doctrine.[131] The Grand Maneuvers of 1912 and 1913 had revealed serious deficiencies in training, material, and command. Time and training might have allowed for a more sophisticated interpretation

[128] Louis de Grandmaision, *Two Conférences faites aux officiers de l'état-major de l'armée*; quoted in Porch, *March*, p. 228.

[129] Keiger, *Poincaré*, p. 186.

[130] Joffre, *Mémoires*, vol. 1, p. 34.

[131] *Règlement sur la conduite des grandes unités* (October 1913), *Règlement sur le service des armées en campagne* (2 December 1913), *Réglement de manouevre de l'infanterie* (20 April 1914).

of Joffre's ideas, but "war broke out before the important work of reju-
venating the high command had been completed." Poorly trained officers
would seize upon the offensive as the panacea for every situation, and
French soldiers would take literally every exhortation to attack.[132]

Even more disconcerting than Joffre's nonchalance in the face of deficiencies in infantry training was his handling of problems with the artillery. In the model 1897 75 mm gun, France had the world's finest light
field piece.[133] French gunners believed that the 75's light weight (a mere
1205 kg), mobility, accuracy, and phenomenal rate of fire made it an ideal
tool for close support of infantry assaults on a mobile battlefield.[134] Given
contemporary artillery spotting and fire direction techniques, French artillerymen saw little benefit in long-range, indirect fire gunnery. Instead,
in its own version of the "cult of the bayonet," French artillery would
advance so close on the heels of the infantry that the carriage of the 75
mm mounted a metal shield to deflect enemy rifle bullets.

The defects of the French 75 mm were consequences of its virtues.
All would be well if the Germans could be persuaded to attack on
level ground, but, as Joffre observed during the 1912 maneuvers, a flat-
trajectory piece was of little value in the uneven terrain of Lorraine on
which French and German forces were likely to meet.[135] The gun's light
and inexpensive 7.2 kg round packed a minimal punch and was worthless against fortifications. Germany, by contrast, put its faith in medium-
caliber howitzers – low velocity, high trajectory, long range, indirect fire
ordnance – all of this rejected as too heavy by French experts.

The synergy between France's 75 mm field gun and its army's offensive doctrine left little room for other artillery.[136] Larger howitzers would
merely complicate ammunition supply and reduce mobility in return for
apparently unnecessary increases in range and projectile weight. Moreover, new weapons would strain France's limited financial and manpower

---

[132] Joffre, *Mémoires*, vol. 1, pp. 37–40. Doise and Vaïsse, *Diplomatie*, p. 198.

[133] Its revolutionary recoil system gave the piece a theoretical rate of fire of twenty-four
rounds per minute at an effective range of 6,500 m. Germany's Krupp 77 mm gun, by
comparison, fired eight rounds a minute.

[134] James E. Hicks, *French Military Weapons, 1777–1938* (New Milford, Conn., 1964),
p. 169. Light guns could shift positions and targets rapidly, and a flat trajectory produced
a better spread of shrapnel than did the parabolic arc of a howitzer. Every French infantry
corps had 120 of these remarkable weapons, against a German corps' allotment of 108
inferior Krupp 77 mm guns.

[135] Joffre, *Mémoires*, vol. 1, p. 38.

[136] For a denial that offensive doctrine explains the French failure to built heavy artillery,
see Porch, *March*, pp. 232–7.

resources. Perhaps only heavy guns and howitzers could assault fortresses, but Joffre had little faith in such operations. In any case, French artillerymen felt little pressure to develop a procurement program given the army's conviction that the French legislature would not pay for the new guns or for the extra soldiers to man them.

Advocate of the offensive though he was, Joffre felt skeptical about the claims of the 75. From 1910, in his capacity as director of services of the rear, Joffre argued for medium field artillery comparable to that of the German Army (which the French would eventually acquire in 1916).[137] Concerns about inadequate artillery should have given Joffre pause, but, instead, in January 1914 this consistent advocate of medium field guns executed a remarkable *volte face* by reporting to the Conseil Supérieur de la Guerre that, while heavier artillery would be nice to have, it was hardly indispensable. The French would do well enough with current armament. Though knowing that "our inferiority could not escape anyone," Joffre took this unrealistically positive tone to support French (and undoubtedly Russian) morale.[138]

The army, like the government, depended on the Franco-Russian alliance. Some historians have denied that French soldiers felt any assurance about what Russia would do. For example, Gerd Krumeich dismisses Joffre's claims to have based his offensive plans on Russian promises as "a retrospective euphemism": "The fact that only a few days before the outbreak of the First World War French Army officers and politicians were by no means convinced that Russia was actually prepared to launch the main offensive against Germany – and not Austria! – proves just how fragile the 1911 agreements were considered to be."[139] Similarly, Samuel R. Williamson describes the Russians as "secretive with the French about their intentions" and points out that the British, though not allied with France, were more forthcoming about their military plans.[140]

Joffre's *Mémoires* explains his confidence in the Russian alliance. Not only were there regular staff talks between the two armies, but he and

---

[137] Joffre, *Mémoires*, vol. 1, p. 2. The excellent 155 GPF howitzer of 1916 had a range of 18,000 m and a rate of fire of three rounds a minute; Doise and Vaïsse, *Diplomatie*, p. 199.

[138] Joffre, *Mémoires*, vol. 1, pp. 72–3.

[139] Krumeich, *Armaments*, p. 23.

[140] Williamson, *Politics of Grand Strategy*, pp. 138, 223. Williamson describes the Quai d'Orsay as "taking Russian help for granted," but does not ask why it did so; also, "Joffre," p. 137. His disparaging comparison between the informal and frequent Franco-British exchanges and the "high-level and formal" Franco-Russian meetings is not persuasive; ibid., p. 147.

Grand Duke Nicholas Nikolaevich developed a personal friendship at their first meeting in France in September 1912. The grand duke's subsequent hospitality to Joffre during the Russian maneuvers of August 1913 far exceeded obligatory courtesy. Over the period of three weeks Nikolai and Joffre had "numerous conversations" about the importance of a rapid Russian offensive, and, Joffre reports, he assured his ally that "it was essential to bring relief to our front at any price."[141] In between these meetings, there were other conversations both in France and Russia.[142]

Joffre's trust was vindicated by the wartime actions of the grand duke, then commander-in-chief of the Russian Army, who advanced his forces on the fifteenth day after mobilization, six weeks before his reserves were fully deployed. Indeed, in a telegram received by Joffre on 7 August 1914, Nikolai announced that his headquarters would fly the tricolor alongside his personal flag.[143]

There are two obvious parallels between French diplomatic and military actions in July 1914. First, the requirements of the Franco-Russian relationship overrode all other considerations and, indeed, obviated the need for major decisions. Second, the two parties proceeded independently of one another. Absence of communication between army and government – and within branches of the army – may have contributed to the rigidity of French policy in 1914. In particular, the army's uncertainty about diplomatic events may have led it to exaggerate the importance of sustaining the Russian alliance.

Typical of French government practice was the Foreign Ministry's refusal to share diplomatic plans with soldiers or even with the political leadership of the War Ministry. Thus, the Quai d'Orsay "guarded its information jealously and simply refused to communicate information to

---

[141] Joffre, *Mémoires*, vol. 1, pp. 130–1. A special relationship between Joffre and Nikolai would not have been the first example of the role of friendship in fostering Franco-Russian understanding. George Kennan has demonstrated the extent to which that alliance emerged from personal interactions between chiefs of staff Nikolai Obruchev and Raoul le Mouton de Boisdeffre (and their wives). The French and Russian chiefs of staff, Generals Dubail and Gilinski, had visited each other's countries in 1911 and 1912, respectively; Doise and Vaïsse, *Diplomatie*, pp. 201–2. At the French maneuvers of 1912 the Russian grand duchess collected Alsatian soil and a thistle to plant in Russia and told General Laguiche that "when we return again to France, this country will be yours." Louis Garros, "En marge de l'alliance franco-russe, 1901–1914," *Revue historique de l'armée* 6 (1950): 30.

[142] Garros, "En marge de l'alliance," pp. 34–40.

[143] Joffre, *Mémoires*, vol. 1, p. 243.

politicians it considered incompetent."[144] Thanks to the Foreign Ministry's failure to inform military leaders about the Franco-Italian convention of 1902, for a period of seven years the army unnecessarily stationed two corps to deal with a nonexistent Italian threat.[145] The War Ministry, showing a similar concern, kept from the Foreign Ministry the details of the Franco-British staff talks.

Joffre believed that the army ought to be briefed on foreign policy *before* drafting its war plans, but Premier Caillaux was "unwilling" to share his government's views.[146] Joffre described a Conseil Supérieur de la Guerre meeting of 11 October 1911 in which he and War Minister Millerand argued with Foreign Minister Justin de Selves over whether the army had any right to information from the Quai d'Orsay. When President Armand Fallières supported Joffre's request for diplomatic guidance during the military planning process, Caillaux, newly arrived at the meeting, literally told him to "shut up."[147] Joffre succeeded in getting several Quai d'Orsay assessments of other countries' likely policies, most notably, the prediction that Germany would move her army through Belgian territory regardless of that country's neutrality.[148] The civilian authority provided no clear statement, however, on such issues as its attitude toward the problem of Belgian neutrality and Britain's expected contribution to any French military effort.

Some of the most notorious disputes occurred in the realm of intelligence, where vital information was squandered as ammunition in intramural conflicts. Astonishingly, France lost "her single most valuable source of foreign intelligence" in 1911 when Caillaux revealed to the Germans the cryptographic successes of the "rival" Foreign Ministry. Conflicts between the Sureté Générale and the Quai d'Orsay and between the War Ministry and its own cryptography section further impeded French intelligence assessment.[149]

Cooperation fell short even within the General Staff, whose Second (intelligence) and Third (operations) bureaus showed no greater fraternity than did the war and foreign ministries. Far from exchanging intelligence and planning information in a mutual effort to improve both, the two bureaus appeared driven to thwart one another. British liaison

[144] Hayne, *French Foreign Office*, p. 35.
[145] Joffre, *Mémoires*, vol. 1, p. 104; Keiger, *France*, p. 126.
[146] Williamson, *Politics of Grand Strategy*, p. 211.
[147] Joffre, *Mémoires*, vol. 1, pp. 105–6; Williamson, *Politics of Grand Strategy*, p. 209.
[148] Joffre, *Mémoires*, vol. 1, p. 111. This information, of course, he chose to ignore.
[149] Andrew, "France and the German Menace," pp. 130–1.

officer Sir Edward Spears lamented, "Who will ever know what harm was done by the often unconscious adoption of a thesis by the 3ème Bureau just because the opposition point of view was advanced by the 2ème."[150]

The twin themes of the centrality of the Russian alliance and the lack of candor in French policy making appear once again in the story of the three-year military service bill passed on 19 July 1913. Universal two-year service had become law on 21 March 1905 and, along with the twenty-six-year reserve obligation, remained for the majority of Frenchmen the maximum acceptable military obligation. Officially, proposals in 1913 for an extra year of service reflected a temporary need to match the German Army's 1912 expansion.[151] Only on those terms was the extended military service tolerable to the left.[152] Although they exploited the immediate German threat in arguing for the third year of active service, the authors of the three-year law, in fact, were less interested in the army's size than in improving its training, particularly in the artillery and cavalry, and in having more troops available for immediate offensive action.[153] The three-year service did not affect the total number of French soldiers; but it did, however, increase the ratio of active to reserve troops, thereby improving France's offensive capability.

Because three-year service did not increase the army's size, it was unnecessary as long as the high command envisioned a slow, defensive campaign in which reservists would gradually be assimilated into French formations for the eventual counterattack. The short war assumed by Plan XVII, however, called for a larger number of active duty troops ready for an immediate offensive.[154] There would be no time to incorporate even half-trained reservists into active units, let alone to toughen their feet for the long march into Germany. Given the manpower requirements of Plan XVII, it is hardly surprising that its acceptance by the Conseil Supérieur de la Guerre on 18 April 1913 coincided with military lobbying for three-year service. Nor can one believe that the backers

---

[150] Ibid., p. 141. The most violent interdepartmental skirmish included an attempt by War Minister Messimy to strangle his naval counterpart, Gauthier, in a cabinet meeting.

[151] Joffre reported that the 1912 law gave the Germans 657,000 active soldiers to France's 519,000 and allowed her to call up 511,000 reservists in 1912 instead of the 456,000 called up in 1909; Joffre, *Mémoires*, vol. 1, p. 136.

[152] That it was to be financed by a progressive income tax also made it palatable to the Left but not to the Right; Krumeich, *Armaments*, pp. 138–9.

[153] Becker, "Les Trois Ans," p. 8.

[154] As Joffre put it, by increasing the percentage of active-duty troops, "our units would obviously have considerable offensive power"; Krumeich, *Armaments*, p. 49.

of the legislation would have been satisfied with a temporary increase. Three-year service remained necessary as long as France committed to Plan XVII.

France's left-leaning electorate did not want to hear that the unpopular third year of military service was necessary for offensive operations.[155] Equally unpalatable was the suspicion that the Three-Year Law was being imposed on France by Russia as part of a deal made by Poincaré on his first trip to St. Petersburg.[156] Forced to acknowledge the connection between three-year service and the Dual Alliance, the leftwing Doumergue/Caillaux government, which took power in December 1913, adopted the line that the best possible defense for France was a Russian Army capable of deterring German adventurism, and that French military reforms were a means of encouraging the Russians to do the same.[157]

Left-wing fears about Russian pressure were entirely justified. In February 1914, Prime Minister Doumergue acknowledged to Tsar Nicholas II that the Three-Year Law was an essential component of the Dual Alliance, the "loyal application" of which concerned both Russia and France.[158] In June 1914, a Russian journal described France's retention of the Three-Year Law as being as much an obligation of the alliance as were Russian military reforms and railroad construction.[159] Those Russians who opposed the Dual Alliance used French domestic opposition to the Three-Year Law as an argument to shift to a Russo-German axis.[160]

French politicians could not admit the inextricable interweaving of the Franco-Russian Dual Alliance, Russian military reforms, and France's military service law. Frenchmen on the left accepted the extra year of military service only as a temporary response to Germany's recent military legislation. Louis Barthou and Poincaré had achieved the Three-Year Law

---

[155] Caillaux's dominant wing of the Radical Socialist Party "regarded the defence bill as at best a provisional shelter against a German attack and not as an essential element of French alliance policy"; ibid., p. 144.

[156] Wright, *Poincaré*, pp. 120–1.

[157] Indeed, Paléologue informed Doumergue that Russia had passed a military law increasing the 1917 contingent from 1,280,000 to 1,700,000; *DDF*, D.n. 128, 21 May 1914, p. 409.

[158] The tsar's statement was on 29 January 1914 and Doumergue's probably in February; see Krumeich, *Armaments*, pp. 171, 213; Becker, "Les Trois Ans," p. 12.

[159] "*La Russie est Prête: La France doit l'être également,*" *La Gazette de la Bourse*, quoted in Doulcet to Bourgois, D.n. 154 13 June 1914 (*DDF*, vol. 10, pp. 542–3).

[160] Paléologue to Viviani, T.n.212, 27 June 1914 (*DDF*, vol. 10, pp. 641–2).

under false pretenses and, had war not intervened, might well have lost it to the antimilitarist majority produced by the 1914 elections.[161]

The story of the Three-Year Law is that of French decision making in microcosm. The few choices available to the French government were not suitable for public discussion. Though military and political policies led to the same conclusions, with all roads leading to St. Petersburg, the effect was less one of coherence than of desperation. Paul Cambon's description of the impotence of French policy in late July 1914 – "The situation is very serious and we cannot see any way of controlling events" – was true long before the July Crisis.[162]

## Conclusion

In the final analysis, French diplomatic decisions mattered rather little in July 1914. Almost regardless of what it did, France would be dragged into an unwanted war. But the decision-making process remains important nonetheless. To the extent that French choices had any impact at all, its support for Russia made war more likely rather than less. Worried about its alliances and military conventions, France feared that any hesitation would erode its fragile understandings with Russia and Great Britain. In this atmosphere of uncertainty and fear ("nothing firm from St. Petersburg, nothing firm from Paris"), French leaders did not weigh alternatives but desperately seized upon those dangerous choices that brought some clarity to the situation.[163] Supporting Russia risked war, but it also brought hopes of alliance solidarity, firmer military agreements, and a more effective national defense.

Soldiers working under different circumstances also found themselves constrained to a single, desperate course of action. Compared with the confusing world of politics and diplomacy, that of the military planners was relatively straightforward. Friendly military assets were quantifiable. Relatively good information was available about German capabilities and intentions. Even if French military leaders did not confront the implications of the Schlieffen plan, they could have recognized the dangers inherent in their inflexible commitment to Plan XVII. They refused to take

---

[161] But see above, note 19, for Keiger's argument suggesting that the electorate's hostility to the three-year law has been exaggerated.
[162] Paul Cambon to Bienvenue-Martin, T.n., 24 July 1914, *DDF*, vol. 11, pp. 641–2.
[163] The quotation in the parentheses is from Poincaré, his view from *La France* as he steamed home from Russia; Poincaré, vol. 4, *L'Union sacrée*, pp. 315, 321.

advantage of the greater predictability of their world. As committed as their political masters were to the Russian alliance, French military leaders could not put that alliance at risk by evaluating the military assumptions behind the promised offensive. Fear of the probable answers – and of their impact on French alliance policy – discouraged questions. Joffre had remarked in 1913 that "fear is the beginning of wisdom."[164] It is hard to say whether in 1914 France felt too little fear or too much.

[164] Joffre, *Mémoires*, vol. 1, p. 54.

# 8

# Great Britain

## J. Paul Harris

For the British, the First World War has particular significance. It is by far the bloodiest conflict in the nation's history.[1] It resulted in a dramatic decline in Great Britain's economic strength and a great, if more gradual, diminution in its international standing.[2] Perhaps for these reasons it remains something of a national obsession, the intensity of which has, if anything, increased in recent years.

Yet for all the war's prominence in national consciousness, the British debate on its origins, especially when compared with that in Germany, has been desultory and muted.[3] The British are still horrified by their losses and have tended to regard the competence of much of their military leadership as at least open to question.[4] But they generally feel that they have little need to reproach themselves over the war's causation. Since 1918, indeed, few historians of any nationality have accused the British of having instigated the war. Great Britain was not directly involved in

---

[1] Approximately 744,000 servicemen from Great Britain and Ireland were killed in the war; 14,661 merchant seamen died and 1,117 civilians were killed in air raids. War deaths for the British Empire as a whole amounted to some 947,000. W. N. Medlicott, *Contemporary England 1914–1964* (London, 1978), p. 73.

[2] For the effects of the war on the British economy, see P. J. Cain and A. G. Hopkins, *British Imperialism: Crisis and Reconstruction 1914–1990* (London, 1993), pp. 31–48. See also Kathleen Burk, *Britain, America and the Sinews of War* (London, 1985), p. 223.

[3] John W. Langdon, *July 1914: The Long Debate, 1918–1990* (New York, 1991), provides excellent coverage of the debate on the war guilt issue in the various different countries.

[4] The day in the history of the war that most fascinates the British public is 1 July 1916, the bloodiest in British military history. One of the most acclaimed popular books on the war is Martin Middlebrook, *The First Day on the Somme* (London, 1971), which has gone through numerous reprints.

the quarrel in the Balkans that triggered it, and it is undeniable that the British government tried hard to defuse the crisis, offering mediation.[5]

Particularly since the publication of David Lloyd George's memoirs in the 1930s, some people have argued that Sir Edward Grey, the British foreign secretary, was culpable for failing to deter German aggression. According to this analysis, Grey might have faced Germany down had he categorically declared, in July 1914, Great Britain's readiness to go to war if France were attacked.[6] However, even without reference to extenuating circumstances (to be examined later in this essay), which help account for Grey's seeming passivity for most of that fateful month, an allegation of reluctance to threaten force appears less than damning. It is surely more reasonable to attribute blame to statesmen whose readiness both to threaten and to employ violence was all too great.

Any assessment of Great Britain's part in the origins of the First World War must address four basic questions:

1. Why had Britain's relationship with Germany become so severely strained by 1914?
2. How was it that Britain became increasingly aligned, in the decade preceding the war, with France and Russia – powers that had long been considered its most dangerous competitors?
3. Was it possible for the British government, during the crisis of July 1914, to have prevented a general European war?
4. Who eventually made the British decision to enter war and why?

To these may be added one further:

5. Should Great Britain, despite its agreements with France and Russia, have kept out of the war?

Each of these questions is, of course, very complex in itself, and a relatively brief treatment cannot provide exhaustive discussion of any of them.

## Developments Prior to 1914

In the last quarter of the nineteenth century, Great Britain's position in the world depended critically upon a balance of power on the Continent.[7]

---

[5] On British efforts at mediation, see Luigi Albertini, *The Origins of the War of 1914*, 3 vols. (London and New York, 1952–7), vol. 2, pp. 390–465.
[6] David Lloyd George, *War Memoirs*, 6 vols. (London, 1933), vol. 1, ch. 3.
[7] A. J. P. Taylor, *The Struggle for Mastery in Europe 1848–1918* (Oxford, 1954), p. 303.

Britain did a substantial proportion of its trade with Europe and it was important that no continental state should be in a position to sever or seriously constrain this commerce, still less to offer a serious threat to the home islands or the empire. Since 1815, however, a balance had been maintained without the British having to enter into any long-term alliance. Lord Salisbury, the British statesman with the greatest experience in foreign policy, continued to believe, until the turn of the century, that it was possible to protect the national interest by reliance on economic and naval strength, combined with astute diplomacy, without entering into long-term commitments to other powers.[8] The notion that it might be necessary, in order to check German ambitions, for Britain to align itself, on a long-term basis, with one or more continental powers only began to take root more than thirty years after the creation of the Reich. Even then it developed very gradually and tentatively.[9] In the 1890s France and Russia were generally considered the most serious threats to the British empire. As late as the early 1900s, an Anglo-German treaty seemed a possibility, though Salisbury, who had considerable reservations about the German kaiser, Wilhelm II, wanted, as usual, the benefits of friendly relations without the binding commitment of a formal treaty.[10]

Some members of Salisbury's government, however, began to doubt that the aging prime minister's policy of avoiding formal alliances was any longer valid. Joseph Chamberlain was the most prominent of these. An industrialist, Chamberlain was conscious of Britain's relative industrial decline and wished to expand the empire as an assured market for British goods. He was acutely aware, however, of the multiple military and naval challenges that the British faced overseas and believed it necessary to reduce these to manageable proportions. Seeing France and Russia as the main threats, he obtained permission from Salisbury to approach the United States and Germany for alliances.[11]

American policy makers were civil but noncommittal. Chamberlain's extended flirtation with Germany between spring 1898 and autumn 1901 succeeded only in establishing a very profound mistrust of that country's rulers in British government circles. The ultimate failure to produce

---

[8] J. A. S. Grenville, *Lord Salisbury and Foreign Policy: The Close of the Nineteenth Century* (London, 1964), pp. 434–40; C. H. D. Howard, *Splendid Isolation* (London, 1967), pp. 1–19; James Joll, *The Origins of the First World War* (London, 1992), p. 50.

[9] Zara Steiner, *Britain and the Origins of the First World War* (London, 1977), pp. 1–19.

[10] Taylor, *Struggle*, pp. 332–3, and 397; and E. B. Carroll, *Germany and the Great Powers 1866–1914* (New York, 1938), p. 312.

[11] Steiner, *Britain and the Origins*, pp. 24–5.

an Anglo-German treaty stemmed from reservations on both sides. But by late 1901, the British government and public opinion were, not unreasonably, tending toward the belief that the kaiser's government was duplicitous, unreliable, and rather hostile to British interests.[12]

The kaiser's government was now following a new course in foreign policy, a course that became known as *Weltpolitik*. Never very clearly defined, broadly it meant trying to expand Germany's possessions and influence, especially in the world outside Europe.[13] This was bound to cause concern for the British.

To support his *Weltpolitik*, the kaiser decided, under the influence of Admiral Alfred von Tirpitz, state secretary of the Imperial Navy Office from 1897, and with the close cooperation of Bernhard von Bülow, the state secretary of the Foreign Office, to create a battle fleet specifically designed to take on the Royal Navy in the North Sea. "For only when we can hold our mailed fist in his face," the kaiser argued, "will the British lion draw back."[14] Thus, while the British were seeking an alliance with Germany, German leaders were in the process of creating an instrument to threaten the British. By October 1902, Lord Selborne, first lord of the admiralty, warned his cabinet colleagues that the German fleet was being carefully constructed "from the point of view of . . . war with us."[15] By 1905, powerful voices in Britain, including that of the first sea lord, Admiral Sir John Fisher, were calling for a preemptive naval strike.[16]

German policymakers felt able to antagonize the British with impunity partly because they had convinced themselves that Britain's disputes with

---

[12] Lord Newton, *Lord Lansdowne: A Biography* (London, 1928), pp. 206–8. And for a comprehensive study, Paul M. Kennedy, *The Rise of Anglo-German Antagonism 1860–1914* (London, 1980).

[13] On the development of *Weltpolitik*, see Fritz Fischer, *Germany's Aims in the First World War* (New York, 1967), pp. 3–49; Gordon Craig, *Germany 1866–1945* (Oxford, 1978), pp. 224–50; Thomas A. Kohut, *Wilhelm II and the Germans: A Study in Leadership* (New York, 1991), pp. 177–98.

[14] Quotation from the kaiser is from Kennedy, *The Rise of Anglo-German Antagonism*, p. 224. On the beginnings of German naval expansion, see E. L. Woodward, *Great Britain and the German Navy* (London, 1964), pp. 19–53; and Paul M. Kennedy, "The Development of German Naval Operations Plans against England 1896–1914," *English Historical Review* 89 (1974): 48–76. On the crucial (and very complex) issue of the kaiser's attitude to Great Britain, a good modern account is Kohut, *Wilhelm II*, pp. 199–223.

[15] George Monger, *The End of Isolation: British Foreign Policy 1900–1907* (London, 1963), p. 82.

[16] Paul Kennedy, *The Realities behind Diplomacy: Background Influences on British External Policy 1865–1980* (London, 1981), p. 115.

France and Russia were too deep to permit accommodation, still less partnership, with those powers.[17] British policy makers, however, were aware even before the outbreak of the South African War in October 1899 that they faced a multitude of threats that, in combination, might prove too great for their resources. They were beginning to sense what Paul Kennedy has called "overstrain" and were trying to reduce risks by making deals with other powers.[18] The conflict on the veldt generated strongly anti-British currents of public opinion on the Continent.[19] This catalyst intensified British anxieties and led to the search for accommodations.[20] Since Germany had rejected Britain's overtures, it followed that the British would turn to Germany's enemies.

Even before the end of the South African War, Lord Lansdowne, who had succeeded Salisbury at the Foreign Office in 1900, had concluded a treaty with an emerging power. From the British point of view, the aims of the Anglo-Japanese alliance of 1902 were to limit Russian expansion in China and to prevent the Royal Navy in the Far East from being overwhelmed by a Franco-Russian naval combination. This formal alliance contained obligations to support a foreign power with armed forces in some circumstances. Some contemporaries therefore saw it as a radical departure in British foreign policy.[21] Though British fear of the combined power of France and Russia was one of the grounds for the Anglo-Japanese Treaty, this did not prevent the British commencing serious negotiations with France shortly afterward.

The Russo-Japanese War, beginning in February 1904 with a Japanese attack on Port Arthur, further alarmed Britain. The conditions of both the Anglo-Japanese alliance and the Franco-Russian alliance bound their signatories to aid each other in the event of war against two or more enemies. If France joined on the Russian side or Britain joined on the Japanese side, the British and the French would thus end up fighting each other. Since neither Lansdowne nor Théophile Delcassé, his French opposite, wished to see that, the negotiations became an urgent matter. The

---

[17] Newton, *Lansdowne*, pp. 207–8.

[18] Paul Kennedy, *The Rise and Fall of the Great Powers: Economic Change and Military Conflict from 1500 to 2000* (London, 1988), p. 698.

[19] Newton, *Lansdowne*, pp. 196, 210, 211.

[20] Samuel R. Williamson, Jr., *The Politics of Grand Strategy: Britain and France Prepare for War* (Cambridge, Mass., 1969), p. 2; and Howard, *Splendid Isolation*, p. 64.

[21] Ian Nish, *The Anglo-Japanese Alliance: The Diplomacy of Two Island Empires, 1894–1907* (London, 1966), p. 209; Newton, *Lansdowne*, pp. 218–29; Monger, *The End of Isolation*, pp. 46–66.

Anglo-French *entente* was signed on 8 April 1904, two months after the outbreak of war between Japan and Russia. On paper it was an agreement on colonies, spheres of interest, and fishing rights. It committed neither partner to military action in any set of circumstances. But by reducing the potential for conflict in several parts of the world, it seemed dramatically to reduce Britain's strategic problems.[22]

In December 1905, Arthur Balfour's Unionist government, of which Lansdowne had been part, fell. The French were fortunate in the choice of the new British foreign secretary, Sir Edward Grey. A landed aristocrat and a member of the "Liberal Imperialist" branch of the party, Grey was convinced of the need to maintain a balance of power on the Continent. He believed, more strongly than had Lansdowne, in the long-term German threat to British interests. Grey authorized military and naval staff talks with the French and at the international conference on Morocco held at Algeciras, Spain, in January 1906, gave the French considerable support. The Germans received only modest backing from Austria-Hungary and none from Italy and, not being prepared to resort to war, suffered a humiliating diplomatic defeat.

One important result of the crisis was a strengthening of the *entente*. In February 1906 Grey wrote:

If there is a war between France and Germany, it will be very difficult for us to keep out of it. The *Entente* and still more the constant and emphatic demonstrations of affection (official, naval, political, commercial and in the Press) have created in France a belief that we shall support them in war.... If this expectation is disappointed the French will never forgive us.... On the other hand the prospect of a European war and of our being involved in it is horrible.[23]

Grey's reading of these matters would not change, in essentials, between February 1906 and August 1914. Grey allowed unofficial and highly secret talks between the French and the recently established British General Staff to continue, though these were not frequent or detailed before 1910. The staff talks, together with remarks made to French politicians and diplomats by Grey, encouraged a French expectation of British military support in the event of blatant German aggression.[24]

---

[22] Steiner, *Britain and the Origins*, pp. 30–31; Kennedy, *Realities*, pp. 121–3.

[23] Keith Robbins, *Sir Edward Grey: A Biography of Lord Grey of Fallodon* (London, 1971), pp. 142–52; and G. P. Gooch and Harold Temperley, eds., *British Documents on the Origins of the War, 1898–1914*, 11 vols. (London, 1926–1938), vol. 3, no. 299, p. 266. Hereafter cited as *B.D.*

[24] Robbins, *Grey*, pp. 154–297. On the very gradual, hesitant development of a Continental role for the British army, see John Gooch, *The Plans of War: The General Staff and the*

Senior officials of the Foreign Office, while not ultimate decision makers, did inevitably influence policy. By the end of the first Moroccan crisis,
a substantial proportion of them had developed strongly anti-German attitudes. The most detailed exposition of their anxieties about Germany
was contained in a memorandum of 1 January 1907, written by Eyre
Crowe, senior clerk in the Western Department. Crowe was no mindless
Germanophobe. He felt that it "would be neither just nor politic to ignore
the claims to a healthy expansion which a vigorous and growing country like Germany has a right to assert." The British, accordingly, should
reassure the Germans of their basic benevolence. If the Germans found
means "peacefully and honourably to increase [their] trade and shipping,
to gain coaling stations or other harbours ... or to gain concessions for
the employment of German capital or industries," the British should not
get in their way. But he believed that in cases in which the Germans chose
to adopt coercive methods it would be a great mistake to appease them.
Though a life-long Liberal, Crowe came to despise the Liberal Cabinets
of 1906–14, including Sir Edward Grey, for what he perceived as their
irresolute attitude to Germany.

The next episode in the division of Europe into two armed camps
came with the signature of an Anglo-Russian *entente* on 31 August 1907.
The idea of a rapprochement with Russia had been widely accepted
in British policy-making circles for many years, Grey, for example,
having favored it since the mid-1890s. The basic idea was that, by
defining and agreeing upon spheres of influence, the risk of minor
incidents resulting in unnecessary war would be reduced. Lower levels of
tension might diminish the need for certain kinds of military and naval
deployment, allowing resources to be concentrated where they were
really needed, and thus diminishing, again borrowing Kennedy's term,
"overstrain."

The Russians had for a long time been difficult to persuade. But the
shock of defeat in the Russo-Japanese War and the accompanying costs
dramatically altered the incentives. By that time, the First Moroccan
Crisis, coupled with continued German naval building, had increased
British fears of German intentions. In Foreign Office thinking, therefore,

*British Military Strategy c. 1900–1916* (London, 1974), pp. 278–98. On the details of
Franco-British negotiations, see Williamson, *Grand Strategy*, pp. 59–329. On the vexing
question of British Cabinet knowledge of the Anglo-French staff talks, see J. W. Coogan
and P. F. Coogan, "The British Cabinet and the Anglo-French Staff Talks, 1905–1914:
Who Knew What and When Did He Know It?," *Journal of British Studies* 24 (1985):
110–31.

a possible agreement with the Russians now developed a distinct anti-German slant. As Grey put it on 20 February 1906, "An *entente* between Russia, France and ourselves would be absolutely secure. If it is necessary to check Germany it could then be done."[25] As with the Anglo-French *entente*, the agreement signed by Britain and Russia was also a settlement of imperial spheres of influence (in this case in relation to Persia, Afghanistan, and Tibet). There was no obligation for either power to provide military support to the other in any set of circumstances.[26]

The Moroccan crisis of 1911 brought a further deterioration of the Anglo-German relationship. Austrian interests were not directly involved, and the Germans received no support from that quarter; nor did they receive any from Italy. As the crisis developed, British leaders recognized that both the French and the Germans were viewing it as a test of strength of the *entente*. On this occasion, the Germans backed down before really testing the British cabinet's resolve. Germany acquired some strips of territory in Central Africa, but the informed German public recognized that, in relation to the magnitude and implications of the confrontation, these gains were very modest.[27] On the other hand, the Agadir crisis forced the Asquith government to consider the possibility of a major European war, and most ministers found the prospect appalling.[28]

Between February 1912 and the crisis of July 1914, it appeared that Britain's relations with Germany were improving. Before the end of 1912, Tirpitz was forced to scale down his naval building program, and the British were thus reassured that they could maintain a substantial degree of superiority over the Germans at sea. The related matter of colonial rivalry also became less troublesome. The Germans' relative reasonableness in these years may not have been due to any real change of heart, but it did prove possible, with regard to southern Africa, the Middle East, and the Balkans, for the British to negotiate and even, to some degree, to cooperate with them.

Various conflicts involving the Ottoman Empire also were resolved in these years. During the Balkan crises of 1912 and 1913, Grey worked with the Germans to prevent a clash between Austria-Hungary and Russia that might have become a general European war. He acted the part of honest

[25] B.D., vol. 3, no. 299, p. 267.
[26] B. Williams, "Great Britain and Russia 1905–1907," in F. H. Hinsley, ed., *British Foreign Policy under Sir Edward Grey* (Cambridge, 1977), pp. 143–7.
[27] Albertini, *Origins of the War*, vol. 1, pp. 332–4.
[28] Robbins, *Grey*, pp. 244–54; Kennedy, *Realities*, p. 132.

broker with great skill and his performance was widely regarded as the greatest personal triumph of his career.[29]

In June 1914, a fortnight before the murder of Archduke Franz Ferdinand, Britain and Germany arrived at a fairly wide-ranging agreement concerning their economic interests in Mesopotamia. Thus, for the British government, the assassination was set against the background of generally improving Anglo-German relations.[30] Few informed persons in Britain, therefore, found it possible to believe that a crisis following the assassination could result in war with Germany.

### The British Constitution: The Power to Make War

We must now look at the British reaction to the continental crisis that followed the assassination and see how the British decision for war was made. In Britain the right to make foreign policy and to declare war was part of the royal prerogative – the power of the crown to act independently of parliament. By custom and precedent, however, the monarch's ministers and in particular the prime minister – the custodian of much of the royal prerogative – were, by the early twentieth century, expected to exercise these powers on the monarch's behalf.[31]

The position of prime minister was absolutely critical to the whole British system of government. A politician became prime minister by being invited by the monarch to form a government. The individual thus selected would then form a cabinet, which would have collective responsibility for all the government's acts. But by the early twentieth century, the monarch, when inviting a politician to become prime minister, was normally no longer exercising a personal choice. Rather, the monarch was obliged to pick a party leader capable of leading a majority in the House of Commons, and there was normally only one such person.[32]

A British government with the committed support of both houses of parliament (the House of Commons and the House of Lords) had,

---

[29] Grey, *Twenty-Five Years*, vol. 1, pp. 249–77; Robbins, *Grey*, pp. 255–70.

[30] Steiner, *Britain and the Origins*, pp. 107–9; W. S. Churchill, *The World Crisis, 1911–1914* (London, 1923), pp. 178–9. For the essential falseness of the apparent improvement in Anglo-German relations in these years, see R. J. Crampton, *The Hollow Détente* (London, 1979), pp. 167–80.

[31] A. V. Dicey, *Introduction to the Study of the Law of the Constitution*, 10th ed. (London, 1959), pp. 464–5.

[32] On the selection of the prime minister and his constitutional position, see Sir Ivor Jennings, *Cabinet Government* (Cambridge, 1951), pp. 20–5, 160–208; on the collective responsibility principle in cabinet government, see pp. 257–69.

in accordance with a crucial constitutional doctrine known as the "sovereignty of Parliament," practically unlimited political and legal power.[33] Without the backing of a majority in the House of Commons (the popularly elected chamber, also known as "the Commons" or "the House"), however, it was virtually impossible to govern at all. The government was not obliged to submit the decision to go to war to a Commons vote. But if the Commons generally disapproved of being taken into a war, members could demand a "confidence motion." If the Commons voted that it had no confidence in the government, the government was obliged (by a well-established constitutional convention) to resign, or at least to hold a general election (an election for all Commons seats) without delay.[34] The Commons had the "power of the purse," the right to control the raising of taxes and government expenditure.[35] No government could wage war without spending much public money and, in the British system, the Commons had to approve that expenditure.[36] Only a prime minister in an advanced state of insanity would, therefore, deliberately lead the country into a major war without being fairly certain of the support of the House.

Though the House would not divide on party lines on all issues, in general a prime minister would expect to have the support of his own party in that chamber. The first step toward keeping his own party united behind him in the Commons was to preserve its cohesion in the cabinet. The cabinet was simply a group of the most important government ministers, chosen by the prime minister and regarded as having collective responsibility for all the actions of the government. Its members were normally drawn from both Houses of Parliament. It did not have a fixed number of members; its size and composition were up to the prime minister. It would have been considered grossly abnormal for the prime minister not to include in the cabinet the heads of the greatest government departments, including the chancellor of the exchequer (the politician who was departmental head of the treasury) and the foreign secretary. But it was also normal to include people holding posts such as lord privy seal and

---

[33] For a lengthy discussion of the concept of the sovereignty of parliament, see Dicey, *Law of the Constitution*, pp. xxxiv–xcvi.

[34] On the principle that a government losing the support of the House of Commons must resign, see ibid., pp. 449–50; and Jennings, *Cabinet Government*, p. 420.

[35] For a discussion of the financial control function of the House of Commons, see Frank Stacey, *The Government of Modern Britain* (London, 1968), pp. 131–47.

[36] On the Commons' control of finance, see J. Harvey and L. Bather, *The British Constitution and Politics* (London, 1985), pp. 185–96; Sir Ivor Jennings, *Parliament* (Cambridge, 1969), ch. 9.

lord president of the council, which had ceased to carry much administrative responsibility. The occupants of such posts, not being preoccupied
by departmental matters, would have time for the widest consideration
of policy issues.[37]

Up to the outbreak of the First World War, the cabinet did business in
a very informal way. The prime minister set a loose agenda and chaired
meetings. Minutes were not taken; historians are dependent on contemporary letters and diaries for knowledge of what was said. There were no
formal votes. The prime minister would try to achieve consensus behind
major policies. If a minister felt he could not accept responsibility for a
policy adopted, he was free to resign, indeed, honor-bound to do so. Yet
the resignation of a high proportion of cabinet ministers at the same time
on the same issue would constitute a massive political crisis for a prime
minister. He would be quite entitled to replace those who resigned, but he
might not be able to do so without fracturing his party and jeopardizing
his all-important Commons majority.[38] This was a prospect that, as we
shall see, confronted H. H. Asquith in late July and in the first couple of
days of August 1914.

It is also important to appreciate the party politics of this period –
British governments being formed out of generally well-disciplined parliamentary parties, backed by sophisticated nationwide organizations. The
Liberal Party was in power in 1914, as it had been since the resignation of Arthur Balfour's Unionist government in December 1905. The
Liberal leader was H. H. Asquith, prime minister since 1908. The Liberal
Party stood for domestic reform and free trade. It was, for the most part,
somewhat more dubious than the Unionists about the morality of imperialism, and many members were reluctant to spend heavily on the armed
forces. (A relatively small group of "Liberal Imperialists," which included
Asquith and Grey, was, however, more positive about the empire and more
attentive to defense requirements than the bulk of the party.) The Liberals
were allied to an emerging Labour Party representing trade-union and
working-class interests.[39]

The Unionist Party, led in 1914 by Andrew Bonar Law, was formed
from a marriage between the Conservatives and the Liberal Unionists
(who favored some domestic reform but not Irish Home Rule). Most

[37] Jennings, *Cabinet Government*, pp. 52–71.
[38] Ibid, pp. 210–69; John P. Mackintosh, *The British Cabinet* (London, 1968), pp. 298–344.
[39] For discussion of the Liberal Party and the meaning of Liberalism in the Edwardian
period, see Roy Jenkins, *Asquith* (London, 1964), pp. 113–64; and Malcolm Pearse and
Geoffrey Stuart, *British Political History 1867–1990* (London, 1992), pp. 185–211.

Unionists were more socially conservative than were the Liberals. In general, they were in favor of protective tariffs for British industry, proud of the empire, and more willing to spend money on the armed services than was the bulk of the governing Liberal Party.[40]

The clearest division between the parties was, however, over Ireland. The Liberals, allied to a substantial Irish Nationalist Party in the Commons, wanted to give Ireland "Home Rule": its own parliament and the right to manage its own internal affairs. The Unionist Party wished to preserve the union between Great Britain and Ireland or at least to exclude the northeast of Ireland, known as Ulster, where there was a good deal of Protestantism and Unionism, from the provisions of the Home Rule bill. When the July continental crisis started, a massive internal crisis over Home Rule had been in progress for months. The two crises then ran concurrently, the Home Rule crisis lasting a few weeks into the war.[41]

In 1914, the Liberals, in alliance with Labour members of Parliament and the Irish Nationalists, controlled the Commons. But the Unionists controlled the House of Lords.[42] The Lords consisted mostly of landed aristocrats sitting by hereditary right. But it also contained a growing number of recently ennobled plutocrats and, in addition, a group of appointed judges known as the law lords, the most senior of these being the lord chancellor. Though the powers of the House of Lords had been significantly reduced by the Parliament Act of 1911, it still had the right to delay nonfinancial legislation initiated in the Commons and was currently doing precisely that with the government's Home Rule bill. Home Rule was causing one of the most dangerous political-constitutional crises in Britain since the 1830s.[43]

---

[40] Probably the best discussion of the Unionist Party and Unionism at this period is John Ramsden, *The Age of Balfour and Baldwin 1902–1940* (London, 1978), pp. ix–90.

[41] R. C. K. Ensor, *England: 1870–1914* (Oxford, 1936), pp. 450–6, 473–81. In September 1914, both the British parties and the principal Irish leaders agreed to shelve their differences over Ireland for the duration of the greater struggle. But on 31 August 1914, Asquith noted, "The Irish on both sides are giving me a lot of trouble at a difficult moment. I sometimes wish we could submerge the whole lot of them and their island for, say, ten years, under the waves of the Atlantic." Herbert Henry Asquith, *Memories and Reflections: 1852–1927*, 2 vols. (London, 1928), vol. 2, p. 29. It is a sentiment that must have been privately echoed by several British prime ministers since 1914. In Asquith's case it was followed by much more charitable feelings when, in September, the Home Rule crisis appeared to have been resolved. Ibid., pp. 32–3, 36–9.

[42] Ramsden, *Age of Balfour and Baldwin*, pp. 27–33.

[43] For a balanced account of the Home Rule crisis from the point of view of the British monarch, see Harold Nicolson, *George V* (London, 1952), pp. 209–43. For a more general account, see Ensor, *England*, pp. 450–81.

Ireland was on the brink of civil war. Paramilitary groups on both sides of the Home Rule issue had armed themselves and were actively drilling and training. The Unionist Party had strong links with the Ulster Volunteer Force, a unionist paramilitary group in the northern part of the country.[44] The bulk of British army officers were Unionists and some had felt sufficiently disaffected to mount a sort of officers' mutiny, known as the "Curragh Incident," in March 1914.[45]

## The July Crisis

In these circumstances, Asquith's cabinet's reaction to the European crisis that followed the Sarajevo assassinations was somewhat slow and, until very late, quite ineffectual. In addition to its preoccupation with Ireland, two main reasons for this may be given. First, Grey appears to have been slow to realize the danger of the situation. The initial response of the Austrian government to the assassinations seemed to him "neither alarmist nor extreme." By mid-July, reports coming from the British ambassador in Vienna of a likely Austrian hard line with Serbia did stimulate his concern. But he was not sufficiently alarmed to draw these to the attention of the cabinet. It was not until 23 July, when the Austrian ambassador in London informed him of the text of the Austrian ultimatum to Serbia, that he fully grasped the imminent danger of European war. Until 28 July, moreover, when the Germans rejected his proposals for mediation, he still held out some hope that they would use their influence to restrain the Austrians.[46]

The other main cause of the cabinet's ineffectiveness for most of the crisis was that it was deeply divided. A small minority was prepared to take a committed stand beside France and Russia – to the point of war, if necessary – to preserve the balance of power on the Continent. But as late as 1 August, the majority of cabinet ministers would not commit themselves to going to war in any eventuality.[47]

---

[44] On the internal state of Ireland at this time, see R. F. Foster, *Modern Ireland 1600–1972* (London, 1988), pp. 461–71. On British Unionist links with the Protestant paramilitary in Ulster, see Ramsden, *Age of Balfour and Baldwin*, pp. 82–4.

[45] For a documented account of the Curragh affair, see Ian F. Beckett, *The Army and the Curragh Incident, 1914* (London, 1986), pp. 1–29.

[46] Grey, *Twenty-Five Years*, vol. 1, pp. 308–21. On British complacency in the early part of the crisis, see also Michael Brock, "Britain Enters the War," in R. J. W. Evans and Hartmut Pogge von Strandmann, eds., *The Coming of the First World War* (Oxford, 1988), pp. 164–7.

[47] Keith Wilson, "Britain," in Wilson, ed., *Decisions for War* (London, 1995), pp. 189–94.

On the afternoon of 24 July, Grey first alerted the cabinet to the risk of a European war. That body had spent most of a lengthy meeting desperately trying to stave off the outbreak of civil war in Ireland. The only way of doing this seemed to be to partition the country between the predominantly Unionist-Protestant northeast and the predominantly Catholic-Nationalist rest of the country. But where exactly should the country be divided? The cabinet, in Winston Churchill's famous phrase, "toiled around the muddy fields of [the Irish counties of] Fermanagh and Tyrone" without reaching any definite conclusion. The meeting was about to break up when, again in Churchill's words, "the quiet, grave tones of Sir Edward Grey's voice" were heard reading the Austrian note to Serbia that he had received at the Foreign Office.

This note was clearly an ultimatum; but it was an ultimatum such as had never been penned in modern times. As the reading proceeded it seemed absolutely impossible that any State in the world could accept it, or that any acceptance, however abject would satisfy the aggressor. The parishes of Fermanagh and Tyrone faded back into the mists and squalls of Ireland, and a strange light began immediately, but by perceptible gradations, to fall and grow upon the map of Europe.[48]

Grey was initially inclined to take a hopeful view of German intentions in this crisis. One reason for this was his own apparent success in negotiating with them the previous year to defuse the international tension following the Second Balkan War. Another possible and connected reason was the cordial relationship that he enjoyed with Prince Karl Max von Lichnowsky, the German ambassador in London. Lichnowsky was an aristocrat, an Anglophile with fairly liberal views, and a man of culture with impeccably good manners. Up to 24 July, Grey seems to have been inclined to regard him almost as a colleague.[49] Lichnowsky reported to Berlin a conversation he had with Grey that evening in which Grey stated: "The danger of a European war, should Austria invade Serbian territory would become immediate. The results of such a war between

---

[48] Churchill, *World Crisis 1911–1914*, pp. 192–3.
[49] On Grey's feelings about the European climate, Anglo-German relations, and his own relationship with Lichnowsky, see Grey, *Twenty-Five Years*, vol. 1, pp. 271–307. On Lichnowsky's personality, see Harold Nicolson, *Sir Arthur Nicolson, Bart, First Lord Carnock* (London, 1930), p. 391; and Harry F. Young, *Prince Lichnowsky and the Great War* (Athens, Ga., 1977), pp. 1–32. For Lichnowsky's account of the July Crisis, see Lichnowsky, *My Mission to London 1912–14* (London, n.d.), pp. 31–40. Lichnowsky appears to have been intensely and genuinely Anglophile. He thought that his own government behaved irresponsibly during the July crisis and felt that it was entirely understandable that the entire world outside Germany blamed Germany for the war. Ibid., p. 40.

four nations – [Grey] expressly emphasized the number four, and meant
by it Russia, Austria-Hungary, Germany and France – would be absolutely
incalculable."[50]

That formulation, it appears, gave German policy makers some
grounds for hope, at least for about forty-eight hours, that the British
would stay out of any war that resulted. It is inconceivable that Grey intended to give that impression. Not having expected the Austro-Serbian
dispute to lead to any kind of war, however, he had not thought through
Great Britain's likely response. During his meeting with Lichnowsky on
24 July, Grey seems to have been thinking aloud – a dangerous thing to do
in the presence of a representative of an opposing power during a crisis.
But in this particular crisis, Grey was only just beginning to realize that
Germany was, indeed, a hostile power trying to bring on a war and not a
partner for peace.

Over the next couple of days, the Russian government made it clear to
Grey that it could not stand aside in the event of an Austrian invasion of
Serbia. Grey came under considerable pressure from the Russians and the
French to declare, to both them and the Germans, Britain's position in the
event of a general European war.[51] By 26 July, Grey appears to have made
up his mind what the British position should be – though he could not
be sure that the cabinet would follow his advice. Sir Arthur Nicolson, the
permanent under-secretary at the Foreign Office, and Sir William Tyrell,
Grey's private secretary, had strong words with Lichnowsky that evening.
Grey spoke to Lichnowsky directly the following day, 27 July. The foreign
secretary succeeded in convincing the ambassador that, in the event of a
general European war, Britain would align itself with France and Russia.
Lichnowsky relayed this message to Berlin.[52]

But a more encouraging subsequent report may have reduced the
impact of Lichnowsky's communication on the kaiser. Prince Henry of
Prussia, Wilhelm's younger brother, had been yachting at Cowes, but felt
compelled to return home when he realized the magnitude of the European
crisis. Before doing so, however, he briefly called at Buckingham Palace,

---

[50] Lichnowsky to Jagow, 24 July 1914. Printed in translation in Imanuel Geiss, ed.,
*July 1914: The Outbreak of the First World War: Selected Documents* (New York, 1967),
no. 57, pp. 183–4.

[51] Wilson, "Britain," p. 184.

[52] Lichnowsky to Jagow, 27 July 1914. Geiss, ed., *July 1914*, no. 99, pp. 240–1. On the role
of Tyrell in British foreign policy at this period, see E. T. Corp, "Sir William Tyrell: The
*Eminence Grise* of the British Foreign Office, 1912–15," *Historical Journal* 25 (1982):
697–708.

on Sunday, 26 July. There he had a conversation with King George V. Shortly after his arrival at Kiel on 28 July, Henry wrote to the kaiser, quoting George as saying: "We shall try all we can to keep out of this and shall remain neutral." There is evidence to suggest that George V had indeed made an unguarded remark to Prince Henry – expressing the hope that the crisis would allow Britain to remain neutral, if not actually giving an assurance of British neutrality. The kaiser, however, seems to have seized on this second-hand assurance. The word of a monarch was good enough for him, he claimed.[53] Wilhelm appears to have ignored not only the possibility that his brother had misinterpreted an informal remark, but also the difference between the constitutional positions of the German emperor and the British king. George V might wish his country to remain at peace. He could not guarantee that it would.

At a cabinet meeting on the morning of 29 July, Grey presented his view of the European situation and tried to persuade his colleagues to make a commitment to support Belgium and France in the event of an attack by Germany. In particular, he produced copies of a report written by the law officers of the crown in 1870, at the time of the Franco-Prussian War, indicating that the Treaty of London of 1839 obliged Great Britain to defend Belgian neutrality. Though supported by the prime minister, Asquith, and the first lord of the admiralty, Churchill, he met strong resistance from the majority. Most of the ministers present rejected the view that Great Britain was obliged to defend Belgian neutrality by force of arms. The cabinet would not commit itself in advance to any course of action in any particular set of circumstances and merely decided not to decide.[54]

On the afternoon of 29 July, Grey, in a desperately weak position, played for time. He was generally honest with the French, telling their ambassador, Paul Cambon, that the cabinet had not yet decided what to do in the event of a Franco-German war. He indicated that the ultimate British decision might depend on whether the Germans violated Belgian neutrality and also on the state of public opinion in Britain.[55] He tried a tougher statement on Lichnowsky saying that if Germany became involved in a war with France, it would not be possible for the British

[53] Harold Nicolson, *King George V, His Life and Reign* (London, 1952), pp. 245–6.
[54] Wilson, "Britain," pp. 188–9.
[55] Ibid, pp. 189–90; Grey to Bertie, 29 July 1914, *B.D.*, vol. 11, no. 283, p. 180. Asquith, *Memories*, p. 7.

government "to stand aside and wait for any length of time."[56] The kaiser dismissed this as bluff.[57] At this precise moment in the crisis, as Keith Wilson points out, he was quite right to do so.[58]

Bethmann Hollweg approached Sir Edward Goschen, the British ambassador in Berlin, on the evening of 29 July, with an offer that, if the British remained neutral, the Germans would restore Belgian integrity after the war and would annex no French territory except colonies. Grey was driven to fury by what he regarded as a shameless "attempt on the part of Germany to buy our neutrality." He rejected the overture on 30 July, even before mentioning it to the cabinet. There was no meeting of the cabinet on 30 July, but the following day Grey informed his colleagues of Bethmann's approach. It brought little response, even though it clearly indicated Germany's intention to attack France.[59]

In the absence of formal minutes and formal votes, our knowledge of what was said at the critical cabinet meetings, and of the positions that individuals adopted at different stages in the debate, is incomplete. It is, of course, even more difficult to know precisely what was going on in people's heads. From contemporary diaries and letters, however, historians have assessed that on Friday, 31 July, the nineteen men who composed the cabinet were divided into three unequal groups. The largest, those still undecided, seems to have included Asquith (prime minister), Lloyd George (chancellor of the Exchequer), Haldane (lord chancellor), Lord Crewe (lord privy seal), Reginald McKenna (home secretary), and Herbert Samuel (president of the Local Government Board). The second group, those favoring an immediate declaration of neutrality, included John Morley (secretary of state for India), John Burns (president of the Board of Trade), Sir John Simon (attorney-general), the Earl of Beauchamp (lord president of the council), and Charles Hobhouse (postmaster general). Only Grey and Churchill, the third group, were definitely in favor of intervention in a general European war.[60]

Morley spoke strongly against intervention on the side of Russia, and his arguments seemed to have much support.[61] Grey threatened to resign if "an out-and-out uncompromising policy of non-intervention" were

[56] Lichnowsky to Jagow, 29 July 1914. In Geiss, ed., *July 1914*, no. 130, pp. 288–90.
[57] Kaiser's note on Lichnowsky to Jagow, 29 July 1914. In Geiss, ed., *July 1914*, no. 130, p. 290.
[58] Wilson, "Britain," p. 190.
[59] Goschen to Grey, 29 July 1914. In Geiss, ed., *July 1914*, no. 139, pp. 300–1.
[60] Wilson, "Britain," p. 191.
[61] D. Hamer, *Morley: Liberal Intellectual in Politics* (Oxford, 1968), p. 367.

adopted. Asquith feared the immediate break-up of the cabinet, a contingency that was avoided only by putting off any decision. Grey managed to secure the cabinet's agreement formally to ask both the French and the German governments to give a guarantee that they would respect Belgian neutrality, provided that the other power did so.[62] The Foreign Office dispatched these requests to the German and French governments at 5:30 P.M. on 31 July. A positive reply from the French arrived at 2:15 A.M. on 1 August. The Germans, on the other hand, replied that they could give no such assurance, as to do so would reveal details of their war plans.[63]

On the morning of 1 August, Grey's position was still desperately weak and intensely embarrassing. He wanted to show solidarity with France and Russia, but the majority of the cabinet wished to stay out of the war at virtually any price. The Austro-Serbian-Russian dispute in the Balkans, in itself, involved no vital British interest, and it seemed very unlikely that the cabinet would be prepared to fight a war in support of Serbia or Russia. Grey still hoped to preserve France from German attack. That morning he suggested to Lichnowsky that if Germany did not attack France, Britain would remain neutral, regardless of what was going on further east. Lichnowsky leapt at this offer, guaranteeing, on his own authority, that Germany would not attack France even before reporting Grey's offer to the kaiser.[64] Grey, perhaps unsure of the worth of Lichnowsky's guarantee, did not pass it on to his cabinet colleagues.

At a meeting commencing about midday on 1 August, the cabinet heard the responses of the French and German governments to the question that had been sent to them the previous evening about Belgium. Though the Germans had refused to guarantee that they would respect the neutrality of that country, the majority of the cabinet remained opposed to making any substantial and immediate intervention in the unfolding European crisis. Grey eventually managed to get the agreement of his colleagues to communicate to the German ambassador that "if there were a violation of the neutrality of Belgium by one combatant while the other respected it, it would be extremely difficult to restrain public opinion in this country."

[62] Asquith to Venetia Stanley, 31 July 1914. In M. Brock and E. Brock, eds., *H. H. Asquith: Letters to Venetia Stanley* (Oxford, 1982), p. 191.
[63] B.D., vol. 9, nos. 382 and 383, pp. 234–5.
[64] Lichnowsky to Jagow, 1 August 1914. In Geiss, ed., *July 1914*, no. 170, p. 343. Wilson, "Britain," pp. 194–5.

But he had to threaten resignation to gain even this much and, as a quid pro quo, he and Asquith were forced to agree that the British Expeditionary Force would not be sent to France. Lichnowsky passed this tepid British warning on the Belgian neutrality issue to the German Foreign Office that evening.[65]

Earlier the same day, 1 August, however, Lichnowsky had passed on to Berlin Grey's offer to guarantee French neutrality if the Germans would not attack France.[66] The kaiser was initially very enthusiastic about this. Grey's proposal appeared, after all, to offer the breakup of the Franco-Russian alliance and to give Austria and Germany a free hand in the Balkans and eastern Europe, respectively. Austria could destroy Serbia and Germany could shatter Russian military power while the states of western Europe stood back and watched.[67] At 7:02 P.M. on 1 August, the kaiser dispatched a telegram to George V stating that he had just received "the communication from your Government offering French neutrality under the guarantee of Great Britain." Wilhelm assured George that Germany would refrain from attacking France if France remained neutral and if France's neutrality were "guaranteed by the British Fleet and Army."[68]

Grey was summoned to Buckingham Palace later that Saturday evening to help frame a reply to the kaiser's telegram. Grey had, in fact, no assurance from the French that they were prepared to remain neutral in the event of a Russo-German war, and he seems at this point to have decided to allow this trial balloon to fall to earth. Grey drafted a reply to the kaiser in pencil on a scrap of paper. "I think," replied the king to the kaiser, "there must be some misunderstanding of a suggestion that passed in friendly conversation between Prince Lichnowsky and Sir Edward Grey."[69] Neither the British nor the Germans pursued the scheme of Franco-German nonaggression after 1 August.[70]

---

[65] Wilson, "Britain," pp. 191–2. Lichnowsky to Jagow, 1 August 1914. In Geiss, ed., *July 1914*, no. 174, p. 345.

[66] Lichnowsky to Jagow, 1 August 1914. In Geiss, ed., *July 1914*, no. 170, p. 343.

[67] Ibid., pp. 336–7; Albertini, *Origins of the War*, vol. 3, p. 381.

[68] Nicolson, *George V*, p. 247.

[69] Albertini, *Origins of the War*, vol. 3, pp. 174–9, 381; Nicolson, *George V*, p. 247.

[70] Lichnowsky to Jagow, 1 August 1914. In Geiss, ed., *July 1914*, no. 174, p. 345. The "misunderstanding" of 1 August is an extremely critical incident in the crisis in terms of what it reveals about both British and German motivations. The clearest explanation of the British side of the affair is in Wilson, "Britain," pp. 194–7. Older accounts include H. F. Young, "The Misunderstanding of August 1, 1914," *Journal of Modern History* 48 (1976): 644–5; and S. J. Valone, "'There must be some misunderstanding': Sir Edward Grey's Diplomacy of August 1, 1914," *Journal of British Studies* 27 (1988): 405–24.

Saturday, 1 August, was, of course, a critical date in the crisis. News reached London that evening that Germany had declared war on Russia, converting the Balkan war that had started on 28 July, when Austria attacked Serbia, into a European war. Germany and France had begun to mobilize their armies, and it seemed to Grey that a German invasion of Belgium and France was only a matter of time. At some point on Saturday evening, Grey decided to confront the neutralists in the cabinet the next morning and to carry out his threat of resignation if they opted for neutrality.[71]

Until 2 August, it appeared that sentiment amongst cabinet ministers was still far more neutralist than interventionist. But something happened that Sunday morning that strengthened the hands of the interventionists. Asquith received a note from Bonar Law, the leader of the Unionist Party, and from Lansdowne, the Unionist spokesman on foreign policy, offering "unhesitating support" for the government in any measures it considered necessary to support France and Russia. The Unionist note to Asquith resulted, at least in part, from action taken by Winston Churchill on the evening of 30 July. A former Conservative, Churchill had informed his former colleague, F. E. Smith, that the cabinet was split over the developing European crisis. He asked for more information on Unionist attitudes to the "supreme issue" of whether or not to support Britain's *entente* partners. The following evening, 31 July, Churchill received a note from Smith assuring him that the Unionist leadership favored intervention.[72]

Two cabinet meetings were held on Sunday, 2 August: the first from 11 A.M. until 2 P.M., the second from 6:30 till 8 P.M. Grey put his cards on the table. He said that he was "outraged by the way in which Germany and Austria have played with the most vital interests of civilization, had put aside all attempts at accommodation made by himself and others, and while continuing to negotiate had marched steadily towards war." Grey wanted the cabinet to declare straightaway in favor of intervention. But the majority was not yet ready to do this. The most that Grey could obtain was agreement to inform the French government that if the German fleet undertook hostile operations against French coasts or shipping in the Channel or the North Sea, the British fleet would give France all

---

[71] Wilson, "Britain," p. 194; B. Wasserstein, *Herbert Samuel: A Political Life* (Oxford, 1992), pp. 162–3.

[72] Churchill, *World Crisis, 1911–1914*, pp. 214–18. The director of military operations, General Sir Henry Wilson, may also have had some hand in rallying the Unionist leadership in support of intervention at this juncture. Albertini, *Origins of the War*, vol. 3, pp. 396–9.

the protection in its power. Even this modest concession required Grey's threat of resignation and insistence by Asquith that he would go if Grey did. This very limited step was too much for Burns and Morley, who Samuel thought certain to resign.[73]

That the bulk of the cabinet held together through the crisis appears to have been due in great measure to the efforts of one of its most junior members. This was Samuel, one of the "undecideds," who thought the imminent war would be "the most horrible catastrophe since the abominations of the Napoleonic time, and in many respects worse." Samuel wished, as his biographer expresses it, to place "the onus of provoking any [British] intervention on Germany." Two sets of circumstances, Samuel argued, would justify Britain's declaring war. The first would be a German naval descent on the north coast of France. The second scenario would be a German action that threatened the existence of Belgium as an independent state. A limited violation of Belgian neutrality – the passage of German troops through the Ardennes, for example – would not have been sufficient to justify British intervention. A full-scale German invasion of Belgium, on the other hand, would be sufficient cause. Britain had recognized Belgium's independence and neutrality by treaty in 1839 and was considered to have some responsibility for protecting that country, though not perhaps an automatic obligation to go to war in its defense.[74]

At the morning cabinet meeting of 2 August, during informal meetings with groups of ministers over lunch and later that afternoon, and again during the evening cabinet, Samuel pressed his case that Britain should be prepared to go to war in the circumstances outlined, but in those alone. One of his objectives was to hold the cabinet together. If it split, he believed, the result would be either a Unionist government or a coalition government, either of which would take Britain into the war.[75] Asquith drove this point home at one of the cabinet meetings that day – we cannot be quite sure which – when he read to his colleagues Bonar Law's letter of support for intervention.[76]

[73] Wasserstein, *Samuel*, p. 162; Wilson, "Britain," p. 139.
[74] Wasserstein, *Samuel*, pp. 161–3; Roy Jenkins, *Asquith* (London, 1964), p. 328; Wilson, "Britain," p. 199. For a fuller discussion of the British belief in the possibility of a German march through the Ardennes, leaving the rest of Belgium alone, see Brock, "Britain Enters," in Evans and Strandmann, eds., *Coming of the First World War*, pp. 149–54.
[75] Wasserstein, *Samuel*, p. 163.
[76] Runciman reported Asquith as reading the Unionist letter to the morning cabinet of 2 August. Cameron Hazlehurst, *Politicians and the War, July 1914 to May 1915: A*

Perhaps because Samuel's formula seemed to remove some of the burden of decision from individual ministers and perhaps also because it offered the prospect of the government holding together and remaining in office, the majority ultimately went along with it.[77] At their evening meeting on 2 August, the cabinet heard that the Germans had violated the neutrality of Luxembourg. At the same meeting, Grey was authorized to tell the House of Commons the following day that if the Germans substantially violated Belgian neutrality, the British would be compelled to take action.[78] It appeared that in such an eventuality most of the cabinet would stay together, though Burns and Morley were determined to go. At this point Samuel cherished hopes that

Germany will neither send her fleet down the Channel nor invade Belgium, and we shall be able to keep England at peace while rendering France the greatest of services – the protection of her north coasts from the sea and the protection of her 150 miles of frontier with Belgium. If we achieve this without firing a shot, we shall have accomplished a brilliant stroke of policy.... If we do not accomplish it, it will be an action of Germany's, and not of ours which will cause the failure and my conscience will be easy in embarking on the war....[79]

All the major Liberal newspapers, with the partial exception of the *Westminster Gazette*, were neutralist up to the end of July and, to that point, no popular enthusiasm for war was evident. Yet the evidence both of the press and of street demonstrations suggested that, from the beginning of August, British public opinion was shifting in favor of intervention – seeing the Germans as the aggressors and expecting that Great Britain would stand by her *entente* partners. An antiwar demonstration held in Trafalgar Square on the afternoon of 2 August received noticeably little support.[80] As Lloyd George relates in his memoirs, the prowar feeling was, by this stage, a good deal more vociferous:

I shall never forget the warlike crowds that thronged Whitehall and poured into Downing Street, whilst the Cabinet was deliberating on the alternatives of peace or war.... On Monday afternoon I walked with Mr. Asquith to the House of Commons to hear Grey's famous speech. The crowd was so dense that ... had it not been for police assistance we could not have walked a yard.... It was

*Prologue to the Triumph of Lloyd George* (London, 1971), p. 93. But Churchill recalled that he did not discover the existence of the letter until lunchtime. Churchill, *World Crisis 1911–1914*, p. 218.

[77] Wasserstein, *Samuel*, p. 163.
[78] Wilson, "Britain," p. 179; Brock and Brock, *Asquith*, p. 143.
[79] Wasserstein, *Samuel*, p. 163.
[80] Brock and Brock, *Asquith*, p. 143.

distinctly a pro-war demonstration.... The threatened invasion of Belgium had
set the nation on fire from sea to sea.[81]

The late but apparently quite pronounced shift in popular sentiment
probably had a strong influence on some ministers, and especially on
Lloyd George.[82] There can, moreover, be little doubt that an attachment
to office caused others who abhorred war to the bottom of their Liberal
souls to remain in a war government. The Unionists were waiting in the
wings to form a coalition with interventionist Liberal ministers or, indeed,
a government of their own. With the British public apparently prepared
to lend such a government electoral support, resignation would not
have helped the careers of ambitious politicians like Samuel and Simon.
Asquith may have been influenced by the apparent shift in public opinion.
He had remained undecided until a relatively late stage in the crisis and
had noted on 31 July that "our actions must depend upon the course of
events including the Belgian question and the direction of public opinion
here."[83]

Yet it cannot be said that the British cabinet entered the war lightly. It
did so with great reluctance, indeed with a deep sense of dread. By the time
the next cabinet meeting was held, 11 A.M. to 2 P.M. on 3 August, the
German government had demanded free passage for its troops through
Belgium and the Belgians had decided to resist. There were rumors that
the German invasion of Belgium had already begun (though it did not
actually commence in any force until the following morning) and the
atmosphere was highly charged. As Samuel put it: "The Cabinet was
very moving. Most of us could hardly speak at all for emotion.... The
world is on the verge of a great catastrophe."[84] Simon and Beauchamp
tendered their resignations, adding to those of Burns and Morley the
previous day. But Asquith and Lloyd George ultimately prevailed upon
Simon and Beauchamp to remain.[85]

At 3 P.M. that same afternoon, Grey delivered a momentous speech
to the House of Commons. He argued the importance of defending
Belgian neutrality and asked whether it would be in British interests

[81] Lloyd George, *Memoirs*, vol. 1, pp. 64–70. The quotation is from pp. 65–6.
[82] The influence of public opinion on Lloyd George is discussed in Albertini, *Origins of the War*, vol. 3, pp. 482–3. Keith Wilson draws the same conclusion in "Britain," pp. 181–2. For a more sympathetic analysis of Lloyd George's motives, see John Grigg, *Lloyd George: From Peace to War 1912–1916* (London, 1985), pp. 127–48.
[83] Wilson, "Britain," p. 199. Asquith quoting from contemporary notes of 31 July in Asquith, *Memories*, p. 7.
[84] Wasserstein, *Samuel*, p. 164.
[85] Jenkins, *Asquith*, pp. 328–9.

for France to be "in a struggle of life and death, beaten to her knees, [losing] her position as a great Power ... subordinate to the power of one greater than herself." Would it be tolerable for "the whole of the West of Europe opposite to us ... [to be] under the domination of a single Power?" He argued that if the British allowed, without fighting, the violation of Belgium and the subjugation of France "our moral position would be such as have lost us all respect." The House received the speech well.

After he had finished speaking but before he left the House, Grey received a formal note from the Belgians announcing that at 7 P.M. the previous evening the Germans had demanded the right of passage of their troops through Belgium and that the Belgians had decided to resist. After this note had been read to the House, Grey remarked in his memoirs, "[T]here can have been no doubt left in any mind that war was certain and inevitable."[86]

At a further cabinet meeting on the evening of 3 August, it was decided to send a message to the German government, via the British ambassador, Goschen, asking it to withdraw its demand to pass troops through Belgium. Such a telegram, very moderately worded, was dispatched from the Foreign Office at 9:30 the following morning. Grey's tardiness in this respect has never been adequately explained.[87]

Definite reports of German violation of Belgian neutrality were presented at the cabinet on 4 August. Asquith and Grey decided to issue an ultimatum to expire at midnight German time (11 P.M. British time). If the Germans had not announced their intention to desist by that time, the British "would be obliged to take all steps in their power necessary to uphold the neutrality of Belgium." Whether the cabinet explicitly sanctioned the sending of the ultimatum is not clear, but neither does it seem important.[88] There can be no doubt that the ultimatum had been implicitly sanctioned. The second cabinet of 2 August and the first of 3 August had authorized Grey to tell the Commons that a full-scale German invasion of Belgium would constitute grounds for British intervention in the European war.

---

[86] Albertini, *Origins of the War*, vol. 3, pp. 486–7; Grey, *Twenty-Five Years*, vol. 2, pp. 16–17.

[87] Albertini, *Origins of the War*, vol. 3, pp. 490–1.

[88] Asquith to Venetia Stanley, 3 and 4 August 1914. In Brock and Brock, *Asquith*, pp. 144–5; Asquith, *Memories*, vol. 2, p. 21; Albertini, *Origins of the War*, vol. 3, p. 490–4. Churchill indicates that the decision to send an ultimatum to Germany was not explicitly made by the cabinet but was done on the authority of the prime minister. Churchill, *World Crisis, 1911–1914*, p. 220.

Goschen received two telegrams from Grey on 4 August, both on the subject of Belgian neutrality, and had two interviews with Gottlieb von Jagow, the German foreign secretary. After receiving, during the afternoon, the second telegram containing the British ultimatum, Goschen had his second interview with Jagow at about 7 P.M., at which he delivered the ultimatum. Jagow made it clear that there was no chance of German withdrawal from Belgium. Goschen next went to see Bethmann Hollweg, who, intensely irritated and emotional, made his famous remark about the British going to war for a "scrap of paper." According to Bethmann Hollweg's account, Goschen was in tears by the end of the interview.[89]

By that time Asquith had, on the afternoon of 4 August, announced the ultimatum to the House of Commons. The House accepted the news, according to Asquith, "very calmly and with good deal of dignity and we got through all the business by half-past four." The Germans sent no reply to the British ultimatum. On the night of 4–5 August, the Foreign Office delivered, in succession, two letters, containing somewhat different versions of the British declaration of war, to Lichnowsky. The first version, delivered around 10 P.M., was drafted on the basis of a false report that Germany had already declared war on Great Britain. When Foreign Office officials realized that a mistake had been made, a second, corrected version, was delivered by Harold Nicolson, the son of the permanent under-secretary, an hour or so later. The young Nicolson retrieved the first, incorrect version, only partly opened and apparently unread, from a sleepless, haggard, and distraught Lichnowsky. Accepting the corrected version from Nicolson, the German ambassador asked him to convey his best wishes to his father. When the British public awoke on the morning of Wednesday, 5 August, their country was at war.[90]

### Assessment

At this point, we may offer answers to four of the five questions raised early in this chapter. First, the extremely difficult relations between Great Britain and Germany that brought the threat of war by 1911 were largely the result of the exceptionally ambitious, intermittently aggressive, generally crude, blustering, and incompetent conduct of German foreign policy under Kaiser Wilhelm II. This may seem a somewhat one-sided and simplistic historical interpretation. There were, indeed, some underlying,

---

[89] Albertini, *Origins of the War*, vol. 3, pp. 494–501; Asquith, *Memories*, vol. 2, p. 21.
[90] Nicolson, *Sir Arthur Nicolson*, pp. 423–6; Albertini, *Origins of the War*, vol. 3, p. 500–1.

practically unavoidable sources of tension between Britain and Germany – the most obvious of these economic competition and the ideological differences. In themselves, however, these did not preclude amicable relations.

The British industrial dominance of the early Victorian period was certainly a thing of the past. British industrialists were intensely aware of German competition, and some of them wanted the protection of the same sorts of tariffs that their German counterparts enjoyed. Industrial competition was not, however, what brought the two countries near to the brink of war in 1911 or pushed them over it in 1914. British industry, after all, also experienced serious competition from the Americans. Many British industrialists and entrepreneurs were, moreover, doing very good business with Germany. Twenty-two of the forty prewar international producer cartels were Anglo-German, and between 1904 and 1914 Britain became Germany's best customer and Germany Britain's second best.[91]

As two of Britain's most eminent economic historians have pointed out, British industrialists exerted relatively little influence on Britain's policy-making elite compared with the class of "gentlemanly capitalists" – the great financiers of the City of London.[92] The city in 1914 was terrified of war. The leading financiers believed that a major European conflict would lead to Britain's economic ruin – a fear shared by the foreign secretary. Grey had been considerably influenced by Norman Angell's book *The Great Illusion*. Angell argued that war rarely paid, even for the victor, and that the degree of economic interdependence between nations was now such that a major European war would be disastrous for the Continent as a whole. Whatever triggered the British declaration of war in 1914, it was not the wishes of the nation's "finance capitalists."[93]

From the creation of the German Reich, some ideological tensions had existed between Britain and Germany, this being especially noticeable when Britain had a Liberal government. But ideological tension did not necessarily give rise to poor relations. Britain had an *entente* with Russia, a

---

[91] Steiner, *Britain and the Origins*, pp. 62–64.

[92] This is the fundamental argument of Cain and Hopkins, *British Imperialism*. For a summary of the "gentlemanly capitalism" thesis, see *British Imperialism*, vol. 1, pp. 3–52.

[93] Asquith to Venetia Stanley, 30 and 31 July 1914. In Brock and Brock, *Asquith*, pp. 136, 138; Asquith, *Memories*, p. 7; Norman Angell, *The Great Illusion: A Study of the Relation of Military Power to National Advantage* (London, 1913). Grey actually read Angell's book under its earlier title, *Europe's Optical Illusion* (London, 1909); see Robbins, *Sir Edward Grey*, p. 244. For further discussion of the City's hostile attitude to the war, see Albertini, *Origins of the War*, vol. 3, pp. 374–7, and Chapter 15 below.

country even less liberal than Germany.[94] Rather, the Germans by building
their High Sea Fleet had quite knowingly and deliberately antagonized
the British. The fleet was an instrument specifically designed to coerce the
British rather than to defend any established German interest, and British
policy makers realized this.[95] That the kaiser and his ministers had scarcely
any idea of what they wanted to coerce the British into doing is beside
the point – except that it indicates German incompetence in the conduct
of foreign policy. By 1912, the British were winning the naval race, and,
equally clearly, the Germans could not use their fleet to coerce the British
into doing anything. For the time being, the Germans were placing much
less emphasis on expansion overseas and thus, *in the short term*, presented
no credible threat to the British Empire. Both the German and the British
governments recognized this fact, a recognition that permitted a limited
rapprochement between 1912 and 1914.[96]

Germany's failure in the naval competition was a direct result of the
military balance on the Continent. The Germans had massive military
commitments there that the British, in normal times, did not share. The
Germans could not afford to maintain an army big enough successfully
to fight Russia and France simultaneously (with only second-rate military
support from the Austrians and perhaps none from the Italians) while at
the same time outbuilding the Royal Navy. If, however, the Germans had
been able to overturn the balance of power on the Continent, shattering French and Russian military power and establishing hegemony there,
the consequences for the British might have been extremely adverse. The
Germans might have permitted only such British trade with continental
Europe as would not have competed with their own – and British and
German trade competed in many areas. Given control of much of the
economic resources of the Continent, moreover, there was every reason
to fear that the Germans might revive their more grandiose aspirations
for a "place in the sun." Disregarding British interests, they might back
up these aspirations with preponderant sea power.[97]

Why did the British establish *ententes* with France and Russia and why
did Grey and the Foreign Office attach such importance to preserving them

[94] British Liberal ideological misgivings about the *entente* with Russia are mentioned in
Kennedy, *Realities*, pp. 126–7.
[95] Kennedy, *Anglo-German Antagonism*, p. 224.
[96] S. M. Lynn-Jones, "Détente and Deterrence," in Steven E. Miller et al., eds., *Military
Strategy and the Origins of the First World War* (Princeton, 1991), pp. 169–79; Geiss,
ed., *July 1914*, p. 38; Kennedy, *Realities*, pp. 135–6.
[97] Kennedy, *Realities*, p. 139.

in the crisis of 1914? The *entente* with France had, on the British side, originally been motivated mainly by anxiety about imperial "overstrain." There was certainly no intention on the part of Lord Lansdowne to become involved in a sort of quasialliance against Germany. Even in 1914, as indicated earlier, the *entente* did not commit the British to military involvement on the continent.[98]

But crass, incompetent attempts by German leaders to break the *entente* during the Moroccan crises gave that agreement greater importance in British foreign policy than was originally intended. This led to a defense relationship of sorts, if not a fully committed one. A decade or more before 1907, some members of the British Foreign Office were actively considering an agreement with Russia, also as a means of reducing imperial overstrain. By the time that *entente* was formulated, however, in the aftermath of the First Moroccan Crisis, it had already become, in Grey's mind, part of a system of maintaining a balance of power on the Continent and thus keeping Germany in check.[99] Grey's wish to prevent the Germans from smashing France and Russia in 1914 and thus destroying the balance of power on the Continent (as would have happened if Britain had not intervened), was a rational policy. It could be defended quite logically in terms of Britain's self-interest, leaving aside the moral commitment that, after a decade of fairly close relations with them, Grey certainly felt to the French.[100]

Might the British cabinet have prevented a European war if it had acted more decisively during the crisis? That is conceivable; the German decision makers were a nervous lot and were extremely anxious to avoid British involvement. But Lloyd George's attempt to blame Grey for British ineffectiveness during the crisis is, as Keith Wilson has pointed out, a piece of the grossest hypocrisy, a shameful accusation by one who, for all his undoubted talents, was to bring much shame on British public life.[101] To be sure, Grey only gradually realized the precise character of German intentions. But in the absence of high-grade diplomatic intelligence of the sort

---

[98] Niall Ferguson argues against the existence of a definite military commitment to France in "Kaiser's Economic Union," in Ferguson, ed., *Virtual History: Alternatives and Counterfactuals* (London, 1997), pp. 261–2. For Asquith's view that there was no definite British military commitment to France, see Asquith to Venetia Stanley, 2 August 1914; in Brock and Brock, *Asquith*, p. 146. See also Keith M. Wilson, *The Policy of the Entente: Essays on the Determinants of British Foreign Policy, 1904–1914* (Cambridge, 1985), p. 134.

[99] *B.D.*, vol. 3, no. 299, p. 267.

[100] For Grey's view of the commitment to France, see Wilson, *Policy of the Entente*, p. 123.

[101] Wilson, "Britain," pp. 175–82.

that the British gained through interception of signals and cryptanalysis during the war, he cannot altogether be blamed for this.[102]

By 24 July, Grey was aware of the gravity of the situation. From that point onward the slowness of the British response stemmed primarily from the extreme reluctance of the majority of the cabinet to follow Grey's advice and to take a strong line in support of France and Russia. It was the neutralists and those like Lloyd George, who could not make their minds up, who made any clear, unambiguous declaration of British support impossible. Anything that Grey said to deter the Germans that did not have the committed support of the great majority of the cabinet behind it could only be bluff – and in this crisis bluffs were likely to be detected and called.[103]

Who actually made the British decision for war? With strict constitutional propriety, Asquith's cabinet made the decision. The House of Commons could have stopped British intervention by bringing the government down, but the leaders of both major parties favored intervention, and Members of Parliament followed their leaders. The cabinet did not act in unison. As sometimes happens with a jury considering a verdict, a resolute minority eventually won over a reluctant majority. The prime mover was Grey, who, from the outset, was vociferously supported by Churchill.[104] Asquith was far from enthusiastic about intervention but trusted Grey's judgment in foreign policy and provided the much-needed support. Nearly all the others eventually went along.

The cabinet's motives were mixed. Grey was consistent in his adherence to the *entente* with France (though rather less so to the one with Russia) and in his wish to prevent Germany dominating the Continent. Churchill and Asquith each ultimately endorsed Grey's position, though Churchill

---

[102] On the Foreign Office's lack of a "black chamber" to intercept and decode foreign signals and on the very primitive and amateurish nature of the British Secret Service at this period, see Christopher Andrew, *Secret Service: The Making of the British Intelligence Community* (London, 1985), pp. 136–7.

[103] This was the case with Grey's attempt to bluff the Germans on 29 July 1914, as pointed out in Wilson, "Britain," p. 190.

[104] On Churchill's support for Grey, see Asquith to Venetia Stanley, 28 July and 1 August 1914. In Brock and Brock, *Asquith*, pp. 129, 139. See also Jenkins, *Asquith*, p. 327. Churchill's commitment to intervention helps account for the speedy response of the Royal Navy to the crisis. The First Fleet was dispatched to its war base at Scapa Flow on the night of 29 July and had taken up battle positions in the North Sea by 31 July. Williamson, *Grand Strategy*, p. 361. These precautions in themselves did not, however, commit the British to any particular course of action and had no apparent influence on the unfolding of the continental crisis.

did so with far greater enthusiasm than the prime minister. The rest of the cabinet was much less sure that intervention was justified. The German violation of Belgian neutrality helped persuade them. In the case of some ministers, the desire to retain their jobs at a time when resignation would likely have resulted in a coalition or Unionist government was probably an important factor.

In striking contrast to what occurred in Austria-Hungary, Russia, and Germany, the views of military men had little direct influence on the government's handling of the crisis of July–August 1914. It is true that there had been intermittent staff talks with the French since 1906. It is also true that by the late summer of 1911, the General Staff had worked out plans for the dispatch of six infantry divisions and a cavalry division for the support of France. At an important meeting of the Committee of Imperial Defence on 23 August 1911, ministers, including Asquith, while not giving these plans wholehearted endorsement, had thought them far more realistic than wild, ill-considered naval proposals for an amphibious assault on Heligoland. From that time onward, British strategic thinking had an increasingly continentalist tendency.[105] But a tendency in grand strategic thinking does not amount to a binding commitment.

It seems clear that members of the General Staff – especially General Sir Henry Wilson, the director of military operations – had assured their French opposite numbers that, in the event of a German attack, they would do everything possible to ensure that France would have substantial British military support. It is also evident that Grey had privately given the French a similar assurance. But it is equally certain that the French had no binding, written promise of military help from anyone in Britain.[106] So grave was the emergency in which the French found themselves by late July 1914 that, had they possessed such a promise, they would surely have produced it, however embarrassing it might have proved to some of their British friends.

Neither Wilson nor Grey had, indeed, the power to commit the cabinet to any particular course of action in advance. Even the prime minister

---

[105] The Committee of Imperial Defence, established in 1902, was a forum for discussion of defense matters between cabinet ministers and representatives of the two armed services. On Anglo-French staff talks and the CID meeting of 23 August 1911, see Williamson, *Grand Strategy*, pp. 59–88, 167–204.

[106] On Grey's personal feeling of commitment to France, see Wilson, "Britain," p. 198. Williamson, *Grand Strategy*, p. 331, concludes: "Strictly speaking, the Cabinet was under no obligation to give military assistance to France, nor had it ever given verbal assurances to this effect; it was only obligated to consult in times of danger."

did not have such power. Asquith could not have taken the country to war if he could not have found ministers to serve under him in a war government. Nor could he reasonably have done so without the consent of a majority in the House of Commons, for it would have to vote the necessary money. The French, moreover, would have been very ignorant of the British constitution and very naive about the practical workings of the British political system had they been unaware of these matters. Cambon's rather calm behavior in late July 1914, when Grey told him how uncertain the cabinet was about its response in particular eventualities, suggests that he, for one, was neither ignorant nor naive in these respects.[107]

During late July and early August 1914, most members of the cabinet certainly did not speak and act as if they believed themselves committed in advance by promises made by army officers (or by the foreign secretary). The cabinet collectively did not consult the service chiefs during the crisis. General Wilson recorded on 28 July that "no military opinion has been asked for by this Cabinet, who are deciding on a question of war."[108]

For much of the critical period from 23 July to Britain's entry into the war on 4 August, the leaders of the General Staff were not even officially informed of the cabinet's deliberations. On 2 August, Field Marshal Sir John French is reported to have telephoned Lord Riddell of the Newspaper Proprietors' Association and asked, "Can you tell me old chap, whether we are going to be in this war? If so, are we going to put an army on the Continent and, if we are, who is going to command it?"[109] Far from considering itself bound to enter the war by General Staff contingency plans for the dispatch of the expeditionary force, the cabinet decided to send the expeditionary force to the Continent only two days after Britain entered the war. At the same time, it decided that two of the infantry divisions that the General Staff had earmarked for the Continent would be retained at home and only four infantry divisions and a cavalry division sent.[110]

---

[107] On Cambon's calm, see Wilson, "Britain," p. 190.

[108] Sir Charles E. Callwell, *Field Marshal Sir Henry Wilson*, 2 vols. (London, 1927), vol. 1, p. 153.

[109] Lord Riddell, *Lord Riddell's War Diary* (London, 1933), p. 6. On French's activities at this period, see Gerald French, *The Life of Sir John French, First Earl of Ypres* (London, 1931), pp. 191–201.

[110] Haldane to Arthur Balfour, 6 August 1914. Quoted in Sir Frederick Maurice, *Haldane 1856–1915: The Life of Viscount Haldane of Cloan K.T., O.M.* (London, 1937), p. 359; Williamson, *Grand Strategy*, pp. 361–6.

If the General Staff had any influence on the decision for war, it was an indirect influence, exerted through Unionist leaders. Wilson kept himself informed of what was going on in the cabinet through two Foreign Office officials, Nicolson and Crowe. An ardent Unionist, he passed this information on to the Unionist leaders. Though the Unionists had, in Churchill, a better source for what was going on in the cabinet than the director of military operations, Wilson's first biographer gives him credit for rallying the Unionist leaders in London during the weekend of 1–2 August.[111] It was on the night of 1 August that Bonar Law and Lansdowne drafted the note, delivered to Asquith on the morning of 2 August, that offered their support for British entry into the war. As we have seen, there is some reason to believe that this note played a significant role in keeping most of Asquith's cabinet together in support of British intervention. How much responsibility Wilson really had for rallying the Unionist leaders in this emergency is, however, difficult to establish.[112]

Senior civil servants do not appear to have played a significant role in the decision, except, perhaps, by helping to shape Grey's outlook in the years preceding the crisis and by their contacts, direct and indirect (through Wilson), with the Unionist leaders. Grey appears to have told senior Foreign Office officials such as Nicolson and Crowe very little of what he was thinking in late July and early August. So much was this the case that Crowe considered him cowardly and indecisive when he was actually straining every nerve to secure British support for France.[113]

What part did George V play in the British decision for war? It is clear that, until a late stage in the crisis, the king's instincts were pacific and neutralist – like those of most of his ministers and the majority of his people. By 4 August, however, George V had concluded that German behavior had made British involvement inevitable. As he later told the American ambassador, "My God Mr. Page, what else could we do?"[114] In the twentieth century, it would have been almost impossible for a British monarch to prevent a declaration of war by a prime minister supported by the bulk of the cabinet and the great majority in the House of Commons.

[111] On Wilson's militant Unionism, see Ramsden, *Age of Balfour and Baldwin*, p. 115. On his role during the weekend of 1–2 August 1914, see Callwell, *Wilson*, p. 155.
[112] Albertini shows awareness of the claims made about Wilson's role in rallying the Unionists. Although he does not altogether dismiss this role, he somewhat plays it down. Albertini, *Origins of the War*, vol. 3, pp. 397–9.
[113] Wilson, "Britain,", pp. 207, n. 108; and 200.
[114] Nicolson, *George V*, p. 247.

But the monarchy is supposed to be a national rallying point in wartime. Conducting a war that the monarch was known personally to oppose would, therefore, have presented problems. In 1914, however, no such issue arose. George V gave wholehearted support to the war effort.[115]

We must now attempt to answer the fifth and last of the questions set near the beginning of this chapter. Should Great Britain, despite the *ententes*, have remained neutral? Two historians, Niall Ferguson and John Charmley, have recently (and independently) suggested that a policy of neutrality should have been adopted. Ferguson explicitly suggests a brighter counterfactual twentieth century for Britain and Europe as a whole had the majority of cabinet ministers remained true to their pacific instincts. He accepts that without British involvement the Germans would have won the war, probably in 1914, but imagines Great Britain living quite amicably with a German-dominated "Kaiser's European Union."[116] It is impossible to disprove a counterfactual hypothesis. But it is just as easy to conceive of a rather less appealing "Kaiser's New European Order" (with room for development into a "Kaiser's New World Order"), one with which Great Britain might have had considerable difficulty. A "Kaiser's New World Order" was very much what Grey, Nicolson, and Crowe imagined at the time.

Ferguson's case rests on his belief that the Germans would never have developed such grandiose war aims as outlined in Fritz Fischer's *Germany's Aims in the First World War* had their armed forces been able to win a European war in a few weeks. Swift and decisive victory would have been Germany's, Ferguson argues, had it not been for the involvement of the British Expeditionary Force.[117] But the political elites of Wilhelmine Germany, led by the kaiser, were given, even before the war, to grandiose dreams of power and dominance.[118] To suggest that an easy victory on the Continent would have satiated such desires and dissipated such fantasies seems very optimistic. Is it not equally likely that partial gratification would have nourished and reinforced them?

There appears to be little reason to believe that having overturned the balance of power and made themselves masters of Europe, Germany's rulers would have been inclined to tolerate much dissent from their

[115] Ibid, 248–343.
[116] Ferguson, "Kaiser's Economic Union," pp. 276–80; Ferguson, *The Pity of War* (London, 1998), pp. 433–62; John Charmley, *Splendid Isolation? Britain and the Balance of Power 1874–1914* (London, 1999), pp. 379–401.
[117] Ferguson, "Kaiser's Economic Union," p. 276.
[118] Geiss, ed. *July 1914*, pp. 32–35.

world view or much competition with German industries. A continental hegemony exercised by a Hohenzollern supreme warlord flush with easy victory would probably have had little room for liberalism, democracy, or British trade. Perhaps, as hegemon of the Continent, Wilhelm II would have dropped Alfred Thayer Mahan in favor of Halford Mackinder. But had he wished to make himself master of the North Sea and the eastern Atlantic, who could then have checked him? The concentration of power in his hands would have made it difficult to prevent him becoming lord of the Near East or emperor of Africa had he wished to be so.

Even accepting all in the last two paragraphs, it could still be suggested that things could hardly have worked out worse than they actually did: two catastrophic world wars, the Russian Revolution, and all that flowed from those events. Perhaps not, but who can tell? The usefulness of counterfactual argument has its limits. The main task of the historian is to try to explain why men acted as they did. Grey's decision for intervention in the European war of 1914, ultimately supported, from a mixture of motives, by the great majority of his cabinet colleagues, was honorable and rational in the circumstances of the time. It was entered into with a deep sense of foreboding in the belief that any other course would be both dishonorable in its treatment of Britain's *entente* partners and potentially even more damaging than war to Britain's national interests.[119]

---

[119] Some historians have emphasized the importance of the Anglo-Russian relationship, indicating that fear of Russia was as important as fear of Germany in British calculations in the years leading up to the First World War and even in the July–August crisis. This argument seems first to have been suggested by J. W. Headlam-Morley, editor of volume 11 of the official British documents on the origins of the war (*B.D.*, vol. 11, p. xi). At one stage in his career, Keith Wilson was prepared to endorse this, arguing that Britain went to war with Germany in August 1914 to maintain the Anglo-Russian *entente* and thus preserve her Asian interests from the consequences of its collapse (*Policy of the Entente*, pp. 74–85, 95–9, 115–20). It is undoubtedly true that Russia was a great power capable of threatening British interests in some portions of the globe and that senior Foreign Office civil servants were very keen to maintain amicable relations. But, ultimately, Grey, Asquith, and the cabinet, not civil servants, were responsible for taking Britain to war. Grey, as noted, consulted but little with his senior civil servants during the crisis. His main preoccupation in the latter stages of the crisis was with preserving France from German aggression. In extreme circumstances, such as those that presented themselves on the morning of 1 August, he was prepared to abandon Russia to preserve France. The rest of the cabinet certainly would not have been prepared to see Britain go to war in support of Russian interests. It took a massive German military advance to the west to get Britain into the war, and even then it was touch and go. Had the Germans avoided Belgium, the British might, in effect, have ditched the *entente*.

# 9

## Japan

### Frederick R. Dickinson

The present great disturbance is the divine aid of the new Taishō era for the development of the destiny of Japan.

Marquis Inoue Kaoru, August 1914

## World War I and Japan

Discussions of the Great War rarely turn to East Asia.[1] Far from the Western and Eastern fronts and spared the enormous slaughter, the Asian theater naturally merits less attention than the marred landscapes of Europe. But Asia, particularly Japan, was not as invisible to the main belligerents as most major surveys of the Great War suggest.[2] The Japanese cabinet decided on war against Germany on 8 August, just four days after ally Britain cut ties with Berlin. And when some 50,000 Japanese troops,

---

[1] The author thanks the Mershon Center at the Ohio State University for sponsoring the conference for which this paper was originally drafted. Special praise goes to Richard Hamilton and Holger Herwig for their expert editing and insightful suggestions for revision. The revision, itself, was made possible by the generous support of the Hoover Institution on War, Revolution and Peace, where the author was a National Fellow during the 2000–2001 academic year. All Japanese and Chinese names are rendered here according to local custom, or surname first. All Chinese personal and place names are romanized according to the *pinyin* system, with the more familiar Wade-Giles system noted in parentheses on the first appearance of the term.

[2] The celebrated eight-part PBS series, "The Great War and the Shaping of the 20ᵗʰ Century" (1996) and the accompanying volume by Jay Winter and Blaine Baggett, for example, make only one mention of Japan: "Japan, too, was on the Allied side." Jay Winter and Blaine Baggett, *The Great War and the Shaping of the 20ᵗʰ Century* (New York, 1996), p. 109. Martin Gilbert's 615-page *The First World War: A Complete History* (New York, 1994), devotes sixteen sentences to Japan.

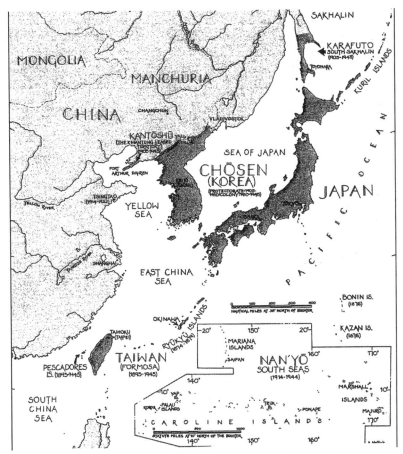

MAP 9.1. Japan and the Pacific. *Source: Cambridge History of Japan*, vol. 6, edited by Peter Duus.

joined by 2,000 British Imperial forces, vanquished 4,920 Germans at Qingdao (Tsingtao), China, on 7 November 1914,[3] East Asia became the only theater of the war that not only met but bettered expectations of a quick victory. The Japanese Navy seized the Marshall, Mariana, and Caroline islands after the German East Asiatic Squadron took flight in August 1914 (see Map 9.1). And Japanese men-of-war protected convoys of Australian and New Zealand troops from the Pacific to Aden.

---

3 Figures from Major K. F. Baldwin, Office of the Chief of Staff, War Department, Military Intelligence Division, "A Brief Account of Japan's Part in the World War" (16 September 1921), p. 4. Stanley K. Hornbeck papers, Box 255, "War Costs and Contributions" file, the Hoover Institution on War, Revolution and Peace.

From February 1917, three Japanese destroyer divisions joined the hunt for German submarines in the Mediterranean.

Throughout the war, both the *entente* and the Central Powers eagerly sought Japanese aid and support. In addition to benefiting from Japanese military action, the *entente* relied upon Japanese shipping, copper, munitions (including 600,000 rifles to Russia), and almost ¥1 billion in loans.[4] Efforts by Allied statesmen to tap Japan's enormous military and financial potential persisted throughout the war, including informal French requests in 1915 for 500,000 Japanese troops to the Balkan peninsula.[5]

The Central Powers were just as eager to stem the flow of Japanese aid to the allies. The German ambassador to Japan, Count Graf von Rex, was so distressed by the prospect of Japanese support of the *entente* that, in an audience with Japanese Foreign Minister Katō Takaaki on 9 August, he broke the chair upon which he was sitting and almost tumbled to the floor.[6] German and Austrian representatives in European capitals approached Japanese representatives several times in the first two years of war over the possibility of a separate peace.[7] In February 1915, the American ambassador to Germany noted that there was much talk in Berlin about the possibility of "Japan's making a separate peace and attacking America."[8]

---

[4] Ibid., p. 6.

[5] Payson Jackson Treat, "Japan, America and the Great War," in World Peace Foundation, *A League of Nations*, vol. 1, no. 8 (December 1918), p. 8. Stanley K. Hornbeck Papers, Box 238, "Japan: War, 'Japan in the War,' by P. J. Treat" file. As late as August 1918, the U.S. State Department, at the urging of the navy, requested that Japan send battle cruisers to aid in the protection of U.S. troop transports to Europe. Letter from Secretary of the Navy Edwin Denby to Secretary of State Charles E. Hughes, 23 September 1921. Stanley K. Hornbeck papers, Box 255, "Japan: War Costs and Contributions" file.

[6] Matsui Keishirō, *Matsui Keishirō jijoden* (Autobiography of Matsui Keishirō) (Tokyo, 1983), p. 79.

[7] Frank Iklé, "Japanese-German Peace Negotiations during World War I," *American History Review*, no. 71 (October 1965): 62–76. The Fourth Russo-Japanese Convention of July 1916 reflected, in part, an Allied desire to strengthen Japan's fidelity to the fight against Germany and can be reasonably considered, in part, as a reaction to these peace feelers. See Frederick R. Dickinson, *War and National Reinvention: Japan in the Great War, 1914–1919* (Cambridge, Mass., 1999), pp. 138–48. Iklé makes the same point about the Anglo-Japanese and Franco-Japanese agreements of early 1917. Iklé, pp. 70–1.

[8] Telegram from Nelson Page to Secretary of State William Jennings Bryan, 26 February 1915, Stanley K. Hornbeck papers, Box 255, "Japan: War Costs and Contributions" file.

## World War I as Opportunity

Why did Japan, so far from the principal theater of conflict, declare war on Germany in August 1914? When elder statesman Inoue Kaoru spoke of the outbreak of war in Europe as "divine aid," he expressed a broad sense of exhilaration in Tokyo. In many ways, the excitement mirrored the longing in European capitals for a renewed sense of national purpose after the profligacy of the *belle époque*. Just as British Prime Minister David Lloyd George hailed the chance to rediscover "the great peaks" of "Honour, Duty, Patriotism," and "Sacrifice," Japanese continental adventurer Ioki Ryōzō praised the "awakening" of Japanese subjects from their petty political battles, worship of money, "anti-state nihilism," "naturalism," and "vulgar sensualism." This was the opportunity, Ioki proclaimed, for a return to "simplicity and purity."[9]

But if Japanese statesmen and subjects identified broadly with the universal quest for stability amidst the growing discontents of the industrial age, they had a specific roster of grievances in mind. They looked fondly upon an earlier age, recently passed, when Japan leapt from the depths of feudalism to join the ranks of the great powers. During the reign of the Meiji emperor (1868–1912), a select group of low-ranking samurai had transformed a disparate coalition of over 270 semiautonomous feudal domains into a modern, unified nation-state, complete with the trappings of a world power: constitutional government, a modern army and navy, and an empire. By 1895, when Japan's armed forces defeated the former cultural and political hegemon of Asia – China – foreign observers hailed Japan as the "pioneer of progress in the Orient."[10] After her surprising military victory over Imperial Russia in 1905, Japan's own statesmen proclaimed to the world the spectacular consummation of a "New Japan."[11]

As the powers, in the aftermath of the Russo-Japanese War, elevated their legations in Tokyo to embassies in honor of Japan's accomplishments, however, the confidence of the heady nation-building days of mid-Meiji began to wane. The anxiety derived, in part, from the increasing individualism and hedonism resulting from the expansion and diffusion of capitalist culture and ideology. As one popular commentator wrote

---

[9] From Lloyd George's Queen's Hall speech, 19 September 1914; cited in Marc Ferro, *The Great War, 1914–1918* (London, 1973), pp. 20–1. Ioki Ryōzō, "Shin kiun o ridō seyo" (Guide the New Trends to Our Benefit), *Nihon oyobi Nihonjin*, 1 January 1915; cited in Banno Junji, *Taishō seihen: 1900-nen taisei no hōkai* (Tokyo, 1994), p. 211.

[10] John L. Stoddard, *John L. Stoddard's Lectures*, 10 vols. (Chicago, 1897), vol. 3, p. 116.

[11] Ōkuma Shigenobu, ed., *Fifty Years of the New Japan*, 2 vols. (New York, 1909).

in 1906, while the latter nineteenth century marked the "golden age of
government authority" in Japan, the contemporary era had replaced the
ethic of *kanson minpi* (respect the officials, despise the people) with *kinson
kanpi* (respect money, despise the officials).[12]

More generally, the crisis of confidence of the post-Russo-Japanese War
years stemmed from the realization that the principal object of the Meiji
era – for Japan to "take its place among the nations of the world" –
had been achieved.[13] That goal had been the national obsession since
the original confrontation with great power imperialism in the 1850s,
which produced the humiliating "unequal treaties."[14] Those treaties had
been abrogated in the Meiji period. And Japan, following the accepted
standards of the Age of Imperialism, had begun projecting its power
abroad: acquiring Taiwan and the Pescadores Islands in 1895 after the
Sino-Japanese War, and southern Sakhalin Island, South Manchuria, and
preponderant influence in Korea after the Russo-Japanese War in 1905.
Japan's metamorphosis into an imperial power, understandably, raised an
obvious question: What next?

Three developments, in particular, raised serious concerns about the
future of the empire after the Russo-Japanese War. First was the outbreak
of revolution in China. Japanese soldiers and statesmen initially welcomed
the disturbance in October 1911, seeing it as an opportunity to increase
Japanese influence on the Continent. The administration of Prince Saionji
Kinmochi tried to mediate a settlement to produce in Beijing a constitutional monarchy along Japanese lines.[15] And the Imperial Army hoped to
send a fresh expedition of Japanese troops to Manchuria.[16] But the civilian cabinet forbade Japanese military involvement there. And it watched
in astonishment as Chinese General Yuan Shikai accepted the mediation
of Britain and founded a republic on the model of the United States.

[12] The commentator was Tokutomi Sohō; cited in Oka Yoshitake, "Generational Conflict
after the Russo-Japanese War," in Tetsuo Najita and J. Victor Koschmann, eds., *Conflict
in Modern Japanese History: The Neglected Tradition* (Princeton, 1982), pp. 198, 202.
[13] This was the proclamation of one of modern Japan's founders, Kido Takayoshi, in 1868.
[14] These were treaties imposed upon Japan by the great powers, which, following the model
of treaties concluded with China after the Opium War, established trade relations with
the outside world on disadvantageous terms. Both Japan and China forfeited the right to
set their own tariffs and to try foreign nationals in domestic courts. See W. G. Beasley,
*Japanese Imperialism, 1894–1945* (Oxford, 1987), ch. 2.
[15] Usui Katsumi, *Nihon to Chūgoku: Taishō jidai* (Japan and China: The Taishō Era)
(Tokyo, 1972), pp. 7–10.
[16] Kitaoka Shin'ichi, *Nihon rikugun to tairiku seisaku* (The Japanese Army and Continental
Policy) (Tokyo, 1978), pp. 93–4.

Having explicitly rejected republican rule for their own state in 1889, Japanese statesmen were appalled. It was, warned Terauchi Masatake, the governor general of Korea, a "serious matter for Japan's National Polity."[17]

Soon after this evidence of Japan's waning influence on the Continent, the emperor, the preeminent symbol of the exalted nation-building era, passed away. All fundamental reforms of the late nineteenth century had been executed in the name of the Meiji emperor. The arrival of the boy monarch in Edo castle in November 1868 marked the official end of the Tokugawa dynasty (1600–1867); the emperor dressed as generalissimo "bestowed" a modern constitution upon his subjects in February 1889; and the image of a hard-working commander-in-chief at imperial headquarters in Hiroshima sustained Japanese troops in their first modern military engagement, against China in 1894. Baron Makino Nobuaki detected a deep "anxiety" gripping the nation after the emperor's death, "as it hit home that a shadow was descending on an exalted age."[18]

No sooner had the throngs of mourners dispersed from their kneeling vigil outside the Imperial Palace than Japan faced the most serious crisis of its short history of constitutional government. Early in December 1912, War Minister Uehara Yūsaku resigned over the cabinet's refusal to fund a long-awaited two-division expansion for the army. Unable to obtain a replacement, the Saionji cabinet fell. When the *genrō* (elder statesmen) nominated one of their own, Lord Keeper of the Privy Seal Katsura Tarō, to succeed Saionji, Japan's politicians cried foul. In February 1913 a coalition of political parties brought down an oligarchic cabinet for the first time in the history of modern Japan. Field Marshal Yamagata Aritomo deplored the tragic "confusion of public sentiment" brought on by the Taishō political crisis.[19]

On the eve of the Great War Japan seemed to have lost its luster as the "pioneer of progress in the Orient." Abroad, it had failed to inspire China to follow its example of constitutional monarchy. At home, the political unity so highly touted by Japan's preeminent statesmen in 1907 – "under one Imperial House and sovereign ... absolutely unexampled in the world" – appeared fragmented beyond recognition.[20]

[17] In a 1911 memorandum to the cabinet; cited in Shinobu Seizaburō, *Taishō seijishi* (Taishō Political History), 4 vols. (Tokyo, 1951), vol. 2, p. 349.
[18] Makino Nobuaki, *Kaisōroku* (Memoirs), 2 vols. (Tokyo, 1978), vol. 2, p. 61.
[19] Itō Takashi, ed., *Taishō shoki Yamagata Aritomo danwa hikki* (Record of Yamagata Aritomo's Conversations in Early Taishō) (Tokyo, 1981), p. 43.
[20] Ōkuma, *Fifty Years of the New Japan*, vol. 1, p. 23.

When Japanese policy makers and opinion leaders learned of general mobilizations in Europe, then, they responded with a sense of relief and enthusiasm. Already in 1887, General Viscount Tani Kanjo had spoken of a potential time of great "confusion" in Europe that would spell opportunity for Japan. At such a distance, Tani reflected, Japan did not have to be "mixed up" in the matter. But the distraction of the great powers would enable the empire to become the "chief nation of the Orient."[21] Indeed, in August 1914, "confusion" in Europe was widely viewed as providing the opportunity to get back on track with Japanese continental aims. Yoshino Sakuzō, soon to gain celebrity as the preeminent champion of democracy in Japan, saw it as "absolutely the most opportune moment" to advance Japan's standing in China.[22] And Marquis Inoue Kaoru welcomed the "solidarity of national unity" that a renewed drive for influence on the Continent would bring.[23]

### Japan Joins the War

Japanese enthusiasm over war in Europe, then, focused on the opportunity to consolidate Japanese interests in Asia. It did not necessarily translate into an immediate call for war against Imperial Germany. Appeals and proposals for a comprehensive agreement with China flooded the administration of Prime Minister Ōkuma Shigenobu (April 1914–October 1916) from all quarters in the first month of the war.[24] But few voices demanded that Japan officially join the fight in Europe.

Tokyo would ultimately declare war in the name of the Anglo-Japanese alliance. But even Foreign Minister Katō Takaaki, the man most responsible for Japanese belligerence, would note that Japan was

---

[21] Quoted in Tyler Dennett, *Americans in Eastern Asia: A Critical Study of the Policy of the United States with Reference to China, Japan and Korea in the 19th Century* (New York, 1922), p. 527.

[22] Yoshino Sakuzō, *Nisshi kōshō ron* (Discourse on the Sino-Japanese Negotiations) (Tokyo, 1915), p. 255; cited in Hirono Yoshihiko, "Yoshino Sakuzō Chūgoku ron oboegaki" (The China Memoranda of Yoshino Sakuzō), *Kyōto daigaku hōgaku ronsō* 121, no. 6 (1987): 48.

[23] Inoue Kaoru kō denki hensankai, *Segai Inoue kō den* (Biography of the Late Lord Inoue), 5 vols. (Tokyo, 1968), vol. 5, p. 367.

[24] Among those petitioning the Ōkuma administration were the chief of the Army General Staff's Second Bureau, Fukuda Masatarō (7 August), Marquis Inoue Kaoru (10 August), Elder Statesman Yamagata Aritomo (15 August), Korea Governor General Terauchi Masatake (mid-August), Vice Minister of War Ōshima Ken'ichi (24 August), Japan's Minister to China, Hioki Eki (26 August), Major General Tanaka Giichi (30 August), Kokumintō party president Inukai Tsuyoshi (7 September), and Guandong Governor General Fukushima Yasumasa (11 September).

not obligated under the alliance to join in the fray.[25] Some members of the cabinet, in fact, hoped to prevent the spread of hostilities to Asia. And the traditional wielders of state power in Japan, the four remaining elder statesmen, worried about potential Japanese losses in a military engagement with Germany.[26] The outcome of a war between Britain and Germany was, in August 1914, by no means certain. Most Japanese military experts and members of the Imperial Army, in fact, gave Germany a better than even chance of victory.[27]

In this context, it is surprising that Tokyo decided on war against Germany only thirty-six hours after receiving a formal request for aid from London. It was, according to one source, like a "force of lightning."[28] Even more remarkable is the fact that the decision was, for all intents and purposes, orchestrated by one man.

Under the 1889 Imperial Constitution (dubbed the "Meiji" constitution," after the reign of Emperor Meiji), all sovereign powers in Japan – executive, legislative, and judicial – resided in the emperor. Imperial rule was, however, an elaborate fiction designed to solidify central control after the toppling of a feudal regime. In reality, the power to govern went to those individuals and institutions with direct ties to the emperor, those that could be said to be acting on his behalf: the Imperial Cabinet, Imperial Diet (parliament), Imperial Army and Navy, Imperial Courts, and the Privy Council. Given the competing demands of these institutions, leadership in Imperial Japan was constantly in flux, depending on the relative strength of these bodies and the individuals who came to dominate them and/or the small body of extraconstitutional advisors surrounding the emperor known as the *genrō*.

As with all other prerogatives, the power to declare war resided with the emperor under the Meiji constitution. In reality, a decision for battle was made through consultation among some combination of imperial advisors: the *genrō*, cabinet, military leaders, and/or Privy Council. At the very least, a declaration of war required a cabinet decision and formal sanction of the emperor.[29]

[25] Katō would note this fact in the 7 August cabinet meeting convened to decide on a declaration of war. Itō Masanori, *Katō Takaaki* (Biography of Katō Takaaki), 2 vols. (Tokyo, 1929), vol. 2, pp. 78–9.
[26] Ibid., pp. 73, 80.
[27] Ibid., p. 82.
[28] Ibid., p. 81.
[29] For a brief overview of Japanese war powers, see Tatsuji Takeuchi, *War and Diplomacy in the Japanese Empire* (New York, 1935), pp. 452–3.

The Japanese decision for war in August 1914 followed only the bare minimum requirements for consultation. On 1 August, Foreign Minister Katō Takaaki instructed the Japanese ambassador to London, Inoue Katsunosuke, to sound out British Foreign Secretary Sir Edward Grey about Britain's proposed response to developments in Europe. Grey said he considered it unlikely that the Anglo-Japanese alliance would be invoked if Britain became involved in the war.[30] Two days later, Katō summoned the British ambassador to Japan, Sir Conyngham Greene, to relay thanks to Grey for his clarification and to offer immediate Japanese assistance in the event of a German attack on Hong Kong or of other acts of aggression in Asia.[31] The following morning, Prime Minister Ōkuma Shigenobu called an extraordinary cabinet session to clarify Japanese official policy on possible hostilities in Asia. In the midst of the meeting, a messenger from Ambassador Greene presented Katō with a telegram from Foreign Secretary Grey outlining Britain's expectation of Japanese aid if Germany attacked Hong Kong or the British concession of Wei-hai-wei in Shandong (Shantung).[32] In response, the cabinet agreed to take "all means necessary" to aid Britain in the event that war spread to East Asia.[33] Katō informed Ambassador Greene that afternoon of the cabinet decision and added that the Japanese Second Battle Fleet, comprising four large cruisers, was lying ready at Sasebo naval base "for immediate action if required."[34]

The formal British request for assistance came on the afternoon of 7 August. Katō responded by presenting an outline of Japan's official response to Prime Minister Ōkuma, who organized another extraordinary cabinet session for 8 P.M. that evening. After four hours of debate, the cabinet decided on war with Germany. The following morning, the foreign minister personally informed the emperor of the decision at the latter's summer residence at Nikkō (north of Tokyo). A special *genrō*-cabinet conference that evening (8 August) delivered the sanction of Japan's elder statesmen. One week later, on 15 August, a second *genrō*-cabinet

[30] Gaimusho, ed., *Nihon gaikō bunsho 1914*, vol. 3, pp. 32–3; Peter Lowe, *Great Britain and Japan, 1911–15* (London, 1969), p. 180.
[31] G. P. Gooch and Harold Temperley, eds., *British Documents on the Origins of the War, 1898–1914*, 11 vols. (London, 1926–38), vol. 11, p. 305.
[32] "Taisen ni dō taisho suru ka, Nichi-Ei kōshō hajimaru" (Anglo-Japanese Negotiations over the Great War Begin), *Tokyo Asahi shinbun*, 5 August 1914, in Taishō nyūsu jiten hensan iinkai, ed., *Taishō nyūsu jiten* (Tokyo, 1986), vol. 1, p. 430. Lowe, *Great Britain and Japan*, p. 180.
[33] Gaimusho, ed., *Nihon gaikō bunsho 1914*, vol. 3, p. 99.
[34] Gooch and Temperley, *British Documents*, vol. 11, pp. 327–8.

conference, this time in the presence of the emperor, approved an ultimatum, drafted by Katō and three of his closest advisors,[35] demanding Germany transfer her Jiaozhou (Kiaochou) concession to Japan.[36]

## One Man's Decision for War

The Japanese decision for war, then, depended largely on the initiative and efforts of Foreign Minister Katō Takaaki. Compared with the Sino- and Russo-Japanese Wars (1894–95 and 1904–5, respectively), the autonomy exhibited by the foreign minister here is remarkable. On both of these earlier occasions, both the *genrō* and members of the military high command had played a critical role in deliberations. In August 1914, however, Katō seized the initiative and presented the elder statesmen and army leadership with a fait accompli.[37] According to those present at the 7 August cabinet meeting, the foreign minister "deflected all doubts, solved all questions and, in every way, decided upon war with Germany on his own."[38]

Katō's coup came at the expense, particularly, of Japan's established elite. Most important among these were the elder statesmen, men who had risen to power by toppling the feudal regime and participating, in their capacity as the new emperor's closest advisors, in the construction of a modern nation-state. These men had wielded enormous influence in the first two decades of the new cabinet system from 1885, occupying most cabinet posts and personally directing the nation's domestic and foreign policies. But due to age and their dwindling numbers, they increasingly yielded to

---

[35] Namely, Minister of Finance Wakatsuki Reijirō, Navy Minister Yashiro Rokurō, and the chief of the Political Affairs Bureau of the Foreign Ministry, Koike Chōzō.

[36] This meeting in the presence of the emperor (the *gozen kaigi*) followed precedent established in the Sino- and Russo-Japanese Wars for granting final imperial sanction of a decision for war. It was delayed for a week in this case because of diplomatic negotiations with Britain over the terms of Japan's military engagement. For detailed coverage of the Anglo-Japanese wrangling over terms, see Lowe, *Great Britain and Japan*, ch. 6. The Jiaozhou concession comprised a 500-square-kilometer area around Jiaozhou Bay, including a series of forts and modern harbor (with an enormous floating dry dock) at Qingdao (Tsingtao), and a railroad connecting Qingdao with Jinan (Tsinan) in central Shandong (Shantung).

[37] The navy leadership, by contrast, seems to have been kept in the loop. See below.

[38] Itō, *Katō Takaaki*, vol. 2, p. 81. Itō attributes these remarks to Finance Minister Wakatsuki Reijirō, Minister of Education Ichiki Kitokurō, and the Chief of the Cabinet Secretariat, Egi Tasuku. Cf. Saitō Seiji, who argues that Katō's actions at the outbreak of the war identify him more as a symbol of general political trends in Japan than as a maverick. Saitō Seiji, "Nichi-Doku Chintao sensō no kaisen gaikō" (Diplomacy at the Outbreak of the Japanese-German War over Qingdao), *Kokusai seiji*, no. 119 (Oct. 1998): 198.

younger statesmen after the Russo-Japanese War. In August 1914, the four remaining *genrō* – Inoue Kaoru, Matsukata Masayoshi, Ōyama Iwao, and Yamagata Aritomo – were all septuagenarians. By 1916, Inoue and Ōyama were dead. At the outbreak of war in Europe, only Yamagata remained a formidable political force by virtue of his leadership of an extensive network of supporters in the civilian and army bureaucracies, known as the "Yamagata faction."

The core of this faction comprised members of the Imperial Army. Most important of this group were the faction's second-in-command, Korea Governor-General Terauchi Masatake, and Yamagata's able assistant and close confidant, Major General Tanaka Giichi. Although neither of these men counted among the inner policy circle in August 1914, both would have a pivotal influence on Japanese foreign policy after Katō's resignation from the cabinet in August 1915.[39] Within the cabinet, there were two civilian members of the Yamagata faction in 1914: Minister of Agriculture and Commerce Ōura Kanetake and Minister of Education Ichiki Kitokurō.

Katō could easily hold his own in this company of potential political rivals. At fifty-four, he was in his prime and already a seasoned veteran of foreign affairs and Japanese bureaucratic politics. As a career bureaucrat in the Foreign Ministry, Katō had served twice in Britain, first as Japanese minister (1894–99), then as ambassador to London (1908–12), and he had enjoyed three brief stints as foreign minister.[40] Katō developed a reputation at an early age for not suffering fools gladly.[41] And as foreign minister, he had always insisted upon pursuing an agenda free from the interference of extracabinet elites such as the elder statemen.[42] In April 1913, Katō's political importance was secured when he became president of the second largest political party in the Imperial Diet, the Rikken Dōshikai (Constitutional Association of Friends). It was a platform from which he would ultimately serve two consecutive terms as prime minister (1924–26).

In addition to being foreign minister and president of the Dōshikai, Katō had significant help from members of the cabinet in his effort to

[39] As vice chief of the Army General Staff, Tanaka would command Japan's approaches to China in 1916. He would subsequently become minister of war (1918–21) and prime minister (1927–29). Terauchi would serve as prime minister between 1916 and 1918.
[40] The dates of Katō's service were October 1900 to June 1901, January to March 1906, and January to February 1913.
[41] He was described by some as "outrageously straightforward" (baka shōjiki) and "argumentative" (kenka zuki). Itō, *Katō Takaaki*, vol. 1, pp. 12, 14.
[42] Ibid., pp. 451–4.

outmaneuver his military-bureaucratic rivals in August 1914. He had, in
fact, hand-picked most of the cabinet ministers himself. As a longtime
champion of "constitutional government," Count Ōkuma had become
prime minister in April 1914 to wide public acclaim. But at seventy-
four years of age, he was past his prime and eager to cede the policy
initiative to Katō, with whom he had been close since the two men
had worked together to renegotiate Japan's unequal treaties in the late
1880s (as foreign minister and secretary, respectively). The Ōkuma cabinet until Katō's resignation in August 1915, then, was very much a Katō
cabinet. In addition to Katō himself, it included three other members
of the Dōshikai party, among whom was Minister of Agriculture and
Commerce Ōura.[43] Although Ōura was a member of the Yamagata faction, in other words, he had served as an elder in the Dōshikai party
since its inception in 1913 and was a mentor to Katō.[44] In the position of justice minister was Ozaki Yukio, who, despite being from the
rival Chūseikai party (Fairness Association), was sympathetic to the cabinet's anti-Seiyūkai, antibureaucratic agenda.[45] He would, in fact, join the
Dōshikai in 1916.

Perhaps the most critical support for Katō in the cabinet after the
outbreak of war came from the two service ministers. Minister of War
Oka Ichinosuke hailed from the same former feudal domain of Chōshū
as Field Marshal Yamagata and owed his rise in the ranks to the elder
statesman. But he proved willing to work with the administration to the
extent that Yamagata and Tanaka would attempt to remove him from
office in 1915.[46] Navy Minister Yashiro Rokurō was a close friend and
confidant of Katō's from the time both men had attended the Western
school in Nagoya in their youth. Katō had handed the Imperial Army a
fait accompli with the cabinet decision for war on 8 August, but, given the
Katō-Yashiro friendship and the coincidence of Katō's actions with navy

43 The other two members of the Dōshikai were Finance Minister Wakatsuki Reijirō (who,
   together with Navy Minister Yashiro and chief of the Political Affairs Bureau of the
   Foreign Ministry, Koike Chōzō, was one of three key Katō confidants with whom, for
   example, the foreign minister consulted in drafting the ultimatum for Germany) and
   Communications Minister Taketomi Tokitoshi.
44 Katō had, in fact, lobbied to have Ōura placed in the more powerful position of home
   minister. Ōura would assume the Home Ministry portfolio in January 1915, from where
   he would successfully manage the March 1915 general election that gave the Dōshikai a
   simple majority in the Lower House for the first time.
45 The Seiyūkai party (Constitutional Association of Political Friends) was the majority
   party in the Imperial Diet from its inception in 1900 until 1915.
46 See Dickinson, *War and National Reinvention*, pp. 103–6.

initiatives, it is likely that the foreign minister coordinated his activities with those of Yashiro and the Imperial Navy in early August.[47]

## War and the Domestic Contest to Redefine the Nation

Given Katō's pivotal role in the Japanese decision for war, a study of the causes of Japanese belligerence must turn first to the motives of the foreign minister. The story begins in the volatile arena of Japanese politics.

The most salient feature of Japanese politics in August 1914 was its turbulence. Largely the product of difficulties in transforming a feudal realm into a modern nation-state in two and a half decades, it was the direct consequence of the obsessive concern to concentrate power. To combat the centrifugal tendencies that threatened the fledgling regime in the 1870s and '80s, modern Japan's founders sought not only political centralization but absolute political hegemony. They placed all sovereignty in the hands of the Japanese emperor. And they created a new ruling class that enjoyed the exclusive right to govern by virtue of its direct tie to this all powerful, but largely symbolic, monarch – the founders themselves as elder statesmen (principally, lower-level samurai from the Satsuma and Chōshū feudal domains), a larger body of both hereditary and appointed peers, and a new civilian and military bureaucracy.

The sanction of a monarch deemed "sacred and inviolable"[48] offered powerful political support for the new regime. But to place all sovereignty in an emperor who did not actually rule created one serious difficulty: unregulated competition within the new ruling circle. Nor did the new system provide a clear mechanism for the transfer of power. From its inception, then, internecine political battles plagued the modern regime. And when Tokyo's most influential leaders, the elder statesmen, began relaxing their

---

[47] On 2 August, for example, Navy Minister Yashiro instructed the commander of the Japanese Second Fleet to make full preparations for a possible military engagement. This was one day after Katō instructed Japan's ambassador to London to gauge Britain's proposed response to developments in Europe and one day before the foreign minister offered Britain's ambassador to Japan immediate Japanese assistance in the event of German aggression in Asia. As we have seen, Katō informed Ambassador Greene on 4 August that the Second Fleet was ready "for immediate action." For details of the Imperial Navy's response to the outbreak of war in Europe, see Hirama Yōichi, *Dai-ichiji sekai taisen to Nihon kaigun* (The Japanese Navy and the First World War) (Tokyo, 1998), ch. 1.

[48] In Article 3 of the Meiji constitution. Hugh Borton, *Japan's Modern Century* (New York, 1955), Appendix IV, p. 491.

grip on power in the twentieth century, Japan faced a formidable question: Who would govern in their stead?

This was the fundamental issue of the Taishō political crisis. Despite the determination of modern Japan's founders that cabinets "have no connections whatever" with political parties, party politicians made steady political gains since their emergence in the 1880s.[49] The political crisis brought the end of oligarchic rule and its replacement by a coalition of political parties. As the exalted Meiji era yielded to Taishō (1912–26), the question of the basic character of Japanese politics, then, came to a head. Did the small circle of samurai from the Satsuma and Chōshū domains retain the right, either directly or through their proxies, to rule the nation? Or, as the liberal journalist Ishibashi Tanzan argued, was the "greatest enterprise" of the Meiji years "the implementation of democratic reform in all political, legal and social systems and thought"?[50]

At the outbreak of war in 1914, Japan was sharply divided on this fundamental constitutional question. On the one hand, members of the Meiji ruling circle – modern Japan's founders, members of the new civilian and military bureaucracies, and elected and appointed peers – struggled desperately to repair the damage done by the Taishō political crisis to their waning political authority. They looked to the "European War" as an opportunity, following the experience of the Sino- and Russo-Japanese Wars, to rouse the nation united behind their command. On the other hand, the victors of the Taishō political crisis, particularly Japan's party politicians, welcomed the opportunity of war to further their efforts to consolidate representative government.

### War as a Bid for British Parliamentarism

Foreign Minister Katō Takaaki's decision for war is best understood within context of this domestic struggle to redefine the Japanese nation. Of course, like most of his contemporaries, Katō considered the war an opportunity to consolidate Japanese gains on the Continent. Before returning from London in January 1913 to become foreign minister for the third time, he discussed Japan's special interests in Manchuria with

---

[49] Quotation from the father of the Meiji constitution, Itō Hirobumi; cited in Robert Scalapino, *Democracy and the Party Movement in Prewar Japan* (Berkeley, 1953), p. 88, n. 131.

[50] "Meiji jidai no igi," *Tōyō jiji*, September 1912; cited in Ishibashi Tanzan, *Tanzan kaisō* (Reminiscences of Tanzan) (Tokyo, 1985), p. 188.

British Foreign Secretary Sir Edward Grey.[51] Katō hoped to negotiate an
extension of the leases on Port Arthur (Lüshun), Dalian (Dairen), and the
South Manchuria and Andong (Antung)-Mukden railways, which were
to expire in ten to twenty-five years.[52] But before talks could begin with
China, the Taishō political crisis forced Prime Minister Katsura out of
office. Katō viewed the outbreak of war in Europe, then, as an ideal
opportunity to complete some unfinished business in China. It was his
"fervent diplomatic wish to strengthen Japan's position in Asia."[53]

But if Katō joined the general rush to expand Japanese continental interests, he also shared with the victors of the Taishō political crisis the hope
that war would sound the death knell to oligarchic politics. Katō was, as
noted above, the president of the Dōshikai. But his battle with the "clique"
rule of the elder statesmen had a history much older than his identification
with party politics. Katō was Japan's preeminent Anglophile. From twelve
years of residence in London, first as an apprentice in Mitsubishi enterprises, then as Japan's representative to the court of St. James's, he had
developed a deep appreciation for British culture and life. The foremost
object of his enthusiasm was the British political system.

Katō found a general concern for politics and willingness to defend
one's rights to be a natural part of British life. He marveled that both
men and women were politically engaged, and that even British coach-
men were knowledgeable about public affairs.[54] Katō saw Britain as the
vanguard of modern society and considered the British idea of citizen-
ship and political responsibility the model toward which to strive. To that
end, he worked tirelessly, as foreign minister and then prime minister,
to bring Japanese politics into conformity with British parliamentarism.
Katō's decision to declare war on Germany was then, in part, a vote for
British parliamentarism. Through swift and unilateral action, he sought
to replace the elder statesmen's traditional prerogative by putting foreign
policy decision making firmly in the hands of the cabinet and Foreign
Ministry.[55]

---

[51] Nagaoka Shinjirō, "Katō Takaaki ron" (Discourse on Katō Takaaki), *Kokusai seiji* 33
(1966): 32.

[52] Japan's leases on Port Arthur, Dalian, and the Andong-Mukden Railway (which connected the South Manchuria Railway to the Korea Railway) were due to expire in 1923.
Her lease on the South Manchuria Railway was up in 1938.

[53] Itō, *Katō Takaaki*, vol. 2, p. 73.

[54] Ibid., vol. 1, pp. 800–4.

[55] According to Katō's biographer, this had been Katō's goal since first assuming the Foreign
Ministry portfolio. Ibid., pp. 451–2.

## War as Defense of the Anglo-Japanese Alliance

Domestic political supremacy, however, did not require a declaration of war. Katō could have strengthened the cabinet and Foreign Ministry, and accomplished the general aim of fortifying Japanese interests in China, simply by controlling the substance and timing of direct negotiations with China. This is, in fact, what he did with the so-called Twenty-One Demands of 1915. Katō himself noted at the 7 August cabinet meeting that Japan could increase her world standing by remaining neutral and simply preserving her strength while the great powers eroded their own power on the battlefield.[56]

The question of why the foreign minister sought a cabinet decision for war remains. His principal motive for defying the domestic momentum for neutrality is to be found again in his relationship with Great Britain. From his twelve years in London, Katō had gained an appreciation not only for British parliamentarism but also for British imperialism. In an age when empires determined the relative standing of national power, Katō carefully observed the actions of the grandfather of modern empires. If his conception of the Japanese polity was progressive, the diplomatic component was quite traditional. For Katō readily subscribed to the world view championed by Britain and followed by Japan in the late nineteenth century.

Japan had engaged China in war over influence in Korea in 1894, with the 1895 Shimonoseki Treaty joining the "treaty port" system pioneered by Britain to ensure economic privileges in China and, from 1902, strengthened its strategic standing through an alliance with London. Katō was an early advocate of the Anglo-Japanese alliance and remained convinced of the continuing utility of the formula that had brought Japan to international prominence. For him, the key to Japan's world standing remained in steadily expanding economic privileges in China and continued association with the world's greatest naval power and largest commercial presence on the Asian continent. Katō's insistence on declaring war against Germany, then, depended largely on his respect for Japan's alliance with Britain. He told the cabinet, on 7 August, that participation in the war made sense "from the alliance friendship from which Britain's request derives."[57] Agreeing to a formal British request for assistance against Germany would serve as a powerful affirmation of the Anglo-Japanese alliance.

[56] Ibid., vol. 2, p. 79.
[57] Ibid.

This version of Japanese intent in August 1914 may surprise students of British policy in East Asia. For, as Peter Lowe and Ian Nish have shown, Anglo-Japanese tensions began to flare in the wake of the Chinese revolution and, more precisely, with Japan's attempt at joint Sino-Japanese management of the iron- and ore-producing Han-Ye-Ping Company in the British sphere of influence in the Yangzi (Yanqtse) Valley.[58] Those tensions intensified at the outbreak of war in Europe when London, surprised by the alacrity with which Japan responded to its request for assistance against German cruisers, withdrew its invitation only four days later. The subsequent diplomatic tussle over the scale of Japanese involvement in the war, according to Nish, was "the first major dispute between allies" and had a decidedly negative effect upon mutual confidence.[59] For many, the episode marks the beginning of a pattern of Japanese behavior during the war that, far from aiding the Allied cause, aimed simply to profit at the expense of the powers' interests in Asia.[60]

### War as Battle against Budding Pan-Asianism in Japan

That Katō's actions of August 1914 rested, rather, on his devotion to the Anglo-Japanese alliance may best be seen by considering the aims of his rival policy makers, men who did not share Katō's enthusiasm for British political institutions or his respect for the Anglo-Japanese alliance. Katō's greatest political rival was elder statesman Yamagata Aritomo. Yamagata was the most powerful of the four founders of Meiji Japan who remained in 1914. He was the father of the Japanese army, architect of Imperial Japan's system of local government, twice prime minister, and president of the Privy Council. Yamagata became the premier kingmaker after the death of oligarchic rival Itō Hirobumi in 1909. Although his actual influence on policy making, like that of his fellow *genrō*, declined

---

[58] See Lowe, *Great Britain and Japan*, and Ian Nish, *Alliance in Decline: A Study in Anglo-Japanese Relations, 1908–23* (London, 1972).

[59] Nish, *Alliance in Decline*, p. 131; and Nish, "Japan," in Keith Wilson, ed., *Decisions for War 1914* (New York: 1995), esp. pp. 212–20. Saitō Seiji has recently reemphasized the exacerbation of Anglo-Japanese tensions as one of the principal legacies of Japan's decision to enter the First World War. Saitō, "Nichi-Doku Chintao sensō no kaisen gaikō."

[60] As William Keylor puts it in subtle, but unmistakable language, "[t]he *effortless absorption* of the former German colonial possessions in Asia and Oceania, when added to the territories and privileges previously obtained as the spoils of victory after wars with China and Russia, enabled Tokyo to direct its *expansionist energies* toward the historic object of Japanese *designs*: China itself." Emphasis added. William Keylor, *The Twentieth-Century World: An International History* (Oxford, 1996), p. 220.

after the Russo-Japanese War, the field marshal retained a decisive say in the formation of each cabinet and certainly expected to be consulted on such important policy matters as a declaration of war.

Like many of his contemporaries, Yamagata viewed the war as an ideal opportunity to expand Japanese influence in China. His was among the many petitions for a comprehensive agreement with China that flooded the Ōkuma administration in August 1914. In his proposal, Yamagata described the hostilities as a "golden opportunity" to correct past missteps in China and develop an "inseparable spirit" (*kyōdō itchi no seishin*) between Tokyo and Beijing.[61]

Like Katō, Yamagata envisioned a domestic political benefit to war in Europe. As the preeminent oligarchic ruler, Yamagata had been on the losing side of the Taishō political crisis. Since that debacle, he and fellow *genrō* Marquis Inoue Kaoru had worked frantically to stem the tide of liberal political change. Together, these men had sponsored the Ōkuma Cabinet to crush the power of the majority party in the Diet, the Seiyūkai. They viewed the "European War," then, as "a rare occasion" to "turn the calamities of domestic and foreign policies into fortunes." They urged Prime Minister Ōkuma to seize the opportunity to effect "national unity" immediately through close cooperation with themselves.[62] They hoped, in other words, for a renaissance of *genrō* power.

As already described, however, Katō assumed the policy initiative immediately after the outbreak of war. Rather than greet a restoration of oligarchic authority, Yamagata and Inoue found themselves on the defensive, fending off the foreign minister's aggressive assault on *genrō* prerogatives. The field marshal's reaction to Katō's 8 August fait accompli was "virtual amazement."[63] He immediately abandoned his campaign to destroy the majority Seiyūkai party to concentrate on the more formidable task of suppressing Katō. Between the Japanese declaration of war and Katō's resignation in August 1915, Yamagata twice assembled the four elder statesmen to directly pressure Prime Minister Ōkuma, first to exclude the foreign minister from policy making, then to remove him from office.[64]

[61] "Opinion on China Policy," 15 August 1914. Found in Ōyama Azusa, comp., *Yamagata Aritomo ikensho* (Written Opinions of Yamagata Aritomo) (Tokyo, 1966), pp. 342–3.
[62] Tokutomi Iichirō, ed. *Kōshaku Yamagata Aritomo den* (Biography of Prince Yamagata Aritomo), 3 vols. (Tokyo, 1969), vol. 3, p. 912.
[63] Itō Takashi, ed., *Taishō shoki Yamagata Aritomo danwa hikki* (Record of Yamagata Aritomo's Conversations in Early Taishō) (Tokyo, 1981), p. 59.
[64] At a 24 September 1914 meeting with Ōkuma, the *genrō* commanded the premier to make the fundamental foreign policy decisions himself in consultation with the elder statesmen.

While Yamagata welcomed Japanese expansion in China, he worried about Katō's control of the continental agenda. He had grave misgivings, moreover, about the foreign minister's decision to wage war against Germany. For, despite the shared concern for enhancing Japanese continental interests, there was a substantive difference between the world view of Katō and Yamagata. If Katō followed the conservative pattern of great power behavior in China since the latter nineteenth century, Yamagata anticipated the unbridled expansionism of a subsequent age. Where Katō considered Japan as one among many powers competing for interests in China, the elder statesman increasingly rejected any limits to Japan's continental presence. His 15 August memo to the cabinet, in fact, called upon China to "trust" Japan politically and accede to "mutual reliance" in economic matters. The field marshal hoped, in essence, to replicate in China the protectorate that Japan had established in Korea only a decade earlier. He urged Prime Minister Ōkuma to have Beijing consult Tokyo on all political and economic problems involving foreign countries.[65]

Yamagata had less interest in the alliance politics of the nineteenth century than in what would become the ideological foundations of Japanese expansionism in the 1930s: pan-Asianism. In place of the alliance with Britain that facilitated Japan's victory in the Russo-Japanese War, the field marshal, increasingly, considered only one policy practical for Japanese survival: an "inseparable spirit" with China, with which Japan shared the "same color and culture" (*dōshoku katsu dōbun*). Such intimate ties would guarantee Japanese independence in an eventual "contest between the yellow and white races."[66]

Although Yamagata had supported the Anglo-Japanese alliance in 1902, he began dissociating himself from the pact soon after the Russo-Japanese War. Britain, of course, belonged to the "white race" against which Japan would ultimately have to take up arms.[67] In the immediate

He was then to "compel the foreign minister to obey," that is, to accept this arrangement. Tokutomi, *Kōshaku Yamagata Aritomo den*, vol. 3, p. 912. At a 25 June 1915 meeting with Ōkuma, the *genrō* would call directly for the removal of Katō from office; Itō, *Katō Takaaki*, vol. 2, p. 48. Yamagata hoped, as well, to "destroy the Dōshikai"; Hara Keiichirō, ed. *Hara Takashi nikki* (Diary of Hara Takashi), 6 vols. (Tokyo, 1981), vol. 4, p. 100 (diary entry of 18 May 1915).

[65] Ōyama, *Yamagata Aritomo ikensho*, p. 343.

[66] Ibid.

[67] In the 8 August *genrō*-cabinet meeting, Yamagata cited Britain's "open discrimination of Indian residents in South Africa and Canada" as evidence of the world trend of "racial war." Itō, *Yamagata danwa hikki*, p. 60.

term, in the context of the field marshal's increasing appetite for continental expansion, Britain's commercial presence in China became clearly
more of an obstacle than a help. Less than two years after Japan had
acquired a sphere of influence in South Manchuria in the Russo-Japanese
War, Yamagata defined Japan's best military strategy on the Continent as
an expansion not northward in Manchuria but south of the Great Wall,
where Britain claimed an exclusive sphere of influence.[68] At the same time,
he betrayed less than full confidence in Japan's formal alliance by insisting
that "the empire will pursue national defense on its own strength. It is
not, by any means, something that we will rely on an ally for."[69] Japan's
difficulties in penetrating Britain's sphere of influence in the Yangzi Valley
after the Chinese Revolution spurred complaints by Yamagata and his fellow elder statesmen of "Britain's oppression of our interests in southern
China."[70] And the field marshal increasingly lamented the decline of pro-
Japanese attitudes in the British government and among British popular
sentiment.[71]

At the outbreak of war in Europe, then, Yamagata's sympathies lay less
with Britain than with Britain's archenemy, Germany. From the 1880s,
the field marshal had looked to Imperial Germany as *the* model in his
construction of the Imperial Army and Japanese system of local government. And he continued to value the "military bearing" of German society
long after his two sojourns in Berlin in 1869 and 1889.[72] In August 1914
Yamagata's daughter lived in Germany, married to the Japanese ambassador in Berlin.[73] And Yamagata confidently predicted victory for the
Central Powers by a 60 to 40 margin.[74] The British, after all, fought half-
heartedly, "as if fighting for someone else's sake," and the French placed
priority on minimizing casualties.[75] "I would like to see [British Foreign

[68] Yamagata's "Basic Plan of National Defense Personal Draft" of October 1906 read,
"From now on, the best means of promoting [Japan's] national prosperity and the happiness of the people is a strategy of guarding the north and advancing south [in China]."
Ōyama, *Yamagata Aritomo ikensho*, p. 300.
[69] Ibid., p. 296.
[70] In a *genrō* conference with the prime minister on 24 September 1914. Tokutomi, *Kōshaku
Yamagata Aritomo den*, vol. 3, p. 917.
[71] Hara, *Hara Takashi nikki*, vol. 4, p. 113 (8 July 1915).
[72] See Roger Hackett, *Yamagata Aritomo in the Rise of Modern Japan, 1838–1922*
(Cambridge, 1971), pp. 52, 75.
[73] Yamagata's daughter was married to Baron Funakoshi Mitsunojō. See Nish, "Japan,"
p. 221.
[74] In a February 1915 memorandum titled "For a Russo-Japanese alliance." Ōyama,
*Yamagata Aritomo ikensho*, p. 346.

Secretary Edward] Grey's face," Yamagata sneered in August 1914, "as the German army poises to march on Paris."[76]

Yamagata's reaction to Katō's fait accompli reflected the strong sense that the foreign minister, in joining the war on the side of Britain, had backed the wrong horse. It was natural for Japan to act on behalf of her formal ally, he allowed at the 8 August *genrō*-cabinet conference. But, he insisted, Japan "should not forget that Germany too is a friendly power." Besides, the final outcome of the war was far from certain. Although German troops were clearly outnumbered on the Western front, they would nevertheless advance to Paris and "seize the heart of France." Japan should make absolutely clear to Berlin, then, that she harbored no grudges against the Reich.[77]

Specialists of Japanese diplomatic history have, in recent years, portrayed Yamagata as a voice of "caution" in Japanese foreign affairs.[78] As evidence, they highlight the field marshal's frequent expressions of respect for the Anglo-Japanese alliance. But such expressions ring hollow in the context of Yamagata's vision of Japan's absolute regional hegemony. Upon closer inspection, many of his utterances reveal not an enduring deference to Britain but unwavering respect for Germany. In the 8 August *genrō*-cabinet conference, for example, the elder statesman spoke of "adhering to the Anglo-Japanese alliance." But this was not meant as a sign of respect for Grey. Rather, he explained, it was important to invoke the alliance to demonstrate to "our friend Germany" that Japan was taking up arms only because of an obligation to Britain.[79] Likewise, combined operations with Britain in China were absolutely necessary "to show that [Japan] is acting reluctantly [in declaring war against the kaiser]."[80]

[75] Hara, *Hara Takashi nikki*, vol. 4, p. 113 (8 July 1915).
[76] Mochizuki Kotarō to Inoue Kaoru, 19 August 1914, in Yamamoto Shirō, ed., *Dai-niji Ōkuma naikaku kankei shiryō* (Documents Relating to the Second Ōkuma Cabinet) (Kyōto, 1979), p. 92.
[77] Itō, *Taishō shoki Yamagata Aritomo danwa hikki*, pp. 59–60.
[78] See, e.g., George Akita and Itō Takashi, "Yamagata Aritomo to 'jinshū kyōsōron" (Yamagata Aritomo's Theory of Racial Conflict) in Kindai Nihon Kenkyūkai, ed., *Nihon gaikō no kiki ninshiki* (Tokyo, 1988), pp. 95–118; Hackett, *Yamagata Aritomo in the Rise of Modern Japan*; and Oka Yoshitake, *Yamagata Aritomo: Meiji Nihon no shōchō* (Yamagata Aritomo: Symbol of Meiji Japan) (Tokyo, 1958).
[79] Itō, *Taishō shoki Yamagata Aritomo danwa hikki*, p. 60; Mochizuki to Inoue, 19 August 1914, in Yamamoto, *Dai-niji Ōkuma naikaku kankei shiryō*, p. 91.
[80] Itō, *Taishō shoki Yamagata Aritomo danwa hikki*, p. 61; Mochizuki to Inoue, 19 August 1914, in Yamamoto, *Dai-niji Ōkuma naikaku kankei shiryō*, p. 91.

## War as Defense against a Japanese-German Alliance?

These sharp differences of opinion over Germany and the Anglo-Japanese alliance raise questions about the Japanese, more precisely, about Katō's motives for declaring war against Germany. Katō jumped at the opportunity, as we have seen, to consolidate Japanese interests abroad and promote British parliamentarism at home. Given the declining enthusiasm for the Anglo-Japanese alliance and glorification of German prowess among other influential circles in Japan, the speed and decisiveness with which the foreign minister responded to London's request for assistance take on added significance. That Katō chose expressly to pursue his domestic and foreign policy aims through a declaration of war rather than simply through direct negotiations with China stemmed primarily from his desire to halt the growing movement in Tokyo to abandon the Anglo-Japanese alliance.

To push the logic even further, one might speculate that Katō mobilized like a "force of lightning" in August 1914 to forestall a contrary move among the Japanese leadership, namely, to join the war with Germany against Britain. Although we have no direct evidence of such a scheme, Katō had ample reason to worry.[81] Several influential Japanese statesmen, after all, had lobbied for a German-Japanese alliance since 1911.

One of them was a bitter political rival, Baron Gotō Shinpei, who had left the management council of the Dōshikai and the party itself in October 1913 after Katō had assumed the party leadership. When Katō subsequently rebuffed Gotō's efforts for a place in the Ōkuma cabinet, Gotō became one of the cabinet's most vocal critics. Gotō originally proposed a German-Japanese alliance after the Chinese Revolution. The turmoil, he noted, was a "golden opportunity" to shift Japanese sights from the declining Britain, which was increasingly plagued by "decrepitude," to focus on the most rapidly rising power in Europe, Imperial Germany.[82] In July 1912, Gotō accompanied Prince Katsura Tarō, who had recently completed a second term as prime minister, to Europe in an apparent bid

---

[81] Katō was, apparently, not the only one with such a concern. In the 7 August cabinet meeting to decide on war with Germany, Justice Minister Ozaki Yukio urged an immediate declaration of war, in part from worry that members of the Imperial Army sympathizing with Germany would sway Japan toward Berlin. Saitō, *Nichi-Doku Chintao sensō no kaisen gaikō*, p. 203, n. 32.

[82] Kobayashi Michihiko, "Nichi-Ro sengo no Nichi-Doku dōmei ron" (Post-Russo-Japanese War Discussion of a German-Japanese Alliance), *Nihon rekishi*, no. 532 (September 1992): 83.

to begin talks with German officials for an alliance. To avoid international attention, the plan was to begin negotiations with German representatives in St. Petersburg. As recounted to Sun Yatsen by Katsura, a German-Japanese pact aimed to "topple British [political and economic] hegemony," in Turkey, India, and China. But Katsura received word of the Meiji emperor's imminent death soon after arriving in the Russian capital and headed for home without beginning discussions.[83]

Meanwhile, influential members of the Imperial Army had contemplated a shift in international loyalties. Most important among these was Tanaka Giichi, who would, in his capacity as vice chief of the Army General Staff in 1916, direct Japan's China policy after Katō's departure from the Foreign Ministry.[84] Tanaka was a protégé of army patriarch Yamagata Aritomo and had made a name for himself through a brilliant stint of operational planning as an army staff officer at Imperial Headquarters during the Russo-Japanese War. One year after the Japanese victory, Tanaka proposed a Russo-Japanese alliance to divide up British possessions in Asia between the partners.[85] On the eve of the Great War, Major General Tanaka Giichi urged a political alliance with Germany to "contain Russia on her Western border."[86]

Tanaka's appeal for a German-Japanese alliance rested, in part, on a respect for Germany that, as mentioned above, was widespread within the Japanese army. Since its creation in the 1880s, the Imperial Army had looked primarily to German military organization and training for inspiration. Japan borrowed from Berlin the idea of a regionally based army corps, a General Staff Office, a General Staff College, even employing Prussian officers to staff Japan's new college. Japanese officers, moreover, regularly traveled to Germany for advanced training.[87]

[83] Tai Kitō (Dai Zhidao), *Nihon ron* (Discourse on Japan), Ichikawa Hiroshi, trans. (Tokyo, 1972), p. 98.

[84] For details of Tanaka's continental schemes as vice chief of the Army General Staff during the war, see Dickinson, *War and National Reinvention*, ch. 4.

[85] Tanaka proposed a transfer of all British concessions in China to Japan and her territory in India to Russia; in "Miscellaneous Notes," 1906. Cited in Tsunoda Jun, *Manshū mondai to kokubō hōshin* (The Manchuria Problem and the National Defense Plan) (Tokyo, 1967), pp. 686–7, 699.

[86] See Tanaka, "Tai-Man shokan (II)" (May 1914). Tanaka Giichi kankei monjo (Papers Relating to Tanaka Giichi), no. 15. Yamaguchi Prefectural Library, Yamaguchi, Japan. Although a photocopy of the original document may be found in the National Diet Library in Tokyo, only the original in Yamaguchi prefecture contains the reference to Germany. I am indebted to Kobayashi Michihiko for bringing this to my attention.

[87] For an in-depth look at the German influence on the Imperial Army, see Ernst L. Presseisen, *Before Aggression: Europeans Prepare the Japanese Army* (Tucson, 1965).

Given this history, and Germany's spectacular rise to world power, there was widespread faith within the Japanese Army in an eventual German victory in Europe. Even after Japan had ejected the kaiser's troops from their Asian base at Qingdao, Tanaka Giichi and mentor Yamagata Aritomo continued to express their admiration. Tanaka viewed the battle of Ypres and subsequent failed Allied counteroffensives in the summer of 1915 as evidence of "the superior power and influence of Germany."[88] And Yamagata proclaimed in January 1916, "It is not Britain from which we should be learning but, in the future, at least for the next few years, Germany."[89]

### War and the Attempt to Control Imperial Army Power

There is, however, no evidence that Japanese generals were anything but delighted by the prospect of military action on the Asian continent, even at the expense of their former instructors. Tanaka, who advocated a political alliance with Germany in May 1914, just as readily recommended large-scale military operations against Germany in China soon after the cabinet decision for war on 8 August.[90] And Japanese officers relieved any disquiet they may have felt about attacking their tutors besieged at the German fortress at Qingdao by sending into the garrison wishes for luck and safety before the assault.[91]

Contrary to Foreign Minister Katō's fears, in other words, members of the Imperial Army were more captivated by the prospect of military action on the Continent than by the comparatively minor question of the target of their attention. Among the new ruling class of Meiji Japan, after all, the army had reaped the greatest benefits from continental expansion. Victory in the Russo-Japanese War granted the army a base in South Manchuria and justified an enormous augmentation of force. The Imperial Army grew from thirteen to nineteen standing divisions after the war, and the 1907 Basic Plan of National Defense called for eventual expansion to twenty-five standing divisions, with a mobilization potential of twice that. Japanese generals became increasingly active on the Continent after

[88] Terauchi Masatake kankei monjo (Papers Relating to Terauchi Masatake), 315–38, Tanaka to Terauchi Masatake, 3 July 1915. National Diet Library, Tokyo.

[89] Hara, *Hara Takashi nikki*, vol. 4, p. 156 (24 January 1916).

[90] Oka Ichinosuke monjo (Papers of Oka Ichinosuke), 7–1, Tanaka to Oka Ichinosuke, August 1914, National Diet Library, Tokyo.

[91] Meiron Harries and Susie Harries, *Soldiers of the Sun: The Rise and Fall of the Imperial Japanese Army* (New York, 1991), pp. 110–11.

1905, sending their own private agents to Beijing and Manchuria and
becoming involved in such schemes as Manchurian independence and gun
running to revolutionary forces during the Chinese revolution. Yamagata
Aritomo hoped to take advantage of the revolutionary turmoil to send two
new divisions to Manchuria. Army General Staff Second Bureau Chief
Utsunomiya Tarō advocated the partition of China.[92]

Japan's generals ultimately failed to take advantage of the Chinese revolution to engineer a massive new level of army power on the Continent.
And their fortunes at home also declined. While the 1907 Basic Plan of
National Defense called for six more divisions for the army's nineteen-
division force, fiscal austerity following the Russo-Japanese War blocked
support for even two new divisions.

The army leadership forced the dissolution of the Saionji cabinet over
its refusal to fund two divisions in 1912. But the subsequent cabinet of
Navy admiral Yamamoto Gonnohyōe sank army fortunes to new depths.
Yamamoto promoted naval expansion while maintaining a cap on army
funding. And he abolished the active-duty rule for the army and navy
ministers that had enabled War Minister Uehara Yūsaku to bring down
the Saionji regime. Finally, the admiral intruded into army sacred ground
in Manchuria by allowing the leadership of the South Manchuria Railway
to pass to the Seiyūkai party. By 1913, in other words, the Imperial Army
stood on the defensive against increasing cabinet and naval encroachments
upon its prerogatives.

The leaders of the Imperial Army, in short, had no reservations about
fighting their former tutors in China. They considered the battle a golden
opportunity to expand their area of operations in China and bolster
their waning political fortunes at home. The governor-general of Korea,
General Terauchi Masatake, noted after Britain's declaration of war simply that "we must eventually determine our attitude toward the belligerent
powers."[93] As soon as Katō decided upon the course, however, he, like
Tanaka Giichi, appealed for a dramatic new level of Imperial Army activity in China. After the fall of Qingdao, he urged Japan's minister to China
that Japanese troops should "share the responsibility" of public peace
in China with Beijing.[94] Vice chief of the Army General Staff Akashi

[92] For the Army response to the Chinese revolution, see Kitaoka, *Nihon rikugun to tairiku seisaku*, pp. 92–100.

[93] Yamamoto Shirō, ed., *Terauchi Masatake nikki* (Diary of Terauchi Masatake) (Kyōto, 1980), p. 635 (diary entry of 5 August 1914).

[94] Akashi Motojirō monjo 32–11, Terauchi to Akashi, 22 August 1914; in Nihon seiji gaikōshi kenkyūkai, ed., "Akashi Motojirō monjo oyobi kadai" (Papers of Akashi Motojirō and topics), *Keiō daigaku hōgaku kenkyū* 58, no. 9 (September 1985): 96.

Motojirō called for an immediate attack on the German concession at Jiaozhou. Otherwise, Russia would seize the territory after her victory over Berlin.[95] At home, Governor General Terauchi hoped that the war would enable Japanese policy makers to "redirect internal discord outward," particularly, away from the heated parliamentary debate over taxes, which threatened army prospects for expansion.[96]

Like Field Marshal Yamagata, the plans of Japanese generals for expansion during the war went well beyond the bounds of great power behavior in China in the latter nineteenth century. Like Yamagata, Major General Tanaka described the war in Europe as a "race war" and envisioned at the center of Japanese diplomacy not the Anglo-Japanese alliance but "intimate" Sino-Japanese relations. His prescription for close ties similarly echoed Yamagata's appeal for China to consult with Japan on all diplomatic matters.[97] But he went further by calling for the removal of Chinese president Yuan Shikai, who, he argued, perpetually conspired with Britain against Japanese interests.[98] As vice chief of the Army General Staff in 1916, Tanaka would commandeer the nation's China policy after Katō's departure from the cabinet and concoct an elaborate scheme for civil war on the continent. The disturbance, he hoped, would serve as a pretext for a major expedition of Japanese troops to China.[99]

General Terauchi described his own strategy for taking advantage of the war as an "Asian Monroe Doctrine." Like Yamagata and Tanaka, he spoke of Japan's particular racial and cultural affinity with China. And the European war was a "race war":

From our perspective as Asians, it is a war between Christians and, if we borrow their words, heathen peoples. Although we will not insist upon excluding Europeans and Americans, it is proper to inform the Westerners that, up to a point, Asia should be under the control of Asians.[100]

Japan should apprise Yuan Shikai of "the situation in Europe and Asia" and convince him to follow Japanese leadership. In this way, Terauchi hoped to restrain the "haughtiness" of the Europeans and establish

[95] Oka Ichinosuke monjo 1-1, Akashi to Oka Ichinosuke, undated. Cited in Kitaoka, *Nihon rikugun to tairiku seisaku*, p. 167.
[96] Gotō Shinpei monjo (Papers of Gotō Shinpei), R-86, Terauchi to Gotō Shinpei, 7 August 1914, National Diet Library, Tokyo.
[97] Oka Ichinosuke monjo 7-1, Tanaka to Oka, August 1914.
[98] Terauchi Masatake kankei monjo 315-24, Tanaka to Terauchi, 12 August 1914.
[99] See Dickinson, *War and National Reinvention*, ch. 4. The scheme would fail with the death of Chinese president Yuan Shikai in June 1916.
[100] Akashi Motojirō monjo 32-11, Terauchi to Akashi, 22 August 1914; in Nihon seiji gaikōshi kenkyūkai, "Akashi Motojirō monjo oyobi kadai," p. 96.

Japanese international authority. "Eventually all of Asia," he urged, "should be under the control of our Emperor."[101]

Given such expansive visions of Japanese power within the Imperial Army, Katō faced a more serious practical problem in declaring war on Germany than the concern over the military's sympathies for the kaiser. He worried that as soon as hostilities began, the army would run away with the wartime agenda, that it would pull the nation into a wildly ambitious scheme of territorial expansion in China. The fact that Katō decided to join the war despite this danger again testifies to his absolute loyalty to the Anglo-Japanese alliance. But once it was decided to join Britain in declaring war against Germany, the foreign minister painstakingly maneuvered to minimize army involvement in Japanese war aims.

Immediately after receiving *genrō* sanction on 8 August of the cabinet's decision for war, Katō met with his three closest confidants at his home.[102] The cabinet had decided to declare war. But Japan did not actually have to *go* to war. The foreign minister solicited advice as to how to avoid the risks of a military engagement. After a lengthy discussion, the four men decided that Japan would issue Germany an ultimatum demanding the cession of Jiaozhou to Japan. If Berlin complied, Katō would accomplish his two principal foreign policy aims – an enhancement of Japanese continental interests and a vote of confidence for the Anglo-Japanese alliance – without a fight. Katō and his advisors set an ultimatum deadline of seven days, rather than the customary forty-eight hours, to allow ample time for a German capitulation.[103]

A surrender was not, of course, forthcoming. Rather, Katō soon faced a situation that he had hoped to avoid: an Imperial Army offensive in China with few obstacles in its path. The foreign minister successfully headed off an attempt by Japanese generals in mid-August to invade Fujian (Fukien) province across the strait from Japan's colony of Taiwan.[104] But he was unable to confine army movements in Shandong province east of Weixian (Weihsien). By 6 October, the Eighteenth Division had occupied the entire

---

[101] Terauchi Masatake kankei monjo 421–3, Terauchi to Sugiyama, 1915.
[102] As noted above, Minister of Finance Wakatsuki Reijirō, Navy Minister Yashiro Rokurō, and the chief of the Political Affairs Bureau of the Foreign Ministry, Koike Chōzō.
[103] Itō, *Katō Takaaki*, vol. 2, pp. 83–5. Austria-Hungary, it will be remembered, gave Serbia forty-eight hours to respond to its ultimatum on 23 July. By contrast, Berlin's ultimatum to Belgium on 2 August, and London's ultimatum to Berlin on 4 August, allowed only twelve hours. Katō's ultimatum to China on 7 May 1915 over the Twenty-One Demands granted forty-eight hours.
[104] Hatano Masaru, *Kindai Ajia no seiji hendō to Nihon no gaikō* (Japanese Diplomacy and Political Change in Modern Asia) (Tokyo, 1995), pp. 205–6.

Shandong Railway to Jinan (Tsinan).[105] But Katō was able to achieve the replacement of operational forces by occupation troops soon after the fall of Qingdao. In so doing, he precluded army maneuvers from threatening his control of negotiations for a comprehensive agreement with China in 1915.[106]

## War and the Imperial Japanese Navy

The Imperial Navy posed much less of a threat to Katō's domestic and foreign policy aims in August 1914 than did the elder statesmen or the Imperial Army. Like Japan's generals, her admirals had greatly benefited from Japanese expansion on the Continent. The war with Russia that brought a substantial growth in Japanese ground forces also justified a large increase in naval tonnage. The 1907 Basic Plan of National Defense that outlined a target of twenty-five standing divisions for the army called for a fleet of sixteen capital ships (the so-called 8-8 fleet) for the navy. The Naval General Staff, then, readily adopted a plan of operations for the Japan Sea two days after the 1 August 1914 German declaration of war on Russia. The plan called for an assault on Qingdao, in concert with the army, aimed at "permanently extinguishing Germany's power in Asia and eliminating its ambition."[107]

But the navy did not share the army's enthusiasm for a military engagement. Although fiscal troubles prevented Japan's admirals, as they had her generals, from fulfilling expansion targets in the Basic Plan of National Defense, since 1911 the navy had received budgetary priority over the army. Nor, understandably, was the navy as interested in a continental agenda as Japanese ground forces. Such an agenda necessarily prioritized the Imperial Army as the first line of national defense.

Although the 1907 Basic Plan justified an enormous maritime expansion program, it defined the navy's principal strategic aim according to Field Marshal Yamagata's preferences, as maintaining the lines of communication and transport to the Asian continent. Japan's admirals fiercely contested this subordinate role. In May 1910 the Naval General Staff stepped outside the 1907 framework to call for an 8-4-8 fleet to

[105] Usui, *Nihon to Chūgoku*, pp. 48–52.
[106] Indeed, General Terauchi would lament Katō's failure to begin negotiations with China before the withdrawal of operational troops from Shandong. Tanaka Giichi kankei monjo, Terauchi to Tanaka, 27 January 1915, National Diet Library, Tokyo.
[107] Hatano, *Kindai Ajia no seiji hendō to Nihon no gaikō*, p. 187.

"accomplish the duty of the first line of defense."[108] Rear Admiral Satō Tetsutarō went further in January 1912, with an appeal for two 8-4 fleets, to be funded by holding the army to its immediate post-Sino-Japanese War strength of nineteen wartime divisions.[109] In response to queries in the Peers budget committee in June 1914, Navy Minister Yashiro Rokurō clarified the navy's complaint about the army's continental aims. To meet current budgetary restrictions, he argued, "we must bear with a minimum of national strength. . . . What I mean by a minimum of national strength is not possessing the will to invade other countries or create potential enemies."[110]

Unlike the Imperial Army, then, the Japanese navy responded to the prospect of war with Germany in August 1914 with hesitation. The above-mentioned plan of operations by the Naval General Staff calling for a joint army-navy offensive at Qingdao did not envision a protracted occupation on the Continent. Rather, it warned against "violating the neutrality of China."[111] Furthermore, this "Operational Outline" represented only one contingency, and a less preferred one for the High Command.

Naval authorities favored a neutral posture toward hostilities in Europe, recognizing "the advantage of keeping an eye on the situation." They argued that Japan was not restricted by the Anglo-Japanese alliance but could determine her attitude based upon her own interests. Their wait-and-see approach clearly rested upon a maritime definition of the Empire's interests. "To maintain peace in the Far East and develop maritime commerce is in Japan's interest and is thus a means to fulfill Japan's national policy," they declared. "Therefore, it is best to first advocate neutrality and propose the cessation of belligerent actions in the Far East."[112]

Navy Minister Yashiro reflected these sentiments when, during the joint *genrō*-cabinet conference of 8 August, he advised that Japan refrain from belligerency. The main portion of the German fleet appeared headed for home via South America, he noted. With a change in the situation thus imminent, the growing consensus within the navy was to await developments.[113] On 13 August, Yashiro urged the cabinet to postpone

[108] Kobayashi Michihiko, " 'Teikoku kokubō hōshin' no dōyō" (The Trembling of the "National Defense Plan"), *Nihon rekishi*, no. 507 (August 1990): 59.

[109] Ibid., p. 61.

[110] Kaigun daijin kanbō, ed., *Kaigun gunbi enkaku* (Development of Naval Armaments) (Tokyo, 1934), p. 179.

[111] Hatano, *Kindai Ajia no seiji hendō to Nihon no gaikō*, p. 187.

[112] Hirama, *Dai-ichiji sekai taisen to Nihon kaigun*, p. 21.

[113] Ibid., p. 22.

a declaration of war and, instead, to send an ultimatum to Germany to restore Qingdao to China and withdraw the German fleet from the China Sea.[114] Beyond the expulsion of the German fleet, in other words, naval leaders perceived few advantages to military action in East Asia in August 1914.

In fact, the disadvantages of hostilities in Asia became increasingly clear to Japan's admirals with the landing of imperial troops in northern Shandong on 2 September. Even before the embarkation, Japan's generals had, as we have seen, shown their enthusiasm for the opportunity provided by the war in Europe by planning an invasion of Fujian province. And they quickly moved after the beginning of their campaign to occupy the entire Shandong Railway to Jinan.

The brisk operation soon impelled naval leaders to revise their initial response to the European War. Until early in September, the Naval General Staff had confined operations at sea to the blockade of Qingdao, the transport of Japanese troops to Shandong, and the surveillance of German ships, postponing a decision on maneuvers in the German South Pacific. But on 12 September, the General Staff drafted an operational plan for the navy to crush the enemy fleet in the Pacific islands and destroy the ground facilities there.[115] The plan initially rejected a prolonged presence in the South Pacific, calling instead for a withdrawal soon after the completion of operations. But with the army rapidly advancing toward a new stronghold in Shandong, Navy Minister Yashiro and Chief of the Naval General Staff, Shimamura Hayao, agreed on 21 September to delete the demand for a quick retreat.[116] One day before facing off with the army in an appeal before the recently established Military Affairs Council for a wartime budget, Yashiro demanded cabinet approval for the "perpetual occupation" of the territories.[117]

The cabinet ultimately authorized only a limited occupation of the Marshalls, Marianas, and Carolines, with the eventual disposal of the territories to be decided at a later date. But by December, Foreign Minister Katō informed the British that Japan desired to maintain the islands in perpetuity.[118] Spurred by the army's drive for a new area of operations

[114] Banno Junji et al., eds, *Takarabe Takeshi nikki* (Diary of Takarabe Takeshi), 2 vols. (Tokyo, 1983), vol. 2, p. 319.
[115] Hatano, *Kindai Ajia no seiji hendō to Nihon no gaikō*, p. 209.
[116] Ibid.
[117] Gaimushō, ed., *Nihon gaikō bunsho: Taishō jidai* (Documents on Japanese Diplomacy: Taishō Period), 36 vols. (Tokyo, 1964–87), 1914, vol. 3, p. 666.
[118] Ibid., p. 676.

on the Continent, the navy embarked upon an assertive campaign in the South Pacific.

## War and the Seiyūkai

If Japanese admirals worried about the domestic political ramifications of Japanese participation in the European War, so too did the Seiyūkai party. The largest force in the Imperial Diet since its founding in 1900, the Seiyūkai had led the "movement to protect constitutional government" that felled the oligarchic cabinet of Katsura Tarō in 1913 and thus threatened the political future of Japan's nonelected elites. It shared with Katō and his Dōshikai party the aim of promoting representative government in Japan.

But Katō and the Seiyūkai were also natural competitors for a portion of the gradually expanding popular franchise. In August 1914, that franchise was restricted to adult males with an annual tax obligation of ten yen, approximately 2.6 percent of the population. But the Imperial Diet was not an insignificant force. It had proven capable of toppling an oligarchic cabinet in 1913. And the Seiyūkai enjoyed an absolute majority of 205 to the Dōshikai's puny 91 seats in the Lower House.[119]

But the true source of Katō's power lay not with his political party. It rested instead in his position as foreign minister. Especially at a time of national crisis such as war, he could use his position as a bully pulpit and do so with devastating effect. This was, undoubtedly, the principal concern of Seiyūkai party leaders in August 1914 as they urged caution in the cabinet response to events unfolding in Europe. Acting upon word of a possible Japanese declaration of war, former finance minister Takahashi Korekiyo paid Prime Minister Ōkuma a visit. To join the war against Germany, he argued, seemed "extreme." Could the administration not find a solution to the situation in Asia through peaceful negotiations with Berlin?[120] Party president Hara Takashi himself signaled his displeasure after receiving confirmation of the decision for war. "The stratagem of fortifying the Cabinet by directing public sentiment outward," he grumbled, "is clear."[121]

---

[119] This was the breakdown in December 1913, The total number of seats in the Lower House was 381. Masumi Junnosuke, *Nihon seijishi* (Japanese Political History), 4 vols. (Tokyo, 1998), vol. 2, p. 250.
[120] Itō, *Katō Takaaki*, vol. 1, pp. 72–3.
[121] Hara, *Hara Takashi nikki*, vol. 4, p. 32 (14 August 1914).

That the party's objection to a declaration of war went no further than concern over the political power of Katō Takaaki is evidenced by the Seiyūkai's public posture after the formal cabinet decision. Despite having discretely urged Ōkuma to consider a peaceful avenue to Japanese aims in August, party leaders in the Thirty-Fourth Diet (4–9 September 1914) condemned not the government's recklessness but its caution. What was the meaning of limiting Japanese demands of Germany to its continental concession of Jiaozhou, queried the Seiyūkai's Ōoka Ikuzō. How about German possessions in the South Pacific, or elsewhere? What was the point of restricting Japan's area of military operations? Was Japan not an independent country? What was the aim of Japan's promise to eventually return Jiaozhou to China? Had Britain not already occupied German territory in the South Pacific?[122]

## War and the Japanese Media

That the Seiyūkai criticized the government for its caution reveals something about the general state of Japanese public opinion through the first year of the Great War. In the Thirty-Fifth Diet (7–25 December 1914), Seiyūkai member Ogawa Heikichi asked what the administration planned to do for Japanese rights in China now that Germany had been vanquished at Qingdao. "It is time to make a dramatic move," he demanded.[123] And when on the eve of the 25 March 1915 election Katō had yet to conclude an agreement with China over the Twenty-One Demands, President Hara Takashi tried to squeeze the most political capital from the failure. "China policy is the core of the Empire's diplomacy," he declared at a 22 March party rally. "One mistake and the repercussions are almost unimaginable."[124] Kokumintō party president Inukai Tsuyoshi went on record as early as 7 September as an enthusiastic champion of a comprehensive new agreement with China. "In order to make this relationship [with China] intimate," he urged the Lower House, "we must form an alliance based upon the most intimate interests of survival."[125]

---

[122] "Gunhi yosan sōkai" (Plenary Session over the Military Budget), *Yomiuri shinbun*, 6 September 1914, in *Shinbun shūsei Taishō hennenshi* (Newspaper Compilation: Chronicles of Taishō), 43 vols. (Tokyo, 1969–81), 1914, vol. 2, p. 389.

[123] Ōtsu Jun'ichirō, *Dai Nihon kenseishi* (Constitutional History of Greater Japan), 10 vols. (Tokyo, 1970), vol. 7, pp. 389–96.

[124] *Tokyo Asahi shinbun*, 23 March 1915, p. 2.

[125] Washio Yoshitsugu, ed., *Inukai Bokudō den* (Biography of Inukai Tsuyoshi), 3 vols. (Tokyo, 1938–39), vol. 2, p. 254.

The national media echoed this parliamentary enthusiasm for the opportunity in the fall of 1914. At first, the liberal newspaper *Tokyo Asahi
shinbun* on 5 August welcomed the outbreak of war and distraction of
powers to Europe as a chance for Japan to curb the emphasis on arms
that had propelled it to world prominence.[126] Only two weeks later, after
the Japanese ultimatum to Germany, it hailed the prospect of a brand new
continental mission. "Imperial [Japanese] subjects," it declared, "will not
be the only ones to rejoice over the warning to deliver Jiaozhou to the
Empire and the extinguishing of German ambitions."[127]

The Japanese cabinet decision for war spurred a series of articles in
the *Ōsaka Mainichi shinbun* that revealed rapidly expanding imperial
ambitions. The 11 August issue urged a Japanese takeover of the "source
of evil in the Far East," German-occupied Jiaozhou.[128] On 12 August, it
spoke of "a critical period in which Japan, as a member of the Anglo-
Japanese alliance, must assume the responsibility of protecting Anglo-
Japanese interests east of India."[129] The message of 13 August was that
"this might be the time for Japan, as an independent empire in the Far
East, to press for what we believe necessary for self-defense, regardless of
our alliance with Britain."[130]

Widespread celebration marked the fall of the German fortress at
Qingdao in November 1914. The *Ōsaka Mainichi shinbun* talked of
"sowing the seeds" that would ensure the future "luxuriant growth"
of Shandong province according to Japanese wishes.[131] And the *Tokyo
Asahi shinbun* welcomed the prospect of increased trade with China,
especially in Shandong, where goods would now travel inland "after
inspection by Japanese [customs officers] and along railroads run by
Japanese."[132]

---

[126] "Ōshū tairan to waga gunbi" (The Great European War and our Military), *Tokyo
Asahi shinbun*, 5 August 1914, in *Shinbun shūsei Taishō hennenshi*, 1914, vol. 2,
p. 259.

[127] "Doitsu to Santō" (Germany and Shandong), *Tokyo Asahi shinbun*, 19 August 1914,
in ibid., p. 317.

[128] "Kagen Kōshūwan" (Jiaozhou, Source of Evil), *Ōsaka Mainichi shinbun*, 11 August
1914, in ibid., pp. 287–8.

[129] "Kiken naru Shina no keisei" (The Dangerous Situation in China), *Ōsaka Mainichi
shinbun*, 12 August 1914, in ibid., p. 291.

[130] "Heiwa o iu mono, heiwa o magotsukaseru" (Those Who Speak Peace, Those Who
Confuse Peace), *Ōsaka Mainichi shinbun*, 13 August 1914, in ibid., p. 296.

[131] "Santō keiei ron" (On the Management of Shandong), *Ōsaka Mainichi shinbun*,
8 November 1914, in ibid., p. 685.

[132] "Chintao kanraku no kekka" (Consequences of the Fall of Qingdao), *Tokyo Asahi
shinbun*, 9 November 1914, in ibid., p. 686.

## Conclusion: Old and New Imperialism in Japan

Analyses of Japan's actions in the First World War generally note that its loyalties between 1914 and 1918 seemed divided. This was the perception in Allied capitals as Japan argued against any limits to its operations against Germany in Asia, negotiated a comprehensive agreement with China on Japanese "rights" on the Continent (the Twenty-One Demands), concluded a treaty with Russia aimed at checking American power in Asia (the 1916 Russo-Japanese convention), refused to send Japanese troops to the European theater, and resorted to autonomous action during the Allied expedition to Siberia. Foreign observers spoke of Japan during the war as the "Germany of the Orient" and as a "military autocracy" that "makes a mock of 'constitutional government.'"[133] In 1917, Americans worried about a possible Japanese alliance with Germany and Mexico aimed at the United States.[134] During the Paris Peace Conference, they suspected clandestine Japanese talks with Germany.[135]

The Japanese did, in fact, pursue their own agenda during the Great War, which, far from aiding the Allied cause, threatened great power interests in Asia. But Japanese war aims do not confirm the assumption of contemporaries that there was a single-mindedness of purpose in Tokyo during the Great War. Nor do they substantiate subsequent scholarly analyses that locate a direct link between aggressive Japanese intent during the 1914–18 years and renewed Japanese belligerence in the 1930s. On the contrary, as the above discussion reveals, much of what fueled Japanese participation in the First World War was political turmoil within Japan. At its most fundamental level, the Japanese decision to declare war on Germany was the work of one man and his advocacy of one side in a turbulent domestic debate over the Japanese national essence.

---

[133] See "Japan is Seen as the Germany of the Orient," *New York Times*, 21 November 1915, sec. 4, p. 16; and Putnam Weale, "Japan's Imperialism," *New York Times*, 7 December 1919, sec. 3, p. 8, respectively.

[134] This was a response to the "Zimmermann note," which came to light in March 1917. Berlin's Foreign Secretary, Alfred Zimmermann, had instructed Germany's minister in Mexico in January 1917 to work on a German-Mexican alliance, and to solicit the support of Japan, against the imminent participation of the United States in the war. The sensational news headlined the American press and inspired a film, Patria, the work of press lord William Randolph Hearst, which depicted Japanese and Mexican troops looting, murdering, and raping as they invaded the United States. For the "Zimmermann note," see Barbara W. Tuchman, *The Zimmermann Telegram* (New York, 1958). For more on the film and Woodrow Wilson's reaction, see Walter LaFeber, *The Clash: U.S.-Japanese Relations Throughout History* (New York, 1997), p. 120.

[135] Russell H. Fifield, *Woodrow Wilson and the Far East* (Hamden, 1965), p. 221, n. 6.

The "whither Japan" debate had been fought ever since the nation's founding in 1868. On the eve of the Great War, the profusion of competing voices could be distilled into two fundamental camps. On the one hand were members of the new ruling class of Meiji Japan: elder statesmen, bureaucrats, soldiers, and elected and appointed peers, those who favored empire, arms, and oligarchic rule. On the other hand were the victors of the Taishō political crisis, particularly the leaders of Japan's political parties. Deprived of any formal voice in the Meiji system, these latter had slowly chipped away at the political supremacy of the elder statesmen and their allies to promote representative government and greater civilian uses of the national budget. Both camps in 1914 agreed on the wisdom of continental expansion as the principal avenue for Japanese international status. And they universally greeted the outbreak of war in Europe as the "golden opportunity" to strengthen Japanese "rights" and influence in China. In addition to the conflict over political arrangements within Japan, however, there was a growing rift over the nature of Japanese power abroad.

In this context, the cabinet's swift decision on 8 August to eject German power from Asia is less a signal of Japan's insatiable appetite for conquest than the strongest expression during the war of Japan's fidelity to the Anglo-Japanese alliance. Rather than fortifying Japan's continental interests through the clearly viable option of neutrality and direct negotiations with China, Katō Takaaki insisted upon Japanese participation in the war "upon the broad foundation of the Anglo-Japanese alliance." Given that the alliance did not require Japanese belligerence, and in the context of widespread predictions, even sympathy, in Tokyo for a German victory, the foreign minister's actions are remarkable.

Katō was Japan's preeminent Anglophile. He insisted on continued close relations with Britain because, from his twelve years of residence in London, he had developed a deep respect for British parliamentarism and an abiding faith in the strategic utility of the Anglo-Japanese alliance. His decision to move quickly in August 1914 also derived from a growing realization that influential members of Japan's established elite did not share his reverence for the British. On the contrary, in their vision of Japanese power in China, these men felt ever less use for the alliance. Instead, they placed increasing faith in "intimate" Sino-Japanese relations to protect Japan in an imagined future apocalyptic "race war."

The link between Japanese aggression in the 1930s and Tokyo's expansion in China in the First World War, then, is complex. Like the Japanese declaration of war in August 1914, the diplomatic event most identified with future continental aggression, the Twenty-One Demands, was the handiwork not of the most belligerent forces in Tokyo, but of Katō Takaaki. Like the declaration of war, the "demands" were the product of a conservative world view. In negotiating a comprehensive agreement for Japanese "rights" in China, Katō did not exceed the bounds of behavior that had governed great power competition in China since the Sino-Japanese War. After China's military defeat in 1895, the powers had scrambled for exclusive rights in "spheres of influence" in China to facilitate commercial intercourse. Likewise, in 1915, Katō negotiated a wide range of principally economic rights in several areas on the Continent.[136]

In their own plans for a comprehensive agreement with China, however, Japan's elder statesmen and members of the Imperial Army, in particular, were moved less by the desire for economic might than by political and territorial gain. In the name of "intimate" Sino-Japanese relations, they advocated the ouster of the Chinese president, fanned civil war on the continent, and planned a major expedition of troops to China. To protect their continental gains from a possible American challenge, they sought not to strengthen the Anglo-Japanese alliance but to conclude a new alliance with Russia. And they leapt at the opportunity in 1918 to flood Siberia with over 50,000 Japanese troops.[137] The most aggressive foreign policy initiatives of the First World War, in other words, were the product of these men, those who exalted the power of Imperial Germany and increasingly viewed Great Britain as an obstacle to their ambitious dreams of an "Asian Monroe Doctrine." The links between the objectives of these men and the military-bureaucratic instigators and promoters of the Manchurian Incident were real.

The First World War was for Japan, as for all the main belligerents, a principal crossroads separating the nineteenth from the twentieth centuries. In political terms, for its powerful promotion of cabinet and Foreign Ministry supremacy in the making of Japanese foreign policy, Katō Takaaki's declaration of war anticipated the dawn of a new age of representative government in interwar Japan. In diplomatic terms, on the other hand, the decision looked backward. It was a product of Japan's turn-of-the-century quest for international status through economic competition in China and alliance with Great Britain. It served, in other words,

---

[136] For more on the conservative nature of the Twenty-One Demands, see Dickinson, *War and National Reinvention*, ch. 3.

[137] For coverage of these initiatives by members of the Yamagata faction during the First World, see ibid., chs. 4,5.

as a check against a more disturbing trend of expansionist fervor based upon the boundless ideal of pan-Asianism.

Katō Takaaki's vision of British parliamentarism and free trade imperialism prevailed in the first year of the war until his resignation in August 1915. And it would triumph again in interwar Japan in the aftermath of Imperial Germany's defeat. But the ambitious militarism and pan-Asianism that Katō so decisively threatened with his declaration of war on Germany in August 1914 would not disappear. It would be cultivated throughout the 1920s by members of Japan's military-bureaucratic elite, who stood to gain politically by its revival. These men would, in fact, fight every gain made by British parliamentarism and free-trade imperialism in 1920s Japan and be ever alert for the opportunity to embark upon an ambitious new path of militarism and territorial expansion. That opportunity would come in an explosion along the South Manchuria Railway in September 1931.

# 10

# The Ottoman Empire

## Ulrich Trumpener

Among the countries that entered the Great War before the end of 1914, the Ottoman (or Turkish) Empire was destined to play a major role in shaping its course and eventual outcome. Despite its economic backwardness and financial penury, this polyglot state of about 22 million people put up a remarkable war effort against the *entente* powers and forced them to divert large numbers of troops and significant naval forces to the newly opened Turkish theaters of war, thus reducing Allied pressure on Germany and her Austro-Hungarian ally for long periods of time. Moreover, by barring Allied shipping through the Black Sea Straits (the Bosphorus and the Dardanelles), the Ottoman armed forces contributed in a major way to Russia's supply shortages and thereby hastened the collapse of the tsarist regime in 1917.[1] In the end, of course, the Ottoman Empire itself collapsed under the strains and stresses of the Great War. Its defeat in the fall of 1918 opened the way for drastic political changes throughout the Middle East: Between 1919 and 1926, a host of new states were to emerge in that region, among them the new Republic of Turkey; Syria and Lebanon (under French mandate); Iraq, Palestine, and "Transjordania" (under British mandates); as well as the future kingdoms of Saudi Arabia and Yemen. The establishment of a "Jewish homeland" in Palestine, as promised by Great Britain in the Balfour Declaration of 1917, would soon become a source of major friction in the Middle

---

[1] For a brief overview of the Ottoman war effort, see Ulrich Trumpener, "Turkey's War," in Hew Strachan, ed., *World War I: A History* (Oxford, 1998), pp. 80–91. See also the pioneering study by Maurice Larcher, *La Guerre turque dans la guerre mondiale* (Paris, 1926).

East and elsewhere whose repercussions are still being felt today, almost ninety years after the Ottomans marched into the last war of their history.[2]

## Antecedents

Often derided as "the sick man of Europe," the tricontinental Ottoman Empire, under pressure from reformist army officers and various other Young Turk groups, had been transformed into a constitutional monarchy during the summer of 1908.[3] After the suppression of a counterrevolutionary coup in April 1909, Sultan Abdülhamid II had been removed from the throne and replaced by his brother Reşad, who would henceforth preside over the empire as Mehmed V, with very clearly defined limitations of his powers.[4]

In the Ottoman Chamber of Deputies, elected during the fall of 1908, the party with the largest number of seats was the so-called Committee of Union and Progress (CUP), an organization that had its headquarters in Salonica.[5] While it was strong in the legislature and usually quite well represented in the cabinet, the CUP's political influence varied considerably during the next four years, and it was only in 1913 that it gained absolute power in the country.[6]

While the overthrow of Abdülhamid's despotic regime in 1908 had initially been greeted with enthusiasm by most of his subjects, Turks and non-Turks alike, some of the policies promoted by the CUP soon aroused suspicion and resentment among some of the ethnic minorities in the empire.[7] In March 1910, a revolt against the government erupted in the

---

[2] On the background of the Balfour Declaration, see Isaiah Friedman, *The Question of Palestine, 1914–1918* (New York, 1973); idem, *Germany, Turkey, and Zionism, 1897–1918* (Oxford, 1977); and the relevant chapters in Egmont Zechlin, *Die deutsche Politik und die Juden im Ersten Weltkrieg* (Göttingen, 1969).

[3] On the Young Turk Revolution, see Ernest E. Ramsaur, Jr., *The Young Turks: Prelude to the Revolution of 1908* (Princeton, 1957); Feroz Ahmad, *The Young Turks: The Committee of Union and Progress in Turkish Politics, 1908–1914* (London, 1969), pp. 1–32; Erik Jan Zürcher, *The Unionist Factor: The Role of the Committee of Union and Progress in the Turkish National Movement, 1905–1926* (Leiden, 1984), chs. 1–2; and Aykut Kansu, *The Revolution of 1908 in Turkey* (Leiden and New York, 1997).

[4] See Victor R. Swenson, "The Military Rising in Istanbul 1909," *Journal of Contemporary History* 5 (1970): 171–84; and Aykut Kansu, *Politics in Post-Revolutionary Turkey, 1908–1913* (Leiden and Boston, 2000), chs. 1–3.

[5] The CUP only moved its offices to Istanbul in 1912.

[6] See Ahmad, *The Young Turks*, chs. 3–5; and Kansu, *Politics*, chs. 4–10.

[7] Aside from the various non-Turkish population groups in the Balkan region (which separated from the Ottoman Empire in 1912/13), the most important ethnic and/or religious "minorities" in the sultan's realm were, in order of size, the Arabs, the Armenians, the

Kosovo area, which required several months to stamp out. In January 1911, another rebellion began in Yemen, forcing the government to transfer troops to that region.[8] Two months later, further disturbances erupted in northern Albania, and it was only after making a number of concessions that the government could restore order there.

Then, in late September 1911, the Kingdom of Italy declared war on the sultan and invaded his Tripolitanian provinces (today's Libya). The small Ottoman garrisons in the region, backed by thousands of native tribesmen, successfully prevented the invaders from penetrating into the interior of the country, but that did not deter the Italian government from proclaiming its annexation on 5 November.[9] Determined not to lose face in the Arab-Islamic world, the Ottoman government, now headed by an experienced elder statesman, Mehmed Said Pasha, sent several energetic staff officers to Libya, where they soon built up more effective defensive positions around the Italian-occupied coastal towns of Tripoli, Benghazi, Derna, and Tobruk. Among the Turkish officers transferred to North Africa at this time was one of the heroes of the 1908 revolt against Abdülhamid's regime, Major Enver Bey, who had previously served as military attaché at the Ottoman embassy in Berlin.[10]

To force the Ottoman government to accept the loss of Libya, the Italians broadened the war in 1912, first by a naval bombardment of the Dardanelles in April and then, in May, by seizing Rhodes and the other islands of the Dodecanese.[11] In the same months, Albanian and other malcontents staged uprisings in several areas of the Balkan peninsula, which in turn led to a political crisis in Istanbul and eventually, in mid-July, to the formation of a new cabinet under Gazi Ahmed Muhtar Pasha.

---

Greeks, the Kurds, and the Jews. On the difficulties in getting an accurate picture of Ottoman demographics, see Kemal H. Karpat, *The Ottoman Population 1830–1914: Ethnic and Social Characteristics* (Madison, Wis., 1985).

[8] To deal with the troubles in Yemen, the chief of the Ottoman General Staff, Ahmed Izzet Pasha (Furgaç), personally took charge of the pacification program there. One of the junior officers on his staff was Adjutant Major Mustafa Ismet (Inönü), a future prime minister and president of Turkey. Names enclosed by parentheses are the surnames that all Turks had to adopt in 1934.

[9] See William C. Askew, *Europe and Italy's Acquisition of Libya* (Durham, N.C., 1942); and Luigi Albertini, *The Origins of the War of 1914*, 3 vols. (London and New York, 1952–57), vol. 1, pp. 340–53.

[10] For a good introduction to Enver's life and career, see Dankwart A. Rustow, "Enwer Pasha," in *Encyclopedia of Islam*, New Series (1960– ), vol. 2, pp. 698–702.

[11] See the detailed commentaries on "Der Italienisch-Türkische Krieg" by Major General Heinrich Imhoff et al., in the German *Militär-Wochenblatt* 96–97 (1911–12): 3624–29, 5–11, 110–15, 245–51, 503–8, 687–92, and passim. See also Albertini, *The Origins*, vol. 1, pp. 353–63.

With this change, the domestic opponents of the CUP regained some of their influence in the country, though they would not enjoy their comeback for very long.[12]

While the Turks were busy dealing with the Italians, several Balkan states were secretly preparing to pounce on the Ottoman Empire as well. On 8 October 1912, the Kingdom of Montenegro declared war on the sultan's realm; ten days later, Bulgaria, Serbia, and Greece officially entered the fray. During the next three weeks, the numerically inferior Ottoman armies in the Balkan Peninsula were defeated in a number of pitched battles, losing control of Macedonia, Epirus, Albania, and most of Thrace. Simultaneously, the Greeks used their fleet to seize numerous islands in the northern Aegean. Reinforcements from Asia Minor eventually allowed the Turks to settle down in a fortified line roughly thirty miles to the west of their capital, Istanbul (or Constantinople, as most westerners called it in those days). Moreover, Ottoman spirits were lifted somewhat by the fact that the garrisons of Edirne (Adrianople), Janina, and Scutari were holding out against the forces besieging them.[13]

When the Ottoman government, now headed by another elderly statesman, Mehmed Kâmil Pasha, agreed to make major territorial concessions during peace talks in London early in 1913, a group of nationalist officers with close ties to the CUP decided to stage another coup d'état. Headed by Enver Bey, they stormed into the grand vizier's office on 23 January and forced him and his cabinet to resign. During the confrontation, the minister of war, General Hüseyin Nâzim Pasha, was shot dead, possibly by accident.[14] This "Babiâli Incident" brought the more radical elements of the CUP closer to power than they had ever been before. While a senior army general with only loose ties to the CUP, Mahmud Şevket Pasha, became the new grand vizier (and minister of war), several other important portfolios were taken over by prominent CUP figures, among them Adil (Arda) (Ministry of the Interior), Prince Said Halim Pasha (Foreign Ministry), and Ahmed Şükrü Bey (Ministry of Education).[15]

---

[12] See Ahmad, *The Young Turks*, ch. 5; and Kansu, *Politics*, chs. 8–9.

[13] See Albertini, *The Origins*, vol. 1, ch. 7; and Béla K. Kiraly and D. Djordjevic, eds., *East Central European Society and the Balkan Wars* (New York, 1987).

[14] Ahmad, *The Young Turks*, pp. 116–20; and Kansu, *Politics*, pp. 434–39.

[15] Şevket Pasha, more than twenty years older than most of the CUP leaders, had a distinguished career behind him, both in the army and as a cabinet minister. As a young officer he had headed an Ottoman team processing weapons purchases from the Mauser company in Oberndorf. Since that time he spoke German fluently, albeit with a heavy Swabian accent.

Less than five months after his appointment as grand vizier, Şevket Pasha was shot down by a band of assassins while he was on his way to the Porte.[16] Under heavy pressure from the CUP, Sultan Mehmed V agreed to make Prince Said Halim Pasha the new grand vizier. Wealthy, intelligent, and well educated, this Egyptian-born grandee had risen rather rapidly in the councils of the CUP, but during his long tenure as grand vizier (until February 1917) his views were often ignored by his colleagues in both the party and the cabinet. More about his role in bringing the Ottoman Empire into the Great War is said below.[17]

By far the strongest and most talented member of Said Halim's new cabinet was a former postal official, Mehmed Talât Bey. A veteran of underground work against Abdülhamid's regime, Talât since 1908 had held important posts in both the government and the party; as minister of the interior he would keep a close eye on the grand vizier and eventually, in 1917, officially succeed him.[18] In December 1913, Major-General Ahmed Cemal Pasha, another senior figure in the CUP, joined the cabinet as minister of public works.[19] A few weeks later, on 4 January 1914, Enver Bey received a double promotion to brigadier general and simultaneously joined the cabinet as minister of war.[20] Barely thirty-two years old, Enver Pasha (as he would henceforth be known) shortly thereafter married one of the sultan's nieces.

It has often been claimed that from early 1914 on, the Ottoman Empire was run by a triumvirate composed of Enver, Talât, and Cemal (who switched from Public Works to the Navy Ministry in March of that year), but that generalization is quite misleading. Indeed, there is ample evidence to support the conclusion that both before and during the Great War the

---

[16] Şevket's murder was probably instigated by prominent opponents of the CUP, but parts of the story remain murky. See Ahmad, *The Young Turks*, pp. 126–30. The Porte is the chief office of the Ottoman Empire.

[17] On the prince's career, see I. M. K. Inal, *Osmanli devrinde son sadriazamlar* (The Last Grand Viziers of the Ottoman Era), 14 vols. (Istanbul, 1940–53), vols. 12–13, pp. 1893–1932.

[18] See ibid., vol. 13, pp. 1933–72; and Ulrich Trumpener, *Germany and the Ottoman Empire, 1914–1918* (Princeton, 1968), pp. 17ff. and passim.

[19] See Dankwart A. Rustow, "Djemal Pasha," in *Encyclopedia of Islam*, N.S., vol. 2, pp. 531ff. Like Said Halim, Talât, and several other CUP leaders, Cemal was assassinated by Armenians in the early 1920s.

[20] His elevation to that important post was facilitated by the fact that he had played a conspicuous role in the recapture of Edirne during the Second Balkan War. Enver's predecessor in the War Ministry, Marshal Ahmed Izzet (Furgaç), was chosen in October 1918 to lead the defeated Ottoman Empire out of the Great War. See Trumpener, *Germany and the Ottoman Empire*, pp. 352–62.

Central Committee of the CUP, the Merkezi Umuni, remained the principal policy-making body in the empire, and that no government minister could take action on any major matter without gaining support from a majority of the committee's members. In the period leading up to Ottoman intervention, two physicians with extensive experience in covert political action, Drs. Bahaeddin Şakir and Selânikli Nazim, appear to have been particularly influential in the committee. Another powerful figure was Midhat Sükrü (Bleda), an erstwhile accountant who also held a seat in the Chamber of Deputies. These men, along with about ten other party functionaries in the Merkezi Umuni, certainly must share a great deal of responsibility for both the foreign and domestic policies of Prince Said Halim's cabinet.[21]

From August 1914 on, the CUP leadership increased its power within the empire as well as its capabilities for covert action abroad through the establishment of a "Special Organization" (Teskilâti Mahsusa). Although it was funded by the War Ministry and directly responsible to Enver Pasha, it is clear that some of its activities went far beyond conventional secret service norms. Indeed, one branch of the Special Organization was involved in promoting the "Turkification" of business and industry within the Ottoman Empire at the expense of its Greek and Armenian citizens. Among the functionaries doing that kind of work was a bank manager in Izmir (Smyrna), Mahmud Celâl (Bayar), who would conclude his colorful political career as the president of Turkey (1950–60).[22] Finally, it should be mentioned that the CUP made excellent use of the press to generate support for its policies. Among the newspapers directly under the control of the party, the *Tanin* was probably the most widely read. Its editor, Hüseyin Cahit (Yalçin), was both a brilliant journalist and a man of action, serving simultaneously in the Chamber of Deputies and as the Ottoman delegate on the council of the Public Debt Administration (an agency representing the foreign creditors of the Porte with extensive control over its tax revenues).[23]

[21] On the functions and membership of the *Merkezi Umuni*, see T. Z. Tunaya, *Türkiyede siyasi partiler 1859–1952* (The Political Parties of Turkey...) (Istanbul, 1952), pp. 195–200; Ahmad,*The Young Turks*, pp. 157–61, 166–81; and Zürcher, *The Unionist Factor*, pp. 35, 38f., 43, 47, 63, 70, 77ff., 88, and 124. Dr. Bahaeddin Şakir fled to Germany in 1918, where he was assassinated by Armenians in 1922; Dr. Nazim was hanged in Ankara four years later for allegedly plotting against President Mustafa Kemal (Atatürk).
[22] See Zürcher, *The Unionist Factor*, pp. 28, 59, 74, 83ff., 123, 129ff., and passim.
[23] A close friend of Talât, Yalçin survived British internment after the Great War and a treason trial in Ankara in 1926. He died in 1957 at age eighty-two.

In addition to its heavy indebtedness to foreign bondholders, the Ottoman Empire on the eve of World War I faced numerous other structural problems. Its transportation system, underdeveloped as it was, was mostly owned by foreign companies, and the same was true with regard to public utilities and several other sectors of the economy. To patriotic Ottomans, another cause for resentment was the refusal of various foreign governments to allow the abrogation of the "capitulations," a series of commercial treaties going back to the sixteenth century that granted a number of privileges to certain categories of foreigners.[24]

While the Balkan Wars of 1912–13 had drastically reduced the sultan's realm in southeastern Europe, the Ottoman government on the eve of World War I still controlled a vast empire in Asia: Anatolia, Mesopotamia (Iraq), Syria, Lebanon, Palestine, the Hijas and some other sections of modern Saudi Arabia, as well as parts of Yemen. Moreover, at least in theory, Egypt was still linked to the Ottoman Empire, even though the actual administration of the country was under British supervision since the 1880s.

Having gone through the loss of numerous territories in both Europe and Africa between 1911 and the spring of 1913, the Ottoman government in May of that year decided that its military establishment needed major changes, and that these reforms should, as often before, be supervised by German army officers. After lengthy discussions with Berlin, agreement was reached on the size and functions of the new mission, and in mid-December 1913 the first contingent of the German reformers arrived in Istanbul. Headed by a recently ennobled cavalry general, Otto Liman von Sanders, the mission was reinforced during the following four months and had roughly seventy members scattered all over the empire by July 1914.[25]

To many contemporary observers, and particularly to the Russian government, the dispatch of the German military mission to the Ottoman Empire looked like a major increase of German power and influence in that country. But such fears were quite unjustified. Indeed, while General

[24] See Donald C. Blaisdell, *European Financial Control in the Ottoman Empire* (New York, 1929); Orhan Conker and Emile Witmeur, *Redressement économique et industrialisation de la nouvelle Turquie* (Paris, 1937); and Osman Nebioglu, *Die Auswirkungen der Kapitulationen auf die türkische Wirtschaft* (Jena, 1941).

[25] See Jehuda L. Wallach, *Anatomie einer Militärhilfe: Die preussisch-deutschen Militärmissionen in der Türkei 1835–1919* (Düsseldorf, 1976), chs. 1–5; and Ulrich Trumpener, "From Entente to Alliance: The German Armed Forces and the Ottoman Empire, 1882–1914," in *Forces Armées et Systèmes d'Alliances* (Montpellier, France, 1984), pp. 477–89.

Liman and his subordinates were busy training and upgrading the Ottoman officer corps and certain "model" regiments, the Porte established contact with the member states of the Triple Entente, probing their willingness to finance the revival of Ottoman strength and even their inclination to conclude an alliance with Turkey. In February 1914, the Ottoman government formally conceded to Russia the authority to "supervise" reforms in the Armenian-populated provinces of eastern Anatolia. Three months later, the powerful minister of the interior, Talât Bey, led an Ottoman delegation to the tsar's summer palace in the Crimea, where he proposed a Russo-Turkish alliance to the Russian foreign minister, Sergei Sazonov. The latter was quite skeptical about the offer and nothing further developed.[26]

In the first half of July, the Ottoman navy minister, General Cemal Pasha, went to Paris for political talks. In a meeting with Pierre de Margerie, a senior official of the French Foreign Ministry, Cemal pointed out that the Ottoman government was willing to establish closer relations with the *entente*, but expected some help in return on the Aegean islands issue (that is, on the status of the islands seized by Greece during the First Balkan War). Since René Viviani, the French premier and foreign minister, was about to leave Paris for a state visit to St. Petersburg, Cemal's invitation also brought no response.[27]

Regarding Great Britain, the CUP regime continued the policy adopted by previous governments, particularly by maintaining close ties in naval matters with that country. Aside from employing a large British naval mission under Rear Admiral Sir Arthur H. Limpus for the improvement of the sultan's fleet, the Porte also had several warships on order in British shipyards.[28]

---

[26] See Albertini, *Origins*, vol. 1, pp. 540–50; R. H. Davison, "The Armenian Crisis, 1912–1914," *American Historical Review* 53 (1948): 481–505; and Marian Kent, ed., *The Great Powers and the End of the Ottoman Empire* (London, 1996), pp. 15ff., 94ff., 161, and passim. Also, the older study by Harry N. Howard, *The Partition of Turkey: A Diplomatic History, 1913–1923* (Norman, Okla., 1931), pp. 71–75.

[27] The ostensible purpose of Cemal's visit was to attend French naval exercises, which he did from 5 to 13 July. He had previously been instrumental in ordering six destroyers and two submarines from French shipyards. See Jacques Thobie, *Intérêts et impérialisme français dans l'empire ottoman (1895–1914)* (Paris, 1977), pp. 684–9.

[28] Cf. Arthur J. Marder, *From the Dreadnought to Scapa Flow: The Royal Navy in the Fisher Era*, 5 vols. (London, 1961–70), vol. 1, p. 302; Allan Cunningham, "The Wrong Horse? A Study of Anglo-Turkish Relations before the First World War," *St. Antony's Papers No. 17* (London, 1965), pp. 56–76; and Feroz Ahmad, "Great Britain's Relations with the Young Turks, 1908–1914," *Middle Eastern Studies* 2 (1966): 302–29. One ship, the dreadnought *Sultan Osman*, was ready for delivery in late July 1914.

## The July Crisis

Inasmuch as the Porte's various overtures to the *entente* had produced no tangible results, the CUP regime in the latter part of July 1914 approached the German government with an offer of closer ties. As Enver Pasha informed the German ambassador in Istanbul, Hans Baron von Wangenheim, on 22 July, the Ottoman Empire needed "support from one of the Great Power groups." While a minority of his CUP associates "favored an alliance with Russia and France" because the Triple Entente bloc was stronger in the Mediterranean region than the German-led Triple Alliance group, Enver, as well as Prince Said Halim, Talât, Halil Bey (Mentese) (the president of the Chamber of Deputies), and a majority in the party's central committee preferred to link up with the Reich. With remarkable frankness, Enver further explained that their option was based on two considerations: They did not like the risk of having the Ottoman Empire become "Russia's vassal," and they were also convinced that Germany and her allies were militarily stronger than the *entente* powers and would therefore prevail in a world war.[29]

Although Wangenheim reacted rather coolly to Enver's offer, Kaiser Wilhelm II ruled two days later that in view of the tense international situation, the Ottoman interest in a closer connection with the Triple Alliance group should be accommodated. During the next few days, negotiations regarding the scope and nature of the proposed Ottoman alignment with the Reich were initiated in Istanbul, and on 28 July, the day Austria-Hungary declared war on Serbia, a formal Ottoman alliance proposal was presented to the German government. After some modifications had been inserted, the German chancellor, Theobald von Bethmann Hollweg, advised Wangenheim on the evening of 31 July that he was authorized to sign the treaty *if* he was sure that the Turks could, and would, "undertake some action against Russia" that was more than a mere gesture. In consonance with these instructions, the ambassador on the next day invited both Enver Pasha and General Liman to his office to review the plans and capabilities of the Ottoman army. The three men eventually agreed that the Ottoman divisions in eastern Anatolia would initially adopt a defensive posture, while the bulk of the army would be deployed in Thrace for

[29] See Albertini, *Origins*, vol. 3, pp. 607–23; and Trumpener, *Germany and the Ottoman Empire*, pp. 15ff., 19ff. Halil Bey had held senior positions in both the CUP and the cabinet since 1909; in October 1915 he would officially succeed Prince Said Halim as foreign minister.

a joint offensive with the Bulgarians against southern Russia or, possibly, for action against Greece.[30]

Even though this "plan" was rather vague on several key issues – neither Bulgaria's willingness to cooperate nor Romania's willingness to allow Ottoman and/or Bulgarian troops to march through its territory was as yet known – Wangenheim decided to proceed with the conclusion of the treaty. On the afternoon of 2 August, he and Prince Said Halim signed the document on behalf of their respective governments, though both of them, it appears, were fully aware of the fact that it would take a long time, at least four weeks, to complete the mobilization and deployment of the Ottoman army.[31] Within the next twenty-four hours, the Porte ordered general mobilization, but it also issued a declaration of Ottoman neutrality in the rapidly expanding European war.

Reflecting the haste with which the alliance had been cobbled together, the treaty called for the Ottoman Empire's intervention on Germany's side if the latter became involved in hostilities with Russia in connection with the Austro-Serbian conflict – a contingency that, of course, had already become a reality by 2 August. Other clauses of the treaty stipulated that General Liman's military mission was to have "an effective influence on the general direction" of the Ottoman army, that the Reich would help to protect the territorial integrity of the sultan's realm, and that this "secret" treaty would remain in effect beyond the year 1918 unless it was renounced by either party.[32]

Two days after the Porte had issued its declaration of neutrality, on 5 August, Enver Pasha told the Russian military attaché in Istanbul that the recently ordered mobilization of the Ottoman army was by no means directed against Russia. Indeed, the Porte was prepared to thin out its troops along the Transcaucasian border with Russia and to use its forces instead in southeastern Europe to neutralize "this or that Balkan State which might intend to move against Russia." Moreover, Ottoman troops might even become available to assist other Balkan countries

[30] See Trumpener, *Germany and the Ottoman Empire*, pp. 15ff., 23f.; and idem, "Liman von Sanders and the German-Ottoman Alliance," *Journal of Contemporary History* 1 (1966): 181ff.

[31] It will be noted that both the Porte and the kaiser's government preferred to deal with each other through Baron von Wangenheim rather than through the Ottoman ambassador in Berlin, General Mahmud Muhtar Pasha. The latter was both disliked and distrusted by Enver Pasha and other CUP figures. He was removed from his post in July 1915 and then took up residence in Switzerland.

[32] The full text of the treaty may be found in *Die deutschen Dokumente zum Kriegsausbruch*, compiled by Karl Kautsky (Berlin, 1919), no. 733.

"against Austria," provided that the Russians, in turn, helped the Ottoman Empire in regaining possession of the Aegean islands (from Greece) and of Western Thrace (from Bulgaria).[33]

Enver Pasha's overture to the Russians, which he repeated a few days later, may seem rather strange at first sight, but it actually made sense in several ways. To begin with, his statement provided a perfect cover story for the planned concentration of Ottoman troops in eastern Thrace. Second, a negative response from the Russian government would strengthen the case against those CUP elements both in the Central Committee and the cabinet that still leaned toward an alignment with the *entente* powers. Even in the unlikely event that St. Petersburg proved willing to meet Enver's conditions, nothing would be lost; indeed, it would greatly enhance the Porte's bargaining position vis-à-vis Berlin.[34]

That the CUP regime was in a bargaining mood was first brought home to the Germans at one o'clock in the morning of 6 August, when Prince Said Halim summoned Baron von Wangenheim to his office. According to the grand vizier, his cabinet had just decided, "unanimously," to open the Dardanelles to both the German Mediterranean Squadron (the modern battle cruiser *Goeben* and the light cruiser *Breslau*) and any Austro-Hungarian warships that might accompany them, though the Ottoman Empire would definitely maintain its status as a neutral country. Well aware of the precarious situation in which the two German cruisers found themselves at that time, the grand vizier then asked Wangenheim whether he was prepared to pledge Germany's acceptance of the following six proposals:

1. Germany promises its assistance in the abolition of the capitulations.

2. Germany agrees to lend its support in regard to the indispensable understandings with Romania and Bulgaria, and it will see to it that Turkey secures a fair agreement with Bulgaria with reference to possible spoils of war.

3. Germany will not conclude peace unless Turkish territories which may be occupied by its enemies in the course of the war are evacuated.

---

[33] See Howard, *The Partition*, pp. 96–102; and C. Jay Smith, Jr., *The Russian Struggle for Power, 1914–1917* (New York, 1956), pp. 69–76.

[34] It is clear from German records that Enver informed Wangenheim of his contacts with the Russians, albeit with some delay.

4. Should Greece enter the war and be defeated by Turkey, Germany will see to it that the Aegean islands are returned.
5. Germany will secure for Turkey a small correction of its eastern border, which shall place Turkey into direct contact with the Muslims of Russia.
6. Germany will see to it that Turkey receives an appropriate war indemnity.

Fearful lest he endanger the rescue of the German cruisers by "protracted discussions," Wangenheim immediately accepted the grand vizier's proposals and later in the day confirmed the agreement in writing. As he subsequently pointed out to his superiors in Berlin, most of the promises he had made would come into play only if the Central Powers won the war "decisively," and the German government thereupon formally approved the deal.[35]

The agreement of 6 August marked a definite improvement in the Porte's diplomatic position. Unlike the alliance treaty signed four days earlier, the new agreement formally assured the Ottoman Empire of certain tangible gains after victory once it entered the war on Germany's side. On 9 August, while Wangenheim and other Germans in Istanbul were impatiently waiting for the arrival of the *Goeben* and *Breslau* at the mouth of the Dardanelles, the grand vizier politely informed the ambassador that the Bucharest government had proposed the conclusion of an Ottoman-Greek-Romanian "neutrality pact," and that under certain circumstances the Porte might decide to enter into such an arrangement. In that case, he added, the secret alliance with Germany would "of course remain in effect," though it would be necessary to convert the *Goeben* into an Ottoman ship "by means of a fictitious sale."[36]

As soon as these propositions became known in Berlin, Bethmann Hollweg wired back to Istanbul that none of them was acceptable, and that every effort should be made to bring both the Ottoman Empire and Bulgaria into the war. That demand was highly unrealistic, for by this time the governments of both of these states had ample reasons to postpone any overt action. The entry of the British Empire into the war as well as

[35] See Trumpener, *Germany and the Ottoman Empire*, pp. 27–9. On the voyage of the *Goeben* and *Breslau* from the western Mediterranean to the Dardanelles, see Hermann Lorey, ed., *Der Krieg in den türkischen Gewässern*, 2 vols. (Berlin, 1928–38), vol. 1, pp. 1–21; and Ulrich Trumpener, "The Escape of the *Goeben* and *Breslau*: A Reassessment," *Canadian Journal of History* 7 (1971): 171–87.
[36] Trumpener, *Germany and the Ottoman Empire*, pp. 29ff.

Italy's and Romania's refusal to fight on the side of the Central Powers had visibly shifted the power balance in the Mediterranean region and the Balkans; both Istanbul and Sofia were receiving strong warnings from the *entente* bloc not to do anything foolhardy under these circumstances.[37]

Contrary to Berlin's expectation, the arrival of the German Mediterranean Squadron at the Dardanelles, on the afternoon of 10 August, did not immediately strengthen its hand vis-à-vis the Porte. While Enver Pasha, after some hesitation, authorized the Dardanelles command to admit the German cruisers into the Straits, Prince Said Halim soon thereafter made it clear to Wangenheim that he, and the rest of the cabinet, objected to the squadron's "premature" arrival. No progress had been made in lining up the Bulgarians, and if the *entente* decided to declare war because of the cruisers' presence in the Straits, Bulgaria might "exploit Turkey's engagement elsewhere and march on Constantinople." After prolonged arguments with Wangenheim, the grand vizier eventually offered the following "compromise": While the two cruisers would be allowed to stay in some "remote spot" in the Sea of Marmara, the Porte would insist on turning them into Ottoman property through a fictitious purchase.[38] Before Berlin had time to react to this proposal, the Porte issued a public statement that the two German cruisers had been bought "for eighty million Marks." A few days later, on 16 August, a solemn ceremony was staged near the Golden Horn, during which Cemal Pasha officially welcomed the ships, and their crews, into the sultan's navy. The *Goeben* was formally renamed *Yavuz Sultan Selim*, the *Breslau* became the *Midilli*, all German sailors donned fezzes, and the squadron's leader, Rear Admiral Wilhelm Souchon, was officially entrusted with the command of the entire Ottoman fleet.[39]

Public opinion in the Ottoman Empire was elated over the "acquisition" of the two ships, all the more so since earlier in the month two dreadnoughts that had been ordered from British shipyards (and already paid for by the Porte) had been requisitioned by the Royal Navy.[40]

---

[37] On Bulgaria's attempts to bargain with both belligerent camps, see Wolfgang-Uwe Friedrich, *Bulgarien and die Mächte 1913–1915* (Stuttgart, 1985), pp. 106–29; and Chapter 12 below.

[38] Trumpener, *Germany and the Ottoman Empire*, pp. 30ff.

[39] Ibid., pp. 31ff. De facto, the *Goeben* remained a German ship until the end of the war. Subsequently, she served as the flagship of the Turkish navy for several decades.

[40] Cf. W. W. Gottlieb, *Studies in Secret Diplomacy during the First World War* (London, 1957), pp. 42ff.; and Yusuf Hikmet Bayur, *Türk Inkilâbi Tarihi*, 3 vols. in 9 parts (Ankara, 1940–67), vol. 3/1, pp. 65–74.

However, both Wangenheim and his Austro-Hungarian colleague in Istanbul, Johann Margrave von Pallavicini, recognized that the Ottoman Empire was simply not ready for war, and they so informed their superiors in Berlin and Vienna.[41]

During the next three weeks (while the German invasion of France *seemed* to be progressing very satisfactorily), Berlin repeatedly appealed to the Porte to join the war effort of the Central Powers, but not even Enver Pasha could be persuaded that the time for action had come. While the minister of the interior, Talât Bey, had long talks with the Bulgarian premier, Vasil Radoslavov, all he brought home from Sofia was an agreement that the two countries would help each other if either one was attacked. Moreover, Admiral Souchon and a number of other Germans quickly came to the conclusion that the Dardanelles defenses were in woeful shape, thus making Ottoman intervention far too risky for the time being. To remedy that situation, Berlin agreed to send roughly 700 sailors and coast defense specialists to Turkey. Headed by Admiral Guido von Usedom, these men arrived at the straits at the beginning of September and began their remedial tasks.[42]

On 8 September, to the complete surprise of its allies, the Porte announced to the world that it had decided to abrogate the capitulatory privileges of all foreign powers. Intent on placating hostile reactions from the neutral world, Wangenheim and Pallavicini joined the ambassadors of the *entente* bloc (and of Italy) in signing a formal note of protest against the Porte's resort to unilateral action. Simultaneously, they advised the grand vizier that the Central Powers would not really press the issue for the time being. Three weeks later, on 1 October, the Porte began to implement its program, raising the hitherto foreign-controlled customs duties and closing all foreign post offices in the empire. Most of the other capitulatory privileges were officially canceled shortly thereafter.[43]

On 14 September, after satisfying himself that the defense system at the Dardanelles was getting stronger each day, Enver Pasha authorized Admiral Souchon to take his ships into the Black Sea and to open fire on

---

[41] Parenthetically it should be mentioned that, on 19 August, General Liman von Sanders formally asked the kaiser to permit him and his officers to leave the Ottoman Empire, since they were wasting their time there! See Trumpener, *Germany and the Ottoman Empire*, pp. 32–4.

[42] See ibid., pp. 34–6; Friedrich, *Bulgarien*, pp. 132ff.; and Carl Mühlmann, *Das deutsch-türkische Waffenbündnis im Weltkriege* (Leipzig, 1940), pp. 18–21.

[43] Cf. Bayur, *Türk Inkilâbi Tarihi*, vol. 3/1, pp. 161–71; and Trumpener, *Germany and the Ottoman Empire*, pp. 38ff.

any Russian vessels he might encounter. In thus giving the green light for Ottoman intervention, the war minister certainly exceeded his authority, but he seems to have had sufficient backing in the CUP's Central Committee to venture down that path. However, before Admiral Souchon could act on Enver's *carte blanche*, the grand vizier arranged a showdown on this issue in the cabinet and emerged triumphant. With practically everyone against him, Enver eventually agreed to withdraw his directive.[44]

Frustrated on the Black Sea front, the Ottoman war minister bided his time for about a week and then struck his next blow. Apparently with at least some backing in the CUP Central Committee, he ordered the Dardanelles closed to all foreign ships, effective 26 September. During the following days, new mine fields and antisubmarine nets were laid across the straits. While the grand vizier assured the *entente* governments that the waterway would be reopened as soon as Britain and France withdrew their warships from the vicinity of the Dardanelles, Talât on 2 October made it clear to Wangenheim that the straits would remain closed, *entente* protests and threats notwithstanding.[45]

A few days later, Enver Pasha advised the German ambassador that both Talât and Halil Bey had moved closer to his own position – intervention in the near future – and so had the "overwhelming" majority of the CUP Central Committee. If the grand vizier and some of his anti-interventionist colleagues, notably, the finance minister, Mehmed Cavid Bey, persisted in their attitude, they would ultimately be overruled. Cemal Pasha, according to Enver, was leaning toward intervention, but more needed to be done to obtain his unconditional support.[46] Ottoman entry into the war, the war minister concluded, might come fairly soon, even by mid-October, provided that adequate gold supplies were furnished by Germany without further delay.[47]

Requests for a gold loan of five million Turkish pounds had first been made in late September, but so far Berlin had insisted that 95 percent of that amount could be paid out only *after* the Turks had become fully

[44] See ibid., pp. 39ff.
[45] Cf. Bayur, *Türk Inkilâbi Tarihi*, vol. 3/1, pp. 92–4; and Trumpener, *Germany and the Ottoman Empire*, pp. 46ff.
[46] See ibid., pp. 47ff. Cavid Bey, possibly the most brilliant of the CUP leaders, was a vigorous defender of Ottoman economic and financial interests both before and during the Great War. He was hanged in Ankara in 1926 on trumped-up treason charges.
[47] Given the chronic financial problems of the Ottoman Empire, including the involvement of a *foreign* bank in the issue of its paper currency, it was recognized by everyone that a bullion reserve was vital for any future war effort. In other words, this was *not* a bribe, as some critics would later charge.

involved in the war. To expedite matters, Enver, accompanied by Talât, Halil, and Cemal, called on Wangenheim on 11 October for a strategy conference. The upshot of their meeting was that they would send Souchon's ships into action against the Russians as soon as at least 40 percent of the gold loan had arrived in the Ottoman capital; if the grand vizier refused to sanction Ottoman intervention, he would be induced to resign.[48]

In response to these pledges, Berlin on the next day dispatched one million Turkish pounds in gold coins on a special train. Routed through Austria-Hungary, Romania, and Bulgaria, the shipment reached Istanbul on the evening of 16 October. A second shipment, dispatched on the following day, arrived in the Ottoman capital on 21 October, despite Russian diplomatic efforts in Bucharest to block its transit through Romania.[49]

Once the gold had arrived, Enver transmitted an action plan to German imperial headquarters, confirming previous pledges by his interventionist group: Hostilities would be opened by naval action against the Russians in the Black Sea, while the bulk of the Ottoman army would remain assembled in Thrace for future joint operations with the Bulgarians against Serbia and/or Russia. The latter operation, though, depended on Romania's cooperation, which was quite unlikely, as the Porte knew all too well. An advance against Egypt (which the Germans had urged on Enver since August) would require at least six more weeks to prepare and involve at most two Ottoman corps.[50]

Before General Erich von Falkenhayn, the acting chief of the German Supreme Army Command (OHL), had a chance to express his agreement with Enver's plan, Enver notified Baron von Wangenheim that both Talât and Halil were no longer sure that Ottoman intervention was desirable under the present circumstances. The next day, presumably after considerable discussion, Talât swung back to Enver's side, while Halil, still unconvinced, made it known that he would personally go to Berlin to explain why the Ottoman Empire should stay out of the war for the time being.[51]

---

[48] See Trumpener, *Germany and the Ottoman Empire*, pp. 48–50.

[49] Ibid., pp. 50f. Well aware of the purpose of these gold transfers, the Russian Foreign Ministry promptly put out an alert that an Ottoman attack on Russia might occur "within the next few days."

[50] See ibid., pp. 51f.

[51] After working together in negotiations with Bulgaria in Sofia (in August) and with Romania and Greece in Bucharest (in August and September), Talât and Halil seem to have become fairly close allies on major policy issues. See Trumpener, *Germany and the Ottoman Empire*, pp. 53ff.; and George B. Leon, *Greece and the Great Powers, 1914–1917* (Thessaloniki, 1974), pp. 50–5.

Despite these complications, Enver Pasha, in his newly acquired role as "deputy commander-in-chief,"[52] on 24 October issued a directive to Admiral Souchon that he should take the Ottoman fleet into the Black Sea for training exercises and attack the Russian fleet if a "suitable opportunity" presented itself. Simultaneously, Navy Minister Cemal Pasha dispatched a secret order to the senior Ottoman officers of the fleet that the German admiral was entitled to receive their strict compliance with his directives.[53]

Two days after receipt of these instructions, on 27 October, the Ottoman fleet steamed out of the Bosporus. Once the ships were at sea, Souchon informed the senior German and Ottoman officers under his command that they were on a mission of war. Deviating from his original plan, which had called for a high-seas encounter with the Russian fleet in advance of any attacks on the Russian coast, the admiral ordered an *immediate* assault on the enemy's ports and coastal installations. His decision in this matter made sense from an operational point of view, but it also produced needless political embarrassment for Enver and his interventionist colleagues in the cabinet, all of whom had expected a less provocative initiation of hostilities, that is, a manufactured incident in open waters.[54]

By and large, the coastal raids were carried out in consonance with Souchon's instructions. Early on 29 October, several ports and other targets on the Russian coast were shelled, mines were dropped in major shipping lanes, and some Russian ships were sunk. A few hours later, Souchon notified Istanbul by wireless that, in response to continuous Russian interference with the training exercises of the Ottoman fleet on the previous day, "hostilities have been opened today."[55]

The news of Souchon's raid provoked a major crisis in the Ottoman cabinet as well as heated debates in the Central Committee of the CUP. While many details of the ensuing power struggle are still obscure today, it is clear that Prince Said Halim put up a valiant effort to prevent any further hostile acts (and to make amends to Russia for what had already happened); that he was backed most energetically by the finance minister,

---

[52] He had assumed that title on 21 October, making him de facto the supreme commander of all the Ottoman armed forces. De jure, the sultan retained that power.

[53] See Trumpener, *Germany and the Ottoman Empire*, pp. 54ff.; and Gotthard Jäschke, "Zum Eintritt der Türkei in den Weltkrieg," *Die Welt des Islams*, New Series, 19 (1979), pp. 223–5.

[54] See Lorey, ed., *Der Krieg*, vol. 1, pp. 46–56; Trumpener, *Germany and the Ottoman Empire*, p. 55; and Bayur, *Türk Inkilâbi Tarihi*, vol. 3/1, pp. 237–9.

[55] See ibid.

Cavid Bey; that several other ministers threatened to resign in protest; and that the antiinterventionist members of the Central Committee argued vigorously against Enver Pasha and his supporters' policies. After almost four days of wrangling, the interventionists came out on top, but only after making a number of concessions to their opponents. One of these was the dispatch of a conciliatory note to Petrograd (on 1 November); another was an appeal to Berlin to agree to a major revision of the existing alliance treaty, by granting better guarantees for the future and more concessions than Germany had thus far conceded to the Porte.[56]

On 2 November, the same day that Wangenheim was informed of these developments, the Russian government formally declared war on the Ottoman Empire. During the next forty-eight hours, Cavid Bey and three other ministers resigned from the cabinet; but Prince Said Halim stayed on as the grand vizier, possibly in deference to the expressed will of the CUP Central Committee.[57]

## Conclusion

The decision of the CUP regime (or at least of its most influential members) in July 1914 to throw in their lot with Germany and the intervention of the Ottomans in the Great War three months later sealed the fate of their empire. Contrary to the hopes of its proponents, the alliance with the Reich aligned the Ottoman Empire with a power bloc that was materially weaker than the opposing side and would ultimately lose the war. It is small wonder, then, that for many years thereafter, the official Turkish view of the CUP regime would be highly critical, depicting Enver Pasha and his interventionist colleagues as reckless adventurers or even servile helpmates of German imperialism. More recently, though, these harsh verdicts have been replaced by more moderate judgments. Indeed, it is widely held today that most of the men who took the sultan's realm into the Great War were good patriots, albeit misguided ones.

Recent suggestions that the CUP regime entered that war to promote the "modernization" of the Ottoman Empire and to enhance its status as a "European" state seem rather far-fetched. Indeed, if the Ottoman

---

[56] See Trumpener, *Germany and the Ottoman Empire*, pp. 55–61; and Bayur, *Türk Inkilâbi Tarihi*, vol. 3/1, pp. 241–57.

[57] See ibid., pp. 258–9 and passim. Despite his withdrawal from the cabinet, Cavid Bey remained a powerful figure behind the scene, conducting most of the financial and economic negotiations with Berlin and Vienna during the next two years. He reentered the cabinet as finance minister when Talât became the grand vizier (10 February 1917).

interventionists agreed on anything, it was that their country should regain some of its lost territories and expand further into Asia – into Transcaucasia, the Caspian region, and beyond. Moreover, most of them also hoped that participation in the war would facilitate the administrative "centralization" of the sultan's realm, particularly, by whittling down the remaining privileges of its various ethnic and religious minorities. In the case of the Armenian communities in the eastern provinces of the empire, that policy would be implemented in 1915 with a degree of ruthlessness that shocked the world. The "Greek Problem," on the other hand, would be solved only in the aftermath of the Greco-Turkish War (1919–22), when Athens and Ankara agreed on a major population exchange between the two countries. As for the "Kurdish Question," it was never resolved at all and is still very much an issue today.

The impact of Ottoman participation in the First World War has been the subject of considerable debate. While many historians regard the fighting in most of the Turkish theaters of war as mere sideshows, a good case can be made for the thesis that the Allies allotted a disproportionately large portion of their human and material resources to these "sideshows" and thereby enabled Germany to prolong her military struggle with the *entente* powers by at least one year and possibly even more.

# Italy

## Richard F. Hamilton and Holger H. Herwig

I could be wrong, but I see our situation towards Austria as insecure: ... one spark, the death of the old emperor, the succession of the new who is openly hostile to us, can provoke a conflict, however contrary to the interests of the two countries.

Paolo Spingardi, Minister of War, 1911

Richard Bosworth, a leading specialist, describes Italy in 1914 as "the Least of the Great Powers."[1] Italy's allies, Austria-Hungary and Germany, paid it scant attention that July. Vienna and Berlin excluded Rome from their policy discussions in the aftermath of the murder of Archduke Franz Ferdinand. And they did not inform the Italians of the terms of the ultimatum Vienna handed Belgrade on 23 July. Austria-Hungary, from the start, discounted the likelihood of Italian military support for the Triple Alliance. Germany feared that any information passed on to Rome would quickly find its way to St. Petersburg. During those four weeks, neither Austria-Hungary nor Germany treated Italy as a valued ally, much less as a great power.

Italy's first response to the war was a declaration of neutrality, this announced on 3 August 1914. That decision was largely the work of one man, Foreign Minister Antonio di San Giuliano. Italy at that point was the Continent's largest neutral nation. Both sides in the struggle, accordingly, competed for its support, encouraging either continued neutrality or active participation. Italy's leaders, from the start, welcomed these offers and

---

[1] R. J. B. Bosworth, *Italy, the Least of the Great Powers: Italian Foreign Policy before the First World War* (London, 1979).

for some nine months prepared for combat and weighed the options. This period, called the *intervento*, ended with the second response, the decision to enter the war on the side of Britain and France in May 1915.[2]

## Antecedents

In 1861, Italy ceased to be a mere "geographical expression." Through the "national resurrection" of the *risorgimento* and with the military assistance of Napoleon III, it became a constitutional monarchy presided over by the House of Savoy, the royal family of the kingdom of Sardinia. Five years later, Prussia's victory over Austria brought Venetia into the new state. And in 1870, the Franco-Prussian War allowed the taking of Rome and the last of the Papal states. Rome then became the new capital, but Pope Pius IX refused to recognize the Kingdom of Italy, which he denounced as the "Subalpine usurper." Instead, the pontiff locked himself into the Vatican, ending a millennium and a half of papal rule over Rome.[3] Nor did he recognize the new Italian Law of Guaranties, which accorded the pope all the honors and immunities of a sovereign, the right to appoint bishops, and a compensation of 3.5 million lire per annum for the lost territories.[4] At that point, a high proportion of Italy's tiny electorate, approximately 1 percent of the population, was said to have been anticlerical. As a consequence, relations between the Italian state and the Vatican – the so-called Roman question – remained a very problematic issue.[5]

The new kingdom had just under 27 million people. It was the sixth largest state in Europe. Its population was located largely in the towns, villages, and rural areas. The biggest city, Naples, did not reach 700,000

[2] A cautionary note: In 1957, Alberto Monticone published an article dealing with the "intervento" that contained a letter from Salandra to Sonnino, dated 16 March 1915. The letter reviewed Italy's position at that time and, among other things, contained the following sentence: "Ma allo stato attuale delle cose *noi due soli* [his emphasis] non possiamo assolutamente giocare la terrible carta." From his "Salandra e Sonnino verso la decisione dell' intervento," *Rivista di studi politici internazionali* 24 (1957): 64–89, esp. p. 69. "We two alone," he declares, absolutely cannot play this terrible card. A subsequent account, one citing Monticone as its source, reports the exchange as follows: "Salandra e altrettanto se non più esplicito: *'noi due soli ...'* dovremo decidere" – we two alone will have to decide. This is from Brunello Vigezzi, *Da Giolitti a Salandra* (Florence, 1969), p. 59. The latter reading has been taken over in a couple of English-language sources.
[3] Christopher Seton-Watson, *Italy from Liberalism to Fascism 1870–1925* (London, 1967), pp. 6–11.
[4] See the "Law of the Papal Guaranties" of 13 May 1871 in Walter Farleigh Dodd, *Modern Constitutions*, 2 vols. (Chicago and London, 1909), vol. 2, pp. 16–17.
[5] Eamon Duffy, *Saints and Sinners: A History of the Popes* (New Haven, Conn., 1997), pp. 232–3.

until 1911. Italy had a high birth rate, but also a high rate of emigration. About eight million people emigrated between 1876 and 1905; another six million would follow in the next decade. The more than 500 million lire sent home by the emigrants helped to balance the national budget before 1914. There was also a return flow, with almost two million returnees arriving in the decade before the Great War. The 1911 census put the population at just under 35 million.[6]

Italy's economy was mainly agrarian. In 1911, some 55 percent of the economically active population was engaged in agriculture. The agrarian sector was rife with bitter class hatred. On the one side stood the landowners and the *signori*, their agents and lawyers, and the merchants and bureaucrats of the small towns; on the other side stood the landless laborers (*braccianti*) of the lower Po Valley, the Roman Campagna, Sicily, and the Neapolitan provinces. They and their families accounted for more than half of the rural population.[7]

There was, to be sure, a growing industrial sector: an automobile industry at Turin, ship building in Genoa, and a small iron industry based on Elba. With German and Swiss assistance, great advances had been made in producing hydroelectric power, but Italy possessed no oil and little coal, most of this a very low grade. Its chemical industry was minuscule, its ports "neither safe nor modern," and technical and commercial education almost nonexistent. Italy was not a major beneficiary of the second industrial revolution that swept central Europe by 1870.[8]

After 1861, Italy was governed according to the Sardinian constitution of 1848. Although in spirit based on the liberal constitutions of France (1830) and Belgium (1831), the Albertine Statuto assured royal dominance. Article 2 accorded Italy a "representative monarchical form of government." Article 3 stated that the legislative power was to be "exercised collectively by the King and the two Chambers, the Senate and the Chamber of Deputies." But the Italian king had more power than most constitutional monarchs did. Under Article 5, he held the so-called war powers: "The King alone has the executive power. He is the supreme head of the state, commands all the armed forces by sea and land, declares war, makes treaties of peace, of alliance ..." Article 7 decreed that only the monarch could "sanction and promulgate laws." And Article 65

---

[6] See R. J. B. Bosworth, *Italy and the Wider World 1860–1960* (London and New York, 1996), pp. 114ff.

[7] B. R. Mitchell, *International Historical Statistics: Europe, 1750–1988* (New York, 1992), pp. 6, 149; and Seton-Watson, *Italy from Liberalism to Fascism*, pp. 22–7.

[8] Ibid., pp. 18–22.

stated tersely: "The King appoints and dismisses his Ministers." [9] He was
not obliged to follow the advice of his ministers, who were responsible
to him and not to parliament, and he had the right to appoint members
of the Senate. The suffrage was gradually extended, but until the June
1911 reform, was still restricted to about 7 percent of the population.
At that point, in a major reform, the vote was given to all literate males
of age twenty-one or more. The illiterate males were given the vote on
completion of military service or on reaching age thirty.

In July 1914, the sweeping powers accorded the occupant of the
Quirinale rested with Vittorio Emanuele III. A tiny man who did not
"look a king," the monarch suffered constant barbs about his diminutive
stature from Kaiser Wilhelm II of Germany. The king was cynical and sarcastic toward his soldiers and diplomats and detested the Roman Church
to the point that he ate meat on Fridays and rarely went to mass. Despite
his sweeping constitutional powers, he took little part in the actual
running of the government beyond offering advice, in effect, delegating
power to his ministers. In May 1915, the German ambassador asked the
king directly about Italy's imminent decision. He replied: "Speak with
my ministers, I am a parliamentary King like the King of England and
not like the Emperor Wilhelm or the Emperor Franz Joseph. It's up to
my ministers to make such decisions." [10] Bosworth states that Vittorio
Emanuele III "confined his politics to pedantry ... and to malice." [11] A
more serious problem was the king's mental state during the July Crisis.
Bosworth reports he "was close to a nervous breakdown with scandal-
mongers ascribing his problems variously to the Queen's pregnancy, to
'neurasthenia,' 'meningitis,' or 'attacks of madness and similar things.' " [12]

[9] See Albert P. Blaustein and Gisbert H. Flanz, eds., *Constitutions of the Countries of the World: Italy* (Dobbs Ferry, N.Y., 1987), pp. 1–10; Dodd, *Modern Constitutions*, vol. 2, pp. 5–16; Shephard B. Clough and Salvatore Saladino, *A History of Modern Italy: Documents, Readings, and Commentary* (New York and London, 1968), pp. 66–70; and Denis Mack Smith, *Modern Italy: A Political History* (Ann Arbor, 1997), pp. 27ff.

[10] Renzi, *Shadow of the Sword*, p. 100. Given the just-reviewed constitutional provisions, however, it is clear that monarchist Italy was "closer to the autocratic government of Tsarist Russia than to the western democracies"; from Denis Mack Smith, *Italy and Its Monarchy* (New Haven, 1989), p. 222. In September 1914, when asked by another cabinet member, Salandra said the king would leave the neutrality decision to his government: "He does not wish to decide. He will accept the decision of the government, whatever it may be. If it is for war, he has told me that he will go to war, following the tradition of his dynasty."

[11] R. J. B. Bosworth, *Italy and the Approach of the First World War* (London and Basingstoke, 1983), p. 21.

[12] Bosworth, *Least of the Great Powers*, p. 14. See also Mack Smith, *Modern Italy*, pp. 191–2; and his *Italy and Its Monarchy*, pp. 198–9.

To shore up its fragile "great power" status, Italy in May 1882 joined
Austria-Hungary and Germany in the Triple Alliance in the wake of a
putative French move on Tunis. Otto von Bismarck privately denounced
the Italian leaders, referring to them as jackals, drawn by the "odor of
corruption and calamity" and always ready "to attack anybody from
the rear and make off with a bit of plunder." The iron chancellor nevertheless welcomed the chance to tie Rome to Berlin by treaty.[13] In the
process, he hoped to use Italy to keep France and Russia in check. Italy,
for her part, became Germany's ally because "no other country wanted
her."[14]

The alliance was defensive, designed to shield the signatories from attack by "two or more Great Powers." In February 1887, the treaty was
renewed, with the important addition of a new article that offered "reciprocal compensation for every advantage, territorial or other," that one
power might garner "in the regions of the Balkans or of the Ottoman
coasts and islands in the Adriatic and in the Aegean Sea." In the third
treaty of the Triple Alliance of May 1891, that statement became en-
shrined as Article VII.[15] It would be of great importance in July 1914.
Additionally, in January 1888, the Italian and German army staffs signed
a separate convention wherein Rome promised to send six army corps
and three cavalry divisions to the Rhine in case of a joint war against
France.

The Triple Alliance, in the words of one expert, "rested uneasily on
matters stated and unstated, on myth and on reality."[16] It settled none
of the outstanding differences between Rome and Vienna – especially not
those involving the *terra irredenta*, Italy's "unredeemed lands," which
were mostly in Austrian hands. First and foremost, the irredentists wished
to complete the *risorgimento* by gaining Trentino-Alto Adige (the Alpine
watershed northwest of Venice) and Trieste, a port city on the Adriatic. In
terms of ethnicity, these claims were mixed. In 1910, there were 800,000
Italians in the Austro-Hungarian Empire. The largest segment was located
in the Trentino (97 percent of 374,000 total population). Immediately
to the north, in Alto Adige (for Austrians, Süd-Tirol), they formed only
9 percent of the 238,000 total.[17] Over 60 percent of Trieste was made

[13] Cited in Otto Pflanze, *Bismarck and the Development of Germany*, vol. 3: *The Period of Fortification, 1880–1898* (Princeton, 1990), p. 85.
[14] Bosworth, *Least of the Great Powers*, p. 198.
[15] See Alfred Franzis Pribram, ed., *The Secret Treaties of Austria-Hungary*, 2 vols. (New York, 1967), vol. 1, pp. 109, 155.
[16] Bosworth, *Italy and the Approach*, p. 58.
[17] Seton-Watson, *Italy from Liberalism to Fascism*, p. 353.

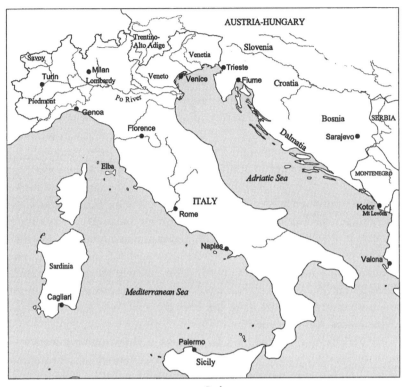

MAP 11.1. Italy, 1914

up of Italians, the rest being Slovenes, Croats, and some German-speaking Austrians. The city's hinterland was overwhelmingly Slovenian (see Map 11.1).[18]

In addition to lands in the Austro-Hungarian Empire, Italy's leaders (and various nationalist spokesmen) showed interest in Corsica, Malta, Nice, Savoy, Montenegro, Albania, Asia Minor, and, most especially, northern Africa. In the Mediterranean, Italian aspirations ran head-on into British and French interests. From 1888 to 1898, Italy and France had fought a bitter tariff war. Rome remained suspicious of French designs in North Africa, beyond Morocco and Tunis. But on 30 June 1902, two days after renewing the Triple Alliance, the Italian foreign minister, Giulio

---

[18] For the highly complex issue of ethnic populations, see Kent Roberts Greenfield, "The Italian Nationality Problem of the Austrian Empire: The Early Period of Austrian Rule," *Austrian History Yearbook* 3 (1967): 503–22; and John W. Cole, *The Hidden Frontier: Ecology and Ethnicity in an Alpine Valley* (New York, 1974).

Prinetti, in a secret exchange of notes with the French ambassador to
Rome, Camille Barrère, obtained agreement that Morocco would fall into
the French, and Tripoli-Cyrenaica into the Italian, sphere of interest. Italy
also promised neutrality if France were attacked by one or two powers;
France offered reciprocal neutrality in similar circumstances. The Prinetti-
Barrère Agreement posed an obvious problem. Denis Mack Smith refers
to Italy's "simultaneous and hardly compatible relations with both of the
main rival alliances in Europe."[19] But since the agreement was secret and
remained so for some years, the implications did not surface immediately.

The dominant figure in Italian politics in this period was Giovanni
Giolitti, a man of unusual abilities who, between 1891 and 1921, served
five times as prime minister. He controlled a sprawling centrist party and,
with exceptional negotiating skills, put together his governing coalitions.
Giolitti's political practice required both electoral manipulation and questionable political deals, and his coalition arrangements, accordingly, were
often tenuous. One aspect of Giolitti's "system" was the strategic retreat.
When things became difficult he would give up office, turning affairs over
to some less capable lieutenant, but with the expectation of returning to
office at some quieter time.[20]

In 1911, Italy celebrated the Cinquantennio, the fiftieth anniversary of
the *risorgimento*, with a wave of patriotic and nationalistic demonstrations. Giolitti sought to quiet his vociferous opponents (to "unify the nation") with a new imperialist venture. On 29 September, Italy invaded the
Ottoman provinces of Tripolitania and Cyrenaica (the cherished "Garden
of the Hesperides") with an expeditionary corps of 44,000 troops under
General Carlo Caneva. On 9 November, Giolitti announced the annexation of what later would be called Libya. The Chamber of Deputies gave
its blessings to this action in February 1912.[21] In November 1912, a new
Ministry of Colonies was established to administer the former Ottoman
possessions, this under the direction of Ferdinando Martini.

But the campaign proved both lengthy and costly. The Turkish garrison withdrew inland, aided and abetted by Arab guerilla forces soon
numbering 25,000 men. The Italian army, the Regio Esercito, still smart-
ing from its defeat at the hands of the Ethiopian Emperor Menelik II

[19] Seton-Watson, *Italy from Liberalism to Fascism*, pp. 329–31; Mack Smith, *Italy and Its
Monarchy*, pp. 195–6.
[20] For a discussion of Giolitti's "system," see Renzi, *Shadow of the Sword*, pp. 45–9.
[21] Ibid., pp. 366–70; Mack Smith, *Modern Italy*, pp. 242–9; and John Whittam, *The Politics
of the Italian Army, 1861–1918* (London, 1977), ch. 11.

at Adowa in March 1896, proceeded cautiously. Rome had to send out 100,000 soldiers to press its invasion. Costs swelled to double the original estimate, and by 1914 had reached about 1.7 billion lire. Victory over the Bedouin in Libya was achieved only in 1932.

In the course of this war, the Italian navy, the Regia Marina, seized thirteen islands of the Dodecanese, including the most important, Rhodes. This, in turn, brought a demand for compensation under Article VII of the Triple Alliance (1891) from the Austro-Hungarians – who blithely ignored the fact that they had offered Italy none after their annexation of Bosnia-Herzegovina in 1908. Giolitti carried the day by insisting ingenuously that the islands of the eastern Aegean were Asiatic, and by assuring Kaiser Wilhelm II of Germany that the occupation was only temporary.

Important for future events is that the government – basically Giolitti and his foreign minister, San Giuliano – ran the war in Libya by way of direct orders to General Caneva, thus bypassing the chief of the General Staff, General Alberto Pollio, as well as the king's chief aide, General Ugo Brusati.[22] Pollio, who had been appointed staff chief in 1908, had studied at the military academies at Naples and Turin as well as at the Scuola di Guerra. He had risen rapidly through the ranks and his career had been closely tied to the General Staff. Those biographical facts taken in combination with an impressive intellect and his writing of books – one on Napoleon I (1901) and the other on the Battle of Custozza (1903) – made him a suspect academic to many commanders, to the men "schooled in battle."[23]

Italy's struggle with the Ottomans, as seen in previous chapters, allowed several Balkan states to also take up arms against "the sick man of Europe." Indeed, Italy escaped the wrath of the European powers over its rapacious actions in Libya mainly because of the two Balkan wars of 1912–13.[24] In both of those wars, Vienna seriously considered using armed force against Serbia to keep that nation's ambitions in the Balkans in check. Specifically, the Habsburg government sought to deny Serbia

---

[22] For a comprehensive overview, see Brian R. Sullivan, "The Strategy of the Decisive Weight: Italy, 1882–1922," in Williamson Murray, MacGregor Knox, and Alvin Bernstein, eds., *The Making of Strategy: Rulers, States, and War* (Cambridge, 1994), pp. 325–7.

[23] Whittam, *Politics of the Italian Army*, pp. 159–60.

[24] See William C. Askew, *Europe and Italy's Acquisition of Libya* (Durham, N.C., 1942); and Luigi Albertini, *The Origins of the War of 1914*, 3 vols. (London and New York, 1952–7), vol. 1, pp. 340–63.

access to the Adriatic Sea by forcing Montenegro to cede its coastline to Albania. The General Staff demanded that the Dual Monarchy be given Mount Lovčen to protect a future naval base in the Gulf of Kotor.[25] Both times, Rome declared it would not feel bound by the terms of the Triple Alliance to aid Austria-Hungary in those efforts.

Italy avoided censure by two of the major powers for its Libyan venture by hurriedly renewing the Triple Alliance on 5 December 1912 – eighteen months ahead of schedule and for a period of fourteen years. German-Italian military discussions began that same month, during which General Pollio promised Helmuth von Moltke, the chief of the German General Staff, that "as soon as the *casus foederis* was established, Italy would mobilize all her forces and would take the offensive in the Alps without delay." He also promised that Italian troops would be landed in the south of France. In addition, the Italian navy would engage in joint action to block any movement of French reinforcements from North Africa. The 1888 Triple Alliance called for Italian forces to be sent to the Rhine to fight alongside German forces in case of a war with France.

In the course of those December 1912 discussions, however, the Italian representative, Colonel Vittorio Zupelli, told Moltke that because of the Libyan involvement, Germany could not count on any Italian troops being sent to the Rhine. Shortly thereafter, in January 1913, the German quartermaster-general, Alfred von Waldersee, visited Rome and Vienna to discuss matters. Pollio reviewed Italy's troop commitments: five corps for the Alps and another five for "a possible landing" in southern France. He agreed in principle that any troops not needed there would be made available for service on the Rhine. After further discussion, he "promised to make a full army available for service on the Rhine, after he got the approval of the king and the political leaders."[26]

A steady exchange of information and mutual visitations to firm up and detail their arrangements continued through to the summer of 1914. Italy's military leaders reiterated their commitments for the Rhine, in March 1914 agreeing that the Third Army would be present and would serve under direct German command. In April, Italian, German, and Austrian general staff railroad specialists met to plan the movement of three Italian army corps through Habsburg territory.

---

[25] The mountain and the gulf were located in Bosnia-Herzegovina, then ruled by Austria-Hungary. Seton-Watson, *Italy from Liberalism to Fascism*, pp. 404–10.

[26] Michael Palumbo, "German-Italian Military Relations on the Eve of World War I," *Central European History* 12 (December 1979): 346–9.

Italy's military leaders provided strong assurances of their good faith and, although some doubts remained, German leaders trusted them, counting on an involvement that, by their estimates, would occupy some twenty French divisions. The meetings climaxed in 1913, when King Vittorio Emanuele III attended the Kiel Regatta. Pollio, Moltke, and Franz Conrad von Hötzendorf, the Habsburg chief of staff, attended the German maneuvers in Silesia and they again reviewed their arrangements. The Germans were not optimistic about the likely outcome of these Italian efforts. But their key concern was that they occupy or divert French forces. An energetic engagement by the Italians, Moltke thought, would mean "almost certain success" for the German operation.[27]

The optimism of Germany's leaders in the first months of 1914 was based, in great measure, on the assurances and promises of Italy's military leaders. But a serious problem appeared in this connection: Italy's governance was characterized by a very dysfunctional compartmentalization, by an unwillingness to share information or even to inquire about the plans and operations of related departments. Italy's Foreign Ministry, for example, did not inform the nation's generals and admirals of the terms of the Triple Alliance. John Gooch writes that following renewal of the Triple Alliance, Pollio, in "accordance with Italian practice . . . was kept entirely in the dark about it and had no idea whether it contained any undertaking to support Austria-Hungary." Elsewhere, Gooch refers to "the customary gulf in Italian civil-military relations." One result was that, late in July 1914, while the political leaders were planning neutrality, the new chief of the General Staff spent his first days in office working to meet Italy's "obligations under the Triple Alliance," specifically, planning the attack on France. No politicians had "consulted him, and no one disabused him."[28]

One reason for this extreme compartmentalization was an attitude prevalent among the civilian leaders, described by one scholar as "repeatedly and scathingly dismissive of the army." Giolitti declared, in May 1915, that "the generals are worth little; they came out of the ranks

[27] Ibid., pp. 350–2, and, Moltke's statement, p. 348.
[28] John Gooch, *Army, State and Society in Italy, 1870–1915* (New York, 1989), pp. 149, 156, and 158. Sullivan reports that Pollio "apparently never learned of the 1902 neutrality agreement with France," in his "Strategy of Decisive Weight," p. 322. For more on the pathology, see John Gooch, "Italy before 1915: The Quandary of the Vulnerable," in Ernest R. May, ed., *Knowing One's Enemies: Intelligence Assessment before the Two World Wars* (Princeton, 1984), ch. 8, esp. pp. 207, 211; and Mack Smith, *Italy and Its Monarchy*, pp. 200–1.

at a time when families sent their most stupid sons into the army because they did not know what to do with them."[29] The nation's army and naval officers simply were not part of the inner power circle. Chief of the General Staff Pollio, the man charged with developing military plans, was forbidden to communicate directly with cabinet members – because he was a subordinate of the minister of war. The military leaders of Berlin and Vienna were not aware of that compartmentalization. They believed that, like themselves, their Italian counterparts played an integral role in their nation's policy making.

In the final prewar flurry of agreements with Berlin and Vienna, Italy's military leaders pledged to cooperate with Germany and Austria-Hungary at sea and on land in the event of a war with the *entente* powers. Both King Vittorio Emanuele III and General Pollio again and again promised to transport at least three army corps, one-quarter of the Italian army, to the Rhine in case of war between the Triple Alliance and the Triple Entente. Further, Pollio assured the Germans that his troops would deploy in Alsace within four weeks of mobilization – under direct German command. At Vienna, he secured agreement to send them to the Rhine by rail via Innsbruck and Villach in Austria. He also discussed with his Habsburg counterpart, Conrad von Hötzendorf, the possible use of Italian troops against Russia.[30] As late as April 1914, Pollio offered the Austrians, by way of the German military attaché in Rome, forces to help them against both Russia and Serbia![31] That the Austro-Hungarian railway system could never have handled these extra burdens apparently escaped both Pollio and Hötzendorf.

To put teeth into these promises, the chief of staff in May 1914 requested funding for four separate armaments projects. In addition to the regular military expenditures of 511 million lire per annum, his extraordinary requests ranged from a *programma massimo* of 551 million lire to a *programma ultraminimo* of 198 million. As well, Pollio pointed to Italy's shortage of all branches of artillery (heavy, field, horse, mountain, and fortress) and argued that the nation needed ten new divisions and 30,000

[29] Gooch, *Army, State and Society*, p. 173. For more, see Bosworth, *Least of the Great Powers*, p. 22. There was, moreover, a sharp division of labor between the two top military leaders. The war minister was charged with troop readiness (fitness, uniforms, weapons, etc.); the chief of the General Staff with war plans and with operations.
[30] Sullivan, "Strategy of Decisive Weight," p. 321.
[31] Wolfgang Foerster, "Die Deutsch-Italienische Militärkonvention," *Kriegsschuldfrage* 5 (May 1927): 402.

more conscripts per year just to keep pace with Austria-Hungary.[32] The war minister, Domenico Grandi, painfully aware that the costs of the Libyan venture had yet to be covered, remained noncommittal.

Despite all the official declarations of Triple Alliance solidarity, the arrangement, as of 1914, was more an appearance than a binding reality. For most Italian irredentists, Austria-Hungary remained the archenemy. The previous war minister, Paolo Spingardi, could hardly be accused of hyperbole when in 1911 he depicted Italo-Austrian relations as "insecure" and as susceptible to "conflict" following a single "spark."[33]

### The Decision Makers

The king, as indicated, had an enormous grant of powers under the Italian constitution. But for all practical purposes, Vittorio Emanuele III was "an absentee ruler" who delegated those powers to others. "Signs of positive interventions by him into foreign affairs," Bosworth reports, "are rare."[34] The most obvious "others," those who would deal with an international crisis, were the prime minister and the foreign minister. The politics of the Italian Kingdom up to this point had been rather chaotic, with many changes of government and much difficult negotiation to find viable coalitions. The dominant figure in the previous decades, as stated earlier, was Giolitti. Facing serious difficulties, largely over the Libyan engagement, he gave up office in March 1914 for what his enemies termed a "calculated political vacation."[35] He was replaced by Antonio Salandra, who had served previously, once as minister of agriculture and twice as finance minister, all for brief periods. Salandra had very limited experience in international affairs and according to William Renzi "had demonstrated no particular talent for statecraft."[36]

It is not surprising, therefore, that these matters fell largely to Foreign Minister San Giuliano, a Giolitti holdover. Salandra was not entirely pleased with the choice, but the king, in an exceptional move, insisted that he be continued in that office.[37] Although "off stage" during the war

[32] Gooch, *Army, State and Society*, pp. 153–4.
[33] Bosworth, *Italy and the Approach*, p. 66. Spingardi's full statement is cited in the epigraph to this chapter.
[34] Bosworth, *Least of the Great Powers*, p. 17.
[35] Mack Smith, *Modern Italy*, p. 255. Giolitti served still another term as premier, from June 1920 to July 1921.
[36] Renzi, *Shadow of the Sword*, p. 49.
[37] Mack Smith, *Italy and Its Monarchy*, p. 198.

years, Giolitti still headed the largest party in parliament and, as seen below, continued to influence the nation's affairs. One might expect the minister of war and perhaps the chief of staff to participate in discussions of foreign affairs and international crises. At the beginning of 1914, that would have meant Count Grandi and General Pollio. But, as seen, the incumbents in those two offices were systematically excluded from the key political discussions.

Some geographic difficulties and some "facts of life" added to the decision-making problems. The king "preferred to keep distant from the political hustle of Rome, spending much of his time on his estates at Castelporziano or in Piedmont."[38] San Giuliano spent much of his time at Fiuggi, a spa that was a two-hour drive to the east of Rome. Although continuing his work, he was, in fact, dying. "Sometimes," Mack Smith reports, "the foreign minister complained of an inability to sleep or eat, and ambassadors found him 'too ill to work.' He had to be regularly sedated with narcotics that must have affected his judgement, and before coming into Rome for meetings with Salandra had to take counter-injections that made him highly excitable."[39] The end came in mid-October.

Another "fact of life" affected decision making at the onset of the crisis. The chief of staff, Pollio, had a heart attack on the day Archduke Franz Ferdinand was assassinated. Misdiagnosed as a gastric ailment, he was given a purgative. He died on 1 July. The selection of a successor proceeded slowly and erratically. Almost four weeks passed, this in the midst of the crisis, before General Luigi Cadorna was installed in his place. The four responsible generals were divided over the two likely successors and the final choice was left to the king. Appointed on 20 July, Cadorna was installed in office a week later, on 27 July.

## The July Crisis: The Neutrality Decision

The "one spark" that War Minister Spingardi had feared in 1911 turned out to be the assassination of Franz Ferdinand, an ardent opponent of cooperation with Italy. For the members of the Triple Alliance, it brought the greatest crisis since 1882. And it caught Italy, now ruled by Prime Minister Salandra, in the throes of the "Red Week" of June 1914. Peasant *jacqueries* broke out in Emilia and the Romagna, where landless *braccianti* had founded cooperatives to secure better pay and more employment. In

---

[38] Bosworth, *Least of the Great Powers*, p. 14.
[39] Mack Smith, *Italy and Its Monarchy*, p. 199.

a wave of strikes and political upheavals, shops were looted, churches assaulted, villas sacked, railroad tracks dug up, and telephone poles torn down. Barricades were raised at Rome and elsewhere. At Ancona there were protests against military service, and the town proclaimed itself an independent commune; others quickly followed that example. Red flags flew from a number of city halls. Benito Mussolini, editor of the Milan socialist newspaper *Avanti!*, reveled in the violence. Landowners responded by forming mobile squads of "volunteers" for the "defense of order." Eventually, the government called out 10,000 conscripts to restore order.[40]

News of the Sarajevo murder reached Rome on the afternoon of 28 June. The nation's leaders expressed outrage and ordered appropriate memorial ceremonies, but otherwise there was an unmistakable sense of relief: A dangerous and potentially powerful opponent to Rome had been removed. The Italian General Staff received the news, but Pollio's heart attack, combined with the generally benign reading of the event, meant that no action was taken. Parliament began its normal summer recess on 5 July and was not recalled until December, thus removing one source of difficulty in the subsequent months of crisis. The Austrian embassy held memorial services on 7 July, but then, for a week or so, "the murder was all but forgotten."[41]

The new chief of staff, General Cadorna, a Piedmontese aristocrat, suffered from a major persecution complex and was convinced that Freemasons and Jews had blocked his promotion in the past. The compartmentalization problem meant he was uninformed about the "larger political issues" facing the nation. On the day of his installation, he assured the German military attaché that he would carry out all of the staff arrangements made by Pollio, and he reminded the chief of the German General Staff, Moltke, of the bond that united the Triple Alliance partners.[42] There was still another serious difficulty: "[H]e trusted no one but maintained an absolute faith in his own strategic abilities."[43]

Cadorna, understandably, offered more than words. He ordered the four army corps on the French border to recall their effectives, canceled all leaves and furloughs, reprovisioned storehouses and dispatched fortress

[40] See Seton-Watson, *Italy from Liberalism to Fascism*, pp. 393–5; Mack Smith, *Modern Italy*, pp. 256–7.
[41] Renzi, *Shadow of the Sword*, pp. 59–60.
[42] Gooch, *Army, State and Society*, p. 157.
[43] Ibid.

artillery to the Mediterranean Alps, and brought the three army corps destined for the Rhine up to full strength.[44] Cadorna, however, knew little of the realities of Italian diplomacy or of the army's readiness for a major European war. In 1914, Italy had some 345,000 men under arms.[45] But in July 1914, about 60,000 soldiers remained in Libya. Tons of ammunition, clothing, and foodstuffs likewise had been diverted to the new colony, as had some of the nation's most modern field, mountain, and fortress artillery.[46] In March 1914, Pollio had warned the government about the army's sad state of readiness: There existed a severe shortage of 13,500 officers and about as many noncommissioned officers. Ten of Italy's thirty-six regiments of field artillery existed on paper only. The army lacked 200,000 sets of uniforms. Three months later, Prime Minister Salandra, no champion of the Regio Esercito, learned that full equipment was available for only 730,000 of the 1,260,000 men of the fully mobilized army.[47] There was, in short, no possibility of an immediate involvement.

The Italian navy viewed the July Crisis even more pessimistically. Its policies were dominated by Vice Admiral Paolo Thaon di Revel, the naval chief of General Staff. The son of a noble Piedmontese cabinet minister, Revel possessed ferocious energy and an authoritarian temperament. He could be stubborn and single-minded when it came to upholding Italy's vital interests – as he saw them. On 1 August 1914, he warned the government that the British and French had a 14 percent advantage over the naval forces of the Triple Alliance, rising to 26 percent when two new French dreadnoughts entered service in the next few months. Specifically, the Capo di Stato Maggiore feared that the Regia Marina could protect neither Italy's coastal cities (Genoa, Naples, Palermo) nor its land communications against *entente* naval forces. Most of the country's rail lines ran along the coastline of the Adriatic or the Mediterranean and were thus vulnerable to naval bombardment.[48] After 1912, Italy's ability to communicate with the so-called Fourth Shore, with Libya or with its colonies beyond Suez, was at the sufferance of *entente* naval forces.

[44] Palumbo, "German-Italian Military Relations," pp. 362–3.
[45] David Stevenson, *Armaments and the Coming of War: Europe, 1904–1914* (Oxford, 1996), pp. 2–7.
[46] Gooch, *Army, State and Society*, pp. 147–8.
[47] Ibid., p. 160; Sullivan, "Strategy of Decisive Weight," p. 330; and Whittam, *Politics of the Italian Army*, chs. 11 and 12.
[48] Paul G. Halpern, *The Naval War in the Mediterranean, 1914–1918* (London, 1987), p. 9; and Gooch, "Italy before 1915," pp. 218–27.

Italy also faced a virtually insurmountable economic problem. Britain in 1913 supplied 90 percent of Italy's annual imports of about 10.8 million tons of coal. Loss of that coal, obviously, would paralyze Italian industry.[49] While Germany in 1913 mined 220 million tons of coal, most of that would be used at home or, in case of war, exported to Austria-Hungary. The German railway system, moreover, would be taxed fully during mobilization and the Alps would be a major physical impediment to large-scale transfers of coal to Italy. In short, there existed a deep chasm between Triple Alliance planning and Italian military and economic realities.

Italy's naval situation in the Mediterranean, however, was not entirely hopeless. In July 1914 it had available three modern dreadnoughts; another would be ready in April 1915 and two more in May 1915 and March 1916. Austria-Hungary had two new dreadnoughts in service, with a third recently commissioned and a fourth to be completed in November 1915. The German Mediterranean Squadron consisted of the new battle cruiser *Goeben* and the light cruiser *Breslau*. According to the naval convention of June 1913, in case of war this force of potentially five capital ships was to be placed under the command of the Austrian Admiral Anton Haus. Its primary mission would be to prevent French troops in North Africa from reaching metropolitan France. By contrast, the British, having withdrawn their battleships in July 1912, had but three battle cruisers in the Mediterranean, the French a mere two dreadnoughts (with two more scheduled for completion later that year). That comparison of forces represents a "best case" scenario. But, as the Italian leaders knew, those Triple Alliance commitments were, as Paul Halpern puts it, "slightly unreal. The realities of the Austro-Italian antagonism remained and both navies realized that they were just as likely to be at war with each other instead of allies and planned accordingly."[50]

The immediate decision facing Italy's government – whether to join with the Alliance or to remain neutral – was made largely by Prime Minister Salandra and Foreign Minister San Giuliano.[51] Because of Salandra's inexperience in foreign affairs, the decision was due mostly to the efforts of the foreign minister. A cynical Sicilian aristocrat, San Giuliano argued

[49] On coal, see Shephard B. Clough, *The Economic History of Modern Italy* (New York and London, 1964), pp. 75, 84. Also, Gianni Toniolo, *An Economic History of Liberal Italy 1850–1918* (London and New York, 1990), ch. 10.
[50] Halpern, *Naval War*, pp. 2–8.
[51] Renzi, *Shadow of the Sword*, ch. 4; Whittam, *Politics of the Italian Army*, ch. 12.

that Italy should prepare militarily and await developments. In the meantime, his prescribed course for Italy was one of "courageous serenity."[52]
Already in failing health, San Giuliano retreated to Fiuggi to work out
the details of Italy's response. There he shared the waters with the chatty
German ambassador, Hans von Flotow. From the latter, San Giuliano
learned by 16 July that Vienna was prepared to use force against Serbia.
The next day, he learned that Austria-Hungary, supported by Germany,
was preparing an ultimatum with conditions unacceptable to Serbia.[53]

San Giuliano was moved by several considerations. First, he (as well
as many members of the cabinet) was well aware of Italy's military weakness and of the fact that its vital coal imports could be jeopardized by
an Anglo-French naval blockade. Second, he knew that the harvest, expected to be 10 percent below average, was not yet complete. Third, he
feared that the riots of "Red Week" might well flare up again, especially
if war loomed on the horizon. Fourth, he had learned from Flotow's in-
discretions and Italian intelligence that Germany intended fully to back
whatever play its Viennese ally planned for the Serbs. Fifth, he chose to
avoid direct contact with the Austro-Hungarians, fearing it might jeop-
ardize Italy's chance for compensation under Article VII of the Triple
Alliance. According to Christopher Seton-Watson, the hope for territorial
compensation dominated Salandra's thoughts. Thus, he turned to Berlin
in hopes of indirectly pressuring Vienna to offer the Trentino, Valona, or
southern Albania as compensation.[54]

Germany had no problems with offering Italy extensive concessions
in the Austrian border regions. Between 15 and 30 July 1914, various
leaders in Berlin – Chancellor Theobald von Bethmann Hollweg, Foreign
Secretary Gottlieb von Jagow, and Chief of the General Staff von Moltke –
urged Vienna to secure Italian military support by way of compensations.
But Vienna stood firm, refusing, in the words of Kaiser Franz Joseph, to
allow itself to be "pulled to pieces like an artichoke."[55]

---

[52] See Clough and Saladino, *History of Modern Italy*, p. 306.

[53] Bosworth, *Least of Great Powers*, p. 386. For details, dates, sources, and further transmission of the Austro-Hungarian and German plans for Serbia, see Renzi, *Shadow of
the Sword*, pp. 61–2. By 21 July, the Italian leaders knew the essentials of the Dual
Monarchy's impending actions and had transmitted them elsewhere, most importantly
to their ambassador in St. Petersburg. That information had been intercepted by others
and, from that point, was known to the Russian and French leaders. See the discussion
in Kiesling, "France," Chapter 7.

[54] Seton-Watson, *Italy from Liberalism to Fascism*, pp. 413–14.

[55] Cited in Holger H. Herwig, *The First World War: Germany and Austria-Hungary 1914–
1918* (London, 1997), p. 150.

For most of July, Berlin and Vienna kept Rome in the dark concerning their policies. Wilhelm II continued to take Italian military assistance for granted if a European war developed. Vittorio Emanuele III had promised Germany "every last man" if it came to war in Europe; Pollio had repeated that promise in February 1914. In Vienna, few if any among the coterie of decision makers took Italian participation seriously. Still, to make certain that Italy could not demand compensation in the coming action against Serbia, the final decision for war reached at a special Crown Council in Vienna on 19 July specifically ruled out the annexation of Serbian territory.[56]

Vienna delivered its ultimatum to Serbia at 6 P.M. on 23 July. Approximately two hours earlier, the Austro-Hungarian chargé d'affaires in Rome drove to Fiuggi and presented "a communication" to San Giuliano. It told of the ultimatum, of "a certain number of requests," and the forty-eight-hour time limit but gave no details about the contents. Shortly before noon the next day, the chargé presented the specific demands but did so at the Foreign Ministry in Rome, even though he knew San Giuliano was in Fiuggi where he had been joined by Salandra. The information was immediately telephoned to them, but by then the document had been published by the Stefani News Agency, the telephone message thus confirming what they had already seen.

The two men discussed matters for several hours. San Giuliano judged Vienna's actions to be aggressive. Rome had not been consulted beforehand, as stipulated in the Triple Alliance treaty, and therefore the *casus foederis* did not exist. The two agreed, however, that if Austria-Hungary provided "suitable compensation," Italy might still join on the side of their allies. Article VII and compensation, in short, were introduced from the beginning of the crisis. Telegrams reporting their position went to Italy's ambassadors in Berlin and Vienna, allowing them to open the discussions. Those conclusions were also transmitted to Vittorio Emanuele III, who at that point was off in Piedmont.[57]

Three days later, on 26 July, the foreign minister laid out his policy in a letter to Prime Minister Salandra: "No immediate decisions are required, indeed they would be extremely dangerous. We must for the moment

---

[56] See ibid., p. 17.

[57] Renzi, *Shadow of the Sword*, pp. 67–70. These few sentences cannot begin to describe the complexities of these two days. Telegrams were sent to officials at home and abroad; concern was expressed about public reactions. The German ambassador was present in Fiuggi when Salandra and San Giuliano received the official statement. His reaction: "Vraiment, c'est en peu fort."

leave everyone, at home and abroad, in doubt as to our attitude and our decisions, and in this way try to obtain some positive advantage."[58] San Giuliano advised the members of the government to work in silence, to be deliberate, and to remain away from Rome as much as possible. Austria-Hungary declared war on Serbia on 28 July 1914. Vittorio Emanuele III returned to Rome that day, but left again the next morning as if to signal that nothing of importance was about to transpire. On 29 July, General Cadorna, kept in the dark by San Giuliano and the cabinet concerning the state of diplomatic affairs, requested permission from the king to dispatch the Third Army to the Rhine, as per the most recent understandings with Germany and Austria-Hungary. The Italian navy, meanwhile, was making plans to rendezvous with Austro-Hungarian and German naval units off Medina, Sicily.

At this point an immediate decision was required: either to join with their allies or to remain neutral. Salandra and San Giuliano instituted a new governing arrangement at this point, one that might be described as cabinet government. The cabinet had met three times earlier in the month, but despite the evident crisis, the rigid compartmentalization still prevailed, which meant "no serious discussion of foreign affairs." San Giuliano was not even present at the last two meetings. The cabinet met again, at 10 A.M. on 31 July, now to consider the pressing question.

San Giuliano, aided by Salandra, reviewed the situation. The foreign minister "stressed that Italian public opinion opposed war, and that in no event could Italy participate in a conflict against Britain." He concluded: "Fortunately, the casus foederis of the alliance does not exist. Neither the letter nor the spirit of the Triple Alliance obliges us in this instance to aid Germany and Austria." There appears to have been little discussion and no dispute. Renzi's laconic summary is that the cabinet "in effect agreed that neutrality was the only possible policy." That decision, he adds, was tentative, since the king, still away from Rome, had yet to approve it.[59] Still another step remained, namely, to determine the character of the public announcement.

---

[58] Cited in Seton-Watson, *Italy from Liberalism to Fascism*, p. 415.

[59] Renzi, *Shadow of the Sword*, pp. 78–9; Gooch, *Army, State and Society*, p. 158; Bosworth, *Least of Great Powers*, p. 396. The cabinet vote was a formality, not a legal requirement; the aim apparently was to give greater legitimacy to the decision. Beyond noting the fact, the major sources cited here pay the meeting no attention. No mention is made of divisions or dissent. Apart from the persons mentioned in the text, the participants are not named. It was very different from the experience of the British cabinet.

A flurry of communication followed – by Italy's leaders, by the Alliance powers, and by some *entente* leaders seeking a clear and prompt declaration. The cabinet met again the next morning, 1 August. A majority still favored an immediate declaration, but one member successfully argued for postponement. The ministers approved some measures of military preparation – so that the "declaration of neutrality does not appear to be the result of weakness." On Sunday, 2 August, the king returned to Rome and "immediately approved" a declaration of neutrality. The cabinet met again later that day to discuss the content of the forthcoming communiqué. Agreement on the text was reached and the decision was ratified, thus making Italy, for the moment, a neutral nation.[60] The text was made public the next day.

Leaders in Berlin and Vienna, not surprisingly, were outraged by this decision. Kaiser Wilhelm II fumed about the incompetence of German diplomacy and complained that the Reich's allies were falling away "like rotten apples" even before the war had begun. General von Moltke spoke of revenge for what he called "Italy's felony." "May God now grant us victory," he wrote his counterpart in Vienna, "so that later you can settle accounts with these scoundrels." Conrad von Hötzendorf, in turn, blamed the situation on his Foreign Ministry's failure in the past to deal with the "snake" Italy. "Our future lies in the Balkans; our barrier is Italy; we must finally settle accounts with Italy."[61] Strong feelings are one thing; however, "the letter" of the agreement is something else. Legally, Italy was on solid ground: No *casus foederis* existed in July 1914, as no "two or more Great Powers nonsignatory to the present Treaty" had attacked or even seriously threatened Austria-Hungary.

The decision for neutrality appears to have been very popular with the nation's citizens. Renzi writes that public opinion in general was ill informed, but that "there can be no doubt that the great majority favored a pacific policy."[62] Italy's peasants and farm laborers, "who constituted the vast bulk of the army and would inevitably suffer most casualties, were

[60] Renzi, *Shadow of the Sword*, pp. 79–81. That same day, "for some obscure reason, even after the government had decided to remain neutral, the king ... informed the army that their preparations for war against France should proceed." Mack Smith, *Italy and Its Monarchy*, p. 200.

[61] Cited in Herwig, *The First World War*, p. 32.

[62] Renzi, *Shadow of the Sword*, p. 75. This is, obviously, a judgmental call, the conclusion of a well-informed researcher. Elsewhere, he summarized the opinion of Martini, a cabinet member: "The public was decidedly against participation in the conflict" (p. 80).

reported as strongly opposed to fighting."[63] The Revolutionary Socialists, speaking for "the workers," issued strong antiwar pronouncements. The secretary of the American embassy wrote that, virtually without exception, "the entire press of Italy" desired only continued peace."[64]

Business and financial leaders also desired peace, wishing an end to the violence of "Red Week" and a restoration of productivity. Giovanni Agnelli of Fiat had contracts with Britain, Russia, and Germany. Gino Olivetti of Confindustria saw war as "a monstrous phenomenon" that would lead only to the "brutal destruction of men and wealth." The captains of Italy's hydroelectric industry, heavily dependent on German and Swiss technology, and those of its southern shipping industry, which feared French economic rivalry, were not among the hawks in 1914.[65]

We have no serious evidence showing that big business, the press, or special interest groups influenced the decision. The decision makers proceeded independently, having little contact with any domestic groups outside of their own narrow circle. There were nationalistic pressure groups – the Italian Navy League, Dante Alighieri Society, the Geographical Society, and the Italian Colonial Institute – but they never developed into mass societies capable of shaping government policy. Most, in fact, required government subsidies merely to survive. Their members came from the court, diplomacy, commerce, politics, and the intelligentsia, and their memberships often overlapped.[66] Intervention was favored by some intellectuals, middle-class professionals, bureaucrats, layers, and journalists, but at this point their efforts, clearly, had no significant impact.

Italy's leaders, as seen, considered many factors before deciding for neutrality. Among these were the lack of military preparedness, the hazards of naval war, the dependence on imported coal, the threat of domestic disturbance, and the possibility of territorial gains. Assigning weight to the factors is a highly speculative enterprise. At one point, San Giuliano told Kajetan Mérey von Kapos-Mére, the Austrian ambassador to Italy, that "the Ministry of the Interior believed that a general mobilization might itself provoke revolt." Renzi concludes that this "basic public sentiment

[63] Mack Smith, *Italy and Its Monarchy*, p. 208.
[64] Renzi, *Shadow of the Sword*, p. 74. For more detail, see Bosworth, *Italy and the Approach*, pp. 46–8, 108.
[65] Bosworth, *Italy and the Approach*, pp. 81–2, 125–6.
[66] Ibid., p. 48.

against intervention was the first and perhaps the most important fact which dictated Italian neutrality."[67]

Several days after the decision for neutrality, San Giuliano mused over his options. In an ideal world, Austria-Hungary would be beaten in the Adriatic and surrender Trieste; France would be beaten on land and surrender Savoy or Nice or Corsica or Tunis to Italy.[68] But he would not live to see the outcome; San Giuliano died of severe gout at Rome on 16 October 1914.

## The *intervento*

San Giuliano's last recommendation was a "policy of temporization." It was, effectively, a "wait and see" policy. Unlike the five major powers, where the decisions for war were taken in at best several weeks (or at worst in a few days), Italy's leaders had much time for thought, negotiation, and their "considered judgment," taking nine months before deciding to intervene on the side of the *entente*. This period, known as the *intervento*, is filled with activity and events, basically to encourage a decision either for continued neutrality or for participation on one side or the other. It is, accordingly, a much more complicated narrative than those about the decisions of the five major powers.

Paying no attention to Giuliano's recommendation, General Cadorna, an instant convert from the pro-Alliance policy, called for immediate intervention in support of the *entente*. But the political leaders, with some aid from Grandi, successfully opposed that plan, pointing to the serious, long-hidden deficiencies of the Italian military. For most of Italy's leaders, Austria-Hungary, still in possession of *Italia irredenta* (Trentino, Trieste, and Fiume) was the prime target. The German victory over the Russians at Tannenberg on 26–30 August, however, relieved the pressure on the Dual Monarchy and, understandably, generated some caution. The prospect of an easy Alliance victory was dimmed by the outcome of the Marne campaign in early September. It became apparent also that Italy could not mobilize prior to the onset of winter due to staff planning deficiencies and the lack of winter uniforms. That fact forced the postponing of

---

[67] Renzi, *Shadow of the Sword*, p. 75. The statement appears in a telegram, Mérey to Berchtold, 3 August 1914. That might provide an honest indication of the foreign minister's reading of things. Or, of course, it might be a plausible excuse, an assertion of helplessness versus the threat of the "aroused masses."

[68] Ibid., p. 62; Bosworth, *Least of Great Powers*, p. 397.

any intervention until the spring. Those seven or eight months would allow time for three tasks: to upgrade the military, to plan an intervention, and to solicit and negotiate terms from both contenders. Intervention, of course, was not the only option to be considered. Continued neutrality was also a negotiable offering, one that would be virtually costless. But the rewards for intervention, other things equal, would be considerably greater.

The negotiation of terms required a sense that Italy represent a plausible threat, that it could, somehow, make a difference in the military outcome. But faced with continuing difficulties in Libya, a struggle that erupted again in July 1914, forcing a withdrawal to coastal bases, Italy's "weight" was not clear and obvious. This was a persistent problem for Italy's leaders. The recent domestic disturbances also entered into the considerations of those potential allies. A general mobilization could bring renewed insurgency, requiring use of troops in Italian cities.

Italy also faced a serious domestic political problem. The military deficiencies had been hidden, and, making matters worse, parliament had been lied to, having been assured both of the army's recovery and its readiness. One consequence of this scandal was Grandi's expulsion from office. He was replaced by General Vittorio Zupelli, previously the deputy chief of staff, who now developed and implemented a training program. Political and military leaders worked better than before, but as seen below, that did not prevent several disastrous planning failures.[69] Bypassing the parliament, which was in recess, the enormous financial requirements were met, at Salandra's bidding, through "liberal use of the royal signature," that is, through "the prerogative of royal decree."[70]

On the death of San Giuliano, Salandra temporarily took over the direction of Italy's foreign affairs. It was during this period that the prime minister made a serious error, using an unfortunate expression to describe and justify his policies – *sacro egoismo*. It would be used against Italy and its policies for some time thereafter. Overwhelmed by the tasks, Salandra chose Sidney Sonnino as his new foreign minister. Sonnino was from a wealthy Tuscan family, a politician who had served four decades in parliament. His family history was unusual: He was born in Pisa of a Jewish-Italian father and Scottish mother, both of whom were Protestants. He was a member of the Anglican Church. His outlook and preparation were also unusual: He was "handicapped by inflexibility and intellectual

---

[69] Gooch, *Army, State and Society*, pp. 159–64.
[70] Renzi, *Shadow of the Sword*, p. 108.

intolerance," a serious failing when combined with limited experience in foreign affairs.[71] Recognizing that Italy could make no move before the spring, Sonnino, within days of taking office, pursued the negotiations with London, Berlin, and Vienna, which would last for the next six months.

Italy was a very high-priority concern for both the Alliance and the *entente*. It was by far the most populous of the remaining European neutrals. And its army, although an uncertain factor, was sizable, close to 1.4 million in 1910, of which 600,000 were front-line troops.[72] It could obviously "make a difference" depending on whether several hundred thousand men were moved against Austria-Hungary or against France. Both sides, accordingly, undertook major efforts to achieve their preferred outcome.

The negotiations had a peculiar asymmetrical character. High on the agenda of wished-for territories were the Trentino and Trieste. But the Dual Monarchy, as seen, went to war to stem the losses experienced over several previous decades and, understandably, was very reluctant to give even more. Germany urged the concession, seeing it as a small price to avoid Italian involvement and the opening of another front. A linked consideration was the possible involvement of Romania, seeking to gain its *irredenta*, lands that were also in Austro-Hungarian hands.

Germany's chancellor, Bethmann Hollweg, was preoccupied with these questions. From the beginning, his secretary Kurt Riezler reports, he resented the "pride, stubbornness, and stupidity, as if sent by the gods" with which Vienna refused "the necessary territorial concessions" to Rome and Bucharest.[73] The Italian ambitions, however, went far beyond those modest properties to include the Alto Adige (German-speaking Süd-Tirol), the Isonzo frontier, Istria, the Dalmatian coast, Albania, the Dodecanese, and a share of the Turkish empire. Achieving those goals, much of which ran counter to Serbian aspirations, would require wider and more complicated negotiation.[74]

[71] Geoffrey A. Haywood, *Failure of a Dream* (Florence, 1999), p. 5; and Renzi, *Shadow of the Sword*, pp. 104–5.

[72] Whittam, *Politics of the Italian Army*, p. 160.

[73] Konrad H. Jarausch, *The Enigmatic Chancellor: Bethmann Hollweg and the Hubris of Imperial Germany* (New Haven, 1973), pp. 239–40.

[74] Gooch, *Army, State and Society*, p. 165. If successful, those territories would give Italy control of the entire Adriatic. The Dalmatian coast had (and has) a largely Slavic population. It had once belonged to Venice, and Italian populations were still present in several coastal cities.

Parliament met briefly in early December for the first time since the outbreak of the war. Salandra made some changes in his cabinet, which parliament confirmed. Giolitti arrived and "spoke in support of the government, pointedly praising the policy of neutrality" and, at the same time, rejected German and Austrian claims of betrayal. Giolitti's forces gave substantial backing to the government, in effect supporting the current policy, neutrality, the vote being 413 to 49. Ten days later, the Senate gave the government unanimous support. Following that very public declaration, parliament adjourned, Giolitti returned to Piedmont, and the private efforts to secure intervention continued.[75]

On 11 December 1914, Count Leopold Berchtold, the Austrian foreign minister, told Giuseppe d'Avarna, the Italian ambassador, that Vienna was "entirely unwilling" to discuss any compensation under the Article VII. In mid-December, Prince Bernhard von Bülow, the former German chancellor, arrived in Rome as ambassador. He had served in that post from 1893 to 1897, spoke fluent Italian, and had an Italian wife, the stepdaughter of a former premier. He put forth suggestions that Austria might yield the Trentino in exchange for Italy's neutrality. But there could be no yielding on Trieste; the Dual Monarchy's only major port was its indispensable "lung."[76]

Many pages would be needed to summarize the Alliance efforts to influence Italy. There were press subsidies, but these were accepted by small-circulation newspapers, their combined circulation less than that of the interventionist *Corriere della Sera*. Those efforts were hopelessly inept and also heavily burdened by the problem of the Belgian incursion, a theme much emphasized by *entente* sources. Bülow provided lavish entertainment in his private residence, the Villa Malta, to win over Rome's "social aristocracy." Through intermediaries, he was in fairly regular communication with Giolitti. The German government awarded contracts to firms that favored neutrality. The influential Banca Commerciale was Bülow's "single greatest economic weapon." It had German and Swiss-German management and "penetrated every level of the Italian economy." The services of Matthias Erzberger, a prominent Catholic politician and head of the Center Party, were enlisted. He was sent five million lire, which was used to bribe deputies and some neutralists within the cabinet. Some of that money came into the Vatican. A Bavarian priest, Rudolf Gerlach, serving as the pope's private secretary, was a very

[75] Seton-Watson, *Italy from Liberalism to Fascism*, pp. 427–8.
[76] Renzi, *Shadow of the Sword*, pp. 167–8.

active "agent in German pay." All of these efforts, however, were to no avail.[77]

The *entente* effort was even more extensive. The prominent socialist Benito Mussolini, editor of *Avanti!*, abandoned party, newspaper, and neutralism, and in mid-November brought out a new publication, *Il Popolo d'Italia*. This appears to have been financed in part by two Italian industrial groups, Fiat and Ansaldo, and by the French government and private sources. In February 1916, the director of the French Bureau de la Presse in Rome, a propaganda agency that sought to influence Italian publications, reported that Mussolini was "completely in our hands" and that he had "rendered us great service in the spring of 1915."[78] Many other journalists, Renzi reports, were "in the pay of the Entente" and "disseminated interventionist propaganda during the spring of 1915." Public lectures were another means; Belgian speakers reported, with lantern slides, on German atrocities. The French painter Albert Besnard returned to Rome and engaged in interventionist activities. Among other things, he arranged for Auguste Rodin to sculpt a bust of the pope, Benedict XV, this providing an opportunity during which, the artist reported, "we have spoken of the war and I have spoken the truth to the pope." The pope, who favored Catholic Austria-Hungary and advocated continued neutrality, broke off the sittings.[79]

The discussions in London, meanwhile, were bogged down over a question of sequence. Italy wanted territorial assurances prior to involvement; Britain wished the commitment first. During the fall and winter months, the resolution of this issue was not an urgent concern. On 21 December, Cadorna completed his plan for an attack on Austria-Hungary. It would, on paper at least, bring Italian troops into the heart of Slovenia within forty-five days, this in preparation for "a drive on Vienna."[80] At a cabinet meeting in late January 1915, Zupelli declared that the army could not move before mid-April.

The date of mobilization was pivotal in any negotiation, timing being central to any concerted effort. The date of Italy's involvement gained

---

[77] Ibid., ch. 9. All of the quotations here are from Renzi's chapter, entitled "German and Austrian Propaganda and Espionage in Italy."

[78] Ibid., pp. 138–43. For more detail, see Renzi's ch. 8, "Entente Propaganda and Influence in Italy." Seton-Watson's account differs in some respects, most importantly on the date of the French (and Belgian) subsidies to *Il Popolo d'Italia*, which, he says, began only in May 1915; *Italy from Liberalism to Fascism*, p. 441.

[79] Renzi, *Shadow of the Sword*, pp. 151–3.

[80] Ibid., pp. 165–8. Cadorna was informed by very credible sources about the difficulties, about the near-impossibility of this plan, but gave those observations "no notice whatsoever."

significance when, toward the end of February, Sonnino learned of the likely Allied move on the Dardanelles. Italy's negotiating position would, accordingly, be considerably enhanced by an early declaration. Joining after the anticipated easy victory over the Ottomans would obviously be of negligible value. On 4 March, Guglielmo Imperiali, the Italian ambassador to Britain, opened discussions with Sir Edward Grey, presenting his country's territorial demands. Grey's interest increased significantly after a mid-March military setback. Italy's entry would shift the balance, especially if other Balkan nations joined at the same time. Grey thought that Italy's entry "probably would, in a comparatively short time, effect the collapse of German and Austro-Hungarian resistance." It would be, he said, "the turning-point of the war."[81]

Recognizing the changed situation, Austria now shifted position and offered to concede the entire Trentino.[82] In mid-April, General Erich von Falkenhayn, the German chief of staff, obviously concerned, tried intimidation to block Italy's impending move. He provided his reading of the military situation and told the Italians of the difficulties and losses they would face should they join with the *entente*.

On 26 April, representatives of Britain, Italy, Russia, and France signed the Pact of London. The terms were simple: Italy would enter the war on the *entente* side by 26 May, this in exchange for a generous promise of territories plus a loan of £50 million (under "equitable conditions") to be issued on the London market. The Germans tried a last-minute threat – namely, that Field Marshal Paul von Hindenburg, the victor of the Battle of Tannenberg, would lead German forces against Italy. The Austrians now agreed to negotiation. But by then, it was too late. Sonnino felt he could not again shift course.[83]

---

[81] Ibid., p. 201. And, for a comprehensive review, ch. 11. The turning-point quotation appears, among other places, in Seton-Watson, *Italy from Liberalism to Fascism*, p. 430.

[82] Ibid., pp. 179–91. It would take many pages to cover all of the complex events leading up to this shift. Berchtold, the Austro-Hungarian foreign minister, was forced out of office in mid-January for agreeing to some modest territorial concessions. Bethmann, the German chancellor, was "utterly downcast" and "nearly despaired of a solution." A decisive factor leading to Austria-Hungary's yielding was another exchange of territory: "[T]he unprecedented offer of compensation in Upper Silesia . . . in the interest of common victory." From Jarausch, *Enigmatic Chancellor*, pp. 240–1.

[83] Renzi, *Shadow of the Sword*, ch. 11; and, for the terms of the pact, Clough and Saladino, *History of Modern Italy*, pp. 308–11. For these events from the British side, see Keith Robbins, *Sir Edward Grey* (London, 1971), pp. 304–9. Although frequently called the Treaty of London in English-language sources, the terms treaty and convention were avoided "lest approval of the French Chamber be necessary"; from Renzi, *Shadow of the Sword*, p. 211.

By signing the London Pact, Italy's leaders were, in effect, giving a promissory note. Fulfilling that promise, actually taking the nation into the war, brought a major political crisis. The Triple Alliance had to be renounced (for a brief period, from 26 April to 4 May, Italy was allied with both sides); and the new tie with the *entente* had to be announced and justified. Most serious of all, the commitment for Italy's entry into the war had to be made public and justified. This posed an obvious problem, since most Italians still approved the current policy, that is, neutrality.[84]

In mid-April, Salandra sent a dispatch to Italy's prefects asking them to sound out and report on the state of public opinion in the event of Italy's intervention. The vast majority of these reports indicated, with many variations of argument, strong neutralist sentiment. Over fifty replies had come in by 26 April, the date of the signing. Renzi concludes that when the king, Salandra, and Sonnino authorized the signature of the Pact of London, there could have been no doubt in their minds that the overwhelming majority of Italians "would have stayed Imperiali's hand [the actual signer] had a plebiscite been held on the issue of war or peace." Seton-Watson adds an important further observation: "They give a general impression of a country with little desire to go to war but unlikely to offer active opposition."[85]

Vittorio Emanuele III was very anxious during the following month and several times spoke of abdication. Parliament was scheduled to meet on 12 May, but to allow more time for preparation, that event was postponed to the 20th. The cabinet met on the 12th and Salandra, seeking some wider legitimacy for the decision, provided a comprehensive review of developments. The cabinet met again the next day for further discussion. Salandra had canvassed the major party leaders and reported, not surprisingly, overwhelming neutralist sentiment. After much discussion, he proposed the government's resignation, and the cabinet agreed. This news brought consternation throughout Italy and, of course, in all *entente* capitals. Three days later, the king asked Salandra to continue.

Mass meetings, demonstrations, and riots occurred at this time. Seton-Watson reports that the "universities, both professors and students, set the pace and the revolutionary interventionists were prominent." In Florence,

---

[84] For a brief overview, see Mack Smith, *Italy and Its Monarchy*, pp. 209–14; for more detail, see Renzi, *Shadow of the Sword*, chs. 13 and 14.

[85] Ibid., pp. 240–1; Seton-Watson, *Italy from Liberalism to Fascism*, pp. 441–2, n. 3. At about the same time, Barrère, the French ambassador, sent the following report to Delcassé: "Today war would not only be accepted but would be generally popular" (Renzi, *Shadow of the Sword*, p. 231).

Bologna, Genoa, and other cities, "brawls between rival demonstrations brought bloodshed and thousands of arrests. Leading neutralists were threatened and Austrian consulates attacked." Mussolini urged people to occupy the streets and remain there to impose their will on the monarchy. His slogans were "War or revolution" and "War on the frontier or war at home." The interventionists were still a minority but were more aggressive and better organized. Except in Turin, they "created an impression of superior strength."

Gabriele D'Annunzio, poet and demagogue, returned from his "exile" in France, arriving in Rome on 12 May to be welcomed by a massive crowd of nearly 100,000. In his first address, from his hotel balcony, he told them: "For three days a stink of treason has been suffocating us.... Romans, sweep away all the filth, chuck all the garbage back into the sewer.... Friends, it is no longer time for talk but for action." The next day he declared: "If it is a crime to incite citizens to violence, I shall boast of this crime.... Form platoons, form citizens' patrols." A thousand students, led by some professors, tried to storm the parliament building and then searched the streets "for friends of Giolitti to assault." Troops were called out to protect persons and property. The demagogues quickly termed these *le radiose giornate* – "the Radiant Days" – pointing to these events as evidence of "massive" support for intervention.[86]

The Cabinet met again on 17 and 18 May and approved a measure for submission to the parliament that would vest "full financial powers in the government in the event of war." On 20 May, in two secret ballots, one procedural, the other substantive, parliament backed the government, giving it overwhelming majorities. In the second of these, the decisive ballot, the vote was 407 to 74, most of the latter from Revolutionary Socialists. The body was recessed sine die "amidst the singing of the Garibaldi Hymn and a final outburst of enthusiasm for war."[87] The next day, the Senate gave the measure unanimous approval. Salandra and Sonnino were given ovations.

Mack Smith suggests that intimidation was one factor accounting for the conversion. Some deputies and senators, he feels, "were simply afraid of being attacked by the mob." Some were moved by concern for government patronage. Some were worried about the monarchy, a negative vote

---

[86] Seton-Watson, *Italy from Liberalism to Fascism*, pp. 445–8; and Mack Smith, *Italy and Its Monarchy*, pp. 212–13. English-language sources generally refer to these days as "Radiant May."

[87] Renzi, *Shadow of the Sword*, pp. 260–1.

being seen possibly as a challenge to the king. In the preceding fortnight, in their search for a way out, both the king and Salandra met with Giolitti. The former prime minister felt his return to office at this time would be inopportune, declined the invitation, and suggested several other options, none of which succeeded. Giolitti left Rome before parliament met. But before leaving, he instructed his followers, who formed by far the largest party, to "save the honour of the country by putting up no opposition" to the new direction, to the intervention.[88]

Mobilization was ordered on 22 May. Austria-Hungary was sent an ultimatum the next day. And on 24 May, Italy was at war. With time, much more than Cadorna had anticipated, Italy assembled thirty-five divisions, some 400,000 men, along the Austrian border, the most difficult front in Europe. By the end of the year, four Italian offensives had been halted. Italy had yet to cross the Isonzo River.

Italy's intervention was intended to be part of a larger effort, with other Balkan nations, most importantly, Romania, supposed to move at the same time. The Romanian case (which is discussed in detail in the next chapter) was a close match to that of Italy. Romania had also joined the Triple Alliance, but its leaders also vacillated, looking for more favorable terms. Their interest was in Transylvania, a part of the Dual Monarchy with a Romanian population. A similarity existed also in the relations between the Alliance partners, Italy's leaders treating Romania with some deprecation or indifference. The Romanian premier, Ionu Brătianu, had already achieved a major success, Russia having promised Transylvania in exchange for its neutrality. In the spring of 1915, Brătianu saw little additional gain from involvement and, accordingly, "was not to be budged from neutrality."[89]

Article 2 of the London pact required Italy's "pursuit of the war jointly with France, Great Britain, and Russia against all of their enemies." But in May 1915, Italy declared war against and fought only Austria-Hungary. Italy declared war on the Ottomans in August and on Bulgaria in October. The new allies insistently reminded Italy's leaders of a further obligation,

[88] Mack Smith, *Italy and Its Monarchy*, p. 213; see also Seton-Watson, *Italy from Liberalism to Fascism*, pp. 447–8.
[89] See Chapter 12 of this work for further discussion. More than a year later, in August 1916, in a markedly different military situation, Brătianu did bring his nation into the war on the side of the *entente*. Again, the complexities are not easily summarized. For brief overviews, see H. James Burgwyn, "A Diplomacy Aborted: Italy and Romania Go Their Separate Ways in May, 1915: A Reasssessment," *East European Quarterly* 21 (1987): 305–18; and Renzi, *Shadow of the Sword*, pp. 128–35.

but despite much urging, Italy's leaders did not declare against Germany until 28 August 1916, fifteen months later.[90]

## Conclusion

The Italian case differs from the experience of the five major European powers in that the process of decision was spread over some nine months. And in sharp contrast to the experience of those five, where time did not allow it, in Italy much attention was given to discovering the attitudes of "the public" and developing some kind of response. The purpose of that effort, however, was not to respond to popular sentiment but rather to thwart the will of "the masses." As Renzi puts it, a "small minority of essentially conservative leaders had superimposed their will over that of the nation as a whole."[91] Salandra, clearly no democrat, felt no obligation to any expressions of mass opinion. In his memoirs he describes Italy's elites and masses as follows: "Those who spoke and wrote – that is, the active minorities which in every great country carry along with them the mentally inert majority...." In his view, it was right and proper that the interventionist elites should set the nation's direction.[92]

The process has implications for several of the theories reviewed in Chapter 1, specifically, for those assuming some kind of "bottom up" influence. It simply did not work that way. The two key proponents, the men who more than any others brought Italy to war, were Salandra and Sonnino. Their efforts did require the consent of Vittorio Emanuele III, clearly a willing collaborator. The instigators of the "Radiant Days," the nationalist demagogues, played an important role. Salandra gave credit to the press. "Without the newspapers," he wrote later, "Italy's intervention would perhaps have been impossible." Especially important was *Corriere della Sera*, Italy's most influential newspaper. Luigi Albertini, the editor, was a leading opponent of Giolitti, a man who worked closely with Salandra and Sonnino. The newspaper was neutralist in 1914, but as Albertini wrote on 4 August, "Neutrality is merely a starting-point." Involvement would allow Italy to achieve its "aspirations in the struggle for a better world."[93] The support for intervention generated by this

[90] Seton-Watson, *Italy from Liberalism to Fascism*, pp. 454–5, 459.
[91] Renzi, *Shadow of the Sword*, p. 264.
[92] Clough and Saladino, *History of Modern Italy*, p. 306.
[93] Seton-Watson, *Italy from Liberalism to Fascism*, pp. 441, 252, 424.

newspaper would be exerted by upper- and upper-middle-class readers, certainly not by "the masses." The move to war could have been blocked in the legislature, but, probably due to Giolitti's recommendation, that did not happen.

One might assume that a determined coterie would plan and coordinate policies with great care, and that some evident rationality would govern or guide their judgments. But both assumptions are unwarranted readings, or, put differently, are insistent, unfounded inferences. In the Italian case, one had a monarch, a man vested with exceptional powers, who was somewhat "out of touch." His "withdrawal" put the war powers into the hands of the two key civilian ministers who then made the basic decision. One would assume that those ministers would work closely with the two key military leaders, carefully coordinating policies and timing. But that was not the case, either.

Gooch reports that "Cadorna did not explain his strategic presuppositions to the politicians and they never bothered to explore them." He provides some clues to account for the decision-making pathologies:

Cadorna's amazing strategic vision of a march on Vienna, and his complete disregard of the realities of trench warfare, were the product of a unique personality in a position of unquestioned and unquestionable authority. No group existed to challenge his assumptions and no doctrine had been established through which to assess them. The Italian general staff, unlike its German counterpart, was a small bureaucratic secretariat whose skills and training were narrowly functional.... Cadorna's scheme met no institutional or intellectual obstruction.[94]

Vittorio Emanuele III's Order of the Day, his address to the troops about to do battle, gives some sense of the "realism" guiding his judgments: "Favored by the terrain and by careful preparations [the Austrians] will put up a tough resistance, but your unquenchable dash will, without doubt, overcome them."[95]

Italy's involvement in the war, from the start, is best described as a series of disasters. The distinctive compartmentalization problem reviewed here at several points appeared again in grievous form. On 5 May, Cadorna learned – from a chance overheard conversation – that the nation was pledged to enter the war by 26 May at the latest, that is, in three weeks. The military plans were presumably well developed and the troops ready for engagement. But planning deficiencies were evident from the start. Moving the troops to the front took forty-eight days, more than twice

[94] Gooch, *Army, State and Society*, p. 170.
[95] Ibid.

the twenty-three stipulated in the plan. Cadorna's grand plan assumed a coordinated attack with Russians, Serbians, and possibly Romanians moving on Austria-Hungary from all sides. The coordination – what there was of it – was late and inadequate. Romania, as indicated, chose to stay out. Russia experienced a serious defeat at Gorlice beginning on 4 May and, in the weeks following, retreated along its entire western frontier, from Courland, Lithuania, Poland, and Galicia. The numbers of casualties and those taken prisoner were enormous. In those same weeks, the allies at Gallipoli also experienced defeat. For the moment, then, Italy stood virtually alone, the "great opportunity" having evaporated. Still another disaster was to follow, that of Caporetto.[96]

[96] Seton-Watson, *Italy from Liberalism to Fascism*, pp. 450–504.

# 12

# Bulgaria, Romania, and Greece

## Richard C. Hall

With Montenegro and Serbia engaged in the First World War from its outbreak, three other southeastern European countries hovered on the periphery of the fighting: Bulgaria, Romania, and Greece. Since, like Italy, all three harbored desires to realize their nationalist aspirations at the expense of their neighbors, they could not ignore the opportunities presented by the war. With the fighting raging elsewhere in Europe between the two great power alliance systems, affiliation with one or the other side promised substantial benefits. Before acting, each remaining Balkan nation had to determine which side offered the greatest gains and the most likely chance of victory. At the same time, the two warring alliance systems, the *entente* (France, Great Britain, and Russia) and the Central Powers (Austria-Hungary and Germany) sought any possible advantage in the Balkans. The interest of both blocs in this region increased after the fighting had deadlocked elsewhere.

Bulgaria, Romania, and Greece, like their Serbian neighbor, had cast off Ottoman rule in the nineteenth century. All three regarded their borders as temporary, because significant numbers of their conationals lived close by under foreign rule. All three devoted much of their national energy and treasure toward the establishment of large national states based on historical and ethnic claims, on occasion resorting to war for this purpose. Bulgaria fought Serbia successfully to this end in 1885; Greece the Ottoman Empire unsuccessfully in 1897. In the recent Balkan Wars of 1912–13, all three countries participated to further their nationalist aims. The victories of Greece and Romania, and the defeat of Bulgaria, only intensified these nationalist strivings. In the aftermath of the Balkan Wars, the Greeks and Romanians sought to retain and even expand their gains, and the Bulgarians endeavored to obtain revenge and to restore their national aspirations.

Except for a ten-year period from 1885 to 1895, Bulgaria enjoyed the patronage of Russia since 1878. From 1882 on, Romania had a formal alliance with Austria-Hungary, and through that arrangement to the Triple Alliance. Greece lacked the direct support of any great power, although after the marriage in 1889 of Crown Prince Constantine to Sophia Hohenzollern, the sister of Kaiser Wilhelm II, Germany developed a benevolent attitude. This pro-Greek stance on the part of Germany increased after Constantine's accession to the throne in 1913, and to a degree was reciprocated by the pro-German attitude of the new Greek king.

## Bulgaria

The Bulgarian decision to intervene in the First World War was predicated upon its catastrophic defeat in the Balkan Wars. Bulgaria possessed political and social structures similar to those of Serbia. The king (tsar) lacked a secure throne. Tsar Ferdinand, née Coburg, was the scion of an Austro-German house and the grandson of Louis Philippe of France; he came to Bulgaria after a coup originating in the army in 1886 deposed his popular predecessor, Alexander Battenberg. As in most European monarchies at that time, the constitutional monarch, in this case the distinctly unmilitary Ferdinand, was commander-in-chief of the Bulgarian Army. He, however, did not completely dominate it.

After Bulgaria's liberation from the Ottoman Empire by Russian forces in 1878, it focused on the inclusion of all Bulgarians in a single state. The ephemeral Treaty of San Stefano in March 1878 concluding the Russo-Turkish War accomplished this. The Treaty of Berlin in July of that year, however, revised the San Stefano arrangement and returned much Bulgarian territory to direct or indirect Ottoman rule. This alteration of the Balkan settlement occurred because of Austro-Hungarian and British concerns that a large Bulgaria would serve as a base from which Russia could dominate the region. Thereafter, Bulgarian governments sought to restore the San Stefano borders, which included most of Thrace and Macedonia. In particular, Bulgarian policy focused on the problem of Macedonia.

Macedonia is an area of extremely mixed population.[1] The Slavic element predominates, but Albanians, Turks, Roma, Vlachs, Greeks, and

---

[1] On the role of Macedonia in Balkan affairs in the last quarter of the nineteenth century to 1914, see Hugh Poulton, *Who Are the Macedonians?* (Bloomington, 1995), pp. 48–77.

others also live there. After the Treaty of Berlin, Sofia governments sought to unify this region with Bulgaria. The only issue was whether to accomplish this with or without the assistance of the Russian liberators. Russophiles contended that Russian help offered the best opportunity for the restoration of a San Stefano Bulgaria. Russophobes, however, weary of maladroit Russian interference in Bulgarian affairs, increasingly perceived the Triple Alliance powers, especially Austria-Hungary, as Bulgaria's great power sponsors. The terms *russophile* and *russophobe* were not official party designations; rather, they signified the orientation of virtually all Bulgarian politicians.

Both the Greeks and the Serbs rejected Bulgarian claims to Macedonia and vied with Bulgaria for the hearts and minds of the population through religious and educational efforts. Also, all three Balkan states supported guerilla units in Macedonia, which battled the Ottoman authorities as well as each other. Even the Romanians made an appearance in the Macedonian arena, expressing their interest by funding schools for the Vlach minority, whose Latin-based language is closely related to Romanian.

Most of the Bulgarian political class had been educated abroad. Ivan Geshov, the Bulgarian prime minister during the Balkan Wars, studied in Manchester, England. His successor, Stoyan Danev, attended law school in Prague. The prime minister who led Bulgaria into the First World War in 1915, Vasil Radoslavov, received his education in Heidelberg. No matter where they studied, these Bulgarian politicians were convinced nationalists. Geshov and Danev were russophiles; Radoslavov was russophobe.

The identification of the vast majority of the population in the Balkan countries – the peasant masses – with the national ideal was by no means certain. Since the departure of the Ottomans in the nineteenth century, Bulgarian peasants, like those in Serbia, were mainly owners of small plots of land. They had little influence on policy (a circumstance shared by the peasantry of Greece, Romania, and Serbia). Their perceptions of national interests were (and are) difficult to evaluate. Clearly, the idea of "Greater Bulgaria" (or "Greater Greece," or "Greater Romania") did not mesmerize everyone. Just before the outbreak of the First Balkan War, the Bulgarian Agrarian Party leader Aleksandŭr Stamboliski eloquently stated his opposition to the impending conflict:

We are not seeking war with Turkey, because we know how the horrible consequences are borne by working peasants, who fill the barracks and who will sacrifice the most capable of their children on the battlefield. We are not seeking war because we do not know, nor can we know, what kind of diplomatic, financial and military circumstances Bulgaria has arranged. We are not seeking war, because we do not wish to be responsible for an outright adventure. We do not want a war, because we are expressing the opinions and convictions of an enormous agrarian class.[2]

Nevertheless, the Bulgarian peasantry responded to the government's call to arms in 1912, 1913, and 1915 with stolid acquiescence. Their disaffection became evident with the disorders in the Bulgarian Army in the spring and summer of 1913, and was manifest in the military collapse of Bulgaria and revolt in the autumn of 1918. The peasantry of the other Balkan states likewise acquiesced in the call to arms in the Balkan Wars and in the First World War.

Two secret societies advocated direct action in pursuit of Bulgarian national aspirations. The Supreme Macedonian Committee (Supremist) was formed in 1895 out of several older organizations. It advocated the annexation of Macedonia by Sofia and received political and material support from the Bulgarian Army. Through the Supremists, the Bulgarian government and military attempted, not always successfully, to influence the Macedonian movement. A competing society, the Internal Macedonian Revolutionary Organization (IMRO) was formed in 1893. It operated relatively independently of the Sofia government. Its members advocated autonomy for Macedonia within a Balkan federation with the slogan "Macedonia for the Macedonians."[3] This idea, however, threatened the goal of a "greater Bulgaria."

Macedonians assassinated former Prime Minister Stefan Stambulov in 1895 because his government had been too friendly to the Ottoman Empire. After the failure of a major Macedonian uprising in 1903, these groups fragmented further into competitive factions. No single group could claim overall authority in Macedonian affairs, a diffusion that made control of these factions by the Bulgarian tsar, government, or military impossible. It also greatly obfuscated the actions of both factions so that neither the Supremists nor IMRO could receive clear responsibility for subsequent "Macedonian" actions in Macedonia.

Even as the Bulgarian government prepared for war against the Ottoman Empire after concluding an alliance with Serbia in March 1912, the activities of Macedonian revolutionaries threatened to force peremptory action.[4] On 1 August 1912, a bomb exploded in the marketplace of

---

[2] Nikola Petkov, *Aleksandar Stambolijski, njegova lichnost i ideje* (Belgrade, 1933), p. 130.

[3] On the Macedonian organizations, see Duncan Perry, *The Politics of Terror: The Macedonian Revolutionary Movements 1893–1903* (Durham, N.C., 1988).

[4] For the details of the Bulgaro-Serb treaty, see Chapter 3.

the Macedonian town of Kochana.[5] In response, vengeful Turks massacred more than 100 Macedonians. Demonstrators throughout Bulgaria demanded immediate action by the Sofia government. Prime Minister Geshov soon managed to calm the situation. At this point, war was premature, since the final military arrangements were still incomplete. The Kochana incident, however, demonstrated the ability of nongovernmental organizations to preempt policy and even to provoke war.

In the First Balkan War, the Bulgarians achieved great victories over Ottoman armies in Thrace. Under terms of the March 1912 alliance with Serbia and subsequent agreements, however, the conquest of the main goal of Bulgarian aspirations, Macedonia, was left to Serbia. Bulgarian troops had to confront the main Ottoman force in eastern Thrace. Consequently, Serbian forces were in control of most of Macedonia by the end of 1912. When the Serbs refused to abide by the terms of the March 1912 alliance and evacuate Macedonia in the spring of 1913, the Bulgarians prepared to fight their erstwhile allies. With the conclusion of the Treaty of London on 30 May 1913, the Bulgarians transferred the bulk of their army from Thrace to their southwestern frontiers positioned there to enforce their claims to Macedonia against the Greeks and Serbs. Throughout June 1913, tensions rose among the Balkan allies. Because he was unable to reach a settlement with the Serbs, Geshov, the main architect of the Balkan League, resigned as Bulgarian prime minister at the end of May. Stoyan Danev, a zealous russophile, replaced him at the beginning of June. Danev later remembered, "I hoped I could compel the Serbs to accept the arbitration agreement. I would suffer the consequences for what might happen if they snipped off part of Macedonia. I did not intend to yield, because we had signed the agreement of 1912. At last we had to act."[6] The new Bulgarian government insisted on maintaining the March 1912 treaty.

Reluctantly, Foreign Minister Sergei Sazonov agreed on 15 June 1913 to uphold the Russian promise to arbitrate the Bulgarian-Serbian dispute.[7] Meanwhile, the situation in Bulgaria became critical. The mostly peasant

---

[5] Narodno sŭbranie, *Doklad na parlamentarnata izpitatelna komisiya*, 4 vols. (Sofia, 1918) (hereafter referred to as DPIK), p. 35, no. 1; pp. 35–6, no. 2; pp. 37–40, no. 8; pp. 40–1, no. 9. All dates are given according to the Gregorian Calendar (new style) unless otherwise indicated as being from the Julian Calendar, then in use in Bulgaria, Greece, and Serbia (old style, or os).

[6] Narodno sŭbranie, *Prilozhenie kŭm tom pŭrvi ot doklada na parlamentarnata izpitatelna komisiya* (Sofia, 1918) (hereafter referred to as *Prilozhenie*) (Danev), p. 104.

[7] DPIK, vol. 1, p. 502, no. 166; *Prilozhenie* (Danev), pp. 76–7.

soldiers of the Bulgarian Army, who had been at arms since the previous autumn, were becoming restive. They were exhausted and wanted to go home. The Bulgarian commander, Lieutenant General Mihail Savov, demanded that the government either fight the Serbs for Macedonia or allow the army to disperse.[8] Under this pressure, Danev insisted that the Russians act within a week. At first, Sazonov refused to accept a deadline and denounced all agreements with Bulgaria.[9] After a round of hurried diplomacy, the Bulgarians and Russians appeared to resolve their quarrel. But before the Russian arbitration could proceed, fighting began in Macedonia.

A limited Bulgarian attack against Serbian troops on 29 June precipitated the Second Balkan War. General Savov, who had ordered the attacks, later justified them by insisting, "In the first days of June everyone, with only rare exception, was for the war, because no one, given the partition of Macedonia, wanted to *sign the death warrant of the national ideal.*"[10] Tsar Ferdinand's degree of complicity in the decision to attack remains obscure. Macedonian bands had threatened Ferdinand and Danev with assassination if Bulgaria agreed to Russian arbitration.[11] With the Bulgarian Army in some disarray, the impetus for the attack came from General Savov and the Bulgarian military, not Ferdinand. The Bulgarian tsar certainly knew of and approved of the order. Danev later claimed that he was unaware of the attack order, although Savov insisted that the prime minister knew about it.[12] Nevertheless, the order cannot have come as a complete surprise to Danev, given his bellicose demeanor. Danev remained in close contact with Savov throughout this crisis.

The Bulgarian attack on Serbian positions on the night of 29–30 June 1913 demonstrated the ability of the military and the nationalist societies to dictate policy. The position of the Sofia government in June 1913 was

---

[8] Bŭlgarska akademiya naukite (Sofia), arkiv na Petŭr Abrashev (hereafter referred to as BAN), 51-I-18–334; *Prilozhenie* (Savov), pp. 267, 277. Technically, Tsar Ferdinand was the commander-in-chief of the Bulgarian Army, and General Savov the deputy commander.

[9] DPIK, vol. 1, pp. 532–3, no. 205.

[10] General M. Savov, "General Savov govori," *Dnevnik* no. 4002, 7 November 1913 os. Emphasis in the original.

[11] A. Toshev, *Balkanskite voini*, 2 vols. (Plovdiv, 1929–31), vol. 2, p. 473; Carnegie Endowment for International Peace, *Report of the International Commission to Inquire into the Causes and Conduct of the Balkan Wars* (Washington, D.C., 1914), p. 67.

[12] Narodno sŭbranie, *Dnevnitsi (stenografski) na sedemnadestoto obiknoveno narodno sŭbranie: Pŭrva redovna sesiya* (Sofia, 1914). Speech of St. Danev, 5 May 1914 os, p. 652; BAN 51-I-18–397, 398.

not unlike that of the Belgrade government in June 1914. In both cases, the government had to assume responsibility for actions taken by more aggressive elements within the military establishment. The difference was that in 1913 the Bulgarian attack was directed against two other Balkan states, while in 1914 the Serbian terrorist action had as its target a great power, Austria-Hungary.

The result of General Savov's orders was war with Greece and Serbia. Both of Bulgaria's erstwhile allies had awaited the opportunity to settle the Macedonian issue by force of arms. The attacks of 29–30 June allowed them to present themselves to the great powers as the victims of Bulgarian aggression. The Serbian and Greek armies deflected the Bulgarian attacks and counterattacked into Bulgaria. Just as their army began to contain these onslaughts and to resume the offensive, another disaster doomed the Bulgarians.

Because of the overwhelming Bulgarian victories in Thrace in the First Balkan War, the Romanian government sought compensation in Bulgarian (southern) Dobrudzha. The Romanians wanted to prevent the development of a potential threat in a powerful Bulgaria. After great power arbitration failed to deliver a satisfactory portion of Dobrudzha to Romania at the St. Petersburg ambassadors conference in April 1913, and with the Bulgarian Army totally engaged against the Greeks and Serbs, the Romanian Army crossed the Danube and moved into Bulgaria on 11 July 1913. At the same time, the Ottoman Army, perceiving the opportunity, reversed its defeat of the previous March by seizing Adrianople. The invasion of Romanian forces from the north and Ottoman forces from the southeast ensured a catastrophic defeat for Bulgaria.

In these calamitous circumstances, and in the absence of any assistance from St. Petersburg, Danev's russophile government resigned. The failure of the Russians to help their Bulgarian clients in the hour of need completely discredited Danev's government and his pro-Russian positions. A russophobe government, led by Vasil Radoslavov, replaced it and immediately sued for peace. The subsequent peace treaties, one signed at Bucharest on 10 August by Bulgaria, the former allies, and Romania, and another at Constantinople by Bulgaria and the Ottoman Empire on 29 September, deprived Bulgaria of most of Macedonia as well as southern Dobrudzha and eastern Thrace.[13]

---

[13] For the terms of the Treaty of Bucharest, see B. D. Kesiyakov, *Prinos kŭm diplomaticheskata istoriya na Bŭlgariya*, 4 vols. (Sofia, 1925), vol. 1, pp. 155–8; for the Treaty of Constantinople see ibid., pp. 158–9.

The Balkan Wars, begun in such glory, had ended in catastrophe for Bulgaria. Its armies had decisively defeated the former Ottoman masters, only to falter against its onetime Greek and Serbian allies. For Bulgaria, the Treaty of Bucharest was an unmitigated disaster. One member of the Bulgarian delegation at Bucharest, General Ivan Fichev, later wrote of the signing of the treaty: "This day must be the day of the deepest sorrow of the Bulgarian nation."[14] Despite the sacrifice of so many Bulgarian lives and so much material in the two Balkan Wars, the Bulgarians saw Macedonia, which they envisioned as their national goal, partitioned between Greece and Serbia.

They had also received confirmation that their Russian liberators no longer protected their interests. Bulgarian Prime Minister Radoslavov explained this situation to Alexander Savinski, who in January 1914 assumed the position of Russian minister in Sofia. "At Bucharest, we clearly realized that Russia had turned away from us; a word from Schebeko would have been enough for us to obtain Macedonia and Kavala. That word was not spoken, and therefore we find ourselves in our present melancholy position."[15] The russophobe Radoslavov government now looked to the Triple Alliance to support Bulgarian claims to Macedonia.

Most Bulgarian political and military leaders refused to consider the Treaty of Bucharest as final. As a result of the catastrophe, refugees from Macedonia, southern Dobrudzha and Thrace flooded into Bulgaria, further strengthening demands to reverse the Bucharest verdict. Bulgaria was too exhausted from the efforts of the First and Second Balkan Wars to attempt any immediate revision.[16] Nevertheless, as early as the autumn of 1913, the Bulgarians began to sponsor and shelter Macedonian guerrillas fighting against Serbian rule.

The assassination of Archduke Franz Ferdinand in June 1914 aroused the apprehensions of Tsar Ferdinand, himself the object of assassination rumors the year before. He feared that Macedonian or Serbian secret

---

[14] Ivan Fichev, *Balkanskata voina 1912–1913, prezhivelitsi, belezhki i dokumenti* (Sofia, 1940), p. 473.

[15] Otto Hoetzsch, ed., *Die internationalen Beziehungen im Zeitalter des Imperialismus: Dokumente aus den Archiven der zarischen und der provisorischen Regierungen* (Berlin, 1942) (hereafter referred to as RD), ser. 1, vol. 4, no. 311. Nikolai N. Schebeko was the Russian minister in Romania during the negotiations for the Treaty of Bucharest. Kavala is an Aegean port east of Salonika.

[16] In the two Balkan Wars the Bulgarians lost a total of 56,000 dead and 110,000 wounded. See Richard C. Hall, *The Balkan Wars, Prelude to the First World War* (London and New York, 2000), p. 135.

societies might make an attempt on his life.[17] Ferdinand's concerns were exaggerated, but they demonstrated his appreciation of the power wielded by the secret societies.

The onset of general war in Europe during the summer of 1914 presented Bulgaria with a clash of loyalties as well as an opportunity to revise the Treaty of Bucharest. General Franz Conrad von Hötzendorf, the chief of the Austro-Hungarian General Staff, urged the Bulgarians to attack Serbia, insisting, on 29 July, that "there is no more favorable moment than today."[18] Yet many Bulgarians remained strong russophiles. At the outbreak of the war, the Bulgarian minister in St. Petersburg, the Balkan War hero Lieutenant General Radko Dimitriev, resigned his post to accept a commission in the Russian Army. Other Bulgarians also volunteered to serve in the Russian Army. A political ally of Radoslavov explained the dilemma for Bulgaria at the beginning of the war this way: "Our natural place was with Russia. Yet after 1885, ... and the Bucharest Peace Treaty, how could Bulgaria take Serbia's side?"[19]

For the time being, Radoslavov maintained Bulgarian neutrality, insisting that the country needed time to recover from the Balkan Wars.[20] Sofia concentrated its attentions on Serbian Macedonia, the same area promised to Bulgaria by the March 1912 treaty. An active guerilla campaign against the Serbs in Macedonia ensued from August 1914.[21] While the general European war offered the Bulgarians the opportunity to rectify the judgment of Bucharest, their immediate policies, while anti-Serbian, did not yet commit them to either of the warring coalitions.

In an effort to obtain the national objective in Macedonia, Bulgaria negotiated with both warring alliances. Although favoring the Central Powers, Radoslavov wavered according to their successes and failures

[17] RD, ser. 1, vol. 4, no. 219.
[18] Archive of Tsar Ferdinand of Bulgaria, Hoover Institute, Stanford, California, 50-1 1914, telegram of Lieutenant Colonel Tantilov, Bulgarian military attaché in Vienna, to Sofia, 29 July 1914. Conrad's entreaty belied Austrian claims of wanting only a limited war.
[19] P. Peshev, *Istoricheskite sŭbitiya i zhivota mi, ot navecherieto na osvobozhdenieto ni do dnes* (Sofia, 1925), p. 197. In 1885 the Serbs attacked Bulgaria, and after suffering a defeat, were rescued by Austro-Hungarian threats of intervention.
[20] Ministerstvo na vŭnshinite raboti i na izpovedaniyata, *Diplomaticheski dokumenti po namesata na Bŭlgariya v Evropeiskata voina*, 2 vols. (Sofia, 1920–21) (hereafter referred to as DD), vol. 1, nos. 225, 226, 227, 228; Ministero delgli affari esteri, Commissiona per la publicazione de documenti diplomatici, *I Documenti diplomatici italiani* (Rome, 1964) (hereafter referred to as ID), vol. 4, book 12, no. 510.
[21] Dimitŭr G. Gotsev, *Natsionalno-osvoboditelnata borba v Makedoniya 1912–1915* (Sofia, 1981), p. 145.

on the battlefield. After the Russian capture of the Austro-Hungarian fortress of Przemysl and the Anglo-French landings on both sides of the Dardanelles in the spring of 1915, Radoslavov expressed interest in co-operating with the *entente*.[22] After some dithering, on 29 May 1915 the *entente* promised Bulgaria most of Macedonia and eastern Thrace at the end of the war, provided that Serbia received Bosnia.[23] The offer came too late. The Russians were already in retreat in Galicia, and the British remained stuck on the beaches after their landings at Gallipoli. The de-feats of the *entente* powers adversely affected their position in Sofia. As one Bulgarian historian has noted, the "the russophile policy was deeply wounded" by the Russian defeats that spring and summer.[24] Following the Russian setbacks, the Sofia government's interest in the *entente* waned.

The *entente* labored under another disadvantage in Sofia. Serbian re-luctance to concede any part of Macedonia greatly hampered the efforts of London and Paris to persuade Sofia to remain neutral, let alone join in an attack on the Ottoman Empire. Serbian Prime Minister Nikola Pashich's empty assurance that "Bulgaria will benefit from its present neutral con-duct" held little allure for the Bulgarian government.[25]

No such obstacle impeded the blandishments of the Central Powers. They promised Bulgaria the immediate occupation of all Macedonia. In spring of 1915, Radoslavov insisted, "Bulgaria cannot and will not be denied its historical and ethnographic rights. It cannot be without Macedonia, for which it has shed so much blood."[26] After victories in Galicia and at Gallipoli in the summer of 1915, the Central Powers ap-peared to be in a better position to help Bulgaria's leaders obtain their national aims. Tsar Ferdinand was inclined toward the Central Powers. He was, as noted, an Austro-German prince by birth, and he also seems to have harbored a somewhat paranoid concern that an *entente* victory would mean the end of the Coburg dynasty in Bulgaria.[27]

The German promise to participate in an attack upon Serbia was the de-cisive factor in persuading Ferdinand and Radoslavov to join the Central Powers.[28] Such a powerful ally was certain to crush Serbia and deliver

---

[22] RD, ser. 2, vol. 7, part 2, no. 503; Vasil Radoslavov, *Dnevni belezhki 1914–1916*, Ivan Ilchev, ed. (Sofia, 1993), p. 125.

[23] ID, vol. 5, book 4, no. 9; RD, ser. 2, vol. 8, part 1, no. 38; Vasil Radoslavov (Radoslawoff), *Bulgarien und die Weltkrise* (Berlin, 1923), p. 154.

[24] Simeon Damyanov, Bulgariya *vův Frenskata politika, 1878–1918* (Sofia, 1985), p. 427.

[25] DD, vol. 1, no. 415.

[26] Ibid., no. 798.

[27] ID, vol. 5, book 1, nos. 840, 923; Radoslavov, *Dnevni belezheki*, p. 96.

[28] See Richard C. Hall, *Bulgaria's Road to the First World War* (Boulder, 1996), p. 302.

Macedonia to Bulgaria. It was, clearly, the best opportunity to reverse the Treaty of Bucharest and finally obtain the national objective. Tsar Ferdinand, in his Manifesto to the Bulgarian People of 14–15 October 1915, announcing Bulgaria's entry into the war on the side of the Central Powers, stated: "Both warring sides recognize the great injustice, which was inflicted upon us by the division of Macedonia. And both warring sides are agreed that the greater part of it needs to belong to Bulgaria."[29] With this assertion, Bulgaria began the third of four unsuccessful wars for Macedonia over a period of thirty years.

Some Bulgarians still objected to participation in the war. Together with other Bulgarian political party leaders, the Agrarian Party leader Alexandŭr Stamboliski met with Ferdinand as Bulgaria was poised to enter the war. The peasant leader warned the tsar, "[I]f you choose to follow your course, you should think first of your head."[30] For this impertinence, Stamboliski spent most of the war in jail.

The Bulgarian decision to intervene on the side of the Central Powers appeared justified at the time. Berlin and Vienna promised Sofia the immediate annexation of all of Serbian-held Macedonia. Bulgarian troops had only to take it. Also at that point, the Central Powers appeared to be winning the war. The time seemed propitious to act.

In the ensuing conflict, Bulgarian troops attacking from the east together with Austro-Hungarian and Germans soldiers invading from the north quickly overwhelmed the Serbs and occupied their country. At the beginning of 1916, Austria-Hungary overran Montenegro. In the course of the war, Bulgarian troops in Greece, Macedonia, and Romania faced British, French, and Romanian soldiers, among others. They even encountered Russian troops around Salonika and in the Dobrudzha. Ultimately, Bulgarian arms failed again. The armistice of 29 September 1918 brought an exhausted Bulgaria further human, material, and territorial losses and more dispirited refugees.

### Romania

Bulgaria's entry into the war on the side of the Central Powers surrounded Romania with belligerents, all of whom had reason to regard Romania with suspicion and antipathy. Over the previous three years, Romania had

---

[29] Hristo Hristov, ed., *Bŭlgarska voenna istoriya. Podbrani izvori i dokumenti* (Sofia, 1986), vol. 3, no. 50, "Manifest kŭm Bŭlgarskiya narod za obyavyavane na voina na Sŭrbiya."

[30] John D. Bell, *Peasants in Power: Alexander Stamboliski and the Bulgarian National Union, 1899–1932* (Princeton, 1977), p. 120.

been a faithless ally to Austria-Hungary, a covetous irredentist to Russia, and a treacherous opportunist to Bulgaria. Those unneighborly attitudes imperiled the position of Romania in the Balkan Peninsula.

By participating in the defeat of Bulgaria during the Second Balkan War and acquiring southern Dobrudzha, the Bucharest government enforced its self-proclaimed mission as the "gendarme of the Balkans." This triumph occurred without combat casualties, although many soldiers died from sickness, primarily cholera. It established Romania as the dominant regional power in the Balkan Peninsula, and enabled the Romanian government to concentrate its foreign policy on its three irredentist aspirations. To the west, the Romanian objective was Hungarian-controlled Transylvania, which had a large self-aware Romanian population made increasingly restive by strictures imposed by Budapest. To the north, the goal was Bukovina, where a large Romanian population languished under the benign neglect of Austrian rule. In the east, the object of interest was Russian-held Bessarabia, where the Romanian population was much less developed economically and nationally than in Transylvania. The Bucharest government had no clear indications, however, that the Romanian populations of any of these areas sought inclusion in a Greater Romania. No activist organizations comparable to the Macedonian and Serbian secret societies existed in any of these regions, or in the Romanian kingdom itself.

The Romanian political system stood on a much narrower social basis than those of its southeastern European neighbors. A land-owning aristocracy retained control of most of the agricultural properties in the country, while a small educated urban class ran most of its banking and commercial establishments. They, together with the German-born Hohenzollern king Carol I, dominated the political system.

As in the other southeastern European countries, the king's role was important in Romanian political affairs. Between 1881 and 1914, every government supported by the king won at the polls.[31] In foreign policy issues, the Conservative Party leaned toward the Triple Alliance, while the Liberal Party favored the *entente*, although these inclinations were by no means absolute. The prospect of gains from the European conflict completely fragmented the Conservative Party, but left the Liberal Party largely intact. In the summer of 1914, the Liberal Party leader Ion Brătianu was the Romanian prime minister. Brătianu had studied civil engineering in France, but had mainly pursued a political career. The Romanian Army

---

[31] Keith Hitchens, *Rumania 1866–1914* (Oxford, 1994), p. 94.

was dedicated to nationalist goals but, unlike the Bulgarian and Serbian militaries, remained firmly under government control.[32]

The peasant majority, mostly landless, demonstrated its regard for its debased circumstances in a bloody revolt in 1907. This effort brought 11,000 dead and much destruction, but little real change. The government in Bucharest recognized that the pursuit of a nationalist agenda in the Second Balkan War and in the First World War served to some degree as a diversion from the more immediate goals of the peasantry. Even so, the Romanian peasants, who as in the other Balkan countries formed the vast majority of the military conscripts, stolidly answered the calls to duty in 1913 and 1916.

King Carol had overseen the negotiations for Romania's treaty with Austria-Hungary in 1883. This connection to the Triple Alliance was the mainstay of Romanian foreign policy through the deterioration of events in the Balkans beginning in 1912. As recently as 5 February 1913, the Romanian government had renewed the treaty with Austria-Hungary.[33] In the aftermath of the Balkan Wars, the Russians, who had lost their Bulgarian connection, flirted with Romania. To this end, Tsar Nicholas II visited the Romanian Black Sea port of Constanţa in the first week of June 1914, and exchanged complements with King Carol. Nothing further developed, however. One tangible result of the Russian attempt to detach Romania from the Triple Alliance was the further alienation of the jealous Bulgarians.[34]

At first during the July Crisis of 1914, Romanian policy wavered. King Carol assured the Austro-Hungarian ambassador that in the event of a general war, Romania would side with the Triple Alliance.[35] At the same time, Brătianu asserted Romania's determination, together with Greece, to preserve the Bucharest peace settlement.[36] This assertion was directed

---

[32] See Colonel Dr. Vasile Alexandrescu, "The Romanian Army's Adherence to the Ideal of Making the Unitary Romanian State," in Colonel Dr. A. G. Savu, *The Army and the Romanian Society* (Bucharest, 1980), pp. 114–15.

[33] Karl Kautsky, ed., *Die Deutschen Dokumente zum Kriegsausbruch*, 4 vols. (Charlottenburg, 1919), vol. 4, app. 3.

[34] Another consequence: The tsar's visit thoroughly alarmed Austria-Hungary's leaders. On this, see Chapter 4 above.

[35] Ministerium des K. und K. Hauses und des Äussern, *Österreich-Ungarns Aussenpolitik: Von der bosnischen Krise 1908 bis zum Kriegsausbruch 1914; diplomatische Aktenstücke des österreichisch-ungarischen Ministeriums des Äussern*, Ludwig Bittner and Hans Uebersberger, eds., 8 vols. (Vienna, 1930) (hereafter referred to as ÖUA), vol. 8, no. 10589.

[36] G. P. Gooch and Harold Temperley, eds., *British Documents on the Origins of the War 1898–1914*, 11 vols. (London, 1927), vol. 11, nos. 316, 371.

against Bulgarian revisionism. Romania could not allow Bulgaria to take advantage of Serbia's indisposition at the end of July 1914 to overturn the Peace of Bucharest. To this end, the Romanian and Greek government made a joint declaration in Sofia.[37] The deteriorating situation in Europe, however, forced the Romanian government to take additional action. A Crown Council met at the royal palace at Sinaia near the capital on 3 August 1914 to consider Bucharest's options. Only a few muted voices from the Conservative Party, most notably that of Petre Carp, a landowner from Moldavia, joined together with King Carol to advocate loyalty to the treaty with Austria-Hungary. The Conservatives favored the Triple Alliance because of its superior strength and because of fears of Russian Pan-Slavism.[38]

News of the defection of Italy from the Triple Alliance destroyed what little credibility these arguments had maintained. A German offer of Bessarabia in return for adherence to the Central Powers failed to entice the Romanian government.[39] Finally, a moderate Conservative leader, Alexandru Marghiloman, persuaded the king that the conditions for action specified in the treaty did not exist.[40] At the conclusion of the council, the German-born king, who at the time already was sick with the illness that would kill him, lamented, "Gentlemen, you cannot imagine how bitter it is to find oneself isolated in a country of which one is not a native."[41] On the other hand, Carol may well have perceived in these circumstances a means to avoid responsibility.[42]

Underlying the Romanian declaration of neutrality was a pervasive spirit of realism, dictated by geography. Fealty to the Austro-Hungarian alliance would ensure the hostility of Russia on Romania's eastern frontier. A tilt toward the *entente* could incur the wrath of Austria-Hungary on

---

[37] ÖUA, vol. 8, nos. 10876, 11018.

[38] Ministère des Affaires étrangères, *Documents diplomatiques français 1871–1914*, 41 vols. (Paris, 1929–59) (hereafter referred to as DDF), 3rd ser., vol. 11, no. 633.

[39] Kautsky, *Die Deutschen Dokumente*, vol. 3, nos. 506, 582. Brătianu thought that Romania could retain Bessarabia only if Russia were weakened by additional territorial losses to Germany and Austria-Hungary. The Germans thought that the Bulgarians and Ottomans might help the Romanians conquer Bessarabia. Ibid., vol. 4, pp. 795, 830.

[40] Glenn E. Torrey, "Alexandru Marghiloman of Romania: A War Leader," in Bela K. Király and Albert A. Nofi, eds., *East Central European War Leaders: Civilian and Military* (Boulder, 1988), p. 96; Kautsky, *Die Deutschen Dokumente*, vol. 4, no. 811.

[41] R. W. Seton-Watson, *A History of the Roumanians from Roman Times to the Completion of Unity* (Cambridge, Eng., 1934), pp. 476–7.

[42] Glenn E. Torrey, "Romania and the Belligerents 1914–1916," in Glenn E. Torrey, *Romania and World War I* (Portland, Ore., 1998), p. 10.

Romania's western borders. The European war would enable Romania to realize at least part of its irredentist goals, and at the same time profit economically. To profit from the war however, the Romanians, like their Bulgarian neighbors, first had to determine who would win.

The death of King Carol in October 1914 left foreign policy firmly in the hands of Brătianu.[43] While Romania ostensibly maintained a neutral position in the war, Brătianu initiated negotiations with the *entente* to obtain guarantees of Habsburg territory. Soon after the king's death, the Romanians signed an agreement in St. Petersburg that promised them Russian support for the annexation of those Habsburg territories with a majority of Romanian inhabitants in return for benevolent neutrality.[44] This was a sensible move. Located up against Austria-Hungary and relatively isolated from the *entente* powers, Romania had scant opportunity for any military action. Its situation in the initial period of the war reversed that of Bulgaria, which although neutral, tilted toward the Central Powers.

Not all Romanians were enthusiastic about joining the war on the side of the *entente*. Large estate owners prospered by selling their grain to the Central Powers. The war enabled them to realize substantial profits.[45] Also, many Romanians living in Moldavia, next door to Russia, lacked ardor for joining an alliance directed against their large and powerful neighbor.

When the Italians entered the war on the side of the *entente* in May 1915, they provided Bucharest with a precedent for switching loyalties and an incentive for negotiating further with the now strengthened *entente*. Bulgaria's intervention on the side of the Central Powers in October 1915 intensified the danger on Romania's southern frontier. The German-Austrian-Bulgarian defeat of Serbia later that autumn further imperiled Bucharest. As a result of these developments, military talks between the Romanians and *entente* assumed a new urgency.[46]

With the opening of the German offensive at Verdun in February 1916, Romania assumed an even greater importance for the *entente*. The

---

43 Glenn E. Torrey, "Romania's Decision to Intervene," in Bela K. Király and Nandor F. Dreisziger, eds., *East Central European Society in World War I* (New York, 1985), p. 206.

44 Alfred J. Rieber, "Russian Diplomacy and Rumania," in Alexander Dallin et al., eds., *Russian Diplomacy and Eastern Europe 1914–1917* (New York, 1963), p. 250.

45 Charles J. Vopicka, *Secrets of the Balkans* (Chicago, 1921), pp. 80–1.

46 E. Adamov, ed., *Die Europäischen Mächte und die Türkei während des Weltkrieges: Konstantinople und die Meerengen* (Dresden, 1930), vol. 2, no. 197.

French sought to counter the Germans by applying pressure against the Central Powers in the east; specifically, they wanted the Romanians to attack Austria-Hungary to supplement an *entente* offensive planned in Macedonia. The apparent success of the Brusilov offensive in June 1916 offered the Bucharest government the opportunity to accommodate the French and, more important, to realize its nationalist goals. While Russian troops were overrunning Austro-Hungarian positions in Galicia, British and French staff officers planned an offensive at Salonika, which would distract the Bulgarians and enable Romania to enter the war without fear of attack from the south. General Joseph Joffre, the commander-in-chief of the French Army, optimistically predicted, "The neutralization of the Bulgarian Army will allow Romania to enter the fray and precipitate the resolution of the war."[47] *Entente* pressure on Bucharest increased. At the end of June 1916, London and Paris warned Bucharest to join the war or risk losing the prospect of obtaining Transylvania and Bukovina.[48] At the same time, nationalist societies, energized by the apparent defeat of Austria-Hungary, clamored for intervention on the side of the *entente*.[49]

With the Austro-Hungarian Army evidently in retreat in the East, and the Bulgarian Army apparently fully engaged around Salonika, the time appeared propitious for intervention. Brătianu attempted to use the opportunity to lever material benefits from the *entente* for the underequipped Romanian Army.[50] This delayed the realization of a formal arrangement for over a month. Brătianu finally signed a military convention with Britain and France on 17 August 1916.[51] At a Crown Council ten days later, he explained the decision to enter the war to King Ferdinand, who had succeeded his uncle Carol in October 1914, and to leading politicians from the Liberal and Conservative parties. Some Conservatives, notably Marghiloman, refrained from active opposition to intervention. Others, however, rejected Brătianu's reasoning. Petru Carp thundered, "I wish that you will be conquered because your victory will be the ruin of the country!"[52] Nevertheless, with the support of the king, the Brătianu

[47] Ministerère de la Guerre, État-Major de la Armée, Service Historique, *Les Armées français dans la Grande Guerre*, 9 vols. (Paris, 1923) (hereafter referred to as AFGG), vol. 8, book 1, annex 3, no. 1349.
[48] Hitchens, *Rumania*, p. 261. See also AFGG, vol. 8, book 1, annex 3, nos. 1352, 1359.
[49] Colonel Dr. Vasile Alexandrescu, *Romania in World War I* (Bucharest, 1985), p. 14.
[50] AFGG, vol. 8, book 1, annex 3, no. 1368.
[51] Ibid., nos. 1457, 1458, 1482; Fredrich Stieve, ed., *Der Diplomatische Schriftwechsel Iswolskis 1914–1917: Im Auftrage des Auswärtigen Amt* (Berlin, 1926), no. 301.
[52] Sherman David Spector, *Rumania at the Paris Peace Conference* (New York, 1962), p. 38.

government declared war on Austria-Hungary on 27 August 1916. King Ferdinand stated:

Although I am a member of the Hohenzollern family, I am the King of Roumania first, and therefore I have to do what my subjects wish to. I perceive that the majority of the people are asking that Roumania enter the war on the side of the Entente, and I therefore state to you that I am prepared to comply with their wish.[53]

This statement was rather disingenuous, since "the people" had not demanded war. Rather, it was Liberal politicians, under considerable pressure from the *entente*, who had decided that the time was right to intervene.

Given Romania's geographic location between warring Austria-Hungary and Russia, and with a hostile Bulgaria to the south, Brătianu's initial caution was appropriate. After King Carol's death, Brătianu had a domestic consensus to support a policy of pro-*entente* neutrality. He was unable to maintain this equilibrium, however. His own nationalist inclinations together with *entente* coercion led him to act in the summer of 1916.

Initially, the Romanian Army achieved some successes against weak Austro-Hungarian resistance in Transylvania. The force of the Russian offensive, however, was largely spent by the time Romania entered the war. Contrary to General Joffre's expectations, the *entente* offensive north of Salonika not only failed to achieve a war-winning breakthrough on the Balkan front but was unable to prevent the Bulgarians from participating in a punishing action against Romania. Consequently, a massive counterattack by the Central Powers in September – including Austro-Hungarian and German forces in Transylvania, and Bulgarian, German, and Ottoman troops moving into the Dobrudzha and across the Danube – overwhelmed the Romanians. In December, the Central Powers occupied Bucharest and the major Black Sea port Constanţa.

The remaining Romanian forces retreated to northern Moldavia, but the Russian revolutions of 1917 soon isolated them. Romania had to acknowledge defeat. A change of government brought the Conservative Party leader Marghiloman to power. He signed the Treaty of Bucharest with the Central Powers on 7 May 1918, which took Romania out of the war. On 10 November 1918, with the defeat of the Central Powers assured, Romania returned to the war on the side of the *entente* and gained the benefits and rewards of its victory.

[53] Vopicka, *Secrets of the Balkans*, p. 86.

## Greece

The Greek decision to enter the First World War was the most difficult and convoluted of any country in southeastern Europe. Strong domestic political elements both favored and opposed intervention. At the same time, the warring alliance systems exerted considerable influence within the country. The resulting pressures on the Greek political establishment delayed Greek entry into the war until 1917.

Unlike Bulgaria and Serbia, Greece lacked social extremes arising from property, title, or wealth. Unlike Bulgaria and Romania, Greece had not enjoyed the patronage of a great power before the war. The maritime aspect of the Greek economy and the large Greek diaspora did, however, establish strong connections to western Europe and beyond. These circumstances complicated the political situation at the beginning of the war.

Since the end of Ottoman rule in 1829, Athens had consistently pursued a nationalist agenda of acquiring those areas where Greek populations resided under foreign control. The unification of such areas with Greece constituted the *megale idea*: the unification of all Greeks in one state. To realize this "great idea," Greek foreign policy focused on the increasingly decrepit Ottoman Empire. Concerned by the possible consequences of reform under the Young Turk regime, the Greek government turned to Bulgaria. In March 1911, the Sofia government received a proposal for mutual action against the Ottomans.[54] This overture eventually led to the inclusion of Greece in the loose Balkan Alliance of 1912. The Greeks achieved considerable military success against the Ottomans in the First Balkan War of 1912–13, and then against their erstwhile Bulgarian allies in the Second Balkan War of 1913.

Greek territory increased by 70 percent and the Greek population by two million after the Balkan Wars. Athens also concluded an alliance with Belgrade on 1 June 1913 on the eve of the Second Balkan War.[55] These gains, however, brought with them Ottoman and Bulgarian enemies determined on redress. Still, Greek national aspirations were not yet exhausted. Besides Cyprus, then under British control, and the Dodecanese under Italian control, these national goals included areas of Albania and Bulgaria, but mainly parts of the Ottoman Empire.

At the outbreak of First World War, many Greeks, notably the anglophile Prime Minister Eleutherios Venizelos, favored the *entente*.

---

[54] RD, ser. 3, vol. 1, part 2, no. 587.
[55] Édouard Driault and Michel Lhéritier, *Histoire diplomatique de la Grèce de 1821 a nos jours,* vol. 5: *La Grèce et la Grande Guerre De la Révolution turque au Traité de Lausanne (1908–1923)* (Paris, 1926), pp. 115–20.

Venizelos, a native of Crete and a graduate of Athens University, was the leader of the Liberal Party and the dominant Greek political personality at the beginning of the twentieth century. He came to power in 1910 after a 1909 military coup cleared away the political debris of the previous inept government.[56] After guiding Greece to success in the Balkan Wars, Venizelos saw the outbreak of the European war as an opportunity to utilize the power of the *entente* to realize the *megale idea*. As early as 2 August 1914, he made his sympathies clear, stating, "If the European situation results in a general conflict, *whatever happens* Greece will not be found on the side *opposed* to the Entente."[57] This prediction, however, would not be realized for almost three years.

At the same time, the prime minister indicated to the Serbs that Greece would not uphold the terms of the alliance with Serbia. He informed Belgrade: "The Royal [Greek] government considers that it fulfills all its responsibilities of friendship and alliance by its decision to maintain, in regard to Serbia, a very benevolent neutrality, and to be prepared to repel any aggression undertaken by Bulgaria against Serbia."[58] Together with the Romanians, the Greeks warned the Bulgarians against any attempt to overturn the Treaty of Bucharest.[59] Like the Romanians, the Greeks declined to uphold their alliance commitments. They saw little to gain from a war against Austria-Hungary.

As the fighting spread, the Venizelos government stayed neutral. Greece remained exhausted from the Balkan Wars. Additionally, Greece was deeply committed in southern Albania (northern Epirus). There, Greek irregulars fought Albanians in a savage war similar to that being fought simultaneously in northern Albania between Albanian and Serbian forces.[60]

Serious obstacles to Venizelos's sympathies for the *entente* existed within Greece. King Constantine, who was of Danish origin and who had received a German education, sympathized with his brother-in-law, the German kaiser. So did many senior army officers, including the German-educated chief of staff, General Ioannis Metaxas.[61] Kaiser Wilhelm II's personal intercession in the negotiations for the Treaty of Bucharest in

---

[56] On the 1909 military coup, see S. Victor Papacosma, *The Military in Greek Politics: The 1909 Coup d'Etat* (Kent, Ohio, 1977).

[57] DDF, 3rd ser., vol. 11, no. 577. Emphasis in original.

[58] Driault and Lhéritier, *Histoire diplomatique de la Grèce*, vol. 5, p. 162.

[59] ÖUA, vol. 8, nos. 11017, 11018.

[60] See N. Petsalis-Diomidis, *Greece at the Paris Peace Conference 1919* (Thessaloniki, 1978), pp. 25–8.

[61] General Metaxas, a member of the family famous for its brandy, would exercise dictatorial power in Greece from 1936 until his death in January 1941.

1913 had been instrumental in securing the Thracian port of Kavala for Greece.[62] King Constantine enjoyed some prestige because he had commanded the victorious Greek Army during the Balkan Wars while General Metaxas had overseen the staff work.

Initially, the Germans did make some attempt to persuade Greece to join the Central Powers, promising territory in Albania and Serbia in exchange for intervention.[63] There was little inclination in Greece to pursue this course of action, however, because Greece's political leaders' aims focused on the Ottoman Empire. The dominance of the British Navy in the eastern Mediterranean precluded an overtly hostile attitude toward the *entente*. Thus, Constantine and many general staff officers favored a neutral position in the war.

The Ottoman Empire's entry into the war on the side of the Central Powers in November 1914 both simplified and complicated the Greek position. On the one hand, nationalist goals within the Ottoman Empire now appeared attainable on the side of the *entente*. On the other hand, Greek intervention on the side of the *entente* risked attacks from Bulgaria, still precariously neutral, and from the Ottomans themselves. At the same time, the British incurred some bad feeling when upon the Ottoman entry into the war, they annexed Cyprus, formally under Ottoman rule but under British occupation since 1878. Cyprus had been for some time a part of the Greek irredenta, and many Greeks still sought its inclusion in their nation.

The Anglo-French attack on the Dardanelles beginning in February 1915 brought the fighting close to Greek territory and increased Athens's importance for the *entente*. In a note of 23 January 1915, British Foreign Minister Sir Edward Grey offered Venizelos extensive territories in Asia Minor in return for Greek help for Serbia and for the pending Dardanelles campaign.[64] This note set in motion a course of events that would ultimately culminate in the Anatolian disaster of 1922.[65] King Constantine and the General Staff opposed sending a Greek army to Serbia and adopting a policy of annexing part of Asia Minor. In two memoranda written at the end of January 1915, General Metaxas warned that any intervention in Asia Minor was beyond the resources of the Greek

[62] E. C. Helmreich, *The Diplomacy of the Balkan Wars 1912–1913* (New York, 1969), pp. 391–2; A. A. Pallis, *Greece's Anatolian Venture – and After* (London, 1937), pp. 180–1. See also n. 14.

[63] Petsalis-Diomidis, *Greece at the Paris Peace Conference*, p. 40.

[64] Driault and Lhèritier, *Histoire diplomatique de la Grèce*, vol. 5, p. 176.

[65] Pallis, *Greece's Anatolian Venture*, p. 19.

Army.[66] With its army engaged in Asia Minor, Greece would be vulnerable to a Bulgarian attack. Russian interests in annexing Constantinople and its environs further complicated the question of Athens's entry into the war. Russian Foreign Minister Sergei Sazonov warned on 5 March 1915: "Because of political and religious reasons the possibility of the Greek flag at Constantinople produces in Russia a sharp impression of disquiet and irritation."[67] Under these circumstances, the realization of the British offer was problematic.

At the same time, with the Dardanelles campaign ongoing, Bulgaria's proximity to the Ottoman capital at Constantinople made it strategically more useful to *entente* planners than was Greece. Sofia received considerable attention from London and Paris during this time. With the *entente* in disarray regarding its policy toward Athens, the possibility of Greek intervention in the Dardanelles campaign passed. Consequently, Venizelos resigned on 6 March 1915.

The new government, appointed by the king, brought a hardening of the division in Greek politics, the so-called national schism (*ethnikos dikhasmos*).[68] Therein, those Greeks, led by Venizelos, who favored intervention in the war on the side of the *entente* opposed those, led by King Constantine, who advocated neutrality. Venizelos's victory in the parliamentary elections of June 1915 and his subsequent return to power as prime minister that August only intensified the division.

Italy's entry into the war on the side of the *entente* in May 1915 further complicated the issue of Greek intervention. The Italians sought some of the same territories in Asia Minor that nationalist Greeks considered part of their irredenta. Moreover, Greek claims to southern Albania conflicted with Italian designs to make all of Albania a protectorate.[69] Because of these issues, the Italians were not strong advocates of Greek intervention.

Soon after Venizelos resumed office, the Bulgarian Army mobilized against Serbia on 24 September 1915. In response, the Greek prime minister agreed on 3 October 1915 to the landing of *entente* troops at Salonika (Thessaloniki), on the condition that they leave Greek sovereignty intact and not occupy Macedonia only to turn it over to Bulgaria.[70] Venizelos

[66] Ibid., pp. 22–5.
[67] Driault and Lhèritier, *Histoire diplomatique de la Grèce*, vol. 5, p. 181.
[68] See Richard Clogg, *A Short History of Modern Greece* (Cambridge, 1986), p. 107.
[69] On the Greek-Italian discord over Asia Minor and Albania, see Petsalis-Diomidis, *Greece at the Paris Peace Conference*, pp. 47–50.
[70] E. Adamov, ed., *Die Europäischen Mächte und Griechenland während des Weltkrieges* (Dresden, 1932), nos. 20, 21. On the genesis of the *entente* landings in Salonika, see Alan Palmer, *The Gardeners of Salonika* (New York, 1965), pp. 19–36.

feared that London and Paris might still consider Sofia a more useful ally than Athens. British and French troops began to disembark at Salonika on 5 October in an effort to assist the endangered Serbs. That same day, Venizelos again resigned because King Constantine held him responsible for the *entente*'s occupation of northern Greece. Elections held that December, boycotted by Venizelos and his followers, returned a neutralist-royalist government to power. By this time, Serbia's defeat had brought Bulgarian and German troops to Greece's northern frontier and confined the British and French to the vicinity of Salonika.

The continuing *entente* presence at Salonika and its January 1916 occupation of Corfu to secure an evacuation base for the defeated Serbian Army trekking across Albania further aggravated relations with Greece. The allies' arrogant behavior caused a backlash in popular opinion, and thus worked against Venizelos's intentions.[71]

In turn, the Greek government antagonized the *entente* by refusing passage across its territory by the Serbian troops retreating from the Central Powers' invasion of their country. The Athens government further irritated London and Paris when it ordered the garrison of the important border defenses at Fort Duppel on the Struma River north of Salonika to surrender to Bulgarian troops on 26 May 1916. Control of the fort opened up much of northern Greece to the Central Powers. That summer, the Bulgarians utilized this advantage to occupy much of southern and eastern Macedonia, including Kavala, Drama, and Seres. The situation became extremely muddled as both warring alliances violated Greek neutrality.

Under these circumstances, the interventionist party decided to act. On 30 August 1916 a cabal of pro-*entente* Greek officers, with the knowledge and encouragement of Venizelos, launched a coup in Salonika.[72] Ottoman officers had carried out the coup against their government, which established the Young Turk regime in Constantinople and precipitated many of these events in the Balkans, in that same city only eight years earlier. After touring the Aegean Islands to gather support, Venizelos joined the officers in Salonika on 9 October. There he established a separate Greek

---

[71] Driault and Lhèritier, *Histoire diplomatique de la Grèce*, vol. 5, pp. 240–1. Serb officers sitting at a banquet with French officers in Salonika toasting, "Salonika as the capital of Serbia, as the great Serbian port on the Aegean," produced an especially poor impression. Obviously, alcohol consumption was a factor in this indiscretion.

[72] The actual timing of the coup appears to have taken Venizelos by surprise. See Thanos Veremis, *The Military in Greek Politics From Independence to Democracy* (Montreal, 1997), pp. 53–7.

government and army. The national schism had produced a legitimate Greek government in Athens under King Constantine, which favored a neutral course, and an alternative Greek government in Salonika led by Venizelos, which advocated intervention in the war on the side of the *entente*.

Confident of the Salonika regime's support, British and French troops landed in Athens in December 1916 to coerce the legitimist government into capitulation. These landings met strong opposition from loyal Greek army units as well as armed civilians. After taking heavy casualties, the *entente* troops had to withdraw. A French report conceded the strength of the legitimist resistance: "The balance sheet for the allies and especially for France is most humiliating."[73]

Having failed at armed intervention, Britain and France imposed a naval blockade around legitimist Greece, which by this time consisted mainly of the Peloponnesus and southern Thessaly. At the same time, they slowly increased their physical occupation of Greece. With Russia slipping into civil and military disarray, the Balkan front in stalemate, and the Americans still months away from appearing in force, the *entente* attempted to strengthen its position in southeastern Europe. Finally, on 10 June 1917, the French demanded the abdication of King Constantine within twenty-four hours and prepared to occupy Athens.[74] Confronted with overwhelming force, the king complied with the ultimatum. In his announcement of departure on 12 June, Constantine warned his followers against any further resistance. "The slightest action, even though undertaken for the best of purposes, would now lead to great catastrophe."[75] His second son Alexander succeeded him, and immediately acquiesced in the formation of a united government restored in Athens under Venizelos. Greece duly declared war on the Central Powers on 30 June 1917, the final European state to enter the First World War.

Venizelos had decided in the first days of August 1914 to favor the *entente*. King Constantine and elements in the General Staff, however, supported a neutral stance as the best course. The resulting schism in Greek policy lasted for three years. During that time, armies from both belligerent sides intruded on Greek territory. Moreover, the Greek state physically

---

[73] AFGG, vol. 7, book 2, annex 2, no. 1126.

[74] Adamov, *Die Europäischen Mächte und Griechenland*, nos. 378, 379, 380.

[75] Ibid., no. 386. On the abdication of King Constantine, see George B. Leontaritis, *Greece and the First World War: From Neutrality to Intervention, 1917–1918* (Boulder, 1990) pp. 3–43.

divided, with one government in Athens and another in Salonika. Finally, a combination of nationalist enthusiasm and direct *entente* intervention forced Greece into the First World War. After the end of the war in 1918, pursuit of the *megale idea* led Greek troops deep into Anatolia. There they would suffer catastrophic defeats in 1921 and 1922 that finally ended hopes for realizing that goal.


## Conclusions

A comprehensive examination of the First World War and southeastern Europe must consider expanded physical and chronological parameters. Especially important in this regard was the role of Bulgaria in the events from March 1912 to October 1915, but the actions of Romania and Greece were also significant. In this extended arena, the direct preconditions for the First World War in Southeastern Europe and indeed in all Europe began with the signing of the March 1912 treaty between Bulgaria and Serbia under Russian aegis. This arrangement provided for mutual assistance against the Habsburg as well as Ottoman empires. The treaty emphasized Belgrade's anti-Austrian orientation and any reaction to this orientation on the part of Austria-Hungary. The fighting erupted in October 1912, when the Balkan alliance confronted the Porte. Less than two years later, the conflict spread over much of the rest of Europe.

The decisions to intervene in the First World War in Bulgaria, Romania, and Greece were based on the same considerations that had led these countries to participate in the Balkan Wars. All sought to realize their national aspirations. The victories of the First Balkan War and the catastrophic defeat of the Second Balkan War had added urgency to Bulgaria's acquisition of Macedonia, but precluded an immediate entry into the war. In the summer of 1914, Belgrade held most of Macedonia. And Serbia was firmly ensconced, by force of circumstances, on the side of the *entente*. This meant that Bulgaria, despite a tradition of russophilia, was likely to join the Central Powers unless Britain, France, and Russia could pressure the Serbs to surrender Macedonia. The Central Powers could guarantee Bulgaria immediate possession of all of Macedonia, and the *entente* could not. This brought Bulgaria into the war on the side of the Central Powers in October 1915.

For Romania, participation in the war was more problematic. Its national aspirations to acquire Austro-Hungarian Bukovina and Transylvania as well as Russian Bessarabia were divided between the warring powers. This permitted the government in Bucharest a certain freedom of negotiation, but it also ensured the direct enmity of whichever side the Romanian government decided to act against. Acquisition of the large Romanian-populated areas of Austria-Hungary proved more attractive than the annexation of a backward corner of the Russian Empire. When the Romanians finally acceded to *entente* pressures and promises, however, their opportunity for success had largely passed.

For Greece, the question was not which side to join, but whether to intervene in the war on the side of the *entente*. Vulnerability to the British Navy precluded direct Greek participation on the side of the Central Powers. The issue of intervention produced a rift in Greek politics, which resulted in a division of the country into a prointerventionist north governed from Salonika and a proneutral south centered on Athens. The political division between pro-*entente* interventionists and pro–Central Powers neutralists facilitated the intrusion of both warring alliances onto Greek soil. The northern part of the country as well as the capital became battlefields. This situation continued for almost a year, until the Anglo-French ultimatum forced King Constantine to leave the country. Under these circumstances, the Greeks were fortunate to avoid overt civil war.

Neutrality offered tangible benefits for each of these three countries. Their economies, damaged during the Balkan Wars, grew from the sale of foodstuffs and raw materials to the warring sides. Bulgaria might well have obtained at least some of Macedonia at the end of the war by simply remaining neutral. Not many political leaders in these countries seemed to recognize the value of neutrality. The Bulgarian peasant leader Stamboliski, the Romanian Conservative politician Marghiloman, and the Greek King Constantine were among the relatively few opponents of intervention in their countries. None of them, however, was able to prevail against the combination of nationalist expectations and great power demands for intervention.

The decisions to go to war in Bulgaria, Romania, and Greece were difficult and prolonged. Domestic differences over which side to join complicated the decisions in Bulgaria and Romania. Also, the governments in both of these countries wanted, understandably, to determine the likely victor before committing themselves. In Greece, the great powers, increasingly desperate to break the war's military stalemate, played an important role in forcing decisions to intervene by exerting great pressure in Sofia, Bucharest, and especially Athens. In no case, however, did the great powers force the leading politicians – Radoslavov, Brătianu, and Venizelos – to act against their inclinations. Great power pressure was significant only in determining the timing of the intervention in Bulgaria and Romania.

In Greece, this pressure was much more overt, and resulted in the suppression of those elements opposed to intervention.

The political and military leaders of Bulgaria, Romania, and Greece decided to intervene in the First World War because they assumed that victory would largely complete the process of national unification for their countries, and that as a result of this, national unification, political power, and economic development would ensue. Other elites in these countries had little impact on the foreign policy and military decision-making process. The nationalist expectations proved to be illusory. Entry into the First World War caused great hardship in both Bulgaria and Romania. Scarcely recovered from the material and human losses of the Balkan Wars, the Bulgarians performed valuable service to the Central Powers by containing *entente* forces north of Salonika. This enabled the Bulgarians to control most of Macedonia for the duration of the fighting. By war's end the Bulgarian forces were exhausted and the defeat again deprived them of Macedonia. Subsequently, in 1941, the Bulgarians occupied Macedonia once more, only to lose it again at the end of the war.

Romanian intervention in the First World War brought defeat and foreign occupation. Even though, in a remarkable turn of events, the Romanians realized their goals of unification with Transylvania and Bessarabia after the end of the war, this triumph brought them little prosperity or stability. Little over twenty years after the realization of a Greater Romania, the country again underwent the disasters of military defeat and foreign occupation, losing in the process Bessarabia, northern Bukovina, and southern Dobrodzha.

Greece's pursuit of a nationalist agenda gained only Bulgaria's Aegean seaboard in western Thrace at the end of the First World War. Four years later, this same impulse resulted in catastrophic military defeat in Asia Minor and in the flight of the Greek population there, forever ending the realization of the *megale idea*.

Whether nationalist expectations in the First World War were disappointed (as in the case of Bulgaria), fulfilled (as with Romania), or deferred (as for Greece), all three failed to develop politically and economically in the war's aftermath. The pursuit of nationalist agendas in southeastern Europe in the twentieth century succeeded only in causing destruction and disappointment. The pursuit of those agendas made further conflict in this region likely.

# 13

## The United States

### John Milton Cooper, Jr.

In April 1917, the United States entered World War I on the side of the Allies. Ever since then, people have been arguing about why this happened and what to make of it. Most of the combatants who have entered the fray have been Americans. These verbal warriors have included not only historians, but also journalists and other writers and even, at times, politicians. Their conflict grew most intense, curiously, not immediately following the war nor in the first decade afterward. Rather, it was in the 1930s, as Americans confronted the breakdown of international order and the approach of what became World War II, that intervention in World War I retrospectively became a hot political and intellectual issue. Since that time, the argument has largely subsided and has usually involved only a coterie of historians. During all of these decades, few people on the other side of the Atlantic have taken much interest in the subject, with a few interesting and significant exceptions from time to time among certain Britons and more recently among the Germans.[1]

Remarkably, for an argument that lasted so long and once involved so much passion, this one took place within a constricted conceptual framework. That framework really consisted of two propositions. One was that the only point worthy of contention was approval or condemnation of intervention. Was it a good thing or a bad thing? Did it spring from noble

---

[1] For examples of German interest in American intervention, see Klaus Schwabe, *Woodrow Wilson, Revolutionary Diplomacy, and Peacemaking, 1918–1919: Missionary Diplomacy and the Realities of Power* (Chapel Hill, N.C., 1985), and Reinhard Doerries, *Imperial Challenge: Ambassador Count Bernstorff and German-American Relations, 1908–1917* (Chapel Hill, N.C., 1989). Both of these books were published in the United States as supplementary volumes to *The Papers of Woodrow Wilson*, edited by Arthur S. Link.

or sordid motives? Did it bode well or ill for the future of the United States and the world? As in any effort to grapple with a historical event that remained fraught with later contemporary relevance, asking such questions was unavoidable. Many of the interpretations advanced in attempts to answer those questions were interesting and well taken, although they were often highly colored with emotion and value judgments.[2]

The other proposition that defined the argument about this event was denigration of the role of individual actors. Passionate partisans on both sides of the debate over the wisdom and morality of intervention tended to believe as a matter of course that great forces of history, diplomacy, geopolitics, economics, and culture largely shaped what happened. With rare exceptions, these interpreters viewed individual decision makers as witting or unwitting, honest or devious agents of those great forces. It would be pejorative to call the argument over American entry into World War I a tempest in a teapot, but it has been a storm that raged within the bounds of a virtual consensus.

My main interpretative task in viewing the event at the beginning of a new millennium is two-fold. First, I think it is worthwhile to look again over some of the terrain of previous argument as it has involved attribution of larger influences on the historical actors. Second, and more important, I believe it is imperative to examine the validity of this conceptual framework.

## Historical Background and Interpretations

Viewed from an extended historical perspective, American intervention in World War I might not seem especially noteworthy. On the contrary, it might appear anomalous if the United States *not* been drawn into that conflict. During the preceding four centuries, inhabitants of the transatlantic settlements in North America and the indigenous peoples surrounding them had found themselves drawn into all the general European wars that had erupted in nearly every generation, broken only by the "long peace" after 1815. American extensions of those conflicts had even acquired names of their own, such as the "War of Jenkins' Ear" (War of

---

[2] For two excellent essays on the historiography of American intervention, see Richard W. Leopold, "The Problem of American Intervention, 1917: An Historical Retrospect," *World Politics* 2 (April 1950): 405–25; and Daniel W. Smith, "National Interest and American Intervention, 1917: An Historiographical Appraisal," *Journal of American History* 52 (June 1965): 5–24.

Austrian Succession) and the "French and Indian War" (Seven Years' War). The American Revolution had succeeded in large measure because the Americans were able to entice France and Spain into resuming their recent strife against Britain. The wars of the French Revolution had involved the new United States in limited, undeclared maritime conflict with France, and the Napoleonic Wars had drawn the nation into a full-fledged, declared war against Britain, the War of 1812. With such a long line of historical precedents, it is tempting to conclude that strong odds favored the United States becoming a participant also in this first general European war of the twentieth century.

As in earlier conflicts, the main belligerents reflexively involved Americans by using their naval forces to wage economic warfare against each other. Once more, they sought to blockade their adversaries' overseas trade by stopping and sometimes sinking American vessels bound for enemy ports and by seizing cargoes and confiscating property suspected of having hostile destinations. In World War I, as earlier, the United States found itself caught in the classic dilemma of neutral nations during a large-scale war. Such nations must either submit to the exactions of the belligerents, thereby sacrificing interest and honor in order to stay at peace, or they must stand up for interest and honor by risking war with one side or the other. This situation offered an eerie repetition of what had happened just over a century earlier, and the resemblance was not lost on Americans at the time. In the fall of 1914, President Woodrow Wilson, who was a historian, told his confidant, Colonel Edward M. House, "Madison [James Madison, president during the War of 1812] and I are the only two Princeton men that have become President. The circumstances of the war 1812 and now run parallel. I sincerely hope they will not go further."[3]

But if historical precedents might seem to favor American entry into this war, those precedents did not require that the Allies would benefit from such intervention. The 1812 parallel that President Wilson noted and feared involved being drawn into war with Britain, one of the principal Allies. Thanks to British control of the seas, American contacts

---

[3] Entry, 30 September 1914, Diary of Edward M. House, in Arthur S. Link, ed., *The Papers of Woodrow Wilson*, 69 vols. (Princeton, N.J., 1979), vol. 31, p. 109. The German military attache in Washington and future chancellor, Franz von Papen, had hatched various schemes to sabotage American munitions factories, for which he was expelled from the United States, and also to mount an invasion of Canada using cowboys and Irish-Americans. See Martin Kitchen, "Militarische Unternehmungen gegen Kanada im Ersten Weltkrieg," in *Militärgeschichtliche Mitteilungen* (1970): 27–36.

and relations with the belligerents during the first six months of the war were strictly with the Allies, mainly with Britain. Nor were those contacts entirely salutary. The Allied blockade of the Central Powers and neighboring neutral nations wrought hardship in sensitive export sectors of the American economy, particularly cotton. Inasmuch as Wilson's was a Democratic administration whose strongest political base lay in the South, anti-British political pressure could be particularly potent. Conversely, the largest, wealthiest, and best-organized ethnic group in the country had ties to the principal belligerent of the Central Powers, Germany. Hardworking, disciplined, often highly educated, German-Americans attracted both admiration and envy as what a later generation would call a "model minority," and such cultural institutions as universities and symphony orchestras were German imports. In addition, many members of another potent though not so well-organized ethnic group, Irish-Americans, held an ancient grudge against Britain, an attitude that received powerful reinforcement with the suppression of the Easter Rising in 1916.[4]

Why then, it might be asked, with such powerful forces of precedent, economics, and culture working against Britain and the Allies, did the United States go to war on their side? The answer that was usually given in the long-running argument over intervention was that the forces on the other side were more powerful still. The century of peace between America and Britain after the War of 1812 had slowly spawned a diplomatic rapprochement based mainly upon British appeasement of American aggrandizement in the Western Hemisphere and acceptance of rising American naval power and expansion in Asia. Correspondingly, since the 1890s a tiny band of geopolitically savvy Americans, which included Alfred Thayer Mahan, Theodore Roosevelt, and Henry Cabot Lodge, had recognized that the two countries held a common interest in maintaining the international balance of power and that the United States profited from British naval supremacy, especially in the Atlantic. For such strategic-minded Americans, therefore, an Allied defeat and a weakening of British

---

[4] German influence had a specific vehicle to make itself felt. From early in the war, the German-American Alliance, a national federation of grassroots groups previously financed by the brewing interests to fight against prohibition, fell under the control of the German embassy and became a lobby to promote pro-German policies, especially an embargo on sales of arms and munitions to the Allies. On this effort, see Clifton J. Child, "German-American Attempts to Prevent the Exportation of Munitions of War, 1914–1915," *Mississippi Valley Historical Review* 25 (December 1938): 351–68, and Arthur S. Link, *Wilson: The Struggle for Neutrality* (Princeton, N.J., 1960), pp. 161–6. On Irish-Americans, see William M. Leary, Jr., "Woodrow Wilson, Irish Americans, and the Election of 1916," *Journal of American History* 54 (June 1967): 57–72.

seapower would constitute a security threat to the United States. Such considerations, the influential political commentator Walter Lippmann once argued, were really what impelled the United States to intervene as it did in 1917.[5]

Culture reinforced strategy, so this argument went. The passage of time since the American Revolution and War of 1812 had gradually eroded traditional Anglophobia. In its place, sentimental Anglophilia slowly burgeoned, based upon the common language and shared literary heritage, which dominated American education, despite German influences, and held strong attractions for social and cultural elites, most of whom traced their ancestry back to England, Scotland, and Wales. Moreover, as American wealth proliferated with the industrial revolution, children of transatlantic plutocrats occasionally intermarried with the British aristocracy. The First Lord of the Admiralty in 1914, Winston Churchill, had an American mother, while his cousin, the Duke of Marlborough, had been married to the heiress Consuelo Vanderbilt. On an immediate and popular level, the German "rape of Belgium" in 1914, allegedly exaggerated by clever British propaganda, made the Allies and especially the English-speaking countries stand in American eyes as defenders of freedom and civilization against autocracy and barbarism.

Finally, if such ties of geopolitics and culture were not enough, economics exerted an inexorable pull. Both Britain's control of the seas and its dependence on overseas trade quickly turned the United States, which had the largest industrial and agricultural economy in the world, into the Allies' supply house, especially for munitions and foodstuffs. The vast, urgent demand for American products necessitated borrowing on a huge scale by the British on behalf of themselves and the Allies, mainly through J. P. Morgan and Company. That borrowing soon turned the United States into the Allies' banker as well. By 1917, the British had exhausted their sources of collateral and faced a credit crisis that could have crimped or possibly even cut their overseas lifeline of supplies. Such fears, some have argued, were what really prompted the United States to intervene in 1917. It was to save the Allies from financial collapse or, as some left-wing critics jeered, "to save the Morgan loan."[6]

---

[5] For Lippmann's argument, see *U.S. Foreign Policy: Shield of the Republic* (Boston, 1943), pp. 33–9.

[6] On the financial influences, see John Milton Cooper, Jr., "The Command of Gold Reversed: American Loans to Britain, 1915–1917," *Pacific Historical Review* 45 (May 1976): 209–30.

Given such relentless stress on great forces, it is easy to see why individual actors would get short shrift in the argument over intervention. By and large, the principal American decision makers in these events have come to be depicted as pawns in a grand historical chess game. The main contention about their roles has consisted of whether they knew what they were doing and whether they were open and honest about their thought and motives. In the 1930s, when "revisionists" deplored intervention as wrong, arguing among themselves about whether it was folly or crime, Wilson seemed to be either deluded or dishonest in his two-and-a-half-year maintenance of neutrality and in his subsequent justification of intervention. In their view, this son of an English-born mother who was admittedly a cultural Anglophile and an admirer of British parliamentarism could never have been anything but pro-Allied at heart. Furthermore, as the historical detectives of that decade delighted in discovering, his closest advisors, Colonel House and Secretary of State Robert Lansing, were covertly pro-Allied, while his ambassador in London, Walter Hines Page, wrote weekly screeds admonishing the president to side with Britain and the Allies. To these interpreters, the pursuit of neutrality between 1914 and 1917 was either a charade to hoodwink a war-wary public or a holding action until the Allies' impending financial collapse required dropping the mask of nonbelligerence.

If Wilson looked more like a knave to those "revisionists," he looked like a fool to their "realist" successors. To critics such as Lippmann and later George F. Kennan, the fault in American policy toward the war lay in not getting in on the Allied side sooner. To them, it was Wilson's belligerent critics such as Roosevelt and Lodge who correctly recognized America's strategic interest in an Allied victory and wanted to do whatever they could to assure that outcome to the war. To them, such advisors as House and Lansing appeared to be benevolent conspirators bent on saving Wilson from the consequences of his ignorance of what was really at stake and his quasipacifist meddling in the war. Even when the president did the right thing by their lights, they saw him as acting perilously late, when the Allies were teetering on the brink of disaster, and having the wrong reasons and justifications. Rather than acknowledge the nation's vital interest in an Allied victory and form a strategic alliance, Wilson foolishly beclouded the issue with idealistic rhetoric about democracy, a nonpunitive peace, and international reforms to prevent future wars.[7]

[7] For Kennan's version of this interpretation, see *American Diplomacy, 1900–1950* (New York, Mentor edition, 1952), pp. 50–65.

### Great Forces at Work?

That constitutes the major terrain of more than eight decades of argument over why America went to war on the Allied side in 1917. Small wonder that individuals do not seem to count for much. This would seem to be a clear-cut case of the great forces working their will in spite of the people who happened to be on the scene at the time. The most important question to ask is whether such a view of the roles played by these individuals is correct. But before that question can be addressed, questions have to be raised about whether the great forces ascribed really operated in the ways that most interpreters have seen them doing. On examination, each of those forces appears to have at best problematical links with what actually happened. The historical precedents prove to be the weakest of all. Besides apparently favoring an American stance against rather than alongside the Allies, those precedents were dated and tenuous. A lot had happened in the century since the Napoleonic wars, on both sides of the Atlantic. The intervening industrial revolution had likewise revolutionized warfare, as the slaughter on the Western Front quickly showed. Those same processes and other events had transformed the United States from a small, struggling, newly independent federation of states into a large, populous centralized nation and an economic giant. Furthermore, important though it might be in certain places, foreign trade counted for comparatively little in this new twentieth-century economy, while maritime shipping had withered into a minor industry. Blockades and economic warfare by European powers, therefore, touched far fewer Americans in their livelihoods and pocketbooks than they had done a century earlier.

Another historical influence, if not precedent, similarly militated against American involvement in World War I. This was the tradition of diplomatic isolation, or noninvolvement in power politics, outside the Western Hemisphere. First laid down in George Washington's warning against "permanent alliances" and Thomas Jefferson's ban on "entangling alliances," this isolationist policy had sprung from the determination of the nation's founders to extricate themselves from the imbroglios that could involve the United States in foreign wars. Thanks in part to a change in focus of European power politics and the absence of general wars after 1815, this policy had succeeded and hardened into largely unchallenged dogma. Even men such as Roosevelt and Lodge, who wanted to abandon isolation and plunge the United States into the great power game, did not directly challenge this tradition. Threats of involvement in World War I would breathe new life into isolationist attitudes as a buttress to strong antiinterventionist sentiment.[8]

The problem with the geopolitical forces is that they were neither widely nor urgently recognized enough to influence anyone's views. Few people outside Roosevelt's immediate circle of friends and associates subscribed to such strategic views, and Wilson's pro-Allied advisors appear to have given little weight to the balance of power. Even Roosevelt himself based his passionate partisanship of the Allies on moral rather than strategic grounds. He subscribed to a more sophisticated version of the popular revulsion over Belgium, and he based his fervent interventionism, which he never explicitly advocated in public, on yearning to have his countrymen share in what he saw as the uplifting, ennobling experience of the war. Furthermore, in order for the strategic argument for joining the Allies to have an impact, people had to believe that the Allies might lose. Thanks to British secrecy and optimistic propaganda, no one in America at the beginning of 1917 had any inkling of what dire straits they were in, not Roosevelt and his friends and not Lippmann, who later made so much of this argument.

Culture does not help explain actions, either. Anglophilia among elites was diffuse and abstract and gave rise to scant interventionist sentiment. As well as public opinion can be gauged, popular anti-German sentiment over Belgium was neither so widespread nor so strongly felt as later interpreters imagined. According to a nationwide poll of newspaper editors conducted in the fall of 1914 by the magazine *Literary Digest*, about half declared themselves impartial between the belligerent camps; broken down regionally, that figure rose to three-quarters in the Midwest and West. Nor should pro-Allied attitudes be confused with interventionist sentiment. In April 1915, the British ambassador in Washington told the foreign secretary, "It is, I think, useless and misleading to depend on these people for help or practical sympathy...." Later, in 1916, even detached pro-Allied attitudes waned in reaction to such high-handed British practices as stopping and opening the mails and blacklisting American businesses and, even more, out of revulsion toward British brutality in Ireland. For the British and, by extension, the Allies, Ireland besmirched

---

[8] Unaccountably, neither early isolationist policies nor twentieth-century isolationism have received the attention that they deserve. By far the best treatment of the early policies is Felix Gilbert, *To the Farewell Address: Ideas of Early American Foreign Policy* (Princeton, N.J., 1961), and, at the risk of immodesty, for the twentieth-century incarnation in this context I recommend John Milton Cooper, Jr., *The Vanity of Power: American Isolationism and the First World War, 1914–1917* (Westport, Conn., 1969).

their moral standing in American eyes the way Belgium had done earlier for the Germans. When the United States finally did enter the war in 1917, as seen below, the newspapers' "plague-o'-both-your-houses" dismissals of the belligerents were more frequent than at any time since the outbreak of the war.[9]

Of all the great forces, economics would seem to have the clearest connection with intervention, but this also evaporates under scrutiny. British secrecy likewise effectively masked knowledge of their financial plight, not only in the United States but also among their adversaries. After the war, the Treasury's brilliant young expert on war finance, John Maynard Keynes, was amazed to discover that his German opposite numbers had had no inkling of how bad off the British had been. The only influential person who seems to have grasped the Allies' precarious financial situation was President Wilson, and he used his insight not to aid them but to threaten them as part of his peace offensive at the end of 1916. Moreover, even if the Allies' desperate fix had become widely known, their financial agents on Wall Street lacked political influence with Wilson and his Democratic Party, whom they had hotly opposed in the 1916 election. Nor would an Allied financial collapse have necessarily done much economic damage to the United States. All of the loans before 1917 were secured, and the Allied war orders were competing with rising domestic demand to superheat a booming economy.[10]

In the last analysis, the machinations of great forces do a far better job of explaining why the United States almost did *not* enter World War I rather than why it intervened on the side of the Allies. Here was a big, geographically removed nation with a largely self-sufficient economy and a polyglot population, many of whose most recently arrived members had ties and feelings on opposing sides in the war. A tradition of diplomatic isolation and a century of nearly unbroken uninvolvement in overseas affairs had made foreign policy only a minor and intermittent concern in the nation's politics. Furthermore, as nearly every observer at the time and every scholar since then has noted, the great majority of the population

---

[9] The poll of newspaper editors is in *Literary Digest* 49 (14 November 1914): 939–41, 974–8. Sir Cecil Spring Rice to Sir Edward Grey, 16 April 1915, in Stephen Gwynn, ed., *The Letters and Friendships of Sir Cecil Spring Rice* (Boston, 1929), vol. 2, p. 262.

[10] On Keynes's discovery, see Keynes, "Notes on Exchange Control," 24 September 1939, in Elizabeth Johnson, ed., *The Collected Works of John Maynard Keynes*, 30 vols. (London, 1971), vol. 16, p. 212; on Wilson's financial threats, see Arthur S. Link, *Wilson: Campaigns for Progressivism and Peace* (Princeton, N.J., 1965), pp. 200–6, and Cooper, "Command of Gold," pp. 221–6.

showed no appetite for intervention right up until April 1917, and a large minority opposed intervention under any circumstances.[11] Contrary to the usual line of argument, it is indeed noteworthy that the United States did intervene in World War I. Great forces do not suffice to carry out this major task of historical explanation.

## Individual Actors Abroad

What does suffice to explain American intervention is the element that has lain outside the conceptual framework of most interpretations: individual actors and their decisions. This is one instance where the old saw "It takes two to make a fight" does apply. The two decision-making coteries stood on opposite sides of the Atlantic, in Germany and in the United States. The German group created the situation to which the Americans had to respond. American intervention on the side of the Allies could not have happened if the Germans had not initiated submarine warfare. Without those attacks, there would have been no remotely plausible grounds for the United States to enter the war.

This German action revolved around two decisions. The first decision, which came at the beginning of 1915, was to commence submarine warfare against Allied and neutral shipping and to sink those ships without warning. The second decision, which came in January 1917, was to resume and expand submarine warfare. The first decision created the necessary preconditions for the second, which supplied the indispensable precipitant to American intervention.

Historians of Germany are much better qualified than I am to interpret these decisions, but I can make a few observations about them. First, in both decisions, the major factors do not seem to have been great historical forces or influences but, rather, mundane matters such as human credulity, stupidity, stubbornness, inattention, willfulness, and wishful thinking. Of the two, the first decision evidently stemmed almost entirely from those failings, with little to be said in its favor. The standard U-boat in 1915 was a small, vulnerable, slow-moving craft with a limited cruising range. Germany had a total of twenty-nine of these craft, of which no more than a third could be deployed at one time. It was the height of folly to imagine that such a weak weapon could inflict serious damage on Britain's maritime supply lines. The German threat in February 1915 to

---

[11] On public opinion in 1917, see Link, *Wilson: Campaigns for Progressivism and Peace*, pp. 415–19, and Cooper, *Vanity of Power*, pp. 190–2.

sink all shipping headed for Allied ports was a colossal bluff, and the imperial government appears to have decided for this action through a light-hearted desire to try out a new piece of military technology.[12]

But that was not the worst aspect of this decision. This act of folly bordered on being criminal because it did the only thing that might conceivably cause war with the United States. At the beginning of 1915, thanks to British dominance on the seas, Germany and the United States had virtually no contact with each other, other than diplomacy. Direct trade between them had ground to a halt, and British blockades were also stopping shipping through ports in neutral countries neighboring Germany, particularly Rotterdam. Furthermore, the British had cut all of Germany's undersea cables, thereby hampering contacts with the United States, which then had to go through neighboring neutral countries.[13] Historically, German-American relations had been correct though distant, and nothing had ever arisen to provoke significant friction or hostility. Now, for the sake of a fantasy, the Germans were reaching out to do the only thing that might bring the largest neutral and richest nation in the world into the war against them. A year later, in the spring of 1916, after a year-long diplomatic fencing match with the Americans over the submarine, cooler heads temporarily prevailed in Berlin and some restraints followed. Even those belated restrictions, however, owed little to fear of American intervention, which the Germans discounted militarily, but reflected only an elementary recognition that there were too few submarines yet operational to have a chance to cut the Allies' overseas lifeline of food and munitions.

The second submarine decision undid that restraint. This decision was both better and worse than the first. It was better in the sense that it appeared to embrace sound military calculations. German shipyards had been working overtime, and submarine advocates could now argue that there were enough of them to accomplish the goal of severing Allied supply lines. Actually, as Holger Herwig has shown, those advocates falsified their data, greatly exaggerating both the numbers and firepower that were deployable. Even so, the unlimited submarine campaign of 1917 did sink significant tonnage, and it might have knocked Britain out of the war except for countermeasures adopted by the British. Most authorities credit

---

[12] On the number of U-boats and their deployability, see Bernd Stegemann, *Die Deutsche Marinepolitik, 1916–1918* (Berlin, 1970), p. 26.

[13] Paul M. Kennedy, "Imperial Cable Communication and Strategy, 1870–1914," *English Historical Review* 86 (1971): 740–52.

the fortuitous Allied adoption of the convoy system, which provided some defense against the submarine, with foiling the Germans' plans. Others, most notably Mancur Olson, argue that more vigorous prosecution of industrial and agricultural policies by Lloyd George's new coalition government after December 1916 offset the effectivenss of the submarine campaign, together with more massive and efficiently delivered supplies from the United States.[14]

This decision was worse than the first, however, because there was nothing absentminded or lighthearted about it. On 9 January 1917, the only Imperial Council of the war met at Pless in Silesia to consider a renewed submarine campaign. The emperor had already privately sided with the submarine advocates, and after impatiently listening to opposing arguments, he ordered unrestricted submarine warfare to commence on 1 February. This time, there was no question that the German decision makers knew exactly what they were doing. They were under no illusions that this move would almost certainly bring the Americans into the war against them. Ten days after this meeting, the foreign minister dispatched the infamous Zimmermann Telegram, which offered Mexico an alliance with Germany and recovery of the "lost provinces" of Texas, New Mexico, and Arizona in the likely event of war with the United States. These decision makers were confident that they could win the war long before the militarily unprepared Americans could make any difference.[15]

What is shocking about their decision is that they ignored both diplomatic hints that an expanded but still limited submarine campaign might not provoke American intervention and some evidence of Britain's financial difficulties. Despite Keynes's later discovery of German ignorance of the Allies' economic situation, some policy makers in Berlin knew enough to discount its importance. In some memoranda they pooh-poohed any

---

[14] See Herwig, "Total Rhetoric, Limited War: Germany's U-Boat Campaign, 1917–1918," in Roger Chickering and Stig Foerster, eds., *Great War, Total War: Combat and Mobilization on the Western Front, 1914–1918* (New York, 2000), pp. 189–206, and Olson, *The Economics of Wartime Shortage: A History of British Food Supplies in the Napoleonic Wars and World Wars I and II* (Durham, N.C., 1963), pp. 82–97. Olson concludes, "Even if the submarine blockade had been much more tactically effective and had lasted much longer, Britain could have survived and the Allies could still have won the war." Ibid., p. 111. On the convoy, he argues that it deserves "only part" of the credit for foiling the submarine campaign, "and perhaps the smaller part." Ibid., p. 115. These assessments remain controversial.

[15] For a description of the meeting at Pless, which quotes extensively from eyewitness accounts, see Link, *Wilson: Campaigns for Progressivism and Peace*, pp. 243–7.

influence from financial factors as compared with the exciting prospect of sweeping military victory. One British historian, Patrick, Lord Devlin, has concluded that these German decision makers willfully discounted economic factors in their zeal for armed triumph, and he has speculated that they would have made the same decision even with full knowledge of Britain's financial plight. I agree and have compared this decision to Edmund Burke's characterization of the French Revolution as "a fond election of evil." Through both ignorance and willfulness, these German decision makers were doing the one thing that would save the Allies from financial collapse and a supply disaster. In view of the military setbacks that the Allies would suffer in 1917, especially in Russia and Italy, such a turn of events would almost certainly have been the proverbial straw that broke the camel's back. It is difficult to escape the conclusion they rightfully earned and richly deserved their defeat in 1918.[16]

### Individual Actors at Home

Despite all the provocation that the Germans gave, it required an American response to bring intervention to pass. Nothing was foreordained about what that response might be – not at the beginning of 1915, not in the months that followed, not even in 1917. In many ways, submarine warfare offered odd and unsatisfying reasons for plunging America into the conflagration of World War I. Inasmuch as the nation's merchant marine had shrunk to a minuscule size, few ships involved in this combat flew the stars and stripes. Only in February and March 1915, at the outset of submarine warfare, and again in 1917, with the unrestricted campaign, were any American ships attacked or sunk. In between, strict orders from the German naval command forbade assaults on American vessels, and, despite their grumbling about the difficulty of identifying ships at sea, U-boat commanders were able to follow those orders.

The main matter of contention involved the safety of American citizens who were on board Allied, mainly British, ships as passengers and crew. There were not many people involved. Few Americans worked as merchant officers and seamen under any flag. The outbreak of the war itself had curtailed transatlantic travel, and many of those who persisted in crossing the ocean were wealthy, privileged folk. Broader issues of freedom of navigation in wartime and regard for civilian safety entered into

---

[16] See Devlin, *Too Proud to Fight: Woodrow Wilson's Neutrality* (New York, 1975), pp. 626–33, and Cooper, "Command of Gold," p. 229.

the diplomatic disputes, as did questions of national prestige or "honor." But, at bottom, a huge disparity yawned between cause and effect, between the small number of Americans whom submarine warfare actually touched and the enormity of the conflict. As antiinterventionists never ceased to ask, why should the peace and happiness of a hundred million people be sacrificed for the sake of a few hundred pampered, selfish persons who insisted on endangering themselves?

The American system of government and the accidents of contemporary politics dovetailed to foist primary, at times exclusive, responsibility for the American response to submarine warfare onto a single person. This was the president, Woodrow Wilson. A small minority among the interpreters of intervention in World War I has long insisted upon his overweening importance. The British were the first to stress his crucial role. In 1923, Winston Churchill gave a classic statement of this argument when he wrote, "It seems no exaggeration to pronounce that the action of the United States with its repercussions on the history of the world depended, during the awful period of Armageddon, upon the workings of this man's mind and spirit to the exclusion of almost every other factor; and that he played a part in the fate of nations incomparably more direct and personal than any other man." Half a century later, his countryman, Lord Devlin, published a massive book examining and supporting that proposition, entitled *Too Proud to Fight: Woodrow Wilson's Neutrality*. In the meantime, in the United States Wilson's greatest biographer and editor of the monumental edition of his papers, Arthur S. Link, had been advancing similar arguments. Some other Americans in more recent years, myself included, have also followed this line of argument.[17]

Still, this remains the minority point of view. Perhaps the overweening importance and often exclusivity of Wilson's role explain why comparatively few interpreters have been willing to adhere to this position. As with the submarine issue, the disparity between cause and effect is unsettling. How could something so momentous for the United States and the world, something so earth-shaking as entry into the most terrible war up to that time, hinge upon just one man? Plainly, great influences had to have some effect, particularly in framing the choices before decision makers. Plainly, other people had to participate in the events: a few others as advisors and critics, and multitudes of others as voters who put leaders in office and

---

[17] Churchill, *The World Crisis* (London, 1923), vol. 3, p. 229. The works of Devlin and Link are cited in notes above.

as followers who supported or opposed the decisions that were made. Moreover under the American Constitution, only Congress can declare war, by majority vote of both houses – which meant that several hundred other elected officials had to share in the decision.[18] Yet, when all such allowances are taken into account and all such background influences are noted, Wilson remains at the center, directing the nation's response.

A mundane reason accounted for Wilson's solitary role during the first year and a quarter of the war. Congress was out of session for all but three months between August 1914 and the end of 1915. The war broke out just as a marathon session devoted to domestic reform was rushing to adjourn before the off-year elections in November 1914. The three-month "lame duck" session between December 1914 and March 1915 predictably did little and dealt with nothing related to the war except for unsuccessful efforts by Wilson to buy interned German ships and by German-Americans to embargo arms and munitions sales to the Allies. Thereafter, until the next Congress, elected in 1914, convened in December 1915, Wilson acted on his own, and these nine months witnessed the first American dealings with submarine warfare.[19]

This president's basic approach to dealing with not only the submarine but also the war and foreign policy in general fell into two radically different phases. The dividing point between them came in May 1915, with the sinking of the *Lusitania*. Like nearly every American president of that era and later, Wilson was a foreign policy neophyte. Just after his election in 1912, he had casually remarked to a friend, "It would be an irony of fate if my administration had to deal with foreign problems, for all my preparation has been in domestic matters."[20] That irony of fate had begun to befall Wilson early, especially with painful, protracted dealings with the revolution in Mexico. By and large, however, he had been able to concentrate on domestic affairs during his first year and a half in office, and he had racked up an awesome record of legislative accomplishment. In foreign affairs, both before and for a while after the outbreak of the world war, Wilson acted the same way that he did in domestic affairs.

---

[18] The relevant portion of the Constitution, Article I, section 8, paragraph 11, reads: "The Congress shall have power: ... to declare war, grant letters of marque and reprisal and make rules concerning captures on land and water...."

[19] The Twentieth Amendment to the Constitution, ratified in 1933, changed the congressional calendar to convene on 3 January following its election and also changed the date of the presidential inauguration to 20 January.

[20] Wilson quoted in Ray Stannard Baker interview with Edward Grant Conklin, 19 June 1925, Ray Stannard Baker Papers, Library of Congress.

He was a genuinely collegial leader, who sought advice from his principal advisors and delegated a great deal of authority to them.

The secretary of state, three-time Democratic presidential nominee William Jennings Bryan, possessed an independent power base and felt free to weigh in with advice and take initiatives of his own. Critics often sneered at Bryan as an inexperienced, inept, and woolly-headed diplomatist, but he was one of only two leading American politicians before World War I who had an established reputation in foreign affairs (the other was Theodore Roosevelt).[21] Despite differences in temperament and background, Wilson and Bryan got on well and worked together harmoniously. The president had two other main advisors in foreign affairs. One was the second-ranking officer in the state department, who held the title of "Counselor," Robert Lansing. He was an experienced international lawyer and was related by marriage to a former Republican secretary of state. The other advisor was Colonel House, a wealthy Texan who held no office but enjoyed a close personal friendship with Wilson. The American ambassadors in the major belligerent capitals were a mixed lot. The envoys in Paris and Berlin, William C. Sharp and James W. Gerard, respectively, were financial contributors to the Democratic Party who were not expected to do much more than convey messages back and forth. The envoy in London, Walter Hines Page, was a former magazine editor and an old friend and political backer of Wilson's, but he had become an ardent admirer of the British before the war and soon turned himself into a shrill, uncritical partisan of the Allies. The ambassadors of the major belligerent powers in Washington – Count Johann von Bernstorff of Germany, Jules Jusserand of France, and Sir Cecil Spring Rice of Britain – were able, experienced diplomats, but none of them ever grew close to the president.[22]

During the first nine months of the war, Wilson practiced foreign policy as usual. Affirming neutrality was a virtually automatic procedure, although the president did speak out to urge Americans to be "neutral in fact

[21] This characterization of Wilson's relationship with Bryan differs from the well-known portrait of the two men as ignorant, clumsy, moralistic practitioners of "missionary diplomacy," in Arthur S. Link, *Woodrow Wilson and the Progressive Era, 1910–1917* (New York, 1954). More recent scholarship has treated that characterization as greatly overdrawn, especially as applied to Wilson. Link himself quietly dropped this emphasis when he examined Wilson's foreign policy in the three volumes of his full-scale biography that treated the period from 1914 to 1917.

[22] Among the ambassadors in Washington, Spring Rice suffered from the additional handicap of being a close friend of Theodore Roosevelt, who was a leading political opponent of Wilson's and, as the war unfolded, a harsh critic of his foreign policies.

as well as in name, . . . impartial in thought as well as in action." At first, he allowed Bryan to forbid loans to belligerents, but when it became clear that this ban would hamper foreign trade, he quietly reversed the action, with Bryan's consent. The first major issue for the United States to arise out of the war involved whether to challenge the Allies' expanded block-ade practices in the fall of 1914. With the agreement of all his advisors, Wilson declined to mount a full-fledged diplomatic challenge and adopted a wait-and-see attitude. Both the Germans and historical "revisionists" later denounced this acquiescence as a pro-Allied tilt. For Lansing and House, who wanted to see that the United States did not hamper the Al-lied war effort, those charges may have contained a grain of truth, but Bryan, who harbored no such sentiments, fully agreed with this decision. Wilson wished to avoid repeating what he and most historians regarded as the mistakes that had led to the War of 1812. But the most important motive behind this decision was a desire to avoid unnecessary trouble. Furthermore, because Germany had not yet entered into this arena of war with the submarine, these American policy makers correctly viewed this as a matter strictly between themselves and the British.[23]

Germany's opening of submarine warfare in February 1915 did not change Wilson's approach to foreign policy. The initial American response – to hold the Germans to "strict accountability" for any American losses of life and property – adopted Lansing's harsh-sounding phrase but only after consultation and approval by Bryan and Wilson. In fact, "strict accountability" sounded stronger than it was, because there were no sanctions threatened for failure to comply.[24] Two poles of thought about the problem quickly formed within the administration. Lansing took a hard line against acquiescence in any kind of attacks by submarines, while Bryan sought a face-saving way to avoid trouble such as forbidding or warning Americans against travel on belligerent vessels. Wilson favored neither approach but looked instead for a middle way. In the face of sporadic attacks on American ships and the endangering of

[23] Wilson statement to the press, 18 August 1914, in Link, ed., *Papers of Wilson*, vol. 30, p. 394. On these decisons, see Link, *Wilson: Struggle for Neutrality*, pp. 62–4, 126–9, 132–6. The Germans would soon justify submarine warfare as a retaliation for the Allied blockade, and American revisionists would lay blame on Wilson for having acquiesced in that blockade. Actually, German submarine warfare was an offensive proposition and would almost certainly have been adopted regardless of what the Allies did or did not do in the way of blockade.

[24] On "strict accountability" and the early discussions, see Link, *Wilson: Struggle for Neu-trality*, pp. 320–4, and Ernest R. May, *The World War and American Isolation, 1914–1917* (Cambridge, Mass., 1959), pp. 136–48.

a few citizens and killing of one of them onboard belligerent ships, the president tried to brace the country for some kind of trouble. In April, he stated publicly, "[O]ur whole duty, for the present, at any rate, is summed up in this motto: 'America first.' Let us think of America before we think of Europe, in order that America may be fit to be Europe's friend when the day of tested friendship comes."[25]

## Woodrow Wilson's Neutrality

What did change Wilson's approach to foreign policy was the sinking of the *Lusitania*. In the course of a few hours on the afternoon of 7 May 1915, the country's whole relation to the war changed as the news of the great British liner's sinking reached America. Wilson's first response was again to counsel calm. "There is such a thing as a man being too proud to fight," he suggested publicly. "There is such a thing as a nation being so right that it does not need to convince others by force that it is right." Wilson almost instantly retracted that statement, although not because Roosevelt and other pro-Allied stalwarts lambasted it as cowardly. Rather, he recognized that the sinking of the *Lusitania*, which had killed 128 Americans among the nearly 1,200 lives lost, had totally altered the context of foreign policy.

The popular response was not belligerent. Out of 1,000 newspaper editors who took part in a telegraphic poll, only six called for war. But now public consciousness was aroused, and how to respond to submarine warfare was burgeoning into a major political issue. Wilson grasped the essence of this new situation when he told Bryan, "I wish with all my heart that I saw a way to carry out the double wish of our people, to maintain a firm front in respect of what we demand of Germany and yet do nothing that might by any possibility involve us in the war."[26]

From this point on, Wilson took virtually complete charge of foreign policy toward the war. The occasion for his taking control of foreign affairs was Bryan's decision to resign as secretary of state on 9 June 1915,

[25] Wilson speech of 20 April 1915, in Link, ed., *Papers of Wilson*, vol. 33, p. 38. House took little part in these discussions mostly because he was in Europe on one of his informal diplomatic missions.

[26] Wilson speech of 10 May 1915, in Link, ed., *Papers of Wilson*, vol. 33, p. 149; Wilson to Bryan, 7 June 1915, ibid., p. 349. On the impact of the sinking of the *Lusitania*, see John Milton Cooper, Jr., "The Shock of Recognition: The Impact of World War I on America," *Virginia Quarterly Review* 76 (Autumn 2000): 574–7.

rather than incur what he regarded as wrongful risks of war in Wilson's demands on Germany. Accepting Bryan's resignation took courage on Wilson's part. The secretary of state still stood high in the Democratic Party, and the party's congressional leaders had recently informed him that they would not support any belligerent response to the sinking of the *Lusitania*.[27] At first, Wilson evidently wanted to find someone of comparable stature to replace Bryan. William Gibbs McAdoo, who was both secretary of the treasury and Wilson's son-in-law, told Colonel House that Wilson balked at appointing Lansing because "he did not think he was big enough." House agreed but made a virtue of that inadequacy. Lansing, he told Wilson, "could be used to better advantage than a stronger man.... I think the most important thing is to get a man with not too many ideas of his own and one that will be guided by you without unnecessary argument...." Whether because of this advice or not, Wilson did name Lansing as Bryan's successor, and he did act the way that the colonel suggested.[28]

The ever-devious House was almost certainly making a play to increase his own influence. In their last conversation before his resignation, Bryan told Wilson, "Colonel House has been Secretary of State, not I, and I have never had your full confidence." But things did not go House's way, either. His star was already falling in Wilson's eyes. Someone else had replaced him as an intimate advisor with whom the president could share his innermost thoughts. This was Edith Bolling Galt, whom Wilson had begun courting in the spring of 1915 and whom he married in December. The future second Mrs. Wilson took an instant dislike to the Texas colonel and began to undermine his influence. Wilson would continue to use House as a negotiator, and he allowed him to pursue his scheme to mediate the war that culminated in the House-Grey Memorandum of February 1916. Yet, as earlier, Wilson seems to have indulged House more than he relied upon him. For example, at the place in the House-Grey Memorandum that stated that if a joint effort at mediation by the United States and Britain failed, the president inserted the fateful word "probably"

---

[27] The Democratic congressional leaders' nonbelligerent stand was conveyed to Bryan by Senator Thomas Martin and Representative Hal Flood, both of Virginia, who had canvassed some of their party colleagues and found unanimous opposition to war over the *Lusitania*. For the Democratic congressional leaders' warning to Wilson, see Bryan to Wilson, 4 June 1915, in Link, ed., *Papers of Wilson*, vol. 33, p. 337. Wilson made his comment about the "double wish" in reply to this letter.

[28] Entry, 14 June 1915, House Diary, ibid., p. 397; House to Wilson, 16 June 1915, ibid., p. 409.

in the statement that America would then enter the war on the Allied side. No one but Wilson was dictating what American policy would be.[29]

That policy continued to be the attempt to carry out Americans' "double wish." For almost a year following the sinking of the *Lusitania*, Wilson engaged in a protracted, frustrating diplomatic sparring match with the Germans over submarine warfare. In August 1915, after an attack on another passenger liner, he informally threatened to break diplomatic relations – a likely prelude to war – unless such attacks without warning stopped. The Germans agreed to cease attacks on passenger ships, but they resisted demands to apologize and give compensation for the sinking of the *Lusitania* and not to attack freighters. Meanwhile, Wilson, reversing previous Democratic policy, now advocated a major buildup in the army and navy, thereby stealing political thunder from quasibelligerent critics like Roosevelt. He also allowed Lansing to float an ill-conceived and fruitless proposal to tie German moderation of submarine warfare to British disarmament of merchant vessels. Matters came to a head in March 1916, when a U-boat attacked an English Channel steamer, the *Sussex*, wounding several Americans. Wilson responded with a formal threat to sever relations, and this move prompted the Germans to restrict submarine warfare by pledging not to attack merchant vessels without warning. It was a diplomatic triumph for Wilson.[30]

This victory was doubly sweet because he was winning on other fronts as well. In the political arena at home, Bryan chose to fight Wilson over both submarine policy and military "preparedness," as the issue was then called, as well as generally for control of the Democratic Party. Wilson carried the day on both issues by prevailing on showdown votes in Congress on Bryan's idea of warning citizens not to travel on belligerent ships and by adroitly compromising and arousing public opinion over preparedness. The payoff to Wilson's newly won mastery of his party came with his uncontested renomination for president by the

---

[29] Entry, 24 June 1915, House Diary, ibid., p. 409. For the text of the House-Grey Memorandum, see ibid., vol. 36, p. 180, n. 2, and for Wilson's insertion of "probably" see entry, 6 March 1916, House Diary, ibid., p. 262. There is much that is still unclear and mysterious about this incident. See also John Milton Cooper, Jr., "The British Response to the House-Grey Memorandum: New Evidence and New Questions," *Journal of American History* 59 (April 1973): 958–71.

[30] The fullest accounts of Wilson's diplomacy during this time are in Link, *Wilson: Confusions and Crises* (Princeton, N.J., 1964). One of the Americans involved in the attack on the *Sussex* was the future diplomatic historian Samuel Flagg Bemis, who later became a strong isolationist.

Democrats and the united, enthusiastic campaign that they waged for his reelection in 1916. That November, Wilson became the first Democrat since Andrew Jackson to win a second consecutive term. One of the slogans in that campaign was "He Kept Us Out of War," but on examination the peace issue seems to have played a smaller role in the outcome than domestic reform concerns and the troubles of the Republican opposition.[31]

By the time of the election, Wilson was receiving warnings that the German restraint in submarine warfare might soon be ended. He took the danger of renewed diplomatic crisis so seriously that, in the event that he lost the election, he secretly outlined steps to have his opponent, Charles Evans Hughes, succeed him at once and avoid the four-month interregnum until the next inauguration on 4 March 1917. Under the law of succession then in force, the secretary of state stood second in line, and Wilson planned to appoint Hughes to that post and then, having secured the resignation of the vice-president, resign himself and thereby make Hughes president immediately.

Instead, once his own victory was assured, Wilson moved boldly to moot any renewed submarine threat by bringing the war to an end. In December 1916 and January 1917, he mounted a peace offensive on multiple fronts. Besides jerking the financial chain to soften up the British, he dispatched a public diplomatic note to all the belligerents, asking them to state their peace terms, offering mediation, and promising American membership in a postwar league of nations empowered to maintain peace. Boldly disregarding both hostile and lukewarm responses from Europe and a plot by Lansing to derail the effort, Wilson unveiled his grand design for world peace and order on 22 January 1917. This was when he delivered the speech in which he called for a nonpunitive, compromise settlement to the war – "a peace without victory." He also specified terms such as restoration of Alsace and Lorraine to France, an independent Poland, a restored and indemnified Belgium, and freedom of the seas – all to be later parts of his Fourteen Points – and he again pledged American membership and leadership in a league of nations.[32]

---

[31] On Wilson's political battles and reelection, see ibid. and Link, *Wilson: Campaigns for Progressivism and Peace*. Also, again at the risk of immodesty, I suggest, John Milton Cooper, Jr., *The Warrior and the Priest: Woodrow Wilson and Theodore Roosevelt* (Cambridge, Mass., 1983), esp. pp. 255–7, 298–302.

[32] The plan to resign and install Hughes is detailed in Link, *Wilson: Campaigns for Progressivism and Peace*, 154–6. The other events of these months are ably covered in this volume.

## The Decision to Intervene

The Germans, however, had already decided to resume and expand submarine warfare. This move precipitated the final crisis that led to intervention.[33] But even now that was not the only possible outcome, at least not as long as the decision lay in Wilson's hands. If others could have made the decision, the German move would have instantly brought the United States into the war. Roosevelt and Lodge, whom Wilson's call for "peace without victory" had enraged, could now come out of the closet as full-throated interventionists. Lansing and, more cautiously, House likewise urged war upon the president, as did several cabinet members. But the president did not buy their arguments. He broke relations with Germany at the beginning of February, but in a speech to Congress explaining the action he held out an olive branch, affirming, "We do not desire any hostile conflict.... We shall not believe that they [the Germans] are hostile to us unless and until we are obliged to believe it...." As a defensive measure, Wilson proposed legislation to arm American ships. The measure passed overwhelmingly in the House, but a Senate filibuster led by such antiinterventionists as Robert M. La Follette of Wisconsin and George W. Norris of Nebraska prevented passage before the expiration of Congress. Wilson denounced those opponents as a "little group of willful men, representing no opinion but their own," and, backed by a legal opinion from the attorney general, he issued an executive order to arm the ships.[34]

Those strong words and deeds did not mean, however, that Wilson was ready to go to war yet. Events were coming in a rush. The publication of the Zimmermann telegram, which British intelligence agents operatives had intercepted and artfully disclosed after covering their tracks, caused a sensation. Submarine attacks now hit American ships, two of which

---

[33] Because of the many events coming in these months, a brief chronology may be helpful: 9 January: German decision to resume and widen submarine warfare; 19 January: Zimmermann telegram dispatched to Mexico (and immediately intercepted by the British); 31 January: Public announcement of resumption of submarine warfare, to begin the next day; 3 February: United States breaks diplomatic relations with Germany; 26 February: American women killed in sinking of British passenger liner; 28 February: Zimmermann telegram published in the United States; 1 March: House of Representatives passes armed ships bill; 2–4 March: Senate filibuster prevents passage of armed ships bill; 4 March: Wilson inaugurated for second term as president; Wilson arms ships by executive order; 20 March: Cabinet discusses options; 21 March: Wilson asks for joint session of Congress; 2 April: Wilson addresses the joint session; 4 April: Senate passes war resolution, 82–6; 6 April: House passes war resolution, 373–50.

[34] Wilson speech to Congress, 13 February 1917, in Link, ed., *Papers of Wilson*, vol. 41, pp. 111–12; statement to press, 4 March 1917, ibid., p. 320.

were sunk in February, and two American women passengers died when a U-boat sank a British liner. Their deaths prompted expressions of editorial outrage. The overthrow of the tsarist regime in Russia removed a big contradiction to Allied claims to be fighting for democracy. In response, interventionist sentiment grew in America, though not by leaps and bounds. Every indication still showed substantial opposition to war and a majority of people evidently clinging to the "double wish." Congressional opinion mirrored those divisions. When Congress met in April 1917, three widely separated observers – a peace activist, a second-term congressman, and the British ambassador – all reported that the president could carry majorities in both houses with him for any foreign policy course he chose. Contrary to the fulminations of war hawks like Roosevelt, an outraged public was not forcing a reluctant Wilson into war.[35]

Reluctant he was. As late as the third week in March, just before he called Congress into special session, the president showed unmistakably how unwarlike he felt. On March 19, he had a long talk with Frank Cobb, a leading Democratic newspaper editor, in which he declared, "It [war] would mean that we should lose our heads along with the rest and stop weighing right and wrong. It would mean that a majority of people in this hemisphere would go war mad. ... a declaration of war would mean that Germany would be beaten and so badly beaten that there would be a dictated peace, a victorious peace. ... Once lead this people into war, and they'll forget there ever was such a thing as tolerance. To fight you must be brutal and ruthless, and the spirit of ruthless brutality will enter into the very fibre of our national life. ... If there is any alternative, for God's sake let's take it!"[36]

At a cabinet meeting the next day, March 20, Wilson answered one member's assertion that Congress and the public demanded war, "I do not care for popular demand. I want to do right, whether popular or not." At that meeting, all the members recommended war, some enthusiastically, such as Lansing and McAdoo, and others reluctantly, most notably, Secretary of the Navy Josephus Daniels, an old friend and former political

[35] For the estimates of congressional opinion, see David Starr Jordan to Jessie Jordan, 6 April 1917, David Starr Jordan Papers, Hoover Institution for the Study of War, Peace and Revolution, Stanford University; Fiorello H. La Guardia, *The Making of an Insurgent: An Autobiography, 1882–1919* (Philadelphia, 1948), 138, 140; Spring Rice to Arthur J. Balfour, 23 March 1917, in Gwinn, ed., *Letters and Friendships of Spring Rice*, vol. 2, p. 387.

[36] Wilson quoted in John L. Heaton, ed., *Cobb of "The World": A Leader in Liberalism* (New York, 1924), pp. 268–70.

cohort of Bryan's. Daniels's reluctance did not spring from any advice from his senior commanders, nor did the detached attitude of Secretary of War Newton D. Baker. Oddly perhaps, the views of senior military advisors about the advisability of intervention do not seem to have entered at all into Wilson's decision making, although he did ask Daniels to consult with his admirals about possible naval cooperation with Britain. At the end of this cabinet meeting, Wilson greeted the secretaries' unanimity with the noncommittal remark: "Well, gentlemen, I think that there is no doubt as to what your advice is. I thank you." When Lansing pressed him to call Congress into session to be ready to declare war, he replied, "Oh, I think I will sleep on it." The next day he did issue the call for Congress to meet on April 2, but he gave no indication about what actions he might recommend.[37]

Why, then, feeling the way he did, did Wilson choose intervention? The man who decided to take the United States into World War I was making some of the most eloquent arguments against what he was about to do. This apparent contradiction created an aura of mystery about Wilson's decision that has never disappeared. He added to the mystery by taking no one except Mrs. Wilson into his confidence. When the president went to Capitol Hill to address a joint session of Congress on the night of 2 April 1917, no one except himself and his wife knew what he was going to say. Those circumstances made Wilson's decision seem more mysterious than it really was. He decided to go to war through a combination of mundane calculation, tragic choice, and philosophical reflection – all of which he explained clearly when he spoke to Congress that night.

Woodrow Wilson's war address ranks among the three or four greatest presidential speeches in American history.[38] It is a work of somber eloquence. Warning the members of Congress of the "serious, very serious choices of policy to be made," Wilson began with a dry, factual recitation of what had happened since the resumption of submarine warfare, gradually raising the emotional temperature until he called the German actions "a warfare against mankind ... a war against all nations." In the face of this challenge, Americans must make their choice "with a moderation of counsel and a temperateness of judgment.... We must put excited feeling away. Our motive will not be revenge or the victorious

[37] Entry, 20 March 1917, Josephus Daniels Diary, in Link, ed., *Papers of Wilson*, vol. 41, p. 445; Lansing, "Memorandum of the Cabinet Meeting, 2:30–5 p.m., Tuesday, 20 March 1917," ibid., pp. 444–5.
[38] Wilson speech of 2 April 1917, ibid., pp. 519–27.

assertion of physical might of the nation, but only a vindication of right, of human right, of which we are only a single champion." He had tried armed neutrality, but the Germans' response had made that policy "worse than ineffectual: it is likely only to produce what it was meant to prevent; it is practically certain to draw us into the war without either the rights or the effectiveness of belligerents." On the basis of that simple calculation – the United States was in the war, anyway, and therefore should enjoy whatever advantages true belligerency might bring – Wilson asked Congress to declare that a state of war existed between the United States and Germany.

Wilson also stressed his "profound sense of the solemn and even tragical character" of the step he was taking and declared he was still seeking the kind of settlement to the war and new world order that he had outlined in the "peace without victory" speech. "Our object now, as then," Wilson insisted, "is to vindicate the principles of peace and justice in the life of the world as against selfish and autocratic power and to set up amongst the really free peoples of the world such a concert of purpose and of action as will henceforth ensure the observance of those principles." In expounding on those noble purposes, Wilson's rhetoric sometimes verged on militant assertions of righteousness, but that was not its dominant tone. Instead, he maintained that Americans had no quarrel with the German people, only with their autocratic government, and that they would fight "without rancour ... without passion ... with proud punctilio."

Wilson explicated his vision of careful, limited commitment to a non-punitive peace in the most famous and usually misquoted sentence of the speech: "The world must be made safe for democracy." Because Wilson was a punctilious stylist and the last American president to write his own speeches, it is safe to presume that he chose to use the passive voice deliberately. He was not saying that the United States would or could make the world safe for democracy. He made this point clear three sentences later when he declared, "We are but one of the champions of the rights of mankind. We shall be satisfied when those rights have been made as secure as the faith and the freedom of nations can make them." This oddly downbeat way to lead a nation into war sprang from Wilson's conflicted desires and his recognition of the terrible risk that he was taking. He still yearned to build a "peace without victory," but now he believed that he had no choice but to try to do that through what he had deplored to Frank Cobb as "a dictated peace, a victorious peace."

The somber tone infected even the final, stirring peroration with which Wilson, like all orators then and now, closed his speech. "It is a distressing and oppressive duty, Gentlemen of the Congress," he began, "which I have performed in thus addressing you. There are, it may be, many months of fiery trial and sacrifice ahead of us. It is a fearful thing to lead this great peaceful people into war, into the most terrible and disastrous of all wars, civilization itself seeming to be in the balance." Then, warming to the argument, Wilson asserted that "the right is more precious than peace" and that Americans would be fighting "for democracy, . . . for a universal dominion of right by such a concert of free peoples as shall bring peace and safety to all nations and make the world at last free. To such a task we can dedicate our lives and our fortunes, everything that we are and everything that we have, with the pride of those who know that the day has come when America is privileged to spend her blood and her might for the principles that gave her birth and happiness and the peace which she has treasured." This was an appropriately American call to arms, echoing the signers of the Declaration of Independence's pledge of "our lives, our fortunes, and our sacred honor."

Any other speaker would have ended the speech there, on such a stirring note. But Wilson added a final sentence: "God helping her, she can do no other." Few among Wilson's listeners in the Capitol or among those who read the speech in the newspapers the next day failed to recognize those words. Despite recent large-scale immigration of Roman Catholics, Protestantism remained by far the strongest religious and cultural force in America, and those words were a paraphrase of Martin Luther's declaration to the Diet of Worms: "God helping me, I can do no other." Some observers suspected that Wilson was appealing to German-American Lutherans by ending the speech this way.

Such a consideration may have crossed his mind, but it is much more likely that he included those words because of the philosophical reflection that underlay the whole speech. Wilson was casting the United States in the role of a righteous nation in a sinful world, just as Luther had cast Christian believers as righteous persons in a sinful world. How, Luther had asked, should Christians conduct themselves in this world? As humans tainted by original sin, they could not avoid sin. Instead, Luther argued, in seeking to do God's will, as imperfectly as anyone could perceive God's will, Christians must "sin boldly." This was the analogy that Wilson was drawing. He knew that the war was filled with the worst of human sin, but even his nation could not avoid contamination by such sin. Therefore, the best course for America, in his view, was to "sin boldly" by entering the war, to take the risk that as a victor this nation could shape a better, more just peace and try to prevent such conflagrations from ever happening again. "This man's mind and spirit" did play the ultimate role in bringing the United States into World War I.[39]

Only one step remained to consummate American intervention. True to the observers' estimates, Wilson carried majorities in both houses of Congress with him for war. In the Senate, only six members opposed the war resolution, while in the House there were fifty votes against the measure. Actually, those numbers were high for such votes. No other American war in the twentieth century would have so many dissenting voices raised in Congress at the outset. For comparable opposition, it is necessary to look back at earlier conflicts such as the War of 1812 and the Mexican-American War, both of which had sharply divided the country from the beginning. Nor did these numbers fully reflect the doubts and opposition that still persisted regarding intervention. The small band of opposing senators included eloquent, principled critics such as La Follette and Norris. In the House, the Democratic majority leader, Claude Kitchin of North Carolina, broke with his party to oppose the war, as did the first woman elected to Congress, Jeannette Rankin of Montana. A substantial number of the dissenting votes in both houses came from the Midwest. There was some correlation with concentrations of German-Americans, but the strongest correlation was with left-leaning politics, particularly anti–big business "progressive" insurgency of the kind championed by La Follette and Norris. The lone Socialist in Congress, Representative Meyer London of New York, also voted against the war resolution.[40]

Among the congressmen and senators who spoke in favor of the war resolution, many expressed reluctance and believed little more than money, ships, and supplies would have to come from the United Sates. Aside from Roosevelt and other war hawks, few wanted to see a large-scale commitment of ground forces on the Western Front or imagined that such operations would be necessary. Significantly, too, no one expressed any sense that American intervention would make a critical difference in the outcome of the war. Nobody recognized that this move was likely to save the Allies from defeat.

In the last analysis, there is a simple answer to the question, "Why did the United States enter World War I when it did and as it did?" The answer is, "Because Woodrow Wilson chose to take the United States in."

---

[39] So far as I know, this interpretation of Wilson's decision is originally mine. See Cooper, *Warrior and Priest*, 322–3.

[40] On the debates and votes on the war resolution, see Link, *Wilson: Campaigns for Progressivism and Peace*, pp. 426–31, and Cooper, *Vanity of Power*, pp. 196–208, 235–8.

It is true that great forces of geopolitics, strategy, culture, and economics shaped the context in which he made his decision. It is true that the opinions of others – small numbers of them among his advisors and critics, larger numbers in Congress, and multitudes among the public – counted in his decision. Wilson's decision to intervene was a close, risky thing, a calculation of costs and benefits and a reflection on the human condition that could easily have taken him in a different direction. In the end, his decision was the critical factor. He and he alone took the United States into World War I.

# 14

# Why Did It Happen?

## Holger H. Herwig

The answer to that question regarding the origins of World War I is to be found in the circumstances of four of the five major European powers: Austria-Hungary, Germany, Russia, and France. In each of the four "cases," the decision-making coterie saw their nation as in decline or at least as seriously threatened. To halt the decline or to block the threat, the decision makers felt that some demonstration of strength was imperative. It was the sense of threat and the resultant need to address that decline that led them to the key decision, namely, to participate in the coming war. Our view, in short, is that these strategic considerations were paramount.

### The Major Powers

Austria, once the commanding central European presence, the state that had defeated and pushed back the Ottomans, found itself tagged as the second "sick man of Europe." This empire had been trounced by Napoleon, yet in alliance with other powers appeared among the victors and, for another half-century, dominated continental Europe. But then came the serious threats of revolutions in 1848–49, necessitating being "saved" by Russian intervention. Thereafter came a cluster of defeats, these at the hands of Italian nationalists, allied briefly in 1859 to the France of Napoleon III. This debacle was followed closely by defeat at the hands of Prussia in 1866. Reflecting the instabilities of a multinational society, the empire, in the Compromise of 1867, was forced to divide sovereignty and to reorganize as Austria-Hungary. An important Balkan satellite, Serbia, was lost in 1903 as a result of a coup d'état. Then a series of defeats and/or embarrassments followed in the Balkans. It appeared as if "the Serbs" and others were going to repeat the Italian *risorgimento*. This effort was, if anything, even more serious, threatening the breakaway of many ethnic groups within the Dual Monarchy. A "Greater Serbia" would provide an example for others, for Romanians, Poles, and Czechs. The string of losses and the imminent threat of still more led the top leaders to a now-or-never conclusion: The empire must react; it must end the Serbian threat, or else, like the Ottomans, it would proceed to an ultimate decline. When the time came for "the decision," the empire's leaders, as explained in Chapter 4, directed their troops to the South, to defeat "upstart" Serbia.

Germany's leaders also felt that their empire was threatened. Their image, as defined in Chapter 5, was one of "encirclement," the prime focus being the Franco-Russian alliance, but with Britain always in mind. Austria-Hungary, their loyal ally, was a weak and declining power; Italy, their other ally, was perceived as both weak and unreliable. Watching Russia's economic and military recovery after the Russo-Japanese War of 1905–6, Germany's leaders sensed that they were destined to experience a decline relative to Russia and France. For the decision makers, especially those of the military, the solution was a preemptive war. For them, too, timing was essential: It was "now or never." All of this, incidentally, is spelled out in the opening pages of Fritz Fischer's *Griff nach der Weltmacht* – a separate and distinct agenda from the famous thesis about Germany's world power (*Weltmacht*) aspirations.

By 1912–14, Germany pursued two separate agendas, one defensive, one offensive. The prime concern was defensive, to shore up the gains of 1871, to preserve and if possible to enhance its position of "semihegemony" in Europe.[1] This agenda suggested the need for a preemptive strike against France and Russia. The other agenda, the *Weltmacht* aims – power in Africa and Asia – was not part of that calculus; it was offensive and beyond the European metropole. While both agendas appeared in official discussions – both before and after August 1914 – Berlin never set a priority. As a result, its policies proved troubling to outsiders, part fantasy, part legitimate. The July Crisis of 1914 would force Berlin to choose.

In striking contrast to its Habsburg ally, Germany followed its longstanding operations plan, pushing its forces first into France, then, it was hoped, into Russia. Although we regularly talk of World War I in the

---

[1] Ludwig Dehio, *Deutschland und die Weltpolitik im 20. Jahrhundert* (Frankfurt, 1961), p. 13; in English, *Germany and World Politics in the Twentieth Century* (London, 1959), pp. 11–13. Dehio argued that after unification, Germany was caught in a position between hegemony and balance of power.

singular, it is important to note that two wars were "in process" by early August: the Austro-Serbian war in the Balkans and the German war in Belgium and France. In a matter of days, however, Austrian-Hungarian forces would be called out of the Balkans and sent to the Galician front, a third war, effectively to serve in the "German war."

Russia also was in a troubled state by 1914, having faced some six decades of defeat, beginning with the Crimean War of 1853–56. Russia won the Turkish War of 1877–78, to be sure, but lost decisively in the peace imposed by the other powers. Then came the Russo-Japanese War of 1905–6 and internal revolution. In 1908, Russia was humiliated by the Austro-Hungarian power play in Bosnia-Herzegovina and the German ultimatum to accept the Habsburg annexation. Thereafter, Russian leaders struggled both to rearm and to reorganize their land and sea forces, and to industrialize the empire without surrendering power to the forces demanding political and social reform. To outsiders, the ambitious Russian reform programs seemed a direct threat. By 1914, many continental political leaders sensed that the nation had regained strength, economically and militarily, and, accordingly, that the incentives had now changed. As seen in Chapter 6, a frequently repeated justification offered by Russian leaders during the July Crisis was that the empire had to demonstrate strength or capacity, otherwise its standing as a great power would be ended.

France, like Austria, also had been a major European power. Four world wars had been fought to contain its expansion, in Europe and overseas. France had been defeated in the last of those struggles, the Napoleonic wars of 1803–15, and had lost many of its overseas holdings. But then, in the course of the nineteenth century, it had gained a "second empire," in Algeria, Tunisia, Equatorial Africa, and Indo-China. France had scored some military victories by mid-century, in the Crimean War and in support of Piedmont-Sardinia's independence struggles against Austria. But then came a humiliating loss: Napoleon III's attempt from 1863 to 1867 to establish a Catholic and Latin empire in Mexico under Archduke Maximilian von Habsburg (!) ended in defeat at Puebla. Much worse, closer to home, was the serious and humiliating defeat by Prussia and the other German states in 1870–71, which soon led to the establishment of a much larger, unified, and stronger Germany – as well as to the loss of much of Alsace-Lorraine. Security against this new Germany was uppermost in the minds and hearts of the leaders of the new Republic. But over time, they forgot the "gap in the Vosges," and cries of "revenge" for 1871 abated.

Otto von Bismarck's aims were to keep France isolated (without allies) and to encourage colonial distraction. For several decades, France did "stand alone." After Bismarck's dismissal in 1890, however, the new German leaders dropped the Russian connection (the Reinsurance Treaty of 1887), allowing the Russo-French links of 1892 and 1894. France now had a strong ally on Germany's eastern flank. Its key aim was to fasten the bonds and to encourage Russian military plans that would serve France's needs. That meant to speed Russia's mobilization, to concentrate its forces quickly for attack on Germany in case of war. By 1914, as spelled out in Chapter 7, French foreign policy centered on its links with the Russian alliance.

Thus, it is fair to state that the various foreign policy decisions made by the four continental powers before 1914 were based on what might be termed defensive considerations, that is, on the concern, as the leaders saw it, to protect or to prop up an enfeebled or threatened state. Put differently, the concern was to fend off further threats to the state's power and prestige.

That positive statement of "the cause" also had an important negative: Territorial expansion was not a key consideration. Austria-Hungary, for the reasons indicated in Chapter 4, explicitly disclaimed any interest in annexing Serbia. Russia had no immediate targets (East Prussia or Austrian Poland) at that point. Coming to the defense of Serbia would perhaps garner Russia Slavic allies in the years to come, but new possessions were not a war "cause."

The Dardanelles was always a general European security concern, and in July 1914 preventing German dominance there was a pressing issue for London, Paris, and St. Petersburg. Germany actually stood to lose its overseas possessions as a result of a general European war; that was an easy prediction, the probability of loss escalating dramatically with Britain's involvement. For France, one can always point to Alsace and Lorraine as ultimate aspirations. But in July 1914, the prime concern was fending off the likely imminent German attack, French leaders knowing at least the broad outlines of the Schlieffen plan.

Great Britain, the fifth European power, was not directly threatened as in case of the other four. Historically, Britain had stood secure behind the "moat" of the English Channel and the guns of the Royal Navy. It coveted no European territory, and, as argued in Chapter 8, its primary concern was to keep the continental markets (and especially the German ones) open to its industry and banking. But ever since the wars of Louis XIV and Napoleon I, British policy had been to maintain a balance of power in Europe. London had shown time and again that it would tolerate no hegemon on the Continent.

Beyond the four major powers most immediately involved in the decision to resort to war in 1914 – Austria-Hungary, Germany, Russia, and France – and the one tangentially involved – Great Britain – the others, the late entrants, were dealers and negotiators. They solicited terms, judged the likely winners, and, based on those calculations, joined the fray. The contrasting goals of the major powers and the late entrants is striking. The former, as indicated, were largely defensive, basically, as they saw it, protecting a threatened enterprise. The late entrants, with one important exception, were expansionists, offering intervention in exchange for some territorial gains (and, possibly, some prestige or recognition).

## The Lesser Powers

The first of the so-called lesser powers to enter the European war was Japan. Allied with Great Britain since 1902, Japan had no vital interests at stake in the European power struggle. But those European powers did claim large pieces of real estate in the Far East, either as outright colonies or as so-called leaseholds. Japan's leaders spied a golden chance to strengthen their "rights" and influence in China. Political leaders of all stripes in Tokyo saw a policy of continental expansion as the principal avenue to international status. Japan's decision on 8 August 1914 to eject German power from Asia was an expression of its fidelity to the Anglo-Japanese alliance and, more important, an opportunity for territorial outreach. At the domestic level, it was a triumph for the leaders of political parties that doggedly sought to promote representative government and greater civilian uses of the national budget – over the established Meiji ruling class of elder statesmen, bureaucrats, soldiers, and peers. In both cases, as suggested in Chapter 9, the decision for war was the triumph of one man, Foreign Minister Katō Takaaki.

The Porte was the second lesser power to enter the war. Indeed, the Ottoman Empire provides important background for the 1914 readings by the leaders of the four continental powers. The empire had been in manifest decline for more than a century, bits and pieces having been lost since Napoleon III's venture into the area. It had been tagged as "the sick man of Europe," and the consequences of that sickness were visible for all to see; other nations believed that they could, more or less at will, pick up some of those pieces. France took a piece, Tunisia. Italy took another, Libya. And in 1913, the states of the Balkan League defeated the empire and took more of the pieces. In August 1914, as Europe formally engaged in a general war, there was little that the exhausted Ottomans could do militarily. Their initial and strongest incentive was to stay out of the fray. But then, as argued in Chapter 10, with the German offer first of a treaty of alliance and then of two warships, the Young Turks who had seized power in 1905 decided for war on the side of the Central Powers. Therewith, the Great War spilled into the Middle East. And therewith, in the views of two disparate men such as David Lloyd George and Erich Ludendorff, it enabled Germany to prolong the war by two years.[2]

National aspirations and territorial aggrandizement drove the agendas in four other capitals of the lesser powers: Athens, Bucharest, Rome, and Sofia. After declining in July 1914 to maintain a moral commitment of at least "benevolent neutrality" to the Triple Alliance of 1882, Italian leaders from July to September 1914, as shown in Chapter 11, repeatedly debated entry into the war on both sides. For much of the winter or 1914–15 – the so-called *intervento* – these leaders sought to discern the outcome of the conflict and negotiated with both warring coalitions what Italy might receive for its intervention. In April 1915, they negotiated highly favorable terms of alliance with London and Paris, but in May parliamentary, labor, Catholic, and Socialist opposition as well as passive hostility among the peasantry blocked such a declaration of war against the Central Powers. Still, later that same month, on 25 May 1915, King Vittorio Emanuele III declared war against Austria-Hungary alone. Italian leaders had carefully weighed their options and eventually opted for war on the side of the *entente* as being in the nation's best interest, which now was described, much to the nation's detriment, as the *sacro egoismo*.

The Italian decision to enter the war energized Bulgaria. Tsar Ferdinand, the scion of the German house of Coburg, and his prime minister, Vasil Radoslavov, shared "Greater Bulgaria" aspirations, which translated into claims to Macedonia against Greece and Serbia. For the first few months of the war, Ferdinand and Radoslavov wavered, eagerly following the battlefield fortunes of both sides. But, as suggested in Chapter 12, when the Central Powers in the spring of 1915 promised Bulgaria the immediate occupation of all Macedonia, Radoslavov accepted the offer as his golden chance to make good Bulgaria's "historical and ethnographic rights" to the region. Tsar Ferdinand's Manifesto to the Bulgarian People

---

[2] F. A. K. Yasamee, "Ottoman Empire," in Keith Wilson, ed., *Decisions for War 1914* (London, 1995), p. 229.

on 14–15 October 1915 announced Sofia's entry into the war on the side of the Central Powers.

Romania, allied to Austria-Hungary and Germany since 1883 and to Italy since 1888, like Italy and Bulgaria pursued tortuous negotiations before finally entering the war. Its national aspirations in Bukovina and Transylvania on the one hand, and Bessarabia, on the other, were divided between the warring powers. But the ascent of the Liberal Party in the summer of 1914 and the death of the German-born King Carol in October 1914 tilted the balance away from Berlin and Vienna. Italy's entry into the war on the side of the *entente* powers in May 1915 and the success of the Russian Brusilov offensive in June 1916 proved to be the decisive driving forces.[3] Already in the summer of 1915, Romania had secured from Russia assent to the annexation of large parts of Hungary and Bukovina. And when the *entente*, a year later, confronted Romania with the choice of either joining the war or risk losing those prospects of territorial expansion, Prime Minister Ion Brătianu on 27 August 1917 committed the nation to war. That was a rational decision based on expected gains.

The political establishment of Greece was badly divided from the first days of the war. While the Liberal and anglophile Prime Minister Eleutherios Venizelos favored the *entente*, King Constantine sympathized with his brother-in-law, Kaiser Wilhelm II. Greek nationalist aspirations focused on the Ottoman Empire, but the British annexation of Cyprus, part of the Greek irredenta, upset many Greeks. The allied attack on the Dardanelles in February 1915 brought the war closer to home, and divided the Athens power structure further. While Venizelos was receptive to British offers of an alliance and extensive territories in Asia Minor, the Greek Army argued that any intervention in Asia Minor on behalf of hard-pressed Serbia was beyond its resources. Political turmoil dogged Athenian politics throughout the rest of 1915 and into 1916. In October 1915, Venizelos agreed to the landing of *entente* troops at Salonika, and in January 1916, witnessed their occupation of Corfu. In December 1916 British and French troops landed at Athens, only to be confronted by Greek forces and eventually forced to withdraw. An allied naval blockade of Greece and a French ultimatum to King Constantine to abdicate finally proved decisive: On

[3] On the Romanian-Italian connection in 1914–15, see Glenn E. Torrey, "The Romanian-Italian Agreement of 23 September 1914," in Torrey, ed., *Romania and World War I: A Collection of Studies* (Oxford and Portland, Ore., 1998), pp. 75–93; and H. James Burgwyn, "A Diplomacy Aborted: Italy and Romania Go Their Separate Ways in May 1915," *East European Quarterly* 21 (September 1987): 305–18.

30 June 1917, Greece became the last European state to enter the war. It had taken this step through a combination of nationalist enthusiasm and direct *entente* intervention and blackmail.

The last major power to enter the war, the United States, was driven by none of the reasons listed above. During the "long peace" after the War of 1812, American leaders had concentrated their energies on domestic policies. In the realm of foreign policy, diplomatic isolation or noninvolvement in power politics beyond the Western Hemisphere, became tradition. First laid down in George Washington's caution against "permanent alliances" and in Thomas Jefferson's warning against "entangling alliances," this tradition had become an almost unchallenged dogma. As late as 1912, Woodrow Wilson casually remarked that "all my preparation has been in domestic matters" and suggested that it would be "an irony of fate if my administration had to deal with foreign problems."[4]

A tiny band of geopolitically savvy Americans, including Alfred Thayer Mahan, Theodore Roosevelt, and Henry Cabot Lodge, developed the notion that a weakening of British sea power and a concomitant rise of German sea power could constitute a security threat to the United States. But they remained shrill voices in the wilderness. When war came in 1914, the United States found itself caught in the classic dilemma of neutral nations during a large-scale war. For three years, Wilson kept the nation out of the conflict. His policy of intervention, as analyzed in Chapter 13, came about reluctantly and largely because of the incredible German blunder of submarine warfare against allied as well as neutral shipping.

### On the Causes

This book is about the essence of decision making in July 1914. Ten authors have contributed their expertise on *why* first the major European powers (Austria-Hungary, France, Germany, Great Britain, and Russia), then a host of lesser or peripheral powers (Bulgaria, Italy, Japan, Romania, Serbia, and Turkey), and finally the world's major neutral power (the United States), felt the recourse to arms to be in the national interest. In all cases, the contributors have looked at a variety of common, critical issues. With which individuals and groups did "the war powers" rest? Who were the actual decision makers? What influences came into play as they reached their momentous decisions? And by which process was the decision for war arrived at?

---

[4] Wilson in Ray Stannard Baker interview with Edward Grant Conklin, 19 June 1925. Ray Stannard Baker Papers, Library of Congress, Washington, D.C. Cited in Chapter 13.

Our findings are grouped into three observations. First, World War I was the result of decisions taken by the leaders of the five major nations. Second, in each of those nations the decision to go to war was made primarily by a small coterie of senior civilian and military leaders. And third, any explanation for the war's origins must center on the considerations that moved those five groups of decision makers.

The case for decision making by individuals, by a small coterie, makes contingency highly likely. Put differently, possibilities for diverse choices and outcomes were omnipresent. Misinformation, misjudgment of intentions and consequences, the press of time, the fear of being left behind, weak nerves, and ego strength all played their part in the final decision-making processes. But choices, we stress, were present in all cases. The issues at stake and the decision-making process were complex and complicated. And they often were beset with doubt, uncertainty, and fear. To put it in the words of a very young Winston S. Churchill: "Antiquated War Offices, weak, incompetent or arrogant Commanders, untrustworthy allies, hostile neutrals, malignant Fortune, ugly surprises, awful miscalculations – all take their seat at the Council Board on the morrow of a declaration of war."[5] In short, the proverbial "fog of war" was present in Vienna and Berlin, as it was in Paris, St. Petersburg, and London.

The "big causes," by themselves, did not cause the war. To be sure, the system of secret alliances, militarism, nationalism, imperialism, social Darwinism, and the domestic strains, to name but half a dozen of the more often-touted causes, had all contributed toward forming the *mentalité*, the assumptions (both spoken and unspoken) of the "men of 1914."[6] There is no doubt that most senior policy makers in 1914 gave some consideration to expansion, imperialism, nationalism, armaments, and mass opinion. But we argue that the actual decisions to go to war were a matrix of extemporizations, of choices based on assessments of recent events, of alliance needs, of power and prestige, of immediate opportunities, and of survival. It does injustice to the "men of 1914" to suggest that they were all merely agents – willing or unwilling – of some grand, impersonal design. Those who nevertheless argue a determined history, who point to powerful structural factors, and who deny the role of individuals should read Lamar Cecil's comprehensive two-volume biography of Wilhelm II – and then, we suggest, write a statement defending their position.[7]

---

[5] Winston S. Churchill, *My Early Life: A Roving Commission* (London, 1989), p. 246.

[6] See James Joll, *1914: The Unspoken Assumptions* (London, 1968).

[7] Lamar Cecil, *Wilhelm II: Prince and Emperor, 1859–1900* (Chapel Hill, N.C., 1989); and *Wilhelm II: Emperor and Exile, 1900–1941* (Chapel Hill, N.C., 1996).

As well, we suggest that such "atmospheric" depictions of the war's causes carry the danger of relativizing. Was there no difference in decision making among senior leaders in Vienna, Berlin, Paris, St. Petersburg, and London? And what of those in Tokyo, Constantinople, and Washington? The relativizing argument – the assumption of shared responsibility – raises the basic question of focus and fairness. It also raises the first of the causes reviewed in Chapter 1, the notion of inadvertence.

This is the so-called slide-into-war thesis, an easy analogy first enunciated by David Lloyd George, namely, that European leaders had "slithered" over the brink into the "cauldron of war." The evidence reviewed in the previous chapters simply does not support this claim. In each of the countries studied in this volume, a coterie of no more than about a dozen civilian and military rulers weighed their options, calculated their chances, and then made the decision for war. No dark, overpowering, informal, yet irresistible forces brought on what George F. Kennan called "*the* great seminal catastrophe of this century."[8] It was, in each case, the work of human beings. Each of the chapters reports intention as opposed to inadvertence.

A more complicated inadvertence argument, one going beyond the easy analogy, is that of the "calculated risk." The decision makers planned a limited war, the argument goes, one in which astute deterrence policies would discourage any wider involvement. But then, it is claimed, the prudent calculations somehow – inadvertently – proved mistaken, and a general war resulted. An element of equivalence also appears in this connection, usually as applied to Austria-Hungary, Germany, and Russia. But, as seen in the previous chapters, many key decision makers knew the risk, knew that wider involvement was probable, yet proceeded to take the next steps. Put differently, fully aware of the likely consequences, they initiated policies they knew were likely to bring on the catastrophe.

The European crisis began in Vienna. Sensing a Serbian threat behind the assassination of Archduke Franz Ferdinand on 28 June 1914, Habsburg leaders feared that the Sarajevo crisis might possibly constitute the final act in the disintegration of the empire. A Common Council of Ministers met on 7 July to consider the Dual Monarchy's options. With the momentary dissent of Hungarian Minister-President István Tisza, Habsburg leaders ranging from Foreign Minister Count Leopold Berchtold to Chief of the General Staff Franz Conrad von Hötzendorf,

---

[8] George F. Kennan, *The Decline of Bismarck's European Order: Franco-Russian Relations, 1875–1890* (Princeton, 1979), p. 3.

and from Common Finance Minister Leon von Biliński to War Minister Alexander von Krobatin, accepted the danger that a military strike against Serbia could well bring about a general European war. Yet they decided quickly on the need for a "punitive expedition" against Serbia. There was no serious discussion of a localized war, none of the "calculated risk." Berchtold counseled an aggressive policy, "even though our operations against Serbia should bring about the great war."[9] The very existence of the Council of Ministers and its deliberations for war further argues against any suggestion of an inadvertent "slide" into war.

Eight days later, Count Alexander Hoyos, Berchtold's *chef de cabinet* and the man entrusted with securing Germany's "blank check" to back such a contingency, put it perhaps most bluntly: "It is immaterial to us whether the world war comes out of this."[10] General Conrad von Hötzendorf confided his innermost feeling of the coming European struggle to his mistress, Virginie "Gina" von Reininghaus: "It will be a hopeless struggle, but nevertheless it must be because such an ancient monarchy and such an ancient army cannot perish ingloriously."[11] When the likelihood of a Russian intervention on the side of Serbia was raised at the Foreign Ministry, Section Chief János Forgách laconically commented: "Well then, it [the European war] will just have to come."[12] And even the aged Kaiser Franz Joseph, the monarch with whom the "war powers" ultimately rested, accepted the risk of a general European war.[13] "If we must go under," he confided to Conrad von Hötzendorf, "we better go under decently."[14] War, a general European war, Graydon A. Tunstall argues, is what the senior leadership coterie in Vienna expected and was prepared to undertake.

There was little additional input into that decision. The Austrian parliament had been prorogued by Minister-President Count Karl Stürgkh and did not meet to take up the issue of war or peace. Public opinion and the

---

[9] *Protokolle des Gemeinsamen Ministerrates der Österreichisch-Ungarischen Monarchie (1914–1918)* (Budapest, 1966), pp. 141–50. See Chapter 4.

[10] Cited in Fritz Fellner, ed., *Schicksalsjahre Österreichs 1908–1919: Das politische Tagebuch Josef Redlichs,* 2 vols. (Graz and Cologne, 1953–54), vol. 1, p. 237.

[11] Gina Conrad von Hötzendorf, *Mein Leben mit Conrad von Hötzendorf: Sein geistiges Vermächtnis* (Leipzig, 1935), p. 114.

[12] Rudolf Sieghart, *Die letzten Jahrzehnte einer Grossmacht: Menschen, Völker, Probleme des Habsburger-Reichs* (Berlin, 1932), p. 174.

[13] Article 5 of the Fundamental Law of December 1867 stated: "The Emperor shall have supreme command of the armed force, shall declare war, and conclude peace." Walter Fairleigh Dodd, *Modern Constitutions,* 2 vols. (Chicago, 1909), vol. 1, p. 88.

[14] Gina von Hötzendorf, *Mein Leben mit Conrad,* p. 118.

press were informed by the government; they did not take the lead on the matter. Neither bankers nor industrialists were consulted. Most of them, as seen in the next chapter, favored peace and feared war as a disruptive force. Ambassadors to foreign capitals by and large followed the directives of the Foreign Ministry in Vienna. In short, the decision for war was taken basically by about half a dozen ministers and generals. That Austro-Hungarian decision was the first, the decisive step on the road to war.

Recognizing that a "punitive action" against Serbia would likely bring a Russian intervention, Habsburg leaders quickly moved to secure support from their German ally – the Hoyos mission to Berlin. Kaiser Wilhelm II and Chancellor von Bethmann Hollweg on 5 July agreed to back Austria-Hungary's planned offensive against Serbia. The kaiser, with whom the war powers rested, informed Count Hoyos as well as the Austro-Hungarian ambassador to Berlin, Count László Szögyény-Marich, that Vienna could count on "Germany's full support," even if "serious European complications" – a diplomatic euphemism for war – resulted.[15] In fact, Wilhelm II counseled the Austrians not to "delay the action" against Serbia, and he informed Hoyos that Germany fully expected war with Russia and for years had made all preparations with this in mind. Bethmann Hollweg likewise pressed Vienna to move aggressively against Belgrade and described this as the "best and most radical solution" to the empire's Balkan troubles.[16] Helmuth von Moltke, the chief of the German General Staff, had stated as early as 1911 that he believed a general European war to be inevitable, and during the July Crisis constantly pressed the case for war. "To wait any longer," the general had lectured Conrad von Hötzendorf in May 1914, "meant a diminishing of our chances."[17] At the Foreign Office, Under-Secretary of State Arthur Zimmermann already on 5 July stated that the chances of war stood at 90 percent. If a calculation, it represents an extremely high level of risk.

As Holger H. Herwig shows, the kaiser's decision to back the Viennese ally – the so-called blank check – was shared with a small coterie of four or five men in July 1914. On the afternoon of the 5th, Wilhelm II reviewed

[15] Article 11 of the Constitution of 1871 gave the emperor the power "to declare war and to conclude peace,...to enter into alliances and other treaties with foreign countries." Dodd, *Modern Constitutions*, vol. 1, pp. 330–1. A declaration of war required the consent of the Bundesrath.
[16] Cited in Fritz Fischer, *Griff nach der Weltmacht: Die Kriegszielpolitik des kaiserlichen Deutschland 1914/18* (Düsseldorf, 1964), pp. 63–4. See Chapter 5.
[17] Cited in Franz Conrad von Hötzendorf, *Aus meiner Dienstzeit 1908–1918*, 5 vols. (Vienna, Leipzig, and Munich, 1921), vol. 4, p. 670.

his discussions with the Austrians with the Prussian war minister, General Erich von Falkenhayn, and with the chief of his Military Cabinet, General Moriz von Lyncker. The four considered the question of possible Russian intervention in an Austro-Serbian war and accepted the risk, even though this might lead to a general war. If one adds Bethmann Hollweg and Zimmermann to this group, then the decision for war was taken by six men. That decision was not, as the historian Fritz Fischer spectacularly claimed four decades ago, a "bid for world power" but, rather, a nervous, indeed panicked, "leap into the dark" (Bethmann Hollweg) to secure the Reich's position of semihegemony on the Continent. There was no direct input from parliamentary deputies, bankers, industrialists, or the popular press.

The German agreement to the Austro-Hungarian request makes Germany the second actor in the drama of July 1914. A German "no" would have ended the move toward war. But German leaders, moved by "strategic" considerations and fearing their state's loss of position vis-à-vis the growing power of the two "enemies" on their flanks, provided the needed backing. Berlin was not contractually obligated under the terms of the 1878 Dual Alliance, discussed below, to hand Vienna the blank check. But leaders in Berlin simply decided that the Austrian request for assistance constituted the *casus foederis*, the time for their "now-or-never" engagement.

The Russian reaction to events in Vienna and Berlin was key. If Russia had said "no" to any war in Europe, what remained would have been the Austro-Serbian venture, effectively a third Balkan war. But Foreign Minister S. D. Sazonov, as early as 11 July, had demanded that Russia "fulfill her historic mission" and defend Serbia, a threatened "Slavonic nation." To do otherwise, he argued, would transform Russia into a "decadent State" and a "second-place" power.[18] Agriculture Minister A. V. Krivoshein, effectively the leader of the cabinet, claimed that "opinion," both public and parliamentary, demanded war.[19] War Minister V. A. Sukhomlinov and Chief of the General Staff N. N. Ianushkevich likewise demanded a "bold" policy. For Russian leaders, the governing consideration was as simple as it was dangerous: To have stood by while Austria-Hungary defeated Serbia would have meant another humiliation, another demonstration of Russian impotence. No ally, and certainly not

[18] Cited in David MacLaren McDonald, *United Government and Foreign Policy in Russia 1900–1914* (Cambridge, Mass., 1992), p. 204. See Chapter 6.
[19] Ibid., pp. 204–5.

the French, would have been impressed by such indifference. Potential future allies would have been alienated. Thus, Russia chose to confront Austria-Hungary, the protagonist-perpetrator of the July Crisis.

But Russia could not choose the "small war" it hoped to fight. Since the days of Adjutant General Nikolai Obruchev, there was no illusion in St. Petersburg that a war involving the major powers could be localized.[20] The decision to block Austria-Hungary in its Serbian venture, Russian leaders knew, would likely bring German intervention and hence force St. Petersburg to a simultaneous move against Germany. And that move, they knew, would bring Germany's action against France.

Indeed, just as Russia could not leave Serbia at the mercy of Austria-Hungary, so Germany could not leave Austria-Hungary at the mercy of Russia. To stand aside would mean for Germany abandoning its main ally, leaving it to be overwhelmed by Russian forces. Such a course meant humiliation for Germany. Even worse, it meant perilous strategic exposure. Germany would remain "encircled" as before, only now without any credible ally. Especially given the implications of Russia's Great Program of rearmament, German leaders in July 1914 believed that they had to move against Russia.

Despite the immense risks and the enormous costs (even for a smaller war), Russia's leaders chose to engage. In fact, the Russian Army's Schedule 19A comprised a single, integrated, general mobilization. When Sazonov was informed of the severity of the Austro-Hungarian note to Serbia on 24 July, his comment was, "*C'est la guerre européenne.*"[21] On 30 July 1914, the "sacred and inviolable" Tsar Nicholas II made use of his constitutional war powers.[22] Again, no "slide," no "calculated risk."

David Alan Rich rejects the established view that St. Petersburg had little inkling of the crisis that was unfolding after the murder at Sarajevo. Senior Russian planners were well informed of events through their interception and decoding of foreign diplomatic cables, their penetration of the Austro-Hungarian General Staff, and their agents in foreign capitals. That the Council of Ministers from the start deemed general war as the inevitable outcome of the Balkan crisis argues for the seriousness

---

[20] See Obruchev's statement on this in Henry Kissinger, *Diplomacy* (New York, 1994), pp. 202–3. Also, Chapter 1 above.

[21] Otto Hoetzsch, ed., *Die Internationalen Beziehungen im Zeitalter des Imperialismus: Dokumente aus den Archiven der Zarischen und der Provosorischen Regierung* (Berlin, 1933–43), Reihe I, vol. 5, p. 25.

[22] Article 4 of the Fundamental Laws of the Russian Empire of May 1906 allowed the tsar to "wield the supreme autocratic power"; Article 13 the right "to declare war and conclude peace." Dodd, *Modern Constitutions*, vol. 2, pp. 183–4.

and sophistication of their analyses. And from their French ally as well as their observers at German maneuvers, Russian planners also had correctly detected the strategic contours of the Schlieffen plan.

The sequence just spelled out makes it appear, as Luigi Albertini suggested nearly half a century ago, that Russian decision makers bore a major responsibility for enlarging the war, for its transformation from a Balkan to a European venture. But that conclusion would be mistaken, as it ignores the outlooks and choices of Germany's leaders. The men in Berlin, as indicated above, had decided for war, "now or never," in any case.

There was even less "calculation" or "slide" in the French case. With President Raymond Poincaré and Premier/Foreign Minister René Viviani literally out at sea on the battleship *France* during a state visit to Russia from 16 to 29 July, a virtual foreign policy power vacuum existed in Paris. Neither War Minister Adolph Messimy nor Finance Minister Jean-Baptiste Bienvenu-Martin possessed the power to commit the nation to war. Technically speaking, the war powers rested with the president, but his orders had to be countersigned by a minister, and he could declare war only with the consent of the Senate and the Chamber of Deputies.[23] In July 1914, there was no meeting of the Council of Ministers, which had the authority to mobilize the armed forces. Nor was there a military conference at which French leaders debated the relative merits of war and peace. The professional diplomats at the Quai d'Orsay were generally anti-German; the ambassadors operated independent fiefdoms. President Poincaré exercised an influence over French foreign policy far exceeding his constitutional authority, greatly influencing the selection of foreign ministers and, in the case of his close friend Maurice Paléologue, also that of ambassadors. All had come to accept three stable elements of French policy: national pride, fear of Germany, and peace through strength.

The imperative of French policy in 1914, Eugenia C. Kiesling suggests, was simple and clear: to preserve the tie to St. Petersburg at all cost. France could not afford to "decide" whether to stand by Russia. While Premier Viviani publicly avowed that his policy was to "resolve the conflict ... in the interest of the general peace," he nevertheless described France as "entirely ready to support the action of the [Russian] imperial government."[24] France's ambassador to St. Petersburg,

---

[23] See Articles 3, 8, and 9 of the "Constitutional Law" of February 1875 in ibid., vol. 1, pp. 286–93.
[24] Viviani to Paléologue, 27 July 1914. In *Documents diplomatiques français*, 47 vols. (Paris, 1929–59), vol. 10, p. 138. Cited in Chapter 7.

Paléologue, throughout the July Crisis counseled an aggressive stance on the part of France and Russia, including if need be recourse to war. On 25 July and again on 28 July, Paléologue assured Russian Foreign Minister Sazonov of "unequivocal French support."[25] Poincaré's commitment to the Russian alliance was so firm that, in the words of one historian, he pursued it even at the cost of "connivance in dishonesty and blackmail."[26]

Absent from the list of key players in France in 1914 are many of the usual suspects, such as military planners, arms manufacturers, journalists, and public pressure groups, who represented the abstract forces of militarism, capitalism, and nationalism. In Kiesling's words, "None of these ... had a role in the French decision-making in 1914 or influenced the men who did." The decision for war was thus easy and it once again involved less than half a dozen players.

Across the English Channel, the cabinet never did decide to go to war. On 29 July, Foreign Secretary Sir Edward Grey addressed a "critical cabinet" on the issue of war in Europe. One member summarized the result as follows: "Situation seriously reviewed from all points of view. It was decided not to decide."[27] Prime Minister Herbert Asquith opined on 2 August that three-quarters of the Liberal Party in the House of Commons "are for absolute non-interference at any price."[28] No military advice was sought, no counsel given. Grey operated in "singular independence," carefully weighed his options, and, when all attempts to mediate the Serbian dispute had evaporated, moved toward war. Still, the only decisions taken by the ministers at the crucial cabinet meeting of 3 August were: Two of them chose to resign, two chose to resign and then retract, and the rest remained in office. Yet again, J. Paul Harris argues, there was no input from or consultation with the popular press, public opinion, or banking circles in The City. And yet again, there were no illusions about localizing the European conflict. Chaos and confusion may have reigned supreme, but there was no inadvertent "slide" into war.

[25] See Frederick L. Schuman, *War and Diplomacy in the French Republic: An Inquiry into Political Motivations and the Control of Foreign Policy* (New York, 1969), pp. 219–20; and Imanuel Geiss, ed., *July 1914: The Outbreak of the First World War: Selected Documents* (New York, 1967), p. 295.

[26] Schuman, *War and Diplomacy*, p. 204.

[27] Cited in Zara S. Steiner, *Britain and the Origins of the First World War* (New York, 1977), p. 224. See Chapter 8.

[28] Ibid., p. 232.

In fact, British policy had been consistent over the last third of the nineteenth century. Britain was interested in maintaining the balance of power on the Continent, in making sure that no European power was in position to sever or seriously to constrain its seaborne commerce, and in being in position to rebuff any serious threat to the home islands or to the Empire. Grey may have misjudged the seriousness of the initial phase of the July Crisis, but he quickly recovered and made a commitment to the defense of Belgium and France, in large part to block Germany from seizing any of the French Channel or Atlantic ports.

With strict constitutional propriety, the decision for war was made by the Asquith cabinet, with the consent of parliament. But the cabinet did not act in unison; rather, it was swayed, in the end, by a resolute minority. The prime mover was Grey, aided vociferously by First Lord of the Admiralty Winston S. Churchill. Asquith was less enthusiastic about a continental commitment, but trusted Grey's professional judgment. The rest of the cabinet eventually went along with that move toward war. In fact, Germany's violation of Belgian neutrality and Chancellor von Bethmann Hollweg's ill-chosen words about the 1839 Articles constituting but "a scrap of paper" did much to persuade them. Again, decision making by coterie.

The final major contracting power, Italy, constituted perhaps the exception to our argument. To be sure, there was no "slide" into war.[29] King Vittorio Emanuele III and Chief of the General Staff Alberto Pollio had repeatedly assured the Germans that, according to the terms of the third Triple Alliance treaty of 1891, they could count on Italy's "every last man" if it came to war in Europe.[30] At the moment of decision, however, Italy declined to support her alliance partners, Austria-Hungary and Germany. Italian policy in 1914, in the words of Richard Bosworth, was made by "one man alone," and that man was Foreign Minister Antonio di San Giuliano.[31] On 31 July, San Giuliano informed the cabinet that "neither the spirit nor the letter of the Triple Alliance force us to join in this case with Germany and Austria."[32] And it was San Giuliano who in

---

[29] Richard Bosworth, *Italy and the Approach of the First World War* (London and Basingstoke, 1983), p. 33, states: "There can be no defence for a case that Italy 'slithered into war.'"

[30] John Gooch, *Army, State and Society in Italy, 1870–1915* (New York, 1989), pp. 152–5. See Chapter 11.

[31] Bosworth, *Italy and the Approach*, p. 122.

[32] Cited in R. J. B. Bosworth, *Italy, the Least of the Great Powers: Italian Foreign Policy before the First World War* (Cambridge, 1979), p. 395.

August-September 1914 (just before his death in October) mapped out the "well sign-posted paths to intervention" on the side of the *entente*.[33] These "sign posts" consisted of the territorial annexation of the Trentino and Trieste, parts of Istria, the Dalmatian Islands, and Valona. Thus, in the Italian case, Richard F. Hamilton and Holger H. Herwig argue, there existed in 1915 a well-defined "calculus" although not of the kind the German policy advisor Kurt Riezler had in mind.[34]

Of all the powers discussed, Italy was the one case of a nation committed by alliance to a course of action that ran counter to its national interests and the national mood. Most politically aware Italians saw Austria-Hungary as the primary enemy. The country's economy was ill prepared for war. Social unrest, especially in the "red belt" of the Romagna, threatened domestic stability. Given these conditions, Prime Minister Antonio Salandra and his new foreign minister, Sidney Sonnino, "Italy's worst-ever Foreign Minister," moved the government's policy ever closer to that of Britain and France. They carried with them the cabinet, the Chamber of Deputies, and, eventually, the king.[35] In the end, San Giuliano's power and persuasion prompted the Italian government first to ignore the 1882 alliance, then to proclaim neutrality; thereafter, Salandra and Sonnino made the decision to enter the war for anticipated spoils. Italy's entry in World War I was truly decision making by coterie.

With regard to what we call the lesser or peripheral participants, the decision for war in most cases was taken by a coterie of senior leaders; in some (like Japan) by an individual leader. At the Porte, as Ulrich Trumpener argues, a handful of Young Turk leaders, including Minister of War Enver Bey, Minister of the Interior Mehmed Talât Bey, Minister of the Navy Ahmed Cemal Pasha, Premier and Foreign Minister Mehmed Said Halim, and President of the House of Deputies Halil Bey, on 2 August 1914 negotiated and signed a secret alliance with Germany.[36] The rest of the cabinet, the parliament, Ambassador Mahmud Muhtar at Berlin,

---

[33] Bosworth, *Italy and the Approach*, pp. 132–3.

[34] "Wars will no longer be fought," Riezler had argued on the eve of the Great War, "but calculated." J. J. Ruedorffer [Kurt Riezler], *Grundzüge der Weltpolitik der Gegenwart* (Stuttgart and Berlin, 1914). See also Chapter 5.

[35] Under Articles 4 and 5 of the Piedmontese Constitution of 1848, the "sacred and inviolable" king alone held "the executive power," was the "supreme head of state," commanded "all land and naval forces," "declares war," and "makes treaties." Dodd, *Modern Constitutions*, vol. 2, p. 5. The "worst-ever" claim is by Bosworth, *Italy and the Approach*, p. 134.

[36] The standard work remains Ulrich Trumpener, *Germany and the Ottoman Empire, 1914–1918* (New York, 1989). See Chapter 10.

and, most likely, Sultan Mehmed V were kept in the dark. This coterie of Young Turk leaders weighed their options and then decided that the recourse to arms on the side of Germany would best serve the nation. While many of them, like Ottoman politicians and intellectuals, preferred to side with Britain and France, in the final analysis neither London nor Paris offered acceptable terms of alliance; Germany became their last and unavoidable choice. Enver Bey perhaps put the case for the Young Turk leaders in deciding to join Germany most clearly: They did not like the risk of having the Ottoman Empire become "Russia's vassal," and they were also convinced that Germany and its allies were militarily stronger than the *entente* powers and would therefore prevail in the world war.

But the Ottoman entry into the war stemmed also from the Ottoman elites' search for economic independence. Once leaders at the Porte became convinced that the German tie offered them freedom from the British and French financial "capitulations," they agreed to an alliance with Berlin. Again, there was no "slide" into war, no surrender to impersonal and irresistible forces. Rather, there was bold calculation by a coterie of Young Turks that the road to recognition and to financial independence ran through Berlin. The fact that Berlin was negotiating with the Porte to secure its entry into a possible European war at the very time that Vienna was issuing its ultimatum to Belgrade speaks volumes against the "slide" thesis, as does the subsequent dispatch of two gold trains from Berlin to Constantinople and Rear Admiral Wilhelm Souchon's aggressive naval actions off Odessa.

In the Balkans, the decisions for war likewise rested with a small coterie of senior advisors, mainly princes or kings, politicians, and military leaders. In Serbia, given that Crown Prince Alexander had assumed the position of regent only on 24 June 1914, the crisis was handled directly by Prime Minister Nikola Pashich (Pašić). Since the bloody murder of King Alexander in 1903, Serbia had shifted its loyalties to Russia in the hope of securing backing for the creation of a "Greater Serbia," by arms if need be. Serb leaders saw this greater nation as the necessary precondition for economic and political success. In their paths stood first and foremost the Ottoman Empire, and, especially after its annexation of Bosnia-Herzegovina in 1908, the Austro-Hungarian Empire. Apart from Russia, Serb leaders also established shadowy relations with a number of secret societies, which were manned in large part by reserve officers and which had close links to the military establishment. These included, but were not limited to, Union or Death (Ujedinjenie ili Smrt), popularly known as the Black Hand (Tsrna Ruka). The society's leader, Colonel

Dragutin Dimitrijevich ("Apis"), in 1913 became head of Serbian military intelligence.

Prime Minister Pashich, while recognizing that "anarchistic elements" may well have had a hand in the assassination at Sarajevo on 28 June 1914, nevertheless was reluctant to identify the Black Hand as perpetrator of the act for fear of thereby exposing the interconnection among the civilian and military decision-making bodies in Belgrade. In the end, fully aware that Serbia was still recovering from the losses of the two Balkan Wars, he decided not to go to war but, rather, to leave the onus for declaring war with Vienna. Failure to obtain clear commitments of support from St. Petersburg undoubtedly also played a role in this decision. As Richard C. Hall argues, the murder at Sarajevo "caused" nothing; rather, it was the use made of the killings, especially by Vienna, that set Europe on a course toward war. Far from "sliding" into armed conflict, Pashich, recognizing the immediacy of war, moved the government to the southern city of Nish and ordered the military to initiate basic precautions.[37]

With regard to Bulgaria, senior decision makers (king, politicians, military) once again determined the recourse to arms. And as in the case of Serbia, secret societies (the "Supreme Macedonian Committee" and the "Internal Macedonian Revolutionary Committee") spearheaded the drive for a "Greater Bulgaria." Tsar Ferdinand and Minister-President Vasil Radoslavov at first declared that Bulgaria would remain neutral in the European war. But in October 1915, they sided with the Central Powers to assert what Radoslavov termed Bulgaria's "rights" in Macedonia. Bulgaria saw therein the best chance to reverse its defeat in the Second Balkan War and to regain much-sought-after Macedonian territory.[38] It was decision by coterie; the aim, immediate territorial gain.

In Romania, the road to war was dictated by King Carol I and Prime Minister Ion Brătianu, supported by a land-owning aristocracy and a small educated urban class. There were no secret societies at work in Romania or in the territories that she coveted, and, unlike elsewhere in the Balkans, the military remained under government control. A member of the Triple Alliance since 1888, Romania, like Italy, in 1914 opted for neutrality. A "pervasive spirit of opportunism," Richard C. Hall states, led Bucharest in August 1915 to opt for the *entente* in return for three

[37] Alex N. Dragnich, *Serbia, Nikola Pašić and Yugoslavia* (New Brunswick, N.J., 1971). Also see Chapter 3.

[38] Richard C. Hall, *Bulgaria's Road to the First World War* (Boulder, Colo., 1996). Also, see Chapter 12.

irredentist objectives: the annexation of Hungarian-controlled Transylvania, of the Bukovina, and of Bessarabia.[39] Together, they would allow Bucharest to proclaim a "Greater Romania." The lust for irredentist gains at the expense of Austria-Hungary, rather than an innocent "slide," thus brought Romania into the war.

The Greek case, Richard C. Hall suggests, was too interwoven with domestic intrigues, personal agendas, and great power intervention to allow a clear-cut path to war to be identified. Greece in June 1917 was the last European state to enter the war – and then only after tortuous political turmoil, *entente* invasion, Anglo-French blockade, and the forced abdication of King Constantine. Still, in the final analysis, the decision for war can be traced to a single determined leader: Prime Minister Eleutherios Venizelos.

Beyond continental Europe and the Ottoman Empire, tough, aggressive senior decision makers also charted the course toward war. In Japan, the European war brought relief and joy. What senior leaders termed the great "confusion" would spell opportunity for Japan, an opportunity to become the "chief nation of the Orient." On 8 August 1914, the cabinet approved Japanese participation in the war alongside Great Britain. That decision was the work primarily of one man, Foreign Minister Katō Takaaki. In what Frederick R. Dickinson describes as a "complete usurpation of the foreign policy prerogative," in August 1914, Katō, after consulting with just a handful of his closest advisors in the Foreign Ministry, took the *genrō*, or elder statesmen, completely by surprise.[40] There was no input from the public, the popular press, or financial and industrial circles. And far from being a "slide" into war, Japan's entry into that conflict was the product of the machinations of its foreign minister.

Katō's action was the result of a complex set of conditions peculiar to Japan. In part, it played out against a turbulent domestic political battle to define the national essence that had absorbed Japanese energies since the island's "opening" to the modern world in 1853. In part, it was a vote of confidence for the Anglo-Japanese Alliance of 1902 as well as the foreign minister's bid to promote British parliamentarism at

[39] Glenn E. Torrey, *Romania and World War I* (Portland, Ore., 1998).

[40] Frederick R. Dickinson, *War and National Reinvention: Japan in the Great War, 1914–1919* (Cambridge, Mass., 1999). Also, see Chapter 9. The almost limitless powers of the "sacred and inviolable" emperor under the Constitution of February 1889 to "command the army and navy" (Article 11), and to "declare war, make peace, and conclude treaties" (Article 13) did not come into play in 1914. Dodd, *Modern Constitutions*, vol. 2, pp. 24–5.

home. In part, it was an element in Katō's struggle against what Dickinson calls the "battle against budding Pan-Asianism in Japan," that is, against the wildly ambitious schemes for territorial expansion in China promoted especially by senior military leaders. And finally, it was a masterstroke to ensure Katō's control of the foreign policy decision-making process.

Last but not least, the United States entered the war in April 1917 in large measure also because of one man: Woodrow Wilson. Having attempted for the first three years of the war to influence its course and outcome through diplomatic means, the president finally ran out of alternatives after Germany's initiation of unrestricted submarine warfare on 1 February 1917.[41]

John M. Cooper first examines, and then rejects, the customary arguments of scholars that "powerful forces" such as precedent, economics, culture, geopolitics, and popular opinion brought about the American decision to enter the war. He suggests instead that these "powerful forces" were but "background influences" and that they acted on the side of nonintervention. Rather, "Wilson remains at the center. He and, in certain critical respects, he alone cast America's lot for entry into World War I." With Congress out of session for all but three months between August 1914 and the end of 1915, the president acted on his own, with complete faith in his enormous self-assurance.

Germany's submarine offensive determined America's eventual response. The sinking of the British liner *Lusitania* on 7 May 1915, with the loss of 128 Americans, changed the nation's relation to the war. William Jennings Bryan's decision to resign as secretary of state on 9 June 1915 allowed Wilson to take charge of foreign policy. That policy was defined by a tradition of diplomatic isolation and a century of noninvolvement in overseas affairs. It was also shaped by the president's reading of what Cooper calls the "double wish" of the American people: to remain firm in the face of the German threat and yet to do nothing that might propel the United States into the war. Berlin's decision to begin unrestricted submarine warfare on 1 February 1917 caused Wilson to opt for war, to "take the risk that as a victor this nation could shape a better, more just peace and try to prevent such conflagrations from ever happening again." In proper constitutionality, the president presented his case to Congress, which held the war powers. But in the end, Cooper argues, Wilson's role

---

[41] Thomas J. Knock, *To End All Wars: Woodrow Wilson and the Quest for World Order* (Princeton, 1995). See also Chapter 13.

was critical: "He and he alone took the United States into World War I." However one evaluates Wilson's handling of the European crisis, few serious scholars would accuse the president of a "slide" into war.

During the war, arguments of intention, of sinister premeditation were dominant, these basically being arguments of aggressive purpose. A year or two after the end of the war, a sea change occurred and arguments of inadvertence – no one wanted war – were given increasingly wide approval. Both arguments were basically political in character, serving as an aid first in the conduct of the war, and then in the conduct of the peace. Since little serious documentation was available at that point, the actual bases of the decision making were essentially unknown. The most striking instance of the shift in usages appears in the case of David Lloyd George, who, in a less than a year, changed from a committed intentionalist to become the principal author of the nonjudgmental slide thesis. In January 1920, he demanded that Kaiser Wilhelm II be formally tried as a war criminal, perhaps at Dover Castle. Then, in December of that year, he made a famous speech in which he argued that the nations had "glided, or rather staggered and stumbled" into war.[42] As late as 1936, Lloyd George still maintained, "No sovereign or leading statesman in any of the belligerent countries sought or desired war – certainly not a European war."[43] The "slide" thesis renders careful reexamination of the July Crisis unnecessary: no motive, no intention, no responsibility. We suggest instead a consistent pattern, multiple instances of moves for engagement; and we argue that the very essence of decision making is human input by way of choice.

And so it was in 1914. For decades, European leaders had "gamed" the likely scenario for war on the Continent. In each case, they rejected the notion that a war could be localized or isolated. In each case, they recognized the danger of diplomatic escalation leading to armed conflict. In each case, they knew the dangers inherent in a general European war. In each case, they accepted those risks and dangers in July and August, and they decided for war with the full expectation of winning and thereby solving the difficulties that prompted them to consider armed conflict in the first place. That is what made the July Crisis radically different from previous crises, such as the two Moroccan wars, the two Balkan wars, and the Tripolitanian war.

---

[42] Cecil, *Wilhelm II*, vol. 2, p. 299; A. Lentin, *Lloyd George, Woodrow Wilson and the Guilt of Germany: An Essay in the Pre-History of Appeasement* (Leicester, 1984), p. 143.

[43] David Lloyd George, *War Memoirs*, 6 vols. (London, 1933–6), vol. 6, p. 3346.

ct, there was a surprising single-mindedness of purpose in the deci-
akers of 1914. They recognized almost to a man that the strategic
ient of perceived decline or threat demanded the call to arms. In
short order, the murder of Archduke Franz Ferdinand receded from the
forefront of their considerations. Instead, the leaders in Vienna and Berlin,
St. Petersburg and Paris, persisted in their view that war alone could resolve their perceived precarious positions in the European concert. And
when two monarchs, Wilhelm II and Nicholas II, at the last moment tried
to pull back from the precipice, the coteries in Berlin and St. Petersburg
forced them back on course.

The "slide" thesis is also rendered spurious by the various actions, especially in the three critical capitals – Vienna, Berlin, and St. Petersburg – to
block possible mediation of the crisis. Foreign Minister Berchtold as
early as 3 July boldly informed the German ambassador, Heinrich von
Tschirschky, of his government's need for a *"final and fundamental
reckoning"* with Serbia. Kaiser Wilhelm II at Berlin endorsed that initiative with the terse marginalia, "now or never." Vienna refused a state
funeral for Archduke Franz Ferdinand in part because such a formal gathering might have offered the crowned heads of Europe an opportunity to
discuss and perhaps to coordinate their responses to the assassination at
Sarajevo. Vienna was determined to strike out against Belgrade; Berlin
seconded that initiative. And once Russia had decided to block the proposed Habsburg "punitive expedition" against Serbia by way of mobilization, Foreign Minister Sazonov forestalled further discussion and possible
resolution of the crisis by instructing General Ianushkevich, the chief of
the General Staff, to smash his telephone!

Perhaps the last words on the "slide" thesis should go to one of
the pivotal players, the chief of the German General Staff. Already in
March 1913, General von Moltke confided to the Italian military attaché
Germany's intention to violate Belgian neutrality in case of war. The next
war, Moltke stated, would be between France and Germany. In brutal
terms, he allowed that this war would be "a question of life or death for
us. We shall stop at nothing to gain our end. In the struggle for existence,
one does not bother about the means one employs."[44] And in retirement
in June 1915, Moltke in a private letter to Field Marshal Colmar von der
Goltz spoke openly of "this war which I prepared and initiated."[45] No
drift, no slide.

---

[44] Gooch, *Army, State and Society*, p. 149.
[45] Cited in John C. G. Röhl, "Germany," in Wilson, ed., *Decisions for War 1914*, p. 27.

## On the Argument of the Alliances

The second major argument spelled out in Chapter 1 is the claim that the alliance system "caused" the war. It too is an argument of inadvertence: No one planned it that way; it "just so happened" that general war proved the consequence of those obligations.

As laid out in Chapter 1, the alliances were first and foremost defensive. None called for any of the contracting powers to behave as they did in July 1914. None triggered the *casus foederis*. Only one treaty, the Franco-Russian convention of 1892, included specific military measures. At the most extreme interpretation of alliance adherence, the treaties required "benevolent neutrality" of their signatories. Not a single major leader, to the best of our knowledge, argued the recourse to war on the basis of the "alliance system."

All the treaties of the Triple Alliance and of the Triple Alliance with Romania became active only if one of the contracting powers was forced to resort to war "without direct provocation on their part." Given these antecedent events, it is clear that none of the treaties required engagement in July 1914. The decisions to resort to war, beginning with Vienna, were made entirely independent of treaty stipulations. In all cases, the strategic argument – the need to halt a perceived decline or to block a serious threat – proved decisive. Men made the choice for war not according to formal contractual obligations but, rather, according to presumed national interests and needs.

The basic lesson with regard to the alliance systems is that the literal terms of the alliances counted for little; the interpretation, uses, and actions of the key decision makers counted for much. An earlier episode provides a good example. In 1850, Austria and Prussia were on the verge of war in a struggle over Hesse-Kassel. Austria had occupied that state to enforce the elector's authority over an uncooperative parliament, an action that greatly annoyed Prussia. In a heated discussion, one German leader argued that the issue was "purely juridical." Austria had acted in accordance with the constitution of the German Confederation, which was still "the valid law" in Germany. Otto von Bismarck, then a member of the Prussian legislature, responded by stating that he recognized "no law in foreign affairs, only convenience." Later that year, in a public statement, Bismarck put his position, *Realpolitik*, more forcefully:

Why do large states go to war nowadays? The only sound basis for a large state is its egoism and not romanticism: this is what distinguishes a large state necessarily from a small one. It is not worthy of a large state to fight for a thing that is not

484

.t. Just show me an objective worth a war, gentlemen, and I will
6

ı: Treaties are words on paper, words that by themselves
: no determinative impact.[47] They are not golden tablets, cast
r eternity. They are bound by time and circumstance. They
must ᴅᴇ ı the national interest of their signatories to have any value.
They are upheld only insofar as they serve those national interests. To
be sure, the age-old argument of alliance determinism assumes an effective international rule of law and honorable alliance partners. But most
experts in international affairs would count those as among the most
naive hypotheses imaginable. We suggest instead that a more intelligent
reading of the events of July 1914 might have caused a different opinion as to whether the entire Balkans were worth the bones of millions of
grenadiers – Pomeranian or otherwise.

---

[46] Cited in Otto Pflanze, *Bismarck and the Development of Germany*, vol. 1: *The Period of Unification, 1815–1871* (Princeton, 1990), pp. 72–3.

[47] This was made clearest perhaps in December 1908 by Vittorio Emanuele III, who spoke openly to foreign diplomats "of the utter worthlessness of treaties or any agreements written on paper. They are worth the value of the paper." The Italian king placed his faith only "in bayonets and cannon." Cited in Bosworth, *Italy, the Least of the Great Powers*, p. 377; also William A. Renzi, "Italy's Neutrality and Entrance into the Great War: A Reexamination," *American Historical Review* 73 (June 1968): 1414.

# 15

# On the Origins of the Catastrophe

## Richard F. Hamilton

The aim of this chapter is to provide the rudiments of a theory, something intermediate between the Big Causes and Ultimate Particularism. The initial task is to provide a brief portrait of the decision-making coteries, two types of which are easily discerned: those chosen by the dynasts and those chosen by party leaders. This account also reviews the constitutional question, indicating how the key groups came to be so empowered. And it considers how those groups saw the world, indicating the rationales that led to their key policy decisions. We are dealing with patterns of small group dynamics, basically with a social psychology of leadership.

We then consider a third segment, one not present among the decision makers, namely, "the bourgeoisie," the leaders of business and finance. As opposed to notions of a commonality of views, a sharp divergence is seen. Rather than string-pulling or behind-the-scenes operators, we have frustrated and helpless magnates (although once the decision was made, they were willing to go along, willing to "do their part"). This finding indicates the need for consideration of an important counterfactual argument: If business had been dominant, if "the bourgeoisie" had been in power, the war would not have happened. Put differently, the war happened because premodern elites, the dynasts, were still in power. The key question, then, is: How could the elites of Austria-Hungary, Russia, and Germany have made the decisions that, from the start, would clearly have such formidable consequences? How could they justify their moves?

## Theoretical Options

Alexis de Tocqueville was quoted in Chapter 1, specifically, his comments on how history would be written in democracies. His prediction, put simply, was that historians would come to focus on "big causes." That claim has been amply confirmed in some eighty years of review and comment on the origins of the Great War. Tocqueville made a parallel claim, that the previous style of history, the focus on individuals and their linkages, would be disdained. Decades later, that approach would be dismissed as hardly worth discussion. For the cognoscenti, it was "old Namier-style prosopography." For commentators seeking "powerful" generalizations, Namier's approach (or that of Ranke) seemed hopeless, providing a welter of detail and no end of chance or contingent events.

The descriptive terms in that reference to Namier – "old" and "style" – are inappropriate for scholarly work, since times and fashions, by themselves, have no bearing on the key question, that of empirical adequacy. Following that guideline, one should also avoid the fictive generalization, the declaration not capable of testing, such as, for example, those about "mass" opinion prior to the appearance of serious cross-sectional surveys, or statements that purport to indicate preferences, intensities, and impacts. Following Tocqueville's lead, our preference is to look for the useful generalization. "Useful" in this context means a generalization that can be empirically verified or refuted. One should look for the general pattern within the welter of individual events. Should none be found, the researcher should indicate that result. One should also – an obvious correlate – be willing to signal the contributions of individual actors.[1] The exclusion of that possibility, its rejection as a Rankean heresy, is a kind of prejudice, the a priori exclusion of an obvious option. An easy example: Nicholas II could have said "no" to the mobilization on 31 July 1914.

One theoretical framework that appears to be useful in this connection is the elitist perspective. As opposed to the notion of a single cohesive ruling class – "the aristocracy" or "the bourgeoisie" – this view sees modern societies having different institutional sectors, each with its own specialized leadership group.[2] Those leadership groups differ in size and character, as may be easily seen in the political, economic, religious, military, and intellectual sectors. A given elite might consist of a thousand individuals,

---

[1] For an important case study, see Henry Ashby Turner, Jr., *Hitler's Thirty Days to Power: January 1933* (Reading, Mass., 1996).
[2] G. Lowell Field and John Higley, *Elitism* (London, 1980), esp. p. 20.

but only a handful could be directly involved in government decision making, hence our focus on subsets, on the small groups or coteries.

One central underlying assumption of the elitist perspective is that apart from infrequent revolutionary episodes, "the masses" do not participate in the governance of nations.[3] In contrast to the assumptions of Marxism or of the mass society theory, the masses are effectively "out of it." Voluntary associations appeared in the course of the nineteenth century, but they typically enrolled a "thin layer" of upper- and upper-middle class citizens. They made demands and attempted to influence, but they did not manage the day-to-day affairs of government. Governance was much more complicated in 1914 than in 1815. But decision making was still, as always, the work of "the few." The key questions, accordingly, are: Whose rule? or, in this context, Which elites, which coteries? and, With what consequences?

Constitutional arrangements, formal and informal, stipulate or provide guidelines indicating which elites shall rule. Those arrangements, typically, are the result of elite settlements, compromises worked out by powerful groups seeking to end dangerous or threatening contention. An "identity of interest" would be an easy read-in, but an elite settlement might end a serious struggle, even though the differences in viewpoint persist, as with the 1689 English settlement or with the 1867 Austro-Hungarian arrangement.

A constitution, it should be noted, may make precise specifications (allocations of powers), but even the best statement is subject to informal modification. A strong-willed monarch could easily include others in the process or could exclude some authorized participants. Likewise, a strong party leader might make substantial modifications in the official constitutional design. A weak-willed monarch might have extraordinary powers under the constitution but choose not to rule, leaving the "affairs of state" to favored ministers, as was the case with Vittorio Emanuele III. A sudden death, natural or otherwise, would instantly remove a decision maker and dramatically restructure "the forces" present within a ruling

[3] The most familiar accounts of those revolutionary episodes grossly distort the actual events. Karl Marx has it that "the workers" of Paris rose in arms in June 1848 in an attempt to take power, this in the first of the modern class struggles. A detailed study of the event revealed a markedly different history. Most Paris workers, the majority, did not participate; most sat it out. The insurgent workers, moreover, had "reformist" aims, seeking to retain a threatened job-creation program. See Michael Traugott, *Armies of the Poor* (Princeton, 1985); and Richard F. Hamilton, *The Bourgeois Epoch: Marx and Engels on Britain, France, and Germany* (Chapel Hill, 1991), ch. 3.

coterie. That was clearly the case with Gavrilo Princip's "removal" of Franz Ferdinand.

## Institutional Developments: Change and Continuity

In the course of the eighteenth and nineteenth centuries, the societies of western Europe were substantially transformed, developing ever more complex social arrangements and creating new elites. The new economic arrangements, those of industrial capitalism, were built into what for centuries had been agrarian societies. A dramatic growth of cities occurred, these being the primary centers of the new economy. Gradually, over the nineteenth century, the masses received primary schooling: For the first time in human history, people, the overwhelming majority of them, were taught the basics of reading, writing, and arithmetic. The presence of literate masses made possible another important development: large-circulation newspapers, magazines, and popular books. The masses in 1800 or 1700 or in any of the previous centuries would have had a very limited understanding of the world outside their villages. Their descendants in 1900 would have had a much greater knowledge of their societies and of the world.

That "much greater knowledge," however, would have been very limited, a pathetic achievement as compared with that possessed by another recently emerging group: the intellectuals, who "were educated," taught the various elites and the masses, and produced the content of the new "mass media." The intellectuals and their audiences, a very thin layer located for the most part in the upper-middle classes, would have influence like no other groups in previous history.

Those changes were associated, in one way or another, with a major intellectual movement, one that came to be called liberalism.[4] The basic ideas were that people, generally, should be free to do things not previously permitted and that this freedom would bring substantial improvements in the human condition, for individuals and for the collectivity. The initial demand, accordingly, was for the removal of restraints or restrictions. This "liberation" would occur in the economic, social, and political realms. The emphases, understandably, differed. Businessmen (many of them) sought economic freedom; religious and ethnic minorities sought

---

[4] For a brief summary, see Richard F. Hamilton, *Marxism, Revisionism, and Leninism* (Westport, Conn., 2000), ch. 1.

social liberation, an ending of discrimination; intellectuals sought freedom of expression, basically, freedom from the censor.

The liberal movement brought wider and more insistent demands for participation in public affairs. An informed (or enlightened) citizenry was no longer quiescent, no longer showing unquestioning respect and deference to traditional leaders, especially those who owed their position to the accidents of birth. The principal demands were for the extension of suffrage and for vesting an elected legislature with power. The movement also brought advocacy groups, ones that made ever more insistent demands on "the ruling classes." One of the freedoms demanded, understandably, was freedom of association. The extension of that freedom allowed the appearance of formally organized political parties – liberal, conservative, socialist, and religious – and also of pressure groups. Traditional rulers, the monarchs and their supportive aristocracies, clearly, faced ever more serious challenges. For them, governance was becoming ever more complicated.[5]

This review of the dramatic changes, of the many new developments, is somewhat misleading in that it gives no indication of the continued existence, and importance, of the previous social arrangements. Modern industry was making significant advances, but agrarian economies continued to be present and important in some countries until well into the twentieth century. Great cities did appear, beginning with London and Paris, but most people, especially on the continent, continued to live in the towns and villages. In 1910, only a little more than one-fifth of the population in economically advanced Germany lived in cities of 100,000 or more, while more than half were located in communities of 5,000 or less.[6] Mass education did appear, but for most people,

[5] That "participation in government" – the extension of suffrage and increase of powers for an elected legislature – does not alter the basic elitist argument: that governance, actual rule, is the work of a few, of a coterie. When "the socialists" took office in Britain in 1945, for example, that did not mean working-class rule. It meant rule by Labour Party leaders, by a new and different coterie. The policies they instituted differed substantially from those of previous leadership groups. See Peter Hennessy, *Never Again: Britain 1945–1951* (New York, 1993); and, more generally, the important work of Robert Michels, *Political Parties*, trans. Eden and Cedar Paul (1915; Glencoe, Ill., 1949).

[6] J. Scott Keltie, *The Statesman's Year-Book* (London, 1914), p. 889. In France in 1911, only one in seven lived in cities of 100,000 or more; more than three-fifths lived in communities of 5,000 or less. Ibid., p. 814. Austria-Hungary at that point has been described as "an insufficiently developed agrarian state." In Austria, 53 percent of the labor force was engaged in agriculture (vs. 23 percent in industry and trade). In the Hungarian "half" of the empire, the equivalent figures were 69 and 13; from Eduard März, *Austrian Banking*

as indicated, the amount was limited, the quality poor, and the impacts uncertain.[7]

Many accounts of the newly aroused masses, as indicated, focus on Vienna, Berlin, and Paris. They portray "people" there passing time in the coffeehouses, reading newspapers and discussing the events of the day. But most people in those European nations were still living in the towns and villages and most were still involved in, or linked to, the agrarian economy. Most of them, probably, never set foot in a coffeehouse. There is, in short, a serious sampling problem with those accounts. The authors are describing urban intelligentsia, an exceptionally literate group (and one generously endowed with leisure time) that made up probably less than 1 percent of the total population, and treating that curious collection as typical of the entire adult population. Most adults in those societies probably spent more time in churches than in coffeehouses.[8]

The base of power of the traditional rulers, the monarchs and aristocracies, would normally be in the premodern sector, in the agrarian economy and in the towns and villages. In those settings they would ordinarily be supported by an established church and its clergy. That traditional base of power, although clearly in relative decline, was still substantial. Armies were recruited, very disproportionately and by preference, from the farms, villages, and towns. Biased suffrage arrangements and unreformed districts artificially extended the lives of those old regimes. The sources of power in those regimes differed substantially from the bases of the liberal or progressive insurgents. The monarchical regimes depended on deference, on a trained belief in the legitimacy of the handed-down arrangements. For the liberals, that meant regimes based on ignorance, on stubborn prejudice. But the steady advance of "reason," the liberals knew, would eventually erode such views.

Another question of incidence, of frequency should be noted: Modern industry, urbanization, mass education, and intellectual development

---

*and Financial Policy: Creditanstalt as a Turning Point, 1913–1923*, trans. Charles Kessler (London, 1984), p. 16.

[7] For a brief summary of the institutional history, see Richard F. Hamilton, *Mass Society, Pluralism, and Bureaucracy* (Westport, Conn., 2001), ch. 4.

[8] Did the farmers, after a day at the plow, leave the fields for newspaper reading and discussion in the coffee houses? Would the workers, after ten hours of physically demanding factory work, go off to the coffee houses? And did their wives leave house and family for an hour or two of rest and relaxation? Was cost not a factor? Would desperately poor families have the money for such diversions? On the question of cafés versus churches, social historians pay much attention to the former but, typically, are indifferent to the latter.

were most advanced in western Europe, less so in central Europe, and least in eastern Europe. A commonplace observation, but one worth a reminder, is that similar west-to-east variations appeared with respect to governing arrangements. Constitutional restraints, checks on absolute authority, were instituted earlier in western Europe. As seen in the review of the powers of George V, Wilhelm II, and Nicholas II, the extent or impact of those checks was greatest in Britain, least in Russia. Paul M. Kennedy, reviewing the German case, concluded that "Wilhelm's powers were closer to, and probably greater than, those of George III than of Edward VII."[9]

All five major powers in 1914 were constitutional regimes, meaning that the four monarchs and the one president were subject to some legal or, in the case of Britain, some agreed-upon limits to their power. But that categorical formulation, as indicated, hides significant differences. Austria-Hungary, Russia, and Germany had written constitutions, but all three left important powers in the hands of the monarchy, most importantly, the power of declaring war. Those three, moreover, were not parliamentary regimes, since the ministers, in all three empires, were chosen by the monarch. The ministers were responsible to the monarch and, when no longer in favor, could be dismissed by him. The governing coterie, in short, consisted of the monarch and his ministers. The elected legislative bodies provided the principal check on the monarch's power. Their members could initiate legislation and, if they found a majority, could refuse the monarch's initiatives.[10] The legislature's most important limit on the executive's power was financial, namely, the power of the purse. While an important achievement, that formal power on some occasions was not easily exercised. If the empire faced a hostile or threatening power, a vote against a military budget could be a very problematic move.

With all of the major social developments of the age running against them, the authoritarian leaders recognized that "time was running out." Britain's Hanoverian kings recognized the "tide of events," compromised,

---

[9] In his *Rise of the Anglo-German Antagonism 1860–1914* (London, 1980), p. 404.

[10] These few sentences cannot indicate the complexities of three constitutions. The Russian constitution of 1906 announced the tsar's "supreme autocratic power." One clause stipulated that "[t]he initiative in all legislative measures belongs to the Emperor." A later clause declared: "The Council of the Empire and the Imperial Duma ... have the right to propose the amendment or repeal of existing laws or the enactment of new laws, with the exception of the fundamental laws of the Empire, the initiative for the revision of which belongs exclusively to the Emperor." From Walter Fairleigh Dodd, *Modern Constitutions*, 2 vols. (Chicago, 1909), vol. 2, pp. 183, 192.

and accepted the new developments. But the authoritarian rulers on the continent continued the fight. Kaiser Wilhelm's first speech after his accession in 1888 was a message addressed to the Prussian army. He spoke of the death of his grandfather and father, emphasizing their ties and those of many other Hohenzollern ancestors with the army and its glorious heritage. His conclusion reads: "Thus we belong together – I and the army – were born for one another, and thus we will remain together forever, whether, through God's will, in peace or war." Not too surprisingly, he and some of his ministers considered the use of the military, of a *coup d'état*, to stop or reverse the pervasive tendencies.[11]

France, the most progressive of the major powers, had a republican regime, the third in its history, after several tries at other arrangements. The president named a premier, who chose cabinet members from among the parties represented in the legislature. The premier and his government were responsible to, and could be removed by, a vote of that legislature. The government could also be voted out in a subsequent election. Formal constitutional arrangements are one thing; the actual practice could be quite another. Formally, the premier headed the government. But in midyear 1914, as seen, President Poincaré was clearly the de facto head of the government.

Great Britain was nominally a constitutional monarchy, but its king was a figurehead with very limited powers. Officially, the monarch called on a party leader to form a government. That leader, the prime minister, in turn chose the other cabinet members from among the elected members of his party. That government was responsible to parliament, not the king. It could be removed by a no-confidence vote in parliament, or, of course, it could be voted out in the next general election. The cabinet, as seen, was empowered to take the nation into war.

### Dynastic Elites

Those constitutional arrangements specified which office holders were authorized to make the decisions of July and August 1914.[12] In

---

[11] The message appears in *Schulthess' Europäischer Geschichtskalender* (Nördlingen, 1889), new series, vol. 4, pp. 94–5. For their consideration of a possible overthrow, see Michael Stürmer, "Staatsstreichgedanken im Bismarckreich," *Historische Zeitschrift* 209 (1967): 566–615; and Egmont Zechlin, *Staatsstreichpläne Bismarcks und Wilhelms II, 1890–1894* (Stuttgart and Berlin, 1929), pt. 1.

[12] This formulation is perhaps misleading, since by themselves words on paper do not ordinarily determine anything. The arrangements were established by various elites at some

Austria-Hungary, Germany, and Russia, the decision-making coterie consisted of the monarch and his chosen ministers. Among the latter one would find a prime minister, a minister of foreign affairs, a finance minister, a minister of the interior (police), and so on. Those ministers were usually civilians. In addition, one would find the war minister, possibly the head of the General Staff, and the minister of the navy. Even for these people, the chosen ones, no hard and fast rules determined participation. Much depended on the ego strength (and whim) of the ruler who could make ad hoc decisions about inclusion. Influence could also be exerted in the opposite direction. A capable (or tactically adept) subordinate could ingratiate himself and might, possibly, change the monarch's mind on some issue. But it was a chancy business, given the monarch's "last word" and the deference expected of subordinates.

Something needs to be said about the formative experiences of those decision makers. Most of them were drawn from the aristocracy. While an accurate statement, that clue is misleading. Most aristocrats were landowners, persons involved in agriculture and estate management. The civilian ministers left the estates at an early age, might have studied law, and then would have undergone a long apprenticeship moving up the ranks within the government. The military ministers joined the forces at an early age and normally spent their entire lives there. The estate-owning aristocrat, the inheritor, was the de facto ruler within his domain. The aristocrats in government, in contrast, were subordinates during their entire professional careers. Many were tough-minded, many of them arrogant, but all, to some degree at least, had to "play the courtier." This was especially the case at the topmost level, for those directly responsible to the monarch.

The training of monarchs, what might be called the social psychology of monarchy, has been generally neglected by both the historical and social sciences. Heirs apparent are subjected to one of the most unusual child-rearing programs in the entire repertory. Given the careers for which they are destined, they are typically subjected to very demanding and insistent routines, this in the palace nursery under the direction of carefully chosen tutors. Later, in the early teens, the male inheritors were given a military rank and assigned to a unit under the supervision of some trusted officer. Here the young man would find some easy-going companions who, not

prior point. Those agreements were still in place, still honored, still generally accepted at the time of the 1914 crisis.

surprisingly, were deferential, supportive, and very helpful in attending to his needs and wishes.

That early training, accordingly, involved two sharply contrasting experiences. Initially, there was the set of heavy, unyielding demands. Two of the heirs, Frederick (later called "the Great") and crown prince Alexei (son of Peter the Great), found it so oppressive they ran away from home (with horrendous consequences). Rudolf, the son of Emperor Franz Joseph and Empress Elisabeth, committed suicide. Edward backed away from his very demanding parents, Queen Victoria and Prince Albert; Wilhelm backed away from his very demanding parents, Friedrich and Vicky (Victoria's daughter). Both of the disaffected sons, Edward and Wilhelm, sought and found more pliant, more supportive companions elsewhere. In the course of growing up, the heirs gradually discovered an exceptionally permissive environment, one in which almost all wishes would be granted. Given their early experience, many of the heirs identified with the military, feeling "at home" with the men, traditions, and values of this institution.

Coming of age within that exceptionally permissive environment gave rise to two problematic character traits. Few of those companions would challenge the prospective monarch, neither contradicting nor correcting his utterances. For him, accordingly, there would be no serious "reality testing." One result would be an unusual assurance, or certainty, about the validity of his judgments. With no controlling logic to govern his thinking, another result was irresolution, vacillation, continuous, and unpredictable change of positions. Both pathologies were found, in especially egregious form, in the mental processes of Kaiser Wilhelm II.

Finally, something needs to be said about the outlooks, mind-sets, or *mentalités* of the monarchs. Given their training, given the focus on the state, it should come as no surprise that the national interest would figure prominently in their thinking. The power, prestige, or influence of the nation, on the continent and in the world, had a central place in their thinking – as may be seen in the justifications they offered during the 1914 crisis. That expression, "national interest," is misleading in its suggestion of realism, as if one were dealing with an objective reality (such as troop strength, industrial capacity, or food supplies). In fact, however, those interests are definitions, declarations of perceived needs and of appropriate actions, plus some ordering of priorities. In some instances, those needs are declared to be urgent imperatives. A striking feature of the coteries of the three threatened monarchical powers is the high degree of consensus evidenced with respect to "the imperatives" presented by the July Crisis. All three coteries "recognized" that a demonstration of their nation's power was necessary. And all three signaled they were willing to take enormous chances or, more precisely, willing to pay enormous costs for the sake of that aim.

## Party Elites

The decision-making coteries in Britain and France had a strikingly different composition. The members were, basically, party leaders, men heading the dominant party or party coalitions plus some others who had shown some degree of competence, enough for them to be entrusted with cabinet positions. The war and naval ministries in Britain were usually headed by civilians. In France, those offices were usually held by members of the military, but there they had little say in governance. The chiefs of staff were not ordinarily members of the governing coterie. France, of course, had no monarch. The British monarch was, essentially, "off stage." One indication of the difference here: Wilhelm initiated much of "the action" in the July Crisis, including an important last-minute message to Nicholas. In Britain, Asquith and Tyrrell, Grey's secretary, initiated a similar last-minute letter to the tsar, getting the king out of bed for this late-night effort.

The British and French decision makers came to their positions through routes that differed significantly from the paths of three dynastic coteries. All of them were elected officials, members of parliament or of the National Assembly. An individual's presence among the decision makers depended on three processes: first, that his party won favor with the voters; second, that it was chosen to form the government; and third, that the party leader (or leaders) then chose that individual for a cabinet position. Ordinarily, the successful official would have held several cabinet positions, being promoted to more demanding posts as he accumulated experience. Asquith, a prosperous lawyer, was elected to parliament in 1886. He was named as Home Secretary by Gladstone in 1892. The return of the Conservatives in 1895 put him in the opposition until the change of government in late 1905 followed by the sweeping Liberal victory in 1906. At that point he was named, by Campbell-Bannerman, to be Chancellor of the Exchequer. Two years later, following a heart attack, the prime minister resigned and Asquith, at age fifty-five, took his place.

For the British and French ruling coteries, party and party advantage were high-priority continuing concerns. They, too, like the dynastic coteries, like rulers everywhere, would be concerned with "the national interest." But their definitions of that interest differed substantially from the obsessive concerns of the dynastic regimes. One difference deserves special emphasis: In Britain and France, military elites were not ordinarily part of the ruling coterie. Asquith, Grey, and Lloyd George had no military experience. No prestige-obsessed monarch was present in their decision-making circle and there was no Conrad or Moltke insistently pressing military needs and objectives. In contrast to the obsessive concern with power, prestige, and military affairs in the monarchic regimes, one biographer reports that Asquith, at least in the early years of his government, "was generally lax about defence issues." He regarded the Committee of Imperial Defence, established in 1903, "with indifference and only on occasion set it to work on central issues." This Liberal government chose for its central tasks an important series of domestic reforms.[13] Lloyd George describes those efforts in his memoirs, pointing to "a series of controversies on home affairs, each of which raised more passion than any dispute ... within living memory." He also points up an important correlate: "During the eight years that preceded the war, the Cabinet devoted a ridiculously small percentage of its time to a consideration of foreign affairs." Some ministers, those who attended the Committee of Imperial Defence, were familiar with "certain aspects of foreign policy" but "the Cabinet as a whole were never called into genuine consultation upon the fundamental aspects of the foreign situation."[14]

The French and British strategic concerns were markedly different from those of the "threatened" powers. These two nations reacted to events rather than initiating them. The French leaders knew, long prior to the fact, of the German plan to attack, leaving them a basic choice: to resist or to concede. Since the latter was never a serious option, the key choices remaining, as Kiesling reports, involved "presentation." The principal task was to influence events so as to yield the most positive reading, for French citizens and for audiences elsewhere; basically, show France as the victim of unprovoked aggression. The German threat provided the agenda and set the basic directions for the French cabinet. Under Poincaré's direction, a consensus was achieved on the major policies. Because of the direct threat, that consensus was achieved with much greater ease than in the case of Britain.

Unlike France, Britain was not directly threatened in that "distant" struggle. Germany's leaders, in fact, were desperately providing assurances, doing all they could to discourage its intervention. For many

---

[13] George H. Cassar, *Asquith as War Leader* (London, 1994), pp. 6 and 4.
[14] David Lloyd George, *War Memoirs, 1914–1915* (Boston, 1933), pp. 43–4.

Liberals, war was an alien, inappropriate procedure, one that had no proper place in the modern age. That view was an integral part of the liberal world view, a heritage going back at least as far as Adam Smith.[15] As seen, it was a view shared by a substantial minority of the cabinet. The party leaders who argued for intervention were constrained both by constitutional and party considerations. They could not initiate anything without substantial cabinet support. And that support was not available until Germany moved into Belgium and into France. Here, too, as in France, there was an important "style" element. For public consumption, most especially in the case of Lloyd George, emphasis was placed on the violation of Belgian neutrality. The cabinet discussions, however, centered on France.[16] Britain could not let France fall; it could not allow German dominance on the continent. That was the view advanced by Asquith, Grey, Churchill, and, later, by Lloyd George. The German advance across the Meuse, belatedly, brought a majority of the cabinet to accept their view, that intervention was necessary. Their justification, their rationale was to maintain the continental balance of power.

### Business Elites: The Bourgeoisie

An agreement that a given coterie will rule is obviously an agreement that other coteries will not, that they would be excluded. Concretely, that means the choice of a monarchical or party coterie excludes industrial and financial leaders, press lords, religious leaders, labor leaders, heads of advocacy groups, intellectuals, and so on. That conclusion, effectively a truism, is substantiated in the previous chapters, where, with rare exception, those other groups simply do not appear.

The exclusion of other coteries, to be sure, does not necessarily mean opposition or even indifference. Collusion is an easy and often-alleged possibility. Those in power, for example, are sometimes said to be acting in the interest of other groups. Or, in another familiar image, those others, working behind the scenes are said to be pulling the strings. That presumed identity of interests, supposedly, explained the bourgeoisie's acceptance of arrangements led by old regime elites. In its most familiar formulation, those "in power" were acting in the interests of industrialists, bankers, or,

---

[15] A. J. A. Morris, *Radicalism against War* (London, 1972); and Michael Howard, *War and the Liberal Conscience* (London, 1978).
[16] Bentley Brinkerhoff Gilbert, *David Lloyd George: A Political Life*, vol. 2: *Organizer of Victory 1912–1916* (Columbus, Ohio, 1992), p. 109.

more generally, of the bourgeoisie.[17] The argument, as applied to World
War I, would go as follows: Industrialists were seeking raw materials
and new markets; bankers were looking overseas for new investment opportunities. When blocked in those endeavors by the other powers, war
was the "obvious" or "necessary" solution. In this reading, the choice
of *Weltpolitik* and, specifically, the choice of war by Wilhelm, Bethmann
Holweg, Moltke, and a few others served the needs of Germany's business
interests.

While plausible, one should recognize the immediate difficulties. Since
with rare exception, alternative arguments are always possible, one must
look for evidence to allow assessment of the competing offerings. The key
questions here: Do we have documentary evidence showing that business
groups shared and supported the views of the decision-making coteries?
Do we have evidence demonstrating their influence with the governing coteries? If we do not, then obviously we should look for such evidence and,
at the same time, we should consider those other hypotheses, the other
"plausible logics."[18] One immediate possibility would be that "business"
generally did not want war. Put simply: War would be bad for business.
A case in point: In September 1914, Jack Morgan, head of the famous
banking house, saw the war bringing "the most appalling destruction of
values in securities which has ever been seen in this country."[19]

One distinctive characteristic of the accounts provided in the preceding chapters is the absence of business elites, of "the bourgeoisie." There
were no bankers or financiers, no industrial magnates, no representatives of commercial interests, no press lords, and no arms manufacturers
among the decision makers. If they were "operating behind the scenes,"
if they were "pulling the strings," that should be evident somewhere in

---

[17] For a critique and commentary on the most famous of these representations, see Richard F.
Hamilton, *The Bourgeois Epoch: Marx and Engels on Britain, France, and Germany*
(Chapel Hill, 1991).
[18] For a useful statement on this subject, see T. C. Chamberlin, "The Method of Multiple
Working Hypotheses," *Science* 148 (1965): 754–9.
[19] Ron Chernow, *The House of Morgan* (New York, 1990), p. 185. In the 1930s, Joseph
Kennedy was one of the richest men in America, an entrepreneur and speculator in many
fields. Later, when serving as ambassador to Britain, he formed a close friendship with
the prime minister, Neville Chamberlain. The two were "of one mind" on the necessity
of avoiding war. One prime concern for Kennedy was familial: "I have four boys and
I don't want them to be killed in a foreign war." He also "dreaded the economic and
political consequences of war." A friend reported that "Joe thought war was irrational
and debasing. War destroyed capital. What could be worse than that?" From Richard
J. Whalen, *The Founding Father: The Story of Joseph P. Kennedy* (New York, 1964),
p. 234.

the extensive documentary record. Big-business representatives do figure prominently beginning with the first weeks of the war. They would oversee the sudden demands for weapons, munitions, vehicles, uniforms, and so forth. But those activities occur after the fact, after the decision for war had been made. In that initial decision making, however, in the choice of war, their voices were absent. The bankers and industrialists of all participating nations did of course have opinions, and in one way or another their views were communicated. But here one discovers lessons for which most school-trained intellectuals are not prepared.

The decision for war in the Dual Monarchy, as seen, was made by a coterie consisting of the monarch, his ministers, and his military leaders. The literature on the decision, reviewed in Chapter 5, reports practically no representation from business and financial leaders. One might think this was due to laggard development, advanced capitalism not yet having made its appearance. But that conclusion would be erroneous. Both industry and finance were developing rapidly within the Dual Monarchy.[20]

We have some hard evidence attesting to the attitudes of investors generally. This would include businessmen, bankers, some wealthy aristocrats, and some wealthy middle-class retirees. In the days immediately following the assassination, one author reports, the Vienna Bourse "viewed the situation with some uneasiness ... but without intense alarm." Traders, it is said, assumed "the need for peace in the Monarchy had increased" and that little change in government policy was expected. Stock prices, accordingly, "dropped but little." But then, the calling of a meeting of the Council of Ministers on 7 July "had a depressing effect on the market." Although the substance of those discussions was not known, the meeting itself resulted in a "sharp fall in values," these reaching levels lower than they had known since the outbreak of the First Balkan War. The subsequent publication of the note to Serbia, it is said, "wrought havoc on the Bourse." Investors, clearly, did not see war as serving their interests.[21]

---

[20] Richard L. Rudolph, *Banking and Industrialization in Austria-Hungary* (Cambridge, 1976); Bernard Michel, *Banques et banquiers en autriche au debut du 20e siècle* (Paris, 1976); Clive Trebilcock, *The Industrialization of the Continental Powers 1780–1914* (London, 1981), ch. 5; and März, *Austrian Banking*.

[21] Jonathan French Scott, *Five Weeks: The Surge of Public Opinion on the Eve of the Great War in New York* (New York, 1927), pp. 48–9. Nathaniel Rothschild, head of the London branch of the banking house, commented on the crisis in a message to the Paris house: "All the foreign Banks and particularly the German ones took a very large amount of money out of the [Vienna] stock exchange today." From Niall Ferguson, *The House of Rothschild: The World's Banker 1849–1998* (New York, 1998), p. 432. Stock market

Bernard Michel provides a detailed picture of the relationship between "the banks" and "the government" in Austria-Hungary. The Dual
Monarchy, he points out, avoided "the wave of militarism" that broke
over Germany, opposition to that course being found, more than anywhere else, from the major banks (*"la grande bourgeoisie bancaire"*).[22] In
the eyes of the financial bourgeoisie, "the army constituted a reserved domain of the aristocracy, a world totally foreign to the banking universe."
Banks had ties with arms manufacturers – Skoda and Vitkovice are
mentioned – but it was the firms that maintained the relationships with the
military, not the banks. The bankers, Michel reports, were "profoundly
pacifist," not hiding "their hostility to every warlike enterprise." And as
for their governmental contacts, he writes that "the bankers exercise no
real influence on the aristocratic Ministry of Foreign Affairs. The diplomats live in a totally different universe from theirs, one in which they [the
bankers] are rarely admitted."[23]

März confirms those judgments and adds other supporting evidence.
His summary conclusion is that: "The financial world's most prominent
representatives were as good as debarred from influence on the nation's
foreign affairs. These remained the province of the dynasty and a small
exclusive group of the higher nobility...." Rudolf Sieghart had held an
important position in the government (he was in charge of the Office of
the Council of Ministers) prior to his appointment as governor of the
Creditanstalt. But those connections yielded little information and less
influence. His view was that "hostilities could, indeed must, be avoided."
His account provides a striking contrast between this banker's mindset
and that of the "small exclusive group" setting policy: "To the last moment I did not believe that war would happen. I could not imagine that
Austria-Hungary, of all the Great Powers that with the weakest periphery, with an exposed situation on several fronts, and with the magnetic
attraction exercised by numerous nations beyond its borders on their
co-nationals inside them, would plunge into so risky an adventure. I
still do not understand the folly of the erstwhile rulers, and least of all

movements provide a useful index to the views of investors, many of them members of
"the bourgeoisie." Those movements constitute a sensitive "public opinion poll" for the
views of investors. But they are rarely reported in accounts of the war's origins. The
general public in many settings, so it is said, reacted with jubilation or euphoria. For
investors, the predominant reaction appears to have been consternation.

[22] Michel, *Banques*, p. 363. My translations.
[23] Ibid., p. 364.

their childish faith that Austria-Hungary would be dealing solely with Serbia."[24]

The year 1914 seemed very promising for the Austrian bankers, who at this point anticipated "peace and general reconciliation." They were collaborating with "French capital" and "German capital of the Reich" in the Balkans. In the entanglement of interests there, Michel declares, banking capital ignored the political blocs. That truth, he added, had never been clearer than on the eve of the war. For the Austrian banks, 1914 was the year of reconciliation with French capital, the Paris markets about to be opened to Austrian securities. On 20 July, the Austrian banker negotiating in Paris announced that Viviani favored a financial rapprochement with Vienna and that the Austrian loan would be sold in French markets that autumn. Michel's conclusion: "[I]f the banks had had as their sole objective their own interests and their profits, they had to declare themselves against the war."[25] The bankers, Michel reports, were upset by the murders of Franz Ferdinand and his wife. At a memorial ceremony held at the Credit Anstalt on 1 July, the archduke was referred to as "the prince of peace." Even on that occasion, the words spoken stressed conciliation and contained no suggestion of hatred or vengeance. The Serbs were not even mentioned.[26]

"The decision to intervene," Michel concludes, "was taken in the military and diplomatic circles and in the Common Council of Ministers which was staffed, almost exclusively, by the nobility. It was not the capitalists or the bankers who had to choose between peace and war, but the Austria of the aristocrats." This theme is elaborated on at length, detailing the aristocratic presence among the decision makers, all of this put in contrast to the "inability of the bankers" to intervene. "None of them," Michel declares, "appears to have been consulted and no name of a banker, no mention of influence by the press, or that of the bourse appears in the official documents." His summary conclusion reads: "It was the Austria of the diplomats and the generals, not the Austria of the bankers, who, at the end of July 1914, pulled central Europe into the war."[27]

---

[24] Quoted in März, *Austrian Banking*, p. 103. For the original, see Rudolf Sieghart, *Die letzten Jahrzehnte einer Grossmacht* (Berlin, 1932), p. 168.

[25] Michel, *Banques*, p. 366.

[26] Ibid., p. 367.

[27] Ibid., pp. 367, 369. This rich source contains much more information and documentation on banks, bankers, and their relations with the press and with political

More information is available on the German business leaders. For them, too, their presence and contacts with the decision-making coteries are best described as fugitive. The key question is, What was the character of the contacts between the political leaders and big business?

We may begin with an instructive case study, that of Albert Ballin, the manager of the Hamburg-American Line. Called the HAPAG, it was the world's largest shipping firm, one which for obvious reasons would be central to any German *Weltpolitik*.[28] Ballin knew and "drew close to" the Kaiser. He "was the only Jew, and one of the few businessmen, whom William saw regularly and whose friendship he obviously valued and enjoyed." But there was a problem in that Ballin was Jewish and Wilhelm was an anti-Semite.[29]

Ballin was called upon by the decision makers in the course of the July 1914 crisis. Rumors had been circulating earlier in the year about Anglo-Russian talks aimed at a military pact, and at this point, as seen, the question of British intentions became a critical issue for Germany's leaders. On 15 July, after Sarajevo and after the Hoyos mission, Jagow wrote to Ballin, thinking he might be able to gain the needed intelligence through his British contacts. Subsequently, it was agreed that Ballin should make a personal visit to Britain. Jagow then added another, more important agenda item: that he undertake extensive probing of "his English friends' views as to what course England would take in the event that the Serbo-Austrian situation led to a general war on the continent."[30]

Ballin arrived in London on 20 July, ostensibly on a business trip, and on the 23rd, the day of the Austro-Hungarian ultimatum, had dinner with Grey, Lord Morley, and Haldane. Two days later, the day of the Serbian reply, he dined with Churchill. The conclusions Ballin drew from

elites. See, esp. ch. 11, "Le vie sociale des banquiers," and ch. 12, "Les banquiers et la politique."

[28] For a wealth of detail on Hamburg, its major firms, and its business leaders, see Niall Ferguson, *Paper and Iron: Hamburg Business and German Politics in the Era of Inflation 1897–1927* (Cambridge, 1995).

[29] For discussion of Wilhelm's relationship with Ballin, see Lamar Cecil, *Albert Ballin: Business and Politics in Imperial Germany, 1888–1918* (Princeton, 1967), pp. 102–9 (quotation on p. 108). For the kaiser's anti-Semitism, see Lamar Cecil, *Wilhelm II*, 2 vols. (Chapel Hill, 1996), vol. 2, pp. 56–7. Some of his utterances: "The Jews are the curse of my country"; "The Jews are the parasites of my Empire." And to Edward Grey in 1907: "They want stamping out." For much more detail, see John C. G. Röhl, *The Kaiser and His Court: Wilhelm II and the Government of Germany* (Cambridge, 1994), ch. 8.

[30] Cecil, *Albert Ballin*, pp. 204–5.

these meetings were generally positive, a reading that reflected his own preferences. He reported to Berlin that no Anglo-Russian agreement had been signed and that British intervention on the continent was unlikely. His British sources subsequently disputed his account of their statements, arguing that Ballin had misread them. Another factor contributing to his optimistic reading was "the manifest pacifism of large segments of the English population" and the fact that "many financial leaders in the City, with whom he probably talked ... were opposed to any involvement in a continental war."[31] Ballin, the business leader, clearly was not directing the political leaders. Just the opposite was happening: They were using him as their agent.[32]

Ballin's reaction to the war was one of shock. It was, Cecil writes, "a war he loathed." Ballin now regretted the many things he might have done differently. He felt he should have argued more strenuously against Tirpitz's naval plan, one which "could only end in war." In 1915, commenting on naval and commercial realities, he declared that his ships "did not need the protection of a German fleet." At that point, he recognized his contribution, and those of other business leaders, to the catastrophe: "I should have emphatically said so to the Kaiser. But I could never summon the courage to do so.... We were all too weak toward the Kaiser. No one wished to disturb his childlike, happy optimism, which could shift at once into an almost helpless depression if anyone criticized one of his pet projects [*Lieblings-Themen*]. And among these, the fleet was the greatest. Now we have the result of our lack of courage!"[33]

Britain's declaration of war was a disaster for the firm. For the Hamburg-America Line, Cecil writes, there seemed little to do but "to create a moth ball fleet and station it permanently on the Elbe."[34] Almost half of HAPAG's 25,554 employees were called for military service. Some 4,000, those stationed abroad or at sea when war began, were interned. Ballin's principal task at this point was to provide for the families

---

[31] Ibid., pp. 206–8.

[32] Ballin was used by Germany's political leaders on a later occasion, this for propaganda purposes, for an attempt to shift blame away from Germany. The effort was exposed causing him some embarrassment. For this, see Henry Wickham Steed, *Through Thirty Years, 1892–1922* (Garden City, N.Y., 1924), p. 26.

[33] Cecil, *Albert Ballin*, p. 212.

[34] Ibid., p. 214. Many of HAPAG's ships were at sea or in ports elsewhere and, as a result, never reached the Elbe. Half of the American soldiers "transported to France by the U.S. Navy sailed on converted German liners"; from Holger H. Herwig, "Total Rhetoric, Limited War: Germany's U-Boat Campaign," in Roger Chickering and Stig Förster, eds., *Great War, Total War* (Cambridge, 2000), ch. 10, p. 193, n. 18.

of those called to the military and for the 8,000 remaining employees. In late August, Ballin said, "[M]y life's work lies in shreds."[35]

In December that year, Ballin told Chancellor von Bethmann Hollweg to his face: "I have spent my entire life building up something which has been of immense value to the German Reich, and then you come along with a couple of others and destroy it all." Ballin "rejected all Bethmann's protestations and excuses as fairy tales which he should be ashamed to tell."[36] On the first anniversary of the July Crisis, Ballin told Jagow that he, the foreign secretary, "must carry the terrible responsibility for the stage-management of this war which is costing Germany generations of splendid people and is throwing it back 100 years." In 1916, Ballin refused to meet Jagow on the grounds that he "wanted to have nothing further to do with a man who bore the responsibility for this whole dreadful disaster and for the deaths of so many hundreds of thousands of men."[37]

Ballin clearly saw the political and economic elites as having markedly different interests and aims. The growing antagonism between Germany and England, in his view, was not the work of merchants and traders but was due to "misguided princes, ambitious admirals, and inept diplomats." He recognized that economic competition sometimes created friction and bad feelings, but thought those problems soluble were it not for the contest in armaments. The clash came "because of the expansionist naval program pursued by Admiral Tirpitz and his confederates in Berlin...."[38]

Max Warburg was the head of a major family-owned banking house that, like HAPAG, was also based in Hamburg. Ballin and Warburg knew each other and had many ties. Ballin put Warburg on HAPAG's board of directors and also on the board of Blohm and Voss, the nation's leading shipbuilder. Ballin helped arrange Warburg's first meeting with the kaiser,

---

[35] Cecil, *Albert Ballin*, pp. 214–15. Eighty-three HAPAG ships were caught in neutral ports, 35 of them in the United States. Their maintenance cost the firm two to three million marks a month; see pp. 218–19.

[36] Quoted in John C. G. Röhl, "Germany," in Keith Wilson, *Decisions for War 1914* (New York, 1995), ch. 2, p. 28. He was quoting from Theodor Wolff, *Tagebücher 1914–1919*, Bernd Sösemann, ed. (Boppard, 1984).

[37] Röhl, p. 28.

[38] Cecil, *Albert Ballin*, p. 166. These are Cecil's quotations. On the afternoon of 8 November 1918, revolutionaries, then in control of Hamburg, threatened Ballin "with arrest and bodily harm." Obviously shaken, he walked home and there "swallowed a large number of sleeping tablets." The efforts of his physician and a nearby clinic could not save him; he died a few hours later. His friends were divided, whether it was an accidental death (an ulcer aggravated by the pills) or a suicide. Ibid., p. 345. Ferguson reads the death as a suicide in *Iron and Paper*, p. 156.

in 1903, at the behest of the chancellor, Prince Bülow, who thought it "desirable, perhaps even necessary" that the kaiser receive a lecture on a needed financial reform. A series of such meetings followed, but the kaiser's relationship with Warburg was never as close as that with Ballin. The banker was rather outspoken; he did not show the proper deference. Warburg and the kaiser met each year after the regatta dinner in Cuxhaven. In addition, on one occasion, Warburg was invited to the palace in Berlin. That appears to have been the extent of their contact: some ten after-dinner meetings plus the Berlin visit.[39]

Warburg spoke with the kaiser, again after a Cuxhaven dinner, on 21 June 1914, a week before the assassination of Franz Ferdinand. Wilhelm was disturbed by the Russian arms efforts and by the construction of railroads there, seeing these as preparation for a war that could break out in 1916. He wondered if it would not be better to "cut loose" (*loszuschlagen*) instead of waiting. Much disturbed by these views, Warburg replied that he saw things differently, that "Germany will become stronger with every year of peace. Waiting can bring us only advantage."[40]

Warburg's meetings with the kaiser involved discussions of finances, an area in which businessmen would obviously have some expertise. But with respect to international relations, in particular, the events leading up to the Great War, we find no business involvement. Prince von Bülow, the man who initiated the Warburg contact, reported in his memoirs that Germany's decisions leading up to the war were taken in "hermetically sealed rooms in the Foreign Office, without once consulting a diplomat of experience, or any intelligent businessman informed on international economics. Albert Ballin, Max Warburg, and others – all might have been asked."[41] Lamar Cecil's two-volume biography of Wilhelm contains no index reference to Warburg.

A consideration of business influence must also consider the relationship between Kaiser Wilhelm and the Krupps, owners of Germany's leading arms manufacturing firm and the nation's richest family, richer even than the kaiser. Friedrich Krupp (called Fritz) and the kaiser developed a close relationship, with the latter being a regular visitor at Villa Hügel,

---

[39] Max M. Warburg, *Aus Meinen Aufzeichnungen* (Glückstadt, 1952), pp. 30–1.
[40] Ibid., p. 29.
[41] As quoted in Ron Chernow, *The Warburgs: The Twentieth-Century Odyssey of a Remarkable Jewish Family* (New York, 1993), p. 153. For the original, von Bülow, *Memoirs*, vol. 3, p. 198.

the industrialist's estate in Essen. The relationship was very one-sided and, on occasion, troubled by serious differences. Their first meeting, in 1890, was initiated by Krupp, who wished to see some changes in the young ruler's recently announced social policies. Granted an audience, the industrialist raged against the Kaiser's *Sozialprogramm*. The Kaiser, however, "wouldn't budge."[42] Later, during the Boxer Rebellion, it was discovered that German forces had been fired on by guns produced by Krupp. The outraged Kaiser sent Fritz a telegram: "This is no time, when I am sending my soldiers into battle against the yellow beasts, to try to make money out of so serious a situation."[43] The relationship cooled for a month or so but then revived.

Krupp supported Admiral Tirpitz's naval expansion program, "contributing heavily" to the Navy League. The firm bought a shipyard in Kiel and built nine battleships, five light cruisers, and thirty-three destroyers "for Tirpitz." But again, as in the Boxer episode, the economics and technology of the weapons industry had unexpected consequences. Through a "primitive munitions trust" with an American firm, Krupp received $45 per ton for armor plate "used in the fleets of England, France, Japan, Italy, and the United States."[44]

Some years later, on the evening of 6 July 1914, just after the critical Hoyos meeting and just before setting off for his northern voyage, the Kaiser met with Fritz's successor, Gustav Krupp von Bohlen und Halbach. As Fritz Fischer reports, the Kaiser "communicated to him" the crucial conversations and their result. Wilhelm, it will be noted, was telling the industrialist, after the fact, what had been done. He then added that "he would declare war immediately if Russia mobilized." The conversation appears to have been largely one-way. The major lesson, one repeated three times, was that this time he, the Kaiser, would not weaken: "This time I will not cave in." Fischer gives no indication that Krupp provided any advice.[45]

Hugo Stinnes (1870–1924), another major figure in the German business world, was also based in the Ruhr, and his initial efforts were also in coal and steel. Later he acquired a major producer of electric

---

[42] William Manchester, *The Arms of Krupp 1587–1968* (Boston, 1968), pp. 210–11. Lamar Cecil's two-volume biography of the Kaiser contains only two minor passing mentions of the Krupps, one of them in connection with sailing and yachts. Another important source that makes only passing references to the man is Röhl, *Kaiser and His Court*.

[43] Manchester, *Arms of Krupp*, p. 217.

[44] Ibid., pp. 221–4.

[45] Fritz Fischer, *Griff nach der Weltmacht* (Düsseldorf, 1964), p. 65; and, also Fischer, *Krieg der Illusionen* (Düsseldorf, 1969), p. 692.

power, and still later he was involved in commercial shipping. Stinnes had holdings in Luxembourg, French Lorraine, Normandy, Belgium, Wales, St. Petersburg, and the Ottoman Empire. Prior to the war, Gerald Feldman points out, there was "a remarkable lack of militarism and imperialism in Stinnes's behavior." Despite the many international difficulties, he "invested a great deal in his Russian facilities . . . using the floating docks and barges there to sell [English] coal to the Russian navy."[46] He did take extensive precautionary measures to protect his foreign properties in the event of war, basically through ownership by trusted foreign nationals. But his basic expectation, expressed to Heinrich Class, the Pan-German leader, was that the peaceful economic expansion would continue, to his benefit and that of Germany. Class reports his comments as follows: "Let things develop quietly for three or four years and Germany will be the uncontested economic ruler of Europe. The French have remained behind us; they are a nation of *petite rentiers*. And the English are too work-shy and without the courage to undertake new enterprises. Otherwise, there is no one in Europe that can compete with us. Therefore, only three or four years of peace, and I can assure you the silent attainment of German predominance in Europe."[47]

Stinnes's business policies, Gerald Feldman writes, were "geared toward a long period of peace." In the summer of 1913, he wrote his wife of his hope that "the people in the Balkans will soon settle down. . . . Then one can hope for a decade of peace. . . ." At that point he "acquired new mining interests in . . . Yorkshire and Nottinghamshire with the obligation to develop the mining interests involved." Early in 1914, his firm "signed a contract specifying prices for the sale of this coal to branches of the Stinnes firm throughout Europe and the Near East." Stinnes was very poorly informed about the political developments during the July crisis. On the 22nd, his son wrote from London reporting that "the relationship between Germany and England gets better from day to day. The Conservatives as well as the Liberals are in a very friendly mood to Germany." On the 28th, Stinnes and his colleagues were still "hopeful that the war between Austria-Hungary and Serbia would be localized."[48]

---

[46] Gerald D. Feldman, "Hugo Stinnes and the Prospect of War before 1914," in Manfred Boemeke, Roger Chickering, and Stig Förster, eds., *Anticipating Total War* (Cambridge, 1999), ch. 4 (quotation on p. 81).

[47] Ibid., p. 84. For the original, Heinrich Class, *Wider den Strom: Vom Werden und Wachsen der nationalen Opposition im alten Reich* (Leipzig, 1932), pp. 217–18.

[48] Feldman, "Hugo Stinnes," pp. 85–6, 91. Much relevant information in these themes appears on pp. 86–90, these reviewing the relationship of economic and political elites

Feldman sees Stinnes as "an important case" and senses also that his "behavior and attitudes ... appear to be typical." His conclusions, somewhat abbreviated, are that

the great industrialists and the great bankers showed very little interest in preparing for war and did not want to think about it. Excessive military expenditure, high taxes, and reduced credit were all viewed as threats to economic development and prosperity.... [When] they did think about war, it was as a potential social and economic catastrophe that might be bearable if it were of short duration. The great chemical industrialist Carl Duisberg, who, like Stinnes, was to end up heavily engaged in war production and an annexationist, hoped for peace to the last minute and believed that the war would set back German economic development for a decade.... Germany's extraordinary economic growth in the prewar period depended on increasing international trade and interdependence and on international stability.... In the end, politics ruined economics.[49]

Walther Rathenau was a leading executive in the Allgemeine Electrizitäts Gesellschaft, basically, Germany's equivalent of General Electric. In 1915, on the death of Rathenau's father, who founded the firm, he became its head. Rathenau was an industrialist, but that term alone would understate the man's considerable accomplishments. He was also a banker, politician, and intellectual. He was acquainted with the kaiser.[50] Rathenau's diary jumps from 13 March to August of 1914, thus giving no hint of his position or role in the July decision making. In that period, Rathenau wrote seven longer articles, which were published in Vienna's *Neue Freie Presse*, six of them appearing before the outbreak of war. Among the subjects "repeatedly touched" were "the lack of qualities of leadership in Germany." Soon after the beginning of the war, he offered Chancellor Bethmann Hollweg his services, one proposal calling for a customs union between Germany and Austria-Hungary. A union of this kind, he thought, would be desirable for industry and also would reduce "the nationalistic hatred of the states." Those struggles, he believed, were linked to questions of "power, imperialism and expansion." If Europe's "economy merges into a community – and that will happen earlier than we think – politics will merge too. That would not mean world peace,

with respect to the naval program, taxation (paying for armaments), the Morocco crisis, and bank reserves.
[49] Ibid., pp. 92–3.
[50] Hartmut Pogge von Strandmann, ed., *Walter Rathenau: Industrialist, Banker, Intellectual, and Politician: Notes and Diaries 1907–1922* (Oxford, 1985). See pp. 182–3 for a diary entry describing the Kaiser's erratic, one-way conversational style.

nor disarmament, nor slackening, but the moderation of conflicts, the saving of energy and a joint civilization." His proposal for a German-Austrian union was clearly a small step in that direction. The chancellor, faced with many other pressing tasks, passed the memorandum on to Clemens Delbrück, the Secretary of the Interior, who rejected the plan. Among other things, he "did not agree with Rathenau's emphasis on the importance of industry."[51]

Rathenau expressed his doubts about the Great War in a letter to a friend of December 1914: "There is a dissonant note in this war; it is not 1813, not 1866, not 1870. Necessary or not, higher power or not, it did not have to happen as it did here."[52]

In July 1914 in Great Britain, David Lloyd George was Chancellor of the Exchequer and, from that position, was in touch with many leading businessmen. Of all those in the cabinet, he was the most likely to be directly contacted for expression of "the business viewpoint." He reported that on Saturday, the first day of August, "the Governor of the Bank of England called on me, as Chancellor of the Exchequer, to inform me on behalf of the City that the financial and trading interests in the City of London were totally opposed to our intervening in the War."[53]

Lloyd George did not end his narrative with the representations of a single individual claiming to speak on behalf of all his peers. He reviewed two hypotheses, the first being that it was "a war intrigued and organised and dictated by financiers for their own purpose." He responded to this hypothesis with one of the strongest formulations possible: "I was Chancellor of the Exchequer and, as such, I saw Money before the war; I saw it immediately after the outbreak of war; I lived with it for days, and did my best to steady its nerve, for I knew how much depended on restoring its confidence; and I say that Money was a frightened and trembling thing: Money shivered at the prospect. It is a foolish and ignorant libel to call this a financiers' war."[54] The second hypothesis, one put forth "in Germany and amongst the friends of Germany in other lands," holds that the British intervention was due to "a growing jealousy of Germany's

---

[51] Ibid., p. 184. Cecil's biography of Wilhelm has no index reference for Rathenau; Manchester's volume on the Krupps has a single reference to the man, that to the events of 1922.

[52] Quoted in Wolfgang J. Mommsen, *Grossmachtstellung und Weltpolitik* (Frankfurt am Main, 1993), p. 321.

[53] David Lloyd George, *War Memoirs, 1914–1915* (Boston, 1933), vol. 1, p. 61.

[54] Ibid., p. 68.

strength and prosperity." British politicians were presumably eager for "an opportunity to destroy this redoubtable rival." Lloyd George's response is that "big businesses everywhere wanted to keep out of it.... Here were no eager men praying for the hour to arrive when they could strike down a great commercial rival."[55]

Lloyd George is a notoriously unreliable source. But in this case, there is ample evidence attesting to the same conclusion. Asquith, on 30 July, wrote, "The City, [which] is in a terrible state of depression and paralysis, is for the time being all against English intervention." The next day he wrote that "the general opinion at present – particularly strong in the City – is to keep out at almost all costs. They are having a black day there." On the same day, Sir Eyre Crowe, assistant under-secretary in the Foreign Office, wrote of the "panic in the City."[56]

Some striking evidence bearing on the issues discussed here appears in the autobiography of Henry Wickham Steed, the foreign affairs editor of the London *Times*. On 28 July, the *Times* indicated its unambiguous advocacy of intervention, declaring that if the nation's friends were forced into a continental war, "England will ... support them to the full." The lead editorial the next day reiterated the theme, specifying also the key concern, that England cannot "afford to see France crushed by Germany, or the balance of power upset against France...." The financial markets, in all major European capitals, were in disarray, security prices falling dramatically as investors sought to unload their foreign holdings, especially those in likely enemy nations.[57]

On 31 July, the "head of one of the chief financial houses of the City" asked the financial editor of the *Times*, Hugh Chisholm, to call on him. Although unnamed, from internal clues and from other sources the man is easily identified as Lord Nathaniel Rothschild. The banker "denounced" the newspaper's policy and "insisted that the leading articles must cease at once, and that *The Times* should advocate neutrality." Chisholm "resented intensely so gross an impropriety" and consulted with Lord Northcliffe, the paper's owner, and with the editor and Steed. All four men agreed to reject the demand, and the editorial on Saturday, 1 August, again made a strong argument for intervention: "The policy to be adopted by Great Britain in the last resort remains clear and unmistakable.... We

[55] Ibid., p. 69.
[56] H. H. Asquith, *Letters to Venetia Stanley* (New York, 1982), pp. 136–8.
[57] Steed, *Through Thirty Years*, vol. 2, pp. 4–8.

dare not stand aside with folded arms and placidly watch our friends placed in peril of destruction."[58]

That afternoon, Northcliffe conferred with Steed and two other leading members of the firm to discuss the paper's position on these matters. Their discussion was interrupted when Northcliffe was called out for an urgent meeting with some important people who, it turned out, were Rothschild and his younger brother. They had received information that Germany's "overwhelming military and naval strength" was such that if England went to war, "the British Empire would be swept off the face of the earth in a few weeks." They "implored" Northcliffe "to use his influence to keep England neutral." They had made "similar representations" to the Chancellor of the Exchequer, Lloyd George. Earlier, on the 28th, Rothschild had also visited the prime minister. Paul Cambon, the French ambassador, thought some cabinet ministers "had been influenced by ... important men in the City" in favor of neutrality.[59]

The lesson is clear: Britain's leading financiers, the leaders of *Finanzkapital*, were unambiguously opposed to intervention, a position communicated directly to the nation's highest political leaders. Their position was communicated directly on two occasions to Lord Northcliffe, the nation's leading press lord. The business leaders of the nation were saying, "No, don't do it." But the press lord continued his course without change. And the political leaders "did it." It should be noted, moreover, that they did so with impunity. No evident penalties or retribution came from "the City."[60]

The Rothschild firm experienced serious losses as a result of the war. It "lost close to £1.5 million in 1914 – an immense sum equivalent to 23 per cent of its capital." Britain had been the central lender in previous

[58] Ibid., pp. 8–9.

[59] Ibid., 10–11. The visit with Asquith is mentioned in Asquith, *Letters*, p. 131; for Cambon's statement, see Steed, *Through Thirty Years*, vol. 2, p. 14. Rothschild also sent "a personal appeal for peace" to another political leader, Kaiser Wilhelm; Ferguson, *House of Rothschild*, p. 434. Rothschild's attempt to influence the *Times* is reviewed there briefly on p. 433.

[60] One might expect that a leading banker would figure prominently in the memoirs and biographies of the political leaders. Lloyd George's *War Memoirs* give him one fugitive mention (p. 104). Bentley Brinkerhoff Gilbert's biography of Lloyd George makes no mention of the man; *David Lloyd George: A Political Life*, 2 vols. (Columbus, Ohio, 1992), vol. 2. No mention of the Rothschild interventions appears in the following: Keith Robbin, *Sir Edward Grey: A Biography of Lord Grey of Fallodon* (London, 1971); or in George H. Cassar, *Asquith as War Leader* (London, 1994).

wars. In the Great War, that centrality shifted from London to New York. Niall Ferguson summarizes as follows: "[W]hat united the Rothschilds after 1914 was decline – and it was a decline that was to continue for at least half a century."[61]

No discussion of the Great War would be complete without some discussion of the arms merchants, or the Merchants of Death. The Rothschilds had investments in arms manufacturing firms, but they were a small part of the family's total holdings. A war might yield profits in that field, but the losses for their total investments, as just indicated, were immense. An arms manufacturer – such as Krupp – might make a lot of money, but other options are always possible. A firm might sell more armaments at home but lose most or all of its foreign market, leaving a negative balance. The Krupp firm, Manchester reports, was one of the losers: "At the outbreak of the war Krupp had been 130 million marks in the black; the day the chimneys stopped he was 148 million in the red, and the first year of peace was no help – at the end of 1919 the firm had lost another 36 million."[62]

The dominant rationale of the business elites differs considerably from that of the dynasts or the party leaders. Putting profits ahead of national power or prestige and ahead of party advantage, they seek steady economic growth, extending their activities to wherever it appears to be to their advantage. That means they could manufacture, trade, or invest across borders. Other things equal, for them questions of power and prestige would be matters of indifference. Those "other things," however, are never equal, and where those "larger" national issues come into play, most businessmen would be concerned. Both war and the rumors thereof would threaten their foreign activities, reducing profits or, in the extreme case, bringing confiscation of holdings. Increased arms expenditures in peacetime, moreover, would pose some threat to profits in that someone has to pay the costs. Tax increases are usually a source of domestic unrest. Those added taxes might be charged to the businessmen themselves. If charged to others, however, to the middle classes, workers, and/or farmers, higher taxes would mean a reduction of aggregate purchasing power that in turn would mean, for most businesses, reduced profits. The manufacturers of

---

[61] Ferguson, *House of Rothschild*, pp. 436–7.

[62] Manchester, *Arms of Krupp*, p. 321. For an intelligent well-documented review and critique of the British experience, this focused on what the author calls a "literature of vilification," see Clive Trebilcock, "Legends of the British Armament Industry 1890–1914: A Revision," *Journal of Contemporary History* 5 (1970): 3–19; for more detail, see his *The Vickers Brothers: Armaments and Enterprise 1854–1914* (London, 1977).

guns and ammunition might increase their profits, but other firms and the vast majority of businessmen would be among the losers.

Three coteries have been delineated to this point – the dynasts, party leaders, and business leaders – each operating with markedly different assumptions. Those operating assumptions have been given various names, mindsets, *mentalités*, or *Weltanschauungen*. In each instance, we are dealing with a logic or rationale. Some theoretical discussions, unfortunately, limit consideration of such questions by use of the singular, as if a given logic were the unique, patently obvious option. But here we see diverse rationales, each appearing plausible (or logical) to their bearers. Thus, rather than imposing or reading in an "obvious" logic, the tasks for the analyst are to *discover* the rationales being used and to indicate the circumstances making them plausible.

The dynastic coterie – the monarch, ministers, and military – gives precedence to a distinctive conception of the national interest. This group's concern is with the nation's historic territory, with its defense and, perhaps, its extension. Its policies seek, in one way or another, to demonstrate that nation's prestige and power. In the view of this coterie, a threatening or competing "upstart" must be "put down." Austria-Hungary's leaders in July 1914 provide the key example: It was obvious to them that Serbia must be "taught a lesson." Similar orientations were seen in the efforts of German and Russian decision-making coteries, who also recognized the urgent "need" for the defense of the threatened empire.

There are some obvious correlates of this mindset. The dynasts give strong emphasis to autarchy; a proper defense of the territory requires self-sufficiency. Theirs, accordingly, is essentially a fortress mentality. They, understandably, give considerable emphasis to the military, viewing war (or the threat thereof) as proper and legitimate means for achieving their goals. The dynastic decision makers, civilian and military, see the nation's economy as serving the requirements of those higher goals of power and prestige. Their preferred design for the economy emphasizes autarchy as opposed to free trade and interdependence; the economy should provide ample and secure funding for the needs of the fortress. They would, at best, advocate a "national liberalism," as did Friedrich List, rather than the free trade and world markets commended by Adam Smith.

Those dynasts were last seen in 1917–18, some four score years ago. Our history books tell of their various activities and their roles in bringing on the catastrophe. Many accounts talk about the "old regimes" but provide no serious account of their dynamics, that is, how they functioned. The rationale guiding their thinking seems completely foreign to the generations born and trained decades later. The dynasts' views were given plausibility by virtue of long and exclusive training. Its members typically formed a small and isolated group. The monarch was "chosen" by accident of birth. The other members were chosen by him (or on occasion, by her), the criteria being loyalty to the group and its world view and technical ability, that is, ability to implement aspects of the group's program. Within the group, the prevalent nationalist views would be sedulously reinforced; and with equal system, alternative views would be denigrated or excluded. That insularity made possible, protected, and sustained the rationale that made the initial steps toward war possible. That distinctive logic justified the extraordinary risks involved: For the dynasts, it was right and appropriate that, to save the nation, they would hazard the lives, welfare, and property of millions of human beings.

The party leaders, the decision makers in France and Britain, like the dynastic leaders, were also autonomous, proceeding independently of big business. But they were operating on different principles, following a different rationale or logic. They combined concerns for "the national interest" with the requirements of party (or coalition) support. A significant difference appears in this connection: Where the dynasts initiated events, the party leaders were reacting, responding to others' initiatives. The French leaders were responding to the threat of a German attack. The British leaders were also responding, not to direct threat, but to the more extended implications of the July events, to that of a powerful continental hegemon. The British case involved the entire cabinet, which contained several important factions, interventionist, neutralist, and pacifist. In contrast to the high cohesiveness of the dynastic coteries that made quick decisions possible, the British decision to intervene took several weeks.

The third elite delineated here, the leaders of the economy, are often referred to as "the bourgeoisie." In July–August 1914, as seen, these people were not present in the decision-making circles.[63] And, just as important, their urgent demands to avoid war were given no serious attention.

---

[63] For a useful summary portrait of the position of big business in the Kaiser's regime, see Peter Hayes, "German Businessmen and the Crisis of the Empire," in Volker Dürr, Kathy Harms, and Peter Hayes, eds., *Imperial Germany* (Madison, Wis., 1985), pp. 46–61. Between 1900 and 1910, five major industrialists rejected offers of ministerial posts. Businessmen showed "little interest in gaining access to, or even socializing extensively with, the landed nobility." Many of them, the most eminent of the lot, "refused proffered ennoblement." Few of them showed interest in acquiring a country estate. As for political influence, Hayes writes of "the political irrelevance of industrial leaders in the decisive moments of August 1914 and January 1933" (p. 58).

It is an unexpected lesson, since many intellectuals give much emphasis to the power of big business. The logic is easy: Industrialists and the bankers have immense resources; the anxious and deferential politicians, supposedly, must respond to their demands. But in this case, the political leaders, whether dynasts or party chieftains, proceeded with sovereign indifference to their demands and chose war.[64] From one perspective, the limited power of big business is easily explained. Unlike tsar and kaiser, the bourgeoisie would, at any time, have only modest police forces and no army at its disposal. Paraphrasing a famous question, one may ask: How many troops did big business have?[65]

Big business, as seen, was internationalist and, as such, opposed to notions of national autarchy. Their preferred procedures created interdependencies: Steel was exported and grain imported, finished products were exported and raw materials imported, and so forth. This had the consequence, a basic economic truth, of maximizing the "wealth of nations." But that truth ran up against the competing truth: The power-and-prestige preferences of the dynasts that led them to seek protection for both the domestic steel and grain producers in turn meant higher prices and, in the aggregate, less profit.

The decisions made by the dynasts and party leaders in July and August of 1914 brought disaster for many businesses. This disaster was easily foreseen, the implications having been made clear in previous crises.[66] Mobilization removed a large part of the labor force in the firms of all the participating nations. Family incomes were suddenly diminished. And, at the same time, there was instant inflation, led by food prices. For the firms, the transition from peacetime to wartime production was both cumbersome and costly. HAPAG, as seen, lost all ships at sea along with their cargoes.

---

[64] The banker Arthur von Gwinner "had the audacity to point out Germany's dire financial straits" to the kaiser. Wilhelm's reply: "That makes no difference to me." From Holger H. Herwig, *"Luxury" Fleet: The Imperial German Navy 1888–1918* (London, 1980), p. 74.

[65] On 1 April 1933, a Nazi vigilante squad invaded the Berlin headquarters of the Reichsverband der deutschen Industrie, the key organization of German big business. Their protests were to no avail. In May, the organization "voluntarily" dissolved. See Turner, *German Big Business*, pp. 335–6.

[66] See Jon Lawrence, Martin Dean, and Jean-Louis Robert, "The Outbreak of War and the Urban Economy: Paris, Berlin, and London in 1914," *Economic History Review* 45 (1992): 564–93; Jay Winter and Jean-Louis Robert, *Capital Cities at War: Paris, London, Berlin 1914–1919* (Cambridge, 1997); and John Horne, ed., *State, Society, and Mobilization in Europe during the First World War* (Cambridge, 1997).

That interdependence and the consequent pacific implications had a long history in liberal economic thought. Michael Howard has provided a sweeping summary, one which reviews the basic claims from 1500 to 1975. Among those who in one way or another subscribed to this position are: Erasmus, Adam Smith, Immanuel Kant, Thomas Paine, Jeremy Bentham, James Mill, John Stuart Mill, Richard Cobden, John Bright, J. A. Hobson, and, last but not least, Norman Angell. Not mentioned by Howard, but an influential thinker who should certainly be added to the list, is Herbert Spencer. Paine is quoted as follows: "If commerce were permitted to act to the universal extent it is capable, it would extirpate the system of war and produce a revolution in the uncivilised state of governments." In 1848, John Stuart Mill wrote: "It is commerce which is rapidly rendering war obsolete, by strengthening and multiplying the personal interests which act in natural opposition to it."[67] It was this "basic truth" that accounted for the strength of the neutralist and pacifist factions within the Liberal government in 1914.

Modern-day intellectuals, those of the "critical" persuasion, fault those "nineteenth-century liberals" for their belief that "progress" was the dominant tendency in modern experience. Most especially, they are faulted for their belief that liberal practice would put an end to war. Subsequently, armed with "the lessons of history" – the evidence of two major wars – those critical intellectuals, referring knowingly to "the dark side of modernity," charge naivete. But the Great War, as seen, began with decisions made in barely modified old regimes, with "pre-liberal" elites responding to what they saw as a serious threat. For those elites, the recent developments suggested the coming of their "final conflict." The dynastic elites had not learned the liberal lesson or, perhaps better, were either indifferent or opposed to its claims and implications.

If the liberal theorists were providing a flat-out prediction – that economic development would bring peace – or if they were offering an inevitability thesis, they would obviously be mistaken. If, however, they

---

[67] Howard, *War and the Liberal Conscience*: Paine, p. 29, and Mill, p. 37.

There were of course some exceptions to this general liberal outlook. Friedrich List, a national liberal, saw some merit, some progress to be gained through war (p. 49). And Mazzini "preached wars of national liberation. Italy was to be liberated by education and by insurrection." Education, he wrote in 1831, "must ever be directed to teach by example, word and pen the necessity of insurrection.... Insurrection – by means of guerrilla bands – is the true method of warfare for all nations desirous of emancipating themselves from a foreign yoke." His views had considerable influence in eastern Europe. Those national liberation struggles posed serious problems for British liberals who sympathized with oppressed peoples but rejected war as an appropriate means (pp. 49–51 and 54–9).

were offering a conditional statement, namely, that the coming of peace depended on an understanding and appreciation of the basic lesson, they would have a serious point, not at all a naive judgment. Many of them did clearly recognize the conditional character of their conclusion; many pointed to the continuing presence of dynasts and their military specialists, emphasizing that they did not share the views of the liberal enlightenment.[68]

## Other Elites

One should inquire also about the outlooks and behavior of other elites, about other potentially influential groups. What were they doing in August 1914? What impact, if any, did they have? One might give consideration to media magnates, to the press lords. Were they advocates of war or peace? Lord Northcliffe, as seen, advocated British intervention and proceeded on the course, despite strong "business" opposition. Other British newspapers, however, argued for noninvolvement. Some newspapers in Serbia, it was noted, were generous in their provision of provocative content. And those comments were picked up and used for opposite purposes in many newspapers in Austria-Hungary. But elsewhere, there does not appear to have been any strong or consistent press influence. Few commentators have assigned any important role to the press in the shaping of the key decisions. After the fact, however, with rare exception, the press provided legitimation, giving enthusiastic support for the nation's patriotic efforts.

Religious elites had long since disappeared as decision makers in the nations discussed here. Little attention has been paid to the efforts of the

---

[68] Norman Angell's book, *The Great Illusion*, is often cited as the exemplary case of "naive" anticipation. The work sold over two million copies between 1910 and 1913, was translated into 25 languages, and sold another half a million copies in 1939. Angell was awarded the Nobel Peace Prize in 1933. For discussion of this "case," see Howard Weinroth, "Norman Angell and *The Great Illusion*: An Episode in Pre-1914 Pacifism," *Historical Journal* 17 (1974): 551–74. Weinroth does not see that work as a naive production. Its central thesis, "that modern wars are economically irrational," Weinroth reports, "has been misrepresented to read that they are utterly impossible." The work had considerable influence, stimulating peace movements throughout the world, many people having translated the message as an argument of impossibility. One person making that naive reading was Andrew Carnegie, who declared there was no chance of war because "We won't give them the money." The Carnegie Peace Endowment subsidized publication of Angell's work. On this point, see Roland N. Stromberg, *Redemption by War: The Intellectuals and 1914* (Lawrence, Kans., 1982), p. 9.

clergy, whether Roman Catholic, Orthodox, Protestant, or Jewish. Their contributions appear to have been dependent, coming after the fact, after the political leaders had set the nation's course. And their role, too, as far as we can tell, was supportive, arguing the justice of the nation's cause.[69]

Still another elite deserves some attention, a group whose activities in August 1914 have been generally neglected, namely, the intellectuals. Like the bourgeoisie, this group too had been gaining in numbers and influence over the course of the previous century, mostly based in universities. Given intellectuals' self-depictions, their contributions in August of 1914 are rather surprising. In their self-descriptions, they insistently announce their "critical" mission. Intellectuals comment, analyze, criticize, and reject handed-down beliefs, most especially those put forth by "established" authorities.

In a comprehensive review of intellectuals' productions in July and August 1914, Roland N. Stromberg documents a curious phenomenon, namely, "the almost manic bellicosity of the European intellectuals, writers, artists, scientists, at the crucial beginning of the terrible war...."[70] Two striking findings are the near-instant acceptance and defense of their nation's position and exuberant declarations of support, not to be found in any other context. These diverse groups were not decision makers, to be sure, but conceivably they helped to legitimate the effort, generating greater support for the decisions taken than would have been the case otherwise.

A handful of quotations may prove useful. Rudolf Eucken, the creator of the then-fashionable "life philosophy," hailed the war as "a mighty spiritual movement." Max Scheler published a book in 1915, *Der Genius des Krieges und der Deutsch Krieg*, which Stromberg describes as "sheer bellimania," a book that "hailed the war chiefly for renewing human contacts, breaking down the isolation of individuals from their fellows, and inducing a renaissance of belief." Three composers – Scriabin, Berg, and Stravinsky – welcomed the war as "necessary for human progress." Max Weber wrote: "No matter what the outcome will be, this war is great

---

[69] For a brief overview, see Stromberg, *Redemption by War*, pp. 54–7. Few of the general accounts of the war's origins report on the position of the churches, established or otherwise. The spokesmen for the Prince of Peace, one might think, would have something to say on the subject. For background on the German experience, see Helmut Walser Smith, *German Nationalism and Religious Conflict: Culture, Ideology, Politics, 1870–1914* (Princeton, 1995).

[70] Stromberg, *Redemption by War*, p. 5.

and wonderful." Emile Durkheim thought the war would contribute to "reviving the sense of community."[71]

Stromberg offers a third striking finding: the near-unanimity of intellectuals' support for their country's position. Although unaware of the previous decision making, in other words, ignorant of "the facts," they nevertheless proved zealous advocates of the national cause, showing more zeal than even the dynasts. Intellectuals were ecstatic, transported by mystical visions of redemption and community, and glorifying the imminent catastrophe. In those same countries, "the masses" – the people who would pay the costs – reacted with fear, anguish, and concern. As opposed to the other-worldly orientations of those advanced intellectuals, they recognized the imminent realities of pain, suffering, misery, and death.

### The Absent Bourgeoisie

None of the nations discussed in this volume was governed by economic elites, that is, by big business, industrialists, or bankers (*Finanzkapital*). The bourgeoisie was not present among the decision-making coteries. Their wishes rarely appear in the documentary record reporting the decisions for war; and, as seen, they were generally opposed to the war.

For many commentators, the dominance of the bourgeoisie, the ultimate power of big business, is accepted as a fundamental truth. For Marxists, bourgeois rule is a basic premise of the theory. That assumption, curiously, has also been adopted and accepted as an "obvious fact" by many non-Marxists. The absence of a "bourgeois revolution," most strikingly in the dynastic regimes, means that some "saving" explanation must be provided. The easy option is the argument of delay or postponement: Conditions were not yet "ripe," the revolution was still to come. Another argument claims a quiet evolution, basically, a merger, a coming-together of the segments and a consequent sharing of outlooks. After some initial contention, the dynasts, or monarchs and aristocrats, joined with "the bourgeoisie," both now recognizing their common interests. With that assumption, it is easy to believe the policies of the dynasts "reflected" the interests of that other elite, the *grande bourgeoisie*. In Germany, that

---

[71] Ibid., pp. 66, 68, 51, and 53. Weber's descriptions of the war as "great and wonderful" were repeated on at least three occasions; see Marianne Weber, *Max Weber: Ein Lebensbild* (Heidelberg, 1950), pp. 568, 571, and 578–9.

would mean they favored and pressed for *Weltpolitik*.[72] The absence of clear supporting evidence on this point is dealt with through use of a metaphor: Big business was operating *Hinter den Kulissen*, or "behind the scenes."[73]

The limited review of evidence presented in this chapter suggests an important counterfactual conclusion: If big business had been "in power" in 1914, it is likely that its preferences would have prevailed and that the Great War would not have happened. Some evidence bearing on that claim appears also in the later experience.

In 1917–18, three major powers – Austria-Hungary, Germany, and Russia – saw the end of dynastic rule. For the three royal houses – Habsburg, Hohenzollen, and Romanov – the Great War did prove to be "the final conflict." The tsarist regime was replaced by a new-style authoritarian regime, this led by a coterie purporting to represent the interests of workers and peasants. The Habsburgs were expelled, their territories divided up among various successor states.

Following different "dynamics," Italy and Germany saw their governments set aside or removed and replaced by another, new variety of authoritarian regime. In 1922 in Italy, which was one of the victorious powers, the constitutional monarchy was set aside and the government was taken over by the Fascists. Some fifteen years later, Germany's Weimar republic was replaced, and the new regime, like Italy's, was headed by nationalist authoritarians. The key agencies in both regimes were paramilitary organizations, war-trained veterans – the Fasci di Combattimento and the Storm Troops – each arguing an unjust settlement in the previous conflict. The Italians were denied the promised fruits of victory. The Germans, "undefeated in the field," were victims of a "stab in the back."[74] Adolf Hitler and his party, the National Socialists, were often said to be

---

[72] In the first edition of his famous work, Fritz Fischer assigned a prominent role to "big business." Responding to serious criticisms, that reading was substantially modified in his revised third edition.

[73] The use of metaphor is an often-used and easy substitute for investigation, for the presentation of evidence. Another frequent image is that of a marionette. But Ballin, Warburg, and Krupp, as seen, were not "pulling strings." Kaiser Wilhelm was not "their" puppet.

[74] Richard F. Hamilton, *Who Voted for Hitler?* (Princeton, 1982), esp. chs. 13 and 14 (the Italian case is reviewed on pp. 454–8). This explanation clearly rejects the mythic argument about the lower-middle-class basis of fascist movements. The claim is "mythic" because it was never supported, and no compelling relevant evidence was ever presented. From the start, it was a read-in, ultimately, a widely accepted "social construction." For a later review of the case, see my *Social Misconstruction of Reality: Validity and Verification in the Scholarly Community* (New Haven, 1996), chs. 4 and 5.

"agents" representing big business, but that claim has been shown to be erroneous.[75] The operating rationales of these two regimes were similar to those of the dynastic regimes. They too favored autarky; they too were much concerned with the nation's power and prestige; they gave much emphasis to the military; and they advocated national "expansion."

On the other side of the world, Japan continued with its authoritarian regime, basically, a monarchy dominated by a powerful military elite, one that also rejected basic liberal initiatives. Japan's constitution and military institutions were based on prewar German originals, this giving the military elites a substantial voice in policy making.[76]

World War II was initiated by this trio of authoritarian regimes, called the Axis powers, each reaching out, with varying degrees of initial success, to capture a new empire. With some important modifications, to be sure, this war also had its origins in the initiatives of nonliberal coteries. The democracies, those headed by party elites, were again slow and hesitant in their responses; again, they were reactive rather than initiating. The democracies were slow to react to Japan's efforts in China, to Italy in Ethiopia, to the fascist Putsch in Spain, and, most notorious of all, to the initiatives of Hitler's Germany. The first of these was the dictator's repudiation of the Versailles Treaty clauses in March 1935, those limiting Germany's military. The move met with no opposition. Then, a year later, the dictator proceeded to occupation of the Rheinland. This too was unopposed. An instant French response might conceivably have changed the course of history, France having military superiority at that point.[77] One lesson is that like the dynasts, dictators can decide quickly; democracies react slowly. Like the dynasts, moreover, dictators have continuity

---

[75] On the naming of Hitler as *Reichskanzler*, see Turner, *Hitler's Thirty Days*. And for the business role, or the lack thereof, see his *German Big Business and the Rise of Hitler* (New York, 1985). Turner's summary conclusion reads: "The leaders of German big business were ... absorbed and confined men, preoccupied with the management of large, complex organizations. They could at most dabble in politics. They could not commit their energies in a sustained fashion to that sphere of activity, so that they remained part-time amateurs, operating only sporadically, and usually ineffectually, on the periphery of politics. As such, they were sorely-ill-suited to deal with a phenomenon like Nazism" (p. 349).

[76] In 1878, Japan adopted the German general staff system, which made the military head independent of the civil government and gave him direct access to the emperor. See John K. Fairbank, Edwin O. Reischauer, and Albert M. Craig, *East Asia: The Modern Transformation* (Boston, 1965), pp. 294–5.

[77] Gordon A. Craig, *Germany 1866–1945* (New York, 1978), pp. 684–91; and Stephen A. Schuker, "France and the Remilitarization of the Rhineland, 1936," *French Historical Studies* 14 (1986): 299–338.

in office; democracies have frequent and unpredictable governmental turnovers.

The outcome of World War II differed significantly from its predecessor. The "total" victories of 1945 meant that no group within the perpetrating countries could question the result, or, put differently, could construct an unjust-settlement myth. There was no possibility for a *revengiste* movement. After brief periods of occupation, the victorious allies instituted democratic regimes, ones that were managed by political party elites. Those imposed settlements, moreover, removed the military elites and dismantled their institutions. One important consequence is that the new arrangements gave business elites a stronger voice than ever before. In Europe, the new arrangement allowed the development of the Common Market, originally with six members, then, by the year 2000, with fifteen member nations. The plan involved, effectively, a substantial extension of the liberal program. Two principal correlates should also be noted, namely, a substantial increase in the wealth of the participating nations and an extended period of peace. As of 2000, central and western Europe had experienced fifty-five years of peace. For Japan, its new liberal arrangements also brought both wealth and peace.[78]

---

[78] There is a sizable literature dealing with the issues touched on here. For a start, see Dale C. Copeland, "Economic Interdependence and War: A Theory of Trade Expectations," *International Security* 20 (1996): 5–41; John R. Oneal and Bruce M. Russett, "The Classical Liberals Were Right: Democracy, Interdependence, and Conflict, 1950–1985," *International Studies Quarterly* 41 (1997): 267–94; and Spencer R. Weart, *Never at War: Why Democracies Will Not Fight One Another* (New Haven, 1998).

# Appendix A

## *Chronology, 1914*

### Geoffrey P. Megargee

**June**

20    Assassins trained by the "Black Hand" enter Bosnia.

22    The Austrian minister at Bucharest informs Foreign Minister Berchtold that Romania has gone over to the Triple Entente.

28    Archduke Franz Ferdinand is assassinated in Sarajevo.

29    Austrian Chief of the General Staff Conrad proposes immediate mobilization against Serbia.

      Berchtold tells Hungarian Minister-President Tisza that it is time to settle accounts with Serbia.

**July**

1     German publicist Naumann assures Austrian diplomat Hoyos of German support and urges quick action against Serbia.

2     German Ambassador Tschirschky assures Austrian Emperor Franz Joseph of German support in defense of Austria-Hungary's "vital interests."

4     French President Poincaré advises Serbia and Austria-Hungary to stay calm. Russia issues a similar warning to Austria-Hungary.

5     Hoyos arrives in Berlin to confirm German intentions

      Kaiser Wilhelm II confirms German support ("blank check") to Austrian Ambassador Szögyény.

6   Bethmann assures Hoyos and Syögyény of German support no matter what, and urges immediate action.

    German Ambassador Lichnowsky in London reports to British Foreign Secretary Grey on the mood in Berlin: hostile to Serbia, supportive of Austria-Hungary, suspicious of Russia, possibly favoring war now rather than later.

    Wilhelm II departs for three-week cruise; first tells Capelle (acting state secretary of the Navy Office) that he expects no military complications.

7   Hoyos tells Austrian Foreign Minister Berchtold, who informs Conrad, that Germany will back Austria-Hungary even if operations against Serbia "should bring about the great war."

    Austrian Common Council of Ministers agrees, with Tisza dissenting, to force a military confrontation by issuing an ultimatum that Serbia cannot accept.

8   Tisza protests to Franz Joseph that an attack on Serbia will bring about a world war.

    Berchtold meets with Conrad and tells him the ultimatum to go out on 22 July; further, that he and the war minister should go on leave "to keep up an appearance that nothing is going on." The German government takes similar measures.

10  The Common Council of Ministers agrees on the basic points of the ultimatum.

12  Berchtold tells Conrad that the demands will be presented after French leaders Poincaré and Viviani end a state visit to Russia on 23 July.

14  Tschirschky reports to Bethmann on Austrian intentions.

15  Poincaré and Viviani depart France for St. Petersburg.

16  Italian Foreign Minister San Guiliano learns of the Austrian ultimatum and informs his ambassador in St. Petersburg. Russian Foreign Minister Sazonov hears of it shortly thereafter.

19  The Common Council of Ministers in Vienna finalizes the terms of the ultimatum.

An announcement appears in a semiofficial German newspaper calling for localization of the Austro-Serbian dispute.

20 Poincaré and Viviani arrive in Russia.

21 Franz Joseph accepts terms of the ultimatum.

Sazonov tells the German ambassador, Pourtalès, that Russia will not permit Austria-Hungary to move against Serbia.

22 Sazonov warns Austria against drastic action, but Berchtold does not receive the message until after the ultimatum is delivered.

23 Lichnowsky telegrams Berlin that Britain will back Vienna's demands only if they are moderate and reconcilable with the independence of the Serbian state; Britain expects that Germany will press Austria-Hungary to drop any unrealizable demands. Berlin responds that Germany will not interfere in Austria-Hungary's affairs.

Leaders of the German Foreign Office see the text of the Austrian ultimatum and express approval.

23 Poincaré and Viviani depart St. Petersburg.

18:00: The Austrian ultimatum is delivered in Belgrade.

24 The Russian Council of Ministers asks Tsar Nicholas II to agree in principle to partial mobilization against Austria-Hungary.

Sazonov gives Serbian minister Spalaikovic the Council of Ministers' advice not to oppose any Austro-Hungarian invasion, but to wait for action by the great powers.

Pourtalès tells Sazonov that this is a matter for Austria-Hungary and Serbia to settle on their own. Sazanov rejects this suggestion. Savonor indicates to Berlin that Russian intervention is unlikely.

Grey proposes to Lichnowsky that Britain, France, Germany, and Italy mediate between Austria-Hungary and Serbia. Germany circulates a statement in favor of localization.

Austria-Hungary informs Britain that if Serbia does not agree to terms, Austria-Hungary will break off relations and begin military preparations (but not actual operations).

25   01:16: Berlin receives Grey's suggestion from Lichnowsky. The Foreign Office delays transmission to Vienna until 16:00, so that it will arrive after the ultimatum's deadline.

Szögyény passes on the Germans' repeated advice to his government: Attack without delay.

Morning: Grey meets with Lichnowsky, who reports that Berlin is not prepared to hold Vienna back. Lichnowsky suggests mediation between Austria and Russia; Grey accepts. Lichnowsky urges Berlin to follow suit, warning that Britain will fight if France is involved.

Russia announces publicly it "cannot remain indifferent" to any Austro-Serbian dispute.

15:00: Serbia mobilizes.

18:00: Serbia accepts most terms of the ultimatum, requests clarification on some, and rejects only one. The Austrian ambassador sends a prearranged signal to Vienna, then leaves. The Serbian government evacuates the capital.

Austria-Hungary authorizes mobilization, but only against Serbia; Conrad will start preparations on Monday, 27 July, and proclaim mobilization on Tuesday; operations to start 12 August.

France begins military preparations.

Tsar Nicholas II and the Council of Ministers agree on partial mobilization and issue instructions that it will be only against Austria-Hungary. Nicholas proclaims the "period preparatory to war," that is, a "premobilization period."

Sazonov asks Britain to press Austria-Hungary for moderation and to express solidarity with Russia and France. He also asks Serbia to appeal to Britain for mediation. Both parties ignore him.

23:00: Germany accepts Grey's proposal for mediation between Austria-Hungary and Russia, should conflict between them arise.

22:30: Sazonov, via British ambassador Buchanan, to London: Russia will not allow Austria-Hungary to crush Serbia.

23:30: London learns of Serbian mobilization and the breaking of relations between Serbia and Austria-Hungary.

26     Conrad tells Berchtold that an invasion of Serbia is impossible for weeks. Berchtold replies that a declaration of war is necessary, nonetheless.

Chief of the German General Staff Moltke drafts an ultimatum to Belgium and forwards it to Foreign Minister von Jagow. It calls on Belgium to allow German troops to pass through its territory.

France learns of German officers being recalled to their units and institutes similar measures.

Germany presses for localization. Messages to London, Paris, and St. Petersburg emphasize that Vienna has made no territorial claims on Serbia. Britain and France are asked to restrain Russia; Russia is warned that its preparatory military measures could lead to war.

Grey proposes a conference of ambassadors from Britain, Italy, Germany, and France.

The French cabinet requests that Poincaré and Viviani cancel all stops and return to Paris immediately.

27     Replies to Grey's proposal for a four-power conference: France accepts; Italy accepts, but with reservations; Sazonov states he is in contact with Vienna and wants to wait; Germany rejects the idea.

France recalls its troops from Algeria and Morocco. War Minister Messimy presses Russia to invade East Prussia as soon as war breaks out.

Late morning: Grey tells Lichnowsky that Germany must put pressure on Austria-Hungary, which seems only to be seeking a pretext to crush Serbia.

Grey raises the possibility of British intervention for the first time in a cabinet meeting; most other ministers are firmly opposed.

13:00: Wilhelm II arrives back in Berlin from his North Sea cruise.

Jagow again presses Austria-Hungary to act without delay.

16:30: Austria-Hungary notifies Germany it will declare war on 28 July, not 12 August.

20:50: Austrian ambassador Szécsen from Paris tells Vienna that a general war is possible because Vienna's refusal to accept the Serbian reply has made a bad impression.

21:15: The German Foreign Office passes Grey's latest proposal for mediation on to Vienna, but explicitly disassociates itself from the idea, stating it is transmitting it merely to satisfy Grey. Jagow again urges quick action by Austria.

28      Morning: Wilhelm II reads the Serbian reply (late, because Bethmann and Jagow withheld it from him). He believes all cause for war has been removed and instructs the Foreign Office to propose a peace plan to Vienna, which he will mediate. Bethmann withholds the proposal for nearly twelve hours.

Noon: Austria-Hungary declares war on Serbia.

First Lord of the Admiralty Churchill, on receiving word of the Austro-Hungarian declaration, orders the British fleet to its battle bases.

Afternoon: Berchtold rejects the Russian suggestion of direct talks as well as the British suggestion of mediation, based on a (fictitious) opening of hostilities by Serbia.

After 16:00: Sazonov meets with French Ambassador Paléologue, who assures him of support – despite a telegram from Poincaré and Viviani suggesting moderation. Sazonov now thinks war probable.

18:00: Sazonov informs the tsar of Vienna's declaration of war. They decide to leave the option open as to total or partial mobilization.

Moltke, reacting to initial Russian military preparations and the Austro-Hungarian declaration of war, warns Bethmann that Germany will have to monitor the situation carefully and be ready to mobilize.

Evening: Sazonov orders preparation of two decrees: one for total and one for partial mobilization.

22:15: Bethmann sends an altered version of Wilhelm's peace plan to Austria-Hungary, adding that he does not want to give the impression of holding Vienna back.

Late night: Sazonov telegrams his ambassador to Britain that only if Austria-Hungary suspends military action will mediation be acceptable; he appeals to Britain to help with any mediation. He also telegrams the chargé d'affaires in Berlin that the next day Russia will mobilize in districts facing Austria-Hungary; this is no threat to Germany.

Late that night and the next day, Russian generals pressure Sazonov for total mobilization, on the grounds that partial mobilization is not practical.

29    01:00: Nicholas II telegrams Wilhelm II, "in the name of our old friendship," to restrain Austria. At nearly the same time (01:45), the kaiser telegrams the tsar that Germany is urging moderation on Vienna.

Morning: Nicholas II signs two decrees, one for partial and one for full mobilization. His generals press for full mobilization.

Poincaré and Viviani arrive back in France.

Austro-Hungarian gunboats bombard Belgrade.

11:00: Sazonov tells Pourtalès that Russia will order partial mobilization, against Austria-Hungary only, that day. Pourtalès warns that Germany will institute countermeasures.

12:50: Bethmann instructs Ambassador Schoen in Paris to warn France that if it continues to arm, Germany will proclaim a "state of danger of war," a preliminary step to mobilization. A similar warning goes to Russia via Pourtalès.

Early afternoon: Grey tells Lichnowsky that Germany needs to propose some way for the four powers to work toward peace. He warns Lichnowsky privately that Britain would intervene if Germany and France went to war.

16:27: Goschen, the British ambassador to Berlin, sends a telegram to Grey: Austria-Hungary is not willing to accept mediation.

17:00: Jagow meets with Russian Ambassador Sverbeyer, who notifies Jagow of Russia's partial mobilization against Austria-Hungary. Jagow states that Germany must also mobilize.

17:00: French cabinet meeting. Ambassador Schoen interrupts it to deliver the warning about the "state of danger of war."

c. 18:30: Wilhelm II gets word that the British may remain neutral.

Late afternoon to early evening: Sazonov learns that Austria-Hungary is not willing to negotiate; that Germany is threatening to mobilize; and that Austria is bombarding Belgrade.

c. 19:30: Russian Ambassador Izvolskii from Paris tells Sazonov to expect full French support.

c. 20:00: Nicholas II approves general mobilization. Almost immediately, however, he receives a second telegram from Wilhelm II, which he believes holds out hope for peace. He cancels general mobilization and orders partial mobilization instead.

20:30: Nicholas II telegrams Wilhelm II to suggest putting the Austro-Serbian dispute before the Hague International Court.

Austria-Hungary learns of Russian plans to partially mobilize and decides to mobilize against Russia.

c. 22:30: Bethmann offers Ambassador Goschen a set of guarantees in return for British neutrality. Shortly thereafter, Bethmann learns of Grey's early afternoon warning to Lichnowsky.

Late night: The French government receives a telegram from Sazonov, thanking it for the French ambassador's promise of full support. Poincaré and Viviani are alarmed.

30    01:00: Berchtold telegraphs Szögyény to let the Germans know that Russia's partial mobilization, if it continues, will lead to mobilization by Austria-Hungary, which has no intention of stopping its action against Serbia.

02:55: Bethmann presses Austria-Hungary to accept mediation on the basis of the occupation of Belgrade and some other territory. At 03:00, he suggests that Austria-Hungary reopen direct talks with Russia.

07:00: Viviani telegrams Paléologue and instructs him to caution Russia not to provoke Germany.

09:00: Grey receives Bethmann's offer; he rejects it immediately and strongly.

Morning: Wilhelm II concludes that Nicholas II has been lying to him, and drops his offer to mediate, for the moment.

Morning: Tschirschky receives Bethmann's now-sincere pleas for moderation and passes them on to Berchtold; the latter decides to ask Franz Joseph to order general mobilization.

French ambassador Cambon probes Grey regarding mutual actions in the event of German aggression; Grey puts him off, saying that he will answer after the cabinet meeting on 31 July.

Noon: Moltke begins pressing for mobilization.

16:00: Under strong pressure from his generals and Sazonov, Nicholas II again orders full mobilization; the order is issued at 17:00.

17:30: Austrian Military Attaché Bienerth from Berlin telegraphs Conrad: Moltke is urging Austria-Hungary to mobilize against Russia. Moltke follows this up with personal telegram to Conrad, which arrives at 07:45 on 31 July.

19:15: Wilhelm II telegraphs Franz Joseph, suggesting mediation and a halt at Belgrade.

19:35: Grey telegrams Russia: Germany will try to persuade Austria-Hungary not to advance past Belgrade; if Austria-Hungary agrees, Russia needs to halt further military preparations, provided the other powers do the same. This reaches Russia too late, after mobilization is under way.

Evening: Germany demands that Russia cancel all mobilization measures.

21:00: Bethmann sends another telegram to Vienna, urging moderation.

Bethmann continues pressing Wilhelm II's plan until roughly 23:30, when Moltke persuades him that mobilization is necessary.

31     Morning: Grey tells Lichnowsky that if Germany can come up with a proposal for peace that France and Russia reject unreasonably,

then Britain would wash its hands of the affair, but otherwise that if France became involved, Britain would be drawn in.

11:40: Word reaches Berlin of the Russian general mobilization; Germany declares "state of danger of war." Mobilization to follow within forty-eight hours.

Noon: Austria-Hungary mobilizes against Russia; Franz Joseph so informs Wilhelm II.

12:13: Lichnowsky, having spoken with Grey, telegrams Berlin that Britain might adopt a waiting attitude in event of war.

Afternoon: Grey tells Cambon that Britain cannot give a pledge of support to France yet.

15:10–15:30: Telegrams go from Berlin to the ambassadors in London, St. Petersburg, Paris, and Rome: A "state of danger of war" has been proclaimed; the telegram to Russia warns to cease all hostile action against Austria-Hungary within twelve hours or Germany will mobilize; the telegram to Paris asks whether France will remain neutral, and requires a response within eighteen hours; the telegram to London notes the Russian mobilization and the deadline Berlin gave to St. Petersburg; and the telegram to Rome demands Italian support if war comes.

French Chief of Staff Joffre hears of the German query and urges general mobilization.

17:30: Britain asks France and Germany whether they will respect Belgium's neutrality. France answers yes, Germany is vague. Grey is suspicious, but the British cabinet remains divided.

19:00: Belgium decrees 1 August to be the first day of mobilization.

### August

1    c. 11:00: Viviani tells Schoen, in reply to the German inquiry the previous day, that France will "have regard to her own interests" in a war between Russia and the Central Powers.

11:37: Britain receives news that Belgium is mobilizing.

12:52: Berlin telegraphs the text of the declaration of war against Russia to Pourtalès.

Afternoon: Grey warns Lichnowsky that Germany must not violate Belgian neutrality. Lichnowsky asks whether Grey could guarantee British neutrality if Germany *did* respect Belgium; Grey says no.

Afternoon: Grey tells Cambon that France should not count on British support.

15:45: France orders general mobilization for 2 August. Joffre has been pressing for it in a cabinet meeting since 09:00, arguing that Germany is carrying out a de facto mobilization.

17:00: Since Russia has not responded to the German ultimatum, Wilhelm II orders general mobilization. Moltke and Falkenhayn leave with the order.

17:15: Wilhelm II gets word that Britain and France may remain neutral if Germany does not attack France. Moltke and Falkenhayn are called back; Wilhelm II orders mobilization in the West to halt. Moltke demurs. They agree to continue mobilization as planned while awaiting further word, but no attack is to take place in the meantime.

19:00: Germany declares war on Russia.

c. 23:00: Wilhelm II receives word that his earlier hopes for French and British neutrality were misplaced.

After 23:00: French government learns of the German declaration of war on Russia.

23:15: British government learns of the German declaration of war on Russia.

Late night: German troops enter Luxembourg.

1–2     Late night: Bethmann and the service chiefs discuss a declaration of war on France, drafted over previous two days. They decide not to send it for the moment.

2     01:25: Churchill orders mobilization of the fleet.

07:42: Viviani telegraphs Cambon regarding the violation of Luxembourg's neutrality. Cambon goes to Grey, who remains noncommittal.

Border violations by both Germany and France occur. Germany claims that French attacks justify a declaration of war.

Full British naval mobilization goes into effect.

Germany and Turkey sign a treaty of alliance against Russia.

British cabinet in a meeting from 11:00 to nearly 14:00 decides not to allow the German fleet to operate in the Channel. Britain assures France of naval support.

Italy declares itself neutral.

19:00: Germany delivers its ultimatum to Belgium.

3     07:00: Belgium refuses the German demands.

10:55: German minister at Brussels transmits the Belgian refusal to Berlin.

Turkey mobilizes but declares armed neutrality.

15:00: Grey addresses the House of Commons. At the end he reads out summaries of Germany's ultimatum to Belgium and the latter's reply, which he has just received.

c. 19:00: Germany declares war on France.

c. 19:00: British Cabinet decides it will have to intervene if Belgian neutrality is violated. No ultimatum is to be issued until the next morning, however.

22:00: Lichnowsky cables Berlin that Britain is still not considering intervention.

German troops enter Russia.

4     08:00: German troops enter Belgium

09:30: London cables Goschen news of German ultimatum and Belgian reply. Message ends with a mild protest; there is no mention of war.

c. Noon: Belgium appeals to Russia, France, and Britain for help.

14:00: Britain issues an ultimatum to Germany to reaffirm Belgian neutrality by midnight.

c. 19:30: Bethmann tells Goschen that the British action is terrible, "just for a scrap of paper...."

23:00 (midnight German time): Britain declares war on Germany.

5   British Council of War decides to send the Expeditionary Force to France.

6   Austria-Hungary declares war on Russia.

12  Britain and France declare war on Austria.

26  Austria-Hungary declares war on Belgium.

**November**

3   Russia declares war on Turkey.

5   Britain and France declare war on Turkey.

# Appendix B

## *Dramatis Personae*

The following are some of the key players in the July Crisis of 1914. It is not intended to be exhaustive. Rather, the list serves as an aid to readers in case they lose sight of the scores of diplomats, politicians, and soldiers listed throughout the chapters. And while numerous English spellings exist in the historiography of the outbreak of the First World War, especially for Asian, Ottoman, and Slavic names, the form given here is that which the contributors to this book prefer.

### Austria-Hungary

| | |
|---|---|
| Monarch | Emperor/King Franz Joseph |
| Heir Apparent | Archduke Franz Ferdinand |
| Minister-President (Austria) | Count Karl Stürgkh |
| Minister-President (Hungary) | Count István Tisza de Boros-Jenő |
| Foreign Minister | Count Leopold Berchtold von und zu Ungarschitz |
| Minister of War | Ritter Alexander von Krobatin |
| Chief of the General Staff | Baron Franz Conrad von Hötzendorf |
| *Chef de cabinet* | Count Alexander Hoyos |
| Ambassador to Belgrade | Baron Wladimir Giesl von Gieslingen |
| Ambassador to Berlin | Count László Szögyény-Marich |
| Ambassador to Paris | Count Imre Szécsen von Temerin |
| Ambassador to St. Petersburg | Count Friedrich Szápáry von Szápár |

## Bulgaria

| | |
|---|---|
| Monarch | Tsar Ferdinand |
| Minister-President | Ivan Geshov (to 1913); Vasil Radoslavov (1913–18) |
| Chief of the Army | Mihail Savov (1912–13) |
| War Minister | Nikola T. Zhekov (1915) |
| Ambassador to St. Petersburg | Radko Dimitriev |

## France

| | |
|---|---|
| President | Raymond Poincaré |
| Premier and Foreign Minister | René Viviani |
| Minister of War | Adolphe Messimy |
| Minister of Justice | Jean Baptiste Bienvenu-Martin |
| Chief of the General Staff | Joseph Joffre |
| Ambassador to Berlin | Jules Cambon |
| Ambassador to London | Paul Cambon |
| Ambassador to St. Petersburg | Maurice Paléologue |
| Ambassador to Vienna | Alfred Dumaine |

## Germany

| | |
|---|---|
| Monarch | Emperor/King Wilhelm II |
| Chancellor | Theobald von Bethmann Hollweg |
| Foreign Secretary | Gottlieb von Jagow |
| War Minister | Erich von Falkenhayn |
| Chief of the General Staff | Helmuth von Moltke (the Younger) |
| Chief of the Military Cabinet | Moriz von Lyncker |
| State Secretary, Navy Office | Alfred von Tirpitz |
| Ambassador to Constantinople | Hans Wangenheim |
| Ambassador to London | Prince Karl Max von Lichnowsky |
| Ambassador to Paris | Baron Wilhelm von Schoen |
| Ambassador to Rome | Hans von Flotow |
| Ambassador to St. Petersburg | Count Friedrich von Pourtalès |
| Ambassador to Vienna | Heinrich von Tschirschky und Bögendorff |

## Great Britain

| | |
|---|---|
| Monarch | King/Emperor George V |
| Prime Minister | Herbert Henry Asquith |
| Foreign Secretary | Sir Edward Grey |
| First Lord of the Admiralty | Winston S. Churchill |
| Chancellor of the Exchequer | David Lloyd George |
| Ambassador to Berlin | Sir Edward Goschen |
| Ambassador to St. Petersburg | Sir George Buchanan |
| Ambassador to Tokyo | Sir Coyningham Greene |
| Ambassador to Vienna | Sir Maurice de Bunsen |

## Greece

| | |
|---|---|
| Monarch | King Constantine |
| Prime Minister | Eleutherios Venizelos |
| Chief of the General Staff | Ioannis Metaxas |

## Italy

| | |
|---|---|
| Monarch | King Vittorio Emanuele III |
| Prime Minister | Antonio Salandra |
| Foreign Minister | Antonio di San Giuliano (to 1914); Giorgio S. Sonnino (1914–19) |
| Chief of the General Staff | Alberto Pollio (to 1914); Luigi Cadorna (1914–17) |
| Ambassador to Berlin | Giuseppe Duke d'Avarna |
| Ambassador to London | Marchese Guglielmo Imperiali |

## Japan

| | |
|---|---|
| Monarch | Emperor Yoshihito (Taishō) |
| Prime Minister | Ōkuma Shigenobu |
| Foreign Minister | Katō Takaaki |
| Minister of the Navy | Yashiro Rokurō |
| Chief of the Naval General Staff | Shimamura Hayao |
| Vice Chief of the General Staff | Tanaka Giichi; Akashi Motojirō |
| Elder Statesman | Yamagata Aritomo |
| Elder Statesman | Inoue Kaoru |

| Governor General, Korea | Terauchi Masatake |
| Seiyūkai Party President | Hara Takashi |
| Member, House of Peers | Gotō Shinpei |

## Ottoman Empire

| Monarch | Sultan Mehmed V |
| Premier and Foreign Minister | Mehmed Said Halim Pasha |
| Minister of War | Enver Pasha |
| Minister of the Interior | Mehmed Talât Bey |
| Minister of the Navy | Ahmed Cemal Pasha |
| Minister of Finance | Mehmed Cavid Bey |
| President, House of Deputies | Halil Bey |
| Ambassador to Berlin | Mahmud Muhtar Pasha |

## Romania

| Monarch | King Carol I (to October 1914); King Ferdinand (to 1927) |
| Prime Minister | Ion Brătianu |
| Chief of the General Staff | Alexandru Averescu |

## Russia

| Monarch | Tsar Nicholas II |
| Army Commander (August 1914) | Grand Duke Nikolai Nikolaevich |
| Premier | I. L. Goremykin |
| Minister of Foreign Affairs | S. D. Sazonov |
| Finance Minister | V. N. Kokovtsov; Peter Bark |
| Minister of Agriculture | A. V. Krivoshein |
| Minister of War | V. A. Sukhomlinov |
| Chief of the General Staff | N. N. Ianushkevich |
| Quartermaster-General | Yu. N. Danilov |
| Ambassador to Belgrade | N. V. Hartwig |
| Ambassador to Berlin | S. N. Sverbeyev |
| Ambassador to Paris | A. P. Izvolskii |
| Ambassador to Sofia | Aleksandr Savinski |
| Ambassador to Vienna | N. N. Shebeko |

## Serbia

| | |
|---|---|
| Monarch | King Peter Karadjordjević (to 1914); |
| | Prince Regent Alexander (1914 ff.); |
| | King Nikola (Montenegro) |
| Prime Minister | Nikola Paschich (Pašić) |
| Chief of the General Staff | Radomir Putnik |
| Chief of Military Intelligence | Dragutin Dimitrijevich (called "Apis") |
| Assassin of Archduke Franz Ferdinand | Gavrilo Princep |

## United States of America

| | |
|---|---|
| President | Thomas Woodrow Wilson |
| Secretary of State | William Jennings Bryan (1912–15); |
| | Robert Lansing (1915–20) |
| Secretary of War | Lindley M. Garrison (to 1916); |
| | Newton D. Baker (1916 and later) |
| Secretary of the Navy | Josephus Daniels |
| Presidential Advisor | Edward M. House |

# Appendix C

## Suggested Readings

### Anthologies, Readers

Evans, R. J. W., and Hartmut Pogge von Strandmann, eds. *The Coming of the First World War*. Oxford: Clarendon, 1988.

Herwig, Holger H., ed. *The Outbreak of World War I: Causes and Responsibilities*. Boston: Houghton, Mifflin, 1997.

Joll, James. *The Origins of the First World War*. London: Longman, 1984.

Koch, Hansjoachim W., ed. *The Origins of the First World War: Great Power Rivalry and German War Aims*. London: Macmillan, 1984.

Langdon, John W. *July 1914: The Long Debate, 1918–1990*. New York: Berg, 1991.

Remak, Joachim. *The Origins of World War I, 1871–1914*. New York: Holt, Rinehart and Winston, 1976.

Turner, L. C. F., ed. *Origins of the First World War*. New York: Norton, 1967.

### Austria-Hungary

Albertini, Luigi. *The Origins of the War of 1914*. 3 vols. London and New York: Oxford University Press, 1952–57.

Fellner, Fritz. "Austria-Hungary." In Keith Wilson, ed., *Decisions for War 1914*. New York: St. Martin's Press, 1995. Pp. 9–25.

Galántai, József. *Hungary in the First World War*. Budapest: Akadémiai Kradó, 1989.

Herwig, Holger H. *The First World War: Germany and Austria-Hungary 1914–1918*. London: Arnold, 1997.

Leslie, John. "The Antecedents of Austria-Hungary's War Aims, Policies and Policymakers in Vienna and Budapest before and during 1914." In *Wiener Beiträge zur Geschichte der Neuzeit* Bd. 20. Vienna: Verlag für Geschichte und Politik, 1993. Pp. 307–94.

Rumpler, Helmut. "The Foreign Ministry of Austria-Hungary, 1848–1918." In Zara S. Steiner, ed., *The Times Survey of Foreign Ministries of the World.* London: Times Books, 1982. Pp. 49–59.

Shanafelt, Gary W. *The Secret Enemy: Austria-Hungary and the German Alliance, 1914–1918.* New York: Columbia University Press, 1985.

Tunstall, Graydon A., Jr. *Planning for War Against Russia and Serbia: Austro-Hungarian and German Military Strategies, 1871–1914.* New York: Columbia University Press, 1993.

Williamson, Samuel R., Jr. *Austria-Hungary and the Origins of the First World War.* New York: St. Martin's Press, 1991.

———. "Vienna and July 1914: The Origins of the Great War Once More." In S. R. Williamson and P. Pastor, eds., *Essays on World War I: Origins and Prisoners of War.* New York: Columbia University Press, 1983. Pp. 9–36.

## Balkans

Cornwall, Mark. "Serbia." In Keith Wilson, ed., *Decisions for War 1914.* New York: St. Martin's Press, 1995. Pp. 55–96.

Crampton, Richard. *Bulgaria 1878–1918: A History.* New York: Columbia University Press, 1983.

Dallin, Alexander, et al., eds. *Russian Diplomacy and Eastern Europe 1914–1917.* New York: King's Crown Press, 1963.

Dedijer, Vladimir. *The Road to Sarajevo.* New York: Simon and Schuster, 1966.

Dragnich, Alex N. *Serbia, Nikola Pašić, and Yugoslavia.* New Brunswick: Rutgers University Press, 1974.

Hall, Richard C. *Bulgaria's Road to the First World War.* New York: Columbia University Press, 1996.

Helmreich, E. C. *The Diplomacy of the Balkan Wars 1912–1913.* New York: Russell and Russell, 1969.

Hitchens, Keith. *Rumania 1866–1947.* Oxford: Clarendon, 1994.

Leontaritis, George B. *Greece and the First World War: From Neutrality to Intervention, 1917–1918.* New York: Columbia University Press, 1990.

Mackenzie, David. *Apis, the Congenial Conspirator: The Life of Colonel Dragutin T. Dimitrijevich.* New York: Columbia University Press, 1989.

Palmer. Alan, *The Gardeners of Salonika.* New York: Simon and Schuster, 1965.

Perry, Duncan. *The Politics of Terror: The Macedonian Revolutionary Movements 1893–1903.* Durham: Duke University Press, 1988.

Petrovich, Michael Boro. *A History of Modern Serbia, 1804–1918.* 2 vols. New York: Harcourt Brace Jovanovich, 1976.

Petsalis-Diomidis, N. *Greece at the Paris Peace Conference 1919.* Thessaloniki: Institute for Balkan Studies, 1978.

Rossos, Andrew. *Russia and the Balkans 1908–1914.* Toronto: University of Toronto Press, 1981.

Torrey, Glenn E. *Romania and World War I.* Portland: Center for Romanian Studies, 1998.

Treadway, John. *The Falcon and the Eagle: Montenegro and Austria-Hungary 1908–1914.* West Lafayette, Ind.: Purdue University Press, 1983.

## France

Becker, Jean-Jacques. *The Great War and the French People.* Leamington Spa: Berg, 1993.

Hayne, M. B. *The French Foreign Office and the Origins of the First World War, 1898–1914.* Oxford: Clarendon Press, 1993.

Keiger, John V. F. *France and the Origins of the First World War.* New York: St. Martin's Press, 1983.

———. *Raymond Poincaré.* Cambridge, 1997.

Krumeich, Gerd. *Armaments and Politics in France on the Eve of the First World War: The Introduction of Three-Year Conscription 1913–1914.* Leamington Spa and Dover: Berg, 1981.

Lafore, Laurence. *The Long Fuse: An Interpretation of the Origins of World War I.* Philadelphia: Lippincott, 1971.

Luntinen, Pertti. *French Information on the Russian War Plans 1880–1914.* Helsinki: SHS, 1984.

Porch, Douglas. *The March to the Marne: The French Army 1871–1914.* Cambridge: Cambridge University Press, 1981.

Schuman, Frederick L. *War and Diplomacy in the French Republic.* New York: Whittlesey House, 1969.

Stevenson, David. *Armaments and the Coming of War, Europe 1904–1914.* Oxford: Clarendon, 1996.

Williamson, Samuel R., Jr. *The Politics of Grand Strategy: Britain and France Prepare for War, 1904–1914.* Cambridge, Mass.: Harvard University Press, 1969.

Wright, Gordon. *Raymond Poincaré and the French Presidency.* Stanford: Stanford University Press, 1942.

## Germany

Berghahn, Volker R. *Germany and the Approach of War in 1914.* Basingstoke and London: Macmillan, 1993.

Bucholz, Arden. *Moltke, Schlieffen, and Prussian War Planning.* New York and Oxford: Berg, 1991.

Cecil, Lamar. *William II*, vol. 2: *Emperor and Exile, 1900–1941.* Chapel Hill: University of North Carolina Press, 1996.

Fischer, Fritz. *Germany's Aims in the First World War.* New York: Norton, 1976.

———. *War of Illusions: German Policies from 1911 to 1914.* New York: Norton, 1975.

Geiss, Imanuel, ed. *July 1914: The Outbreak of the First World War. Selected Documents.* New York: Norton, 1968.

Herwig, Holger H. *The First World War: Germany and Austria-Hungary 1914–1918.* London: Arnold, 1997.

Herrmann, David G. *The Arming of Europe and the Making of the First World War.* Princeton: Princeton University Press, 1996.

Ritter, Gerhard. *The Sword and the Scepter: The Problem of Militarism in Germany.* 4 vols. Coral Gables: University of Miami Press, 1969–72. See esp. vol. 4.

Röhl, John. *1914: Delusion or Design? The Testimony of Two German Diplomats.* London: Paul Elek, 1973.
Verhey, Jeffrey. *The Spirit of 1914: Militarism, Myth and Mobilization in Germany.* New York: Cambridge University Press, 2000.

## Great Britain

French, David. *British Strategy and War Aims 1914–1916.* London: Allen and Unwin, 1986.
Gooch, John. *The Plans of War: The General Staff and British Military Strategy c. 1900–1916.* London: Routledge and Kegan Paul, 1974.
Hinsley, F. H., ed. *British Foreign Policy under Sir Edward Grey.* Cambridge: Cambridge University Press, 1977.
Joll, James. *The Origins of the First World War,* 2nd ed. London: Longman, 1992.
Neilson, Keith. *Britain and the Last Tsar: British Policy and Russia, 1894–1917.* Oxford: Clarendon, 1995.
Robbins, Keith. *Sir Edward Grey: A Biography of Lord Grey of Fallodon.* London: Cassell, 1971.
Steiner, Zara S. *Britain and the Origins of the First World War.* London: Macmillan, 1977.
Taylor, A. J. P. *The Struggle for Mastery in Europe 1848–1918.* Oxford: Clarendon, 1954.
Wilson, Keith. "Britain." In Keith Wilson, ed., *Decisions for War 1914.* New York: St. Martin's Press, 1995. Pp. 175–208.
Wilson, Keith M. *The Policy of the Entente: Essays on the Determinants of British Foreign Policy, 1904–14.* Cambridge: Cambridge University Press, 1985.

## Italy

Askew, William C. "Italy and the Great Powers before the First World War." In Edward R. Tannenbaum and Emiliana P. Noether, eds., *Modern Italy: A Topical History since 1861.* New York: New York University Press, 1974. Pp. 313–36.
Bosworth, R. J. B. *Italy and the Approach of the First World War.* New York: Macmillan, 1983.
_____. *Italy, the Least of the Great Powers: Italian Foreign Policy before the First World War.* London: Cambridge University Press, 1979.
_____. *Italy and the Wider World 1860–1960.* London and New York: Routledge, 1996.
Chabod, Federico. *Italian Foreign Policy: The Statecraft of the Founders.* Princeton: Princeton University Press, 1996.
Clough, Shephard B., and Salvatore Saladino, eds. *A History of Modern Italy: Documents, Readings and Commentary.* New York and London: Columbia University Press, 1968.
Gooch, John. *Army, State and Society in Italy, 1870–1915.* New York: St. Martin's Press, 1989.

Haywood, Geoffrey A. *Failure of a Dream: Sidney Sonnino and the Rise and Fall of Liberal Italy, 1847–1922.* Florence: L. S. Olschki, 1999.

Lowe, C. J., and F. Marzari. *Italian Foreign Policy 1870–1940.* London: Routledge and Kegan Paul, 1975.

Mack Smith, Denis. *Modern Italy: A Political History.* Ann Arbor: University of Michigan Press, 1997.

Renzi, William A. *In the Shadow of the Sword: Italy's Neutrality and Entrance Into the Great War, 1914–1915.* New York: P. Lang, 1987.

Seton-Watson, Christopher. *Italy from Liberalism to Fascism: 1870–1925.* London: Methuen, 1967.

Sullivan, Brian R. "The Strategy of the Decisive Weight: Italy, 1882–1922." In Williamson Murray, MacGregor Knox, and Alvin Bernstein, eds., *The Making of Strategy: Rulers, States, and War.* Cambridge: Cambridge University Press, 1994. Pp. 307–51.

Whittam, John. *The Politics of the Italian Army, 1861–1918.* London: CroomHelm, 1977.

## Japan

Beasley, W. G. *Japanese Imperialism, 1894–1945.* Oxford: Clarendon, 1987.

Burdick, Charles B. *The Japanese Siege of Tsington: World War I in Asia.* Hamden, Conn.: Archon, 1976.

Dickinson, Frederick R. *War and National Reinvention: Japan in the Great War, 1914–1919.* Cambridge, Mass.: Harvard University Press, 1999.

Hackett, Roger, *Yamagata Aritomo in the Rise of Modern Japan, 1838–1922.* Cambridge, Mass.: Harvard University Press. 1971.

Harries, Meiron, and Susie Harries. *Soldiers of the Sun: The Rise and Fall of the Imperial Japanese Army.* New York: Random House, 1991.

Lowe, Peter. *Great Britain and Japan, 1911–15.* London: Macmillan, 1969.

Nish, Ian. *Alliance in Decline: A Study in Anglo-Japanese Relations, 1908–23.* London: Athlone Press, 1972.

———. "Japan." In Keith Wilson, ed., *Decisions for War 1914.* New York: St. Martin's Press, 1995. Pp. 209–28.

## Ottoman Empire

Ahmad, Feroz. *The Making of Modern Turkey.* London: Routledge, 1993.

Arai, Masami. *Turkish Nationalism in the Young Turk Era.* Leiden: E. J. Brill, 1992.

Karpat, Kemal. *The Ottoman Population, 1830–1914: Ethnic and Social Characteristics.* Madison: University of Wisconsin Press, 1985.

Kent, Marian, ed. *The Great Powers and the End of the Ottoman Empire,* 2nd ed. London: Frank Cass, 1996.

Lewis, Bernard. *The Emergence of Modern Turkey,* 3rd ed. New York: Oxford University Press, 2002.

Shaw, Stanford, and Ezel Kural Shaw. *History of the Ottoman Empire and Modern Turkey.* 2 vols. Cambridge: Cambridge University Press, 1976–77.

Trumpener, Ulrich. *Germany and the Ottoman Empire, 1914–1918.* Princeton: Princeton University Press, 1968.

Turfan, M. Naim. *Rise of the Young Turks: Politics, the Military, and Ottoman Collapse.* London: I. B. Tauris, 1999.

Weber, Frank G. *Eagles on the Crescent: Germany, Austria-Hungary, and the Diplomacy of the Turkish Alliance, 1914–1918.* Ithaca: Cornell University Press, 1970.

Yasamee, F. A. K. "Ottoman Empire." In Keith Wilson, ed., *Decisions for War 1914.* New York: St. Martin's Press, 1995. Pp. 229–68.

Zürcher, Erik Jan. *Turkey: A Modern History.* London: I. B. Tauris, 1993.

## Russia

Fuller, William C. *Civil-Military Conflict in Imperial Russia 1881–1914.* Princeton: Princeton University Press, 1985.

———. *Strategy and Power in Russia, 1600–1914.* New York: Free Press, 1992.

Gatrell, Peter. *Government, Industry, and Rearmament in Russia, 1900–1914.* Cambridge: Cambridge University Press, 1994.

Geyer, Dietrich. *Russian Imperialism: The Interaction of Domestic and Foreign Policy, 1860–1914.* Leamington Spa: Berg, 1987.

Kennan, George F. *The Fateful Alliance: France, Russia, and the Coming of the First World War.* New York: Pantheon, 1984.

LeDonne, John P. *The Russian Empire and the World, 1700–1917: The Geopolitics of Expansion and Containment.* Oxford: Oxford University Press, 1997.

Lieven, D. C. B., *Russia and the Origins of the First World War.* New York: St. Martin's Press, 1983.

Menning, Bruce W. *Bayonets before Bullets: The Imperial Russian Army, 1861–1914.* Bloomington: Indiana University Press, 1992.

Rich, David Alan. *The Tsar's Colonels: Professionalism, Strategy, and Subversion in Late Imperial Russia.* Cambridge, Mass.: Harvard University Press, 1998.

## United States

Ambrosius, Lloyd R. *Wilsonian Statecraft: Theory and Practice of Liberal Internationalism during World War I.* Wilmington: SR Books, 1991.

Calhoun, Frederick S. *Power and Principle: Armed Intervention in Wilsonian Foreign Policy.* Kent: Kent State University Press, 1986.

Cooper, John Milton. *The Vanity of Power: American Isolationism and the First World War, 1914–1917.* Westport, Conn.: Greenwood, 1969.

———. *The Warrior and the Priest: Woodrow Wilson and Theodore Roosevelt.* Cambridge, Mass.: Harvard University Press, 1983.

Gregory, Ross, *The Origins of American Intervention in the First World War.* New York: Norton, 1971.

Knock, Thomas J. *To End All Wars: Woodrow Wilson and the Quest for World Order*. New York: Oxford University Press, 1992.

Link, Arthur S. *The Higher Realism of Woodrow Wilson and Other Essays*. Nashville: Vanderbilt University Press, 1971.

_____. *Wilson: Confusions and Crises*, 1915–1916. Princeton: Princeton University Press, 1964.

_____. *Wilson: The Struggle for Neutrality*, 1914–1915. Princeton: Princeton University Press, 1960.

May, Ernest R. *The World War and American Isolation*. Cambridge, Mass.: Harvard University Press, 1959.

# Index